W9-AUI-558

- Height and weight continue to increase rapidly.
- The body becomes less rounded, more muscular.
- The brain grows larger, neural interconnections continue to develop, and lateralization emerges.
- Gross and fine motor skills advance quickly. Children can throw and catch balls, run, use forks and spoons, and tie shoelaces.
- Children begin to develop handedness.

- Growth becomes slow and steady. Muscles develop, and "baby fat" is lost.
- Gross motor skills (biking, swimming, skating, ball handling) and fine motor skills (writing, typing, fastening buttons) continue to improve.

- Children show egocentric thinking (viewing world from their own perspective) and "centration," a focus on only one aspect of a stimulus.
- Memory, attention span, and symbolic thinking improve, and intuitive thought begins.
- Language (sentence length, vocabulary, syntax, and grammar) improves rapidly.

- Children apply logical operations to problems.
- Understanding of conservation (that changes in shape do not necessarily affect quantity) and transformation (that objects can go through many states without changing) emerge.
- Children can "decenter"–take multiple perspectives into account.
- Memory encoding, storage, and retrieval improve, and control strategies (meta-memory) develop.
- Language pragmatics (social conventions) and metalinguistic awareness (self-monitoring) improve.

- Children develop self concepts, which may be exaggerated.
- A sense of gender and racial identity emerges.
- Children begin to see peers as individuals and form friendships based on trust and shared interests.
- Morality is rule-based and focused on rewards and punishments.
- Play becomes more constructive and cooperative, and social skills become important.

- Children refer to psychological traits to define themselves. Sense of self becomes differentiated.
- Social comparison is used to understand one's standing and identity.
- Self-esteem grows differentiated, and a sense of self-efficacy (an appraisal of what one can and cannot do) develops.
- Children approach moral problems intent on maintaining social respect and accepting what society defines as right.
- Friendship patterns of boys and girls differ. Boys mostly interact with boys in groups, and girls tend to interact singly or in pairs with other girls.

Preoperational stage	Concrete operational stage
Initiative-versus-guilt stage	Industry-versus-inferiority stage
Phallic stage	Latency period
Preconventional morality level	Conventional morality level

DEVELOPMENTAL PSYCHOLOGY HAS GONE INTERACTIVE!

Available Fall 1999

FELDMAN INTERACTIVE student CD-ROM is an "electronic book"— featuring *Author Tip Videos*, *Speaking of Development Videos*, *Theorist Biographies*, enhanced graphics, quizzes, and extensive links to the Internet and our Companion Website: **www.prenhall.com/feldman**

Using FELDMAN INTERACTIVE is easy!

It's as simple as a click of the mouse. To get started on your explorations in developmental psychology with **FELDMAN INTERACTIVE**, put the CD in your CD-ROM drive, and click on *Install*.

YOU'LL NEVER LOOK AT YOUR TEXTBOOK THE SAME WAY AGAIN!

Bookmark important passages of FELDMAN INTERACTIVE for easy access to material you want to review.

Click on one of the many multimedia icons in the margins throughout the FELDMAN INTERACTIVE e-book and launch a video, a quiz, the Companion Website or Weblinks, and many other special features of the e-book.

Highlight important text in FELDMAN INTERACTIVE just like you would in a print book.

Navigation through FELDMAN INTERACTIVE is easy using the **Contents button, the side tabs, the chapter outlines, the arrow keys, and the scroll bar.**

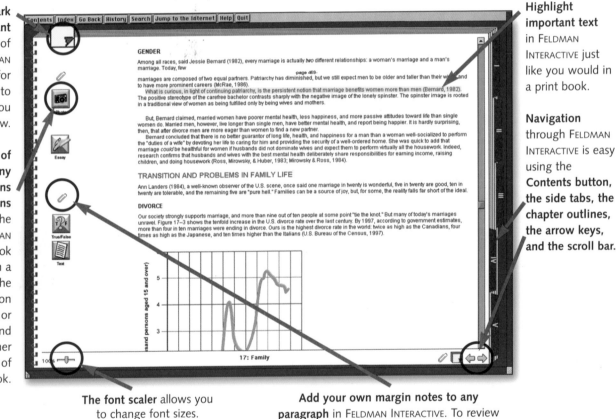

The font scaler allows you to change font sizes.

Add your own margin notes to any paragraph in FELDMAN INTERACTIVE. To review your notes, **simply click on the paperclip** next to the paragraph you've annotated.

For more information on how to use these features, click on the HELP button!

SYSTEM REQUIREMENTS

MACINTOSH: minimum 68040/33MHz, System 7.5 or above, 12mb RAM (16mb recommended), 1mb free HD space, 2x CD-ROM, 640X480 screen resolution, color monitor (thousands of colors required). QuickTime 3.0 installed from CD.

PC: minimum 486/DX25, Windows 3.x (minimum 8mb RAM) or Windows 95/98 (minimum 16mb RAM), 1mb free HD space, 2X CD-ROM, SVGA monitor, thousands of colors, sound and video cards required. For Windows 3.x, Video for Windows installed from CD.

Development Across the Life Span

SECOND EDITION

Robert S. Feldman
University of Massachusetts at Amherst

Prentice Hall
Upper Saddle River, New Jersey 07458

Library of Congress Cataloging-in-Publication Data
Feldman, Robert S. (Robert Stephen),
   Development across the life span / Robert S. Feldman.—2nd ed.
     p.   cm.
   Includes bibliographical references and index.
   ISBN 0-13-087866-9
   1. Developmental psychology.   1. Title.
   BF713.F45   1999
   155—dc21   99-17921
                                      CIP

Editorial Director: *Charlyce Jones Owen*
Editor-in-Chief: *Nancy Roberts*
Executive Editor: *Bill Webber*
Acquisitions Editor: *Jennifer Gilliland*
AVP/Director of Production and Manufacturing: *Barbara Kittle*
Director of Marketing: *Gina Sluss*
Director of Development: *Susanna Lesan*
Senior Managing Editor: *Bonnie Biller*
Assistant Managing Editor/Project Manager: *Mary Rottino*
Development Editor: *Barbara Muller*
Manufacturing Manager: *Nick Sklitsis*
Prepress and Manufacturing Buyer: *Tricia Kenny*
Creative Design Director: *Leslie Osher*
Line Art Coordinator: *Guy Ruggiero*
Interior and Cover Design: *Ximena Tamvakopoulos*
Electronic Illustrations: *Joseph Rattan Design/Mirella Signoretto*
Director, Image Resource Center: *Lori Morris-Nantz*
Photo Research Supervisor: *Melinda Reo*
Image Permission Supervisor: *Kay Dellosa*
Photo Researcher: *Eloise Donnelley*
Editorial Assistant: *Jessica Spillers*

Acknowledgments for copyrighted material may be found beginning
on p. 716, which constitutes an extension of this copyright page.

This book was set in 10/13 Minion and Syntax Black by TSI Graphics
and was printed by RR Donnelley & Sons Co., Roanoke.
The cover was printed by The Lehigh Press, Inc.

Printed in the United States of America
10 9 8 7 6 5 4 3 2 1

ISBN 0-13-087866-9

Prentice-Hall International (UK) Limited, London
Prentice-Hall of Australia Pty. Limited, Sydney
Prentice-Hall Canada, Inc. Toronto
Prentice-Hall Hispanoamericana, S.A., Mexico
Prentice-Hall of India Private Limited, New Delhi
Prentice-Hall of Japan, Inc. Tokyo
Pearson Education Asia Pte. Ltd., Singapore
Editoria Prentice-Hall do Brasil, Ltda., Rio de Janeiro

to my family

Brief Contents

Contents

PART 2 ▪ INFANCY: FORMING THE FOUNDATIONS OF LIFE

4 Physical Development in Infancy 114

PART 3 ■ THE PRESCHOOL YEARS

7 Physical and Cognitive Development in the Preschool Years 214

PART 4 ■ THE MIDDLE CHILDHOOD YEARS

10 Social and Personality Development in Middle Childhood   340

PART 5 ■ ADOLESCENCE

11 Physical and Cognitive Development in Adolescence 376

PART 6 ▪ EARLY ADULTHOOD

PART 7 ■ MIDDLE ADULTHOOD

15 Physical and Cognitive Development in Middle Adulthood   510

16 Social and Personality Development in Middle Adulthood   540

PART 8 ■ LATE ADULTHOOD

17 Physical and Cognitive Development in Late Adulthood   574

PART 9 ■ ENDINGS

19 Death and Dying 640

Preface

This book tells a story: the story of our lives, and our parents' lives, and the lives of our children. It is the story of human beings, and how they get to be the way they are.

Unlike any other area of study, lifespan development speaks to us in a very personal sense. It encompasses the range of human existence from its beginnings at conception to its inevitable ending at death. It is a discipline that deals with ideas and concepts and theories, but one that above all has at its heart people—our fathers and mothers, our friends and acquaintances, our very selves.

Development Across the Life Span, second edition, seeks to capture the discipline in a way that sparks and nurtures and shapes students' interest. It is meant to excite readers about the field and to draw them into its way of looking at the world.

Overview

The Goals of the Book

As it did in its first edition, *Development Across the Life Span,* second edition, seeks to accomplish the following four major goals:

- First and foremost, the book provides a broad, balanced overview of the field. It is designed to introduce readers to the theories, research, and applications that constitute the discipline, examining both the traditional areas of the field as well as more recent innovations.

  The book pays particular attention to the applications of developmentalists. While not slighting theoretical material, the text emphasizes what developmentalists *know*, rather than focusing on unanswered questions. It demonstrates how this knowledge may be applied to real-world problems.

  In sum, the book highlights the interrelationships among theory, research, and application, and it accentuates the scope and diversity of the field. It also illustrates how developmentalists use theory, research, and applications to help solve significant social problems.

- The second major goal of the text is to explicitly tie development to students' lives. The findings of developmentalists have a significant degree of relevance to students, and this text is meant to illustrate how these findings can be applied in a meaningful, practical sense. For instance, applications are presented in a contemporaneous framework. The book includes current news items, timely world events, and contemporary uses of development that are designed to draw readers into the field. Numerous descriptive scenarios and vignettes reflect everyday situations in people's lives, explaining how they relate to development.

- The third goal is to illustrate both the commonalities and diversity of today's multicultural society. Consequently, every chapter has a "Developmental Diversity" section. These features explicitly consider how cultural factors relevant to development both unite and diversify our contemporary, global society. In addition, the book incorporates material relevant to diversity throughout every chapter.

- Finally, the fourth goal of the text is one that underlies the other three: making the field of development engaging, accessible, and interesting to students. Lifespan development is a joy to teach, because so much of it has direct, immediate meaning to our lives. Because all of us are involved in our own developmental paths, we are tied in very personal ways to the content areas covered by the book. *Development Across the Life Span,* then, is meant to engage and nurture this interest, planting a seed that will develop and flourish throughout readers' lifetimes.

In short, the book seeks to provide a broad overview of the field of lifespan development, integrating the theory, research, and applications of the discipline. It is meant to be a book that readers will want to keep in their own personal libraries, one that they will take off the shelf when considering problems related to that most intriguing of questions: how do people get to be the way they are?

Specific Features

CHAPTER-OPENING PROLOGUES

Each chapter begins with a short vignette, describing an individual or situation that is relevant to the basic developmental issues being addressed in the chapter. For instance, the chapter on prenatal development describes the birth of septuplets; one of the chapters on adolescence provides an account of three students' lives; and a chapter on middle adulthood discusses a 47-year-old who returns to college.

PROLOGUE: **MULTIPLICITY**

Kenny and Bobbi McCaughey, parents of septuplets born in Iowa.

O n a warm and sunny day . . . , Kathy Addleman drove from her home in Mason City, Iowa, 130 miles south to the town of Carlisle to check on the pregnancy of her daughter-in-law

LOOKING AHEAD SECTIONS

These opening sections orient readers to the topics to be covered, bridging the opening prologue with the remainder of the chapter and providing orienting questions.

LOOKING AHEAD

It was true: After taking a fertility drug to stimulate pregnancy, Bobbi McCaughey and her husband, Kenny, got more than they bargained for. Kenneth, Brandon, Alexis, Nathan, Joel, Sue, and Kelsey—seven of them—arrived one November afternoon. It was more likely that Bobbi McCaughey would be struck dead by a falling asteroid than conceive and deliver that many children.

Although an extreme case, the conception of the McCaughey septuplets is part of an everyday miracle involved in the first stirrings of all new life. In this chapter, we'll examine what researchers in child development and other scientists have learned about ways that heredity and the environment work in tandem to create and shape human beings. We begin with the basics of heredity, examining how we receive our genetic endowment. We consider a burgeoning area of study, behavioral genetics, that specializes in the consequences of heredity on behavior. The chapter also discusses what happens when genetic factors cause development to go awry, and how such problems are dealt with through genetic counseling and the brave new world of cloning and genetic engineering.

- What is our basic genetic endowment, and how can human development go awry?
- How do the environment and genetics work together to determine human characteristics?
- Which human characteristics are significantly influenced by heredity?
- What happens during the prenatal stages of development?
- What are the threats to the fetal environment and what can be done about them?

DIRECTIONS IN DEVELOPMENT

Each chapter includes a box that describes current developmental research or research issues, applied to everyday problems. For instance, these sections include discussions of gene therapy and cloning, child abuse, bullying, adolescents in cyberspace, the downside of self-esteem, and new approaches to increasing the life span.

Directions in Development

Hello Dolly: Gene Therapy and Cloning

I n all ways she appeared to be an ordinary sheep, not much to look at, with little in the way of personality. But in one way she was far from ordinary, for Dolly, as she was called, was the first animal to be cloned from the cells of an adult. An exact genetic replica of another adult sheep, Dolly was soon followed by other cloned animals who were genetically identical to adults (Pennisi, 1997; Kolata, 1998).

The technological advance that Dolly represents does more than raise ethical questions about the possibility of making genetic replicas of adult humans. It also holds the possibility of correcting genetic flaws even before an individual is born—a procedure that likely will revolutionize medicine in the 21st century.

Already, some forms of gene therapy are being used to correct genetic defects in humans. In *gene therapy*, researchers inject genes that are targeted to correct a particular disease into a patient's blood stream. When the genes arrive at the site of the defective genes that are causing the disease, their presence leads to the production of chemicals that can treat the prob-

Dolly, the cloned sheep, had raised significant ethical questions.

Developmental Diversity

Cultural Differences in Physical Arousal: Might a Culture's Philosophical Outlook Be Determined by Genetics?

The Buddhist philosophy, an inherent part of many Asian cultures, emphasizes harmony and peacefulness, and suggests that one should seek the eradication of human desire. In contrast, some of the traditional philosophies of Western civilization, such as those of Martin Luther and John Calvin, accentuate the importance of controlling the anxiety, fear, and guilt that are thought to be basic parts of the human condition.

Could such philosophical approaches reflect, in part, genetic factors? That is the controversial suggestion made by developmental psychologist Jerome Kagan and his colleagues. They speculate that the underlying temperament of a given society, determined genetically, may predispose people in that society toward a particular philosophy (Kagan, Arcus, & Snidman, 1993).

Kagan bases his admittedly speculative suggestion on well-confirmed findings that show clear differences in temperament between Caucasian and Asian children. For instance, one study that compared 4-month-old infants in China, Ireland, and the United States found several relevant differences. In comparison to the Caucasian American babies and the Irish babies, the

DEVELOPMENTAL DIVERSITY

Every chapter has at least one "Developmental Diversity" section incorporated into the text. These sections highlight issues relevant to the multicultural society in which we live. Examples of these sections include discussions of developing racial and ethnic awareness in childhood, cultural differences in approaches to academic success, cultural differences in health beliefs, gay and lesbian relationships, and cultural constructions of age milestones.

The Informed Consumer of Development

Optimizing the Prenatal Environment

If you are contemplating ever having a child, by this point in the chapter you may be overwhelmed by the number of things that can go wrong. Don't be. Although both genetics and the environment pose their share of risks, in the vast majority of cases, pregnancy and birth proceed without mishap. Moreover, there are several things that women can do to optimize the probability that pregnancy will progress smoothly—both before and during pregnancy. Among them:

■ For women who are planning to become pregnant, several precautions are in order. First, women should have non-emergency X-rays only during the first 2 weeks after their

eating for two. This means that it is more essential than ever to eat regular, well-balanced meals.

■ Do not use alcohol and other drugs. The evidence is clear that many drugs pass directly to the fetus and may cause birth defects. It is also clear that the more one drinks, the greater the risk to the fetus. The best advice: Do not use *any* drug unless directed by a physician.

■ Monitor caffeine intake. Although it is still unclear whether caffeine produces birth defects, it is known that the caffeine found in coffee, tea, and chocolate can pass to the fetus, acting as a stimulant. Because of this, you probably should not drink more than a few cups of coffee a day.

■ Whether pregnant or not, do not smoke. This holds true for mothers, fathers, and anyone else in the vicinity of the pregnant mother, because research suggests that smoke in the fetal environment can affect birth weight.

THE INFORMED CONSUMER OF DEVELOPMENT

Every chapter includes information on specific uses that can be derived from research conducted by developmental investigators. For instance, the text provides concrete information on optimizing the prenatal environment, keeping preschoolers healthy, assessing language development, choosing a day-care provider, using discipline effectively, choosing a career, and caring for people with Alzheimer's disease.

SPEAKING OF DEVELOPMENT

Jeff Milunsky, Geneticist

Education: . . . . Boston University, B.A. in biology; Boston University School of Medicine, M.D.

Position: . . . . Director of Clinical Genetics, Center for Human Genetics, Boston University School of Medicine; Assistant Professor of Pediatrics, Boston University School of Medicine

Home: . . . . West Roxbury, Massachusetts

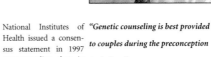

The last 10 years of the 20th century has brought important advances in all areas of medicine, particularly in the field of genetics. Progress in our knowledge of genetics has made the specialty of prenatal genetics possible.

National Institutes of Health issued a consensus statement in 1997 recommending that, in

"Genetic counseling is best provided to couples during the preconception period. . . ."

SPEAKING OF DEVELOPMENT

Each chapter includes an interview with a person working in a field that uses the findings of lifespan development. Among those interviewed are a toy designer, the chief of the marriage and family statistics branch of the U.S. Census Bureau, a former U.S. Secretary of Education, a child-care provider, and a director of senior citizens programs.

COMPANION WEBSITE (CW) LINKS

A new and significant feature in this edition, Companion Website Links are marginal icons indicating material related to a page on the World Wide Web. Readers can refer to the page number on the *Development Across the Life Span* Web page, where hotlinks are provided to the relevant Websites. *The Development Across the Life Span* Website can be found at http://www.prenhall.com/feldman.

bred to have significantly *different* genetic backgrounds on particular traits. Then, by exposing such animals to identical environments, they can determine the role that genetic background plays.

Of course, the drawback to using nonhumans as research subjects is that we cannot be sure how well the findings we obtain can be generalized to people. Still, the opportunities that animal research offers are substantial.

Human Studies: Exploiting Genetic Similarities and Dissimilarities.   Obviously, researchers can't control either the genetic backgrounds or the environments of humans in the way they can with nonhumans. However, nature conveniently has provided the potential to carry out various kinds of "natural" studies—in the form of twins.

Recall that identical, monozygotic twins share an identical genetic code. Because their inherited backgrounds are precisely the same, any variations in their behavior must be due

CW

REVIEW AND RETHINK SECTIONS

Interspersed throughout each chapter are three short recaps of the chapters' main points, followed by questions designed to provoke critical thinking.

REVIEW AND RETHINK

REVIEW

■ In humans, the male sex cell (the sperm) and the female sex cell (the ovum) provide the developing baby with 23 chromosomes each, through which the baby inherits characteristics from both mother and father.

■ A genotype is the underlying combination of genetic material present in an organism, but invisible; a phenotype is the visible trait, the expression of the genotype. Within a range predetermined by the genotype, environmental factors play a significant role in determining the way in which that genotype will be expressed as a phenotype.

RETHINK

■ How might adopted children develop traits similar to those of their adoptive parents? What sorts of traits do you think might be shared or different in adoptive families?

RUNNING GLOSSARY

Key terms are defined in the margins of the page on which the term is presented.

genetic counseling   the discipline that focuses on helping people deal with issues relating to inherited disorders

amniocentesis   the process of identifying genetic defects by examining a small sample of fetal cells drawn by a needle inserted into the amniotic fluid surrounding the unborn fetus

LOOKING BACK

END-OF-CHAPTER MATERIAL

Each chapter ends with Looking Back and a list of key terms and concepts. This material is designed to help students study and retain the information in the chapter. Every chapter also ends with a short epilogue that includes critical-thinking questions relating to the prologue at the opening of the chapter. Because the opening prologues serve as case studies that foreshadow the topics that the chapter will address, these end-of-chapter thought-provoking questions provide a way of tying the chapter together. They also illustrate how the concepts addressed in the chapter can be applied to the real-world situation described in the opening prologue.

Q&A ■ **What is our basic genetic endowment, and how can human development go awry?**

• In human fertilization, ovum and sperm unite to form a single new cell called a zygote, which receives 23 chromosomes from each parent. Within its 46 chromosomes is the genetic blueprint that will guide cell activity for the rest of the individual's life.

• Gregor Mendel discovered an important genetic mechanism that governs the interactions of dominant and recessive genes and their expression in alleles. Traits such as hair and eye color and the presence of phenylketonuria (PKU) are alleles and follow this pattern.

EPILOGUE: MULTIPLICITY

We've discussed the basics of heredity and genetics in this chapter, including the way in which the code of life is transmitted across generations through DNA. We have also seen how genetic transmission can go wrong, and we have discussed ways in which genetic disorders can

KEY TERMS AND CONCEPTS

gametes (p. 46)   *amniocentesis* (p. 56)
fertilization (p. 46)   *chorionic villus sampling (CVS)* (p. 56)
zygote (p. 46)   *ultrasound sonography* (p. 56)

What's New in This Edition?

A considerable number of new topics and areas have been added to the second edition. For example, the coverage of behavioral genetics, cloning, evolutionary approaches, and Vygotsky receive significant new coverage. In addition, a wealth of contemporary research is cited in this edition. Hundreds of new research citations have been added, most from the last few years.

A sampling of topics that have been either newly included or expanded also illustrates the scope of the revision; they include new material on ethnography, gene therapy, new breast-feeding guidelines, automaticity in information processing, the NICHD study on infant care, memory and eyewitness testimony of children, use of Prozac and childhood depression, emotional intelligence, adolescent Internet surfing, the downside of self-esteem, racial and ethnic identity formation, effects of welfare reform, estrogen supplement dilemma, the cultural construction of midlife, increasing the life span, changes in the view of neuronal loss in late adulthood, assisted care living arrangements, theory of mind in late adulthood.

Furthermore, several entirely new features have been added to the second edition. As mentioned earlier, each chapter contains *Companion Website* Links that lead readers to the *Development Across the Life Span website,* where they will be directed to specific websites relevant to the topic being discussed. In addition, every chapter now ends with an Epilogue that includes critical-thinking questions regarding the chapter prologue, tying the material in the chapter together.

Teaching Supports That Accompany the Book

Development Across the Life Span, second edition, is accompanied by a superb set of teaching and learning materials. They include the following:

Instructor's Resource Manual: Prepared by Susan Horton and Gayla Preisser of Mesa Community College, this IRM contains a wealth of teaching tips and creative ideas for new and experienced instructors alike. Each chapter includes: Learning Objectives, Key Terms/Concepts, Chapter Outline, Lecture Suggestions, Cooperative Learning Activities, Critical Thinking Questions/Exercises, Assignment Ideas, Reflective Journal Exercises, Suggested Films and Videos, and Classroom Handouts.

Prentice Hall Color Overhead Transparencies for Human Development: Available in acetate form, or as downloads from our Companion Website, these transparencies will add visual appeal to your discussion of key concepts in Developmental Psychology.

Test Item File: Prepared by Blaine Peden of University of Wisconsin, Eau Claire, this test item file contains over 2000 multiple choice, true/false, and short answer essay questions of varying levels of difficulty as well as factual, conceptual, and applied questions.

Prentice Hall Custom Tests: Available in two platforms, Windows and Macintosh, to allow instructors complete flexibility in building and editing their own customized tests. Advances in the most recent version of the software now allow online testing on a network and the **www**.

Toll-Free Telephone Test Preparation: Prentice Hall offers a telephone test preparation service through which instructors can call a toll-free number and select up to 200 questions from the printed *Test Item File* available with the text. The test, an alternate version, and the answer key are mailed or faxed within hours of the initial request.

Development Across the Life Span Companion Website Faculty Module: Providing online access to key instructor resources, this module of the Companion Website includes Lecture Outlines, Classroom Activity Suggestions, Powerpoint Presentation Slides and downloads of graphics from the text. Visit this site online at ***www.prenhall.com/feldman***.

WebCT: For instructors interested in distance learning, Prentice Hall and WebCT Educational Technologies offer a fully customizable, online course with www Links, online testing, and many other course management features using the popular WebCT online course architecture. See your local Prentice Hall representative or visit our special Demonstration Central website at *www.prenhall.com/demo*.

Video Support Materials

Speaking of Development Videos: Providing students with information about job opportunities in many fields, this exlusive video tape program features interviews with eleven of the professionals highlighted within this text. Each segment visits the individual's workplace, discusses their background in developmental psychology and how it relates to their current job.

ABCNEWS   *ABC News/Prentice Hall Video Libraries:* Consisting of brief segments from award-winning programs such as "Nightline," "20/20," "PrimeTime Live," and "The Health Show," these videos discuss current issues and are a great way to launch your lectures. The following three video libraries are available to adopters of *Development Across the Life Span:*
Human Development 1998
Lifespan Development 1996
Child Development 1995

Student Supplements

Study Guide: Written by Carolyn Meyer, this study guide is designed to help students get the most out of the textbook. Each chapter includes a Study Outline, Learning Objectives, Critical Thinking and Application Questions, a Guided Review, Practice Tests, Key Names, and Key Terms with Definitions.

Development Across the Life Span Companion Website: Written by Lynn Vestal, this online study guide provides unique tools and support that integrate the world wide web into your course. Tied specifically to this text, each chapter includes Multiple Choice, True/False, Fill-In and Short Essay quizzes. Other activities include NetSearch, Web Destination, Chat Room and Bulletin Board. Visit this site online at *www.prenhall.com/feldman*.

Feldman Interactive Student CD-ROM: Available in the Fall, 1999, to purchasers of *Development Across the Life Span,* second edition, *Feldman Interactive* is a multimedia version of the text. Integrated into each chapter of an electronic version of this text are Author Tip Videos, Speaking of Development Videos and Activities, Theorist Biographies, Multiple Choice, True/False, Critical Thinking and Essay Quizzes, enhanced graphics, and direct access to hundreds of websites via our *Development Across the Life Span Companion Website.*

 New York Times Themes of the Time Supplement for Developmental Psychology. In an exclusive arrangement, Prentice Hall and *The New York Times* have joined forces to bring students a complimentary newspaper supplement containing recent articles discussing issues and research.

ACKNOWLEDGMENTS

I am grateful to the following reviewers who provided a wealth of comments, criticism, and encouragement:

Barbara J. Bjorklund, Florida Atlantic University; Stephen D. Brown, Mansfield University; K. Laurie Dickson, Northern Arizona University; Michael Green, University of North Carolina at Charlotte; Charles Kalish, University of Wisconsin at Madison; John A. Piel, University of North Carolina at Charlotte; Edythe H. Schwartz, California State University at Sacramento; and Matthew J. Sharps, California State University at Fresno.

I would also like to acknowledge the reviewers for the first edition: Martin W. Berkowitz, Marquette University; Peter J. Brady, Clark State Community College; Henri Sue Bynam, Indian River Community College; Craig Cowden, Northern Virginia Community College; Robin Desjardin, John Tyler Community College; Robert Frank, Oakton Community College; Robert Hensley, Kirkwood Community College; Russell Isabella, University of Utah; Robert D. Johnson, Arkansas State University; Elaine M. Justice, Old Dominion University; Albert M. Maisto, University of North Carolina at Charlotte; Cynthia Jones Neal, Wheaton College; Sherri Addis Palmer, Northeast Missouri State University; Robert F. Schultz, Fulton-Montgomery Community College; Ralph G. Soney, Western Piedmont Community College; Mary Helen C. Spear, Prince George's Community College; Linda Q. Thede, Kent State University; Frank Vitro, Texas Women's University; and Fred W. Vondracek, Penn State University.

Many others deserve a great deal of thanks. I am indebted to the many people who provided me with a superb education, first at Wesleyan University and later at the University of Wisconsin. Specifically, Karl Scheibe played a pivotal role in my undergraduate education, and the late Vernon Allen acted as mentor and guide through my graduate years. It was in graduate school that I learned about development, being exposed to such experts as Ross Parke, John Balling, Joel Levin, Herb Klausmeier, Frank Hooper, and many others.

My education continued when I became a professor. I am especially grateful to my colleagues at the University of Massachusetts, who make the university such as wonderful place in which to teach and do research.

Several people played central roles in the development of this book. Edward Murphy brought a keen intelligence and editorial eye to the process, and the book has been greatly strengthened by his input. Dan Hrubes and Sara Pollack Levine provided research assistance, and I am thankful for their help. Most of all, John Graiff was essential in juggling and coordinating the multiple aspects of writing this book, and I am very grateful for the central role he played.

I am also grateful to the superb Prentice Hall team that was instrumental in the development of this book. Jennifer Gilliland oversaw the project, always providing support and direction. I am grateful for her enthusiasm, intelligence, and creativity. Bill Webber, Nancy Roberts, and Phil Miller stood behind the project, and I am grateful for their continuing support. Barbara Muller, development editor, prompted and prodded me in her insistent yet always supportive way, always improving the manuscript with her thoughtful suggestions. On the production end of things, Mary Rottino, assistant managing editor and Eloise Donnelley, photo researcher, helped in giving the book its distinctive look. It's a privilege to be part of this world-class team.

I also wish to acknowledge the members of my family, who play such a pivotal role in my life. My brother, Michael; my sister-in-laws and brother-in-laws; my nieces and nephews—all make up an important part of my life. In addition, I am always indebted to the older generation of my family, who led the way in a manner I can only hope to emulate. I will always be obligated to Ethel Radler, Harry Brochstein, and the late Mary Vorwerk. Most of all, the list is headed by my father, the late Saul Feldman, and my terrific mother, Leah Brochstein.

In the end, it is my immediate family who deserves the greatest thanks. My three wonderful children, Jonathan, Joshua, and Sarah, not only are nice, smart, and good-looking, but my pride and joy. And ultimately my wife, Katherine Vorwerk, provides the love and grounding that makes everything worthwhile. I thank them, with all my love.

Robert S. Feldman
University of Massachusetts at Amherst

About the Author

Robert S. Feldman is professor of psychology at the University of Massachusetts in Amherst, where he is Director of Undergraduate Studies and recipient of the College Distinguished Teacher Award. He was educated as an undergraduate at Wesleyan University, from which he graduated with High Honors, and received a M.S. and Ph.D. from the University of Wisconsin in Madison, where he specialized in social and developmental psychology.

Among his more than 100 books, chapters, and articles, he has edited *Development of Nonverbal Behavior in Children* (Springer-Verlag), *Applications of Nonverbal Behavioral Theory and Research* (Erlbaum), and co-edited *Fundamentals of Nonverbal Behavior* (Cambridge University Press). He is the recipient of grants from the National Institute of Mental Health and the National Institute of the Disabilities and Rehabilitation Research, which have supported his research on the development of nonverbal behavior in children. A past Fulbright lecturer and research scholar, he is a Fellow of the American Psychological Association and American Psychological Society.

During the course of nearly two decades as a college instructor, he has taught both undergraduate and graduate courses at Mount Holyoke College, Wesleyan University, Virginia Commonwealth University, in addition to the University of Massachusetts.

Professor Feldman is an avid, if unaccomplished, pianist, and an excellent cook. He has three children, and he and his wife, a psychologist, live in Amherst, Massachusetts, in a home overlooking the Holyoke mountain range.

Development
Across the Life Span

An Introduction
to Lifespan Development

PROLOGUE: VIOLENCE AT SCHOOL

A mother and daughter are reunited following the shootings that left more than a dozen students and a teacher dead at Columbine High School in Littleton, Colorado. The incident raises a variety of issues relating to development across the life span.

When two students went on a rampage at Littleton, Colorado's Columbine High School one bright April morning, the result was shocking. The killers, who targeted blacks and athletes, murdered 13 fellow students and a teacher and planted dozens of bombs around the school. At the end of the shooting spree, they took their own lives.

In retrospect, the signs of impending violence seemed obvious. One of the pair created a Web page containing death threats, and the two had made a video for a class that foreshadowed the massacre. One had a bedroom filled with Nazi and hate literature and explosives. They threatened fellow students, saying, "just wait" to those who made fun of the black trenchcoats they wore as members of the "Trenchcoat Mafia." Minor disagreements with others turned into threats of violence. In a philosophy class, one spoke incessantly about purchasing a gun.

Still, no one could predict the direction their anger would take. As the killers ran through the school, laughing, students hid in storage rooms, offices, and closets to escape the danger. Some students escaped by sheer luck. One of the killers pointed a gun at a potential victim but then inexplicably turned away.

But despite the terror of the situation, the day brought great heroism on the part of many. Students and teachers shielded one another, and people risked their lives to help others. Teacher Chris Mosier led 50 students into a classroom, telling them to lie on the floor. Students helped one another remain calm, quietly praying and offering support to one another.

LOOKING AHEAD   The shooting spree at Columbine High represents many sides of human nature. It also raises a number of significant developmental issues. For example, lifespan developmentalists with different professional emphases would look at the incident in the following ways.

- Developmentalists who investigate behavior at the level of biological functioning would seek to determine whether the incident will produce changes in stress-related hormonal levels.

- Developmentalists who study memory might seek to determine what aspects of the incident will be remembered by the students who witnessed the attack when they are older.

- Developmentalists who study social development may study how the relationships between various groups and cliques in the high school may be related to the incident.

- Developmentalists who study the roots of violence might examine why the perpetrators carried out their attack on the school, seeking to explain the roots of such agression.

- Developmentalists who study the consequences of loss and death might seek to understand the experiences of people who lost family members and loved ones in the attack.

Although their interests take many forms, all these specialists in lifespan development share one concern: understanding the growth and change that occur during the course of life. Taking many differing approaches, developmentalists study how both our biological inheritance from our parents and the environment in which we live jointly affect our behavior.

Some developmentalists focus on explaining how our genetic background can determine not only how we look but also how we behave, how we relate to others—that is, matters of personality. These professionals explore ways to identify how much of our potential as human beings is provided—or limited—by heredity. Other lifespan development specialists look to the environment, exploring ways in which our lives are shaped by the world that we encounter. They investigate the extent to which we are shaped by our early environments, and how our current circumstances influence our behavior in both subtle and evident ways.

Whether they focus on heredity or environment, all developmental specialists acknowledge that neither heredity nor environment alone can account for the full range of human development and change. Instead, our understanding of people's development requires that we look at the joint effects of the interaction of heredity and environment, attempting to grasp how both, in the end, underlie human behavior.

In this chapter, we orient ourselves to the field of lifespan development. We begin with a discussion of the scope of the discipline, illustrating the wide array of topics it covers and the full range of ages it examines, from the moment of conception to death. We also survey the key issues and controversies of the field.

Next, we continue with a consideration of the broad perspectives that developmentalists take, from a focus on people's inner, unconscious lives and the interior operation of their minds to people's outward, overt behavior.

Finally, we discuss the ways developmentalists use research to ask and answer questions. We discuss several research strategies, as well as ethical guidelines for conducting research.

In sum, after reading this chapter, you will be able to answer these questions:

Q

- **What is lifespan development, and what are some of the basic influences on development?**
- **What are the key issues in the field of development?**
- **Which theoretical perspectives have guided lifespan development?**
- **What role do theories and hypotheses play in the study of development?**
- **How are developmental research studies conducted?**

AN ORIENTATION TO LIFESPAN DEVELOPMENT

Have you ever marveled at the way an infant tightly grips your finger with tiny, perfectly formed hands? Or at how a preschooler methodically draws a picture? Or at the way an adolescent can make involved decisions about whom to invite to a party? Or the way a middle-aged politician can deliver a long, flawless speech from memory? Or how an 80-year-old grandfather is able to roughhouse with his grandchild?

If you've ever wondered about such things, you are asking the kinds of questions that scientists in the field of lifespan development pose. **Lifespan development** is the field of study that examines patterns of growth, change, and stability in behavior that occur throughout the entire life span.

Although the definition of the field seems straightforward, the simplicity is somewhat misleading. To understand what development is actually about, we need to look underneath the various parts of the definition.

In its study of growth, change, and stability, lifespan development takes a *scientific* approach. Like members of other scientific disciplines, researchers in lifespan development test their assumptions about the nature and course of human development by applying scientific methods. As we'll see later in the chapter, they develop theories about development, and they use methodical, scientific techniques to validate the accuracy of their assumptions systematically.

Lifespan development focuses on *human* development. Although there are developmentalists who study the course of development in nonhuman species, the vast majority examine growth and change in people. Some seek to understand universal principles of development, whereas others focus on how cultural, racial, and ethnic differences affect the course of development. Still others aim to understand the unique aspects of individuals, looking at the traits and characteristics that differentiate one person from another. Regardless of approach, however, all developmentalists view development as a continuing process throughout the life span.

As developmental specialists focus on the ways people change and grow during their lives, they also consider stability in people's lives. They ask in which areas, and in what periods, people show change and growth, and when and how their behavior reveals consistency and continuity with prior behavior.

Finally, developmentalists assume that the process of development persists throughout every part of people's lives, beginning with the moment of conception and continuing until death. Developmental specialists assume that in some ways people continue to grow and change right up to the end of their lives, whereas in other respects their behavior remains stable. At the same time, developmentalists believe that no particular, single period of life governs all development. Instead, they believe that every period of life contains the potential for both growth and decline in abilities, and that individuals maintain the capacity for substantial growth and change throughout their lives.

lifespan development the field of study that examines patterns of growth, change, and stability in behavior that occur throughout the entire life span

physical development *development involving the body's physical makeup, including the brain, nervous system, muscles, and senses, and the need for food, drink, and sleep*

cognitive development *development involving the ways that growth and change in intellectual capabilities influence a person's behavior*

personality development *development involving the ways that the enduring characteristics that differentiate one person from another change over the life span*

social development *the way in which individuals' interactions with others and their social relationships grow, change, and remain stable over the course of life*

Developmentalists study people across the entire life span.

Characterizing Lifespan Development: The Scope of the Field

Clearly, the definition of lifespan development is broad and the scope of the field is extensive. Consequently, lifespan development specialists cover several quite diverse areas, and a typical developmentalist specializes in two ways: topical area and age range.

Topical Areas in Lifespan Development. Some developmentalists focus on **physical development**, examining the ways in which the body's makeup—the brain, nervous system, muscles, and senses, and the need for food, drink, and sleep—helps determine behavior. For example, one specialist in physical development might examine the effects of malnutrition on the pace of growth in children, whereas another might look at how reaction time changes during adulthood.

Other developmental specialists examine **cognitive development**, seeking to understand how growth and change in intellectual capabilities influence a person's behavior. Cognitive developmentalists examine learning, memory, problem solving, and intelligence. For example, specialists in cognitive development might want to see how intellectual abilities change over the course of life, or whether cultural differences exist in the factors to which people attribute their academic successes and failures.

Finally, some developmental specialists focus on personality and social development. **Personality development** is the study of stability and change in the enduring characteristics that differentiate one person from another over the life span. **Social development** is the way in which individuals' interactions with others and their social relationships grow, change, and remain stable over the course of life. A developmentalist interested in personality development might ask whether there are stable, enduring personality traits throughout the life span, whereas a specialist in social development might examine marriage and divorce during adulthood. (The major approaches are summarized in Table 1-1.)

Age Ranges and Individual Differences. As they specialize in chosen topical areas, developmentalists typically look at particular age ranges. The life span is usually divided into broad age ranges: the prenatal period (the period from conception to birth); infancy and toddlerhood (birth to age 3); the preschool period (ages 3 to 6); middle childhood (ages 6 to 12); adolescence (ages 12 to 20); young adulthood (ages 20 to 40); middle age (ages 40 to 60); and late adulthood (age 60 to death).

Although most lifespan developmentalists accept and employ these broad periods (and they are used to demarcate the major parts of this book), the age ranges themselves are in many ways arbitrary. Although some periods have one clear-cut boundary (infancy begins with birth, the preschool period ends with entry into public school, and adolescence starts with sexual maturity), others don't.

For instance, consider the period of young adulthood, which is typically assumed to begin at age 20. That age, however, is notable only because it marks the end of the teenage period. In fact for many people, such as those enrolled in higher education, the age change from 19 to 20 has little special significance, coming as it does in the middle of the college years. For them, more substantial changes may occur when they leave college and enter the workforce, which is more likely to happen around age 22.

In short, the timing of events in individual people's lives differs substantially. In part, this is a biological fact of life: People mature at different rates and reach developmental milestones at different points. However, environmental factors also play a significant role in determining the age at which a particular event is likely to occur. For example, the typical age of marriage varies substantially from one culture to another, depending in part on the functions that marriage plays in a given culture.

It is important to keep in mind, then, that when developmental specialists discuss age ranges, they are talking about averages—the times when people, on average, reach particular milestones. Some people will reach the milestone earlier, some later, and many—in fact, most—will reach it just around the time of the average. Such variation becomes noteworthy only when children show substantial deviation from the average.

TABLE 1-1

APPROACHES TO LIFESPAN DEVELOPMENT

Orientation	Defining Characteristics	Examples of Questions Asked*
Physical development	Examines how brain, nervous system, muscles, sensory capabilities, needs for food, drink, and sleep affect behavior	What determines the sex of a child? (2) What are the long-term results of premature birth? (3) What are the benefits of breast-feeding? (4) What are the consequences of early or late sexual maturation? (11) What leads to obesity in adulthood? (13) How do adults cope with stress? (15) What are the outward and internal signs of aging? (17) How do we define death? (19)
Cognitive development	Examines intellectual abilities, including learning, memory, problem solving, and intelligence	What are the earliest memories that can be recalled from infancy? (5) What are the consequences of watching television? (7) Do spatial reasoning skills relate to music practice? (7) Are there benefits to bilingualism? (9) How does an adolescent's egocentrism affect his or her view of the world? (11) Are there ethnic and racial differences in intelligence? (9) How does creativity relate to intelligence? (13) Does intelligence decline in late adulthood? (17)
Personality and social development	Examines enduring characteristics that differentiate one person from another, and how interactions with others and social relationships grow and change over the lifetime	Do newborns respond differently to their mothers than to others? (3) What is the best procedure for disciplining children? (8) When does a sense of gender develop? (8) How can we promote cross-race friendships? (10) What are the causes of adolescent suicide? (12) How do we choose a romantic partner? (14) Do the effects of parental divorce last into old age? (18) Do people withdraw from others in late adulthood? (18) What are the stages of confronting death? (19)

*Numbers in parentheses indicate in which chapter the question is addressed.

Furthermore, as people become older, it becomes more likely that they will deviate from the average and exhibit individual differences. In very young children a good part of developmental change is genetically determined and unfolds automatically, making development fairly similar across different children. But as people age, environmental factors become more potent, leading to greater variability and individual differences as time passes.

The Links Between Topics and Ages.   Each of the broad topical areas of lifespan development—physical, cognitive, and social and personality development—plays a role throughout the life span. Consequently, some developmental experts focus on physical development during the prenatal period, and others during adolescence. Some might specialize in social development during the preschool years, whereas others look at social relationships in late adulthood. And still others might take a broader approach, looking at cognitive development through every period of life.

The Context of Development: Taking a Broad Perspective

Considering the course of development in terms of physical, cognitive, and personality and social factors has advantages and disadvantages. It allows us to divide developmental influences into reasonably neat and compact packages. But such a categorization has one serious

BRONFENBRENNER'S APPROACH
TO DEVELOPMENT

Urie Bronfenbrenner's ecological approach
to development offers four levels of the
environment that simultaneously influence
individuals: the macrosystem, exosystem,
mesosystem, and microsystem.

(*Source:* Koop & Krakow, 1982)

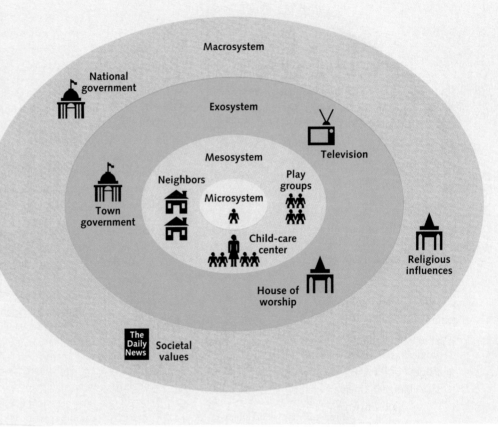

drawback: In the real world, none of these broad influences occurs in isolation from any other. Instead, a constant, ongoing interaction exists between the different types of influence. For instance, what occurs on a cognitive level has repercussions for personality, social, and physical development, and what is happening on a physical level has an impact on cognitive, personality, and social development.

 The Ecological Approach to Development.   In acknowledging the problem with traditional approaches to lifespan development, psychologist Urie Bronfenbrenner (1979, 1989) has proposed an alternative perspective, called the ecological approach. The **ecological approach** suggests that there are four levels of the environment that simultaneously influence individuals. Bronfenbrenner suggests that we cannot fully understand development without considering how a person fits into each of these levels (illustrated in Figure 1-1).

The *microsystem* is the everyday, immediate environment in which people lead their daily lives. Homes, caregivers, friends, and teachers all are examples of the influences that are part of the microsystem.

The *mesosystem* provides connections between the various aspects of the microsystem. Like links in a chain, the mesosystem binds children to parents, students to teachers, employees to bosses, friends to friends. It acknowledges the direct and indirect influences that bind us to one another, such as those that affect a mother who has a bad day at the office and then is short-tempered with her daughter at home.

The *exosystem* represents broader influences, encompassing societal institutions such as local government, the community, schools, places of worship, and the local media. Each of these larger institutions of society can have an immediate, and major, impact on personal development, and each affects how the microsystem and mesosystem operate.

ecological approach   the perspective suggesting that different levels of the environment simultaneously influence individuals

Governmental bodies, such as this state assembly, illustrate the exosystem: societal institutions that influence personal development.

Finally, the *macrosystem* represents the larger cultural influences on an individual. Society in general, types of governments, religious systems, political thought, and other broad, encompassing factors are parts of the macrosystem.

The ecological approach provides several advantages. For one thing, it emphasizes the interconnectedness of the influences on development. Because the various levels are related to one another, a change in one part of the system affects other parts of the system. For instance, a parent's loss of a job (involving the mesosystem) has an impact on a child's microsystem.

Conversely, changes on one environmental level may make little difference if other levels are not also changed. For instance, improving the school environment may have a negligible effect on academic performance if children receive little support for academic success in their home environment. Similarly, the ecological approach illustrates that the influences among different family members are multidirectional. Parents don't just influence their child's behavior—the child also influences the parents' behavior.

Finally, the ecological approach stresses the importance of broad cultural factors that affect development. Researchers in development increasingly look at how membership in cultural and subcultural groups influences behavior. For instance, Western cultures generally tend to be *individualistic*, emphasizing personal identity, uniqueness, freedom, and the worth of the individual. In contrast, Asian cultures are largely *collectivistic*, promoting the idea that the group or society is more important than the individual. As we'll see in Chapter 12, such broad cultural values play an important role in shaping the ways people view the world and behave (Kim et al., 1994; Dent-Read & Zukow-Goldring, 1997; de Mooij, 1998).

Cohort and Normative Influences on Development: Developing with Others in a Social World.   Bob, born in 1947, is a baby boomer; he was born soon after the end of World War II, when an enormous bulge in the birth rate occurred as soldiers returned to the United States from overseas. He was an adolescent at the height of the Civil Rights movement and the beginning of protests against the Vietnam War. His mother, Leah, was born in 1922; she is part of the generation that passed its childhood and teenage years in the shadow of the Great Depression. Bob's son, Jon, was born in 1975. Now starting his first job after graduating from college, he is a member of what has been called Generation X.

These people are in part products of the social times in which they live. Each belongs to a particular **cohort**, a group of people born at around the same time in the same place. Such major social events as wars, economic upturns and depressions, famines, and epidemics (such as the one due to the AIDS virus) work similar influences on members of a particular cohort.

cohort   *a group of people born at around the same time in the same place*

Cohort effects provide an example of **normative history-graded influences**, which are biological and environmental influences associated with a particular historical moment (Baltes, Reese, & Lipsitt, 1980; Baltes, 1987). For instance, people who lived in Oklahoma City, Oklahoma, in 1995 shared both biological and environmental challenges due to the terrorist bombing of the federal building in that city.

Normative history-graded influences contrast with **normative age-graded influences**, biological and environmental influences that are similar for individuals in a particular age group, regardless of when or where they are raised. For example, biological events such as puberty and menopause are universal events that occur at relatively the same time throughout all societies. Similarly, a sociocultural event such as entry into formal education can be considered a normative age-graded influence because it occurs in most cultures around age six.

Development is also affected by normative sociocultural-graded influences. **Normative sociocultural-graded influences** represent the impact of social and cultural factors present at a particular time for a particular individual, depending on such variables as ethnicity, social class, and subcultural membership. For example, sociocultural-graded influences will be considerably different for children who are white and affluent than for children who are members of a minority group and living in poverty.

Finally, nonnormative life events also influence development. **Nonnormative life events** are specific, atypical events that occur in a particular person's life at a time when such events do not happen to most people. For instance, experiencing at an early age the death of both parents, being involved in a serious auto accident, coming down with a deadly disease, or having a physical disability are all nonnormative life events.

KEY ISSUES AND QUESTIONS: DETERMINING THE NATURE—AND NURTURE—OF LIFESPAN DEVELOPMENT

Compared with other sciences, lifespan development is one of the new kids on the block. Although its roots can be traced back to the ancient Egyptians and Greeks, it became established as a separate field only in the late nineteenth and early twentieth centuries.

From the time of its establishment, several key issues and questions have dominated the field. Among the major issues (summarized in Table 1-2) are the nature of developmental change, the importance of critical periods, lifespan approaches versus more focused approaches, and the nature–nurture issue (Kagan, 1994; Parke et al., 1994).

Continuous Change Versus Discontinuous Change. One of the primary issues challenging developmentalists is whether development proceeds in a continuous or discontinuous fashion. In **continuous change**, development is gradual, with achievements at one level building on those of previous levels. Continuous change is quantitative in nature; the basic underlying developmental processes that drive change remain the same over the course of the life span. Continuous change, then, produces changes that are a matter of degree, not of kind.

In contrast, **discontinuous change** occurs in distinct steps or stages. Each stage brings about behavior that is assumed to be qualitatively different from behavior at earlier stages.

Although developmentalists generally believe that most developmental growth is continuous, there are clearly some exceptions. In fact, most developmentalists agree that taking an either/or position on the continuous–discontinuous issue is inappropriate. In this view, some types of developmental change may be continuous, whereas others are discontinuous (Rutter, 1987; Flavell, 1994).

Critical Periods: Gauging the Impact of Environmental Events. If a woman comes down with a case of rubella (German measles) in the 11th week of pregnancy, the consequences for the child she is carrying are likely to be devastating: They include the potential

---

normative history-graded influences *biological and environmental influences associated with a particular historical moment*

normative age-graded influences *biological and environmental influences that are similar for individuals in a particular age group, regardless of when or where they are raised*

normative sociocultural-graded influences *the impact of social and cultural factors present at a particular time for a particular individual, depending on such variables as ethnicity, social class, and subcultural membership*

nonnormative life events *specific, atypical events that occur in a particular person's life at a time when they do not happen to most people*

continuous change *gradual development in which achievements at one level build on those of previous levels*

discontinuous change *development that occurs in distinct steps or stages, with each stage bringing about behavior that is assumed to be qualitatively different from behavior at earlier stages*

TABLE 1-2

MAJOR ISSUES IN LIFESPAN DEVELOPMENT

Issue	Explanation
Continuous change vs. discontinuous change	In continuous change, development is gradual; the achievements at one level build on the previous one. The underlying developmental processes driving the change remain the same over the course of the life span. In contrast, discontinuous change occurs in distinct steps or stages, with each stage bringing about behavior that is assumed to be qualitatively different from that seen at earlier stages.
Critical periods	A critical period is a particular time during development in which a particular event has its greatest consequences. Although early developmental psychologists placed great emphasis on the importance of critical periods, more recent thinking suggests that in many areas individuals may be more malleable than was first thought, particularly in the area of personality and social development.
Lifespan approaches vs. focus on particular periods	Earlier developmental psychologists studying the life span focused attention primarily on the infancy and adolescence periods. Current thinking sees the entire life span as important for a number of reasons, including the discovery that developmental growth and change continue throughout every part of life.
Nature–nurture issue	Nature refers to traits, abilities, and capabilities that are inherited from one's parents. It encompasses any factor that is produced by the predetermined unfolding of genetic information. Nurture, on the other hand, involves the environmental influences that shape behavior. Some may be biological, whereas others are more social in nature. Some influences are a result of larger societal-level factors, such as the socio-economic opportunities available to members of minority groups.

for blindness, deafness, and heart defects. However, if she comes down with the exact same strain of rubella in the 30th week of pregnancy, damage to the child is unlikely.

The differing outcomes of the disease in the two periods demonstrate the concept of critical periods. A **critical period** is a specific time during development when a particular event has its greatest consequences. Critical periods occur when the presence of certain kinds of environmental stimuli are necessary for development to proceed normally.

Although early specialists in lifespan development placed great emphasis on the importance of critical periods, more recent thinking suggests that in many realms individuals may be more malleable than was first thought, particularly in the domain of personality and social development. For instance, rather than permanent damage being caused by a lack of certain kinds of early social experiences, there is increasing evidence that later experiences can overcome earlier deficits. Consequently, more recent formulations speak of **sensitive periods**, rather than critical periods. In a sensitive period, organisms are particularly susceptible to certain kinds of stimuli in their environments. Unlike a critical period, however, the absence of those stimuli does not always produce irreversible consequences (Bornstein, 1989a).

Lifespan Approaches Versus a Focus on Particular Periods. On which part of the life span should developmentalists focus their attention? For early developmentalists, the answers tended to be "infancy" and "adolescence." Most attention was clearly concentrated on those two periods, largely to the exclusion of other parts of the life span.

Today, however, the story is different. Developmentalists now believe the entire life span is important, for several reasons. One is the discovery that developmental growth and change continue during every part of life—as we'll discuss throughout this book.

Furthermore, to understand fully the social influences on people of a given age, we need to understand the people who are in large measure providing those influences. For instance, to understand development in infants, we need to unravel the effects of their

critical period *a specific time during development when a particular event has its greatest consequences and the presence of certain kinds of environmental stimuli are necessary for development to proceed normally*

sensitive period *a point in development when organisms are particularly susceptible to certain kinds of stimuli in their environments, but the absence of those stimuli does not always produce irreversible consequences*

maturation *the predetermined unfolding of genetic information*

parents' ages on their social environments. It is likely that a 15-year-old mother will present parental influences of a very different sort from those presented by a 37-year-old mother. Consequently, infant development is in part a consequence of adult development (Parke, 1989).

Nature Versus Nurture.   One of the enduring questions of development involves how much of people's behavior is due to their genetically determined nature and how much is due to nurture, the physical and social environment in which a child is raised. This issue, which has deep philosophical and historical roots, has dominated much work in lifespan development.

In this context, *nature* refers to traits, abilities, and capacities that are inherited from one's parents. It encompasses any factor that is produced by the predetermined unfolding of genetic information—a process known as **maturation**. These genetic, inherited influences are at work as we move from the one-cell organism that is created at the moment of conception to the billions of cells that make up a fully formed human. Nature influences whether our eyes are blue or brown, whether we have thick hair throughout life or eventually go bald, and how good we are at athletics. Nature allows our brains to develop in such a way that we can read the words on this page.

In contrast, *nurture* refers to the environmental influences that shape behavior. Some of these influences may be biological, such as the impact of a pregnant mother's use of cocaine on her unborn child, or the amount and kind of food available to children. Other environmental influences are more social, such as the ways parents discipline their children and the effects of peer pressure on an adolescent. Finally, some influences are a result of larger, societal-level factors, such as the socioeconomic circumstances in which people find themselves.

If our traits and behavior were determined solely by either nature or nurture, there would probably be little debate regarding the issue. However, for most critical behaviors this is hardly the case. Take, for instance, one of the most controversial arenas: intelligence. As we'll consider in detail in Chapter 9, the question of whether intelligence is determined primarily by inherited, genetic factors—nature—or is shaped by environmental factors—nurture—has caused lively and often bitter arguments. Largely because of its social implications, the issue has spilled out of the scientific arena and into the realm of politics and social policy.

Consider the implications of the issue: If the extent of one's intelligence is primarily determined by heredity and consequently is largely fixed at birth, then efforts to improve intellectual performance later in life may be doomed to failure. In contrast, if intelligence is primarily a result of environmental factors, such as the amount and quality of schooling and stimulation to which one is exposed, then we would expect that an improvement in social conditions could bring about an increase in intelligence.

The issue becomes even more controversial when we try to determine the cause of racial differences in intelligence. For instance, the publication in 1994 of *The Bell Curve*, a book by psychologist Richard Herrnstein and sociologist Charles Murray, raised the issue of the source of differences in IQ scores between whites and African Americans, as measured by traditional tests of intelligence. The controversy concerned whether such differences could be attributed more to nature—the argument of the authors—or nurture—the position taken by many other members of the research community (Herrnstein & Murray, 1994; Nisbett, 1994; Jacoby & Glauberman, 1995; Wachs, 1996).

The ferocity of the debate, and the importance of its resolution, illustrates the significance of issues that involve the nature–nurture question. As we address it in relation to several topical areas throughout this book, we should keep in mind that developmentalists reject the notion that behavior is the result solely of either nature *or* nurture. Instead, the question is one of degree. Furthermore, the interaction of genetic and environmental factors is complex, in part because certain genetically determined traits have not only a direct influence on children's behavior, but an indirect influence in shaping children's *environments* as well. For example, a child who is consistently cranky and who cries a great deal—a trait that may be produced by genetic factors—may influence its environment by making its parents so highly responsive to its insistent crying that they rush to comfort it whenever it cries. Their responsivity to the child's genetically determined behavior consequently becomes an environmental influence on the infant's subsequent development.

In sum, the question of how much of a given behavior is due to nature and how much to nurture is a challenging one. Ultimately, we should consider the two sides of the nature–nurture issue as opposite ends of a continuum, with particular behaviors falling somewhere between the two ends. Moreover, an analogous statement can be made regarding the other controversies that we have considered. For instance, continuous versus discontinuous development is not an either/or proposition; some forms of development fall toward the continuous end of the continuum, whereas others lie closer to the discontinuous end. In short, few statements about development involve either/or absolutes.

REVIEW AND RETHINK

REVIEW

■ Lifespan development, a scientific approach to understanding human growth and change throughout life, encompasses physical, cognitive, and social and personality development.

■ Rather than being distinct categories of development, physical, cognitive, and social and personality development are mutually interactive and influence one another continuously.

■ The ecological approach considers interrelationships among aspects of human development and relationships between the individual and four levels of the environment.

■ Membership in a cohort, based on age and place of birth, subjects people to influences based on historical events (normative history-graded influences). People are also subject to normative age-graded influences (experienced by all people at a given age), normative sociocultural-graded influences (experienced by individuals within particular ethnic, social, or cultural groups), and nonnormative life events (unique to an individual).

■ Four important issues in lifespan development are continuity versus discontinuity in development, the importance of critical periods, whether to focus on certain periods or on the entire life span, and the nature–nurture controversy. Each issue is best seen not as an either/or choice, but as a continuum along which aspects of development can be placed.

RETHINK

■ What sorts of questions would you expect a developmentalist studying cognitive development to ask? How about one studying personality or social development?

■ What are some environmental factors that might influence the timing of human development?

■ How might each of the four elements of the ecological approach influence a major developmental step, such as the decision to marry or not to marry?

theories *explanations and predictions concerning phenomena of interest, providing a framework for understanding the relationships among an organized set of facts or principles*

- What are some events that might have a shared significance for members of your age cohort as normative history-graded influences? How might they produce different effects from events shared by members of different age cohorts?

- Describe one aspect of human development in each area (physical, cognitive, personality and social) that is affected by both nature and nurture.

THEORETICAL PERSPECTIVES

In Europe, there was no concept of "childhood" until the seventeenth century. Instead, children were simply thought of as miniature adults. They were assumed to be subject to the same needs and desires as adults, to have the same vices and virtues as adults, and to warrant no more privileges than adults. They were dressed the same as adults, and their work hours were the same as adults'. Children also received the same punishments for misdeeds. If they stole, they were hanged; if they did well, they could achieve prosperity.

This view of childhood seems wrong-headed now, but at the time it is what passed for lifespan development. From this perspective, there were no differences due to age; except for size, people were assumed to be virtually unchanging, at least on a psychological level, throughout most of the life span (Aries, 1962; Biemiller, 1995; Hwang, Lamb, & Sigel, 1996).

Although, looking back over several centuries, it is easy to reject the medieval view of childhood, it is less clear how to formulate a contemporary substitute. Should our view of development focus on the biological aspects of change, growth, and stability over the life span? The cognitive or social aspects? Or some other factors?

In fact, lifespan development has produced a number of broad conceptual perspectives representing different approaches to development. Each broad perspective encompasses one or more **theories**, explanations and predictions concerning phenomena of interest. A theory provides a framework for understanding the relationships among an organized set of facts or principles.

We all develop theories about development, based on our experience, folklore, and articles in magazines and newspapers. However, theories in lifespan development

Society's view of childhood, and what is appropriate to ask of children, has changed through the ages. These children worked full-time in mines in the early 1900s.

are different. Whereas our own personal theories are built on unverified observations that are developed haphazardly, developmentalists' theories are more formal, based on a systematic integration of prior findings and theorizing. These theories allow developmentalists to summarize and organize prior observations, and they allow them to move beyond existing observations to draw deductions that may not be immediately apparent.

We will consider five major theoretical perspectives used in lifespan development: the psychodynamic, behavioral, cognitive, humanistic, and evolutionary perspectives. Each emphasizes somewhat different aspects of development and steers developmentalists in particular directions. Furthermore, each perspective continues to evolve and change, as befits a growing and dynamic discipline (R. Thomas, 1996).

Sigmund Freud

The Psychodynamic Perspective: Focusing on the Inner Person

When Janet was 6 months old, she was involved in a bloody automobile accident—or so her parents tell her, since she has no conscious recollection of it. Now, however, at age 24, she is having difficulty maintaining relationships, and her therapist is seeking to determine whether her current problems are a result of the earlier accident.

Looking for a such a link might seem a bit far-fetched, but to proponents of the **psychodynamic perspective**, it is not so improbable. Advocates of the psychodynamic perspective believe that behavior is motivated by inner forces, memories, and conflicts that are generally beyond people's awareness and control. These inner forces, which may stem from one's childhood, continually influence behavior throughout the life span.

Freud's Psychoanalytic Theory.   The psychodynamic perspective is most closely associated with a single person and theory: Sigmund Freud and his psychoanalytic theory. Freud, who lived from 1856 to 1939, was a Viennese physician whose revolutionary ideas about the unconscious determinants of behavior ultimately had a profound effect not only on the fields of psychology and psychiatry, but on Western thought in general (Masling & Bornstein, 1996).

Freud's **psychoanalytic theory** suggests that unconscious forces act to determine personality and behavior. To Freud, the *unconscious* is a part of the personality about which a person is unaware. It contains infantile wishes, desires, demands, and needs that are hidden, because of their disturbing nature, from conscious awareness. Freud suggested that the unconscious is responsible for a good part of our everyday behavior.

According to Freud, one's personality has three aspects: id, ego, and superego. The **id** is the raw, unorganized, inborn part of personality that is present at birth. It represents primitive drives related to hunger, sex, aggression, and irrational impulses. These drives are fueled by what Freud called *libido*, or "psychic energy." The id operates according to the *pleasure principle*, in which the goal is to maximize satisfaction and reduce tension.

The **ego** is the part of personality that is rational and reasonable. Providing a reality check for the demands of the id, the ego acts as a buffer between the outside world and the primitive id. The ego operates on the *reality principle*, in which instinctual energy is restrained in order to maintain the safety of the individual and help integrate the person into society.

Finally, Freud proposed that the **superego** represents a person's conscience, incorporating distinctions between right and wrong. It develops around age 5 or 6 and is learned from an individual's parents, teachers, and other significant figures.

In addition to providing an account of the various parts of the personality, Freud also suggested the ways in which personality developed during childhood. He argued that **psychosexual development** occurred as children passed through a series of stages, in which

psychodynamic perspective the approach that states behavior is motivated by inner forces, memories, and conflicts that are generally beyond people's awareness and control

psychoanalytic theory the theory proposed by Freud that suggests that unconscious forces act to determine personality and behavior

id according to Freud, the raw, unorganized, inborn part of personality, present at birth, that represents primitive drives related to hunger, sex, aggression, and irrational impulses

ego according to Freud, the part of personality that is rational and reasonable

superego according to Freud, the aspect of personality that represents a person's conscience, incorporating distinctions between right and wrong

psychosexual development according to Freud, a series of stages that children pass through in which pleasure, or gratification, is focused on a particular biological function and body part

pleasure, or gratification, was focused on a particular biological function and body part. As illustrated in Table 1-3, he suggested that pleasure shifted from the mouth (the *oral stage*) to the anus (the *anal stage*) and eventually to the genitals (the *phallic stage* and the *genital stage*).

According to Freud, if children are unable to gratify themselves sufficiently during a particular stage, or, conversely, if they receive too much gratification, fixation may occur. **Fixation** is behavior reflecting an earlier stage of development due to an unresolved conflict. For instance, fixation at the oral stage might produce an adult unusually absorbed in oral activities—eating, talking, or chewing gum. Freud also argued that fixation was represented through symbolic sorts of oral activities, such as the use of "biting" sarcasm.

TABLE 1-3

FREUD'S AND ERIKSON'S THEORIES

Approximate Age	Freud's Stages of Psychosexual Development	Major Characteristics of Freud's Stages	Erikson's Stages of Psychosocial Development	Positive and Negative Outcomes of Erikson's Stages
Birth to 12–18 months	Oral	Interest in oral gratification from sucking, eating, mouthing, biting	Trust vs. mistrust	*Positive:* Feelings of trust from environmental support *Negative:* Fear and concern regarding others
12–18 months to 3 years	Anal	Gratification from expelling and withholding feces; coming to terms with society's controls relating to toilet training	Autonomy vs. shame and doubt	*Positive:* Self-sufficiency if exploration is encouraged *Negative:* Doubts about self, lack of independence
3 to 5–6 years	Phallic	Interest in the genitals; coming to terms with Oedipal conflict, leading to identification with same-sex parent	Initiative vs. guilt	*Positive:* Discovery of ways to initiate actions *Negative:* Guilt from actions and thoughts
5–6 years to adolescence	Latency	Sexual concerns largely unimportant	Industry vs. inferiority	*Positive:* Development of sense of competence *Negative:* Feelings of inferiority, no sense of mastery
Adolescence to adulthood (Freud) Adolescence (Erikson)	Genital	Reemergence of sexual interests and establishment of mature sexual relationships	Identity vs. role diffusion	*Positive:* Awareness of uniqueness of self, knowledge of role to be followed *Negative:* Inability to identify appropriate roles in life
Early adulthood (Erikson)			Intimacy vs. isolation	*Positive:* Development of loving, sexual relationships and close friendships *Negative:* Fear of relationships with others
Middle adulthood (Erikson)			Generativity vs. stagnation	*Positive:* Sense of contribution to continuity of life *Negative:* Trivialization of one's activities
Late adulthood (Erikson)			Ego-integrity vs. despair	*Positive:* Sense of unity in life's accomplishments *Negative:* Regret over lost opportunities of life

Erikson's Psychosocial Theory. Psychoanalyst Erik Erikson, who lived from 1902 to 1994, provided in his theory of psychosocial development an alternative view of how society and culture both challenge and shape us. **Psychosocial development** encompasses changes in our interactions with and understandings of one another, as well as in our knowledge and understanding of ourselves as members of society (Erikson, 1963).

Erikson's theory suggests that developmental change occurs throughout our lives in eight distinct stages (see Table 1-3). The stages emerge in a fixed pattern and are similar for all people. Erikson argues that each stage presents a crisis or conflict that the individual must resolve. Although no crisis is ever fully resolved, making life increasingly complicated, the individual must at least address the crisis of each stage sufficiently to deal with demands made during the next stage of development.

Unlike Freud, who regards development as relatively complete by adolescence, Erikson suggests that growth and change continue throughout the life span. For instance, as we'll discuss further in Chapter 16, he suggests that during middle adulthood people pass through the *generativity versus stagnation stage*, in which their contributions to family, community, and society can produce either positive feelings about the continuity of life—or a sense of stagnation and disappointment about what they are passing on to future generations.

Erik Erikson

Assessing the Psychodynamic Perspective. It is hard for us to grasp the full significance of psychodynamic theories, represented by Freud's psychoanalytic theory and Erikson's theory of psychosocial development. Freud's introduction of the notion that unconscious influences affect behavior was a monumental accomplishment, and the fact that it seems at all reasonable to us shows how extensively the idea of the unconscious has pervaded thinking in Western cultures. In fact, work by contemporary researchers studying memory and learning suggests that we carry with us memories—of which we are not consciously aware—that have a significant impact on our behavior (Kihlstrom, 1987; Westen, 1990; Jacoby & Kelley, 1992).

Some of the most basic principles of Freud's psychoanalytic theory have been called into question, however, because they have not been validated by subsequent research. In particular, the notion that people pass through stages in childhood that determine their adult personalities has little definitive research support. In addition, because much of Freud's theory was based on a limited population of upper-middle-class Austrians living during a strict, puritanical era, its application to broad, multicultural populations is questionable. Finally, because Freud's theory focuses primarily on male development, it has been criticized as sexist and may be interpreted as devaluing women. For such reasons, many developmentalists question Freud's theory (Guthrie & Lonner, 1986; Brislin, 1993; Crews, 1993).

Erikson's view that development continues throughout the life span is highly important—and has received considerable support (Whitbourne, et al., 1992; Peterson & Stewart, 1993; Hetherington & Weinberger, 1993). However, the theory also has its drawbacks. Like Freud's theory, it focuses more on men's than women's development. It is also vague in some respects, making it difficult for researchers to test rigorously. And, as is the case with psychodynamic theories in general, it is difficult to make definitive predictions about a given individual's behavior using the theory. In sum, then, the psychodynamic perspective provides good descriptions of past behavior, but imprecise predictions of future behavior.

The Behavioral Perspective: Considering the Outer Person

When Elissa Sheehan was three, a large brown dog bit her, and she needed dozens of stitches and several operations. From the time she was bitten, she broke into a sweat whenever she saw a dog, and in fact never enjoyed being around any pet.

To a lifespan development specialist using the behavioral perspective, the explanation for Elissa's behavior is straightforward: She has a learned fear of dogs. Rather than looking inside the organism at unconscious processes, the **behavioral perspective** suggests that the keys to understanding development are observable behavior and outside stimuli in the environment. If we know the stimuli, we can predict the behavior.

psychosocial development the approach that encompasses changes in our interactions with and understandings of one another, as well as in our knowledge and understanding of ourselves as members of society

behavioral perspective the approach that suggests that the keys to understanding development are observable behavior and outside stimuli in the environment

John B. Watson

Behavioral theories reject the notion that people universally pass through a series of stages. Instead, people are assumed to be affected by the environmental stimuli to which they happen to be exposed. Developmental patterns, then, are personal, reflecting a particular set of environmental stimuli, and behavior is the result of continuing exposure to specific factors in the environment. Furthermore, developmental change is viewed in quantitative, rather than qualitative, terms. For instance, behavioral theories hold that advances in problem-solving capabilities as children age are largely a result of greater mental *capacities*, rather than changes in the *kind* of thinking that children are able to bring to bear on a problem.

Classical Conditioning: Stimulus Substitution.

> Give me a dozen healthy infants, well-formed, and my own specified world to bring them up in and I'll guarantee to take any one at random and train him to become any type of specialist I might select—doctor, lawyer, artist, merchant-chief, and yes, even beggar-man and thief, regardless of his talents, penchants, tendencies, abilities. . . . (Watson, 1925)

With these words, John B. Watson, one of the first American psychologists to advocate a behavioral approach, summed up the behavioral perspective. Watson, who lived from 1878 to 1958, believed strongly that we could gain a full understanding of development by carefully studying the stimuli that compose the environment. In fact, he argued that by effectively controlling a person's environment, it was possible to produce virtually any behavior.

As we'll consider further in Chapter 3, **classical conditioning** occurs when an organism learns to respond in a particular way to a neutral stimulus that normally does not evoke that type of response. For instance, pioneering research by Russian psychologist Ivan Pavlov found that if a dog is repeatedly exposed to the pairing of two stimuli, such as the sound of a bell and the presentation of meat, it may learn to react to the bell alone in the same way it reacts to the meat—by salivating and wagging its tail with excitement. Dogs don't typically respond to bells in this way; the behavior is a result of stimulus substitution.

The same process of classical conditioning explains how we learn emotional responses. In the case of dog-bite victim Elissa Sheehan, for instance, one stimulus has been substituted for another: Elissa's unpleasant experience with a particular dog (the initial stimulus) has been transferred to other dogs, and to pets in general.

Operant Conditioning.   In addition to classical conditioning, other types of learning derive from the behavioral perspective. In fact, the learning approach that probably has had the greatest influence is operant conditioning. **Operant conditioning** is a form of learning in which a voluntary response is strengthened or weakened by its association with positive or negative consequences.

In operant conditioning, formulated and championed by psychologist B.F. Skinner (1904–1990), individuals learn to act deliberately on their environments in order to bring about desired consequences (Skinner, 1975). In a sense, then, people *operate* on their environments to bring about a desired state of affairs.

Whether or not children will seek to repeat a behavior depends on whether it is followed by reinforcement. *Reinforcement* is the process by which a stimulus is provided that increases the probability that a preceding behavior will be repeated. Hence, a student is apt to work harder in school if he or she receives good grades; workers are likely to labor harder at their jobs if their efforts are tied to pay increases; and people are more apt to buy lottery tickets if they are reinforced by winning at least occasionally. In addition, *punishment*, the introduction of an unpleasant or painful stimulus or the removal of a desirable stimulus, will decrease the probability that a preceding behavior will occur in the future.

Behavior that is reinforced, then, is more likely to be repeated in the future, whereas behavior that receives no reinforcement or is punished is likely to be discontinued, or, in the language of operant conditioning, *extinguished*. Principles of operant conditioning are used in **behavior modification**, a formal technique for promoting the frequency of desir-

classical conditioning   *a type of learning in which an organism responds in a particular way to a neutral stimulus that normally does not bring about that type of response*

operant conditioning   *a form of learning in which a voluntary response is strengthened or weakened by its association with positive or negative consequences*

behavior modification   *a formal technique for promoting the frequency of desirable behaviors and decreasing the incidence of unwanted ones*

B.F. Skinner

able behaviors and decreasing the incidence of unwanted ones. Behavior modification has been used in a variety of situations, ranging from teaching severely retarded people the rudiments of language to helping people stick to diets (Bellack, Hersen, & Kazdin, 1990; Sulzer-Azaroff & Mayer, 1990; Malott, Whaley, & Malott, 1993).

social-cognitive learning theory *learning by observing the behavior of another person, called a model*

Social-Cognitive Learning Theory: Learning through Imitation. Beavis and Butthead, cartoon characters on MTV, discuss how enjoyable it is to set fires. On at least one occasion, one of them lights the other's hair on fire using matches and an aerosol spray can. Not long after seeing the show, 5-year-old Austin Messner set his bed on fire with a cigarette lighter, starting a blaze that killed his younger sister.

Cause and effect? We can't know for sure, but it certainly seems possible, especially looking at the situation from the perspective of social-cognitive learning theory. According to developmental psychologist Albert Bandura and colleagues, a significant amount of learning is explained by **social-cognitve learning theory**, an approach that emphasizes learning by observing the behavior of another person, called a *model* (Bandura, 1977, 1994).

Social-cognitive learning theory holds that when we see the behavior of a model being rewarded, we are likely to imitate that behavior. For instance, in one classic experiment, children who were afraid of dogs were exposed to a model, nicknamed the "Fearless Peer," who was seen playing happily with a dog (Bandura, Grusec, & Menlove, 1967). After exposure, the children who previously had been afraid were more likely to approach a strange dog than children who had not seen the model.

Bandura suggests that social-cognitive learning proceeds in four steps (Bandura, 1986). First, an observer must pay attention and perceive the most critical features of a model's behavior. Second, the observer must successfully recall the behavior. Third, the observer must reproduce the behavior accurately. Finally, the observer must be motivated to learn and carry out the behavior. Rather than learning being a matter of trial and error, as it is with operant conditioning, in social-cognitive learning theory behavior is learned through observation.

Assessing the Behavioral Perspective. Although they are part of the same general behavioral perspective, classical and operant conditioning on the one hand, and social-cognitive learning theory on the other, disagree in some basic ways (Amsel, 1988). Both classical and operant conditioning consider learning in terms of external stimuli and responses, in which the only important factors are the observable features of the environment. In such an analysis, people and other organisms are "black boxes"; nothing that occurs inside the box is understood—nor much cared about, for that matter.

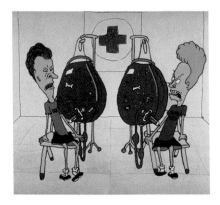

According to social-cognitive learning theory, observation of shows such as *Beavis and Butthead* can produce significant amounts of learning—not all of it positive.

To social-cognitive learning theorists, such an analysis is an oversimplification. They argue that what makes people different from rats and pigeons is mental activity, such as thoughts and expectations. A full understanding of people's development, they maintain, cannot occur without moving beyond external stimuli and responses.

In many ways, social-cognitive learning theory has come to predominate in recent decades over classical and operant conditioning theories. In fact, another perspective that focuses explicitly on internal mental activity has become enormously influential. This is the cognitive approach, which we consider next.

The Cognitive Perspective: Examining the Roots of Understanding

When 3-year-old Jake is asked why it sometimes rains, he answers "so the flowers can grow." When his 11-year-old sister, Lila, is asked the same question, she responds "because of evaporation from the surface of the Earth." And when their cousin Ajima, who is studying meteorology in graduate school, considers the same question, her extended answer includes a discussion of cumulonimbus clouds, the Coriolis effect, and synoptic charts.

To a developmental theorist using the cognitive perspective, the difference in the sophistication of the answers is evidence of a different degree of knowledge and understanding, or cognition. The **cognitive perspective** focuses on the processes that allow people to know, understand, and think about the world.

The cognitive perspective emphasizes how people internally represent and think about the world. By using this perspective, developmental researchers hope to understand how children and adults process information, and how their ways of thinking and understanding affect their behavior. They also seek to learn how cognitive abilities change as people develop, and the degree to which cognitive development represents quantitative and qualitative growth in intellectual abilities.

Piaget's Theory of Cognitive Development.   No single person has had a greater impact on the study of cognitive development than Jean Piaget. A Swiss psychologist who lived from 1896 to 1980, Piaget proposed that all people passed in a fixed sequence through a series of universal stages of cognitive development. In each stage, he suggested that not only did the quantity of information increase, but the quality of knowledge and understanding changed as well. His focus was on the change in cognition that occurred as children moved from one stage to the next (Piaget, 1952, 1962, 1983).

Although we'll consider Piaget's theory in detail beginning in Chapter 5, we can get a broad sense of it now by looking at some of its main features. Piaget suggested that human thinking is arranged into *schemes*, organized patterns that represent behaviors and actions. In infants, such schemes represent concrete behavior—a scheme for sucking, for reaching, and for each separate behavior. In older children, the schemes become more sophisticated and abstract. Schemes are like intellectual computer software that directs and determines how data from the world are looked at and dealt with (Achenbach, 1992).

Piaget suggests that the growth in children's understanding of the world can be explained by two basic principles. **Assimilation** is the process in which people understand an experience in terms of their current stage of cognitive development and way of thinking. In contrast, **accommodation** refers to changes in existing ways of thinking in response to encounters with new stimuli or events.

Assimilation occurs when current ways of thinking about and understanding the world are used to perceive and understand a new experience. For example, a young child who has not yet learned to count will look at a row of buttons that are closely spaced together and say there are fewer buttons in that row than in a row of the same number of buttons that are more spread out. The experience of counting buttons, then, is *assimilated* to already existing schemes that contain the principle "bigger is more."

Later, however, when the child is older and has had sufficient exposure to new experiences, the content of the scheme will undergo change. In understanding that the quantity

---

cognitive perspective   *the approach that focuses on the processes that allow people to know, understand, and think about the world*

assimilation   *the process in which people understand an experience in terms of their current stage of cognitive development and way of thinking*

accommodation   *the process that changes existing ways of thinking in response to encounters with new stimuli or events*

of buttons is identical whether they are spread out or closely spaced, the child has *accommodated* to the experience. Assimilation and accommodation work in tandem to bring about cognitive development.

Assessing Piaget's Theory.   Piaget was without peer in influencing our understanding of cognitive development, and he is one of the towering figures in lifespan development. He provided masterful descriptions of how intellectual growth proceeds during childhood—descriptions that have stood the test of literally thousands of investigations. By and large, then, Piaget's broad view of the sequence of cognitive development is accurate (Gratch & Schatz, 1987).

However, the specifics of the theory, particularly the change in cognitive capabilities over time, have been called into question. For instance, some cognitive skills clearly emerge earlier than Piaget suggested. Furthermore, the universality of Piaget's stages has been disputed. A growing amount of evidence suggests that the emergence of particular cognitive skills occurs according to a different timetable in non-Western cultures. And in every culture, some people never seem to reach Piaget's highest level of cognitive sophistication: formal, logical thought (Rogoff & Chavajay, 1995).

Ultimately, the greatest criticism leveled at the Piagetian perspective is that cognitive development is not necessarily as discontinuous as suggested by Piaget's stage theory. Although Piaget contended that growth proceeds in four distinct stages, in which the quality of cognition differs from one stage to the next, many developmental researchers argue that growth is considerably more continuous. These critics have suggested an alternative perspective, known as the information-processing approach, which focuses on the processes that underlie learning, memory, and thinking throughout the life span.

Information-processing Approaches.   Information processing approaches have become an important alternative to Piagetian approaches. **Information-processing approaches** to cognitive development seek to identify the ways individuals take in, use, and store information. They assume that cognitive growth is typified more by quantitative than qualitative change (Siegler, 1991).

Information-processing approaches grew out of developments in the electronic processing of information, particularly as carried out by computers. They assume that even complex behavior such as learning, remembering, categorizing, and thinking can be broken down into a series of individual, specific steps.

In contrast to Piaget's view that thinking undergoes qualitative advances as children age, information-processing approaches assume that development is marked more by quantitative advances. With age, people are seen to change in their capacities to handle information, as well as in the speed and efficiency of their processing. Furthermore, information-processing approaches suggest that as people age, they are better able to control the nature of processing, and that they change in the strategies they choose to process information.

As we'll see in future chapters, information-processing approaches have become important not only as an alternative to Piagetian approaches, but also as a central part of our understanding of development. They represent an increasingly influential means of studying children's behavior.

Vygotsky's Sociocultural Theory.   To Russian child developmentalist Lev Semenovich Vygotsky, a full understanding of development is impossible without taking into account the culture in which children develop. Vygotsky developed **sociocultural theory**, an approach that emphasizes how cognitive development proceeds as a result of social interactions between members of a culture. To a far greater extent than other approaches, sociocultural explanations of development suggest that culture—a society's beliefs, values, customs, and interests—shapes development (Vygotsky, 1979; 1926/1997; Wertsch & Tulviste, 1992; Beilin, 1996; Daniels, 1996).

Vygotsky, who lived from 1896 to 1934, argued that children's understanding of the world is acquired through their problem-solving interactions with adults and other children. As children play and cooperate with others, they learn what is important in

information-processing approaches the model that seeks to identify the ways individuals take in, use, and store information

sociocultural theory the approach that emphasizes how cognitive development proceeds as a result of social interactions between members of a culture

their society, and at the same time, advance cognitively in their understanding of the world. Consequently, to understand the course of development we must consider what is meaningful to members of a given culture.

Sociocultural theory has become increasingly influential, despite Vygotsky's death more than 60 years ago, because of the growing acknowledgment of the central importance of cultural factors in development. Children do not develop in a cultural vacuum. Instead, their attention is directed by society to certain areas, and as a consequence they develop particular kinds of skills that are an outcome of their cultural environment. Vygotsky was one of the first developmentalists to recognize and acknowledge the importance of culture, and—as today's society becomes increasingly multicultural—sociocultural theory is helping us to understand the rich and varied influences that shape children's development.

The Humanistic Perspective: Concentrating on the Unique Qualities of Human Beings

The special qualities of humans provide the centerpiece of the humanistic perspective, the fourth of the major theories used by lifespan developmentalists. Rejecting the notion that our behavior is largely determined by unconscious processes, by learning from our environment, or by rational cognitive processing, the **humanistic perspective** contends that people have a natural capacity to make decisions about their lives and control their behavior. According to this approach, each individual has the ability and motivation to reach more advanced levels of maturity, and people naturally seek to reach their full potential.

The humanistic perspective emphasizes *free will*, the ability of humans to make choices and come to decisions about their lives. Instead of relying on societal standards, then, people are assumed to be motivated to make their own decisions about what they do with their lives.

Carl Rogers (1971), one of the major proponents of the humanistic perspective, suggests that all people have a need for positive regard that results from an underlying wish to be loved and respected. Because it is other people who provide this positive regard, we become dependent on them. Consequently, our view of ourselves and our self-worth is a reflection of how we think others view us.

Rogers, along with another key figure in the humanistic perspective, Abraham Maslow, suggests that self-actualization is a primary goal in life. *Self-actualization* is a state of self-fulfillment in which people achieve their highest potential in their own unique way. Although the concept initially was deemed to apply to only a few select, famous people, such as Eleanor Roosevelt, Abraham Lincoln, and Albert Einstein, later theorists expanded the concept to apply to any person who realizes his or her own potential and possibilities (Jones & Crandall, 1991; Maslow, 1970, 1987).

Assessing the Humanistic Perspective. The humanistic perspective has not had a major impact on the field of lifespan development. Its lack of influence is primarily due to its inability to identify any sort of broad developmental change that is the result of increasing age or experience. Although some theories suggest that adolescence marks a significant transition period, most humanistic theories are silent on developmental issues.

A further criticism leveled against the humanistic perspective relates to its assumption that people are basically "good." This assumption is vague and largely unverifiable. Furthermore, the key concept of self-actualization has proven difficult to measure objectively. On the other hand, the theory has had some influence, and proponents argue that it highlights aspects of human behavior that other theories ignore (Haymes, Green, & Quinto, 1984; Weiss, 1991; Neher, 1991).

Evolutionary Perspectives: Our Ancestors' Contributions to Behavior

One increasingly influential approach is the evolutionary perspective, the fifth and final developmental perspective that we will consider. The **evolutionary perspective** seeks to identify behavior in today's humans that is the result of our genetic inheritance from our ancestors (Crawford & Krebs, 1997).

humanistic perspective   the theory that contends that people have a natural capacity to make decisions about their lives and control their behavior

evolutionary perspective   the theory that seeks to identify behavior that is a result of our genetic inheritance from our ancestors

Evolutionary approaches grow out of the groundbreaking work of Charles Darwin. In 1859, Darwin argued in his book *On the Origin of Species* that a process of natural selection creates traits in a species that are adaptive to their environment. Using Darwin's arguments, evolutionary approaches contend that our genetic inheritance determines not only such physical traits as skin and eye color, but also certain personality traits and social behaviors. For instance, as we'll discuss further in future chapters, some evolutionary developmentalists suggest that the degree of introversion or sociability that people manifest is influenced by genetic factors (Plomin & McClearn, 1993).

The evolutionary perspective draws heavily on the field of *ethology*, which examines the ways in which our biological makeup influences our behavior. A primary proponent of ethology was Konrad Lorenz (1903–1989), who discovered that newborn geese are genetically preprogrammed to become attached to the first moving object they see after birth. His work, which demonstrated the importance of biological determinants in influencing behavior patterns, ultimately led developmentalists to consider the ways in which human behavior might reflect inborn genetic patterns.

As we'll consider further in Chapter 2, the evolutionary perspective encompasses one of the fastest growing areas within the field of lifespan development: behaviorial genetics. *Behavioral genetics* studies the effects of heredity on behavior; it seeks to understand how we might inherit certain behavioral traits and how the environment influences whether we actually display such traits. Behavioral genetics also considers how genetic factors may produce psychological disorders such as schizophrenia (Bouchard, 1994; Lander & Schork, 1994; Mowry, Nancarrow, & Levinson, 1997).

Although the evolutionary perspective is increasingly visible in the field of lifespan development, it has been subjected to considerable criticism. Some developmentalists are concerned that because of its focus on genetic and biological aspects of behavior, the evolutionary perspective pays insufficient attention to the environmental and social factors involved in producing children's and adults' behavior. Other critics argue that there is no good way to support experimentally theories derived from the evolutionary approach. Still, the evolutionary approach has stimulated a significant amount of research on how our biological inheritance influences at least partially our traits and behaviors (Baltes, 1997; Dent-Read & Zukow-Goldring, 1997; Bjorklund, 1997; Leonard, 1998).

Konrad Lorenz, seen here with geese imprinted to him, considered the ways in which behavior reflects inborn genetic patterns.

Which Approach Is Right? The Wrong Question

We have considered the five major perspectives on development: psychodynamic, behavioral, cognitive, humanistic, and evolutionary—summarized in Table 1-4. It would be natural to wonder which of the five provides the most accurate account of human development.

For several reasons, it is not entirely appropriate to ask which perspective is most accurate. For one thing, each perspective emphasizes somewhat different aspects of development. For instance, the psychodynamic approach emphasizes emotions, motivational conflicts, and unconscious determinants of behavior. In contrast, behavioral perspectives emphasize overt behavior, paying far more attention to what people *do* than what goes on inside their heads, which is deemed largely irrelevant. The cognitive and humanistic perspectives take quite the opposite tack, looking more at what people *think* than at what they do. Finally, the evolutionary perspective focuses on how inherited biological factors underlie development.

Clearly, each perspective is based on its own premises and focuses on different aspects of development. Furthermore, the same developmental phenomenon can be looked at from a number of perspectives simultaneously.

In short, we can think of the different perspectives as analogous to a set of maps of the same general geographical area. One map may contain detailed depictions of roads; another map may show geographical features; another may show political subdivisions, such as cities, towns, and counties; and still another may highlight particular points of interest, such as scenic areas and historical landmarks. Each of the maps is accurate, but each provides a different point of view and way of thinking. No one map is "complete," but by considering them together, we can come to a fuller understanding of the area.

TABLE 1-4

MAJOR PERSPECTIVES ON LIFESPAN DEVELOPMENT

Perspective	Description
Psychodynamic	Advocates of the *psychodynamic perspective* believe that behavior is motivated by inner, unconscious forces, memories, and conflicts over which a person has little awareness and control. The inner forces, which may stem from childhood experiences, continually influence behavior throughout our entire lives. Major proponents: Sigmund Freud and Erik Erikson.
Behavioral	The *behavioral perspective* suggests that the focus of understanding development rests on observable behavior and outside stimuli in the environment. If we know what those stimuli are, we can predict how people will behave. Major proponents: John B. Watson, B.F. Skinner, and Albert Bandura.
Cognitive	The *cognitive perspective* focuses on the processes that allow people to know, understand, and think about the world, and it emphasizes how people internally represent and think about the world. It emphasizes how children and adults process information, and how their ways of thinking and understanding affect their behavior. Major proponents: Jean Piaget and Lev Vygotsky.
Humanistic	The *humanistic perspective* contends that people have a natural capacity to make decisions about their lives and control their behavior. According to this approach, each individual has the ability and motivation to reach more advanced levels of maturity and seeks to reach his or her full potential. The humanistic perspective emphasizes *free will*, the human ability to make choices and come to decisions about one's life. Major proponent: Carl Rogers
Evolutionary	The *evolutionary perspective* suggests that behavior is the result of genetic inheritance from our ancestors. Evolutionary approaches grow out of the groundbreaking work of Charles Darwin. Darwin argues in 1859 in his book *On the Origin of Species* that a process of natural selection creates traits in a species that are adaptive to their environment. Using Darwin's arguments, evolutionary approaches contend that an individual's genetic inheritance determines not only traits such as skin and eye color, but certain personality traits and social behaviors as well. The evolutionary perspective draws heavily on the field of *ethology*, which examines the way behavior is influenced by biological makeup. Major proponent: Konrad Lorenz

In the same way, the various theoretical perspectives provide different ways of looking at development. Considering them together paints a full portrait of the myriad ways human beings change and grow over the course of their lives. However, not all theories and claims derived from the various perspectives are accurate. How do we choose among competing explanations? The answer is *research,* which we consider in the final part of this chapter.

Developmental Diversity

How Culture, Ethnicity, and Race Influence Development

South American Mayan mothers are certain that almost constant contact between themselves and their infant children is necessary for good parenting, and they are physically upset if contact is not possible. They are shocked when they see a North American mother lay her infant down, and they attribute the baby's crying to the poor parenting of the North American. (Morelli et al., 1992)

Two views of parenting are at odds in this passage. Is one correct and the other wrong? Probably not, if we take into consideration the cultural context in which the mothers are operating. In fact, different cultures and subcultures have their own views of appropriate and inappropriate childrearing, just as they have different developmental goals for children (Greenfield, 1995, 1997; Francasso et al., 1997).

Consider, for instance, whether you agree that children should be taught that their classmates' assistance is indispensable to getting good grades in school, or that they should definitely plan to continue their fathers' businesses, or that children should follow their parents' advice in determining their career plans. If you have been raised in the most widespread North American culture, you would likely disagree with all three statements, because they violate the premises of *individualism,* the dominant Western philosophy that emphasizes personal identity, uniqueness, freedom, and the worth of the individual.

On the other hand, if you were raised in a traditional Asian culture, your agreement with the three statements is considerably more likely. The reason? The statements reflect the value orientation known as collectivism. *Collectivism* is the notion that the well-being of the group is more important than that of the individual. People raised in collectivistic cultures tend to emphasize the welfare of the groups to which they belong, sometimes even at the expense of their own personal well-being.

The individualism–collectivism spectrum is one of several dimensions along which cultures differ, and it illustrates differences in the cultural contexts in which people operate. One of the challenges developmentalists face is the need to take different cultural contexts into account.

In addition, they must consider not just broad cultural differences, such as those that separate North American and Asian cultures. They must also take into account finer ethnic, racial, and socioeconomic differences if they are to achieve an understanding of how people change and grow throughout the life span. If developmentalists succeed in doing so, they not only can achieve a better understanding of human development, but also may be able to derive more precise applications for improving the human social condition.

Although the field of lifespan development is increasingly concerned with issues of human diversity, its actual progress in this domain has been slow, and in some ways it has actually regressed. For instance, between 1970 and 1989, only 4.6 percent of the articles published in *Developmental Psychology,* the premier journal of the discipline, focused on African American participants. Moreover, the number of published studies involving African American participants actually declined over that 20-year period (Graham, 1992; MacPhee, Kreutzer, & Fritz, 1994).

Furthermore, members of the research community—as well as society at large—have sometimes used terms such as *race* and *ethnic group* in inappropriate ways. *Race* is a biological concept, which should be employed to refer to classifications based on physical and structural characteristics of species. In contrast, *ethnic group* and *ethnicity* are broader terms, referring to cultural background, nationality, religion, and language.

The concept of race has proved particularly problematic. Although it formally refers to biological factors, race has taken on substantially more meanings—many of them inappropriate—that range from skin color to religion to culture. Moreover, the concept of race is exceedingly imprecise; depending on how it is defined, there are between 3 and 300 races, and no race is biologically pure (Betancourt & Lopez, 1993).

In addition, there is little agreement about which names best reflect different races and ethnic groups. Should the term *African American*—which has geographical and cultural implications—be preferred over *black,* which focuses primarily on race and skin color? Is *Native American* preferable to *Indian?* Is *Hispanic* more appropriate than *Latino?* And how can researchers accurately categorize people with multiracial backgrounds?

The choice of category has important implications for the validity (and usefulness) of research. The choice even has political implications. For example, a recent decision to permit people to identify themselves as "multiracial" on U.S. government forms and in the U.S. Census was controversial (Jones, 1994; Evinger, 1996).

The diversity of America is reflected in these children's faces.

Finally, it is important to keep in mind that race—a biological factor—does not occur independently from environmental and cultural contexts. Consequently, it is impossible to attribute a particular behavior or set of behaviors to race *per se*, without considering the environments in which people are developing.

In short, as the proportion of minorities in U.S. society continues to increase, it becomes crucial to take the complex issues associated with human diversity into account in order to fully understand development (Fowers & Richardson, 1996). In fact, it is only by looking for similarities and differences among various ethnic, cultural, and racial groups that developmental researchers can distinguish principles of development that are universal from ones that are culturally determined. In the years ahead, then, it is likely that lifespan development will move from a discipline that primarily focuses on North American and European development to one that encompasses development around the globe.

REVIEW AND RETHINK

REVIEW

■ Five major theoretical perspectives dominate lifespan development. The psychodynamic perspective looks primarily at the influence of internal, unconscious forces on development. Freud's psychoanalytic theory and Erikson's psychosocial theory are examples.

- A second perspective, the behavioral perspective, focuses on external, observable behaviors as the key to development. Classical conditioning, operant conditioning, and social-cognitive learning theories are examples.

- The third major perspective is the cognitive perspective, which focuses on mental activity. Piaget's stage theory, information-processing approaches, and Vygotsky's sociocultural theory are examples.

- The fourth major perspective is the humanistic perspective. It concentrates on the theory that each individual has the ability and motivation to reach more advanced levels of maturity and that people naturally seek to reach their full potential. The humanistic perspective emphasizes *free will*, the ability of humans to make choices and decisions about their lives.

- Finally, the evolutionary perspective seeks to identify behavior that is a result of our genetic inheritance from our ancestors. Derived from Charles Darwin's theory of natural selection, the evolutionary perspective draws heavily on the field of ethology, which examines the ways in which our biological makeup influences our behavior.

- All five perspectives are valuable and all are partial, with each providing a piece of the total picture. Clearly, each perspective is based on its own premises and focuses on different aspects of development. Furthermore, the same developmental phenomenon can be looked at from a number of perspectives simultaneously.

- Culture and ethnicity also play an important role in development, both broad culture and aspects of culture, such as race, ethnicity, and socioeconomic status.

RETHINK

- How might a person's unconscious affect her or his behavior? How were such behaviors explained before the concept of the unconscious was devised?

- Describe some examples of conditioned responses and reinforcement in everyday life.

- How do the concepts of social learning and modeling relate to the mass media?

- In general, what does each theoretical perspective contribute to our understanding of human development?

- What are some examples of the ways culture (either broad culture or aspects of culture) affects human development?

RESEARCH METHODS

The Egyptians had long believed that they were the most ancient race on earth, and Psamtik [King of Egypt in the 7th century, B.C.], driven by intellectual curiosity, wanted to prove that flattering belief. Like a good psychologist, he began with a hypothesis: If children had no opportunity to learn a language from older people around them, they would spontaneously speak the primal, inborn language of humankind—the natural language of its most ancient people—which, he expected to show, was Egyptian.

   To test his hypothesis, Psamtik commandeered two infants of a lower-class mother and turned them over to a herdsman to bring up in a remote area. They were to be kept in a sequestered cottage, properly fed and cared for, but were never to hear anyone speak so much as a word. The Greek historian Herodotus, who tracked the story down and learned what he calls "the real facts" from priests of Hephaestus in Memphis, says that Psamtik's goal "was to know, after the indistinct babblings of infancy were over, what word they would first articulate."

   The experiment, he tells us, worked. One day, when the children were two years old, they ran up to the herdsman as he opened the door of their cottage and cried out "*Becos!*" Since this meant nothing to him, he paid no attention, but when it happened repeatedly, he sent word to Psamtik, who at once ordered the children brought to him. When he too heard them say it, Psamtik made inquiries and learned that *becos* was the Phrygian word for bread. He concluded that, disappointingly, the Phrygians were an older race than the Egyptians. (Hunt, 1993, pp. 1–2)

With the perspective of several thousand years, we can easily see the shortcomings—both scientific and ethical—in Psamtik's approach. Yet his procedure represents an improvement over mere speculation, and as such is sometimes looked on as the first developmental experiment in recorded history (Hunt, 1993).

Theories and Hypotheses: Posing Developmental Questions

Questions such as those raised by Psamtik lie at the heart of the study of development. Is language innate? What are the effects of malnutrition on later intellectual performance? How do infants form relationships with their parents, and does participation in day care disrupt such relationships? Why are adolescents susceptible to peer pressure? Are there declines in intellectual abilities related to aging?

To resolve such questions, developmentalists rely on the scientific method. The **scientific method** is the process of posing and answering questions using careful, controlled techniques that include systematic, orderly observation and the collection of data.

The scientific method involves the formulation of theories, broad explanations and predictions about phenomena of interest. All of us develop theories about development, based on our experience, folklore, and articles in magazines and newspapers. For instance, many people theorize that there is a crucial bonding period between parent and child immediately after birth, which is a necessary ingredient in forming a lasting parent–child relationship. Without such a bonding period, they assume, the parent–child relationship will be forever compromised (Furnham & Weir, 1996).

Whenever we employ such explanations, we are developing our own theories. However, the theories of developmentalists are different. Whereas our own personal theories are built on unverified observations that are developed unsystematically, developmentalists' theories are more formal, based on a systematic integration of prior findings and theories. These theories allow developmentalists to summarize and organize prior observations, and they enable them to move beyond existing observations to draw deductions that may not be immediately apparent.

Developmental researchers use theories to form hypotheses. A **hypothesis** is a prediction stated in a way that permits it to be tested. For instance, someone who subscribes to the general theory that bonding is a crucial ingredient in the parent–child relationship might derive the more specific hypothesis that adopted children whose adoptive parents never had the chance to bond with them immediately after birth may ultimately have less secure relationships with their adoptive parents. Others might derive other hypotheses, such as that effective bonding occurs only if it lasts for a certain length of time, or that bonding affects the mother–child relationship, but not the father–child relationship. (In case you're wondering: As we'll discuss in Chapter 3, these particular hypotheses have *not* been upheld; there are no long-term reactions to the separation of parent and child immediately after birth, even if the separation lasts several days.)

Choosing a Research Strategy: Answering Questions

Once researchers have chosen a hypothesis to test, they must develop a strategy for testing its validity. Two major categories of research are correlational research and experimental research. **Correlational research** seeks to identify whether an association or relationship between two factors exists. Correlational research is unable to determine whether one factor causes changes in the other. For instance, correlational research could tell us whether an association exists between the number of minutes a mother and her newborn child are together immediately after birth and the quality of the mother–child relationship when the

scientific method   *the process of posing and answering questions using careful, controlled techniques that include systematic, orderly observation and the collection of data*

hypothesis   *a prediction stated in a way that permits it to be tested*

correlational research   *research that seeks to identify whether an association or relationship between two factors exists*

child reaches 2 years of age. Such correlational research indicates whether the two factors are *associated* or *related* to one another, but not whether the initial contact caused the relationship to develop in a particular way.

In contrast, **experimental research** is designed to discover *causal* relationships between various factors. In experimental research, researchers deliberately introduce a change in a situation in order to see the consequences of that change. For instance, a researcher conducting an experiment might vary the number of minutes that mothers and children interact immediately following birth, in an attempt to see whether the amount of bonding time affects the mother–child relationship.

Because experimental research is able to answer questions of causality, it represents the heart of developmental research. However, some research questions cannot be answered through experiments, for either technical or ethical reasons. In fact, a great deal of pioneering developmental research—such as that conducted by Piaget and Vygotsky—employed correlational techniques. Consequently, correlational research remains an important tool in the developmental researcher's toolbox.

experimental research research designed to discover causal relationships between various factors

Correlational Studies

Correlational research examines the relationship between two variables to determine whether they are associated, or *correlated*. For instance, researchers interested in the relationship between televised aggression and subsequent behavior have found that children who watch a good deal of aggression on television—murders, crime shows, shootings, and the like—tend to be more aggressive than those who watch only a little. In other words, the viewing of aggression and actual aggression are strongly associated, or correlated, with one another (Center for Communication & Social Policy, 1998).

But does this mean we can conclude that the viewing of televised aggression *causes* the more aggressive behavior of the viewers? Not at all. Consider some of the other possibilities: It might be that being aggressive in the first place makes children more likely to choose to watch violent programs. In such a case, then, it is the aggressive tendency that causes the viewing behavior, and not the other way around.

Researchers use a wide range of procedures to study human development

Or consider another possibility. Suppose that children who are raised in poverty are more likely to behave aggressively *and* to watch higher levels of aggressive television than those raised in more affluent settings. In this case, it is socioeconomic status that causes *both* the aggressive behavior and the television viewing. (The various possibilities are illustrated in Figure 1-2).

In short, finding that two variables are correlated proves nothing about causality. Although it is possible that the variables are linked causally, this is not necessarily the case.

On the other hand, correlational studies can provide important information. For instance, as we'll see in later chapters, we know from correlational studies that the closer the genetic link between two people, the more highly associated is their intelligence. We have learned that the more parents speak to their young children, the more extensive are the children's vocabularies. And we know from correlational studies that the better the nutrition that infants receive, the fewer the cognitive and social problems they experience later (Pollitt et al., 1993; Plomin, 1994a; Hart & Risley, 1995).

The Correlation Coefficient.   The strength and direction of a relationship between two factors is represented by a mathematical score, called a *correlation coefficient*, that ranges from +1.0 to −1.0. A positive correlation indicates that as the value of one factor increases, it can be predicted that the value of the other will also increase. For instance, if we find that the more calories children eat, the better their school performance, and the fewer calories children eat, the worse their school performance, we have found a positive correlation. (Higher values of the factor "calories" are associated with higher values of the factor "school performance," and lower values of "calories" are associated with lower values of the factor "school performance.") The correlation coefficient, then, would be indicated by a positive number, and the stronger the association between calories and school performance, the closer the number would be to +1.0.

In contrast, a correlation coefficient with a negative value informs us that as the value of one factor increases, the value of the other factor declines. For example, suppose we found that the greater the number of hours adolescents spend speaking on the telephone, the

FIGURE 1-2

FINDING A CORRELATION

Finding a correlation between two factors does not imply that one factor *causes* the other factor to vary. For instance, suppose a study found that viewing television shows with high levels of aggression is correlated with actual aggression in children. The correlation may reflect at least three possibilities: (a) watching television programs containing high levels of aggression causes aggression in viewers; (b) children who behave aggressively choose to watch TV programs with high levels of aggression; or (c) some third factor, such as a child's socioeconomic status, leads both to high viewer aggression and to choosing to watch television programs with high viewer aggression.

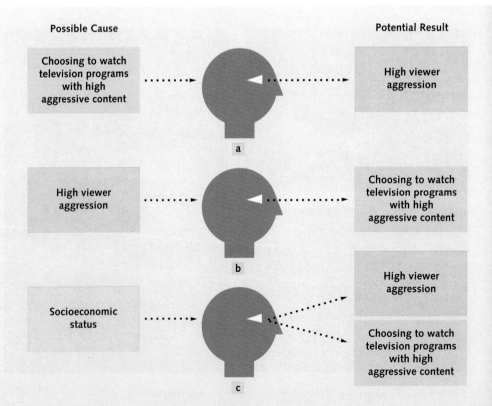

Possible Cause   Potential Result

Choosing to watch television programs with high aggressive content ·······▸ High viewer aggression
a

High viewer aggression ·······▸ Choosing to watch television programs with high aggressive content
b

Socioeconomic status ·······▸ High viewer aggression / Choosing to watch television programs with high aggressive content
c

worse their academic performance is. Such a finding would result in a negative correlation, ranging between 0 and −1. More phone talking is associated with lower performance, and less phone talking is associated with better performance. The stronger the association between talking and school performance, the closer the correlation coefficient will be to −1.

Finally, it is possible that two factors are unrelated to one another. For example, it is unlikely that we would find a correlation between school performance and shoe size. In this case, the lack of a relationship would be indicated by a correlation coefficient close to 0.

It is important to reiterate what we noted earlier: Even if the correlation coefficient involving two variables is very strong, there is no implication that one factor *causes* another factor to vary. It simply means that the two factors are associated with one another in a predictable way.

Types of Correlational Studies.   There are several types of correlational studies. **Naturalistic observation** is the observation of a naturally occurring behavior without intervention in the situation. For instance, an investigator who wishes to learn how often preschool children share toys with one another might observe a classroom over a 3-week period, recording how often the preschoolers spontaneously share with one another. The key point about naturalistic observation is that the investigator simply observes the children, without interfering with the situation whatsoever (Erlandson et al., 1993; Adler & Adler, 1994).

Although naturalistic observation has the advantage of identifying what children do in their "natural habitats," there is an important drawback to the method: Researchers are unable to exert control over factors of interest. For instance, in some cases researchers might find so few naturally occurring instances of the behavior of interest that they are unable to draw any conclusions at all. In addition, children who know they are being watched may modify their behavior as a result of the observation. Consequently, their behavior may not be representative of how they would behave if they were not being watched.

Increasingly, naturalistic observation employs *ethnography*, a method borrowed from the field of anthropology and used to investigate cultural questions. In ethnography, a researcher's goal is to understand a culture's values and attitudes through careful, extended examination. Typically, researchers using ethnography act as *participant observers*, living for a period of weeks, months, or even years in another culture. By carefully observing everyday life and conducting in-depth interviews, researchers are able to obtain a deep understanding of the nature of life within another culture (Fetterman, 1998).

Although ethnographic studies provide a fine-grained view of everyday behavior in another culture, they suffer from several drawbacks. As mentioned, the presence of a participant observer may influence the behavior of the individuals being studied. Furthermore, because only a small number of individuals are studied, it may be hard to generalize the findings to people in other cultures. Finally, ethnographers may misinterpret and misconceive what they are observing, particularly in cultures that are very different from their own (Hammersley, 1992).

Case studies involve extensive, in-depth interviews with a particular individual or small group of individuals. They often are used not just to learn about the individual being interviewed, but also to derive broader principles or draw tentative conclusions that might apply to others. For example, case studies have been conducted on children who display unusual genius and on children who have spent their early years in the wild, apparently without human contact. These case studies have provided important information to researchers, as well as suggesting hypotheses for future investigation.

Surveys represent another sort of correlational research. In **survey research**, people who are chosen to represent some larger population are asked questions about their attitudes, behavior, or thinking on a given topic. For instance, surveys have been conducted about parents' use of punishment on their children and on attitudes toward breast-feeding. From the responses, inferences are drawn regarding the larger population represented by the individuals being surveyed. (An example of the kind of developmental information about children and families that can be obtained from surveys is provided in the "Speaking of Development" box.)

naturalistic observation   *a type of correlational study in which some naturally occurring behavior is observed without intervention in the situation*

case studies   *studies that involve extensive, in-depth interviews with a particular individual or small group of individuals*

survey research   *a type of study in which people who are chosen to represent some larger population are asked questions about their attitudes, behavior, or thinking on a given topic*

Donald J. Hernandez, Family Researcher

Education: . . . .   University of Illinois at Urbana, B.A. in sociology
University of California at Berkeley, M.A. and Ph.D. in sociology

Position: . . . .   Chief of the Marriage and Family Statistics branch of the U.S. Bureau of the Census

Home: . . . .   Silver Spring, Maryland

According to Donald J. Hernandez, when it comes to family life, there wasn't just one American Revolution; there have been five—and counting. Hernandez, who conducts research on the evolution of the family, has uncovered statistics that put into clear perspective where the American family came from, and where it is today. He is the chief of the Marriage and Family Statistics branch of the U.S. Bureau of the Census, and has published his findings in a book entitled *America's Children: Resources from Family, Government and the Economy.*

"In 1940, one in 10 children had a working mother. Today about 60 percent of children have mothers who work for pay."

His findings indicate that over the past 150 years, the family in America has been completely transformed by a series of revolutions. "Three of these revolutions started in the 1800s," he explains. "The first was caused by the rise in non-farm work by the father of the family. In the mid-1800s most families were farm families who worked together on the farm to support themselves. But by the mid-1900s most fathers worked outside the home, earning income to support the family, while the mother's role became that of homemaker.

"Not once in the last 50 years have the majority of children lived in Ozzie and Harriet families."

"During the same period," Hernandez continues, "a second revolution occurred—this one in family size. While most families in the mid-1800s had eight or more children, the figure dropped to two or three children in the 1930s. There was enormous pressure at the time to move off farms and to have fewer children."

The third major change, according to Hernandez, was a marked increase in schooling for America's children. "About half of children aged 5 to 19 were enrolled in school in 1870, but by the 1930s, 95 percent of children 7 to 13, and 79 percent of children 14 to 17, were enrolled."

The next two revolutions involve women's entry into the workforce and, since 1960, the rise of the one-parent, mother-only family. "In 1940, one in 10 children had a working mother. Today about 60 percent of children have mothers who work for pay," he explains. "Similarly, from 1940 to 1960 only 6 to 8 percent of children lived in a mother-only family. As of 1993 the figure was close to 23 percent."

A number of factors have contributed to the changes in the American family, says Hernandez, including the shift of the country's focus from agriculture to industry, new government policies, and the economy.

"There has been an increase of children born into poverty since the late 1970s. This is widely attributed to the rise in one-parent families, but the fact is that the economy and unemployment continue to be major contributors. Parents face many obstacles. They have to deal constantly with economic insecurity. This can lead to divorce. Economic factors have been very important influences on family changes, and on the poverty that results."

One statistic clearly demonstrates that the so-called Ozzie and Harriet family is a myth. Hernandez defines such a family as one in which the father works full-time, the mother is not in the paid labor force, and all the children are born after the parents' only marriage. "Not once in the last 50 years have the majority of children lived in Ozzie and Harriet families," he says. "In 1940, 41 percent of children under one year of age lived in such families. Estimates today indicate that less than one-fourth of children under one year of age live in families that meet the definition."

"To me this was a surprise," Hernandez admits. "When I calculated the statistics, I believed I would find a large majority of Ozzie and Harriet kids, at least in the recent past. But even when Ozzie and Harriet were on television in the 1950s, that's what it was—a myth."

Experiments: Determining Cause and Effect

In an **experiment**, an investigator, called an *experimenter*, typically devises two different experiences for *participants*, or *subjects*. These two different experiences are called treatments. A **treatment** is a procedure applied by an investigator. One group of participants receives one of the treatments, and another group of participants receives either no treatment or an alternative treatment. The group receiving the treatment is known as the **treatment group** (sometimes called the "experimental group"), whereas the no-treatment or alternative-treatment group is called the **control group.**

Although the terminology may seem daunting at first, there is an underlying logic to it that helps sort it out. Think in terms of a medical experiment in which the aim is to test the effectiveness of a new drug. In testing the drug, we wish to see whether the drug successfully *treats* the disease. Consequently, the group that receives the drug would be called the *treatment* group. In comparison, another group of participants would not receive the drug treatment. Instead, they would be part of the no-treatment *control* group.

Similarly, suppose we wish to explore the consequences of exposure to movie violence on viewers' subsequent aggression. We might take a group of adolescents and show them a series of movies that contain a great deal of violent imagery. We would then measure their subsequent aggression. This group would constitute the treatment group. But we would also need another group—a control group. To fulfill this need, we might take a second group of adolescents, show them movies that contain no aggressive imagery, and then measure their subsequent aggression. This would be the control group.

By comparing the amount of aggression displayed by members of the treatment and control groups, we would be able to determine whether exposure to violent imagery produces aggression in viewers. And this is just what a group of researchers found: Running an experiment of this very sort, psychologist Jacques-Philippe Leyens and colleagues at the University of Louvain in Belgium found that the level of aggression rose significantly for the adolescents who had seen the movies containing violence (Leyens et al., 1975).

The central feature of this experiment—and all experiments—is the comparison of the consequences of different treatments. The use of both treatment and control groups allows researchers to rule out the possibility that something other than the experimental manipulation produced the results found in the experiment. For instance, if a control group was not used, experimenters could not be certain that some other factor, such as the time of day the movies were shown, the need to sit still during the movie, or even the mere passage of time, produced the changes that were observed. By employing a control group, then, experimenters can draw accurate conclusions about causes and effects.

The formation of treatment and control groups represents the independent variable in an experiment. The **independent variable** is the variable that researchers manipulate in the experiment. In contrast, the **dependent variable** is the variable that researchers measure in an experiment and expect to change as a result of the experimental manipulation. (One way to remember the difference: A hypothesis predicts how a dependent variable *depends* on the manipulation of the independent variable.) In an experiment studying the effects of taking a drug, for instance, manipulating whether participants receive or don't receive a drug is the independent variable. Measurement of the effectiveness of the drug or no-drug treatment is the dependent variable.

To consider another example, let's take the Belgian study of the consequences of observing filmed aggression on future aggression. In this experiment, the independent variable is the *level of aggressive imagery* viewed by participants—determined by whether they viewed films containing aggressive imagery (the treatment group) or devoid of aggressive imagery (the control group). The dependent variable in the study is what the experimenters expected to vary as a consequence of viewing a film: the *aggressive behavior* shown by participants after they had viewed the films, and measured by the experimenters. Every experiment has an independent and dependent variable.

experiment *a process in which an investigator, called an experimenter, devises two different experiences for subjects or participants*

treatment *a procedure applied by an investigator based on two different experiences devised for participants (See **experiment**)*

treatment group *the group in an experiment that receives the treatment*

control group *the group in an experiment that receives either no treatment or alternative treatment*

independent variable *the variable that researchers manipulate in an experiment*

dependent variable *the variable that researchers measure in an experiment and expect to change as a result of the experimental manipulation*

One critical step in the design of experiments is to assign participants to different treatment groups. The procedure that is used is known as random assignment. In *random assignment*, participants are assigned to different experimental groups or "conditions" on the basis of chance and chance alone. By using this technique, the laws of statistics ensure that there will be equivalence between participant characteristics in the different experimental groups, allowing an experimenter to draw conclusions with confidence (Boruch, 1998).

Given the advantage of experimental research—that it provides a means of determining causality—why aren't experiments always used? The answer is that there are some situations that a researcher, no matter how ingenious, simply cannot control. For instance, no researcher would be able to assign different groups of infants to parents of high and low socioeconomic status in order to learn the effects of such status on subsequent development. Similarly, we cannot control what a group of children watch on television throughout their childhood years in order to learn whether childhood exposure to televised aggression leads to aggressive behavior later in life. Consequently, in situations in which experiments are logistically or ethically impossible, developmentalists employ correlational research.

Choosing a Research Setting.   Deciding *where* to conduct an experiment may be as important as determining *what* to do. In the Belgian experiment on the influence of exposure to media aggression, the researchers used a real-world setting—a group home for boys who had been convicted of juvenile delinquency. They chose the location because it contained adolescents whose normal level of aggression was relatively high, and because they could incorporate showing the films into the everyday life of the home with minimal disruption.

Using a real-world setting like the one in the aggression experiment is the hallmark of a field study. A **field study** is a research investigation carried out in a naturally occurring setting. Field studies may be conducted in preschool classrooms, at community playgrounds, on school buses, or on street corners. Field studies capture behavior in real-life settings, and research participants may behave more naturally than they would if they were brought into a laboratory.

Field studies may be used in both correlational studies and experiments. Typically they employ naturalistic observation, the technique we discussed above in which researchers observe some naturally occurring behavior without intervening or making changes in the situation. For instance, a researcher might examine behavior in a child-care center, or observe mothers interacting with their newborns in a hospital nursery, or view the groupings of adolescents in high school corridors. The crucial point is that researchers who conduct field studies using naturalistic observation do not intervene and change the situation. Instead, they seek to record what they find in as careful and unbiased a manner as possible.

However, it often is difficult to run an experiment in real-world settings, where it is hard to exert control over the situation and environment. Consequently, field studies are more typical of correlational designs than experimental designs, and most developmental research experiments are conducted in laboratory settings. A **laboratory study** is a research investigation conducted in a controlled setting explicitly designed to hold events constant. The laboratory may be a room or building designed for research, as in a university's psychology department. Laboratory studies permit researchers to control the setting, enabling them to learn more clearly how their treatments affect participants.

Theoretical and Applied Research: Complementary Approaches

Developmental researchers typically focus on one of two approaches to research, carrying out either theoretical research or applied research. **Theoretical research** is designed specifically to test some developmental explanation and expand scientific knowledge, whereas **applied research** is meant to provide practical solutions to immediate problems. For instance, if we were interested in the processes of cognitive change during childhood, we might carry out a study that shows how the number of digits that children can remember after one exposure to multidigit numbers increases during childhood—a theoretical approach. Alternatively, we might focus on how children learn by examining ways in which elementary school instruc-

field study   *a research investigation carried out in a naturally occurring setting*

laboratory study   *a research investigation conducted in a controlled setting explicitly designed to hold events constant*

theoretical research   *research designed specifically to test some developmental explanation and expand scientific knowledge*

applied research   *research meant to provide practical solutions to immediate problems*

tors can teach children to remember information more easily. Such a study would represent applied research, because the findings are applied to a particular setting and problem.

Often, the distinctions between theoretical and applied research are blurred. For instance, is a study that examines the consequences of ear infections in infancy on later hearing loss theoretical or applied research? Because such a study may help illuminate the basic processes involved in hearing, it can be considered theoretical. But to the extent that the study helps us to understand how to prevent hearing loss in children and how various medicines may ease the consequences of the infection, it may be considered applied research.

In short, even the most applied research can help advance our theoretical understanding of a particular topical area, and theoretical research can provide concrete solutions to a range of practical problems. In fact, as we discuss in the accompanying "Directions in Development" box, research of both a theoretical and applied nature has played a significant role in shaping and resolving a variety of public policy questions.

Directions in Development

Using Research to Improve Public Policy

Do children benefit from preschool?
What is the best approach to reducing the number of unwed teenage mothers?
Does research support the legalization of marijuana?
Will a series of national educational achievement tests improve scholastic performance?

Each of these questions represents a major national policy issue that can be answered appropriately in only one way: by consulting the results of relevant research studies. By conducting controlled studies, developmental researchers have made a number of important contributions in a variety of areas. Consider, for instance, the variety of ways that public policy issues have been informed by various types of research findings (Lorion et al., 1996; Susman-Stilman et al., 1996):

■ **Asking the right questions.** Research findings can provide a means of determining what questions to ask in the first place. For example, work on children's interactions with caregivers (some of which we'll consider in Chapter 6) has led policymakers to question whether the benefits of infant day care are outweighed by possible deterioration in parent–child bonds.

■ **Writing legislation and laws that improve the lives of children.** A good deal of legislation has been passed based on findings from developmental researchers. For example, research revealed that children with developmental disabilities benefit from exposure to children without special needs. These findings led to the passage of both state and national legislation mandating that children be educated in the least restrictive environment. (As we'll discuss in Chapter 9, the *least restrictive environment* is the educational setting most similar to that of children without special needs; Yell, 1995; Hocutt, 1996.) Similarly, in its 1954 decision ordering the end to school desegregation, the U.S. Supreme Court cited research that showed the detrimental effects of school segregation on minority group members (*Brown v. Board of Education*, 1954).

■ **Developing effective intervention programs.** Research has often helped policymakers and other professionals determine how to implement programs designed to improve the lives of children and adolescents. Research has shaped programs designed to reduce the incidence of unsafe sex among teenagers, to increase the level of prenatal care for pregnant mothers, and to raise class attendance rates in school-age children. The common thread among such programs is that many the details of the programs are built on basic research findings. For example, programs designed to change teenagers' attitudes so that they are more likely to view safer sex as desirable are based on research relating to attitude change.

■ **Program evaluation.** Once a public policy has been implemented, it is necessary to determine whether it has been effective and successful in accomplishing its goals. To do this, researchers employ formal evaluation techniques developed from basic research procedures. For instance, researchers have continually scrutinized the Head Start preschool program, which received massive federal funding, to ensure that it is effective in improving children's academic performance.

In short, research has a substantial impact on public policy related to developmental issues. By building on research findings, developmentalists have worked hand-in-hand with policymakers, and children and adolescents have been the beneficiaries.

Measuring Developmental Change

For developmental researchers, an interest in how people grow and change through childhood and adolescence is central to their discipline. Consequently, one of the thorniest research issues they face concerns the measurement of change and differences over age and time. To solve this problem, researchers have developed three major strategies: longitudinal research, cross-sectional research, and cross-sequential research.

 Longitudinal Studies: Measuring Individual Change.   If you were interested in learning how a child's moral development changes between the ages of 3 and 5, the most direct approach would be to take a group of 3-year-olds and follow them until they were 5, testing them periodically.

Such a strategy illustrates longitudinal research. In **longitudinal research**, the behavior of one or more individuals is measured as the participants in the study age. Longitudinal research measures change over time. By following many individuals over time, researchers can understand the general course of change across some period of life.

The granddaddy of longitudinal studies, which has become a classic, is a study of gifted children begun by Lewis Terman more than 75 years ago. In the study—which has yet to be concluded—a group of 1,500 children with high IQs were tested about every 5 years. Now in their 80s, the participants—who call themselves "Termites"—have provided information on everything from intellectual accomplishment to personality and longevity (Terman & Oden, 1959; Friedman et al., 1995a).

Longitudinal research has also provided great insight into language development. For instance, by tracing how children's vocabularies increase on a day-by-day basis, researchers have been able to understand the processes that underlie the human ability to become competent in using language.

Longitudinal studies can provide a wealth of information about change over time (Bullock, 1995). However, they have several drawbacks. For one thing, they require a tremendous investment of time, because researchers must wait for participants to become older. Furthermore, there is a significant possibility of participant *attrition*, or loss, over the course of the research. Participants may drop out of a study, they may move away, or they may become ill or even die as the research proceeds.

Finally, participants who are observed or tested may become "test-wise" and perform better each time they are assessed as they become more familiar with the procedure. Even if the observations of participants in a study are not terribly intrusive (such as simply recording, over a lengthy period of time, vocabulary increases in infants and preschoolers), experimental participants may be affected by the repeated presence of an experimenter or observer.

Consequently, despite the benefits of longitudinal research, particularly its ability to look at change within individuals, developmental researchers often turn to other methods in conducting research. The alternative they choose most often is the cross-sectional study.

Cross-sectional Studies.   Let's return to the issue of moral development in children 3 to 5 years of age. Instead of using a longitudinal approach and following the same children over several years, we might conduct the study by simultaneously looking at a group of 3-year-olds, 4-year-olds, and 5-year-olds.

Such an approach typifies cross-sectional research. In **cross-sectional research**, people of different ages are compared at the same point in time. Cross-sectional studies provide information about differences in development between different age groups.

Cross-sectional research is considerably more economical in terms of time than longitudinal research: Participants are tested at just one point in time. For instance, Terman's study

---

longitudinal research *research in which the behavior of one or more individuals is measured as the subjects age*

cross-sectional research *research in which people of different ages are compared at the same point in time*

conceivably might have been completed 75 years ago if Terman had simply looked at a group of gifted 15-year-olds, 20-year-olds, 25-year-olds, and so forth, all the way through a group of 80-year-olds. Because the participants would not be periodically tested, there would be no chance that they would become test-wise, and problems of participant attrition would not occur. Why, then, would anyone choose to use a procedure other than cross-sectional research?

The answer is that cross-sectional research brings its own set of difficulties. We can start with cohort effects. Recall that every person belongs to a particular *cohort,* the group of people born at around the same time in the same place. If we find that people of different ages vary along some dimension, it may be due to differences in cohort membership, not age *per se.*

Consider a concrete example: If we find in a correlational study that people who are 15 years old perform better on a test of intelligence than those who are 75 years old, there are several explanations. Although the finding may be due to decreased intelligence in older people, it may also be attributable to cohort differences. The group of 75-year-olds may have had less education when they were younger than the 15-year-olds, because members of the older cohort were less likely to finish high school and attend college than members of the younger one. Or perhaps the older group performed less well because as infants they received less adequate nutrition than members of the younger group. In short, we cannot fully rule out the possibility that differences we find between people of different age groups in cross-sectional studies are due to cohort differences.

Cross-sectional research allows researchers to compare representatives of different age groups at the same time.

Cross-sectional studies also may suffer from *selective dropout,* in which participants in some age groups are more likely to quit participating in a study than others. For example, suppose a study of cognitive development in preschoolers includes a lengthy assessment of cognitive abilities. It is possible that young preschoolers would find the task more difficult and demanding than older preschoolers. As a result, the younger preschoolers would be more likely to discontinue participation in the study than the older preschoolers. If the least competent young preschoolers are the ones who drop out, then the remaining sample of participants in the study will consist of the more competent young preschoolers—together with a broader and more representative sample of older preschoolers. Clearly, the results of such a study would be questionable (Miller, 1998).

Finally, cross-sectional studies have an additional, and more basic, disadvantage: They are unable to inform us about changes in individuals or groups. Although we can establish differences related to age, we cannot fully determine whether such differences are related to change over time.

Cross-sequential Studies.   Because both longitudinal and cross-sectional studies have drawbacks, researchers have turned to some compromise techniques. Among the most frequently employed are cross-sequential studies, which are essentially a combination of longitudinal and cross-sectional studies.

In **cross-sequential studies**, researchers examine a number of different age groups at several points in time. For instance, an investigator interested in children's moral behavior might begin a cross-sequential study by examining the behavior of three groups of children, who were either 3 years old, 4 years old, or 5 years old at the time the study begins. (This is no different from the way a cross-sectional study would be done.)

However, the study wouldn't stop there, but would continue for the next several years. During this period, each of the research participants would be tested annually. Thus, the 3-year-olds would be tested at ages 3, 4, and 5; the 4-year-olds at ages 4, 5, and 6; and the 5-year-olds at ages 5, 6, and 7. Such an approach combines the advantages of

cross-sequential studies *research in which researchers examine a number of different age groups over several points in time*

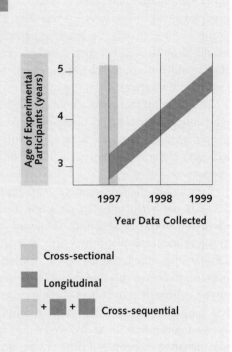

FIGURE 1-3

RESEARCH TECHNIQUES FOR STUDYING DEVELOPMENT

In a *cross-sectional study*, 3-, 4-, and 5-year-olds are compared at a similar point in time (1997). In *longitudinal research*, a set of participants who are 3 years old in 1997 are again studied when they are 4 years old (in 1998). Finally, a *cross-sequential study* combines cross-sectional and longitudinal techniques; here, a group of 3-year-olds would be compared initially in 1997 with 4- and 5-year-olds, but would also be studied 1 and 2 years later, when they themselves were 4 and 5 years old. Although the graph does not illustrate this, researchers carrying out this cross-sequential study might also choose to retest the children who were 4 and 5 in 1997 for the next 2 years.

longitudinal and cross-sectional research, and it permits developmental researchers to tease out the consequences of age *change* versus age *difference*. (The major research techniques for studying development are summarized in Figure 1-3).

Ethics and Research: The Morality of Research

Return, for a moment, to the "study" conducted by Egyptian King Psamtik, in which two children were removed from their mothers and held in isolation in an effort to learn about the roots of language. Clearly, such an experiment raises blatant ethical concerns, and nothing like it would ever be done today.

But sometimes ethical issues are more subtle. For instance, in seeking to understand the roots of aggressive behavior, U.S. government researchers proposed holding a conference in the mid-1990s to examine possible genetic roots of aggression. Based on work conducted by biopsychologists and geneticists, some researchers had begun to raise the possibility that genetic markers might be found that would allow the identification of children as being particularly violence-prone. In such cases, it might be possible to track these violence-prone children and provide interventions that might reduce the likelihood of later violence.

Critics objected strenuously, however. They argued that such identification might lead to a self-fulfilling prophecy. Children labeled as violence-prone might be treated in a way that would actually *cause* them to be more aggressive than if they hadn't been so labeled. Ultimately, under intense political pressure, the conference was canceled (Wright, 1995).

To help researchers deal with such ethical problems, the major organizations of developmentalists, including the Society for Research in Child Development and the American Psychological Association, have developed comprehensive ethical guidelines for researchers. Among the basic principles that must be followed are those involving freedom from harm, informed consent, the use of deception, and maintenance of subjects' privacy (American Psychological Association, 1992; Rosnow et al, 1993; Fisher & Fyrberg, 1994; Gurman, 1994).

Freedom from Harm.   Researchers must protect participants from physical and psychological harm. Their welfare, interests, and rights come before those of researchers. In research, subjects' rights always come first (Sieber, 1998).

Informed Consent.   Researchers must obtain consent from subjects before their participation in a study. If they are above the age of 7, participants must voluntarily agree to be in a study. For those under 18, their parents or guardians must also provide consent.

The requirement for informed consent raises some difficult issues. Suppose, for instance, researchers wish to learn the psychological consequences of abortion on adolescents. Although they may be able to obtain the consent of an adolescent who has had an abortion, the researchers may need to get her parents' permission as well, because she is a minor. But suppose the daughter hasn't told her parents that she has had an abortion. In such a case, the mere request for permission from the parents would violate the privacy of the adolescent—leading to an ethical violation.

Use of Deception.   Although deception to disguise the true purpose of an experiment is permissible, any experiment that uses deception must undergo careful scrutiny by an independent panel before it is conducted. Suppose, for example, we want to know the reaction of subjects to success and failure. It is ethical to tell subjects that they will be playing a game when the true purpose is actually to observe how they respond to doing well or poorly on the task. However, such a procedure is ethical only if it causes no harm to participants, has been approved by a review panel, and ultimately includes a full debriefing for participants when the study is over.

Maintenance of Privacy.   Subjects' privacy must be maintained. If they are videotaped during the course of a study, for example, they must give their permission for the videotapes to be viewed. Furthermore, access to the tapes must be carefully restricted.

The Informed Consumer of Development

Assessing Information on Development

If you immediately comfort crying babies, you'll spoil them.

If you let babies cry without comforting them, they'll be untrusting and clingy as adults.

***

Spanking is one of the best ways to discipline your child.
Never hit your child.

***

If a marriage is unhappy, children are better off if their parents divorce than if they stay together.

No matter how difficult a marriage is, parents should avoid divorce for the sake of their children.

There is no lack of advice on the best way to raise a child or, more generally, to lead one's life. From best-sellers with incomprehensible titles such as *Men Are From Mars, Women Are From Venus* to magazine and newspaper columns that provide advice on every imaginable topic, each of us is exposed to tremendous amounts of information.

Yet not all advice is equally valid. The mere fact that something is in print or on television does not automatically make it legitimate or accurate. Fortunately, there are ways to distinguish when recommendations and suggestions are reasonable, and when they are not. Among the ways of determining whether the advice should be accepted are the following.

■ Consider the source of the advice. Information from established, respected organizations such as the American Medical Association, the American Psychological Association, and the American Academy of Pediatrics are likely to be the result of years of study, and their accuracy is probably high.

■ Determine the credentials of the person providing advice. Information coming from established, acknowledged researchers and experts in a field is likely to be more accurate than that coming from a person whose credentials are obscure.

■ Understand the difference between anecdotal evidence and scientific evidence. Anecdotal evidence is based on one or two instances of a phenomenon, haphazardly discovered or encountered. In contrast, scientific evidence is based on careful, systematic procedures. The evidence has been collected in a methodical, orderly manner.

■ Keep cultural context in mind. Although a pronouncement may be valid in some contexts, it may not be true in all. For example, it is typically assumed that providing infants the freedom to move about and exercise their limbs facilitates their muscular development and mobility. Yet in some cultures, infants' movements are very restricted, and in a few they spend most of their time closely bound to their mothers (Super, 1976; Kaplan & Dove, 1987; Tronick, 1995). Although such infants may show delays in physical development, by late childhood they are indistinguishable from children raised in a less restrictive manner.

■ Don't assume that because many people believe something, it is necessarily true. Scientific evaluation has often proven that some of the most basic presumptions about the effectiveness of various techniques are invalid. For instance, consider DARE, the Drug Abuse Resistance Education antidrug program that is used in about half the school systems in the United States. DARE is designed to prevent the spread of drugs through lectures and question-and-answer sessions run by specially trained police officers. One prob-

lem, though: Careful evaluation has found no evidence that the program works. Teachers, administrators, police officers, and taxpayers who support the program may like it—but it doesn't seem to reduce the use of drugs (Ennett et al., 1994).

In short, the key to evaluating information relating to human development is to maintain a healthy dose of skepticism. No source of information is invariably, unfailingly accurate. By keeping a critical eye on the statements you encounter, you'll be in a better position to determine the very real contributions made by developmentalists to understanding how humans develop over the course of the life span.

REVIEW AND RETHINK

REVIEW

■ Theories in development are systematically derived explanations of facts or phenomena. Theories suggest hypotheses, which are predictions that can be tested.

■ Correlational studies examine relationships between factors without demonstrating causality. Naturalistic observation, case studies, and survey research are types of correlational studies.

■ Experimental research seeks to discover cause-and-effect relationships by the use of a treatment group and a control group. By manipulating the independent variable and observing changes in the dependent variable, researchers find evidence of causal links between variables.

■ Research studies may be conducted in field settings, where participants are subject to natural conditions, or in laboratories, where conditions can be controlled effectively. Studies are traditionally categorized as either theoretical (designed to advance scientific knowledge) or applied (designed to solve practical problems), but the distinction is often unclear.

■ Researchers measure age-related change by longitudinal studies (same subjects at different ages), cross-sectional studies (different-age subjects at one time), and cross-sequential studies (different-age subjects at several times).

■ Developmental researchers follow ethical guidelines relating to such issues as the prevention of harm in subjects, informed consent, the use of deception, and privacy.

RETHINK

■ Formulate a theory about one aspect of human development and a hypothesis that relates to it.

■ What sort of research strategy would be appropriate for investigating each of the statements (about comforting babies, spanking, and divorce) at the beginning of the Informed Consumer box?

■ Would a laboratory or a field setting be most appropriate for each research strategy you identified?

■ Can you think of a correlation between two phenomena related to gender? What are some possible explanations for the correlation? How would you establish causality?

■ What problems might affect a study of age-related changes in sexual attitudes and practices conducted at one time among a cross-section of adults aged 18 to 50?

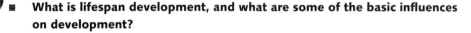

LOOKING BACK

■ **What is lifespan development, and what are some of the basic influences on development?**

- Lifespan development is a scientific approach to questions about growth, change, and stability in the physical, cognitive, and social and personality characteristics at all ages from conception to death.

- The ecological approach to development suggests that four levels of the environment simultaneously affect the individual: the microsystem, the mesosystem, the exosystem, and the macrosystem. The ecological approach stresses the interrelatedness of developmental areas and the importance of broad cultural factors in human development.

- Each individual is subject to normative history-graded influences, normative age-graded influences, normative sociocultural-graded influences, and nonnormative life events.

■ **What are the key issues in the field of development?**

- Four key issues in lifespan development are (1) whether developmental change is continuous or discontinuous; (2) whether development is largely governed by critical periods during which certain influences or experiences must occur for development to be normal; (3) whether to focus on certain important periods in human development or on the entire life span; and (4) the nature–nurture controversy which focuses on the relative importance of genetic versus environmental influences.

■ **Which theoretical perspectives have guided lifespan development?**

- Five major theoretical perspectives currently dominate lifespan development: the psychodynamic perspective (which focuses on inner, largely unconscious forces), the behavioral perspective (which focuses on external, observable actions), the cognitive perspective (which focuses on intellectual, cognitive processes), the humanistic perspective (which focuses on the unique qualities of human beings), and the evolutionary perspective (which focuses on our genetic inheritance).

- The psychodynamic perspective is exemplified by the psychoanalytic theory of Freud and the psychosocial theory of Erikson. Freud focused attention on the unconscious and on stages through which children must pass successfully to avoid harmful fixations. Erikson identified eight distinct stages of development, each characterized by a conflict, or crisis, to work out.

- The behavioral perspective typically concerns stimulus–response learning, exemplified by classical conditioning, the operant conditioning of Skinner, and Bandura's social-cognitive learning theory.

- Within the cognitive perspective, the most notable theorist is Piaget, who identified developmental stages through which all children are assumed to pass. Each stage involves qualitative differences in thinking.

- In contrast, information-processing approaches attribute cognitive growth to quantitative changes in mental processes and capacities. Vygotsky's sociocultural theory emphasizes the central influence on cognitive development exerted by social interactions between members of a culture.

- The humanistic perspective contends that people have a natural capacity to make decisions about their lives and control their behavior. The humanistic perspective emphasizes free will and the natural desire of humans to reach their full potential.

- The evolutionary perspective attributes behavior to genetic inheritance from our ancestors, contending that the genes determine not only traits such as skin and eye color, but certain personality traits and social behaviors as well.

- Culture—both broad and narrow—is another important issue in lifespan development. Many aspects of development are influenced not only by broad cultural differences, but also by ethnic, racial, and socioeconomic differences within a particular culture.

■ **What role do theories and hypotheses play in the study of development?**

- Theories are broad explanations of facts or phenomena of interest, based on a systematic integration of prior findings and theories. Hypotheses are theory-based predictions that can be tested. The process of posing and answering questions systematically is called the scientific method.

- Researchers test hypotheses by correlational research (to determine if two factors are associated) and experimental research (to discover cause-and-effect relationships).

■ **How are developmental research studies conducted?**

- Correlational studies use naturalistic observation, case studies, and survey research to investigate whether certain characteristics of interest are associated with other characteristics. Correlational studies lead to no direct conclusions about cause and effect.

- Typically, experimental research studies are conducted on participants in a treatment group who receive the experimental treatment and a control group who does not. Following the treatment, differences between the two groups can help the experimenter to determine the effects of the treatment. Experiments may be conducted in a laboratory or in a real-world setting.

- To measure change across human ages researchers use longitudinal studies of the same participants over time, cross-sectional studies of different-age participants conducted at one time, and cross-sequential studies of different-age participants at several points in time.

- Ethical guidelines for research include the protection of participants from harm, informed consent of participants, limits on the use of deception, and the maintenance of privacy.

EPILOGUE: VIOLENCE AT SCHOOL

Before we proceed to the next chapter, take a few minutes to reconsider the prologue of this chapter—about the Columbine High School shooting. Based on what you now know about developmental research, answer the following questions.

1. What are some questions that developmentalists who study either physical, cognitive, or personality and social development might ask about the effects of witnessing the attack on the students' future development?

2. How might developmentalists from the psychodynamic, behavioral, and cognitive perspectives explain the reasons why the killers unleashed their deadly attack? What

differences might there be in the questions that would interest them and the studies they might wish to conduct?

3. Formulate one hypothesis about either cognitive or social/personality development regarding the effects on viewers of media reports of the Columbine High School incident.

4. Can you design a correlational study to test the hypothesis you generated in question 3? Can you design an experimental study to test the hypothesis? Try to design both kinds of study, describing the research design, setting, and participants.

KEY TERMS AND CONCEPTS

lifespan development (p. 5)

physical development (p. 6)

cognitive development (p. 6)

personality development (p. 6)

social development (p. 6)

ecological approach (p. 8)

cohort (p. 9)

normative history-graded influences (p. 10)

normative age-graded influences (p. 10)

normative sociocultural-graded influences (p. 10)

nonnormative life events (p. 10)

continuous change (p. 10)

discontinuous change (p. 10)

critical period (p. 11)

sensitive period (p. 11)

maturation (p. 12)

theories (p. 14)

psychodynamic perspective (p. 15)

psychoanalytic theory (p. 15)

id (p. 15)

ego (p. 15)

superego (p. 15)

psychosexual development (p. 15)

fixation (p. 16)

psychosocial development (p. 17)

behavioral perspective (p. 17)

classical conditioning (p. 18)

operant conditioning (p. 18)

behavior modification (p. 18)

social-cognitive learning theory (p. 19)

cognitive perspective (p. 20)

assimilation (p. 20)

accommodation (p. 20)

information-processing approaches (p. 21)

sociocultural theory (p. 21)

humanistic perspective (p. 22)

evolutionary perspective (p. 22)

scientific method (p. 28)

hypothesis (p. 28)

correlational research (p. 28)

experimental research (p. 29)

naturalistic observation (p. 31)

case studies (p. 31)

survey research (p. 31)

experiment (p. 33)

treatment (p. 33)

treatment group (p. 33)

control group (p. 33)

independent variable (p. 33)

dependent variable (p. 33)

field study (p. 34)

laboratory study (p. 34)

theoretical research (p. 34)

applied research (p. 34)

longitudinal research (p. 36)

cross-sectional research (p. 36)

cross-sequential studies (p. 37)

CHAPTER 2

The Start of Life: Genetics and Prenatal Development

PROLOGUE: MULTIPLICITY

Kenny and Bobbi McCaughey, parents of septuplets born in Iowa.

On a warm and sunny day . . . , Kathy Addleman drove from her home in Mason City, Iowa, 130 miles south to the town of Carlisle to check on the pregnancy of her daughter-in-law Bobbi McCaughey. "I asked her if everything was fine and if she was still pregnant," says Addleman, recalling how very ordinary things seemed back then. "And she said, 'Yeah . . . more than one.'

"I looked at her and asked, 'Two?'

"She said, 'More.'

"'Three?'

"'More.'

"I kept going, my eyes getting bigger. She said, 'Seven.' I said, 'No way.'

"Then she said, 'Way.'" (Schindehette, 1997, p. 59)

It was true: After taking a fertility drug to stimulate pregnancy, Bobbi McCaughey and her husband, Kenny, got more than they bargained for. Kenneth, Brandon, Alexis, Nathan, Joel, Sue, and Kelsey—seven of them—arrived one November afternoon. It was more likely that Bobbi McCaughey would be struck dead by a falling asteroid than conceive and deliver that many children.

Although an extreme case, the conception of the McCaughey septuplets is part of an everyday miracle involved in the first stirrings of all new life. In this chapter, we'll examine what researchers in child development and other scientists have learned about ways that heredity and the environment work in tandem to create and shape human beings. We begin with the basics of heredity, examining how we receive our genetic endowment. We consider a burgeoning area of study, behavioral genetics, that specializes in the consequences of heredity on behavior. The chapter also discusses what happens when genetic factors cause development to go awry, and how such problems are dealt with through genetic counseling and the brave new world of cloning and genetic engineering.

Next, we will turn to a discussion of the interaction of heredity and environment. We will also consider the relative influence of genes and environment on a variety of characteristics, including physical traits, intelligence, and even personality.

Finally, we'll focus on the very first stage of development, tracing prenatal growth and change. We'll talk about the stages of the prenatal period, and how the prenatal environment offers both threats to—and the promise of—future growth.

In sum, after reading this chapter, you will be able to answer these questions:

Q

- ■ **What is our basic genetic endowment, and how can human development go awry?**
- ■ **How do the environment and genetics work together to determine human characteristics?**
- ■ **Which human characteristics are significantly influenced by heredity?**
- ■ **What happens during the prenatal stages of development?**
- ■ **What are the threats to the fetal environment and what can be done about them?**

HEREDITY

We humans begin the course of our lives simply.

Like individuals from tens of thousands of other species, we start as a single cell, a tiny speck probably weighing no more than one twenty-millionth of an ounce. But from this humble beginning, human development follows its own unique path, accomplishing a journey that leads to the flowering of humankind's vast potential.

What determines the process that transforms the single cell into something that we can more easily identify as a person? The answer is the human genetic code, transmitted at the moment of conception in the **gametes**, or sex cells, from the mother and father, and embedded in that single, first cell.

Fertilization: The Moment of Conception

When most of us think about the facts of life, we tend to focus on the events that involve the moment when a male's *sperm* cells begin their journey towards a female's *ovum* (egg cell). Yet the act of sex that brings about the potential for conception is both the consequence and the start of a long string of events that precede and follow fertilization. **Fertilization**, or conception, is the process by which a sperm and an ovum—the male and female gametes, respectively—join to form a single new cell, called a **zygote**.

fertilization the process by which a sperm and an ovum—the male and female gametes, respectively—join to form a single new cell

zygote the new cell formed by the process of fertilization

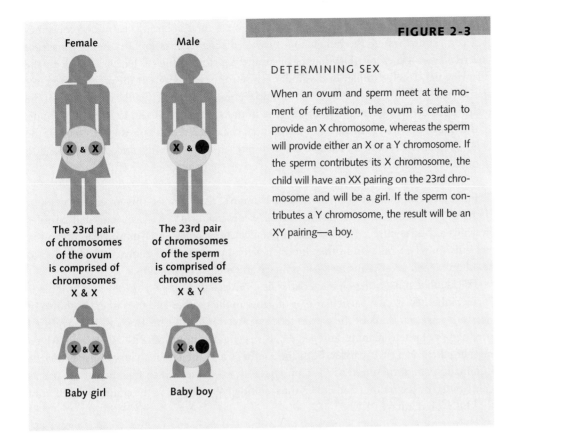

FIGURE 2-3

DETERMINING SEX

When an ovum and sperm meet at the moment of fertilization, the ovum is certain to provide an X chromosome, whereas the sperm will provide either an X or a Y chromosome. If the sperm contributes its X chromosome, the child will have an XX pairing on the 23rd chromosome and will be a girl. If the sperm contributes a Y chromosome, the result will be an XY pairing—a boy.

(but outwardly invisible) in an organism. In contrast, a **phenotype** is the observable trait, the trait that actually is seen.

Although the offspring of the yellow-seeded and green-seeded pea plants all have yellow seeds (i.e., they have a yellow-seeded phenotype), the genotype consists of genetic information relating to both parents.

And what is the nature of the information in the genotype? To answer that question, let's turn from peas to people. In fact, the principles are the same not just for plants and humans, but for the majority of species.

phenotype   *an observable trait; the trait that actually is seen*

Gregor Mendel's pioneering experiments on pea plants provided the foundation for the study of genetics.

Recall that parents transmit genetic information to their offspring via the chromosomes they contribute through the gamete they provide during fertilization. In cases of genes that govern *alleles*—genes for traits that may take alternate forms, such as hair or eye color—the offspring may receive similar or dissimilar genes from each parent. If the offspring receives similar genes, the organism is said to be **homozygous** for the trait. On the other hand, if the offspring receives different forms of the gene from its parents, it is said to be **heterozygous**. In the case of heterozygous alleles, the dominant characteristic is expressed. However, if the child happens to receive a recessive allele from each of its parents, and therefore lacks a dominant characteristic, it will display the recessive characteristic.

Transmission of Genetic Information in Humans.   We can see this process at work in humans by considering the transmission of *phenylketonuria (PKU)*, an inherited disorder in which a child is unable to make use of phenylalanine, an essential amino acid present in proteins found in milk and other foods. If left untreated, PKU allows phenylalanine to build up to toxic levels, causing brain damage and mental retardation.

PKU, unlike most other characteristics, is produced by a single pair of genes in the off-spring, inherited from a particular pair of genes in the mother and the father. As shown in Figure 2-4, we can think of the pair in terms of *P*, a dominant gene that causes the normal production of phenylalanine, and *p*, a recessive gene that produces PKU. In cases in which neither parent is a PKU carrier, both the mother's and the father's pairs of genes are the dominant form, symbolized as *PP*. Consequently, no matter which member of the pair is contributed by the mother and father, the resulting pair of genes in the child will be *PP*, and the child will not have PKU.

However, consider what happens if one of the parents has a recessive *p* gene. In this case, which we can we symbolize as *Pp*, the parent will not have PKU, because the normal *P* gene is dominant. But the recessive gene can be passed down to the child. This is not so bad: If the child has only one recessive gene, it will not suffer from PKU. But what if both parents carry a recessive *p* gene? In this case, although neither parent has the disorder, it is possible for the child to receive a recessive gene from both parents. The child's genotype for PKU then will be *pp*, and it will have the disorder.

Remember, though, that even children whose parents both have the recessive gene for PKU have only a 25 percent chance of inheriting the disorder. Due to the laws of probability, 25 percent of children with *Pp* parents will receive the dominant gene from each parent (*PP*), and 50 percent will receive the dominant gene from one parent and the recessive gene from the other (*Pp* or *pP*). Only the unlucky 25 percent who receive the recessive gene from each parent and end up with the genotype *pp* will suffer from PKU.

The basic principles that explain the transmission of PKU underlie the transmission of all genetic information from parent to child. However, in some respects, the case of PKU is simpler than most cases of genetic transmission. Relatively few traits are governed by a single pair of genes. Instead, most traits are the result of polygenic inheritance. In **polygenic inheritance**, a combination of multiple gene pairs is responsible for the production of a particular trait.

Furthermore, some genes come in several alternate forms, and still others act to modify the way that particular genetic traits (produced by other alleles) are displayed. And some traits, such as blood type, are produced by genes in which neither pair of genes can be classified as purely dominant or recessive. Instead, the trait is expressed in terms of a combination of the two genes—such as type AB blood.

A number of recessive genes, called **X-linked genes**, are located only on the X chromosome. Recall that in females, the 23rd pair of chromosomes is an XX pair, whereas in males it is an XY pair. One result is that males have a higher risk for a variety of X-linked disorders, because males lack a second X chromosome that can counteract the genetic information that produces the disorder. For example, males are significantly more apt to have red-green color blindness, a disorder produced by a set of genes on the X chromosome.

homozygous *inheriting from parents similar genes for a given trait*

heterozygous *inheriting from parents different forms of a gene for a given trait*

polygenic inheritance *inheritance in which a combination of multiple gene pairs is responsible for the production of a particular trait*

X-linked genes *genes that are considered recessive and located only on the X chromosome*

FIGURE 2-4

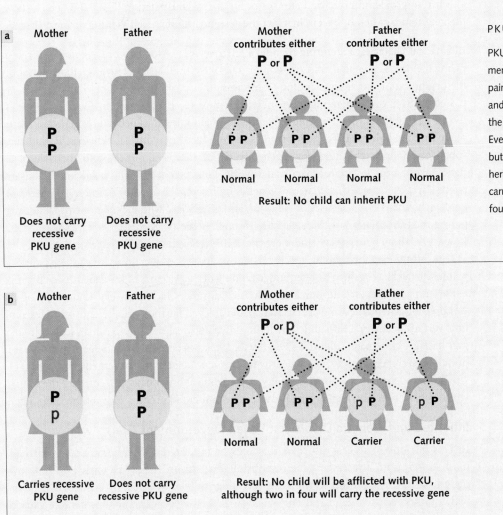

a

Mother | Father

P
P

Does not carry
recessive
PKU gene

P
P

Does not carry
recessive
PKU gene

Mother
contributes either
P or **P**

Father
contributes either
P or **P**

P P
Normal

P P
Normal

P P
Normal

P P
Normal

Result: No child can inherit PKU

b

Mother | Father

P
p

Carries recessive
PKU gene

P
P

Does not carry
recessive PKU gene

Mother
contributes either
P or p

Father
contributes either
P or **P**

P P
Normal

P P
Normal

p P
Carrier

p P
Carrier

Result: No child will be afflicted with PKU,
although two in four will carry the recessive gene

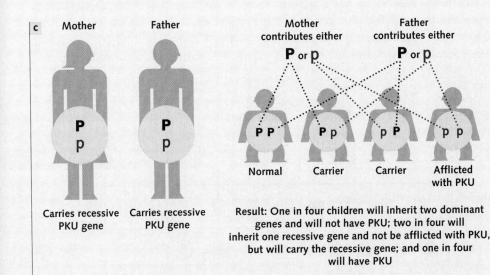

c

Mother | Father

P
p

Carries recessive
PKU gene

P
p

Carries recessive
PKU gene

Mother
contributes either
P or p

Father
contributes either
P or p

P P
Normal

P p
Carrier

p P
Carrier

p p
Afflicted
with PKU

Result: One in four children will inherit two dominant
genes and will not have PKU; two in four will
inherit one recessive gene and not be afflicted with PKU,
but will carry the recessive gene; and one in four
will have PKU

PKU PROBABILITIES

PKU, a disease that causes brain damage and
mental retardation, is produced by a single
pair of genes inherited from one's mother
and father. If neither parent carries a gene for
the disease (a), a child cannot develop PKU.
Even if one parent carries the recessive gene,
but the other doesn't (b), the child cannot inherit the disease. However, if both parents
carry the recessive gene (c), there is a one in
four chance that the child will have PKU.

behavioral genetics *the study of the effects of heredity on behavior*

Similarly, *hemophilia*, a blood disorder, is produced by X-linked genes. Hemophilia has been a recurrent problem in the royal families of Europe, as illustrated in Figure 2-5, which shows the inheritance of hemophilia in many of the descendants of Queen Victoria of Great Britain.

Behavioral Genetics: Extending Mendel's Discoveries.   Mendel's achievements in recognizing the basics of genetic transmission of traits were trailblazing. However, they mark only the beginning of our understanding of the ways that particular sorts of characteristics are passed on from one generation to the next. The most recent approach to deciphering the effect of heredity is through a rapidly burgeoning field known as behavioral genetics. As the name implies, **behavioral genetics** studies the effects of heredity on behavior. Rather than simply examining stable, unchanging characteristics such as hair or eye color, behavioral genetics takes a broader approach, considering how our personality and behavioral habits are affected by genetic factors. Behavioral genetics represents the melding of interests of psychologists, who focus on the causes of behavior, and geneticists, who focus on the processes that permit the transmission of characteristics through heredity (Kimble, 1993; McClearn, 1993; Rowe, 1993; Bouchard, 1994; Lander & Schork, 1994; Segal, Weisfeld, & Weisfeld, 1997).

The promise of behavioral genetics is substantial. For one thing, researchers working within the field have gained a better understanding of the specifics of the genetic code that underlie human behavior and development. Such advances have provided knowledge of the workings of genetics at a molecular and chemical level. Furthermore, scientists are learning how various behavioral difficulties, including psychological disorders such as schizophrenia, may have a genetic basis (Plomin, 1990, 1994b, 1995; Michel & Moore, 1995). Even more important, researchers are seeking to identify how genetic defects may be remedied (Heath et al., 1997). To understand how that possibility might come about, we need to consider the ways in which genetic factors, which normally cause development to proceed so smoothly, may falter.

Inherited and Genetic Disorders: When Development Goes Awry

PKU is just one of several disorders that may be inherited. Like a bomb that is harmless until its fuse is lit, a recessive gene responsible for a disorder may be passed on unknowingly from one generation to the next, revealing itself only when, by chance, it is paired with another recessive gene. It is only when two recessive genes come together like a match and a fuse that the gene will express itself and a child will inherit the genetic disorder.

But there is another way that genes are a source of concern: In some cases, genes become physically damaged. For instance, genes may break down due to wear-and-tear or chance events occurring during the cell division processes of meiosis and mitosis. Sometimes genes, for no known reason, spontaneously change their form, a process called *spontaneous*

FIGURE 2-5

INHERITING HEMOPHILIA

Hemophilia, a blood-clotting disorder, has been an inherited problem throughout the royal families of Europe, as illustrated by the descendants of Queen Victoria of Britain.

(Adapted from Kimball, 1983.)

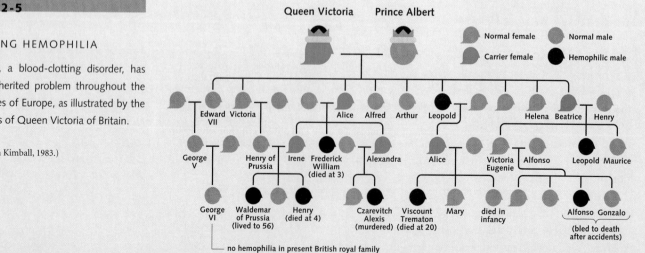

mutation. Alternatively, certain environmental factors, such as exposure to X-rays, may produce a malformation of genetic material. When such damaged genes are passed on to a child, the results can be disastrous in terms of future physical and cognitive development.

In addition to PKU, which occurs once in 10 to 20 thousand births, other inherited and genetic disorders include:

■ *Down syndrome.* As we noted earlier, people have 46 chromosomes, arranged in 23 pairs. One exception is individuals with **Down syndrome**, a disorder produced by the presence of an extra chromosome on the 21st pair. Once referred to as mongolism, Down syndrome is the most frequent cause of mental retardation. It occurs in about 1 out of 500 births, although the risk is much greater in mothers who are unusually young or old (Cicchetti & Beeghly, 1990; Carr, 1995).

■ *Sickle-cell anemia.* Around one-tenth of the African American population carry genes that produce sickle-cell anemia, and 1 African American in 400 actually has the disease. **Sickle-cell anemia** is a blood disorder that gets its name from the shape of the red blood cells in those who have it. Symptoms include poor appetite, stunted growth, swollen stomach, and yellowish eyes. People afflicted with the most severe form of the disease rarely live beyond childhood. However, for those with less severe cases, medical advances have produced significant increases in life expectancy.

■ *Tay-Sachs disease.* Occurring mainly in Jews of Eastern European ancestry, **Tay-Sachs disease** usually causes death before its victims reach school age. There is no treatment for the disorder, which produces blindness and muscle degeneration prior to death.

■ *Klinefelter's syndrome.* One male out of every 400 is born with **Klinefelter's syndrome**, the presence of an extra X chromosome. The resulting XXY complement produces underdeveloped genitals, extreme height, and enlarged breasts. Klinefelter's syndrome is one of a number of genetic abnormalities that result from receiving the improper number of sex chromosomes. For instance, there are disorders produced by an extra Y chromosome (XYY), a missing second chromosome (X0), and three X chromosomes (XXX). Such disorders are typically characterized by problems relating to sexual characteristics and by intellectual deficits (Sorenson, 1992; Sotos, 1997).

The mere fact that a disorder has genetic roots does not mean that environmental factors do not also play a role (Moldin & Gottesman, 1997). Consider, for instance, sickle-cell anemia, which primarily afflicts people of African descent. Because the disease can be fatal in childhood, we'd expect that those who suffer from it would be unlikely to live long enough to pass it on. And this does seem to be true, at least in the United States: Compared with parts of West Africa, the incidence in the United States is much lower.

But why shouldn't the incidence of sickle-cell anemia also be gradually reduced for people in West Africa? This question proved puzzling for many years, until scientists determined that carrying the sickle-cell gene raises immunity to malaria, which is a common disease in West Africa (Allison, 1954). This heightened immunity meant that people with the sickle-cell gene had a genetic advantage (in terms of resistance to malaria) that offset, to some degree, the disadvantage of being a carrier of the sickle-cell gene.

The lesson of sickle-cell anemia is that genetic factors are intertwined with environmental considerations and can't be looked at in isolation. Furthermore, we need to remember that, although we've been focusing on inherited factors that can go awry, in the vast majority of cases the genetic mechanisms with which we are endowed work quite well. Overall, just under 95 percent of children born in the United States are healthy and normal. For the some 250,000 who are born with some sort of physical or mental disorder, appropriate intervention often can help treat and, in some cases, cure the problem.

Moreover, due to advances in behavioral genetics, genetic difficulties increasingly can be forecast, anticipated, and planned for before a child's birth. In fact, as scientists' knowledge regarding the specific location of particular genes expands, predictions of what the genetic future may hold are becoming increasingly exact, as we discuss next (Cook-Deegan, 1994; Plomin, 1995).

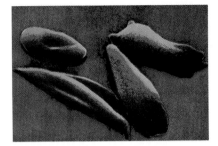

Sickle cell anemia, named for the presence of misshapen red blood cells, is carried in the genes of 1 in 10 African Americans.

Down syndrome *a disorder produced by the presence of an extra chromosome on the 21st pair; once referred to as mongolism*

sickle-cell anemia *a blood disorder that gets its name from the shape of the red blood cells in those who have it*

Tay-Sachs disease *a disorder that produces blindness and muscle degeneration prior to death; there is no treatment*

Klinefelter's syndrome *a disorder resulting from the presence of an extra X chromosome that produces underdeveloped genitals, extreme height, and enlarged breasts*

Genetic Counseling: Predicting the Future from the Genes of the Present

genetic counseling the discipline that focuses on helping people deal with issues relating to inherited disorders

amniocentesis the process of identifying genetic defects by examining a small sample of fetal cells drawn by a needle inserted into the amniotic fluid surrounding the unborn fetus

chorionic villus sampling (CVS) a test used to find genetic defects that involves taking samples of hairlike material that surrounds the embryo

ultrasound sonography a process in which high-frequency sound waves scan the mother's womb to produce an image of the unborn baby, whose size and shape can then be assessed

The last thing Joey Paulowsky needs is another bout with cancer. Only 7 years old, the Dallas native has already fought off leukemia, and now his family worries that Joey could be hit again. The Paulowsky family carries a genetic burden—a rare form of inherited cancer of the thyroid. Deborah, his mother, found a lump in her neck six years ago, and since then one family member has died of the cancer and 10 others have had to have their thyroid glands removed. "Do I have cancer?" Joey asks his mother. "Will it hurt?" The Paulowskys will know the answer next month, when the results of a genetic test will show whether their son carries the family's fateful mutation. (Brownlee, Cook, & Hardigg, 1994, p. 59)

The answer will be delivered by a member of a field that, just a few decades ago, was nonexistent: genetic counseling. **Genetic counseling** focuses on helping people deal with issues relating to inherited disorders.

Genetic counselors use a variety of data in their work (Lindhout, Frets, & Niermeijer, 1991). For instance, couples contemplating having a child may seek to determine the risks involved in a future pregnancy. In such a case, a counselor will take a thorough family history, seeking any familial incidence of birth defects that might indicate a pattern of recessive or X-linked genes. In addition, the counselor will take into account factors such as the age of the mother and father and any previous abnormalities in other children they may have already had.

Typically, genetic counselors suggest a thorough physical examination. Such an exam may identify physical abnormalities that potential parents may have and not be aware of. In addition, samples of blood, skin, and urine may be used to isolate and examine specific chromosomes. Possible genetic defects, such as the presence of an extra sex chromosome, can be identified by assembling a *karyotype*, a chart containing enlarged photos of each of the chromosomes.

If the woman is already pregnant, testing of the unborn child itself is possible. In **amniocentesis**, a small sample of fetal cells is drawn by a tiny needle inserted into the amniotic fluid surrounding the unborn fetus. By analyzing the fetal cells, technicians can identify a variety of genetic defects. In addition, they can determine the sex of the child. Although there is always a danger to the fetus in such an invasive procedure, amniocentesis is generally safe when carried out between the 12th and 16th weeks of pregnancy.

An additional test, **chorionic villus sampling (CVS)**, can be employed even earlier. The test involves taking small samples of hairlike material that surrounds the embryo. CVS can be done between the 8th and 11th weeks of pregnancy. However, because it is riskier than amniocentesis and can identify fewer genetic problems, its use is relatively infrequent.

Other tests that are less invasive and therefore less risky are also possible. For instance, the unborn child may be examined through **ultrasound sonography**, in which high-frequency sound waves are used to bombard the mother's womb. These waves produce a rather indistinct, but useful, image of the unborn baby, whose size and shape can then be assessed. Repeated use of ultrasound sonography can reveal developmental patterns. After the various tests are complete and all possible information is available, the couple will meet with the genetic counselor again. Typically, counselors avoid giving specific recommendations if a problem has been identified. Instead, they lay out the facts and present various options, ranging from doing nothing to taking more drastic steps, such as terminating the pregnancy through abortion. Ultimately, it is the parents who must decide what course of action to follow.

The newest role of genetic counselors involves testing to identify whether an individual is susceptible to future disorders because of genetic abnormalities. For instance, *Huntington's disease*, a devastating, always fatal disorder marked by tremors and intellectual deterioration, typically does not appear until people reach their 40s. However, genetic testing can identify much earlier whether a person carries the flawed gene that produces

CW

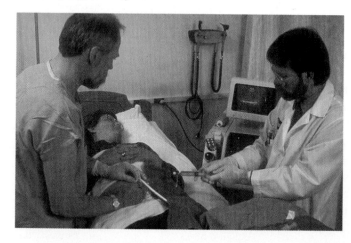

In amniocentesis, a sample of fetal cells is withdrawn from the amniotic sac and used to identify a number of genetic defects.

Huntington's disease. Presumably, people's knowledge that they carry the gene can help them prepare themselves for the future (van 't Spijker & ten Kroode, 1997).

In addition to Huntington's disease, more than 450 disorders can be predicted on the basis of genetic testing (see Table 2-1). Although such testing may bring welcome relief from future worries—if the results are negative—positive results may produce just the opposite effect. In fact, genetic testing raises difficult practical and ethical questions (Lapham, Kozma, & Weiss, 1996; Holtzman et al., 1997; Painter, 1997).

Suppose, for instance, a person who thought she was susceptible to Huntington's disease was tested in her 20s and found that she did not carry the defective gene. Obviously, she would experience tremendous relief. But suppose she found that she did carry the flawed gene and was therefore going to get the disease. She might well experience depression and remorse. In fact, some studies show that 10 percent of people who find they have the flawed gene that leads to Huntington's disease never recover fully on an emotional level (Nowak, 1994a; Groopman, 1998).

Genetic testing is a complicated issue. It rarely provides a simple yes or no answer as to whether an individual will be susceptible to a disorder. Typically it presents a range of probabilities, which many find difficult to interpret. In addition, people are increasingly demanding the latest genetic test, even if evidence is scanty that they are at appreciable medical risk of having a particular disease (Brownlee, Cook, & Hardigg, 1994; Holtzman et al., 1997).

TABLE 2-1

GENETIC TESTS

DNA TESTS AVAILABLE NOW

Disease	Description	Incidence	Cost
Adult polycystic kidney disease	Multiple kidney growths	1 in 1,000	$350
Alpha-1-antitrypsin deficiency	Can cause hepatitis, cirrhosis of the liver, emphysema	1 in 2,000 to 1 in 4,000	$200
Charcot-Marie-Tooth disease	Progressive degeneration of muscles	1 in 2,500	$250–$350
Familial adenomatous polyposos	Colon polyps by age 35, often leading to cancer	1 in 5,000	$1,000
Cystic fibrosis	Lungs clog with mucus; usually fatal by age 40	1 in 2,500 Caucasians	$125–$150
Duchenne/Becker muscular dystrophy	Progressive degeneration of muscles	1 in 3,000 males	$300–$900
Hemophilia	Blood fails to clot properly	1 in 10,000	$250–$350
Fragile X syndrome	Most common cause of inherited mental retardation	1 in 1,250 males; 1 in 2,500 females	$250
Gaucher's disease	Mild to deadly enzyme deficiency	1 in 400 Ashkenazi Jews	$100–$150
Huntington's disease	Lethal neurological deterioration	1 in 10,000 Caucasians	$250–$300
"Lou Gehrig's disease" (ALS)	Fatal degeneration of the nervous system	1 in 50,000, 10% familial	$150–$450
Myotonic dystrophy	Progressive degeneration of muscles	1 in 8,000	$250
Multiple endocrine neoplastia	Endocrine gland tumors	1 in 50,000	$900
Neurofibromatosis	*Café au lait* spots to large tumors	1 in 3,000	$900
Retinoblastoma	Blindness; potentially fatal eye tumors	1 in 20,000	$1,500
Spinal muscular atrophy	Progressive degeneration of muscles	7 in 100,000	$100–$900
Tay-Sachs disease	Lethal childhood neurological disorder	1 in 3,600 Ashkenazi Jews	$150
Thalassemia	Mild to fatal anemia	1 in 100,000	$300

Tests of the Future

Disease	Description	Incidence	Cost
Alzheimer's	Most likely multiple genes involved	4 million cases	Not available
Breast cancer	Five to 10% of all cases are thought to be hereditary	2.6 million cases	Not available
Diabetes	Most likely multiple genes involved	13–14 million cases	Not available
Nonpolyposis colon cancer	Several genes cause up to 20% of all cases	150,000 cases per year	Not available
Manic-depression	Most likely multiple genes involved	2 million cases	Not available

As our understanding of genetics continues to grow, the possibilities for genetic intervention and manipulation increasingly border on what once was science fiction—as we consider in the accompanying "Directions in Development" box about cloning.

Directions in Development

Hello Dolly: Gene Therapy and Cloning

In all ways she appeared to be an ordinary sheep, not much to look at, with little in the way of personality. But in one way she was far from ordinary, for Dolly, as she was called, was the first animal to be cloned from the cells of an adult. An exact genetic replica of another adult sheep, Dolly was soon followed by other cloned animals who were genetically identical to adults (Pennisi, 1997; Kolata, 1998).

The technological advance that Dolly represents does more than raise ethical questions about the possibility of making genetic replicas of adult humans. It also holds the possibility of correcting genetic flaws even before an individual is born—a procedure that likely will revolutionize medicine in the 21st century.

Already, some forms of gene therapy are being used to correct genetic defects in humans. In *gene therapy*, researchers inject genes that are targeted to correct a particular disease into a patient's blood stream. When the genes arrive at the site of the defective genes that are causing the disease, their presence leads to the production of chemicals that can treat the problem. For instance, in the case of cancer, researchers might engineer corrective genes to produce proteins that could kill tumor cells. In other cases, they may add new genes to make up for missing or ineffective cells.

The first patient to receive gene therapy was Ashanti DeSilva, a 4-year-old with a rare, inherited disease called severe combined immunodeficiency (SCID), which caused her immune system to shut down. Consequently, she was continually susceptible to a huge number of infections. To remedy the situation, scientists removed some white blood cells from Ashanti's immune system and inserted nondiseased copies of the defective gene. These nondiseased copies were then injected into her body. Five years later, Ashanti was a normal 9-year-old with no immune-system problems (Anderson, 1995).

Advances in cloning, as exemplified by Dolly, promise to make gene therapy even more useful. In a process called *germ-line gene therapy*, genetic modifications can correct problems not only for unborn individuals, but for future generations as well. In germ-line gene therapy, scientists might "harvest" defective cells soon after conception, removing them from the mother and placing them in a test-tube culture. Gene therapy could be employed to correct the defects in the cells. Next, a corrected cell—a slightly altered clone of the initial cells—could be returned to the

Dolly, the cloned sheep, had raised significant ethical questions.

mother. In a more extreme possibility, cells from one parent might be altered genetically to remove any defects, and this clone could then be permitted to grow. The result would be a clone, genetically identical to the parent except for the lack of the genetic defect. Obviously, such possibilities raise serious ethical questions (Rosenfeld & Curiel, 1996; Mirsky & Rennie, 1997).

The list of diseases currently being treated through gene therapy is still relatively small, although the number is growing. For instance, experiments using gene therapy are now being employed for cystic fibrosis, hemophilia, rheumatoid arthritis, AIDS, and several other diseases. When such treatments will move from the experimental to the routine, however, remains to be seen.

Will cloning, the technology that is making gene therapy possible, one day lead to the ultimate science fiction feat: cloning a complete human being? Some scientists are beginning to think so. For example, Dr. Joseph Schulman, director of the Genetics and IVF Institute in Virginia, suggests that if both a husband and wife are infertile, they might consider cloning both of themselves. "Then they could have one of each," he suggests. Clearly, society needs to think about the ethical and moral consequences of such a feat—and it better begin its thinking soon (Caplan & Venter, 1997; Kolata, 1997; Shapiro, 1997).

The Role of the Environment in Determining the Expression of Genes: From Genotypes to Phenotypes

The expression of particular traits is affected by factors other than genetics alone. The environment also plays a crucial role in determining the degree to which an individual's genotypic potential reaches fruition.

For instance, consider **temperament**, patterns of arousal and emotionality that represent consistent and enduring characteristics in an individual. Suppose we found—as increasing evidence suggests is the case—that a small percentage of children are born with temperaments that produce an unusual degree of physiological reactivity. Having a tendency to shrink from anything unusual, such infants react to novel stimuli with a rapid increase in heartbeat and unusual excitability of the limbic system of the brain (Kagan & Snidman, 1991; Gunnar et al., 1995; DiPietro et al., 1996). Such heightened reactivity to stimuli at the start of life, which seems to be linked to inherited factors, is also likely to cause children, by the time they are 4 or 5, to be considered shy by their parents and teachers. But not always: Some of them behave indistinguishably from their peers at the same age (Rothbart, Ahadi, & Hershey, 1994).

What makes the difference? The answer seems to be the environment in which the children are raised. Children whose parents encourage them to be outgoing by arranging supportive opportunities for them to engage in new activities may overcome their shyness. In contrast, children raised in a stressful environment marked by marital discord or a prolonged illness may be more likely to retain their shyness later in life (Kagan, Arcus, & Snidman, 1993; Pedlow et al., 1993).

Such findings illustrate that many traits represent **multifactorial transmission**, meaning that they are determined by a combination of both genetic and environmental factors. In multifactorial transmission, a genotype provides a particular range within which a phenotype may achieve expression. For instance, people with a genotype that permits them to gain weight easily may never be slim, no matter how much they diet. They may be *relatively* slim, given their genetic heritage, but they may never be able to get beyond a certain degree of thinness (Faith, Johnson, & Allison, 1997). In many cases, then, it is the environment that determines the way in which a particular genotype will be expressed as a phenotype (Wachs, 1992, 1993, 1996; Plomin, 1994c).

On the other hand, certain genotypes are relatively unaffected by environmental factors. In such cases, development follows a preordained pattern, relatively independent of the specific environment in which a person is raised. For instance, research on pregnant women who were severely malnourished during famines caused by World War II found that their children were, on average, unaffected physically or intellectually as adults (Stein et al., 1975). Similarly, no matter how much health food people eat, they are not going to grow beyond certain genetically imposed limitations in height.

Ultimately, of course, it is the unique interaction of inherited and environmental factors that determines people's patterns of development. As developmental psychologist Jerome Kagan writes:

> No human quality, psychological or physiological, is free of the contribution of events both within and outside the organism. . . . [E]very psychological quality is like a pale gray fabric woven from thin black threads, which represent biology, and thin white ones, which represent experience. But it is not possible to detect any quite black or white threads in the gray cloth. (Kagan, Arcus, & Snidman, 1993, p. 209)

Alternative Routes to Pregnancy: Giving Nature a Boost

For some couples, conception presents a major challenge. In fact, some 15 percent of couples suffer from **infertility**, the inability to conceive after 12 to 18 months of trying to become pregnant. Infertility is produced by several causes. In some cases, it is the age of the parents (the older the parents, the more likely infertility will occur); previous use of birth

temperament *patterns of arousal and emotionality that represent consistent and enduring characteristics in an individual*

multifactorial transmission *the determination of traits by a combination of both genetic and environmental factors in which a genotype provides a range within which a phenotype may be expressed*

infertility *the inability to conceive after 12 to 18 months of trying to become pregnant*

Jeff Milunsky, Geneticist

Education: . . . . Boston University, B.A. in biology; Boston University School of Medicine, M.D.

Position: . . . . Director of Clinical Genetics, Center for Human Genetics, Boston University School of Medicine; Assistant Professor of Pediatrics, Boston University School of Medicine

Home: . . . . West Roxbury, Massachusetts

The last 10 years of the 20th century has brought important advances in all areas of medicine, particularly in the field of genetics. Progress in our knowledge of genetics has made the specialty of prenatal genetics possible.

"Genetic counseling is best provided to couples during the preconception period. . . ."

According to Dr. Jeff Milunsky, Director of Clinical Genetics at the Center for Human Genetics at the Boston University School of Medicine, prenatal genetic counseling and treatment are now among the options offered to prospective parents before a pregnancy.

"Genetic counseling is best provided to couples during the preconception period," Milunsky says. "It is of critical importance to get both partners to discuss their family history and their own health. We need to know if they practice any adverse behavior, such as smoking or alcohol abuse, and we need to know about any medications they are taking."

The next step is to establish the ethnic history of both individuals so that the Center can recommend specific carrier tests.

"We inform all couples of their background risks and lay out the chances that the child will have a birth defect, mental retardation, or a genetic disorder."

"Each of us bears a genetic burden," Milunsky says, "and we all carry a handful of harmful genes. Once we determine the couple's ethnicity, we can offer carrier testing for certain disorders."

According to Milunsky, 1 in 30 French Canadians and Ashkenazi Jews carry the specific gene for Tay-Sachs disease. For people of Mediterranean descent, the probability is 1 in 10 they will be carrying the gene for Thalassemia, a form of anemia caused by faulty synthesis of part of the hemoglobin molecule. African Americans have a 1 in 12 probability that the gene for sickle-cell anemia is present, and for Caucasians in general, the probability for the cystic fibrosis gene is 1 in 25.

In addition to diagnosis, the Center offers a number of research-based preventive measures that are now routinely used, according to Milunsky.

"We now recommend multivitamins with folic acid during the preconception period and all the way through the pregnancy. This actually gives about a 70 percent protection rate for certain neural tube defects, specifically spina bifida."

As evidence of the widespread acceptance of genetic testing and the value that is placed on its results, Dr. Milunsky notes that the National Institutes of Health issued a consensus statement in 1997 recommending that, in the context of genetic counseling, all Caucasian couples expecting a child or planning a pregnancy should be offered the cystic fibrosis carrier test.

For couples who come to the Center for Human Genetics with a pregnancy in progress, carrier testing is offered along with additional tests based on maternal age, ultrasound abnormalities, or specific family history of a genetic disorder.

"We inform all couples of their background risks and lay out the chances that the child will have a birth defect, mental retardation, or a genetic disorder. There is approximately a 3 to 4 percent background risk, and added to that would be any risks in their family tree, risks from their own health, or anything currently wrong with the pregnancy.

"If there are ultrasound abnormalities we do further testing, including a material serum triple screen blood test, which is a standard blood test offered to women in all pregnancies," Milunsky says. "Essentially this can reveal a risk for Down syndrome and can also suggest the existence of several other defects."

Once the testing has been completed, the couple decides what to do next, according to Milunsky.

"Prenatally detected fetal abnormalities often influence the mode of delivery," he said. "If they decide to continue the pregnancy of a child who has tested positive for a risk, we work very closely with them and make sure that the doctors are aware of all the problems."

control pills, illicit drugs, or cigarettes; or previous bouts of sexually transmitted diseases. In other cases, men have abnormally low sperm counts, a condition that decreases the chances that a sperm will successfully fertilize an ovum. And still other cases of infertility are a result of the woman's *mother* taking certain drugs during pregnancy.

Whatever the cause of infertility, there are several approaches that provide alternative paths to conception (Colon, 1997). Some difficulties can be corrected through the use of drugs or surgery. Another option may be **artificial insemination**, a procedure in which a physician injects sperm cells directly into a woman's vagina. In some situations, the woman's husband provides the sperm, whereas in others it is an anonymous donor from a sperm bank.

In other cases, in vitro fertilization is employed. **In vitro fertilization (IVF)** is a procedure in which a woman's ova are removed from her ovaries, and a man's sperm are used to fertilize the ova in a laboratory. The fertilized egg is then implanted in either the woman who provided the donor eggs or in a **surrogate mother**, a woman who agrees to carry the child to term. Surrogate mothers may also be used in cases in which a woman who wants children is unable to conceive; the surrogate mother is artificially inseminated by a donor and agrees to give up rights to the infant.

The use of a surrogate mother presents a variety of ethical and legal issues, as well as many emotional concerns. In some cases, surrogate mothers have refused to give up the child after its birth, and in others the surrogate mother has sought to have a role in the child's life. In such cases, the rights of the mother, the father, the surrogate mother, and ultimately the baby are in conflict.

How do children fare who are conceived using emerging reproductive technologies such as in vitro fertilization? Research shows that they do quite well. In fact, one study found that the quality of parenting in families who have used such techniques may even be superior to that in families with naturally conceived children. Furthermore, the later psychological adjustment of children conceived using in vitro fertilization and artificial insemination is no different from that of children conceived using natural techniques (Golombok et al., 1995).

artificial insemination *a process of fertilization in which a physician injects sperm cells directly into a woman's vagina*

in vitro fertilization (IVF) *a procedure in which a woman's ova are removed from her ovaries, and a man's sperm are used to fertilize the ova in a laboratory*

surrogate mother *a woman who agrees to carry a child to term in cases in which the mother who provides the donor eggs is unable to conceive*

REVIEW AND RETHINK

REVIEW

- In humans, the male sex cell (the sperm) and the female sex cell (the ovum) provide the developing baby with 23 chromosomes each, through which the baby inherits characteristics from both mother and father.

- A genotype is the underlying combination of genetic material present in an organism, but invisible; a phenotype is the visible trait, the expression of the genotype. Within a range predetermined by the genotype, environmental factors play a significant role in determining the way in which that genotype will be expressed as a phenotype.

- The field of behavioral genetics, a combination of psychology and genetics, studies the effects of genetics on behavior.

- Several inherited and genetic disorders are due to damaged or mutated genes, including phenylketonuria (PKU), Down syndrome, sickle-cell anemia, Tay-Sachs disease, and Klinefelter's syndrome.

- Genetic counselors use a variety of data and techniques to advise future parents of possible genetic risks to their unborn children.

- Gene therapy, through which genetic flaws are corrected by adding or altering genes, is an emerging field of research and treatment that is based on cloning. Gene therapy is both highly promising and controversial.

■ Among the alternative routes to conception are artificial insemination and in vitro fertilization (IVF).

RETHINK

■ How can the study of identical twins who were separated at birth help researchers determine the effects of genetic and environmental factors on human development? How might you design such a study?

■ How can you inherit some traits from your mother and some from your father? How can you have some traits that are unlike either parent's? How might inherited characteristics "skip a generation," as they are often said to do?

■ How might adopted children develop traits similar to those of their adoptive parents? What sorts of traits do you think might be shared or different in adoptive families?

■ What are some ethical and philosophical questions that surround the issue of genetic counseling? Might it sometimes be unwise to know ahead of time about possible genetically linked disorders that might afflict your child or yourself?

■ What are some examples of how the genotype might limit the expression of the phenotype? How might environment affect the ways in which the genotype is realized as the phenotype?

THE INTERACTION OF HEREDITY AND ENVIRONMENT

Nature versus nurture. Heredity versus environment. Genetic influences versus situational influences. However we choose to state it, each of the previous statements reflects an enduring question about the root causes of human behavior that has intrigued and puzzled developmental researchers. Is behavior produced by inherited, genetic influences, or is it triggered by factors in the environment?

The answer is: There is no answer. As developmental research accumulates, it is becoming increasingly clear that to view behavior as due to *either* genetic *or* environmental factors is inappropriate. A given behavior is not caused just by genetic factors; nor is it caused solely by environmental forces. Instead, as we first discussed in Chapter 1, the behavior is the product of some combination of the two (Rutter et al., 1997). The more appropriate question, then, is *how much* of the behavior is caused by genetic factors, and *how much* by environmental factors. (See, for example, the range of possibilities for the determinants of intelligence, illustrated in Figure 2-6.)

Answering the Nature–Nurture Riddle

Developmental researchers have used several strategies to try to resolve the question of the degree to which traits, characteristics, and behavior are produced by genetic or environmental factors. In seeking a resolution, they have turned to studies involving both human and nonhuman species (Kimble, 1993; Plomin, 1994b; Plomin & McClearn, 1993; Steen, 1996; Wahlsten & Gottlieb, 1997).

Nonhuman Studies: Controlling Both Genetics and Environment.   One approach to understanding the relative contribution of heredity and environment makes use of nonhuman animals. Developing breeds of animals with specific traits that are genetically similar is relatively simple. The people who raise Butterball turkeys for Thanksgiving do it all the time, producing turkeys that grow especially rapidly so that they can be brought to market inexpensively. Similarly, strains of laboratory animals can be bred to share similar genetic backgrounds.

By observing animals with similar genetic backgrounds in different environments, scientists can determine, with reasonable precision, the effects of specific kinds of environmental stimulation. Conversely, researchers can examine groups of animals that have been

FIGURE 2-6

POSSIBLE CAUSES OF INTELLIGENCE

Intelligence is produced by a range of possible causes, spanning the nature–nuture continuum.

Nature				Nurture
Intelligence is provided entirely by genetic factors; environment plays no role. Even a highly enriched environment and excellent education make no difference.	Although largely inherited, intelligence is affected by an extremely enriched or deprived environment.	Intelligence is affected both by a person's genetic endowment and environment. A person genetically predisposed to low intelligence may perform better if raised in an enriched environment or worse in a deprived environment. Similarly, a person genetically predisposed to higher intelligence may perform worse in a deprived environment, or better in an enriched environment.	Although intelligence is largely a result of environment, genetic abnormalities may produce mental retardation.	Intelligence depends entirely on the environment. Genetics plays no role in determining intellectual success.

Possible Causes

bred to have significantly *different* genetic backgrounds on particular traits. Then, by exposing such animals to identical environments, they can determine the role that genetic background plays.

Of course, the drawback to using nonhumans as research subjects is that we cannot be sure how well the findings we obtain can be generalized to people. Still, the opportunities that animal research offers are substantial.

Human Studies: Exploiting Genetic Similarities and Dissimilarities. Obviously, researchers can't control either the genetic backgrounds or the environments of humans in the way they can with nonhumans. However, nature conveniently has provided the potential to carry out various kinds of "natural" studies—in the form of twins.

Recall that identical, monozygotic twins share an identical genetic code. Because their inherited backgrounds are precisely the same, any variations in their behavior must be due entirely to environmental factors.

In a world devoid of ethics, it would be rather simple for researchers to make use of identical twins to draw unequivocal conclusions about the role of nature and nurture. For instance, by separating identical twins at birth and placing them in totally different environments, researchers could assess the impact of environment unambiguously. Obviously, ethical considerations make this impossible. However, there are a fair number of cases in which identical twins are put up for adoption at birth and are raised in substantially different environments. Such instances allow us to draw fairly confident conclusions about the relative contributions of genetics and environment (Lykken et al., 1993; LaBuda, Gottesman, & Pauls, 1993).

Still, the data from monozygotic twins raised in different environments are not always without bias. Adoption agencies typically take the characteristics (and wishes) of birth mothers into account when they place babies in adoptive homes. For instance, children tend to be placed with families of the same race and religion. Consequently, even when monozygotic twins are placed in different adoptive homes, there are often similarities in the two home environments. The consequence is that researchers can't always unambiguously attribute differences in behavior to genetics or environment.

Some traits—like curly hair—have a clear genetic component.

Dizygotic twins, too, present opportunities to learn about the relative contributions of heredity and situational factors. Recall that dizygotic twins are genetically no more similar than siblings in a family born at different times. It is possible to compare behavior within pairs of dizygotic twins with that of pairs of monozygotic twins (who are genetically identical). If monozygotic twins are more similar on a particular trait, on average, than dizygotic twins, we can assume that genetics plays an important role in determining the expression of that trait (e.g., Schulman, Keith, & Seligman, 1993).

Still another approach is to study people who are totally unrelated to one another and who therefore have dissimilar genetic backgrounds, but who share an environmental background. For instance, a family that adopts, at the same time, two very young unrelated children probably will provide them with quite similar environments throughout their childhood. In this case, similarities in the children's characteristics and behavior can be attributed with some confidence to environmental influences (Segal, 1993).

Finally, developmental researchers have examined groups of people in the light of their degree of genetic similarity. For instance, if we find a high association on a particular trait between biological parents and their children, but a weaker association between adoptive parents and their children, we have evidence for the importance of genetics in determining the expression of that trait. On the other hand, if there is a stronger association on a trait between adoptive parents and their children than between biological parents and their children, we have evidence for the importance of the environment in determining that trait. In general, when a particular trait tends to occur at similar levels among genetically similar individuals, but tends to vary more among genetically more distant individuals, we can assume that genetics plays an important role in the development of that trait (Rowe, 1994).

Developmental researchers have used all these approaches, and more, to study the relative impact of genetic and environmental factors. What have they found? Before turning to their specific findings, it is important to state the general conclusion resulting from decades of research: Virtually all traits, characteristics, and behaviors are the joint result of the combination and interaction of nature and nurture. Like love and marriage and horses and carriages, genetic and environmental factors work in tandem, creating the unique individual that each of us is and will become.

Physical Traits: Family Resemblances

When patients entered the examining room of Dr. Cyril Marcus, they didn't realize that sometimes they were actually being treated by his identical twin brother, Dr. Stewart Marcus. So similar in appearance and manner were the twins that even long-time patients were fooled by this admittedly unethical behavior, which occurred in a bizarre case made famous in the film *Dead Ringers*.

Monozygotic twins are merely the most extreme example of the fact that the more genetically similar two people are, the more likely they are to share physical characteristics. Tall parents tend to have tall children, and short ones tend to have short children. Obesity, which is defined as being more than 20 percent above the average weight for a given height, also has a strong genetic component. For example, in one study, pairs of identical twins were put on diets that contained an extra 1,000 calories a day—and ordered not to exercise. Over a 3-month period, the twins gained almost identical amounts of weight. Moreover, different pairs of twins varied substantially in how much weight they gained, with some pairs gaining almost three times as much weight as other pairs (C. Bouchard et al., 1990).

Other, less obvious physical characteristics also show strong genetic influences. For instance, blood pressure, respiration rates, and even the age at which life ends are more similar in closely related individuals than in those who are less genetically similar (Jost & Sontag, 1944; Sorensen et al., 1988; Price & Gottesman, 1991).

Intelligence: More Research, More Controversy

No other issue involving the relative influence of heredity and environment has generated more research than the topic of intelligence. Why? The main reason is that intelligence, generally measured in terms of an IQ score, is a core human characteristic. IQ is strongly related to success in scholastic endeavors and, somewhat less strongly, to other types of achievement.

Let's first consider the degree to which intelligence is related to genetic factors. The answer is unambiguous: Genetics plays a significant role in intelligence. Both overall intelligence and specific subcomponents of intelligence (such as spatial skills, verbal skills, and memory) show strong effects for heredity (Cardon et al., 1992; Pedersen et al., 1992; Cardon & Fulker, 1993; McGue et al., 1993). As can be seen in Figure 2-7, the closer the genetic link between two individuals, the greater the correspondence of their overall IQ scores.

Not only is genetics an important influence on intelligence, but the impact increases with age. For instance, as fraternal (i.e., dizygotic) twins move from infancy to adolescence, their IQ scores become less similar. In contrast, the IQ scores of identical (monozygotic) twins become increasingly similar over the course of time. These opposite patterns suggest the intensifying influence of inherited factors with increasing age (Brody, 1993; McGue et al., 1993; Gottesman, 1997; McClearn et al., 1997; Plomin & Petrill, 1997).

Although heredity clearly plays an important role in intelligence, investigators are much more divided on the question of how to quantify that role. Perhaps the most extreme view is held by psychologist Arthur Jensen, who argues that as much as 80 percent of intelligence is a result of the influence of heredity (Jensen, 1969). Others have suggested more modest figures, ranging from 50 to 70 percent (e.g., Weinberg, 1989; Bouchard et al., 1990; Plomin, DeFries, & McClearn, 1990; Herrnstein & Murray, 1994; Devlin, Daniels, & Roeder, 1997).

Keep in mind, however, that although heredity plays an important role in intelligence, it is hardly the only factor. Even the most extreme estimates of the role of genetics still allow for environmental factors to play a significant role. In fact, in terms of public policy for maximizing people's intellectual success, the issue is not whether primarily hereditary or environmental factors underlie intelligence. Instead, as developmental psychologist Sandra Scarr suggests, we should be asking what can be done to maximize the intellectual development of each individual (Scarr & Carter-Saltzman, 1982; Storfer, 1990; Bouchard, 1997).

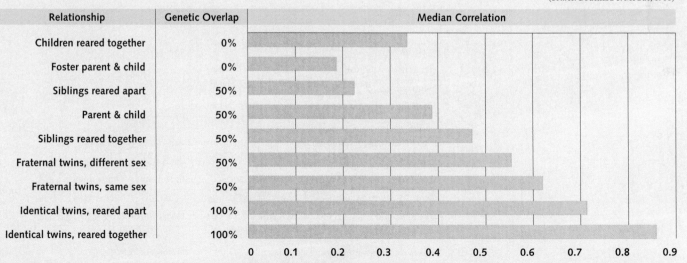

FIGURE 2-7

GENETICS AND IQ

The closer the genetic link between two individuals, the greater the correspondence between their IQ scores.

(*Source:* Bouchard & McGue, 1981)

Relationship	Genetic Overlap	Median Correlation
Children reared together	0%	
Foster parent & child	0%	
Siblings reared apart	50%	
Parent & child	50%	
Siblings reared together	50%	
Fraternal twins, different sex	50%	
Fraternal twins, same sex	50%	
Identical twins, reared apart	100%	
Identical twins, reared together	100%	

Genetic and Environmental Influences on Personality: Born to Be Outgoing?

Although it seems reasonable to most people that such characteristics as race and eye color are inherited, the notion that personality characteristics are affected by genetic factors seems less credible. However, increasing evidence supports the conclusion that at least some personality traits have at least some genetic components (Rowe, 1993; Smith, 1993; Bouchard, 1994; Rowe, 1994).

For example, neuroticism and extroversion are among the personality factors that have been linked most directly to genetic factors. The term *neuroticism*, when considered in the context of personality, refers to the degree of moodiness, touchiness, or sensitivity an individual characteristically displays. In other words, neuroticism reflects emotional reactivity. *Extroversion* is the degree to which a person seeks to be with others, to behave in an outgoing manner, and generally to be sociable (Loehlin, 1992; Bergeman et al., 1993; Plomin, 1994c).

How do we know which personality traits reflect genetics? Some evidence comes from examination of genes. For instance, it appears that a specific gene partially determines risk-taking behavior. According to researchers, a novelty-seeking gene affects the production of the brain chemical dopamine, making some people more prone than others to seek out novel situations and to take risks (Ebstein et al., 1996).

Other evidence for the role of genetics in determining personality traits comes from studies of twins. For instance, in one large-scale study, personality psychologist Auke Tellegen and colleagues studied the personality traits of hundreds of pairs of twins. Because a significant number of the twins were genetically identical but had been raised apart, it

FIGURE 2-8

INHERITING TRAITS

Certain traits are among the personality factors that are related most closely to genetic factors. The higher the percentage, the greater the degree to which the trait reflects the influence of heredity.

(Adapted from Tellegen et al., 1988.)

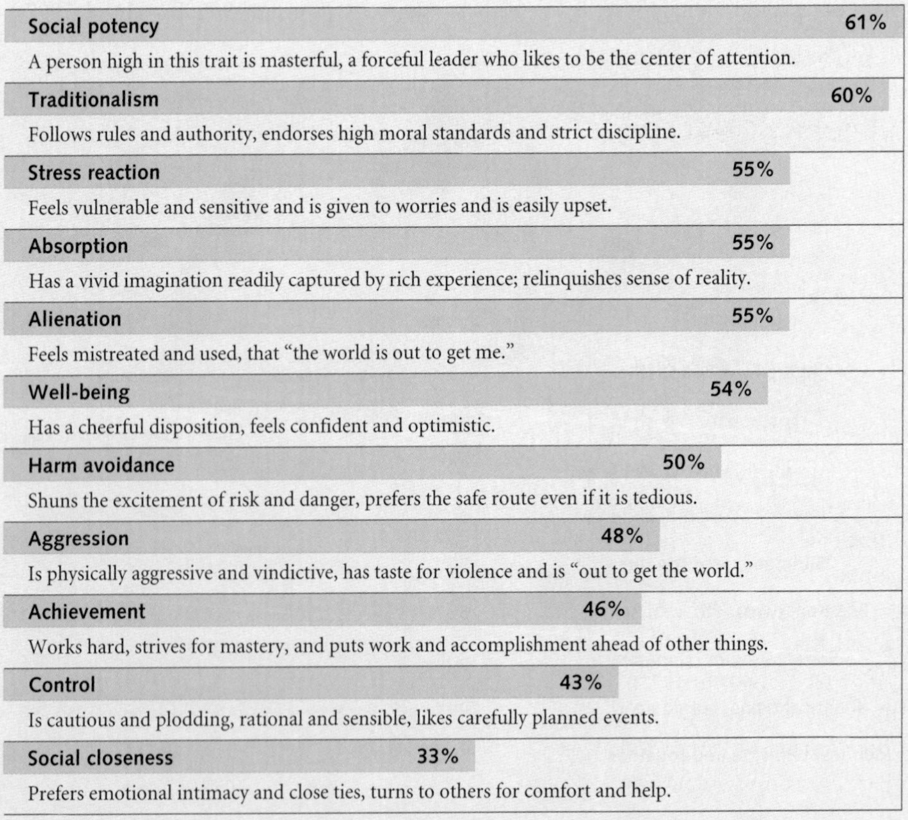

Trait	%
Social potency A person high in this trait is masterful, a forceful leader who likes to be the center of attention.	61%
Traditionalism Follows rules and authority, endorses high moral standards and strict discipline.	60%
Stress reaction Feels vulnerable and sensitive and is given to worries and is easily upset.	55%
Absorption Has a vivid imagination readily captured by rich experience; relinquishes sense of reality.	55%
Alienation Feels mistreated and used, that "the world is out to get me."	55%
Well-being Has a cheerful disposition, feels confident and optimistic.	54%
Harm avoidance Shuns the excitement of risk and danger, prefers the safe route even if it is tedious.	50%
Aggression Is physically aggressive and vindictive, has taste for violence and is "out to get the world."	48%
Achievement Works hard, strives for mastery, and puts work and accomplishment ahead of other things.	46%
Control Is cautious and plodding, rational and sensible, likes carefully planned events.	43%
Social closeness Prefers emotional intimacy and close ties, turns to others for comfort and help.	33%

was possible to determine with some confidence the influence of genetic factors (Tellegen et al., 1988).

Tellegen found that certain traits reflected the contribution of genetics considerably more than others. As you can see in Figure 2-8, social potency (the tendency to be a masterful, forceful leader who enjoys being the center of attention) and traditionalism (strict endorsement of rules and authority) are strongly associated with genetic factors.

Other research has revealed genetic influences on other, less central personality traits. For example, a person's political attitudes, religious interests and values, and even attitudes toward human sexuality seem to have genetic components. Even the amount of television that people watch appears to have a genetic component (Eysenck, 1976; Plomin et al., 1990; Waller et al., 1990; Loehlin, 1992; Coccaro, Bergeman, & McClearn, 1993; Lykken et al., 1993a; Schulman, Keith, & Seligman, 1993).

It may seem far-fetched that factors such as television viewing levels are affected by genetics. Admittedly, it is hardly likely that evolution has provided humans with a gene that controls TV viewing. How, then, could genetics play a role in a behavior that is so purely a part of contemporary life?

The answer comes from considering what is involved in watching television: It is a passive, solitary activity, one that largely precludes involvement in more social activities. Consequently, the influence of genetics may be indirect. For instance, we know that genetics plays an important role in determining a person's general level of extroversion. It may be that people who are relatively extroverted are less likely to watch television, an activity that hinders social involvement with others. On the other hand, a more introverted person may be more apt to watch television largely because it involves only minimal social interaction.

Such reasoning helps illustrate the importance of inherited factors in determining personality. However, it also points out once again the critical interplay between nature and nurture. In homes that have a television set, an individual's personality tendencies that are shaped by genetic factors may be exhibited in a particular way. But in homes that lack a television set, these tendencies may be expressed in quite different behaviors. There is a constant interplay, then, between heredity and environment. In fact, the way in which nature and nurture interact may be reflected not just in the behavior of individuals, but in the very foundations of a culture, as we see next.

"The good news is that you will have a healthy baby girl. The bad news is that she is a congenital liar."

Psychological Disorders: The Role of Genetics and Environment

> Lori Schiller began to hear voices when she was a teenager in summer camp. Without warning, the voices screamed "You must die! Die! Die!" She ran from her bunk into the darkness, where she thought she could get away. Camp counselors found her screaming as she jumped wildly on a trampoline. "I thought I was possessed," she said later. (Bennett, 1992)

In a sense, she *was* possessed: with schizophrenia, one of the severest types of psychological disorder. Normal and happy through childhood, Schiller's world took a tumble during adolescence as she increasingly lost her hold on reality. For the next two decades, she would be in and out of institutions, struggling to ward off the ravages of the disorder.

What was the cause of Schiller's mental disorder? Increasing evidence suggests that schizophrenia is brought about by genetic factors. The disorder runs in families, with some families showing an unusually high incidence. Moreover, the closer the genetic links between someone with schizophrenia and another family member, the more likely it is that the other person will also develop schizophrenia. For instance, a monozygotic twin has close to a 50 percent risk of developing schizophrenia when the other twin develops the disorder (see Figure 2-9). On the other hand, a niece or nephew of a person with schizophrenia has less than a 5 percent chance of developing the disorder (Gottesman, 1991, 1993; Prescott & Gottesman, 1993).

Developmental Diversity

Cultural Differences in Physical Arousal: Might a Culture's Philosophical Outlook Be Determined by Genetics?

The Buddhist philosophy, an inherent part of many Asian cultures, emphasizes harmony and peacefulness, and suggests that one should seek the eradication of human desire. In contrast, some of the traditional philosophies of Western civilization, such as those of Martin Luther and John Calvin, accentuate the importance of controlling the anxiety, fear, and guilt that are thought to be basic parts of the human condition.

Could such philosophical approaches reflect, in part, genetic factors? That is the controversial suggestion made by developmental psychologist Jerome Kagan and his colleagues. They speculate that the underlying temperament of a given society, determined genetically, may predispose people in that society toward a particular philosophy (Kagan, Arcus, & Snidman, 1993).

Kagan bases his admittedly speculative suggestion on well-confirmed findings that show clear differences in temperament between Caucasian and Asian children. For instance, one study that compared 4-month-old infants in China, Ireland, and the United States found several relevant differences. In comparison to the Caucasian American babies and the Irish babies, the Chinese babies had significantly lower motor activity, irritability, and vocalization (see Table 2-2).

Kagan suggests that the Chinese, who enter the world temperamentally calmer, may find Buddhist philosophical notions of serenity more in tune with their natural inclinations. In contrast, Westerners, who are emotionally more volatile and tense, and who report higher levels of guilt, are more likely to be attracted to philosophies that articulate the necessity of controlling the unpleasant feelings that they are more apt to encounter in their everyday experience (Kagan et al., 1994).

This does not mean that one philosophical approach is necessarily better, or worse, than the other. Nor does it mean that either of the temperaments from which the philosophies are thought to spring is superior or inferior to the other. Similarly, we must keep in mind that any single individual within a culture can be more or less temperamentally volatile, and that the range of temperaments found even within a particular culture is vast. Finally, as we noted in our initial discussion of temperament, environmental conditions can have a significant effect on the portion of a person's temperament that is not genetically determined.

Still, the notion that the very basis of culture—its philosophical traditions—may be affected by genetic factors is intriguing. More research is necessary to determine just how the unique interaction of heredity and environment within a given culture may produce a framework for viewing and understanding the world.

TABLE 2-2

MEAN BEHAVIORAL SCORES FOR MOTOR ACTIVITY, CRYING, FRETTING, VOCALIZING, AND SMILING FOR CAUCASIAN AMERICAN, IRISH, AND CHINESE 4-MONTH-OLD INFANTS

Behavior	American	Irish	Chinese
Motor activity	48.6	36.7	11.2
Crying (in seconds)	7.0	2.9	1.1
Fretting (% trials)	10.0	6.0	1.9
Vocalizing (% trials)	31.4	31.1	8.1
Smiling (% trials)	4.1	2.6	3.6

(*Source:* Kagan, Arcus, & Snidman, 1993.)

However, these data also illustrate that genetics alone does not influence the development of the disorder. If genetics were the sole cause, the risk for an identical twin would be 100 percent. Consequently, other factors account for the disorder, ranging from structural abnormalities in the brain to a biochemical imbalance (Iacono & Grove, 1993; Wang et al., 1993).

It also seems that even if individuals harbor a genetic predisposition toward schizophrenia, they are not destined to develop the disorder. Instead, they may inherit an unusual sensitivity

FIGURE 2-9

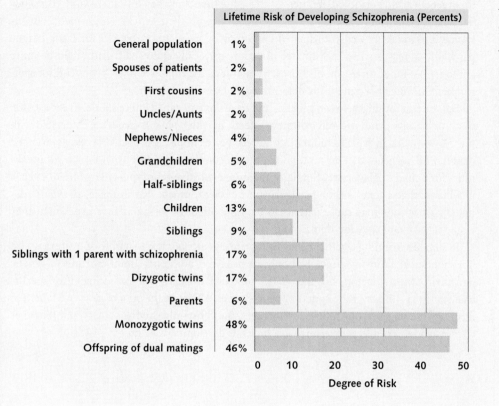

Lifetime Risk of Developing Schizophrenia (Percents)

General population	1%
Spouses of patients	2%
First cousins	2%
Uncles/Aunts	2%
Nephews/Nieces	4%
Grandchildren	5%
Half-siblings	6%
Children	13%
Siblings	9%
Siblings with 1 parent with schizophrenia	17%
Dizygotic twins	17%
Parents	6%
Monozygotic twins	48%
Offspring of dual matings	46%

Degree of Risk

THE GENETICS OF SCHIZOPHRENIA

The psychological disorder of schizophrenia has clear genetic components. The closer the genetic links between someone with schizophrenia and another family member, the more likely it is that the other person will also develop schizophrenia.

(*Source:* Gottesman, 1991.)

to stress in the environment. If stress is low, schizophrenia will not occur. But if stress is sufficiently strong, it will lead to schizophrenia. On the other hand, for someone with a strong genetic predisposition toward the disorder, even relatively weak environmental stressors may lead to schizophrenia (Gottesman, 1991; Fowles, 1992).

Several other psychological disorders have been shown to be related, at least in part, to genetic factors. For instance, major depression, alcoholism, autism, and attention-deficit hyperactivity disorder have significant inherited components (Eaves et al., 1993; McGuffin & Katz, 1993; McGue, 1993; Rutter et al., 1993; Shields, 1973).

The example of schizophrenia and other genetically related psychological disorders also illustrates a fundamental principle regarding the relationship between heredity and environment, one that underlies much of our previous discussion. Specifically, the role of genetics is often to produce preparedness for a future course of development. When and whether a certain behavioral characteristic will actually be displayed depends on the environment. Thus, although a predisposition for schizophrenia may be present at birth, typically people do not show the disorder until adolescence—if at all.

Similarly, certain other kinds of traits are more likely to be displayed as the influence of parents and other socializing factors declines. For example, adopted children may, early in their lives, display traits that are relatively similar to their adoptive parents' traits, given the overwhelming influence of the environment on young children. In contrast, as they get older and their parents' influence declines, genetically influenced traits may begin to manifest themselves as unseen genetic factors begin to play a greater role (Caspi & Moffitt, 1991, 1993, Loehlin, 1992).

According to developmental psychologist Sandra Scarr (1992, 1993), the genetic endowment provided to children by their parents not only determines their genetic characteristics,

Developmental psychologist Sandra Scarr

active genotype–environment effects
situations in which children focus on those aspects of their environment that are most congruent with their genetically determined abilities

passive genotype–environment effects
situations in which parents' genes are associated with the environment in which children are raised

evocative genotype–environment effects
situations in which a child's genes elicit a particular type of environment

but actively influences their environment. Because of **active genotype–environment effects**, children focus on those aspects of their environment that are most congruent with their genetically determined abilities. At the same time, they pay less attention to those aspects of the environment that are less compatible with their genetic endowment. For instance, a particularly well-coordinated child may be more apt to try out for Little League baseball, whereas her less-coordinated but more musically endowed friend might be more apt to try out for an after-school chorus. In each case, the child is actively producing an environment in which her genetically determined abilities can flourish.

But the relationship between genetics and environment can be more subtle. In some cases, there are **passive genotype–environment effects**, in which *parents'* genes are associated with the environment in which children are raised. For example, a particularly sports-oriented parent, who has genes that promote good physical coordination, may provide many opportunities for a child to play sports. Similarly, there are **evocative genotype–environment effects**, in which a child's genes elicit a particular type of environment. For instance, an infant's demanding behavior may cause parents to be more attentive to the infant's needs than they would if the infant were less demanding.

In sum, determining whether behavior is primarily attributable to nature or nurture is a bit like shooting at a moving target. Not only are behaviors and traits a joint outcome of genetic and environmental factors, but the relative influence of genes and environment for specific characteristics shifts over the course of people's lives. Although the pool of genes we inherit at birth sets the stage for our future development, the constantly shifting scenery and the other circumstances in our lives determine just how our development eventually plays out.

REVIEW AND RETHINK

REVIEW

■ Human characteristics and behavior are a joint outcome of genetic and environmental factors. The extent to which a given trait is caused by genetic factors or environmental factors varies from trait to trait and over time.

■ Scientists use both nonhuman and human studies to analyze the different contributions of genetics and environment. Individuals with identical genetic backgrounds and different environmental influences, and conversely, individuals with different genetic backgrounds and highly similar environmental influences are studied to tease out the varying influences of nature and nurture.

■ Genetic influences have been identified in physical characteristics, intelligence, personality traits and behaviors, and psychological disorders.

■ Some developmentalists speculate that entire cultures may be predisposed genetically toward certain types of philosophical viewpoints and attitudes.

■ The complex interaction between genetic and environmental effects may be seen in the active genotype–environment effects of children who tend toward activities and dispositions to which they are genetically predisposed; the passive genotype–environment effects of children who tend toward activities and dispositions that are prominent in their environment because of their parents' traits; and the evocative genotype–environment effects of children whose genetic traits elicit a particular type of environment.

RETHINK

■ How might a different environment from the one you experienced have affected the development of personality characteristics that you believe you inherited from one or both of your parents?

- Do you think dizygotic (i.e., fraternal) twins are likely to be more similar to one another than two siblings born of the same parents at different times? Why? What genetic or environmental factors help determine your answer?

- What sort of study might you design to examine whether "handedness" (the tendency to be either right-handed or left-handed) is determined more by genetics or environment?

- Some people have used the proven genetic basis of intelligence to argue against strenuous educational efforts on behalf of individuals with below-average IQs. Does this viewpoint make sense based on what you have learned about heredity and environment? Why or why not?

- A friend with a schizophrenic sister has just learned that her grandfather also had this disorder. Using your knowledge of the role of genetics and environment, what would you tell your friend about her chances of developing schizophrenia?

germinal stage *the first—and shortest— stage of the prenatal period, which takes place during the first 2 weeks following conception*

PRENATAL GROWTH AND CHANGE

From the moment of conception, development proceeds relentlessly, guided by the complex set of genetic guidelines inherited from the parents, and influenced from the start by environmental factors. Starting as a single cell produced by the alliance of ovum and sperm at the instant of conception, prenatal growth proceeds in an orderly, yet surprisingly rapid, pace (Leavitt & Goldson, 1996).

The Stages of the Prenatal Period: The Onset of Development

The prenatal period consists of three phases: the germinal, embryonic, and fetal stages. They are summarized in Table 2-3.

The Germinal Stage: Fertilization to 2 Weeks. The **germinal stage**, the first—and shortest—stage of the prenatal period, takes place during the first 2 weeks following conception. During the germinal stage, the organism (now called a *blastocyst*) travels toward the *uterus*, where it becomes implanted in the uterus's wall, which is rich in nutrients. The germinal stage is characterized by methodical cell division, which gets off to a quick start: Three days after fertilization, the organism consists of some 32 cells, and by the next day the number doubles. Within a week, it is made up of 100 to 150 cells, and the number rises with increasing rapidity.

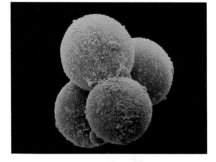

On the second day following fertilization, in the germinal stage, the organism consists of four cells.

TABLE 2-3

STAGES OF THE PRENATAL PERIOD

GERMINAL	EMBRYONIC	FETAL
Fertilization to 2 Weeks	2 Weeks to 8 Weeks	8 Weeks to Birth
The germinal stage is the first and shortest, characterized by methodical cell division and the attachment of the organism to the wall of the uterus. Three days after fertilization the zygote consists of 32 cells, a number that doubles by the next day. Within a week the zygote multiplies to 100–150 cells. The cells become specialized, with some forming a protective layer around the zygote.	The zygote is now designated an embryo. The embryo develops three layers, which ultimately form a different set of structures as development proceeds. The layers are: Ectoderm: Skin, sense organs, brain, spinal cord. Endoderm: Digestive system, liver, respiratory system. Mesoderm: Muscles, blood, circulatory system. The embryo is one inch long.	The fetal stage formally starts when the differentiation of the major organs has occurred. Now called a fetus, the individual grows rapidly as length increases 20 times. At 4 months the fetus weighs an average of 4 ounces; at 7 months, 3 pounds; and at the time of birth the average child weighs just over 7 pounds.

placenta   *a conduit between the mother and fetus, providing nourishment and oxygen via the umbilical cord*

embryonic stage   *the period from 2 to 8 weeks following fertilization during which significant growth occurs in the major organs and body systems*

fetal stage   *the stage that begins at about 8 weeks after conception and continues until birth*

fetus   *a developing child, from 8 weeks after conception until birth*

In addition to increasing in number, the cells of the organism become increasingly specialized. For instance, some cells form a protective layer around the mass of cells, whereas others begin to establish the rudiments of a placenta and umbilical cord. When fully developed, the **placenta** serves as a conduit between the mother and fetus, providing nourishment and oxygen via the *umbilical cord*. In addition, waste materials from the developing child are removed through the umbilical cord.

The Embryonic Stage: 2 Weeks to 8 Weeks.   By the end of the germinal period—just 2 weeks after conception—the organism is firmly secured to the wall of the mother's uterus. At this point, the child is called an *embryo*. The **embryonic stage** is the period from 2 to 8 weeks following fertilization. One of the highlights of this stage is the differentiation and development of the major organs and body systems.

At the beginning of the embryonic stage, the developing child has three distinct layers, each of which will ultimately form a different set of structures as development proceeds. The outer layer of the embryo, the *ectoderm*, will form skin, hair, teeth, sense organs, and the brain and spinal cord. The *endoderm*, the inner layer, produces the digestive system, liver, pancreas, and respiratory system. Sandwiched between the ectoderm and endoderm is the *mesoderm*, from which the muscles, bones, blood, and circulatory system are forged. Every part of the body is formed from these three layers.

An observer looking at an embryo at the end of the embryonic stage would be hard-pressed to identify it as human. Only an inch long, an 8-week-old embryo has what appear to be gills and a tail-like structure. On the other hand, a closer look reveals several familiar features. Rudimentary eyes, nose, lips, and even teeth can be recognized, and the embryo has stubby bulges that will form arms and legs.

CW   **The Fetal Stage: 8 Weeks to Birth.**   It is not until the final period of prenatal development, the fetal stage, that the developing child becomes instantly recognizable. The **fetal stage** starts at about 8 weeks after conception and continues until birth. The fetal stage formally starts when the differentiation of the major organs has occurred.

Now called a **fetus**, the developing child undergoes astoundingly rapid change during the fetal stage. For instance, it increases in length some 20 times, and its proportions change dramatically. At 2 months, around half the fetus is what will ultimately be its head; by 5 months, the head accounts for just over a quarter of its total size (see Figure 2-10). The

FIGURE 2-10

BODY PROPORTIONS

During the fetal period, the proportions of the body change dramatically. At 2 months, the head represents about half the fetus, but by the time of birth, it is one-quarter of its total size.

(*Source*: Robbins, 1929.)

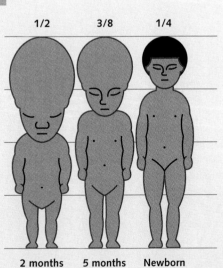

fetus also increases in weight substantially. At 4 months, the fetus weighs an average of about 4 ounces; at 7 months, it weighs about 3 pounds; and at the time of birth the average child weighs just over 7 pounds.

At the same time, the complexity of the organism increases rapidly. Organs become more differentiated and operational. By 3 months, the fetus swallows and urinates. In addition, the interconnections between the different parts of the body become more complex and integrated. Arms develop hands; hands develop fingers; fingers develop nails.

As this is happening, the fetus makes itself known to the outside world. Although mothers may at first be unaware in the earliest stages of pregnancy that they are, in fact, pregnant, the fetus now becomes increasingly active. By 4 months, a mother can feel the movement of her child, and several months later others can feel the baby's kicks through the mother's skin.

During the fetal stage, the fetus develops a wide repertoire of different types of activities (Smotherman & Robinson, 1996). In addition to the kicks that alert its mother to its presence, the fetus can turn, do somersaults, cry, hiccup, clench its fist, open and close its eyes, and suck its thumb. It also is capable of hearing and can even respond to sounds that it hears repeatedly (Lecanuet, Granier-Deferre, & Busnel, 1995). For instance, researchers Anthony DeCasper and Melanie Spence (1986) asked a group of pregnant mothers to read aloud the Dr. Seuss story *The Cat in the Hat* two times a day during the latter months of pregnancy. Three days after the babies were born, they appeared to recognize the story they had heard, responding more to it than to another story that had a different rhythm.

Just as no two adults are alike, no two fetuses are the same. Although development during the prenatal period follows the broad patterns outlined here, there are significant differences in the specific nature of individual fetuses' behavior. Some fetuses are exceedingly active, whereas others are more sedentary. Some spend most of their time sucking their thumbs; others never do this at all. Some have relatively quick heart rates, whereas others' heart rates are slower, with the typical range varying between 120 to 160 beats per minute (Lecanuet et al., 1995; Smotherman & Robinson, 1996).

Such differences in fetal behavior are due in part to genetic characteristics inherited at the moment of fertilization. Other kinds of differences, though, are brought about by the nature of the environment in which the child spends its first 9 months of life. As we will see, there are numerous ways in which the prenatal environment of infants affects their development—in good ways and bad.

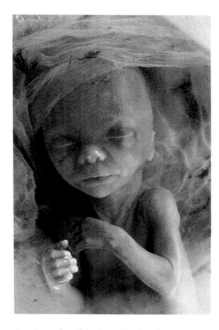

At 12 weeks, this fetus is clearly recognizable as a human.

The Prenatal Environment: Threats to Development

According to the Siriono people of South America, if a pregnant woman eats the meat of certain kinds of animals, she runs the risk of having a child who may act and look like those animals. According to opinions offered on daytime television talk shows such as the Oprah Winfrey show, a pregnant mother should avoid getting angry in order to spare her child from entering the world with anger (Cole, 1990).

Such views are largely the stuff of folklore, although there is some evidence that mothers' anxiety during their pregnancy may effect the sleeping patterns of their fetuses prior to birth. Furthermore, certain aspects of mothers' and fathers' behavior, both before and after conception, can produce lifelong consequences for the child. Some consequences show up immediately, but others, more insidious, may not appear until years after birth. In fact, half aren't apparent before birth (Jacobson et al., 1985; Groome et al., 1995).

Some of the most profound consequences are brought about by teratogenic agents. A **teratogen** is an environmental agent such as a drug, chemical, virus, or other factor that produces a birth defect. Although it is the job of the placenta to keep teratogens from reaching the fetus, the placenta is not entirely successful at this, and probably every fetus is exposed to some teratogens.

The timing of exposure to a teratogen is crucial. At some phases of prenatal development, a certain teratogen may have only a minimal impact. At other periods, however, the

teratogen *an environmental agent such as a virus, drug, chemical, or other factor that produces a birth defect*

same teratogen may have profound consequences. Furthermore, different organ systems are vulnerable to teratogens at different times during development. For example, the brain is most susceptible from 15 to 25 days after conception, whereas the heart is most vulnerable from 20 to 40 days following conception (see Figure 2-11; Needleman & Bellinger, 1994; Bookstein et al., 1996).

Mother's Diet. Most of our knowledge of the environmental factors that affect the developing fetus comes from the study of the mother. For instance, a mother's diet clearly plays an important role in bolstering the development of the fetus. A mother who eats a varied diet high in nutrients is apt to have fewer complications during pregnancy, an easier labor, and a generally healthier baby than a mother whose diet is restricted in nutrients (Brown, 1987; Morgane et al., 1993; Rizzo et al., 1997).

The problem of diet is of immense global concern. In 1992 the World Food Council estimated that there were 550 million hungry people in the world. Even worse, the number of people vulnerable to hunger was thought to be close to one *billion*. Clearly, restrictions in

FIGURE 2-11

TERATOGEN SENSITIVITY

Depending on their state of development, various parts of the body vary in their sensitivity to teratogens.

(*Source:* Moore, 1974.)

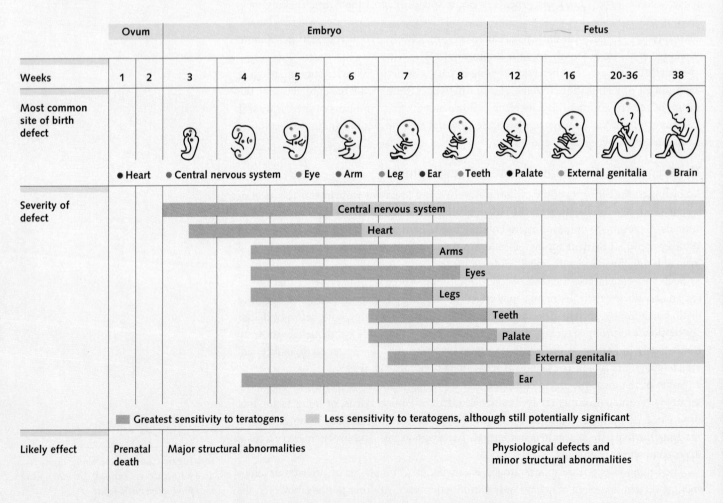

diet that bring about hunger on such a massive scale affect millions of children born to women living in those conditions (United Nations, 1994).

Fortunately, there are ways to counteract the types of maternal malnourishment that affect prenatal development. Dietary supplements given to mothers can reverse some of the problems produced by a poor diet (Crosby, 1991; Prentice, 1991). Furthermore, research shows that babies who were malnourished as fetuses, but who are subsequently raised in enriched environments, can overcome some of the effects of their early malnourishment (Grantham-McGregor et al., 1994). However, the reality is that few of the world's children whose mothers were malnourished *before* their birth are apt to find themselves in enriched environments after birth (Garber, 1981; Zeskind & Ramey, 1981; Ricciuti, 1993).

Mother's Age. With a great deal of medical help from her physicians, Rosanna Della Corta, a 62-year-old woman in Italy, gave birth in 1994. At the time, she was the oldest woman ever known to have become a mother. Most of the media attention, which was substantial, focused on the potential psychological difficulties for a child whose mother would be so atypically old.

However, the mother's advanced age probably had an impact on physical aspects of her pregnancy and birth, as well as potentially on her child's future development. Mothers who give birth when over the age of 30 are at greater risk for a variety of pregnancy and birth complications than younger ones. For instance, they are more apt to give birth prematurely, and their children are more likely to have low birth weights (Berkowitz et al., 1990; Cnattingius, Berendes, & Forman, 1993; Vercellini et al., 1993).

Furthermore, older mothers are considerably more likely to give birth to children with Down syndrome, a form of mental retardation. For mothers over 40, the incidence of Down syndrome is 1 percent; for mothers over 50, the incidence increases to 25 percent (Gaulden, 1992).

The risks involved in pregnancy are greater not only for unusually old mothers, but for atypically young women as well. Women who become pregnant during adolescence—and such pregnancies actually encompass 20 percent of all pregnancies—are more likely to have premature deliveries. Furthermore, the mortality rate of infants born to adolescent mothers is double that for mothers in their 20s.

Keep in mind, though, that the higher mortality rate for younger pregnancies reflects more than just physiological problems related to the mothers' young age. The heightened mortality rate is also a consequence of adverse social and economic factors, which may have set the stage for the adolescent to become pregnant in the first place, and which hamper good prenatal care. Similarly, some researchers argue that older mothers are not automatically at risk for more pregnancy problems. For instance, one study found that when women in their 40s who had not experienced health difficulties were considered, they were no more likely to have prenatal problems than those in their 20s (Ales, Druzin, & Santini, 1990).

Mother's Illness. Depending on when it strikes, an illness in a pregnant woman can have devastating consequences. For instance, the onset of *rubella* (German measles) in the mother prior to the 11th week of pregnancy is likely to cause serious consequences in the baby, including blindness, deafness, heart defects, or brain damage. In later stages of a pregnancy, however, adverse consequences of rubella become increasingly less likely.

Several other diseases may affect a developing fetus, again depending on when the illness is contracted. For instance, *chicken pox* may produce birth defects, and *mumps* may increase the risk of miscarriage.

Some sexually transmitted diseases such as *syphilis* can be transmitted directly to the fetus, who will be born suffering from the disease. In some cases, sexually transmitted diseases such as *gonorrhea* are communicated to the child as it passes through the birth canal to be born.

AIDS (acquired immune deficiency syndrome) is the newest, and probably the deadliest, of the diseases to affect a newborn. Mothers who have the disease or who merely are carriers of the virus may pass it on to their fetuses through the blood that reaches the placenta. If the fetuses contract the disease—and some 30 percent of infants born to mothers with AIDS are born with the virus—they face a devastating path. Many have birth abnormalities, including small, misshapen faces, protruding lips, and brain deterioration. Ninety percent experience neurological symptoms exemplified by intellectual delays and deficits, and loss of motor coordination, facial expressions, and speech. Because AIDS causes a breakdown of the immune system, these babies are extremely susceptible to infection. The long-term prognosis for infants born with AIDS is grim: Although drugs such as AZT may stave off the symptoms of the disease, survival beyond infancy is unusual (Brouwers et al., 1990; Nyhan, 1990; Chin, 1994; Frenkel & Gau, 1994; HMHL, 1994).

Mother's Drug Use.   Mothers' use of many kinds of drugs—both legal and illegal—poses serious risks to the unborn child. Even over-the-counter remedies for common ailments can have surprisingly injurious consequences. For instance, aspirin taken for a headache can lead to bleeding in the fetus. Moreover, impairments in the physical development of 4-year-olds have been linked to the frequent use of aspirin during pregnancy (Barr et al., 1990; Griffith, Azuma, & Chasnoff, 1994).

Even drugs prescribed by medical professionals have sometimes proven to have disastrous consequences. In the 1950s, many women who were told to take *thalidomide* for morning sickness during their pregnancies gave birth to children with stumps instead of arms and legs. Although the physicians who prescribed the drug did not know it, thalidomide inhibited the growth of limbs that normally would have occurred during the first 3 months of pregnancy.

Some drugs taken by mothers cause difficulties in their children literally decades after they were taken. As recently as the 1970s, the artificial hormone *DES (diethylstilbestrol)* was frequently prescribed to prevent miscarriage. Only later was it found that the daughters of mothers who took DES stood a much higher than normal chance of developing a rare form of vaginal or cervical cancer, and had more difficulties during their pregnancies (Herbst, 1981). Sons of the mothers who had taken DES had their own problems, including a higher rate than average of reproductive difficulties (Herbst, 1981).

Illicit drugs may pose equally great, and sometimes even greater, risks for the environments of prenatal children. For one thing, the purity of drugs purchased illegally varies significantly, so drug users can never be quite sure what specifically they are ingesting. Furthermore, the effects of some commonly used illicit drugs can be particularly devastating (DeCristofaro & LaGamma, 1995).

Consider, for instance, the use of *marijuana*. Certainly one of the most commonly used illegal drugs—millions of people in the United States have admitted trying it—marijuana used during pregnancy can restrict the oxygen that reaches the fetus. Its use can lead to infants who are irritable, nervous, and easily disturbed (Feng, 1993).

During the early 1990s, *cocaine* use by pregnant women led to an epidemic of thousands of so-called crack babies. Some estimates put the incidence of children born to mothers who have used cocaine during pregnancy at 1 in 50 (Julien, 1992; Sturner et al., 1992).

Cocaine produces an intense restriction of the arteries leading to the fetus, causing a significant reduction in the flow of blood and oxygen. This process increases the risks of fetal death. At birth, children whose mothers were addicted to cocaine may themselves be addicted to the drug and may have to suffer through the agonies of withdrawal. Even if not addicted, they may be born with significant problems. They are often shorter and weigh less than average, and they may have serious respiratory problems, visible birth defects, or seizures. They behave quite differently from other infants: Their reactions to stimulation are

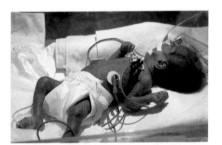

Children born to mothers who were addicted to crack cocaine, so-called crack babies, may themselves be addicted to the drug at birth.

muted, but once they start to cry, it may be nearly impossible to soothe them (Alessandri et al., 1993; Gottwald & Thurman, 1994; Lewis & Bendersky, 1995).

It is difficult to focus on the long-term effects of mothers' cocaine use in isolation, because such drug use is often accompanied by poor nurturing following birth (Richardson & Day, 1994; Myers et al., 1996). However, results of studies of crack babies who are just now entering school are discouraging. These children seem to have difficulty dealing with multiple stimuli and forming close attachments to others (Azuma & Chasnoff, 1993; De-Cristofaro & LaGamma, 1995; Lewis & Bendersky, 1995).

Mother's Use of Alcohol and Tobacco.   A pregnant woman who reasons that having a drink every once in a while or smoking an occasional cigarette has no appreciable effect on her unborn child is, in all likelihood, kidding herself: Increasing evidence suggests that even small amounts of alcohol and nicotine can disrupt the development of the fetus.

Mothers' use of alcohol can have profound consequences for the unborn child. For instance, studies have found that maternal consumption of an average of just two alcoholic drinks a day during pregnancy is associated with lower intelligence in their offspring at age 7. Other research concurs, suggesting that relatively small quantities of alcohol taken during pregnancy can have future adverse effects on children's behavior and psychological functioning (Streissguth, Barr, & Sampson, 1990; Barr et al., 1991; Shriver & Piersel, 1994). Furthermore, the consequences of alcohol ingestion during pregnancy are long-lasting. For example, one study found that 14-year-olds' success on a test involving spatial and visual reasoning was related to their mothers' alcohol consumption during pregnancy. The more the mothers reported drinking, the less accurately their children responded (Hunt et al., 1995).

The children of alcoholics, whose mothers consume substantial quantities of alcohol during pregnancy, are at an even greater risk. Approximately 1 out of every 750 infants is born with **fetal alcohol syndrome (FAS)**, a disorder that may include below-average intelligence and sometimes mental retardation, delayed growth, and facial deformities. FAS is now the primary preventable cause of mental retardation (Able & Sokol, 1987; Streissguth et al., 1991; Feng, 1993).

Because of the risks associated with alcohol, physicians today counsel pregnant women (and even those who are trying to become pregnant) to avoid drinking any alcoholic beverages. In addition, they caution against another practice proven to have an adverse effect on an unborn child: smoking.

Smoking produces several consequences, none good. For starters, smoking reduces the oxygen content and increases the carbon monoxide of the mother's blood, which quickly reduces the oxygen available to the fetus. In addition, the nicotine and other toxins in cigarettes slow the respiration rate of the fetus and speed up its heart.

The ultimate result is an increased possibility of miscarriage and a higher likelihood of death during infancy. In fact, recent estimates suggest that smoking by pregnant women leads to 115,000 miscarriages and the deaths of 5,600 babies in the United States alone each year (Feng, 1993; DiFranza & Lew, 1995).

Smokers are two times as likely as nonsmokers to have babies with an abnormally low birth weight, and smokers' babies tend to be shorter, on average, than those of nonsmokers. Furthermore, women who smoke during pregnancy are 50 percent more likely to have mentally retarded children (Lefkowitz, 1981; Fried & Watkinson, 1990; Drews et al., 1996).

Do Fathers Affect the Prenatal Environment?   It would be easy to reason that once the father has done his part in the sequence of events leading to fertilization, he would have no role in the *prenatal* environment of the fetus. In fact, developmental researchers have in the past generally shared this view, and there is little research investigating fathers' influence on the prenatal environment.

However, it is becoming increasingly clear that fathers' behavior may well influence the prenatal environment. For instance, secondhand smoke from a father's cigarettes may

fetal alcohol syndrome (FAS) *a disorder caused by the mother's consumption of alcohol during pregnancy, potentially resulting in mental retardation and delayed growth in the child*

affect the mother's health, which in turn influences her unborn child. In support of such reasoning, one study found that the greater the level of the father's smoking, the less the child weighed at birth (Lester & Van Theil, 1977; Rubin et al., 1986).

Similarly, associations exist between the development of certain kinds of tumors in a child and the nature of a father's occupation, although the explanation for the relationship is far from clear. It is possible, for instance, that fathers working in high-risk occupations may bring home chemical residuals in their clothing, which later are transmitted to the fetus. Alternatively, the higher risk of tumors may be the result of chromosomal damage brought about by the father's exposure to chemicals. In any case, increasing evidence suggests that fathers, and probably other family members as well, have an impact on the prenatal environment (Campbell et al., 1992).

The Informed Consumer of Development

Optimizing the Prenatal Environment

If you are contemplating ever having a child, by this point in the chapter you may be overwhelmed by the number of things that can go wrong. Don't be. Although both genetics and the environment pose their share of risks, in the vast majority of cases, pregnancy and birth proceed without mishap. Moreover, there are several things that women can do to optimize the probability that pregnancy will progress smoothly—both before and during pregnancy. Among them:

■ For women who are planning to become pregnant, several precautions are in order. First, women should have non-emergency X-rays only during the first 2 weeks after their menstrual periods. Second, women should be vaccinated against rubella (German measles) at least 3, and preferably 6, months before getting pregnant. Finally, women who are planning to become pregnant should avoid the use of birth control pills at least 3 months before trying to conceive because of disruptions to hormonal production caused by the pills.

■ Eat well, both before and during pregnancy (and after, for that matter!). Pregnant mothers are, as the old saying goes, eating for two. This means that it is more essential than ever to eat regular, well-balanced meals.

■ Do not use alcohol and other drugs. The evidence is clear that many drugs pass directly to the fetus and may cause birth defects. It is also clear that the more one drinks, the greater the risk to the fetus. The best advice: Do not use *any* drug unless directed by a physician.

■ Monitor caffeine intake. Although it is still unclear whether caffeine produces birth defects, it is known that the caffeine found in coffee, tea, and chocolate can pass to the fetus, acting as a stimulant. Because of this, you probably should not drink more than a few cups of coffee a day.

■ Whether pregnant or not, do not smoke. This holds true for mothers, fathers, and anyone else in the vicinity of the pregnant mother, because research suggests that smoke in the fetal environment can affect birth weight.

■ Exercise regularly. In most cases, women can maintain their customary exercise level. According to a 1994 advisory from the American College of Obstetricians and Gynecologists, "There are no data in humans to indicate that pregnant women should limit exercise intensity and lower target heart rates because of potential adverse effects" (ACOG, 1994). On the other hand, extreme exercise should be avoided, especially on very hot or very cold days. "No pain, no gain" isn't applicable during pregnancy (Warrick, 1991; Brody, 1994a).

REVIEW AND RETHINK

REVIEW

■ The prenatal period consists of three stages: germinal, embryonic, and fetal.

■ The prenatal environment significantly influences the development of the baby. The diet, age, and illnesses of mothers can affect their babies' health and growth.

■ Mothers' use of drugs, alcohol, and tobacco can adversely affect the health and development of the unborn child. Fathers' and others' behaviors (e.g., smoking) can also affect the health of the unborn child.

■ The vast majority of pregnancies and births proceed without mishap, and pregnant mothers can take positive steps to optimize their babies' chances for normal, healthy development.

RETHINK

■ Based on your knowledge of prenatal development, do you think there is any truth in the opinion that pregnant women should avoid anger in order to spare their children from entering the world angry? Why or why not?

■ Studies show that crack babies who are now entering school have significant difficulty dealing with multiple stimuli and forming close attachments. How might both genetic and environmental influences have combined to produce these results?

■ In addition to avoiding smoking, do you think there are other steps fathers might take to help their unborn children develop normally in the womb? What are they and how might they affect the environment of the unborn child?

■ Based on your knowledge of environmental influences on unborn children, what are some steps parents can take to give the fetus a healthy prenatal environment?

LOOKING BACK

■ **What is our basic genetic endowment, and how can human development go awry?**

• In human fertilization, ovum and sperm unite to form a single new cell called a zygote, which receives 23 chromosomes from each parent. Within its 46 chromosomes is the genetic blueprint that will guide cell activity for the rest of the individual's life.

• Gregor Mendel discovered an important genetic mechanism that governs the interactions of dominant and recessive genes and their expression in alleles. Traits such as hair and eye color and the presence of phenylketonuria (PKU) are alleles and follow this pattern.

• Genes may become physically damaged or may spontaneously mutate. If damaged genes are passed on to the child, the result can be a genetic disorder.

• Behavioral genetics, which studies the genetic basis of human behavior, focuses on personality characteristics and behaviors, and on psychological disorders such as schizophrenia. Researchers are now discovering how to remedy certain genetic defects through gene therapy.

• Genetic counselors use data from tests and other sources to identify potential genetic abnormalities in women and men who plan to have children. Recently, they have begun testing individuals for genetically based disorders that may eventually appear in the individuals themselves.

• Infertility, which occurs in some 15 percent of couples, can be treated by drugs, surgery, artificial insemination, and in vitro fertilization.

- ■ **How do the environment and genetics work together to determine human characteristics?**

  - Behavioral characteristics are often determined by a combination of genetics and environment. Genetically based traits represent a potential, called the genotype, which may be affected by the environment and is ultimately expressed in the phenotype.

  - To work out the different influences of heredity and environment, researchers use nonhuman studies and human studies, particularly of twins.

- ■ **Which human characteristics are significantly influenced by heredity?**

  - Virtually all human traits, characteristics, and behaviors are the result of the combination and interaction of nature and nurture. Many physical characteristics show strong genetic influences. Intelligence contains a strong genetic component, but can be significantly influenced by environmental factors.

  - Some personality traits, including neuroticism and extroversion, have been linked to genetic factors, and even attitudes, values, and interests, have a genetic component. Some personal behaviors may be genetically influenced through the mediation of inherited personality traits.

  - The interaction between genetic and environmental effects has been classified into three types: active genotype–environment effects, passive genotype–environment effects, and evocative genotype–environment effects.

- ■ **What happens during the prenatal stages of development?**

  - The germinal stage (fertilization to 2 weeks) is marked by rapid cell division and specialization, and the attachment of the organism to the wall of the uterus. During the embryonic stage (2 to 8 weeks), the ectoderm, the mesoderm, and endoderm begin to grow and specialize. The fetal stage (8 weeks to birth) is characterized by a rapid increase in complexity and differentiation of the organs. The fetus becomes active and most of its systems operational.

- ■ **What are the threats to the fetal environment and what can be done about them?**

  - Factors in the mother that may affect the unborn child include diet, age, illnesses, and drug, alcohol, and tobacco use. The behaviors of fathers and others in the environment may also affect the health and development of the unborn child.

E P I L O G U E : **MULTIPLICITY**

We've discussed the basics of heredity and genetics in this chapter, including the way in which the code of life is transmitted across generations through DNA. We have also seen how genetic transmission can go wrong, and we have discussed ways in which genetic disorders can be treated—and perhaps prevented—through new interventions such as genetic counseling and gene therapy. One important theme in this chapter has been the interaction between hereditary and environmental factors in the determination of a number of human traits.

Return to the prologue of this chapter—about the McCaughey septuplets—and answer the following questions.

1. Are the McCaughey septuplets likely to be identical septuplets (i.e., from the same original ovum-sperm pairing) or fraternal septuplets (i.e., from more than one original ovum-sperm pairing)? Why? What possibilities exist for some of the septuplets being identical and others being fraternal?

2. If all of the septuplets are fraternal except for one identical pair, what sorts of research studies would it be possible to design to examine the effects of heredity and environment on the children as they grow older? What hypotheses could you generate?

3. Would your research questions be different depending on whether the identical pair of septuplets *knew* or *did not know* that they were identical? Why or why not?

4. Would your research questions differ depending on whether the McCaughey parents *knew* or *did not know* that one pair of their children were identical? Why or why not?

5. What ethical questions would arise regarding any such study of the septuplets (or any other multiple-birth children)?

KEY TERMS AND CONCEPTS

gametes (p. 46)

fertilization (p. 46)

zygote (p. 46)

genes (p. 48)

DNA (deoxyribonucleic acid) (p. 48)

chromosomes (p. 48)

monozygotic twins (p. 48)

dizygotic twins (p. 49)

dominant trait (p. 50)

recessive trait (p. 50)

genotype (p. 50)

phenotype (p. 51)

homozygous (p. 52)

heterozygous (p. 52)

polygenic inheritance (p. 52)

X-linked genes (p. 52)

behavioral genetics (p. 54)

Down syndrome (p. 55)

sickle-cell anemia (p. 55)

Tay-Sachs disease (p. 55)

Klinefelter's syndrome (p. 55)

genetic counseling (p. 56)

amniocentesis (p. 56)

chorionic villus sampling (CVS) (p. 56)

ultrasound sonography (p. 56)

temperament (p. 59)

multifactorial transmission (p. 59)

infertility (p. 59)

artificial insemination (p. 61)

in vitro fertilization (IVF) (p. 61)

surrogate mother (p. 61)

active genotype-environment effects (p. 70)

passive genotype-environment effects (p. 70)

evocative genotype-environment effects (p. 70)

germinal stage (p. 71)

placenta (p. 72)

embryonic stage (p. 72)

fetal stage (p. 72)

fetus (p. 72)

teratogen (p. 73)

fetal alcohol syndrome (FAS) (p. 77)

Birth and the Newborn Infant

PROLOGUE: LABOR OF LOVE

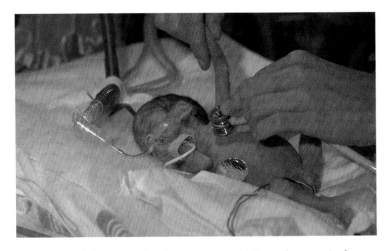

Some preterm infants as early as 18 weeks short of full term have survived.

On the morning of January 7, as Jewel McNeill's labor pains grew stronger and stronger, a nurse came into the delivery room. Did the McNeills have any plans for burying their baby? she asked grimly. Would they want an autopsy? Jewel recalls her using the phrase "disposing of the fetus." Her husband, Michael, noticed a receptacle that looked like a trash can at the bottom of the table. This, he thought, would be his baby's only cradle. According to the hospital's calculations, Jewel was no more than 22 weeks pregnant—18 weeks short of full term. The baby would weigh barely a pound and its lungs would be too undeveloped to sustain life. The doctor told Jewel to start pushing. Better to end the agony. A few minutes later, at exactly 10:08 A.M., Briana Adia-Jewel McNeill was born.

Alive.

Her eyes were open, her arms and legs were wiggling, and she began to cry. To Jewel, it sounded like a cry for help. (Kantrowitz, 1988, p. 62)

LOOKING AHEAD

If Briana had been born only a decade or so earlier, her cry might have been in vain. Yet today, like other infants in the United States who are born early, Briana has a significantly higher chance of survival.

Every birth is tinged with a combination of excitement and some degree of anxiety. In the vast majority of cases delivery goes smoothly, and it is an amazing and joyous moment. Yet the wonder experienced at birth is far overshadowed by the extraordinary nature of newborns themselves. They enter the world with a surprising array of capabilities, ready from the first moments of life outside the womb to respond to the world and the people in it.

This chapter will examine the events that lead to the delivery and birth of a child, and take an initial look at the newborn. We first consider labor and delivery, exploring how the process proceeds as well as several alternative approaches.

We next examine some of the possible complications of birth, investigating the problems that sometimes occur, ranging from premature births to infant mortality. Finally, we consider the extraordinary range of capabilities of newborns. We will look at their physical and perceptual abilities and also at the way they enter the world with the ability to learn and with skills that help form the foundations of their future relationships with others.

In sum, after reading this chapter, you will be able to answer these questions:

Q

- **What is the normal process of labor?**
- **What complications can occur at birth?**
- **What capabilities does the newborn have?**

BIRTH

> Her head was cone-shaped at the top. Although I knew this was due to the normal movement of the head bones as she came through the birth canal and that this would change in a few days, I was still startled. She also had some blood on the top of her head and was damp, a result of the amniotic fluid in which she had spent the last 9 months. There was some white, cheesy substance over her body, which the nurse wiped off just before she placed her in my arms. I could see a bit of downy hair on her ears, but I knew this, too, would disappear before long. Her nose looked a little as if she had been on the losing end of a fistfight: It was squashed into her face, flattened by its trip through the birth canal. But as she seemed to fix her eyes on me and grasped my finger, it was clear that she was nothing short of perfect. (Adapted from Brazelton, 1969)

For those of us accustomed to thinking of newborns in the images of baby food commercials, this portrait of a typical newborn may be surprising. Yet most **neonates**—the term used for newborns—are born resembling this one. Make no mistake, however: Despite their temporary blemishes, babies are a welcome sight to their parents from the moment of their birth.

The neonate's outward appearance is caused by a variety of factors in its journey from the mother's uterus, down the birth canal, and out into the world. We can trace its passage, beginning with the release of the chemicals that initiate the process of labor.

Labor: The Process of Birth Begins

For the average mother, about 266 days after conception, an as-yet-unidentified factor triggers the process that leads to birth. At that point, the hormone *oxytocin* is released by the mother's pituitary gland. When the concentration of oxytocin becomes high enough, the uterus begins periodic contractions (Nathanielsz, 1996).

---

neonates   *the term used for newborns*

During the prenatal period, the uterus, which is composed of muscle tissue, slowly expands as the fetus grows. Although for most of the pregnancy it is inactive, after the fourth month it occasionally contracts in order to ready itself for the eventual delivery. These contractions, called *Braxton-Hicks contractions*, are sometimes called "false labor," due to the fact that they do not necessarily signify that the baby will be born soon.

When birth is actually imminent, the uterus begins to contract intermittently. Its increasingly intense contractions act as if it were a vise, opening and closing to force the head of the fetus against the *cervix*, the neck of the uterus that separates it from the vagina. Eventually, the force of the contractions becomes strong enough to propel the fetus slowly down the birth canal until it enters the world as a newborn (Mittendorf et al., 1990).

Labor proceeds in three stages (see Figure 3-1). In the *first stage of labor*, the uterine contractions initially occur around every 8 to 10 minutes and last about 30 seconds. As labor proceeds, the contractions occur more frequently and last longer. Toward the end of labor, the contractions may occur every 2 minutes and last almost 2 minutes. During the final part of the first stage of labor, the contractions increase to their greatest intensity, a period known as *transition*. The mother's cervix fully opens, eventually expanding enough to allow the baby's head (the widest part of the body) to pass through.

This first stage of labor is the longest. Its duration varies significantly, depending on the mother's age, race, ethnicity, and number of prior pregnancies, plus a variety of other factors involving both the fetus and the mother. Typically, labor takes 16 to 24 hours for first-born children, but there are wide variations. Births of subsequent children usually involve shorter periods of labor.

During the *second stage of labor*, the baby's head starts to move through the cervix and birth canal. During this stage, which typically lasts around 90 minutes, the baby's head emerges more with each contraction, increasing the size of the vaginal opening. Because the area between the vagina and rectum must stretch a good deal, an incision called an

FIGURE 3-1

THE THREE STAGES OF LABOR

Stage 1

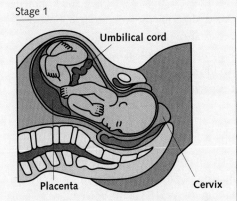

Uterine contractions initially occur every 8 to 10 minutes and last 30 seconds. Toward the end of labor, contractions may occur every 2 minutes and last as long as 2 minutes. As the contractions increase, the cervix, which separates the uterus from the vagina, becomes wider, eventually expanding to allow the baby's head to pass through.

Stage 2

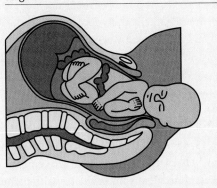

The baby's head starts to move through the cervix and birth canal. Typically lasting around 90 minutes, the second stage ends when the baby has completely left the mother's body.

Stage 3

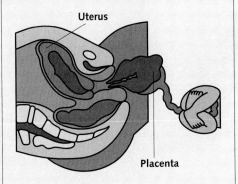

The child's umbilical cord (still attached to the neonate) and the placenta are expelled from the mother. This stage is the quickest and easiest, taking just a few minutes.

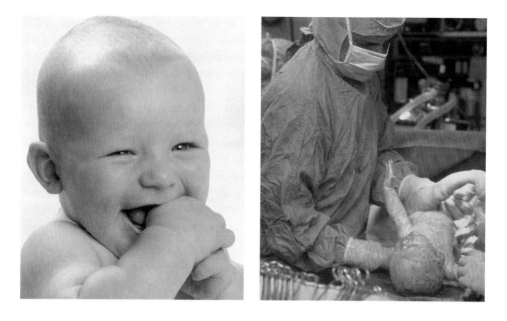

The image of newborns portrayed in commercials differs dramatically from reality.

episiotomy is sometimes made to increase the size of the opening of the vagina. However, this practice has been increasingly criticized in recent years as potentially causing more harm than good, and in developed areas of the world other than the United States episiotomies are uncommon (Klein et al., 1994).

The second stage of labor ends when the baby has completely left the mother's body. Finally, the *third stage of labor* occurs when the child's umbilical cord (still attached to the neonate) and the placenta are expelled from the mother. This stage is the quickest and easiest, taking just a few minutes.

The nature of a woman's reactions to labor reflect, in part, cultural factors. Although there is no evidence that the physiological aspects of labor differ among women of different cultures, expectations about labor and interpretations of its pain do vary significantly from one culture to another (Scopesi, Zanobini, & Carossino, 1997).

For instance, there is a kernel of truth to popular stories of pregnant women in certain societies putting down the tools with which they are tilling their fields, stepping aside and giving birth, and immediately returning to work with their neonates wrapped and bundled on their backs. Accounts of the !Kung people in Africa describe the woman in labor sitting calmly beside a tree and without much ado—or assistance—successfully giving birth to a child and quickly recovering. On the other hand, many societies regard childbirth as dangerous, and some even view it in terms befitting an illness. Such cultural perspectives color the way that people in a given society view the experience of childbirth (Shostak, 1981; Chalmers, Enkin, & Keirse, 1989; Cole, 1992).

Birth: From Fetus to Neonate

The exact moment of birth occurs when the fetus, having left the uterus through the cervix, passes through the vagina to emerge fully from its mother's body. In most cases, babies automatically make the transition from taking in oxygen via the placenta to using their lungs to breathe air. Consequently, as soon as they are outside the mother's body, most newborns spontaneously cry. This helps them clear their lungs and breathe on their own.

What happens next varies from situation to situation and from culture to culture. In Western cultures, health care workers are almost always on hand to assist with the birth. In the United States, 99 percent of births are attended by professional health care workers, but worldwide only about 50 percent of births have professional health care workers in attendance (United Nations, 1990).

---

episiotomy *an incision sometimes made to increase the size of the opening of the vagina to allow the baby to pass*

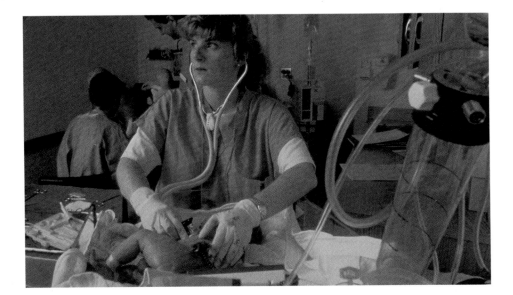

The Apgar scale is used at birth to measure several indications of good health.

The Apgar Scale. In most cases, the newborn infant first undergoes a quick visual inspection. Parents may be counting fingers and toes, but trained health care workers look for something more. Typically, they employ the **Apgar scale**, a standard measurement system that looks for a variety of indications of good health (see Table 3-1). Developed by physician Virginia Apgar in 1953, the scale directs attention to five basic qualities, recalled most easily by using Apgar's name as a guide: *a*ppearance (color), *p*ulse (heart rate), *g*rimace (reflex irritability), *a*ctivity (muscle tone), and *r*espiration (respiratory effort).

Using the scale, health care workers assign the newborn a score ranging from 0 to 2 on each of the five qualities, producing an overall score that can range from 0 to 10. The vast majority of children score 7 or above. The 10 percent of neonates who score under 7 require help to start breathing. Newborns who score under 4 need immediate, lifesaving intervention. Scores that remain between 0 and 3 after 20 minutes indicate that severe problems are likely to be present. On the other hand, most of the components of the Apgar score are based on subjective factors, and parents sometimes place too much emphasis on the specific score (Jepson, Talashek, & Tichy, 1991).

Although low Apgar scores may indicate problems or birth defects that were already present in the fetus, the process of birth itself may sometimes cause difficulties. Among the most profound are those relating to a temporary deprivation of oxygen.

At various junctures during labor, the fetus may not get sufficient oxygen for any of a number of reasons. For instance, the umbilical cord may become pinched during a prolonged

CW

Apgar scale *a standard measurement system that looks for a variety of indications of good health in newborns*

TABLE 3-1

APGAR SCALE

Sign*	0	1	2
Appearance (color)	Blue, pale	Body pink, extremities blue	Entirely pink
Pulse (heart rate)	Absent	Slow (below 100)	Rapid (over 100)
Grimace (reflex irritability)	No response	Grimace	Coughing, sneezing, crying
Activity (muscle tone)	Limp	Weak, inactive	Strong, active
Respiration (breathing)	Absent	Irregular, slow	Good, crying

*Each sign is rated in terms of absence or presence from 0 to 2; highest overall score is 10.
(*Source:* Adapted from Apgar, 1953.)

contraction, thereby cutting off the supply of oxygen to the fetus. The cord may also get wrapped around the neck of the fetus or another part of its body, or an unusual positioning of the fetus within the birth canal may cause the cord to be restricted. It is even possible that the stresses of traveling through the birth canal may cause the baby to grasp the umbilical cord and squeeze it (Bornstein & Lamb, 1992a).

Lack of oxygen for a few seconds is not particularly harmful to the fetus, but deprivation for any longer time may cause serious harm. A restriction of oxygen, or **anoxia**, lasting a few minutes can produce brain damage as unoxygenated brain cells, which never can regenerate, die. Furthermore, anoxia can lead to such an increase in blood pressure that bleeding occurs in the brain.

Physical Appearance and Initial Encounters.   After assessing the newborn's health, health care workers next deal with the remnants of the child's passage through the birth canal. You will recall the description of the thick, greasy substance (like cheese) that covers the newborn. This material, called *vernix*, smooths the passage through the birth canal; it is no longer needed once the child is born and is quickly cleaned away. Newborns' bodies are also covered with a fine, dark fuzz known as *lanugo;* this soon disappears. The newborn's eyelids may be puffy due to an accumulation of fluids during labor, and it may have other blood or fluids on parts of its body.

After cleansing, the newborn is usually returned to the mother and the father, if he is present. The everyday and universal occurrence of childbirth makes it no less miraculous to parents, and most cherish this time to make their first acquaintance with their child.

However, the importance of the initial encounter between parent and child has become a matter of considerable controversy. Some psychologists and physicians argued in the 1970s and early 1980s that **bonding**, the close physical and emotional contact between parent and child during the period immediately following birth, was a crucial ingredient for forming a lasting relationship between parent and child. Their arguments were based in part on research conducted on nonhuman species such as ducklings. This work showed that there was a critical period just after birth when organisms showed a particular readiness to learn, or *imprint*, from other members of their species who happened to be present (Lorenz, 1957).

According to the concept of bonding applied to humans, a critical period begins just after birth and lasts only a few hours. During this period actual skin-to-skin contact between mother and child supposedly leads to deep, emotional bonding (Klaus & Kennell, 1976; deChateau, 1980). The corollary to this assumption is that if circumstances prevent such contact, the bond between mother and child will forever be lacking in some way. Because medical practices prevalent at the time often left little opportunity for sustained mother and child physical contact immediately after birth, the suggestion was received with alarm. The idea was taken seriously and generated a substantial amount of public attention (Eyer, 1992).

There was just one problem: Scientific evidence for the notion was lacking. When developmental researchers carefully reviewed the research literature, they found little support for the idea. Although it does appear that mothers who have early physical contact with their babies are more responsive to them than those who don't have such contact, the difference lasts only a few days. Furthermore, there are no lingering reactions to separations immediately following birth, even separations of several days. Such news is reassuring to parents whose children must receive immediate, intensive medical attention just after birth, as well as to parents who adopt children and are not present at all at their births (Lamb, 1982; Goldberg, 1983; Eyer, 1994; Redshaw, 1997).

Approaches to Childbirth: Where Medicine and Attitudes Meet

Ester Iverem knew herself well enough to know that she didn't like the interaction she had with medical doctors. So she opted for a nurse-midwife at Manhattan's Maternity Center where she was free to use a birthing stool and to have her husband, Nick Chiles, by her side.

anoxia   *a restriction of oxygen to the baby, lasting a few minutes during the birth process, which can produce brain damage*

bonding   *close physical and emotional contact between parent and child during the period immediately following birth, argued by some to affect later relationship strength*

When contractions began, Iverem and Chiles went for a walk, stopping periodically to rock—a motion, she says, "similar to the way children dance when they first learn how, shifting from foot to foot." That helped her work through the really powerful contractions.

"I sat on the birthing chair [a Western version of the traditional African stool, which lies low to the ground and has an opening in the middle for the baby to come through] and Nick was sitting right behind me. When the midwife said 'Push!' the baby's head just went 'pop!,' and out he came." Their son, Mazi (which means "Sir" in Ibo) Iverem Chiles, was placed on Ester's breast while the midwives went to prepare for his routine examination. (Knight, 1994, p. 122)

For something as natural as giving birth, which occurs throughout the nonhuman animal world apparently without much thought, parents in the Western world have developed a variety of strategies—and some very strong opinions. Should the birth take place in a hospital or in the home? Should a physician, a nurse, or a midwife assist? Is the father's presence desirable? Should siblings and other family members be on hand to participate in the birth?

Most of these questions cannot be answered definitively, primarily because the choice of childbirth techniques often comes down to a matter of values and opinions. No single procedure will be effective for all mothers and fathers, and no conclusive research evidence has proven that one procedure is significantly more effective than another.

The abundance of choices is largely due to a reaction to traditional medical practices that had been prevalent in the United States until the early 1970s. Before that time, the typical procedure went something like this: A woman in labor was placed in a room with many other women, all of whom were in various stages of childbirth, and some of whom were screaming in pain. Fathers and other family members were not allowed to be present. Just before delivery, the woman was rolled into a delivery room, where the birth took place. Often she was so drugged that she was not aware of the birth at all.

Physicians argued that such procedures were necessary to ensure the health of the newborn and the mother. However, critics charged that alternatives were available that only would maximize the medical well-being of the participants in the birth, and would represent an emotional and psychological improvement as well (Pascoe, 1993).

Pain and Childbirth.   Any woman who has delivered a baby will agree that childbirth is painful. But exactly how painful is it?

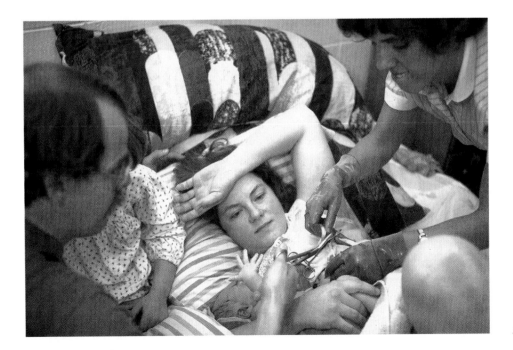

A midwife helps in this home delivery.

Such a question is largely unanswerable. One reason is that pain is a subjective, psychological phenomenon, one that cannot be easily measured. No one is able to answer the question of whether their pain is "greater" or "worse" than someone else's pain, although some studies have tried to quantify it. For instance, in one survey women were asked to rate the pain they experienced during labor on a 1-to-5 scale, with 5 being the most painful (Yarrow, 1992). Nearly half (44 percent) said "5," and an additional one-quarter said "4."

Furthermore, because pain is usually a sign that something is wrong in one's body, we have learned to react to pain with fear and concern. Yet during childbirth, pain is actually a signal that the body is working appropriately—that the contractions that are meant to propel the baby through the birth canal are doing their job. Consequently, the experience of pain during labor is difficult for women in labor to interpret, thereby potentially increasing their anxiety and making the contractions seem even more painful.

Ultimately, the nature of every woman's delivery depends on a complex series of factors. These factors encompass such variables as how much preparation and support she has before and during delivery, her culture's view of pregnancy and delivery, and the specific nature of the delivery itself (Seibel & McCarthy, 1993; Davis-Floyd, 1994; DiMatteo & Kahn, 1997).

Use of Anesthesia and Pain-reducing Drugs. Among the greatest advances of modern medicine is the ongoing discovery of drugs that reduce pain, and today some 80 percent of women receive some form of pain medication during childbirth. However, the use of medication during childbirth is a practice that holds both benefits and pitfalls (Shute, 1997).

About a third of women who receive anesthesia do so in the form of *epidural anesthesia*, which produces numbness from the waist down. Traditional epidurals produce an inability to walk and in some cases prevent women from helping to push the baby out during delivery. However, a newer form of epidural, known as a *walking epidural* or *dual spinal-epidural*, uses smaller needles and a system for administering continuous doses of anesthetic. It permits women to move about more freely during labor and has fewer side effects than traditional epidural anesthesia.

Clearly, drugs hold the promise of greatly reducing, and even eliminating, pain associated with labor, which can be extreme. However, pain reduction comes at a cost: the stronger the drug, the greater its effects on the fetus and neonate. The reason is pharmacologically simple: Drugs administered during labor reach not just the mother but the fetus as well. Because of the small size of the fetus relative to the mother, drug doses that might have only a minimal effect on the mother can have a magnified effect on the fetus.

Many studies have demonstrated the results of the use of anesthesia during delivery. Some consequences are immediate: Anesthetics may temporarily depress the flow of oxygen to the fetus and slow labor (Brackbill, 1979; Hollenbeck et al., 1984; Thorpe et al., 1993). In addition, neonates whose mothers have been anesthetized are less physiologically responsive and show poorer motor control during the first days of life after birth. And the effects may be lasting: Research shows that during the course of the first year, progress in sitting up, standing, and other physical activities is somewhat slower for children whose mothers received drugs during labor (Brackbill & Broman, 1979; Murray et al., 1981; Garbaciak, 1990; Douglas, 1991).

The effects of drugs show up in other, less obvious ways. For example, the use of anesthetics can produce differences in the interactions between mother and child (Scanlon & Hollenbeck, 1983; Hollenbeck et al., 1984). Even after the physical effects of the drugs have worn off and the infants are behaving in the same way as infants whose mothers did not receive drugs, mothers report feeling differently about their babies. There may be several reasons for this difference. It may be that mothers who choose to avoid medication during delivery hold more positive attitudes toward giving birth and toward their babies in the first place. More probably, the presence or absence of drugs in the infants' systems causes

The Informed Consumer of Development

Dealing with Labor

Every woman who is soon to give birth has some fear of labor. Most have heard gripping tales of extended, 48-hour labors or vivid descriptions of the pain that accompanies labor. Still, few mothers would dispute the notion that the rewards of giving birth are worth the effort. Indeed, polls show that almost two-thirds of women report feeling "very positive" about the births of their children (Yarrow, 1992).

There is no single right or wrong way to deal with labor. However, experts suggest several strategies that can help make the process as positive as possible (Salmon, 1993):

■ *Be flexible.* Although you may have carefully worked out beforehand a scenario about what to do during labor, don't feel an obligation to follow through exactly. If a strategy is ineffective, turn to another one.

■ *Communicate with your health care providers.* Let them know what you are experiencing. They may be able to suggest ways to deal with it. By examining you, they will also be able to explain the stage and progress of your labor.

■ *Remember that labor is . . . laborious.* Labor is aptly named: It takes hard work and can be exhausting. Expect that you may become fatigued, but realize that as the final stages of labor occur, you may well find renewed energy, get a "second wind."

■ *Accept your partner's support.* If a spouse or other partner is present, allow that person to make you comfortable and provide support. A partner's encouragement may be critical.

■ *Be realistic and honest about your reactions to pain.* Even if you had planned an unmedicated delivery, realize that you may find the pain difficult to tolerate. At that point, consider the use of drugs. Above all, don't feel that asking for pain medication is a sign of failure. It isn't.

■ *Focus on the big picture.* Keep in mind that labor is part of a process that ultimately leads to an event unmatched in the joy that it can bring.

REVIEW AND RETHINK

REVIEW

■ In the first stage of labor, contractions increase in frequency, duration, and intensity until the baby's head is able to pass through the cervix. In the second stage, the baby moves through the cervix and birth canal and leaves the mother's body. In the third stage, the umbilical cord and placenta emerge.

■ Immediately after birth, birthing attendants usually examine the neonate using a measurement system such as the Apgar scale.

■ Parents today have many birthing options. They may weigh the advantages and disadvantages of anesthetic drugs during birth, and they may choose alternatives to traditional hospital birthing, including the Lamaze method, the Leboyer method, the use of a birthing center, and the use of a midwife.

RETHINK

■ Why might cultural differences exist in expectations and interpretations of labor? Do you think such cultural differences are due primarily to physical or psychological factors?

■ In the United States, professional medical workers or birthing attendants attend 99 percent of births, but worldwide this is the case in only about 50 percent of births. What do you think are some causal factors and implications of this statistic?

■ What arguments have been advanced by those who consider the bonding process—close physical contact between parent and child immediately after birth—an essential ingredient in forming a normal parent–child relationship? Why might some parents have found this position alarming?

preterm infants infants who are born prior to 38 weeks after conception (also known as premature infants)

low-birthweight infants infants that weight less than 2,500 grams (about 5.5 pounds) at birth

small-for-gestational-age infants infants who, because of delayed fetal growth, weigh 90 percent (or less) of the average weight of infants of the same gestational age

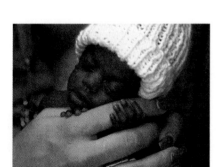

Preterm infants stand a much greater chance of survival today than they did even a decade ago.

■ What are some arguments for and against the use of pain-reducing drugs during birth? What advice would you give a mother-to-be about anesthetics, and why?

■ Which elements of various birthing techniques, including more traditional and less traditional ones, do you think are most likely to contribute to the well-being of the newborn and its family? Why?

BIRTH COMPLICATIONS

In addition to the usual complimentary baby supplies that most hospitals bestow on new mothers, the maternity nurses at Greater Southeast Hospital have become practiced in handing out "grief baskets."

Inside are items memorializing one of [Washington, D.C.'s] grimmest statistics—an infant mortality rate that's more than twice the national average. The baskets contain a photograph of the dead newborn, a snip of its hair, the tiny cap it wore, and a yellow rose. (Thomas, 1994, p. A14)

The infant mortality rate in Washington, D.C., capital of the richest country in the world, is 16.7 deaths per 1,000 births, exceeding the rate of countries such as Sri Lanka, Panama, Chile, and Jamaica. Overall, the United States ranks 22nd in the world in infant mortality, with 7.9 deaths for every 1,000 live births (National Center for Health Statistics, 1993a; Eberstadt, 1994; Singh & Yu, 1995).

Why is infant survival less likely in the United States than in other, less developed countries? To answer this question, we need to consider the problems that can occur during labor and delivery.

Preterm Infants: Too Soon, Too Small

Like Briana McNeill, whose birth was described in the chapter Prologue, some 6 to 7 percent of infants are born earlier than normal. **Preterm infants**, or premature infants, are born prior to 38 weeks after conception. Because they have not had time to develop fully as fetuses, preterm infants are at high risk for illness and death.

The extent of danger faced by preterm babies largely depends on the child's weight at birth, which has great significance as an indicator of the extent of the baby's development. Although the average newborn weighs around 3,400 grams (about 7 1/2 pounds), **low-birthweight infants** weigh less than 2,500 grams (around 5 1/2 pounds). Although only 7 percent of all newborns in the United States fall into the low-birthweight category, they account for the majority of newborn deaths (Gross, Spiker, & Haynes, 1997).

Although most low-birthweight infants are preterm, some are small-for-gestational-age babies. **Small-for-gestational-age infants** are infants who, because of delayed fetal growth, weigh 90 percent (or less) of the average weight of infants of the same gestational age. Small-for-gestational-age infants are sometimes also preterm, but may not be (Meisels & Plunkett, 1988; Shiono & Behrman, 1995).

If the degree of prematurity is not too great and weight at birth is not extremely low, the threat to the child's well-being is relatively minor. In such cases, the main treatment may be to keep the baby in the hospital to gain weight. Additional weight is critical because fat layers help prevent chilling in neonates, who are not particularly efficient at regulating body temperature.

Newborns who are born more prematurely and who have significantly below-average birthweights face a tougher road. For them, simply staying alive is a major task. For instance, low-birthweight infants are highly vulnerable to infection. Furthermore, because their lungs have not had sufficient time to develop completely, premature babies have problems taking in sufficient oxygen. As a consequence, they may experience *respiratory distress syndrome (RDS)*, with potentially fatal consequences.

To deal with respiratory distress syndrome, low-birthweight infants are often placed in incubators, enclosures in which temperature and oxygen content are controlled. The exact amount of oxygen is carefully monitored. Too low a concentration of oxygen will not provide relief, and too high a concentration can damage the delicate retinas of the eyes, leading to permanent blindness.

The immature development of preterm neonates makes them unusually sensitive to stimuli in their environment. They can easily be overwhelmed by the sights, sounds, and sensations they experience, and their breathing may be interrupted or their heart rates may slow. Furthermore, they are often unable to move smoothly; their arm and leg movements are uncoordinated, causing them to jerk about and appear startled. Such behavior is quite disconcerting to parents (T. M. Field, 1990; Doussard-Roosevelt et al., 1997).

Despite the difficulties they experience at birth, the majority of preterm infants develop normally in the long run. However, the tempo of development often proceeds more slowly for preterm children, compared with children born at full term, and more subtle problems sometimes emerge later. For example, by the end of 1 year, only 10 percent of prematurely born infants display significant problems, and only 5 percent are seriously disabled. By the age of 6, however, approximately 38 percent have mild problems that call for special educational interventions. For instance, some preterm children show learning disabilities, behavior disorders, or lower-than-average IQ scores. Others have difficulties with physical coordination. Still, around 60 percent of preterm infants are free of even minor problems (Liaw & Brooks-Gunn, 1993; Cohen, 1995, 1996; Menyuk, Liebergott, & Schultz, 1995; Sykes et al., 1997).

Very-low-birthweight Infants: The Smallest of the Small.   The story is less positive for the most extreme cases of prematurity—very-low-birthweight infants. **Very-low-birthweight infants** weigh less than 1,250 grams (around 2 1/4 pounds) or, regardless of weight, have been in the womb less than 30 weeks.

Very-low-birthweight infants are not only tiny, some fitting easily in the palm of the hand, they hardly seem even to belong to the same species as full-term newborns. Their eyes may be fused shut and their earlobes may look like flaps of skin on the sides of their heads. Their skin is a darkened red color, whatever their race.

Very-low-birthweight babies are in grave danger from the moment they are born due to the immaturity of their organ systems. Before the last two decades, these babies would not have survived outside the mother. However, medical advances have led to a much higher chance of survival, pushing the **age of viability**, the point at which an infant can survive prematurely, to about 24 weeks—some 4 months earlier than the term of a normal delivery. At the same time, such advances have not been without their costs, both developmental and financial.

The physical and cognitive problems experienced by low-birthweight and preterm babies are even more pronounced in very-low-birthweight infants, with astonishing financial consequences. For instance, the costs of keeping very-low-birthweight infants alive are enormous. A 3-month stay in an incubator in an intensive care unit can run hundreds of thousands of dollars, and not infrequently—some 50 percent of the time—the infant ultimately dies, despite massive medical intervention.

Even if a very-low-birthweight preterm infant survives, the medical costs can continue to mount. For instance, one estimate suggests that the average monthly cost of medical care for such infants during the first 3 years of life may be between 3 and 50 times higher than the medical costs for a full-term child. Such astronomical costs have raised significant ethical debate about the advisability of expending substantial financial and human resources in cases in which a positive outcome may be very unlikely (Beckwith & Rodning, 1991; McCormick, 1992; Sung, Vohr, & On, 1993; Hille et al., 1994; Lewit et al., 1995; Wallace et al., 1995).

The difficult issues surrounding very-low-birthweight infants are not likely to diminish in the years ahead. In fact, as medical capabilities progress, the age of viability is likely to be pushed even further back.

Treating Preterm Infants: Effective Interventions.   Developmental researchers are formulating new strategies for dealing with preterm infants in the hope of improving their lives, and emerging evidence suggests that high-quality care can provide protection from

very-low-birthweight infants   *infants who weigh less than 1,250 grams (around 2.25 pounds) or, regardless of weight, have been in the womb less than 30 weeks*

age of viability   *the point at which an infant can survive a premature birth*

some of the risks associated with prematurity. For instance, research shows that children who receive more responsive, stimulating, and organized care are apt to show more positive outcomes than children whose care was not as good (Bradley et al., 1994).

Furthermore, several programs have been designed to lower the risks for preterm infants. For instance, in one successful program, close to 1,000 preterm newborns, each weighing less than 5.5 pounds, were divided into two groups (The Infant Health and Development Program, 1990; Gross, Brooks-Gunn, & Spiker, 1992). Parents of the children in one group received special instruction in their homes from health care experts. During the visit, the parents were given information on health and development and were provided with a program of games and activities meant to improve the cognitive, social, and language skills of their children. In addition, when the children reached 1 year of age, they were placed in a special educational day-care program, with one teacher for every three children. At age 2, the ratio changed to one teacher for every four children.

In comparison to children in the second group—in which the parents received no special training—the children in the treatment group achieved impressive results. Treated children had significantly higher IQ scores than those in the group that received no special treatment. Average IQ scores of the lightest babies, who had weighed less than 4.4 pounds at birth, were more than 13 points higher. Average IQ gains for the heavier babies, who weighed between 4.4 and 5.5 pounds at birth, were not as great—some 7 points higher—but still significant.

Results such as these have important implications for public policy. They suggest that intervention programs to help preterm and low-birth-weight babies should begin with the very start of life. By intervening early, developmental specialists might well diminish—and possibly prevent—future problems.

Causes of Preterm and Low-birthweight Deliveries. Although half of preterm and low-birthweight births are unexplained, several known causes account for the remainder (Goldberg & DiVitto, 1983; Friedman & Sigman, 1992; Radetsky, 1994; Paneth, 1995). In some cases, difficulties relating to the mother's reproductive system cause such births. For instance, mothers carrying twins have unusual stress placed on them, leading to premature labor. In fact, most multiple births are preterm to some degree.

In other cases, preterm and low-birthweight babies are a result of the immaturity of the mother's reproductive system. Young mothers—under the age of 15—are more prone to deliver prematurely than older ones. In addition, a woman who has not had much time between pregnancies is more likely to deliver a preterm or low-birthweight infant than a woman who has given her reproductive system a chance to recover from a prior delivery (DuPlessis, Bell, & Richards, 1997).

Finally, factors that affect the general health of the mother, such as nutrition, level of medical care, amount of stress in the environment, and economic support, all are related to prematurity and low birthweight. Racial factors are also implicated, not because of race per se, but because members of racial minorities have disproportionately lower incomes. For instance, the percentage of low-birthweight infants born to African American mothers is double that for Caucasian American mothers. (A summary of the factors associated with increased risk of low birthweight is shown in Table 3-2; Goldberg & DiVitto, 1983; Kleinman, 1992; National Center for Health Statistics, 1993b; Radetsky, 1994; Cohen, 1995).

Postmature Babies: Too Late, Too Large

One might imagine that a baby who spends extra time in the womb might have some advantages, given the opportunity to continue growth undisturbed by the outside world. Yet the reality is different. **Postmature infants**—those still unborn 2 weeks after the mother's due date—face several risks.

For example, the blood supply from the placenta may become insufficient to nourish the fetus adequately. Consequently, the blood supply to the brain may be decreased, leading to the potential of brain damage. Similarly, labor becomes riskier (for both the child and

---

postmature infants *infants still unborn 2 weeks after the mother's due date*

TABLE 3-2

FACTORS ASSOCIATED WITH INCREASED RISK OF LOW BIRTHWEIGHT

I. *Demographic Risks*
   A. Age (less than 17; over 34)
   B. Race (minority)
   C. Low socioeconomic status
   D. Unmarried
   E. Low level of education

II. *Medical Risks Predating Pregnancy*
   A. Parity (0 or more than 4)
   B. Low weight for height
   C. Genitourinary anomalies/surgery
   D. Selected diseases such as diabetes, chronic hypertension
   E. Nonimmune status for selected infections such as rubella
   F. Poor obstetric history, including previous low-birthweight infant, multiple spontaneous abortions
   G. Maternal genetic factors (such as low maternal weight at own birth)

III. *Medical Risks in Current Pregnancy*
   A. Multiple pregnancy
   B. Poor weight gain
   C. Short interpregnancy interval
   D. Hypotension
   E. Hypertension/preeclampsia/toxemia
   F. Selected infections such as asymptomatic bacteriuria, rubella, and cytomegalovirus
   G. First or second trimester bleeding
   H. Placental problems such as placenta previa, abruptio placentae

I. Hyperemesis
J. Ologohydramnios/polyhydramnios
K. Anemia/abnormal hemoglobin
L. Isoimmunization
M. Fetal anomalies
N. Incompetent cervix
O. Spontaneous premature rupture of membrane

IV. *Behavioral and Environmental Risks*
   A. Smoking
   B. Poor nutritional status
   C. Alcohol and other substance abuse
   D. DES exposure and other toxic exposure, including occupational hazards
   E. High altitude

V. *Health Care Risks*
   A. Absent or inadequate prenatal care
   B. Iatrogenic prematurity

VI. *Evolving Concepts of Risks*
   A. Stress, physical and psychosocial
   B. Uterine irritability
   C. Events triggering uterine contractions
   D. Cervical changes detected before onset of labor
   E. Selected infections such as mycoplasma and chlamydia trachomatis
   F. Inadequate plasma volume expansion
   G. Progesterone deficiency

(*Source:* Adapted from Committee to Study the Prevention of Low Birthweight, 1985.)

the mother) as a fetus who may be equivalent in size to a 1-month-old infant has to make its way through the birth canal (Boylan, 1990).

In some ways, difficulties involving postmature infants are more easily prevented than those involving preterm babies, because medical practitioners can induce labor artificially if the pregnancy continues too long. Not only can certain drugs bring on labor, but physicians also have the option of performing Cesarean deliveries, a form of delivery we consider next.

Cesarean delivery a birth in which the baby is surgically removed from the uterus, rather than traveling through the birth canal

Cesarean Delivery: Intervening in the Process of Birth

As Elena entered her 18th hour of labor, the obstetrician who was monitoring her progress began to look concerned. She told Elena and her husband, Pablo, that the fetal monitor revealed that the fetus's heart rate had begun to repeatedly fall after each contraction. After trying some simple remedies, such as repositioning Elena on her side, the obstetrician came to the conclusion that the fetus was in distress. She told them that the baby should be delivered immediately, and to accomplish that, she would have to carry out a Cesarean delivery.

Elena became one of the almost one million mothers in the United States who have a Cesarean delivery each year. In a **Cesarean delivery**, the baby is surgically removed from the uterus, rather than traveling through the birth canal.

fetal monitors *devices that measure the baby's heartbeat during labor*

Several types of difficulties during the birthing process can lead to Cesarean deliveries. Fetal distress is the most frequent cause. For instance, if the fetus appears to be in some danger, as indicated by a sudden rise in its heart rate or if blood is seen coming from the mother's vagina during labor, a Cesarean may be performed. Cesarean deliveries are also used in some cases of *breech position,* in which the baby is positioned feet first in the birth canal, or *transverse position,* in which the baby lies crosswise in the uterus, or when the baby's head is so large it has trouble moving through the birth canal.

The use of routine **fetal monitors**, devices that measure the baby's heartbeat during labor, has contributed to a soaring rate of Cesarean deliveries. For instance, almost 25 percent of all children in the United States are born in this way, up some 500 percent from the early 1970s (National Center for Health Statistics, 1993). What benefits have resulted from this increase?

According to critics, very few. Other countries have substantially lower rates of Cesarean deliveries (see Figure 3-3), and there is no association between successful birth consequences and the rate of Cesarean deliveries (Notzon, 1990). In addition, Cesarean deliveries carry dangers. A Cesarean is major surgery, and recovery can be relatively lengthy, particularly when compared with a normal delivery. In addition, the risk of maternal infection is higher with Cesarean deliveries (Mutryn, 1993; Shearer, 1993; Fisher, Astbury, & Smith, 1997).

Finally, a Cesarean delivery presents some risks for the baby. Although Cesarean babies are spared the stresses of passing though the birth canal, their relatively easy passage into the world may deter the normal release of certain stress-related hormones into the newborn's bloodstream. Because these hormones help prepare the neonate to deal with the stress of the world outside the womb, their absence may be detrimental to the newborn child. In fact, research indicates that babies who, due to a Cesarean delivery, have not experienced labor are more prone to initial breathing problems upon birth than those who experience at least some labor prior to being born via a Cesarean delivery (Lagercrantz & Slotkin, 1986; Hales, Morgan, & Thurnau, 1993).

FIGURE 3-3

CESAREAN DELIVERIES

The rate at which Cesarean deliveries are performed varies substantially from one country to another.

(*Source:* Notzon, 1990)

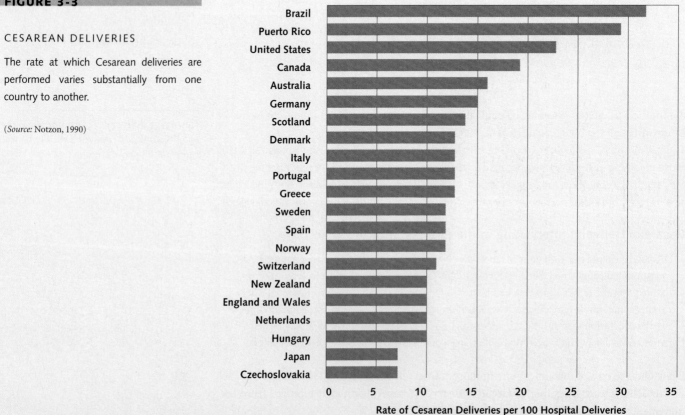

Rate of Cesarean Deliveries per 100 Hospital Deliveries

Due in part to the increase in Cesarean deliveries that results from their use, fetal monitors are no longer employed routinely, in accordance with current recommendations from medical authorities. These experts cite research evidence that the outcomes are no better for newborns who have been monitored than for those who have not been monitored, and that monitors give false alarms regarding the presence of fetal distress with disquieting regularity (Levano et al., 1986; Albers & Krulewitch, 1993). On the other hand, monitors can play a critical role in high-risk pregnancies and in cases of preterm and postmature babies. (For another problem involving birth, see the "Directions in Development" box.)

Directions in Development

Postpartum Depression: Moving from the Heights of Joy to the Depths of Despair

She had been overjoyed when she found out that she was pregnant, and she had spent the months of her pregnancy happily preparing for her baby's arrival. The birth was routine, the baby a healthy, pink-cheeked boy. But only a few days after her son's birth, she sank into the depths of depression. Constantly crying, confused, feeling incapable of caring for her child, she was experiencing unshakable despair.

The diagnosis: a classic case of postpartum depression. *Postpartum depression*, a period of deep depression following the birth of a child, affects some 10 percent of all new mothers. Although it takes several forms, its main symptom is an enduring, deep feeling of sadness and unhappiness, lasting in some cases for months or even years. In about 1 in 500 cases, the symptoms are even worse, evolving into a total break with reality (Walther, 1997).

For mothers who suffer from postpartum depression, the symptoms are bewildering. The onset of depression usually comes as a complete surprise and is typically not linked to anything in their past or present environments. Although there is some evidence relating difficult menstruation with postpartum depression, the relationship is far from firm. Furthermore, mothers who have been clinically depressed at some point in the past, or who have depressed family members, are more apt to become depressed when their child is born. Finally, women who are unprepared for the range of emotions that follow the birth of a child—some positive, some negative—may be more prone to depression. Ultimately, though, research has been unable to pinpoint which women are most likely to suffer from postpartum depression (Brody, 1994b; Murray & Cooper, 1997).

It does seem that postpartum depression is triggered by the pronounced swings in hormone production that occur after birth. For instance, one study found that women who experienced postpartum depression had particularly high levels of progesterone before birth and unusually low levels after birth, compared with mothers who did not suffer postpartum depression (Harris et al., 1994; Harris et al., 1996).

Whatever its cause, maternal depression leaves its marks on the infant. Infants are highly attuned to the moods of their mothers. When depressed mothers interact with their infants, they are likely to display little emotion and act detached and withdrawn. This lack of responsiveness leads infants to display fewer positive emotions and to withdraw from contact not only with their mothers but with other adults as well (Weinberg & Tronick, 1994, 1996; Lundy, Field, & Pickens, 1996).

Given the negative consequences of postpartum depression for both infant and mother, aggressive treatment is warranted—and is often effective. Drugs and therapy are often helpful in alleviating the symptoms. In addition, home visits by nurses who coach depressed mothers on how to interact more effectively with their children have proved effective. Mothers show less depression, and infants show greater emotional involvement as a result (Gelfand & Teti, 1995; Dalton & Holton, 1996).

Infant Mortality and Stillbirth: The Tragedy of Premature Death

The joy that accompanies the birth of a child is completely reversed when a newborn dies. The relative rarity of their occurrence makes infant deaths even harder for parents to bear.

Infant mortality is defined as death within the first year of life. In the 1990s the overall rate in the United States is 8.5 deaths per 1,000 live births. Infant mortality has been declining since the 1960s, and U.S. government officials expect to meet their goal of lowering the overall rate to 7 deaths per 1,000 live births (Wegman, 1993; Guyer et al., 1995).

infant mortality *death within the first year of life*

Sometimes a child does not even live beyond its passage through the birth canal. **Stillbirth**, the delivery of a child who is not alive, occurs in less than 1 delivery out of 100. Sometimes the death is detected before labor begins. In this case, labor is typically induced, or physicians may carry out a Cesarean delivery to remove the body from the mother as soon as possible. In other cases of stillbirth, the baby dies during its travels through the birth canal.

Whether the death is a stillbirth or occurs after the child is born, the loss of a baby is a tragic occurrence. The impact on parents is significant: They move through the same stages of grief and mourning as they experience when an older loved one dies. In fact, the cruel juxtaposition of the first dawning of life and an unnaturally early death may make the death particularly difficult to accept and deal with. Depression is a common aftermath (Brockington, 1992; Thomas, 1995; Finkbeiner, 1996; Lin & Lasker, 1996; McGreal, Evans, & Burrows, 1997).

stillbirth   *the delivery of a child who is not alive, occurring in less than 1 delivery in 100*

Developmental Diversity

Overcoming Racial and Cultural Differences in Infant Mortality

The general decline in the infant mortality rate in the United States over the past several decades masks some significant, and startling, racial differences. In particular, African American babies are more than twice as likely to die before the age of 1 than Caucasian babies (see Figure 3-4). In fact, if current trends continue, by the turn of the century, the mortality rate for African American infants will be three times that for Caucasian infants (National Center for Health Statistics, 1993b; Guyer et al., 1995; Singh et al., 1995).

The overall U.S. rate of infant mortality is higher than the rate in many other countries (see Figure 3-5). The mortality rate in the United States is almost double that of Japan, which has the lowest mortality rate of any country in the world.

Why does the United States fare so poorly in terms of newborn survival? One answer is that the United States has a higher rate of low-birthweight and preterm deliveries than many other

countries. In fact, when U.S. infants are compared with infants of the same weight who are born in countries with lower mortality, the differences in mortality rates disappear (Paneth, 1995; Wilcox et al., 1995).

Another reason for the higher U.S. mortality rate relates to economic diversity. The United States has a higher proportion of people living in poverty than many other countries. Because people in lower economic categories are less likely to have adequate medical care and tend to be less healthy, the relatively high proportion of economically deprived individuals in the United States has an impact on the overall mortality rate (Aved et al., 1993).

Many countries do a significantly better job providing prenatal care to mothers-to-be than the United States. For instance, low-cost and even free care, both before and after delivery, is often available in other countries. Paid maternity leave is frequently provided to pregnant women, lasting in some cases as long as 51 weeks (see Table 3-3). Such opportunities for maternity leave are important: Mothers who spend more time on maternity leave may have better mental health and higher quality interactions with their infants (Hyde et al., 1995; Clark et al., 1997).

In certain European countries, women receive a comprehensive package of services involving general practitioner, obstetrician, and midwife. Pregnant women receive many privileges, such as transportation benefits for visits to health care providers. In Norway, pregnant women may be given living expenses for up to 10 days so they can be close to a hospital when it is time to give birth. And when their babies are born, new mothers receive, for just a small payment, the assistance of trained home helpers (Miller, 1987).

In the United States, the story is very different. The lack of national health care insurance or a national health policy means that prenatal care is often

FIGURE 3-4

RACE AND INFANT MORTALITY

Although infant mortality is dropping for both African American and Caucasian children, the death rate is still twice as high for African American children. These figures show the number of deaths in the first year of life for every 1,000 live births.

(*Source:* National Center for Health Statistics, 1995.)

African American   White

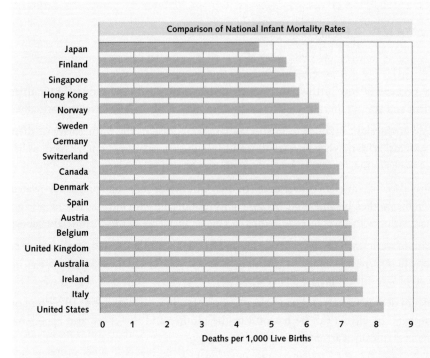

FIGURE 3-5

NATIONALITY AND INFANT
MORTALITY

The rate of infant mortality is higher in the
United States than for other industrialized
countries.

(*Source:* The World Factbook, 1994.)

haphazardly provided to the poor. About one of six pregnant women has insufficient prenatal care. Some 20 percent of Caucasian women and close to 40 percent of African American women who are pregnant receive no prenatal care early in their pregnancies. Five percent of Caucasian mothers and 11 percent of African American mothers do not see a health care provider until the last 3 months of pregnancy; some never see a health care provider at all. In fact, the percentage of pregnant women in the United States who receive virtually no prenatal care has actually increased in the 1990s from earlier decades (National Center for Health Statistics, 1993b; Johnson, Primas, & Coe, 1994; Thomas, 1994).

The ultimate outcome of the deficiency in prenatal services to women with low incomes is the higher likelihood of death for their infants. Yet this unfortunate state of affairs can be changed if greater support is provided. A first step would be to ensure that all economically disadvantaged pregnant women have access to free or inexpensive high-quality medical care from the very beginning of pregnancy. Furthermore, barriers that prevent poor women from receiving such care should be reduced. For instance, programs can be developed that help pay for transportation to a health facility or for the care of older children while the mother is making a health care visit (Aved et al., 1993).

Finally, programs that provide basic education for all mothers-to-be are of paramount importance. Increasing the level of understanding of the potential risks involved in childbearing could prevent many problems before they actually occur (Carnegie Task Force on Meeting the Needs of Young Children, 1994; Fangman et al., 1994).

TABLE 3-3

MATERNITY-LEAVE POLICIES IN OTHER COUNTRIES:
GUARANTEED BY LAW

	Maximum Weeks Allowed	Percent of Salary Replaced
Sweden*	51	90
France	16–38	84
Italy	20	80
Britain	18	90
Canada	15	60
Germany	14	100
Japan	14	60
Netherlands	7	100

*For both parents combined.
(*Source:* Caminiti, 1992.)

REVIEW AND RETHINK

REVIEW

■ Largely because of low birthweight, preterm infants may have substantial difficulties after birth and later in life, although most preterm babies ultimately develop normally.

■ Very-low-birthweight infants are in special danger because of the immaturity of their organ systems. With massive intervention and at high cost, infants who have spent as little as 24 weeks in their mothers' bodies can now be helped to survive.

■ Preterm and low-birthweight deliveries can be caused by health-, age-, and pregnancy-related factors in the mother. Income (and, because of its relationship with income, race) is also an important factor, with lower income leading to a higher incidence of low-birthweight babies.

■ Cesarean deliveries, which occur with unusual frequency in the United States, are performed with postmature babies or when the fetus is in distress, in the wrong position, or unable to progress through the birth canal.

■ Postpartum depression, an enduring, deep feeling of sadness, affects about 10 percent of new mothers. Its effects can be harmful to the mother and the child, and aggressive treatment is typically warranted.

■ Infant mortality rates can be affected by the availability of inexpensive health care and good education programs for mothers-to-be. The infant mortality rate in the United States is higher than the rate in many other countries, and higher for low-income families than higher-income families.

RETHINK

■ What are some ethical considerations relating to the provision of intensive medical care to very-low-birthweight babies? Do you think such interventions should be routine practice? Why or why not?

■ Effective educational programs have been devised for treating preterm infants when they reach school age. What are some public policy implications of this fact? What arguments, pro and con, can be made regarding such efforts?

■ Why do you think the number of Cesarean deliveries has increased dramatically in the United States in recent years? What sort of policy for families and physicians would you design to govern the use of Cesarean procedures?

■ Why do you think the United States lacks educational and health care policies that could reduce infant mortality rates overall and among poorer people? What arguments would you make to change this situation?

THE COMPETENT NEWBORN

In one sense, we are all born too soon. The size of the brain of the average newborn is just one-quarter what it will be at adulthood. In comparison, the brain of the macaque monkey, which is born after just 24 weeks of gestation, is 65 percent of its adult size. Because of the relatively small size of the infant human brain, some observers have suggested that we are propelled out of the womb some 6 to 12 months sooner than we ought to be.

In reality, evolution probably knows best: If we stayed inside our mothers' bodies an additional half-year to a year, our heads would be so large that we'd never manage to get through the birth canal (Schultz, 1969; Gould, 1977; Kotre & Hall, 1990).

The relatively underdeveloped brain of the human newborn helps explain the infant's apparent helplessness. Neonates arrive in the world quite incapable of successfully caring for themselves. Because of this, the earliest views of newborns focused on the things that they could not do, comparing them rather unfavorably to older members of the human species.

Today, however, such beliefs have taken a backseat to more favorable views of the neonate. As developmental researchers have begun to understand more about newborns, they have come to realize that infants enter this world with an astounding array of capabilities.

Physical Competence: Meeting the Demands of a New Environment

The world faced by a neonate is remarkably different from the one it experienced in the womb. Consider, for instance, the significant changes in functioning that the newly born Jamilla Castro, who weighs a robust 8 pounds, 2 ounces at birth, encounters as she begins the first moments of life in her new environment (summarized in Table 3-4).

Jamilla's most immediate task is to bring sufficient air into her body. Inside her mother, air was delivered through the umbilical cord, which also provided a means for the removal of carbon dioxide. The realities of the outside world are different: Once the umbilical cord is cut, Jamilla's respiratory system must begin its lifetime's work.

For Jamilla, the task is automatic. As we noted earlier, most neonates begin to breathe on their own as soon as they are exposed to air. The ability to breathe immediately is a good indication that the respiratory system of the normal neonate is reasonably well developed, despite its lack of rehearsal in the womb.

Neonates emerge from the uterus more practiced in other types of physical activities. For example, newborns such as Jamilla show several **reflexes**—unlearned, organized involuntary responses that occur automatically in the presence of certain stimuli. Some of these reflexes are well rehearsed, having been present for several months before birth. The *sucking reflex* and the *swallowing reflex* permit the neonate to begin right away to ingest food. The *rooting reflex*, which involves turning in the direction of a source of stimulation (such as a light touch) near the mouth, is also related to eating. It guides the infant toward potential sources of food that are near its mouth, such as a mother's nipple.

Not all of the reflexes that are present at birth lead the newborn to seek out desired stimuli such as food. For instance, Jamilla can cough, sneeze, and blink—reflexes that help her to avoid stimuli that are potentially bothersome or hazardous.

Jamilla's sucking and swallowing reflexes, which help her to consume her mother's milk, are coupled with the new-found ability to digest nutriments. The neonate's digestive system initially produces *meconium*, a greenish-black material that is a remnant of the neonate's days as a fetus. The digestive tract immediately begins to process newly ingested nourishment.

Because their livers, a critical component of the digestive system, do not always work effectively at first, almost half of all newborns develop a distinctly yellowish tinge to their

reflexes unlearned, organized involuntary responses that occur automatically in the presence of certain stimuli

TABLE 3-4

JAMILLA CASTRO'S FIRST ENCOUNTERS UPON BIRTH

1. As soon as she is through the birth canal, Jamilla automatically begins to breathe on her own despite no longer being attached to the umbilical cord that provided precious air in the womb.
2. Reflexes—unlearned, organized involuntary responses that occur in the presence of stimuli—begin to take over. Sucking and swallowing reflexes permit Jamilla immediately to ingest food.
3. The rooting reflex, which involves turning in the direction of a source of stimulation, guides Jamilla toward potential sources of food that are near her mouth, such as her mother's nipple.
4. Jamilla begins to cough, sneeze, and blink—reflexes that help her avoid stimuli that are potentially bothersome or hazardous.
5. Her senses of smell and taste are highly developed. Physical activities and sucking increase when she smells peppermint. Her lips pucker when a sour taste is placed on her lips.
6. Objects with colors of blue and green seem to catch Jamilla's attention more than other colors, and she reacts sharply to loud, sudden noises. She will also continue to cry if she hears other newborns cry, but will stop if she hears a recording of her own voice crying.

bodies and eyes. This change in color is a symptom of *neonatal jaundice.* It is most likely to occur in preterm and low-weight neonates, and it is typically not dangerous. Treatment most often consists of placing the baby under fluorescent lights or administering medicine.

Sensory Capabilities: Experiencing the World

Just after Jamilla was born, her father was certain that she looked directly at him. Did she, in fact, see him? This is a hard question to answer for several reasons. For one thing, when sensory experts talk of "seeing," they mean both a sensory reaction due to the stimulation of the visual sensory organs and an interpretation of that stimulation (the distinction, as you might recall from an introductory psychology class, between sensation and perception). Furthermore, as we'll discuss further when we consider sensory capabilities during infancy in Chapter 4, it is tricky, to say the least, to pinpoint the specific sensory skills of newborns who lack the ability to explain what they are experiencing.

Still, we do have some answers to the question of what newborns are capable of seeing and, for that matter, questions about their other sensory capabilities. For example, it is clear that neonates such as Jamilla can see to some extent. Although their visual acuity is not fully developed, newborns actively pay attention to certain types of information in their environment (Haith, 1980, 1991).

For instance, neonates pay closest attention to portions of scenes in their field of vision that are highest in information, such as objects that sharply contrast with the rest of their environment. Furthermore, infants can discriminate different levels of brightness. There is even evidence suggesting that newborns have a sense of size constancy, seemingly aware that objects stay the same size even though the size of the image on the retina varies with distance (Slater, Mattock, & Brown, 1990).

And not only can neonates distinguish different colors, they seem to prefer particular ones. For example, they are able to distinguish between red, green, yellow, and blue, and they take more time staring at blue and green objects—suggesting a partiality for those colors (Adams, Mauer, & Davis, 1986).

Newborns are also clearly capable of hearing. They react to certain kinds of sounds, showing startle reactions to loud, sudden noises, for instance. They also exhibit familiarity with certain sounds. For example, newborns continue to cry when they hear other newborns crying. On the other hand, a crying newborn who hears a recording of its own crying is more likely to stop crying, as if it recognizes the familiar sound (Martin & Clark, 1982).

As with vision, however, the degree of auditory acuity is not as great as it will be later. The auditory system is not completely developed. Moreover, amniotic fluid, which is initially trapped in the middle ear, must drain out before the newborn can fully hear (Reinis & Goldman, 1980).

In addition to sight and hearing, the other senses also function quite adequately in the newborn. It is obvious that newborns are sensitive to touch. For instance, they respond to stimuli such as the hairs of a brush, and they are aware of puffs of air so weak that adults cannot notice them. The senses of smell and taste are also well developed. Newborns suck and increase other physical activity when the odor of peppermint is placed near the nose. They also pucker their lips when a sour taste is placed on them, and respond with suitable facial expressions to other tastes as well. Such findings clearly indicate that the senses of touch, smell, and taste are not only present at birth, but also reasonably sophisticated (Sarnat, 1978; Jacklin, Snow, & Maccoby, 1981; Rosenstein & Oster, 1988; Mistretta, 1990).

In one sense, the sophistication of the sensory systems of newborns such as Jamilla is not surprising. After all, the typical neonate has had 9 months to prepare for his or her encounter with the outside world. As we discussed in Chapter 2, human sensory systems begin their development well before birth. Furthermore, some researchers suggest that the passage through the birth canal places babies in a state of heightened sensory awareness, preparing them for the world that they are about to encounter for the first time (Bornstein & Lamb, 1992b).

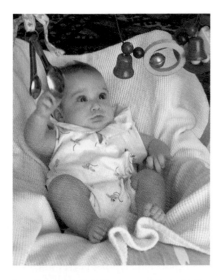

Starting at birth, infants are able to distinguish colors and even show preferences for particular ones.

Early Learning Capabilities

One-month-old Michael Samedi was on a car ride with his family when a thunderstorm suddenly began. The storm rapidly became violent, and flashes of lightning were quickly followed by loud thunderclaps. Michael was clearly disturbed and began to sob. With each new thunderclap, the pitch and fervor of his crying increased. Unfortunately, before very long it wasn't just the sound of the thunder that would raise Michael's anxiety; the sight of the lightning alone was enough to make him cry out in fear. In fact, even as an adult, Michael feels his chest tighten and his stomach churn at the mere sight of lightning.

Classical Conditioning.   The source of Michael's fear is classical conditioning, a basic type of learning first identified by Ivan Pavlov (and first discussed in Chapter 1). In **classical conditioning** an organism learns to respond in a particular way to a neutral stimulus that normally does not bring about that type of response.

You've probably heard of the initial demonstration of classical conditioning, which involved Pavlov's research with dogs, even before we discussed it in Chapter 1. Pavlov discovered that by repeatedly pairing two stimuli, such as the sound of a bell and the arrival of meat, he could make hungry dogs learn to respond (in this case by salivating) not only when the meat was presented, but even when the bell was sounded without the presence of meat (Pavlov, 1927).

The key feature of classical conditioning is stimulus substitution, in which a stimulus that doesn't naturally bring about a particular response is paired with a stimulus that does evoke that response. Repeatedly presenting the two stimuli together results in the second stimulus taking on the properties of the first. In effect, the second stimulus is substituted for the first.

Classical conditioning underlies the learning of both pleasurable and undesired responses. For example, consider Amber Nordstrom, a 3-month-old girl whose older brother Marcus repeatedly stands over her crib, wiggling a doll and lightly tickling her until she smiles. Amber never seems to tire of Marcus's efforts to make her smile, and soon whenever Marcus appears and simply picks up the doll, her lips begin to curl into a smile. Her smile is an example of classical conditioning: The mere arrival of her brother brings the same reaction to the now-conditioned infant as his earlier playing with her doll. On the other hand, Michael Samedi's fear of lightning is also brought about by classical conditioning: The lightning has become a substitute stimulus for thunder, and each stimulus now evokes the response of fear.

One of the earliest examples of the power of classical conditioning in shaping human emotions was demonstrated in the case of an 11-month-old infant called "Little Albert" in the research report documenting the study (Watson & Rayner, 1920). Although he initially adored furry animals and showed no fear of rats, Little Albert learned to fear them when, during a laboratory demonstration, a loud noise was sounded every time he played with a cute and harmless white rat. In fact, the fear generalized to other furry objects, including rabbits and even a Santa Claus mask. (By the way, such a demonstration would be considered unethical today, and it would never be conducted.)

Infants are capable of learning very early through classical conditioning. For instance, 1- and 2-day-old newborns who are stroked on the head just before being given a drop of a sweet-tasting liquid soon learn to suck and to turn their heads at the head-stroking alone (Blass, Ganchrow, & Steiner, 1984). Clearly, classical conditioning is in operation from the time of birth.

Operant Conditioning.   But classical conditioning is not the only mechanism through which infants learn; they also respond to operant conditioning. As we noted in Chapter 1, **operant conditioning** is a form of learning in which a voluntary response is strengthened or weakened, depending on its association with positive or negative consequences. In operant conditioning, infants learn to act deliberately on their environments in order to bring about some desired consequence. An infant who learns that crying in a certain way is apt to bring her parents' immediate attention is displaying operant conditioning.

Like classical conditioning, operant conditioning functions from the earliest days of life. For instance, researchers have found that even newborns readily learn through operant

classical conditioning   *a type of learning in which an organism responds in a particular way to a neutral stimulus that normally does not bring about that type of response*

operant conditioning   *a form of learning in which a voluntary response is strengthened or weakened, depending on its association with positive or negative consequences*

conditioning to keep sucking on a nipple when it permits them to continue hearing their mothers read a story or to listen to music (Butterfield & Siperstein, 1972; DeCasper & Fifer, 1980; Lipsitt, 1986).

Habituation. Probably the most primitive form of learning is habituation. **Habituation** is the decrease in the response to a stimulus that occurs after repeated presentations of the same stimulus. Habituation in infants relies on the fact that the presentation of a novel stimulus typically produces an *orienting response*, in which the infant quiets, becomes attentive, and experiences a slowed heart rate. But when the novelty wears off due to repeated exposure to the stimulus, the infant no longer reacts with an orienting response. However, when a new and different stimulus is presented, the infant once again reacts with an orienting response. When this happens, we can say that the infant has learned to recognize the original stimulus and to distinguish it from others.

Habituation occurs in every sensory system of infants, and researchers have studied the phenomenon in several ways. One is to examine changes in sucking, which stops temporarily when a new stimulus is presented. This reaction is not unlike that of an adult who temporarily puts down his knife and fork when a dinner companion makes an interesting statement to which he wishes to pay particular attention. Other study techniques include measuring heart rate, respiration rate, and the length of time an infant looks at a particular stimulus.

The ability to learn through habituation is clearly present at birth, and it becomes more pronounced over the first 12 weeks of infancy. As a consequence, habituation is linked to physical and cognitive maturation, and difficulties involving habituation signal developmental problems (Rovee-Collier, 1987; Braddock, 1993; Tamis-LaMonda & Bornstein, 1993).

Are There Limits on Learning? Although the three basic processes of learning that we've considered—classical conditioning, operant conditioning, and habituation (summarized in Table 3-5)—are all present at birth, they initially face considerable constraints. According to researchers Marc Bornstein and Michael Lamb (1992a), three factors limit the success of learning during infancy. One is the *behavioral state* of the infant. For learning to occur, infants must be in a sufficiently attentive state to sense, perceive, and recognize the relationship between various stimuli and responses. Without at least a minimal level of attentiveness, learning will not be possible (Papousek & Bernstein, 1969).

Natural constraints on learning are a second limiting factor. Not all behaviors are physically possible for an infant, and infants' perceptual systems, which are not fully developed

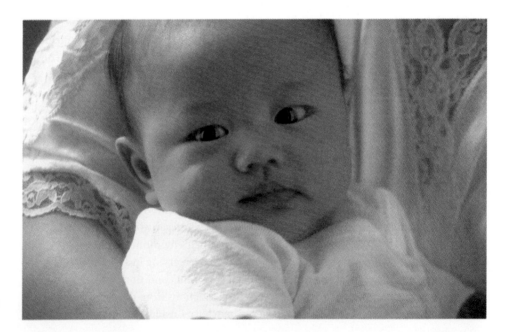

Newborns actively pay attention to their environments.

TABLE 3-5

THREE BASIC PROCESSES OF LEARNING

Type	Description	Example
Classical conditioning	A situation in which an organism learns to respond in a particular way to a neutral stimulus that normally does not bring about that type of response.	One- and two-day-old newborns are stroked on the head just before being given a drop of a sweet-tasting liquid. They soon learn to suck and turn their heads at the head-stroking alone.
Operant conditioning	A form of learning in which a voluntary response is strengthened or weakened, depending on its positive or negative consequences.	An infant who learns that crying in a certain way is apt to bring her parents' immediate attention is displaying operant conditioning.
Habituation	The decrease in the response to a stimulus that occurs after repeated presentations of the same stimulus.	The most primitive form of learning, habituation occurs in every sensory system of infants. It relies on the fact that the presentation of a novel stimulus typically produces an orienting response, in which the infant quiets, becomes attentive, and experiences a slowed heart rate.

at birth, may not be sufficiently refined to respond to, or even notice, a particular stimulus. Consequently, certain types of classical and operant conditioning that are possible with older individuals are ineffective with infants.

Finally, *motivational constraints* may limit learning. For learning to occur, the response involved must not be so taxing on infants that they simply are unmotivated to respond. If the response is too demanding, learning may fail to appear not because the infants haven't learned an association between a stimulus and a response, but because they just don't have the energy or skills to proceed (Rovee-Collier, 1987).

Despite these limitations, infants show great capacities to learn. But just how far do the capabilities of infants extend beyond the basic learning processes? Research on social competence in infants illustrates just how competent infants are in another important regard.

Social Competence: Responding to Others

Soon after Jamilla was born, her older brother looked down at her in her crib and opened his mouth wide, pretending to be surprised. Jamilla's mother, looking on, was amazed when it appeared that Jamilla imitated his expression, opening her mouth as if she too were surprised.

Researchers registered surprise of their own when they first found that newborns did indeed have the capability to imitate others' behavior. Although infants were known to have all the muscles in place to produce facial expressions related to basic emotions, the actual appearance of such expressions was assumed to be largely random.

However, research beginning in the late 1970s suggested a different conclusion. For instance, developmental researchers demonstrated that, when exposed to an adult modeling a behavior that the infant already performed spontaneously, such as opening the mouth or sticking out the tongue, the newborn was apt to imitate the behavior (Meltzoff & Moore, 1977).

Even more exciting were findings from a series of studies conducted by developmental psychologist Tiffany Field and her colleagues (Field, 1982; Field & Walden, 1982; Field et al., 1984). They initially showed that infants could discriminate between such basic facial expressions as happiness, sadness, and surprise. They then exposed newborns to an adult model with a happy, sad, or surprised facial expression. The results were clear: The newborns produced a reasonably accurate imitation of the adult's expression (see Figure 3-6).

Subsequent research, conducted just minutes after birth and in a variety of cultures, has shown that imitative capabilities appear to be a universal characteristic of newborns. Imitative skills are more than a mere curiosity. Effective social interaction with others relies in part on the ability to react to other people in an appropriate manner and to understand the meaning of others' emotional states. Consequently, the imitative capability of newborns provides an important foundation for social interaction later in life (Reissland, 1988; Phillips et al., 1990; Walker-Andrews & Dickson, 1997).

In addition to their imitative abilities, several other aspects of newborns' behavior act as forerunners for more formal types of social interaction that will develop more fully in the future. As shown in Table 3-6, certain characteristics of neonates mesh with parental behavior to help produce a social relationship between child and parent, as well as social relationships with others (Eckerman & Oehler, 1992).

For example, newborns cycle through various **states of arousal**, different degrees of sleep and wakefulness, that range from deep sleep to great agitation. Although immediately after birth these cycles are disrupted, they quickly become more regularized. Caregivers become involved when they seek to aid the infant in transitions from one state to another. For instance, a father who rhythmically rocks his crying daughter in an effort to calm her is engaged in a joint activity that is a prelude to future social interactions of different sorts. Similarly, newborns tend to pay particular attention to their mothers' voices (Hepper, Scott, & Shahidullah, 1993). In turn, parents and others modify their speech when talking to infants, using a different pitch and tempo than they use with older children and adults (DeCasper & Fifer, 1980; Fernald, 1984).

The ultimate outcome of the social interactive capabilities of the newborn infant, and the responses such behavior brings about from parents, is to pave the way for future social interactions. Just as the neonate shows remarkable skills on a physical and perceptual level, then, its social capabilities are no less sophisticated.

states of arousal *different degrees of sleep and wakefulness through which newborns cycle, ranging from deep sleep to great agitation*

Developmental psychologist Tiffany Field

The Informed Consumer of Development

First Encounters: Interacting with a Newborn

If you are the relative or friend of a woman who has just given birth, you may be anticipating your initial encounter with the new baby with some degree of trepidation. In fact, people tend to interact with newborns in very different ways. Some approach newborns gingerly, acting as if they are confronting a representative of an alien society; others show no hesitation in touching and stroking them and hoisting them vigorously into the air.

Is there an optimal way of interacting with newborns? Although there are no hard-and-fast rules, several principles can guide your first encounters with a newborn:

■ *Prepare yourself.* Newborns may look slightly "unfinished." As we discussed earlier, delivery is not an easy experience for a baby: Its head may be misshapen and its nose and ears squashed down. Hairlike material may cover its shoulder blades and spine, its skin may be wrinkled, and its color may be bluish or yellowish. Most of this will change in a few days.

■ *Hold the baby securely.* Keep in mind that newborns have been in the close confines of the womb for 9 months, and they need to become accustomed to the newfound freedom of movement that the world provides. Consequently, they shouldn't be dangled in the air or otherwise treated roughly. In fact, in some Native American cultures, newborns are routinely wrapped up firmly in blankets—a procedure called *swaddling*.

■ *Speak gently.* Because the sense organs of babies are operative even before birth, they can readily hear voices and other sounds in their surroundings. In fact, because the stimulation from their passage through the birth canal may make them particularly sensitive to stimuli, you should take care not to speak too loudly. But do speak to the newborn: As we'll see in the next few chapters, linguistic stimulation is crucial to the development of language skills.

■ *Keep to yourself any suspicions that something may be wrong with the child.* Unless you are a pediatrician or an expert in infant development, you lack the knowledge to make such a pronouncement. Furthermore, what you are seeing may not be a true sample of the baby's behavior, particularly if the mother has received medication during labor. Remember that every baby is different, and that a baby's appearance and behavior on its first day of life will change substantially in just the next few days.

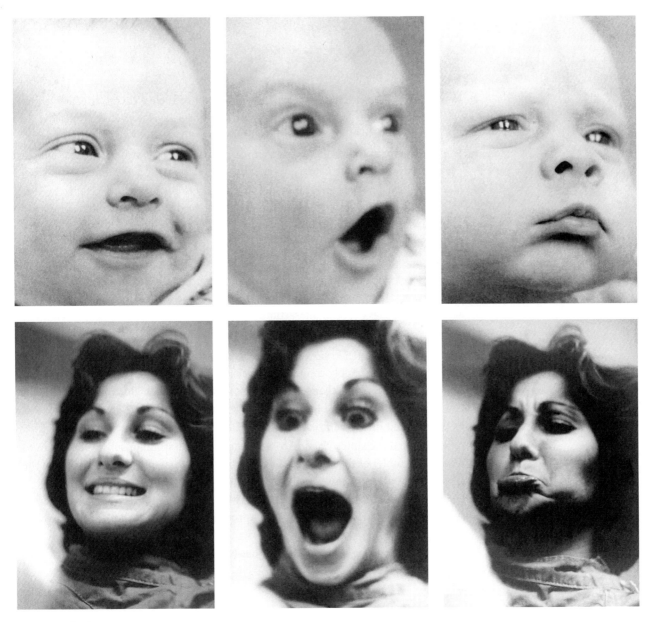

FIGURE 3-6 NONVERBAL IMITATION

This newborn infant is imitating the happy, surprised, and sad expressions of the adult model. (Courtesy of Dr. Tiffany Field.)

TABLE 3-6

FACTORS THAT ENCOURAGE SOCIAL INTERACTION BETWEEN FULL-TERM NEWBORNS AND THEIR PARENTS

Full-Term Newborn	Parent
Has organized states	Helps regulate infant's states
Attends selectively to certain stimuli	Provides these stimuli
Behaves in ways interpretable as specific communicative intent	Searches for communicative intent
Responds systematically to parent's acts	Wants to influence newborn, feel effective
Acts in temporally predictable ways	Adjusts actions to newborn's temporal rhythms
Learns from, adapts to parent's behavior	Acts repetitively and predictably

(*Source*: Eckerman & Oehler, 1992.)

REVIEW AND RETHINK

REVIEW

- Neonates, born with brains that are only a fraction of their ultimate size, are in many ways helpless. Nevertheless, studies of what newborns *can* do, rather than what they *can't* do, have revealed some surprising capabilities.

- Newborns' respiratory and digestive systems begin to function at birth. They come equipped with an array of reflexes to help them eat, swallow, find food, and avoid unpleasant stimuli.

- Newborns' sensory competence includes the ability to distinguish objects in the visual field and to see color differences; the ability to hear and to discern familiar sounds; and sensitivity to touch, odors, and tastes.

- Infants are capable of learning through such simple means as classical conditioning, operant conditioning, and habituation.

- Infants develop the foundations of social competence early. Sophisticated imitative capabilities help them react appropriately to other people's emotional states and to manage the beginnings of social interaction.

RETHINK

- Developmental researchers no longer view the neonate as a helpless, incompetent creature, but rather as a remarkably competent, developing human being. What do you think are some implications of this change in viewpoint for methods of childrearing and child care?

- How do newborns' reflexes help them in their new environment? How might the fetus have developed such organized responses to stimuli?

- According to this chapter, classical conditioning relies on stimulus substitution. Can you think of examples of the use of classical conditioning on adults in everyday life, in such areas as entertainment, advertising, or politics?

- How does the newborn's imitative capability help her or him to develop social competence later in life? In what ways might this process be different or similar for a baby born without sight?

- How should a person who is meeting a newborn for the first time act toward the baby and its parents? Why?

LOOKING BACK

Q & A

■ What is the normal process of labor?

- In the first stage of labor contractions occur about every 8 to 10 minutes, increasing in frequency, duration, and intensity until the mother's cervix expands. In the second stage of labor, which lasts about 90 minutes, the baby begins to move through the cervix and birth canal and ultimately leaves the mother's body. In the third stage of labor, which lasts only a few minutes, the umbilical cord and placenta are expelled from the mother.

- After it emerges, the newborn, or neonate, is usually inspected for irregularities, cleaned, and returned to its mother and father.

■ What complications can occur at birth?

- Preterm, or premature, infants, born less than 38 weeks following conception generally have low birthweight, which can cause chilling, vulnerability to infection, respiratory distress syndrome, and hypersensitivity to environmental stimuli. They may even show adverse effects later in life, including slowed development, learning disabilities, behavior disorders, below-average IQ scores, and problems with physical coordination.

- Very-low-birthweight infants are in special danger because of the immaturity of their organ systems. However, medical advances have pushed the age of viability of the infant back to about 24 weeks following conception.
- Postmature babies, who spend extra time in their mothers' wombs, are also at risk. However, physicians can artificially induce labor or perform a Cesarean delivery to address this situation. Cesarean deliveries are performed when the fetus is in distress, in the wrong position, or unable to progress through the birth canal.
- The infant mortality rate in the United States is higher than the rate in many other countries, and higher for low-income families than higher-income families.
- Postpartum depression, an enduring, deep feeling of sadness, affects about 10 percent of new mothers. In severe cases, its effects can be harmful to the mother and the child, and aggressive treatment may be employed.

■ **What capabilities does the newborn have?**

- Human newborns quickly master breathing through the lungs, and they are equipped with reflexes to help them eat, swallow, find food, and avoid unpleasant stimuli. Their sensory capabilities are also sophisticated.
- From birth, infants learn through such simple means as habituation, classical conditioning and operant conditioning. Newborns are able to imitate the behavior of others, a capability that helps them form social relationships and facilitates the development of social competence.

EPILOGUE: LABOR OF LOVE

Our discussion in this chapter focused on the processes of labor and birth. We looked at the three stages of labor, the first few minutes following birth, and parents' birthing options. We also looked at the complications that can arise during the birthing process and treatments and interventions to deal with them.

Return for a moment to the case of the very premature Briana McNeill, discussed in the Prologue of this chapter and answer the following questions.

1. Briana McNeill was born at 22 weeks. Why was the fact that she was born alive so surprising? Discuss her birth in terms of "the age of viability."
2. Can you describe what Briana probably looked like when she was born and what activities most likely occurred immediately after her birth?
3. What dangers was Briana subject to immediately after birth? What dangers would be likely to continue into her childhood?
4. What ethical considerations affect the decision of whether the high costs of medical interventions for highly premature babies are justifiable? Who should pay those costs?
5. What aspects of the way the hospital treated Briana's delivery would you recommend that the hospital change? Why?

KEY TERMS AND CONCEPTS

neonates (p. 84)
episiotomy (p. 86)
Apgar scale (p. 87)
anoxia (p. 88)
bonding (p. 88)
preterm infants (p. 96)
low-birthweight infants (p. 96)
small-for-gestational-age infants (p. 96)
very-low-birthweight infants (p. 97)
age of viability (p. 97)

postmature infants (p. 98)
Cesarean delivery (p. 99)
fetal monitors (p. 100)
infant mortality (p. 101)
stillbirth (p. 102)
reflexes (p. 105)
classical conditioning (p. 107)
operant conditioning (p. 107)
habituation (p. 108)
states of arousal (p. 110)

INFANCY

Physical Development

PROLOGUE: FIRST STEPS

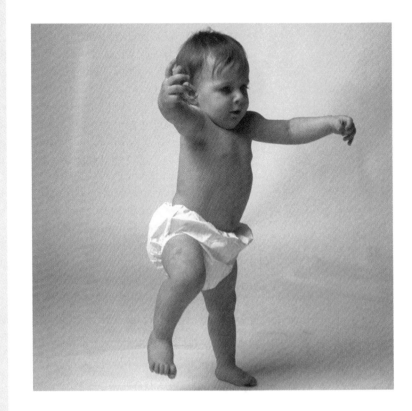

We had initimations that his first steps would not be too far in the future. Josh had previously dragged himself up, and, clutching the side of chairs and tables, managed to progress slowly around our living room. And for the last few weeks, he'd even been able to stand, unmoving, for several moments.

But walking? It seemed too early: Josh was only 10 months old, and the books we consulted suggested that most children would not take their first steps on their own until they were a year old. And our older son, Jon, hadn't walked until he was 14 months of age.

Consequently, when Josh suddenly lunged forward toward the center of the room, taking one awkward step after another away from the safety of the furniture, we were astounded. Despite the appearance that he was about to keel over at any second, he moved one, then two, then three steps forward, until our awe at his accomplishment overtook our ability to count each step.

Josh tottered all the way across the room, finally reaching the other side. Not quite knowing how to stop, he toppled over, landing in a happy heap. It was moment of pure glory.

115

LOOKING AHEAD

Josh's first steps at the age of 10 months capped a succession of milestones that brought him closer to full mobility and caused his parents sheer joy. His accomplishment, however remarkable, was only one of many that characterize the dramatic physical attainments of infancy.

In this chapter we consider physical development during infancy, which starts at birth and continues until the second birthday. We begin by discussing the pace of growth during infancy, noting obvious changes in height and weight, but also less apparent changes in the nervous system. We also consider how infants quickly develop stable patterns in which their basic activities, such as sleeping, eating, and attending to the world, take on some degree of order.

Our discussion then turns to motor development, the development of skills that eventually will allow an infant to roll over, take the first step, and pick up a pin from the floor—skills that ultimately form the basis of later, even more complex behaviors. We start with basic, genetically determined reflexes and consider how even these may be modified through experience. We also discuss the nature and timing of the development of particular physical skills, look at whether their emergence can be speeded up, and consider the importance of early nutrition to their development.

Finally, we explore the development of the senses during infancy. We investigate how several individual sensory systems operate, and we look at how infants sort out data from the sense organs and transform that data into meaningful information.

In sum, after reading this chapter, you will be able to answer these questions:

Q

- How do the human body and nervous system develop?
- How does the environment affect the pattern of development?
- What learning tasks must infants undertake in this period?
- What is the role of nutrition in physical development?
- What sensory capabilities do infants possess?

GROWTH AND STABILITY

The average newborn weighs just over 7 pounds, which is probably less than the weight of the average Thanksgiving turkey. Its length is a mere 20 inches, shorter than a loaf of French bread. It is helpless; if left to fend for itself, it could not survive.

Yet after just a few years, the story is very different. Babies are much larger, they are mobile, and they become increasingly independent. How does this growth happen? We can answer this question first by describing the changes in weight and height that occur over the first 2 years of life, and then by examining some of the principles that underlie and direct that growth.

Physical Growth: The Rapid Advances of Infancy

Over the first 2 years of a human's life, growth occurs at a rapid pace (see Figure 4-1). By the age of 5 months, the average infant's birthweight has doubled to around 15 pounds. By the first birthday, the infant's weight has tripled to about 22 pounds. Although the pace of weight gain slows during the second year, it is still continuous. By the end of its second year, the average child weighs four times its birthweight.

The weight gains of infancy are matched by increased length. By the end of the first year, the typical baby stands a proud 30 inches tall, an average increase from birth of almost a foot. By its second birthday, it usually attains a height of 3 feet.

Not all parts of an infant's body grow at the same rate. For instance, as we saw first in Chapter 2, at birth the head accounts for one-quarter of the newborn's entire body size.

FIGURE 4-1

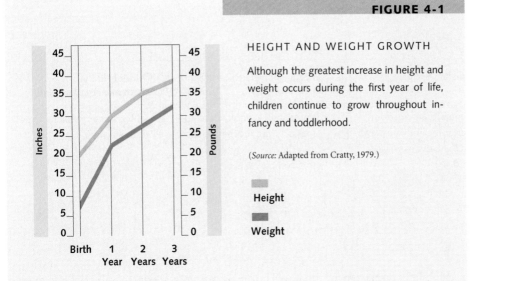

HEIGHT AND WEIGHT GROWTH

Although the greatest increase in height and weight occurs during the first year of life, children continue to grow throughout infancy and toddlerhood.

(*Source:* Adapted from Cratty, 1979.)

During the first 2 years of life, the rest of the body begins to catch up. By the age of 2 the baby's head is only one-fifth of body length, and by adulthood it is only one-eighth (see Figure 4-2). Furthermore, a growing body of evidence suggests that growth is not regular and continuous, as originally thought. Instead, recent research suggests that it occurs in short spurts, separated by periods of days in which there is little or no growth (Lampl et al., 1995).

The disproportionately large size of infants' heads at birth is an example of one of the major principles that govern growth: the cephalocaudal principle, which relates to the direction of growth. According to the **cephalocaudal principle** growth follows a pattern that begins with the head and upper body parts and then proceeds to the rest of the body. Reflecting Greek and Latin roots meaning "head-to-tail," the cephalocaudal growth principle means that we develop

cephalocaudal principle the principle that growth follows a pattern that begins with the head and upper body parts and then proceeds down to the rest of the body

FIGURE 4-2

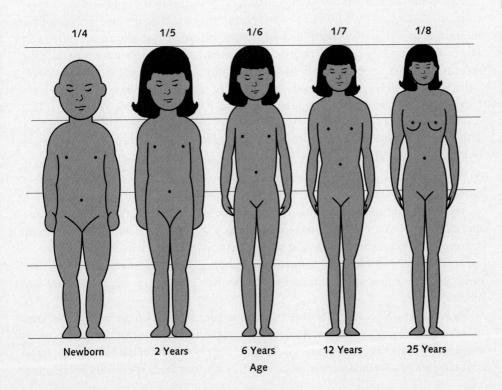

DECREASING PROPORTIONS

At birth, the head represents one-quarter of the neonate's head. By adulthood, the head is only one-eighth the size of the body.

TABLE 4-1

THE MAJOR PRINCIPLES GOVERNING GROWTH

Cephalocaudal principle	Proximodistal principle	Principle of hierarchical integration	Principle of the independence of systems
Growth follows a pattern that begins with the head and upper body parts and then proceeds to the rest of the body. Based on Greek and Latin roots meaning "head-to-tail."	Development proceeds from the center of the body outward. Based on the Latin words for "near" and "far."	Simple skills typically develop separately and independently. Later they are integrated into more complex skills.	Different body systems grow at different rates.

visual abilities (located in the head) well before we master the ability to walk (closer to the end of the body). The cephalocaudal principle operates both prenatally and after birth.

Several other principles (summarized in Table 4-1) help explain the patterns by which growth occurs. According to the **proximodistal principle** development proceeds from the center of the body outward. Based on the Latin words for "near" and "far," the proximodistal principle means that the trunk of the body grows before the extremities of the arms and legs. Similarly, it is only after growth has occurred in the arms and legs that the fingers and toes can grow. Furthermore, the development of the ability to use various parts of the body also follows the proximodistal principle. For instance, the effective use of the arms precedes the ability to use the hands.

Another major principle of growth concerns the way complex skills build on simpler ones. The **principle of hierarchical integration** states that simple skills typically develop separately and independently. Later, however, these simple skills are integrated into more complex ones. Thus, the relatively complex skill of grasping something in the hand cannot be mastered until the developing infant learns how to control—and integrate—the movements of the individual fingers.

Finally, the last major principle of growth is the **principle of the independence of systems**, which suggests that different body systems grow at different rates. This principle means that growth in one system does not necessarily imply that growth is occurring in others. For instance, Figure 4-3 illustrates the patterns of growth for three very different systems: body size, which we've already discussed; the nervous system; and sexual characteristics. As you can see, both the rate and timing of these different aspects of growth are independent (Bornstein & Lamb, 1992a; Bremner, Slater, & Butterworth, 1997).

The Nervous System and Brain: The Foundations of Development

Whatever feelings, movements, and thoughts an infant may experience are brought about by the same complex network: the infant's nervous system. The *nervous system* comprises the brain and the nerves that extend throughout the body.

Although estimates vary, infants are born with between 100 and 200 billion **neurons**, the basic nerve cells of the nervous system. To reach this number, neurons multiply at an amazing rate prior to birth. In fact, at some points in prenatal development, cell division creates some 250,000 additional neurons every minute. This pace is necessary, though: Because virtually no new neurons are created after birth, the number created in the womb is a lifetime's worth.

We can liken the changes that the brain undergoes in its development after birth to the actions of a farmer who, in order to strengthen the vitality of a fruit tree, prunes away unnecessary branches. In the same way, the ultimate capabilities of the brain are brought about in part by a "pruning down" of unnecessary neurons. Neurons that do not become

proximodistal principle   *the principle that development proceeds from the center of the body outward*

principle of hierarchical integration   *the principle that simple skills typically develop separately and independently but are later integrated into more complex skills*

principle of the independence of systems   *the principle that different body systems grow at different rates*

neuron   *the basic nerve cell of the nervous system*

FIGURE 4-3

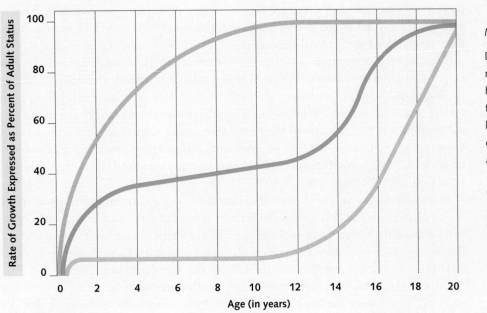

MATURATION RATES

Different body systems mature at different rates. For instance, the nervous system is highly developed during infancy, whereas the development of body size is considerably less developed. The development of sexual characteristics lags even more, maturing at adolescence.

(*Source:* Bornstein & Lamb, 1992a)

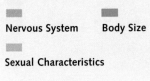

Nervous System   **Body Size**

Sexual Characteristics

interconnected with other neurons as the infant's experience of the world increases become unnecessary. They eventually die out, increasing the efficiency of the nervous system. Unlike most other aspects of growth, then, the development of the nervous system proceeds most effectively through the loss of cells (Black & Greenough, 1986; Lipsitt, 1986; Kolb, 1989, 1995).

Although the creation of neurons stops just after birth, neurons continue to increase in size. Neurons become coated with **myelin**, a fatty substance that helps insulate them and speeds the transmission of nerve impulses. The brain triples its weight in the first 2 years of life, and it reaches more than three-quarters of its adult weight and size by the age of 2. Furthermore, the network of neurons becomes increasingly complex, as illustrated in Figure 4-4 (Conel, 1963). The intricacy of neural connections continues to increase throughout life.

As they grow, neurons become arranged by function. Some move into the **cerebral cortex**, the upper layer of the brain, and others move to *subcortical levels*, which are below the cerebral

myelin   *a fatty substance that helps insulate neurons and speeds the transmission of nerve impulses*

cerebral cortex   *the upper layer of the brain*

FIGURE 4-4

NEURON NETWORKS

Over the first 2 years of life, networks of neurons become increasingly complex and interconnected.

(*Source:* Conel, 1930/1963.)

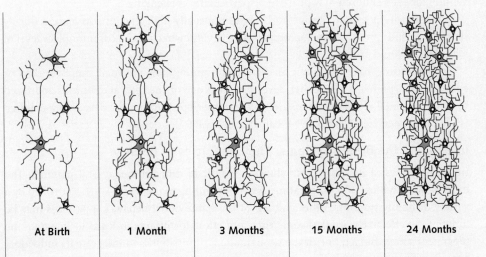

At Birth   1 Month   3 Months   15 Months   24 Months

plasticity   *the degree to which a developing structure or behavior is susceptible to experience*

sensitive period   *a specific, but limited, time, usually early in an organism's life, during which the organism is particularly susceptible to environmental influences relating to some particular facet of development*

cortex. The subcortical levels, which regulate such fundamental activities as breathing and heart rate, are the most fully developed at birth. As time passes, however, the cells in the cerebral cortex, which are responsible for higher-order processes such as thinking and reasoning, become more developed and interconnected.

Brain development, much of which unfolds automatically because of genetically predetermined patterns, is also susceptible to environmental influences. **Plasticity**, the degree to which a developing structure or behavior is susceptible to experience, is relatively great for the brain. For instance, an infant's sensory experience affects both the size of individual neurons and the structure of their interconnections. Consequently, compared with those brought up in more enriched environments, infants raised in severely restricted settings are likely to show differences in brain structure and weight (Rosenzweig & Bennett, 1976; Gottlieb, 1991; Kolb, 1995).

Work with nonhumans has been particularly illuminating in revealing the nature of the brain's plasticity. For instance, some studies have compared rats raised in an unusually visually stimulating environment to those raised in more typical, and less interesting, cages. Results of such research show that areas of the brain associated with vision are both thicker and heavier for the rats reared in enriched settings (Black & Greenough, 1986).

On the other side of the coin, environments that are unusually barren or in some way restricted may impede the brain's development. Again, work with nonhumans provides some intriguing data. In one study kittens were fitted with goggles that restricted their vision so that they could view only vertical lines. When the cats grew up and had their goggles removed, they were unable to see horizontal lines, although they saw vertical lines perfectly well. Analogously, kittens whose goggles restricted their vision of vertical lines early in life were effectively blind to vertical lines during their adulthood—although their vision of horizontal lines was accurate (Hirsch & Spinelli, 1970).

On the other hand, when goggles are placed on older cats who have lived relatively normal kittenhoods, such results are not seen after the goggles are removed. The conclusion is that there is a sensitive period for the development of vision. As we noted in Chapter 1, a **sensitive period** is a specific, but limited, time, usually early in an organism's life, during which the organism is particularly susceptible to environmental influences relating to some particular facet of development. A sensitive period may be associated with a behavior—such as the development of full vision—or with the development of a structure of the body, such as the configuration of the brain.

The existence of sensitive periods raises several important issues. For one thing, it suggests that unless an infant receives a certain level of early environmental stimulation during a sensitive period, it may suffer damage that can never be fully remedied or fail to develop capabilities that can never be acquired later. If this is true, providing successful later intervention for such children may prove to be particularly challenging.

The opposite question also arises: Does an unusually high level of stimulation during sensitive periods produce developmental gains beyond what a more commonplace level of stimulation would provide?

Such questions have no simple answers. Determining how unusually impoverished or enriched environments affect later development is one of the central questions addressed by developmental researchers seeking to maximize opportunities for developing children (Fisher & Lerner, 1994; Lamb, 1994; Lafuente et al., 1997).

Integrating the Bodily Systems: The Life Cycles of Infancy

In the first days of life, the infant shows a jumble of different behavioral patterns. The most basic activities—sleeping, eating, crying, attending to the world—are controlled by a variety of bodily systems. Although each of these individual behavioral patterns may be functioning effectively, it takes some time and effort for infants to learn to integrate the separate systems. In fact, one of the neonate's major missions is to integrate its individual behaviors (Thoman, 1990; Thoman & Whitney, 1990).

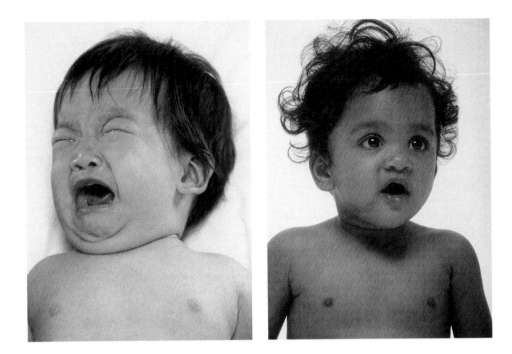

Infants cycle through various states, including crying and alertness. These states are integrated through bodily rhythms.

Rhythms and States.   One of the most important ways that behavior becomes integrated is through the development of various body **rhythms**, repetitive, cyclical patterns of behavior. Some rhythms are immediately obvious, such as the change from wakefulness to sleep. Others are more subtle, but still easily noticeable, such as breathing and sucking patterns. Still other rhythms may require careful observation to be noticed. For instance, newborns may go through periods in which they jerk their legs in a regular pattern every minute or so. Although some of these rhythms are apparent just after birth, others emerge slowly over the first year as the nervous system becomes more integrated (Thelen, 1979; Robertson, 1982; Groome et al., 1997).

One of the major body rhythms is that of an infant's **state**, the degree of awareness it displays to both internal and external stimulation. As can be seen in Table 4-2, such states include various levels of wakeful behaviors, such as alertness, fussing, and crying, and different levels of sleep as well. Each change in state brings about an alteration in the amount of stimulation required to get the infant's attention (Brazelton, 1973; Thoman & Whitney, 1990; Karmel, Gardner, & Magnano, 1991; Balaban, Snidman, & Kagan, 1997).

Some of the different states that infants experience produce changes in electrical activity in the brain. These changes are reflected in different patterns of electrical *brain waves*, which can be measured by a device called an *electroencephalogram*, or *EEG*. Starting at 3 months before birth, these brain-wave patterns change significantly until the infant reaches the age of 3 months, when a more mature pattern emerges and the brain waves stabilize (Parmelee & Sigman, 1983).

Sleep: Perchance to Dream?   At the beginning of infancy, the major state that occupies a baby's time is sleep—much to the relief of exhausted parents, who often regard sleep as a welcome respite from caregiving responsibilities. On average, newborn infants sleep some 16 to 17 hours a day. However, there are wide variations. Some sleep more than 20 hours, whereas others sleep as little as 10 hours a day (Parmalee, Wenner, & Schulz, 1964).

Even though infants sleep a lot, you probably shouldn't ever wish to "sleep like a baby," despite popular wisdom. For one thing, the sleep of infants comes in fits and starts. Rather than covering one long stretch, sleep initially comes in spurts of around 2 hours, followed by periods of wakefulness. Because of this, infants are "out of sync" with the rest of the world, for whom sleep comes at night and wakefulness during the day.

CW

rhythms   *repetitive, cyclical patterns of behavior*

state   *the degree of awareness an infant displays to both internal and external stimulation*

TABLE 4-2

PRIMARY BEHAVIORAL STATES

States	Characteristics	Percentage of Time When Alone in State
Awake States		
Alert	Attentive or scanning, the infant's eyes are open, bright, and shining.	6.7
Nonalert waking	Eyes are usually open, but dull and unfocused. Varied, but typically high motor activity.	2.8
Fuss	Fussing is continuous or intermittent, at low levels.	1.8
Cry	Intense vocalizations occurring singly or in succession.	1.7
Transition States Between Sleep and Waking		
Drowse	Infant's eyes are heavy-lidded, but opening and closing slowly. Low level of motor activity.	4.4
Daze	Open, but glassy and immobile eyes. State occurs between episodes of Alert and Drowse. Low level of activity.	1.0
Sleep–wake transition	Behaviors of both wakefulness and sleep are evident. Generalized motor activity; eyes may be closed, or they open and close rapidly. State occurs when baby is awakening.	1.3
Sleep States		
Active sleep	Eyes close; uneven respiration; intermittent rapid eye movements. Other behaviors: smiles, frowns, grimaces, mouthing, sucking, sighs, and sigh-sobs.	50.3
Quiet sleep	Eyes are closed and respiration is slow and regular. Motor activity limited to occasional startles, sigh-sobs, or rhythmic mouthing.	28.1
Transitional Sleep State		
Active-quiet transition sleep	During this state, which occurs between periods of Active Sleep and Quiet Sleep, the eyes are closed and there is little motor activity. Infant shows mixed behavioral signs of Active Sleep and Quiet Sleep.	1.9

(*Source:* Adapted from Thoman & Whitney, 1990.)

rapid eye movement (REM) sleep
the period of sleep that is found in older children and adults and is associated with dreaming

Luckily for their parents, infants eventually settle into a more adultlike pattern. After a week, babies sleep a bit more at night and are awake for slightly longer periods during the day. Typically, by the age of 16 weeks infants begin to sleep as much as 6 continuous hours at night, and daytime sleep falls into regular naplike patterns. Most infants sleep through the night by the end of the first year, and the total amount of sleep they need each day is down to about 15 hours (Thoman & Whitney, 1989).

Hidden beneath the supposedly tranquil sleep of infants is another cyclic pattern. During periods of sleep, infants' heart rates increase and become irregular, their blood pressure rises, and they begin to breathe more rapidly (Schechtman & Harper, 1991; Ferrari et al., 1994). Sometimes, although not always, their closed eyes begin to move in a back-and-forth pattern, as if they were viewing an action-packed scene. This period of active sleep is similar, although not identical, to the **rapid eye movement**, or **REM**, **sleep**, that is found in older children and adults and is associated with dreaming.

At first, this active, REM-like sleep takes up around one-half of an infant's sleep, compared with just 20 percent of an adult's sleep (see Figure 4-5). However, the quantity of active sleep quickly declines, and by the age of 6 months, amounts to just one-third of total sleep time (Coons & Guilleminault, 1982; Sandyk, 1992).

Infants sleep in spurts, often making them out of sync with the rest of the world.

The appearance of active sleep periods that are similar to REM sleep in adults raises the intriguing question of whether infants dream during those periods. No one knows the answer, although it seems unlikely. First, young infants do not have much to dream about, given their relatively limited experiences. Furthermore, the brain waves of sleeping infants appear to be qualitatively different from those of adults who are dreaming. It is not until the baby reaches 3 or 4 months of age that the wave patterns become similar to those of dreaming adults, suggesting that young infants are not dreaming during active sleep—or at least are not doing so in the same way as adults do (McCall, 1979; Parmelee & Sigman, 1983).

Then what is the function of REM sleep in infants? Although we don't know for certain, some researchers think it provides a means for the brain to stimulate itself—a process called *autostimulation* (Roffwarg, Muzio, & Dement, 1966). Stimulation of the

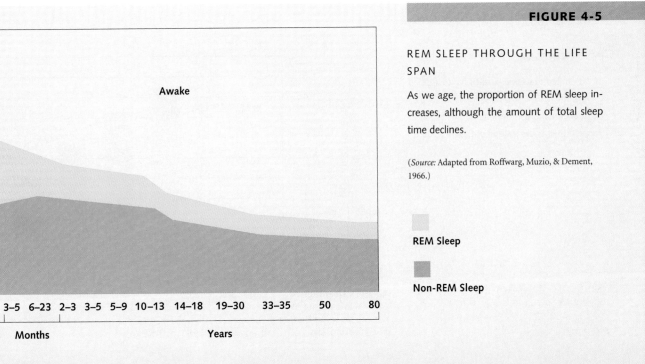

FIGURE 4-5

REM SLEEP THROUGH THE LIFE SPAN

As we age, the proportion of REM sleep increases, although the amount of total sleep time declines.

(*Source:* Adapted from Roffwarg, Muzio, & Dement, 1966.)

REM Sleep

Non-REM Sleep

sudden infant death syndrome (SIDS)
the unexplained death of a seemingly healthy baby

nervous system would be particularly important in infants, who spend so much time sleeping and relatively little in alert states.

Although the patterns that infants show in their wakefulness–sleep cycles seem largely preprogrammed by genetic factors, environmental influences also play a part. For instance, both long- and short-term stressors in infants' environments can affect their sleep patterns. When environmental circumstances keep babies awake, sleep, when at last it comes, is apt to be less active (and quieter) than usual (Halpern, MacLean, & Baumeister, 1995).

Cultural practices also affect the sleep patterns of infants. For example, among the Kipsigis of Africa, infants sleep with their mothers at night and are allowed to nurse whenever they wake. In daytime, they accompany their mothers during daily chores. As a result of these practices, Kipsigis infants do not sleep through the night until much later than babies in Western societies, and, for the first 8 months of life, they seldom sleep longer than 3 hours at a stretch. In comparison, 8-month-old infants in the United States may sleep as long as 8 hours at a time (Boismier, 1977; Super & Harkness, 1982; Cole, 1992; Anders & Taylor, 1994).

SIDS: The Unanticipated Killer.   For a tiny percentage of infants, the rhythm of sleep is interrupted by a deadly affliction: sudden infant death syndrome, or SIDS. **Sudden infant death syndrome (SIDS)** is a disorder in which seemingly healthy infants die in their sleep. Put to bed for a nap or for the night, an infant simply never wakes up.

No known cause has been found to explain SIDS, which strikes about 1 in 1,000 infants in the United States each year. Although it seems to occur when the normal patterns of breathing during sleep are interrupted, scientists have been unable to discover why that might happen. It is clear that infants don't smother or choke; they die a peaceful death, simply ceasing to breathe.

No means for preventing the syndrome have been found. However, as more parents become aware of guidelines from the American Academy of Pediatrics, which suggest that babies sleep on their backs rather than on their sides or stomachs, the numbers of deaths from SIDS has decreased significantly (see Figure 4-6). Still, SIDS is the leading cause of death in children under the age of 1 year (Burns & Lipsitt, 1991; Ponsonby, Dwyer, & Couper, 1997).

Certain factors are associated with an increased risk of SIDS. For instance, boys and African Americans are at greater risk. In addition, low birthweight and low Apgar scores found at birth are associated with SIDS, as is having a mother who smokes during pregnancy (Saugstad, 1997). Some evidence also suggests that a brain defect that affects breathing may

---

FIGURE 4-6

DECLINING RATES OF SIDS

In the United States SIDS rates have dropped by a dramatic 38 percent since 1992 as parents become more informed and put babies to sleep on their backs instead of their stomachs.

(*Source:* National Institute for Child Health & Human Development.)

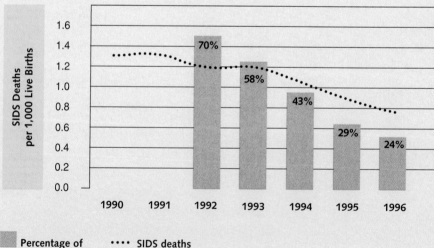

produce SIDS. In a small number of cases, child abuse may be the actual cause, although some researchers contend that abuse may actually account for a relatively high number of deaths. Still, there is no clear-cut factor that explains why some infants die from the syndrome. SIDS is found in children of every race and socioeconomic group and in children who have had no apparent health problems (Burns & Lipsitt, 1991; DiFranza & Lew, 1995; Kinney et al., 1997; Rosen, 1997).

Because parents are unprepared for the death of an infant from SIDS, the event is particularly devastating. Parents often feel guilt, fearing that they were neglectful or somehow contributed to their child's death. Such guilt is unwarranted, because nothing has been identified so far that can prevent SIDS.

REVIEW AND RETHINK

REVIEW

- The major principles of growth are the cephalocaudal principle (growth proceeds from top to bottom), the proximodistal principle (growth proceeds outward), the principle of hierarchical integration (complex skills build on simple skills), and the principle of the independence of systems (different body systems grow at different rates).

- The development of the nervous system entails first the development of billions of neurons, which mostly occurs before birth, and then the formation through the infant's experience of useful interconnections among the neurons.

- Brain development depends on both genetic and environmental factors. Plasticity, the susceptibility of a developing organism to environmental influences, is relatively high for the brain.

- Researchers have identified sensitive periods during the development of body systems and behaviors—limited periods when the organism is particularly susceptible to environmental influences. If environmental influences are disturbed during a sensitive period, development may also be disturbed.

- Babies integrate their individual behaviors by developing rhythms—repetitive, cyclical patterns of behavior. A major rhythm relates to the infant's state—the awareness it displays to internal and external stimulation. Asleep or awake, babies experience various states. Their normal rhythms can be disturbed, as evidenced by sudden infant death syndrome, or SIDS.

RETHINK

- The cephalocaudal principle seems to imply that babies should learn how to talk before they learn how to walk, and yet most babies can walk long before they can form understandable utterances. How does another major growth principle explain this apparent contradiction?

- Research indicates that there is a sensitive period during childhood for normal language acquisition. Persons deprived of normal language stimulation as babies and children may never use language with the same skill as others who were not so deprived. For babies who are born deaf, what are the implications of this research finding, particularly with regard to signed languages?

- This chapter describes sensitive periods during which infants may be either helped or harmed in their development by their exposure to environmental influences. What are the implications of such sensitive periods for public policy relating to infant care?

- What are some cultural influences on infants' daily patterns of behavior that operate in the culture of which you are a part? How do they differ from the influences of other cultures (either within or outside the United States) of which you are aware?

MOTOR DEVELOPMENT

reflexes *unlearned, organized involuntary responses that occur automatically in the presence of certain stimuli*

Suppose you were hired by a genetic engineering firm to redesign newborns and were charged with replacing the current version with a new, more mobile one. The first change you'd probably consider in carrying out this (luckily fictitious) job would be in the conformation and composition of the baby's body.

The shape and proportions of newborn babies are simply not conducive to easy mobility. Their heads are so large and heavy that young infants lack the strength to raise them. Because their limbs are short in relation to the rest of the body, their movements are further impeded. Furthermore, their bodies are mainly fat, with a limited amount of muscle; the result is that they lack strength (Illingworth, 1973).

Fortunately, it doesn't take too long before infants begin to develop a remarkable amount of mobility. In fact, even at birth they have an extensive repertoire of behavioral possibilities brought about by innate reflexes, and their range of motor skills grows rapidly during the first 2 years of life.

Reflexes: Our Inborn Physical Skills

When her father pressed 3-day-old Christina's palm with his finger, she responded by tightly winding her small fist around his finger and grasping it. When he moved his finger upward, she held on so tightly that it seemed he might be able to lift her completely off her crib floor.

The Basic Reflexes.   In fact, her father was right: Christina probably could have been lifted in this way. The reason for her resolute grip was activation of one of the dozens of reflexes with which infants are born. **Reflexes** are unlearned, organized involuntary responses that occur automatically in the presence of certain stimuli. As we first noted in Chapter 2, when we discussed reflexes relating to the intake of food, newborns enter the world with an expansive repertoire of behavioral patterns that, when activated, help them adapt to their new surroundings and serve to protect them.

As we can see from the list of reflexes in Table 4-3, many reflexes clearly represent behavior that has survival value, helping to ensure the well-being of the infant. For instance, the *swimming reflex* makes a baby who is lying face down in a body of water paddle and kick in a sort of swimming motion. The obvious consequence of such behavior is to help the baby move from danger and survive until a caregiver can come to its rescue. Similarly, the *eye-blink reflex* seems designed to protect the eye from too much direct light, which might damage the retina.

Given the protective value of many reflexes, it might seem beneficial for them to remain with us for our entire lives. In fact, some do: The eye-blink reflex remains functional throughout the full life span. On the other hand, quite a few reflexes, such as the swimming reflex, disappear after a few months. Why should this be the case?

Most researchers attribute the gradual disappearance of reflexes to the increase in voluntary control over behavior that occurs as infants become more able to control their

(a)

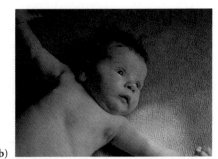

(b)

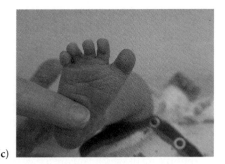

(c)

Infants showing (a) the rooting reflex, (b) the startle reflex, and (c) the Babinski reflex.

TABLE 4-3

SOME BASIC REFLEXES IN INFANTS

Reflex	Approximate age of disappearance	Description	Possible function
Rooting reflex	3 weeks	Neonate's tendency to turn its head toward things that touch its cheek.	Food intake
Stepping reflex	2 months	Movement of legs when held upright with feet touching the floor.	Prepares infants for independent locomotion
Swimming reflex	4–6 months	Infant's tendency to paddle and kick in a sort of swimming motion when lying face down in a body of water.	Avoidance of danger
Moro reflex	6 months	Activated when support for the neck and head is suddenly removed. The arms of the infant are thrust outward and then appear to grasp onto something.	Similar to primates' protection from falling
Babinski reflex	8–12 months	An infant fans out its toes in response to a stroke on the outside of its foot.	Unknown
Startle reflex	Remains in different form	An infant, in response to a sudden noise, flings out its arms, arches its back, and spreads its fingers.	Protection
Eye-blink reflex	Remains	Rapid shutting and opening of eye on exposure to direct light.	Protection of eye from direct light
Sucking reflex	Remains	Infant's tendency to suck at things that touch its lips.	Food intake
Gag reflex	Remains	An infant's reflex to clear its throat.	Prevents choking

muscles. In addition, it may be that reflexes form the foundation for future, more complex behaviors. As these more intricate behaviors become well learned, they subsume the earlier reflexes (Minkowski, 1967; Touwen, 1984; Myklebost & Gottlieb, 1993).

It may even be that the use of reflexes stimulates parts of the brain responsible for more complex behaviors. For example, some researchers argue that exercise of the stepping reflex helps the brain's cortex later develop the ability to walk. As evidence, developmental psychologist Philip R. Zelazo and his colleagues conducted a study in which they provided 2-week-old infants practice in walking for four sessions of 3 minutes each over a 6-week period. The results showed that the children who had the walking practice actually began to walk unaided several months earlier than those who had had no such practice. Zelazo suggests that the training produced stimulation of the stepping reflex, which in turn led to stimulation of the brain's cortex, readying the infant earlier for independent locomotion (Zelazo, Zelazo, & Kolb, 1972; Zelazo, 1983; Zelazo et al., 1993).

Do these findings suggest that parents should make out-of-the-ordinary efforts to stimulate their infant's reflexes? Probably not. Although the evidence shows that intensive practice may produce an earlier appearance of certain motor activities, there is no evidence that the activities are performed qualitatively any better in practiced infants than in unpracticed infants. Furthermore, even when early gains are found, they do not seem to produce ultimately an adult who is more proficient in motor skills.

In fact, structured exercise may do more harm than good: According to the American Academy of Pediatricians, structured exercise for infants may lead to muscle strain, fractured bones, and dislocated limbs, consequences that far outweigh the unproven benefits that may come from the practice (American Academy of Pediatricians, 1988).

The Universality of Reflexes. Although reflexes are, by definition, genetically determined and universal throughout all infants, there are actually some cultural variations in the ways they are displayed. For instance, consider the *Moro reflex*, which is activated when support for the neck and head is suddenly removed. The Moro reflex consists of the infant's arms thrusting outward and then appearing to seek to grasp onto something. Most scientists feel that the Moro reflex represents a leftover response that we humans have inherited from our nonhuman ancestors. The Moro reflex is an extremely useful behavior for monkey babies, who travel about by clinging to their mothers' backs. If they lose their grip, they fall down unless they are able to grasp quickly onto their mother's fur—in a Moro-like reflex (Prechtl, 1982).

Although the Moro reflex is found in all humans, it appears with significantly different vigor in different children. Some differences reflect cultural and ethnic variations. For instance, Caucasian infants show a pronounced response to situations that produce the Moro reflex. Not only do they fling out their arms, but they also cry and respond in a generally agitated manner. In contrast, Navajo babies react to the same situation much more calmly. Their arms do not flail out as much, and they cry only rarely (Freedman, 1979).

In some cases, reflexes can serve as helpful diagnostic tools for pediatricians. Because reflexes emerge and disappear on a regular timetable, their absence—or presence—at a given point of infancy can provide a clue that something may be amiss in an infant's development. (Even for adults, physicians include reflexes in their diagnostic bags of tricks, as anyone knows who has had his or her knee tapped with a rubber mallet to see if the lower leg jerks forward.)

Although some reflexes may be remnants from our prehuman past and seemingly have little usefulness in terms of survival today, they still may serve a very contemporary function. According to some developmental researchers, some reflexes may promote caregiving and nurturance on the part of adults in the vicinity. For instance, Christina's father, who found his daughter gripping his finger tightly when he pressed her palm, probably cares little that she is simply responding with an innate reflex. Instead, he will more likely view his daughter's action as responsiveness to him, a signal perhaps of increasing interest and affection on her part. As we will see in Chapter 6, when we discuss the social and personality development of infants, such apparent responsiveness can help cement the growing social relationship between an infant and its caregivers (Bell & Ainsworth, 1972; Belsky, Rovine, & Taylor, 1984).

Motor Development in Infancy: Landmarks of Physical Achievement

Probably no physical changes are more obvious—and more eagerly anticipated—than the increasing array of motor skills that babies acquire during infancy. Most parents can remember their child's first steps with a sense of pride and awe at how quickly she or he changed from a helpless infant, unable even to roll over, into a person who could navigate quite effectively in the world (Thelen, 1995).

Gross Motor Skills. Even though the motor skills of newborn infants are not terribly sophisticated, at least compared with attainments that will soon appear, infants still are able to accomplish some kinds of movement. For instance, when placed on their stomachs they wiggle their arms and legs and may try to lift their heavy heads. As their strength increases, they are able to push hard enough against the surface on which they are resting to propel their bodies in different directions. They often end up moving backwards rather than forwards, but by the age of 6 months they become

This 5-month-old girl demonstrates her gross motor skills.

FIGURE 4-7

MILESTONES OF MOTOR
DEVELOPMENT

(*Source:* Adapted from Shirley, 1993.)

rather accomplished at moving themselves in particular directions. These initial efforts are the forerunners of crawling, in which they coordinate the motions of their arms and legs and propel themselves forward. Crawling appears typically between 8 and 10 months (Adolph, 1997). (Figure 4-7 provides a summary of some of the milestones of normal motor development.)

Walking comes later. At around the age of 9 months, most infants are able to walk by supporting themselves on furniture, and by the end of the first year of life, many can walk well on their own.

At the same time infants are learning to move around, they are perfecting the ability to remain in a stationary sitting position. At first, babies cannot remain seated upright without support. But they quickly master this ability, and most are able to sit without support by the age of 6 months.

norms *the average performance of a large sample of children of a given age*

Brazelton Neonatal Behavioral Assessment Scale (NBAS) *a measure designed to determine infants' neurological and behavioral responses to their environment*

Fine Motor Skills.   As infants are perfecting their gross motor skills, such as sitting upright and walking, they are also making advances in their finer motor skills (see Table 4-4). For instance, by the age of 3 months, infants show some ability to coordinate the movements of their limbs (Thelen, 1994).

Furthermore, although infants are born with a rudimentary ability to reach toward an object, this ability is neither very sophisticated nor very accurate, and it disappears around the age of 4 weeks. A different, more precise, form of reaching reappears at 4 months. It takes some time for infants to coordinate successful grasping after they reach out, but in fairly short order they are able to reach out and hold onto an object of interest (Mathew & Cook, 1990; Rochat & Goubet, 1995; Berthier, 1996).

The sophistication of fine motor skills continues to grow. By the age of 11 months, infants are able to pick up off the ground objects as small as marbles—presenting care providers with issues of safety, because the place such objects often go next is the mouth. And by the time they are 2 years old, children can carefully hold a cup, bring it to their lips, and take a drink without spilling a drop.

Developmental Norms: Comparing the Individual to the Group: The timing of the milestones that we have been discussing is based on norms. **Norms** represent the average performance of a large sample of children of a given age. They permit comparisons between a particular child's performance on a particular behavior and the average performance of the children in the norm sample.

For instance, one of the most widely used techniques to determine infants' normative standing is the **Brazelton Neonatal Behavior Assessment Scale (NBAS)**, a measure designed to determine infants' neurological and behavioral responses to their environment.

The NBAS provides a supplement to the traditional Apgar test (discussed in Chapter 3) that is given immediately following birth. Taking about 30 minutes to administer, the NBAS includes 27 separate categories of responses that constitute 4 general aspects of infants' behavior: interactions with others (such as alertness and cuddliness), motor behavior, physiological control (such as the ability to be soothed after being upset), and responses to stress (Brazelton, Nugent, & Lester, 1987; Brazelton, 1973, 1990; Davis & Emory, 1995).

Although the norms provided by scales such as the NBAS are useful in making broad generalizations about the timing of various behaviors and skills, they must be interpreted with caution. Because norms are averages, they mask substantial individual differences in the times when children attain various achievements. They also may hide the fact that the sequence in which various behaviors are achieved may differ somewhat from one child to another.

TABLE 4-4

MILESTONES OF FINE MOTOR DEVELOPMENT

Age (months)	Skill
3	Opens hand prominently
3.5	Grasps rattle
8.5	Grasps with thumb and finger
11	Holds crayon adaptively
14	Builds tower of two cubes
16	Places pegs in board
24	Imitates strokes on paper
33	Copies circle

(*Source:* Adapted from Frankenburg et al., 1992)

Developmental Diversity

The Cultural Dimensions of Motor Development

Among the Ache people, who live in the rain forest of South America, infants face an early life of physical restriction. Because the Ache lead a nomadic existence, living in a series of tiny camps in the rain forest, open space is at a premium. Consequently, for the first few years of life, infants spend nearly all their time in direct physical contact with their mothers. Even when they are not physically touching their mothers, they are permitted to venture no more than a few feet away.

***

Infants among the Kipsigis people, who live in a more open environment in rural Kenya, Africa, lead quite a different existence. Their lives are filled with activity and exercise. Parents seek to teach their children to sit up, stand, and walk from the earliest days of infancy. For example, very young infants are placed in shallow holes in the ground designed to keep them in an upright position. Parents begin to teach their children to walk starting at the eighth week of life. The infants are held with their feet touching the ground, and they are pushed forward.

Clearly, the infants in these 2 societies lead very different lives (Super, 1976; Kaplan & Dove, 1987). But do the relative lack of early motoric stimulation for Ache infants and the efforts of the Kipsigis to encourage motoric development really matter?

The answer is both yes and no. Yes, in that Ache infants tend to show delayed motor development, relative both to Kipsigis infants and to children raised in Western societies. Although their social abilities are no different, Ache children tend to begin walking at around 23 months, about a year later than the typical child in the United States. In contrast, Kipsigis children, who are encouraged in their motor development, learn to sit up and walk several weeks earlier, on average, than U.S. children.

In the long run, however, the differences between Ache, Kipsigis, and Western children disappear. By late childhood, there is no evidence of differences in general, overall motor skills among Ache, Kipsigis, and Western children.

Variations in the timing of motor skills seem to depend in part on parental expectations of what is the "appropriate" schedule for the emergence of specific skills. For instance,

one study examined the motor skills of infants who lived in a single city in England, but whose mothers varied in ethnic origin. In the research, English, Jamaican, and Indian mothers' expectations were first assessed regarding several markers of their infants' motor skills. The Jamaican mothers expected their infants to sit and walk significantly earlier than the English and Indian mothers, and the actual emergence of these activities was in line with their expectations. The source of the Jamaican infants' earlier mastery seemed to lie in the treatment of the children by their parents. For instance, Jamaican mothers gave their children practice in stepping quite early in infancy (Hopkins & Westra, 1989, 1990).

In sum, the time at which specific motor skills appear is in part determined by cultural factors. Activities that are an intrinsic part of a culture are more apt to be purposely taught to infants in that culture, leading to the potential of their earlier emergence (Nugent, Lester, & Brazelton, 1989).

It is not all that surprising that children in a given culture who are expected by their parents to master a particular skill, and who are taught components of that skill from an early age, are more likely to be proficient in that skill earlier than children from other cultures with no such expectations and no such training. The larger question, however, is whether the earlier emergence of a basic motor behavior in a given culture has lasting consequences for specific motor skills and for achievements in other domains. On this issue, the jury is still out (Bloch, 1989).

What is clear, however, is that there are certain genetically determined constraints on how early a skill can emerge. It is physically impossible for one-month-old infants to stand and walk, regardless of the encouragement and practice they may get within their culture. Parents who are eager to accelerate their infants' motoric development, then, should be cautioned not to hold overly ambitious goals. In fact, they might well ask themselves whether it matters if an infant acquires a motor skill a few weeks earlier than his or her peers.

The most reasonable answer is "no." Although some parents may take pride in a child who walks earlier than other babies (just as some parents may be concerned over a delay of a few weeks), in the long run the timing of this activity will probably make no difference.

Furthermore, norms are useful only to the extent that they are based on data from a large, heterogeneous, culturally diverse sample of children. Unfortunately, many of the norms on which developmental researchers have traditionally relied have been based on groups of infants who are predominantly Caucasian and from the middle and upper socioeconomic strata (e.g., Gesell, 1946).

This limitation would not be critical if no differences existed in the timing of development in children from different cultural, racial, and social groups. But they do. For example, as a group, African American babies show more rapid motor development than Caucasian babies throughout infancy. Moreover, there are significant variations related to cultural factors, as we discuss next (Werner, 1972; Rosser & Randolph, 1989; Brazelton, 1991).

Nutrition in Infancy: Fueling Motor Development

The rapid physical growth that occurs during infancy is fueled by the nutrients that infants receive. Without proper nutrition, infants not only cannot reach their physical potential, but also may suffer cognitive and social consequences (Pollitt et al., 1993; Pollitt, 1994; Pollitt et al., 1996).

Malnutrition.   *Malnutrition*, the condition of having an improper amount and balance of nutrients, produces several results, none good. For instance, children living in many developing countries, where they are more susceptible to malnourishment and at greater risk for disease than children in more industrialized, affluent countries, begin to show a slower growth rate by the age of 6 months. By the time they reach the age of 2 years, their height and weight are only 95 percent the height and weight of children in more industrialized countries.

Furthermore, children who have been chronically malnourished during infancy later score lower on tests of IQ and tend to do less well in school. These effects may linger even if the children's diet has improved substantially (Barrett & Frank, 1987; Sigman et al., 1989; Gorman & Pollitt, 1992; Grantham-McGregor et al., 1994).

The problem of malnutrition is greatest in underdeveloped countries, where almost 10 percent of infants are severely malnourished. In the Dominican Republic, for instance, 13 percent of children under 3 years of age are underweight, and 21 percent have stunted growth. In other areas, the problem is even worse. In South Asia, for example, almost 60 percent of all children are underweight (World Food Council, 1992; see Figure 4-8).

Problems of malnourishment are not restricted to developing countries, however. In the United States, the richest country in the world, some 14 million children live in poverty, which puts them at risk for malnutrition. In fact, although overall poverty rates are no worse than they were 20 years ago, the poverty rate for children under the age of 3 has increased. Some one-quarter of families who have children 2 years old and younger live in poverty. And, as we can see in Figure 4-9, the rates are even higher for African American and Hispanic families, as well as for single-parent families (Einbinder, 1992; Carnegie Task Force on Meeting the Needs of Young Children, 1994).

Although these children rarely become severely malnourished, due to adequate social safety nets, they remain susceptible to *undernutrition*, in which there is some deficiency in

FIGURE 4-8

UNDERWEIGHT CHILDREN

In developing countries the number of underweight children under the age of 5 years is substantial.

(*Source:* World Food Council, 1992.)

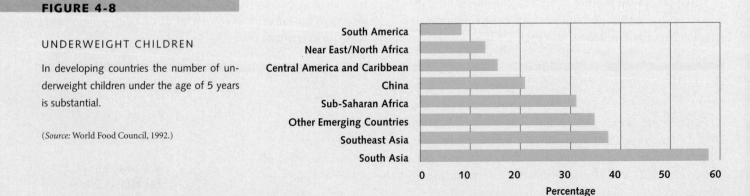

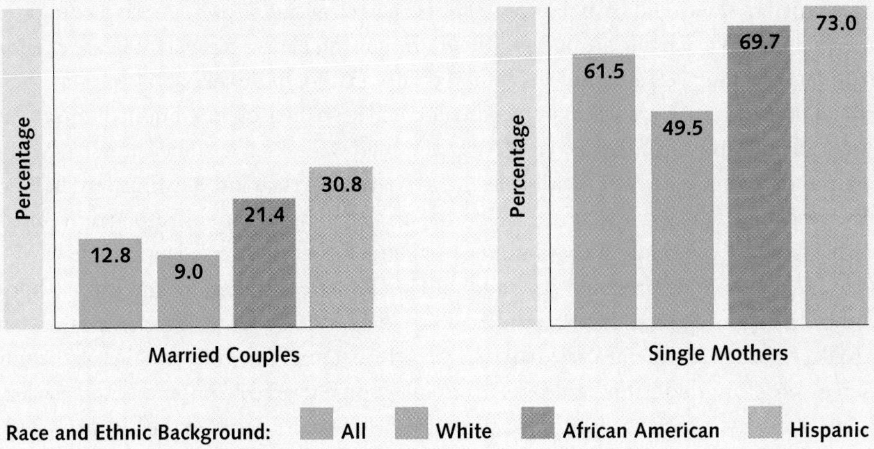

FIGURE 4-9

CHILDREN LIVING IN POVERTY

The incidence of poverty among children under the age of 3 is particularly high in minority and single-parent households. (Figures are shown only for single mothers and not fathers, because 97 percent of all children under 3 who live with a single parent live with their mothers; only 3 percent live with their fathers.)

(*Source:* Einbinder, 1992.)

Married Couples

12.8 9.0 21.4 30.8

Single Mothers

61.5 49.5 69.7 73.0

Race and Ethnic Background: All   White   African American   Hispanic

diet. In fact, some surveys find that as many as a quarter of 1- to 5-year-old children in the United States have diets that fall below the minimum caloric intake recommended by nutritional experts (Barrett & Frank, 1987; U.S. Bureau of the Census, 1992; Pollitt et al., 1996).

Severe malnutrition during infancy may lead to several disorders. Malnutrition during the first year can produce **marasmus**, a disease characterized by the cessation of growth. Marasmus, attributable to a severe deficiency in proteins and calories, causes the body to waste away and ultimately results in death. Older children are susceptible to **kwashiorkor**, a disease in which a child's stomach, limbs, and face swell with water. To a casual observer, it appears that a child with kwashiorkor is actually chubby. However, this is an illusion: The child's body is in fact struggling to make use of the few nutrients that are available.

Although the consequences are not as severe as those of malnutrition, undernutrition also has long-term costs. For instance, there is increasing evidence that cognitive development later in childhood is affected by even mild to moderate undernutrition (Sigman, 1995).

Obesity.   It is clear that malnourishment during infancy has potentially disastrous consequences for an infant. Less clear, however, are the effects of *obesity*, defined as weight greater than 20 percent above the average for a given height. For one thing, there appears to be no correlation between obesity during infancy and obesity at the age of 16 years. (An association does exist between obesity after the age of 6 and adult weight, however.)

Furthermore, although some research suggests that overfeeding during infancy may lead to the creation of unnecessary fat cells, which remain in the body throughout life, it is not clear that an abundance of fat cells necessarily leads to adult obesity. In fact, genetic factors are an important determinant of obesity (Knittle, 1975; C. Bouchard et al., 1990; Fabsitz, Carmelli, & Hewitt, 1992).

In sum, obesity during infancy is not a major concern. However, the societal view that "a fat baby is a healthy baby" is not necessarily correct, either. Rather than focusing on their infant's weight, parents should concentrate on providing appropriate nutrition. At least during infancy, concerns about weight need not be central, as long as infants are provided with an appropriate diet.

Although everyone agrees on the importance of receiving proper nutrition during infancy, just how to reach that goal is a source of controversy. Because infants are not born with the ability to eat or digest solid food, at first they exist solely on a liquid diet. But just what should that liquid be—a mother's breast milk or a formula of commercially processed cow's milk with vitamin additives? The answer has been a major source of contention.

marasmus   *a disease characterized by the cessation of growth*

kwashiorkor   *a disease in which a child's stomach, limbs, and face swell with water*

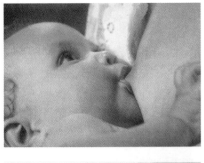

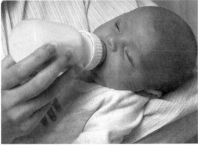

Breast or bottle? Although infants receive adequate nourishment from breast- or bottle-feeding, most authorities agree "breast is best."

Breast or Bottle?

Some 40 years ago, if a mother asked her pediatrician whether breast-feeding or bottle-feeding was better, she would have received a simple and clear-cut answer: Bottle-feeding was the preferred method. Starting around the 1940s, the general belief among child-care experts was that breast-feeding was an obsolete method that put children unnecessarily at risk.

With bottle-feeding, the argument went, parents could keep track of the amount of milk their baby was receiving and could thereby ensure that the child was taking in sufficient nutrients. In contrast, mothers who breast-fed their babies could never be certain just how much milk their infants were getting. Furthermore, use of the bottle was said to help mothers keep their feedings to a rigid schedule of one bottle every 4 hours, at that time the recommended procedure.

Today, however, a mother would get a very different answer to the same question. Child-care authorities agree: For the first 12 months of life, there is no better food for an infant than breast milk (American Academy of Pediatrics, 1997). Breast milk not only contains all the nutrients necessary for growth, but it also seems to offer some degree of immunity to a variety of childhood diseases, such as respiratory and ear infections and diarrhea (see Figure 4-10). Breast milk is more easily digested than cow's milk or formula, and it is sterile, warm, and convenient for the mother to dispense (Eiger, 1987; Howie et al., 1990).

Additional evidence suggests that breast milk has other, more subtle virtues. For instance, several studies have found that breast-fed infants have higher levels of docosahexaenoic acid (DHA) in their brains and retinas than those who have been bottle-fed (Neuringer, 1993). Because research with nonhumans suggests that a deficit of DHA leads to irreversible changes, it is possible—although highly speculative—that higher levels of the chemical may enhance the brain functioning of children who have been breast-fed (Rogan & Gladen, 1993).

Much current work is focused on understanding how other components of breast milk may enhance growth. For instance, some researchers are examining how an epidermal growth factor present in breast milk may advance the development of the digestive and respiratory systems in infants. Furthermore, there is evidence that preterm infants ultimately may do better cognitively as a result of being fed breast milk during infancy (Lucas et al., 1992; Brody, 1994b).

Obviously, breast-feeding is not the solution to every problem faced by infants, and the millions of individuals who have been raised on formula should not be concerned that they have suffered irreparable harm. But it is clear that the popular slogan used by groups advocating the use of breast-feeding is right on target: "Breast is Best."

Breast-feeding may even hold health-related advantages for mothers. For instance, research suggests that women who breast-feed may have lower rates of ovarian cancer and

---

FIGURE 4-10

BREAST MILK ADVANTAGES

One of the advantages to breast milk is that it contains all the nutrients necessary for growth; it also appears to offer some degree of immunity to a variety of childhood diseases.

(*Source:* Pediatrics Electronic Pages, June 1997.)

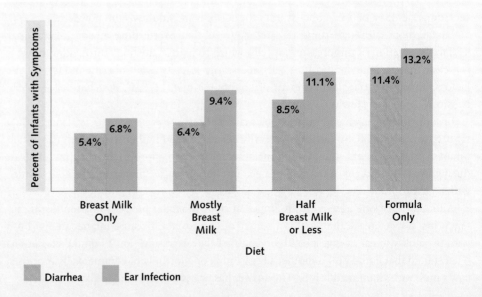

"I forgot to say I was breast-fed."

breast cancer prior to menopause. Furthermore, the hormones produced during breast-feeding help shrink the uteruses of women following birth, enabling their bodies to return more quickly to a prepregnancy state. These hormones also may inhibit ovulation, potentially preventing pregnancy and helping to space the birth of additional children. Breast-feeding even helps mothers react to stress: Research shows that the level of stress hormones is lower in mothers who breast-feed their infants than in those who bottle-feed them (Herbst, 1994; Ross & Yu, 1994; Altemus et al., 1995).

Breast-feeding also offers significant emotional advantages for both mother and child. Most mothers report that the experience of breast-feeding brings about feelings of intimacy and closeness that are incomparable to any other experiences with their infants (Epstein, 1993). At the same time, infants, whose rooting and sucking reflexes are genetically well designed to find nourishment and satisfaction from breast-feeding, seem to be calmed and soothed by the experience (Eiger & Olds, 1987).

Social Patterns in Breast-Feeding.   Although it has several advantages, only about half of all new mothers in the United States employ breast-feeding. This is actually a decline from the peak that was reached in 1982, when almost two-thirds of all new mothers breast-fed their babies. Although recent figures suggest that breast-feeding may once again be on the rise, the decline that occurred in the 1980s was significant (Ross Laboratories, 1993; Ryan, 1997).

Issues of age, social status, and race influence the decision whether to breast-feed. The rates of breast-feeding are highest among women who are older, have better educations, and are of higher socioeconomic status (Richardson & Champion, 1992). Moreover, there are ethnic and racial group differences. For instance, breast-feeding among Caucasian mothers in the United States occurs at a rate almost double that for African American mothers (Maternal and Child Health Bureau, 1994).

If authorities are in agreement about the benefits of breast-feeding, why in so many cases do women not breast-feed? In some cases, they can't. Some women have difficulties producing milk, and others are taking some type of medicine or have an infectious disease such as AIDS that could be passed on to their infants through breast milk. Sometimes infants are too ill to nurse successfully. And in many cases of adoption, where the birth mother is unavailable after giving birth, the adoptive mother has no choice but to bottle-feed.

Sally Ann Lederman, Research Scientist

Education: . . . . Brooklyn College, Brooklyn, New York, B.S. in chemistry; Columbia University, New York, New York, Ph.D. in human nutrition

Position: . . . . Research scientist for the Program in Nutrition Education at Teachers College, Columbia University, New York, New York

Home: . . . . Wayne, New Jersey

The natural act of breast-feeding is older than humankind itself. But its very antiquity works against it in many "modern" societies, especially in the United States, where many women have discarded the practice in favor of bottle-feeding.

"In the United States, cultural and social issues combine with biological factors to discourage women from breast-feeding."

But according to Sally Ann Lederman, a leading expert on nutritional issues related to pregnancy and breast-feeding, the trend has been reversing as women become more aware of the benefits of breast-feeding. Still, Lederman is convinced that more has to be done to encourage women to follow through.

"The American Academy of Pediatrics has suggested that mothers stay away from bottle-feeding for about the first year," Lederman says, "but while the recommendation is encouraging, the behavior has been less so."

One of the main problems is that women do not have either a good understanding of breast-feeding or the proper training to do it right. Many women attempt it, only to give up after a short time—often because of preconceived, but erroneous, notions.

"It has been shown that breast-fed children enjoy greater visual acuity and higher cognitive performance. In some cases, a difference in IQ of almost 10 points has been found, in favor of breast-fed children."

"In the United States, cultural and social issues combine with biological factors to discourage women from breast-feeding," Lederman explains. "You have to do it right for it to succeed, and recent trends have conspired against women learning to do it properly."

"For example, in the last few years there has been an emphasis on releasing a woman from the hospital as soon as possible after she gives birth. This gives her even less time to learn the absolute basics of child care, which would include breast-feeding."

"Breast-feeding isn't easy," Lederman adds. "Oddly enough, it's not entirely natural. Many women give up because they are doing it wrong. For example, they should learn the proper way for the baby to latch onto the breast. It's not a spontaneous action. The baby has to take enough of the nipple, but not the nipple alone."

The natural connection between the dietary needs of the infant and the mother's ability to produce milk is close but not simple. To interpret the link correctly, the mother has to understand the reactions of the infant, according to Lederman. And she has to avoid the temptation to feel guilty over not having enough milk to meet the baby's needs. In fact, a straightforward demand–supply relationship exists between the baby and the milk supply.

"What determines the mother's milk supply is the amount of suckling the baby does," Lederman says. "As the baby grows, it needs more milk and it will suckle more frequently, and in response the mother will produce more milk. After a while the baby will not have to suckle as much. But it's important to understand that if the mother usually nurses 6 times a day, and the baby wants to nurse 8 times a day, this is not because the mother is out of milk."

Lederman also stresses the health advantages that mother's milk offers to the baby compared with bottled formula. Citing recent studies, she notes that the fatty acid pattern that is found in breast milk is beneficial for brain development and neural development in general.

"It has been shown that breast-fed children enjoy greater visual acuity and higher cognitive performance," she notes. "In some cases, a difference in IQ of almost 10 points has been found, in favor of breast-fed children."

"There are so many differences between bottled milk and breast milk that no matter how much the makers of formula attempt to mimic natural milk, it's just not an achievable goal," Lederman concludes.

In other cases, the decision not to breast-feed is based on practical considerations. Women who hold jobs outside the home may not have sufficiently flexible schedules to breast-feed their infants. This problem is particularly true with less affluent women who may have less control over their schedules. Such problems also may account for the lower rate of breast-feeding among mothers of lower socioeconomic status.

Education is also an issue: Some women simply do not receive adequate information and advice regarding the advantages of breast-feeding, and choose to use formula because it seems an appropriate choice. Indeed, some hospitals may inadvertently encourage the use of formula by including it in the gift packets new mothers receive as they leave the hospital.

In developing countries, the use of formula is particularly problematic. Because formula often comes in powdered form that must be mixed with water, local pollution of the water supply can make formula particularly dangerous. Yet until the early 1980s, manufacturers aggressively sold formula in such countries, touting it as the "modern" choice. It took a massive, worldwide boycott of products manufactured by the Nestlé company, a major manufacturer of formula, to end their promotion of bottle-feeding (Fox, 1984). Formula containers now include labels that advertise the benefits of breast-feeding and the dangers associated with bottle-feeding, and free samples are no longer supplied to mothers.

Educational, social, and cultural support for breast-feeding is particularly important. For instance, physicians need to educate their patients about the importance of the practice and to provide specific information on just how to breast-feed. Although breast-feeding is a natural act, mothers require a bit of practice to learn how to hold the baby properly, position the nipple correctly, and deal with such potential problems as sore nipples. (For more on the advantages and difficulties of breast-feeding, see the "Speaking of Development" box.)

Introducing Solid Foods: When and What?

Although pediatricians agree that breast milk is the ideal initial food, at some point infants require more nutriments than breast milk alone can provide. The American Academy of Pediatrics and the American Academy of Family Physicians suggest that babies can start solids at around 6 months, although they aren't needed until 9 to 12 months of age (American Academy of Pediatrics, 1997; American Academy of Family Physicians, 1997).

Solid foods are introduced into an infant's diet gradually, one at a time. Most often cereal comes first, followed by strained fruits. Vegetables typically are introduced next, and ultimately other kinds of food, such as eggs, fish, and meat, are added.

The exact amount of solid foods is hard to specify. In part, it depends on the activity level of the particular infant. Highly active children require more calories than those who are relatively sedentary.

The timing of *weaning*, the cessation of breast-feeding, varies greatly. In developed countries such as the United States, weaning frequently occurs as early as 3 or 4 months. On the other hand, in certain subcultures within the United States, breast-feeding may continue for 2 or 3 years. Recommendations from the American Academy of Pediatrics suggest that infants be fed breast milk for the first 12 months (American Academy of Pediatrics, 1997).

Infants generally start solid foods at around 4 to 6 months, gradually working their way up to a variety of different foods.

REVIEW AND RETHINK

REVIEW

■ Reflexes, which are universal, genetically acquired physical behaviors, have many uses. Some reflexes help the infant survive and remain safe in its new environment, others serve as the basis of later-learned behaviors such as walking, and others seem to help infants and caregivers form intimate social relationships.

- During infancy children achieve a series of landmarks in their physical development. The schedule and order of these landmarks are generally consistent across children. However, significant individual and cultural variations exist, and any norms used to describe the timing of developmental milestones should be regarded with caution.

- Training and cultural expectations can affect the timing of the development of motor skills. Whether such manipulation of the developmental schedule produces lasting effects remains an open question.

- Nutrition strongly affects physical development. Malnutrition, which is a problem especially in developing countries, can slow growth, affect intellectual performance, and cause diseases such as marasmus and kwashiorkor. The victims of undernutrition, which exists even in developed countries, also suffer negative effects.

- The advantages of breast-feeding are numerous, including nutritional, immunological, emotional, and physical benefits for the infant, and physical and emotional benefits for the mother as well. Factors of age, education, socioeconomic status, health, and practicality influence mothers' willingness and ability to breast-feed.

RETHINK

- What are some examples of reflexive behaviors not mentioned in this chapter that are part of your physical repertoire? How are they useful? Are the behaviors you named really innate, automatic reflexes, or are they learned responses?

- In what ways does the practice of training infants to accelerate their motor skill development recall the relationship between genotype and phenotype? What sorts of constraints might there be on the results of such training?

- What advice might you give a friend who is concerned about the fact that her infant is still not walking at 14 months, when every other baby she knows started walking by the first birthday?

- How would you design an experiment to determine whether early development of physical skills produces lasting effects? Why do you think a definitive answer to this question has not yet been found? How would you eliminate factors other than early development from your study?

- Given that malnourishment negatively affects physical growth, how can it also adversely affect IQ scores and school performance, as reported in this chapter?

THE DEVELOPMENT OF THE SENSES

According to William James, one of founding fathers of psychology, the world of the infant is a "blooming, buzzing confusion" (James, 1890/1950). Was he right? In this case, James's wisdom failed him. The newborn's world does lack the clarity and stability that we can distinguish as adults, but day by day the world grows increasingly comprehensible as the infant's ability to sense and perceive the environment develops.

The processes that underlie infants' understanding of the world around them are sensation and perception. **Sensation** is the stimulation of the sense organs, and **perception** is the sorting out, interpretation, analysis, and integration of stimuli involving the sense organs and brain. Sensation is the responsiveness of the sense organs to stimulation, and perception is the interpretation of that stimulation. Sorting out infants' capabilities in the realm of sensation and perception presents a challenge to the ingenuity of investigators.

Visual perception: Seeing the World

From the time of Lee Eng's birth, everyone who met him felt that he gazed at them intently. His eyes seemed to meet those of visitors. They seemed to bore deeply, and knowingly, into the faces of people who were looking at him.

sensation   *the stimulation of the sense organs*

perception   *the sorting out, interpretation, analysis, and integration of stimuli involving the sense organs and brain*

(CW)

How good in fact was Lee's vision, and what, precisely, could he make out of his environment? Quite a bit. According to some estimates, a newborn's distance vision ranges from 20/200 to 20/600, which means that an infant cannot discern visual material beyond 20 feet that an adult with normal vision is able to see from a distance of between 200 and 600 feet (Haith, 1991).

These figures indicate that infants' distance vision is some 10 to 30 times poorer than the average adult's, perhaps suggesting that the vision of infants is inadequate. However, looking at the figures from a different perspective suggests a revised interpretation: The vision of newborns provides the same degree of distance acuity as the uncorrected vision of many adults who wear eyeglasses or contact lenses. (If you wear glasses or contact lenses, remove them to get a sense of what an infant can see of the world.) Furthermore, infants' distance vision grows increasingly acute. By 6 months of age, the average infant's vision is already 20/20—in other words, identical to that of adults (Aslin, 1987; Simons, 1993).

Other visual abilities grow rapidly. For instance, *binocular vision*, the ability to combine the images coming to each eye to see depth and motion, is achieved at around 14 weeks.

Depth perception is a particularly useful ability, as a classic study on the topic indicates. In this study, carried out by developmental psychologists Eleanor Gibson and Richard Walk (1960), infants were placed on a sheet of heavy glass. A checkered pattern appeared under one-half of the glass sheet, making it seem that the infant was on a stable floor. However, in the middle of the glass sheet, the pattern dropped down several feet, forming an apparent "visual cliff." The question Gibson and Walk asked was whether infants would willingly crawl across the cliff when called by their mothers (see Figure 4-11).

The results were unambiguous. Most of the infants in the study, who ranged in age from 6 to 14 months, could not be coaxed over the apparent cliff. Clearly the ability to perceive depth had already developed in most of them by that age. On the other hand, the experiment did not pinpoint when depth perception emerged, because only infants who had already learned to crawl could be tested. But other experiments, in which infants of 2 and 3 months were placed on their stomachs above the apparent floor and above the visual cliff, revealed differences in heart rate between the two positions (Campos, Langer, & Krowitz, 1970).

Still, such findings do not permit us to know whether infants are responding to depth itself, or merely to the *change* in visual stimuli that occurs when they are moved from a lack of depth to depth.

Infants also show clear visual preferences, preferences that are present from birth. For example, when given a choice, infants reliably prefer to look at stimuli that include patterns

FIGURE 4-11   VISUAL CLIFF

The "visual cliff" experiment examines the depth perception of infants. Most infants in the age range of 6 to 14 months cannot be coaxed to cross the cliff, apparently responding to the fact that the patterned area drops several feet.

than to look at simpler stimuli (see Figure 4-12). How do we know? Developmental psychologist Robert Fantz (1963) created a classic test. He built a chamber in which babies could lie on their backs and see pairs of visual stimuli above them. Fantz could determine which of the stimuli the infants were looking at by observing the reflections of the stimuli in their eyes.

Fantz's work was the impetus for a great deal of research on the preferences of infants, most of which points to a critical conclusion: Infants are genetically preprogrammed to prefer particular kinds of stimuli. For instance, just minutes after birth they show preferences for certain colors, shapes, and configurations of various stimuli. Such capabilities may be a reflection of the existence of highly specialized cells in the brain that react to stimuli of a particular pattern, orientation, shape, and direction of movement (Hubel & Wiesel, 1979; Haith, 1991; Gallant, Braun, & VanEssen, 1993; Colombo, 1995).

However, genetics is not the sole determinant of infant visual preferences. Just a few hours after birth, infants have already learned to prefer their own mother's face to other faces. Such findings provide another clear piece of evidence of how heredity and environmental experiences are woven together to determine an infant's capabilities (Field et al., 1984; Pascalis et al., 1995; Gelman & Au, 1996).

Auditory Perception: The World of Sound

What is it about a mother's lullaby that helps soothe a crying, fussy baby? Some clues emerge when we look at the capabilities of infants in the realm of auditory sensation and perception.

It is clear that infants hear from the time of birth—and even before. As we noted in Chapter 3, the ability to hear begins prenatally. Even in the womb, the fetus responds to sounds outside of its mother. Furthermore, infants are born with preferences for particular sound combinations. For example, blends of musical tones with underlying frequencies that are related mathematically as simple proportions are more easily discerned by infants than more complex combinations (Schellenberg & Trehub, 1996).

Because they have had some practice in hearing before birth, it is not surprising that infants have reasonably good auditory perception after they are born. In fact, for certain very high and very low frequencies, infants actually are more sensitive to sound than adults—a sensitivity that seems to increase during the first 2 years of life. On the other hand, infants are initially less sensitive than adults to middle-range frequencies. Eventually, however, their capabilities within the middle range improve (Fenwick & Morrongiello, 1991; Werner & Marean, 1996).

What leads to the improvement during infancy in sensitivity to sounds is not fully clear, although it may be related to the maturation of the nervous system. More puzzling is why, after infancy, children's ability to hear very high and low frequencies gradually declines. One explanation may be that exposure to high levels of noise may diminish capacities at the extreme ranges (Schneider, Trehub, & Bull, 1980; Kryter, 1983; Trehub et al., 1988, 1989).

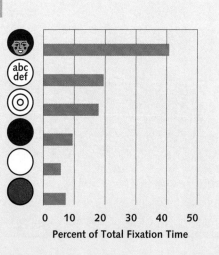

FIGURE 4-12

PREFERRING COMPLEXITY

In a classic experiment, researcher Robert Fantz found that 2- and 3-month-old infants preferred to look at more complex stimuli than simple ones.

(*Source*: Adapted from Fantz, 1961)

Percent of Total Fixation Time

In addition to the ability to detect sound, infants need several other abilities in order to hear effectively. For instance, *sound localization* permits infants to discern the direction from which a sound is emanating. Compared to adults, infants have a slight handicap in this task because effective sound localization requires the use of the slight difference in the times at which a sound reaches our two ears. Because infants' heads are smaller than those of adults, the difference in timing of the arrival of sound at the two ears is less than it is in adults.

However, despite the potential limitation brought about by their smaller heads, infants' sound localization abilities are actually fairly good even at birth, and they reach adult levels of success by the age of one year (Clifton, 1992; Litovsky & Ashmead, 1997). Interestingly, their improvement is not steady: Although we don't know why, the accuracy of sound localization actually declines between birth and 2 months of age, but then begins to increase (Aslin, 1987; Schneider, Bull, & Trehub, 1988; Trehub et al., 1989).

Infant discrimination of groups of different sounds, in terms of their patterns and other acoustical characteristics, is also quite good. For instance, the change of a single note in a six-tone melody can be detected by infants as young as 6 months old. They also react to changes in musical key (Trehub, Thorpe, & Morrongiello, 1985). In sum, they listen with a keen ear to the melodies of lullabies sung to them by their mothers and fathers!

Even more important to their ultimate success in the world, young infants are capable of making the fine discriminations that their future understanding of language will require (Bijeljac-Babic, Bertoncini, & Mehler, 1993). For instance, in one classic study, a group of 1- to 4-month-old infants sucked on nipples that activated a recording of a person saying "ba" every time they sucked (Eimas et al., 1971). At first, their interest in the sound made them suck vigorously. Soon, though, they became acclimated to the sound (through a process called *habituation*, discussed in Chapter 3) and sucked with less energy. On the other hand, when the experimenters changed the sound to "pa," the infants immediately showed new interest and sucked with greater vigor once again. The clear conclusion: Infants as young as 1 month old could make the distinction between the two similar sounds (Eimas et al., 1971; Goodman & Nusbaum, 1994; Miller & Eimas, 1995).

Even more intriguingly, young infants are able to discriminate certain characteristics that differentiate one language from another. By the age of 4½ months, infants are able to discriminate their own names from other, similar-sounding, words. By the age of 5 months, they can distinguish the difference between English and Spanish passages, even when the two are similar in meter, number of syllables, and speed of recitation. In fact, some evidence suggests that even 2-day-olds show preferences for their native language (Bahrick & Pickens, 1988; Moon, Cooper, & Fifer, 1993; Best, 1994; Mandel, Jusczyk, & Pisoni, 1995).

Given their ability to discriminate a difference in speech as slight as the difference between two consonants, it is not surprising that infants can distinguish different people on the basis of voice. In fact, from an early age they show clear preferences for some voices over others. For instance, in one experiment newborns were allowed to suck a nipple that turned on a recording of a human voice reading a story. The infants sucked significantly longer when the voice was that of their mother than when the voice was that of a stranger (DeCasper & Fifer, 1980; Fifer, 1987).

How do such preferences arise? One hypothesis is that prenatal exposure to the mother's voice is the key. As support for this conjecture, researchers point to the fact that newborns do not show a preference for their fathers' voices over other male voices. Furthermore, newborns prefer listening to melodies sung by their mothers before they were born to melodies that were not sung before birth. It seems, then, that the prenatal exposure to their mothers' voices—although muffled by the liquid environment of the womb—helps shape infants' listening preferences (DeCasper & Prescott, 1984; Panneton, 1985).

Smell and Taste

What do infants do when they smell a rotten egg? Pretty much what adults do—crinkle their noses and generally look unhappy. On the other hand, the scent of bananas and butter produces a pleasant reaction on the part of infants (Steiner, 1979).

Infants react to unpleasant tastes from birth.

The sense of smell is so well developed, even among very young infants, that at least some 12- to 18-day-old babies can distinguish their mothers on the basis of smell alone. For instance, in one experiment infants were exposed to the smell of gauze pads worn under the arms of adults the previous evening. Infants who were being breast-fed were able to distinguish their mothers' scent from those of other adults. However, not all infants could do this: Those who were being bottle-fed were unable to make the distinction. Moreover, both breast-fed and bottle-fed infants were unable to distinguish their fathers on the basis of odor (Cernoch & Porter, 1985; Porter, Bologh, & Malkin, 1988; Soussignan et al., 1997).

Taste, like smell, shows surprising sophistication during infancy—in part because the two capabilities are related. Some taste preferences are well developed at birth, such as disgust over bitter tastes. At the same time, infants seem to have an innate sweet tooth—even before they have teeth: Very young infants smile when a sweet-tasting liquid is placed on their tongues. They also suck harder at a bottle if it is sweetened (Crook, 1978, 1987; Steiner, 1979; Rosenstein & Oster, 1988).

Sensitivity to Pain and Touch

When Eli Rosenblatt was 8 days old, he participated in the ancient Jewish ritual of circumcision. As he lay nestled in his father's arms, the foreskin of his penis was removed. Although Eli shrieked in what seemed to his anxious parents as pain, he soon settled down and went back to sleep. Others who had watched the ceremony assured his parents, with great authority, that at Eli's age babies don't really experience pain, at least not in the same way that adults do.

Were Eli's relatives accurate in saying that young infants don't experience pain? In the past, many medical practitioners would have agreed. In fact, because they assumed that infants didn't experience pain in truly bothersome ways, many physicians routinely carried out medical procedures, and even some forms of surgery, without the use of painkillers or anesthesia. Their argument was that the risks from the use of anesthesia outweighed the potential pain that the young infants experienced.

Contemporary Views on Infant Pain. Today, however, it is widely acknowledged that infants are born with the capacity to experience pain. Obviously, no one can be sure if the experience of pain in children is identical to that in adults, any more than we can tell if an adult friend who complains of a headache is experiencing pain that is more or less severe than our own pain when we have a headache.

What we do know is that pain produces signs of distress in infants, such as a rise in heartbeat, sweating, facial expressions indicative of discomfort, and changes in the intensity and tone of crying (Johnston, 1989). Such evidence indicates that infants do, in fact, experience pain. There also seems to be a developmental progression in reactions to pain.

For example, a newborn infant who has her heel pricked for a blood test responds with signs of distress, but it takes her several seconds to show the response. In contrast, only a few months later, the same procedure brings a much more immediate response. It is possible that the delayed reaction in infants is produced by the relatively slower transmission of information within the newborn's nervous system (Porter, Porges, & Marshall, 1988; Bornstein & Lamb, 1992a; Anand & Hickey, 1987, 1992; Axia, Gonichini, & Benini, 1995).

In response to increasing support for the notion that infants experience pain, medical experts now endorse the use of anesthesia and painkillers during surgery for even the youngest infants. According to the American Academy of Pediatrics, painkilling drugs are appropriate in most types of surgery, although minor surgical procedures—such as circumcision—still may be done without their use.

Responding to Touch. It clearly does not take the sting of pain to get an infant's attention. Even the youngest infants respond to gentle touches, such as a soothing caress, which can calm a crying, fussy infant (Stack & Muir, 1992).

In fact, touch is one of the most highly developed sensory systems in a newborn. It is also one of the first to develop; there is evidence that by 32 weeks after conception, the entire body is sensitive to touch. Furthermore, several of the basic reflexes present at birth, such as the rooting reflex, require touch sensitivity to operate: An infant must sense a touch near the mouth in order to seek automatically a nipple to suck (Haith, 1986).

Infants' abilities in the realm of touch are particularly helpful in their efforts to explore the world. Several theorists have suggested that one of the ways children gain information about the world is through touching. For instance, at the age of 6 months, infants are apt to place almost any object in their mouths, apparently taking in data about its configuration from their sensory responses to the feel of it in their mouths (Ruff, 1989). In addition, as we consider in the "Directions in Development" box, touch plays an important therapeutic role for a number of medical conditions.

Multimodal Perception: Combining Individual Sensory Inputs

When Eric Pettigrew was 7 months old, his grandparents presented him with a squeaky rubber doll. As soon as he saw it, he reached out for it, grasped it in his hand, and listened as it squeaked. He seemed delighted with the gift.

One way of considering Eric's sensory reaction to the doll is to focus on each of the senses individually: what the doll looked like to Eric, how it felt in his hand, and what it sounded like. In fact, this approach has dominated the study of sensation and perception in infancy.

However, we might take another approach: We might examine how the various sensory responses are integrated with one another. Instead of looking at each individual sensory response, we could consider how the responses work together and are combined to produce Eric's ultimate reaction. The **multimodal approach to perception** considers how information that is collected by various individual sensory systems is integrated and coordinated.

Although the multimodal approach is a relatively recent innovation in the study of how infants understand their sensory world, it raises some fundamental issues about the development of sensation and perception. For instance, some researchers argue that sensations are initially integrated with one another in the infant, whereas others maintain that the infant's sensory systems are initially separate and that development leads to increasing integration (Rose & Ruff, 1987; Bahrick, 1989; Legerstee, 1990; Streri, 1994; Quinn & Eimas, 1996).

We do not know yet which view is correct. However, it does appear that by an early age infants are able to relate what they have learned about an object through one sensory channel to what they have learned about it through another. For instance, even 1-month-old infants are able to recognize by sight objects that they have previously held in their mouths but never seen (Meltzoff, 1981; Steri & Spelke, 1988). Clearly, some cross-talk between various sensory channels is already possible a month after birth.

The success of infants at multimodal perception is another example of the sophisticated perceptual abilities of infants, which continue to grow throughout the period of infancy. These increasing capabilities are mirrored by the growth of cognitive abilities, which we'll consider in the next chapter.

multimodal approach to perception
the approach that considers how information that is collected by various individual sensory systems is integrated and coordinated

The senses of sight and touch are integrated by infants through multimodal perception.

Touching Moments: The Long-term Benefits of a Gentle Caress

Huddled in his clear Plexiglas incubator at Miami's Jackson Memorial Medical Center, 11-day-old Brandan Owens seems as inaccessible as Snow White in her glass coffin. Born 8 weeks premature, now weighing four pounds, Brandan must live in this artificially warmed environment because his own underdeveloped system cannot yet regulate his body temperature.

Brandan's mother gives a nervous start as Maria Hernandez-Reif of the University of Miami's Touch Research Institute (TRI) reaches through the incubator's portholes and begins to massage the baby. Her hand is larger than Brandan's entire back; as her fingers move in firm downward strokes, the baby's translucent skin looks as if it might tear as easily as tissue paper. Now Hernandez-Reif's fingers stroke an arm as fragile as a twig. She is applying gentle pressure—too light and it tickles, too strong and it hurts. (Colt, 1998, p. 86)

The gentle massage being applied to Brandan won't only soothe him—it may be essential to his future growth. According to a growing body of research with both humans and nonhumans, touch plays an important role in an organism's future development, for it triggers a complex chemical reaction that assists infants in their efforts to survive.

Developmental psychologist Tiffany Field and colleagues have found that gentle massage stimulates the production of certain chemicals in an infant's brain that instigate growth. Periodic massage is also helpful in treating several kinds of medical condi-

tions, including premature delivery and the effects of prenatal exposure to AIDS or cocaine. Furthermore, massage is beneficial for infants and even older children whose mothers are depressed and for those who suffer from burns, cancer, asthma, and a variety of other conditions (Schanberg et al., 1993; Field, 1995a, 1995b; De Roiste & Bushnell, 1996; Scafaldi & Field, 1996).

For example, in one study that illustrated the benefits of massage, a group of preterm infants who were massaged for 15 minutes three times a day gained weight some 50 percent faster than a group of preterm infants of the same age who were not stroked (see Figure 4-13). The massaged infants also were more active and responsive to stimuli. The preterm infants who were massaged were discharged earlier from the hospital, and their medical costs were significantly lower than infants in the unmassaged group (Field, 1988, 1995b).

Not every type of stimulation is successful in producing gains in preterm newborns. Stimulation that is too strong or rough can be harmful; stimulation that is too light can be irritating. Furthermore, in very-low-birthweight infants, too much stimulation can overwhelm infants' efforts to stabilize their internal physiological environments (Lester & Tronick, 1990; Als, 1992; Wheeden et al., 1993).

The same principles also are at work with nonhumans. For example, rats who are licked and groomed by their mothers at higher-than-usual rates during their first 10 days of life show more adaptive physiological reactions when they encounter stress during adulthood. They also explore their environments more, another indication of lower levels of stress. The early licking-and-grooming behavior appears to preprogram hypothalamus, pituitary, and adrenal responses to stress in later life (Liu et al., 1997; Sapolsky, 1997).

Although one wouldn't want to conclude that human parents should mimic the licking-and-grooming behavior of rats, it does seem clear that the right kind of touch can play an important role both in instigating growth and in improving several kinds of medical conditions in human infants. Furthermore, it results in lower anxiety and the production of fewer hormones related to stress. Finally, massage is an economical approach, because parents and grandparents can provide massage therapy with minimal training. And there is an added bonus: The people who provide massage say that that their own feelings of wellness are increased (Field, 1995b).

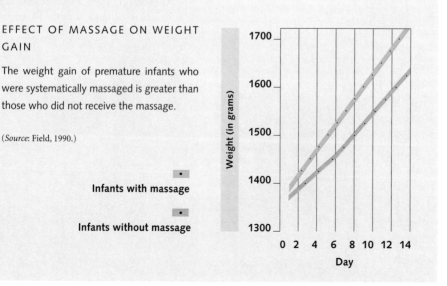

FIGURE 4-13

EFFECT OF MASSAGE ON WEIGHT GAIN

The weight gain of premature infants who were systematically massaged is greater than those who did not receive the massage.

(*Source*: Field, 1990.)

Infants with massage

Infants without massage

The Informed Consumer of Development

Exercising Your Infant's Body and Senses

We've seen how the experiences infants encounter as they grow are reflected in their motor and sensory development. For instance, recall how cultural expectations and environments affect the age at which various physical milestones, such as the first step, occur. Does this suggest that parents are well advised to try to accelerate their infants' timetables?

Although experts disagree, most feel that such acceleration yields little advantage. No data suggest that a child who walks at 10 months ultimately has any advantage over one who walks at 15 months.

On the other hand, it does seem reasonable for parents to ensure that their infants receive some level of physical and sensory stimulation. The goal, according to Jane Clark, an expert in kinesiology (the science of human anatomy and movement), is not to get children to achieve motoric milestones early, but "to raise active, confident children who will become healthy, active adults who feel good about their bodies and who value physical activity for its intrinsic benefits and rewards" (Israeloff, 1991).

There are several specific ways to accomplish this goal:

■ Carry a baby in different positions—in a backpack, in a frontpack, or in a football hold with the infant's head in the palm of your hand and its feet lying on your arm.

■ Let infants explore their environment. Don't contain them too long in a barren environment. Let them crawl or wander around an environment—after first making it "childproof" by removing dangerous objects.

■ Engage in "rough-and-tumble" play. Wrestling, dancing, and rolling around on the floor—if not violent—are activities that are fun and that stimulate older infants' motoric and sensory systems.

■ Let babies touch their food and even play with it. Infancy is too early to start teaching infants very much about table manners.

■ Provide toys that stimulate the senses. For instance, brightly colored, textured toys with movable parts are enjoyable and help hone infants' senses.

■ Above all, don't focus so much on the goal of stimulating an infant's motoric and sensory abilities that you miss out on the joy and wonder of his or her continuing development.

REVIEW AND RETHINK

REVIEW

■ Sensation refers to the activation of the sense organs by external stimuli. Perception is the analysis, interpretation, and integration of sensations.

■ Infants' abilities in the sensory realm are surprisingly well developed at or shortly after birth. Their perceptions through sight, hearing, smell, taste, and touch help them explore and begin to make sense of the world.

■ Very early, infants can see depth and motion, distinguish colors and patterns, localize and discriminate sounds, recognize the sound of their mothers' voices, and discern their mothers by smell alone. Moreover, infants can relate some perceptions received through one sensory channel to those received through another.

■ Infants are sensitive to pain and to touch. Most medical authorities now subscribe to procedures, including anesthesia, that minimize infants' pain. Furthermore, touch is now recognized as playing an important role in development.

■ Parents and caregivers should help infants engage in physical activities that will help them grow into healthy adults who feel confident about their bodies.

RETHINK

■ Given what was said earlier in this chapter about the way the brain and nervous system develop, what sort of sensory environment would probably be most conducive to healthy neural development in the infant? Why?

■ Are the processes of sensation and perception always linked? Is it possible to sense without perceiving? To perceive without sensing? How?

■ This chapter indicated that the nervous system develops by "pruning down" unnecessary neurons that do not form links with other neurons. Do you think an infant's early preference for the sounds of its home language gives evidence that such a process operates in language development? How?

■ The "ba–pa" experiment described in this chapter—in which sucking intensity decreased once babies became used to the "ba" sound, and then increased again when "ba" was changed to "pa"—was used to show that infants can discriminate highly similar sounds. Another conclusion might be that infants prefer novelty. How might a preference for novelty facilitate infant development?

■ Persons who are born without the use of one sense often develop unusual abilities in one or more other senses. Do you think this phenomenon might relate to the argument about whether integration of the senses precedes differentiation, or vice versa? How?

LOOKING BACK

■ How do the human body and nervous system develop?

- Human babies grow rapidly in height and weight, especially during the first 2 years of life.

- The nervous system contains a huge number of neurons, virtually all of which grow before birth. For neurons to survive and become useful, they must form interconnections with other neurons based on the infant's experience of the world.

- Major principles that govern human growth include the cephalocaudal principle, the proximodistal principle, the principle of hierarchical integration, and the principle of the independence of systems.

■ How does the environment affect the pattern of development?

- Brain development, largely predetermined genetically, also contains a strong element of plasticity—a susceptibility to environmental influences.

- Many aspects of development occur during sensitive periods when the organism is particularly susceptible to environmental influences.

■ What learning tasks must infants undertake in this period?

- One of the primary tasks of the infant is the development of rhythms—cyclical patterns that integrate individual behaviors. An important rhythm pertains to the infant's state—the degree of awareness it displays to stimulation.

- Reflexes are unlearned, automatic responses to stimuli that help newborns survive and protect themselves. Some reflexes also have value as the foundation for future, more conscious behaviors.

- The development of gross and fine motor skills proceeds along a generally consistent timetable in normal children with substantial individual and cultural variations.

■ What is the role of nutrition in physical development?

- Adequate nutrition is essential for physical development. Malnutrition and undernutrition affect physical aspects of growth and also may affect IQ and school performance.

- Breast-feeding has distinct advantages over bottle-feeding, including the nutritional completeness of breast milk, its provision of a degree of immunity to certain childhood diseases, and its easy digestibility. In addition, breast-feeding offers significant physical and emotional benefits to both child and mother.

■ **What sensory capabilities do infants possess?**

- Sensation, the stimulation of the sense organs, differs from perception, the interpretation and integration of sensed stimuli.

- Infants' visual and auditory perception are rather well developed, as are the senses of smell and taste. Infants use their highly developed sense of touch to explore and experience the world. In addition, touch plays an important role in the individual's future development, which is only now being understood.

EPILOGUE: FIRST STEPS

In this chapter, we discussed the nature and pace of infants' physical growth and the pace of less obvious growth in the brain and nervous system, and in the regularity of infants' patterns and states. We looked at motor development, the development of basic reflexes into more complex patterns of behavior, the role of environmental influences on the pace and shape of motor development, and the importance of nutrition.

Turn to the prologue of this chapter, about a baby's first steps, and answer these questions.

1. Which principle or principles of growth (i.e., cephalocaudal, proximodistal, hierarchical integration, independence of systems) account for the progression of physical activities that precede Josh's first steps?

2. What conclusions about Josh's future physical and cognitive development can be drawn from the fact that his first steps occurred approximately 2 months early?

3. In walking at 10 months, Josh outpaced his brother Jon by 4 months. Does this fact have any implications for the brothers' comparative physical or cognitive abilities?

4. Do you think anything changed in the environment between the time Jon and Josh were born that might account for their different "first step" schedules? If you were researching this question, what environmental factors would you look for?

5. What cultural factors might help explain why Josh's parents were so pleased and proud of his accomplishment?

KEY TERMS AND CONCEPTS

cephalocaudal principle (p. 117)
proximodistal principle (p. 118)
principle of hierarchical integration (p. 118)
principle of the independence of systems (p. 118)
neuron (p. 118)
myelin (p. 119)
cerebral cortex (p. 119)
plasticity (p. 120)
sensitive period (p. 120)
rhythms (p. 121)
state (p. 121)

rapid eye movement (REM) sleep (p. 122)
sudden infant death syndrome (SIDS) (p. 124)
reflexes (p. 126)
norms (p. 130)
Brazelton Neonatal Behavioral Assessment Scale (NBAS) (p. 130)
marasmus (p. 133)
kwashiorkor (p. 133)
sensation (p. 138)
perception (p. 138)
multimodal approach to perception (p. 143)

CHAPTER 5

Cognitive Development

PROLOGUE: THE FORGOTTEN MEMORIES OF SIMONA YOUNG

Children in this Romanian orphanage had virtually no human contact.

Simona Young was fated to spend her infancy with virtually no human contact. For up to 20 hours each day, she was left alone in a crib in a squalid Romanian orphanage. Cold bottles of milk were propped above her small body, which she clutched to get nourishment. She rocked back and forth, rarely feeling any soothing touch or hearing words of comfort. Alone in her bleak surroundings, she rocked back and forth for hours on end.

Simona's story, however, has a happy ending. After being adopted by a Canadian couple when she was two, Simona's life is now filled with the usual activities of childhood involving friends, classmates, and above all, a loving family. In fact, now, at age six, she can remember almost nothing of her miserable life in the orphanage. It is as if she has entirely forgotten the past. (Blakeslee, 1995, p. C1)

LOOKING AHEAD   Has Simona really forgotten the first 2 years of her life, or do her memories still exist, hidden behind more current—and pleasant—newer recollections? Will she ever recall her past? Will any memories of her infancy be accurate?

Such questions go the heart of the nature of memory in infancy. Clearly, infants remember *some* information, because without memory they would be unable to speak, recognize others, or, more generally, show the enormous advances in cognitive development that routinely occur throughout infancy. Yet it is still not entirely clear how accurate are our earliest recollections, and when—and how—we form our earliest memories.

We address these and related questions in this chapter as we consider cognitive development during the first years of life. To do this, we consider the work of developmental researchers who seek to understand how infants develop their knowledge and understanding of the world. We first discuss the work of Swiss psychologist Jean Piaget, whose theory of developmental stages served as a highly influential impetus for a considerable amount of work on cognitive development. We look at both the limitations and the contributions of this important developmental specialist.

We then turn to the basic processes by which cognitive growth occurs. After considering how learning takes place, we turn to memory in infants and the ways in which infants process, store, and retrieve information. We discuss the controversial issue of the recollection of events that occurred during infancy. We also address individual differences in intelligence.

Finally, we consider language, the medium by which infants develop communication with others. We look at the roots of language in prelinguistic speech and trace the milestones indicating the development of language skills in the progression from first words to first phrases and sentences. We also look at the characteristics of communication addressed to infants, and some surprising universals in such communication across different cultures.

In sum, after reading this chapter, you will be able to answer these questions:

Q

- What are the fundamental features of Piaget's theories of cognitive development?
- How do infants process information?
- How is infant intelligence measured?
- By what processes do children learn to use language?
- How do children influence the language that adults use to address them?

PIAGET'S APPROACH TO COGNITIVE DEVELOPMENT

Action = Knowledge. In certain ways, this equation sums up the view of Swiss psychologist Jean Piaget (1896–1980) of how infants attain an understanding of the world. He argues that infants do not acquire knowledge from facts communicated by others, nor through sensation and perception. Instead, Piaget suggests that knowledge is the product of direct motor behavior. Although subsequent research has challenged many of his basic explanations and propositions, as we discuss later, one of his views remains unquestioned: In significant ways, infants learn by doing (Piaget, 1952, 1962, 1983; Bullinger, 1997).

As we first noted in Chapter 1, Piaget's theory is based on a stage approach to development. He assumes that all children pass through a series of universal stages in a fixed order. He also believes that the quantity of information acquired in each state increases, and—even more importantly—the quality of knowledge and understanding grows as well. Some approaches to cognition focus on the content of an individual's knowledge about the world, such as might be assessed in a traditional intelligence test. In contrast, Piaget's theory suggests that the focus should be on the change in understanding that occurs as the child moves from one stage to another (Montangero, Maurice-Naville, & Cornu-Wells, et al., 1997).

For instance, infants experience changes in knowledge about what can and cannot occur in the world. Consider an infant who, during an experiment, is exposed to an impossible event, such as seeing her mother simultaneously in three identical versions (due to some clever trickery with mirrors). A 3-month-old infant shows no disturbance over the multiple apparitions and in fact will interact happily with each. However, by 5 months of age, the child becomes quite agitated at the sight of multiple mothers. Apparently by this time the child has figured out that she has but one mother, and viewing three at a time is thoroughly alarming (Bower, 1977). To Piaget, such reactions indicate growth in an underlying mastery of principles regarding the way the world operates.

Swiss psychologist Jean Piaget

According to Piaget, such cognitive development occurs in an orderly fashion. Children pass through four major stages as they move from birth through adolescence: sensorimotor, preoperational, concrete operational, and formal operational. Piaget suggests that movement from one stage to the next occurs when a child reaches an appropriate level of physical maturation and is exposed to relevant types of experience. Without such experience, children are assumed to be incapable of reaching their cognitive potential.

Piaget believed that infants have mental structures called **schemes**, organized patterns of sensorimotor functioning, that adapt and change with mental development. Although at first schemes are related to physical activity, as children develop their schemes move to a mental level, reflecting thought. Schemes are similar to computer software: They direct and determine how data from the world are considered and dealt with (Achenbach, 1992).

Schemes are illustrated by the way in which an infant reacts when given a new cloth book. The infant will touch it, mouth it, perhaps try to tear it or bang it on the floor. To Piaget, each of these actions may represent a scheme, and they are the infant's way of gaining knowledge and understanding of the book. Adults, on the other hand, would use a different scheme upon encountering the book. Rather than picking it up and putting it in their mouths or banging it on the floor, they would probably be drawn to the letters on the page, seeking to understand the book through the meaning of the printed words—a very different approach.

In newborns, schemes are primarily limited to reflexes, such as sucking and rooting. Quickly, however, schemes become more sophisticated as infants become more advanced in their motor capabilities—to Piaget, a signal of the potential for more advanced cognitive development.

Piaget contends that two principles underlie the growth in children's schemes: assimilation and accommodation. **Assimilation** is the process in which people understand an experience in terms of their current stage of cognitive development and way of thinking. Assimilation occurs, then, when a stimulus or event is acted on, perceived, and understood in accordance with existing patterns of thought. For example, an infant who tries to suck on any toy in the same way is assimilating the objects to his existing sucking scheme. Similarly, a child who encounters a flying squirrel at a zoo and calls it a "bird" is assimilating the squirrel to his existing scheme of bird.

In contrast, **accommodation** refers to changes in existing ways of thinking that occur in response to encounters with new stimuli or events. When existing ways of behaving, thinking, and understanding become altered to fit or match novel experiences, accommodation takes place. For instance, when a child modifies the way she sucks on a toy according to the particular shape of the toy, she is accommodating her sucking scheme to the special characteristics of the toy. In the same way, a child who sees a flying squirrel and calls it "a bird with a tail" is beginning to accommodate to new knowledge, modifying her scheme of "bird."

scheme an organized pattern of sensorimotor functioning

assimilation the process in which people understand an experience in terms of their current stage of cognitive development and way of thinking

accommodation changes in existing ways of thinking that occur in response to encounters with new stimuli or events

sensorimotor stage (of cognitive development)   *Piaget's initial major stage of cognitive development, which can be broken down into six substages*

Because the sensorimotor stage of development begins at birth and continues until the child is about 2 years old, we consider it here in detail. (In future chapters, we'll discuss development during the other stages.) In considering the specific substages of the sensorimotor period, it may at first appear that they unfold with great regularity, as infants reach a particular age and smoothly proceed into the next substage. However, the reality of cognitive development, Piaget admits, is somewhat different. First, the ages at which infants actually reach a particular stage vary a good deal among different children. The exact timing of a stage reflects an interaction between the infant's level of physical maturation and the social environment in which the child is being raised. Consequently, although Piaget contends that the order of the substages does not change from one child to the next, the timing can and does vary to some degree.

Furthermore, Piaget argues that development is a more gradual process than the demarcation of different stages might seem to imply. Specifically, infants do not go to sleep one night in one substage and wake up the next morning in the next one. Instead, there is a rather steady shift in behavior as a child moves toward the next stage of cognitive development. Infants also pass through periods of transition, in which some aspects of their behavior reflect the next higher stage, and other aspects indicate their current stage (see Figure 5-1).

The Sensorimotor Period: Charting the Course of Early Cognitive Growth

Piaget suggests that the **sensorimotor stage**, the initial major stage of cognitive development, can be broken down into six substages (summarized in Table 5-1).

Substage 1: Simple Reflexes.   The first substage of the sensorimotor period is *Substage 1: Simple reflexes*, encompassing the first month of life. During this time, the various reflexes that determine the infant's interactions with the world are at the center of its cognitive life. For example, the sucking reflex causes the infant to suck at anything placed in its lips. This sucking behavior, according to Piaget, provides the newborn with information about objects—information that paves the way to the next substage of the sensorimotor period.

At same time, some of the reflexes become modified as a result of the infant's experience with the world. For instance, an infant who is being breast-fed, but who also receives supplemental bottles, may begin to make modifications in how it sucks depending on whether the nipple it is sucking is on a breast or a bottle.

FIGURE 5-1

TRANSITIONS

Infants do not suddenly shift from one stage of cognitive development to the next. Instead, Piaget argues that there is a period of transition, in which some behavior reflects one stage, and other behavior reflects the more advanced stage.

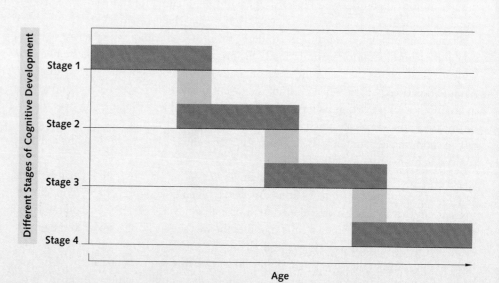

Transition between Stages

TABLE 5-1

PIAGET'S SIX SUBSTAGES OF THE SENSORIMOTOR STAGE

Substage	Age	Description	Example
SUBSTAGE 1: Simple reflexes	First month of life	During this period, the various reflexes that determine the infant's interactions with the world are at the center of its cognitive life.	The sucking reflex causes the infant to suck at anything placed in its lips.
SUBSTAGE 2: First habits and primary circular reactions	From 1 to 4 months	At this age infants begin to coordinate what were separate actions into single, integrated activities.	An infant might combine grasping an object with sucking on it, or staring at something with touching it.
SUBSTAGE 3: Secondary circular reactions	From 4 to 8 months	During this period, infants take major strides in shifting their cognitive horizons beyond themselves and begin to act on the outside world.	A child who repeatedly picks up a rattle in her crib and shakes it in different ways to see how the sound changes is demonstrating her ability to modify her cognitive scheme about shaking rattles.
SUBSTAGE 4: Coordination of secondary circular reactions	From 8 to 12 months	In this stage infants begin to use more calculated approaches to producing events, coordinating several schemes to generate a single act. They achieve object permanence during this stage.	An infant will push one toy out of the way to reach another toy that is lying, partially exposed, under it.
SUBSTAGE 5: Tertiary circular reactions	From 12 to 18 months	At this age infants develop what Piaget regards as the deliberate variation of actions that bring desirable consequences. Rather than just repeating enjoyable activities as in Substage 4, infants appear to carry out miniature experiments to observe the consequences.	A child will drop a toy repeatedly, varying the position from which he dropped it, carefully observing each time to see where it fell.
SUBSTAGE 6: Beginnings of thought	From 18 months to 2 years	The major achievement of Substage 6 is the capacity for mental representation or symbolic thought. Piaget argued that only at this stage can infants imagine where objects that they cannot see might be.	Children can even plot in their heads unseen trajectories of objects, so that if a ball rolls under a piece of furniture, they can figure out where it is likely to emerge on the other side.

Substage 2: First Habits and Primary Circular Reactions. *Substage 2: First habits and primary circular reactions*, the second substage of the sensorimotor period, occurs from 1 to 4 months of age. In this period, infants begin to coordinate what were separate actions into single, integrated activities. For instance, an infant might combine grasping an object with sucking on it, or staring at something with touching it.

If an activity engages children's interests, they may repeat it over and over, simply for the sake of continuing to experience it. A **circular reaction** permits the construction of cognitive schemes through the repetition of a chance motor event. *Primary circular reactions* are schemes reflecting an infant's repetition of interesting or enjoyable actions, just for the enjoyment of doing them. Thus, when an infant first puts his thumb in his mouth and begins to suck, it is a mere chance event. However, when he repeatedly sucks his thumb in the future, it represents a primary circular reaction, which he is repeating because the sensation of sucking is pleasurable.

Substage 3: Secondary Circular Reactions. *Substage 3: Secondary circular reactions* occurs from 4 to 8 months of age. During this period, infants take major strides in shifting their cognitive horizons beyond themselves and begin to act on the outside world. For

circular reaction *an activity that permits the construction of cognitive schemes through the repetition of a chance motor event*

instance, when infants, through chance activities, produce an enjoyable event in their environment, they now seek to repeat that event. A child who repeatedly picks up a rattle in her crib and shakes it in different ways to see how the sound changes is demonstrating her ability to modify her cognitive scheme about shaking rattles. She is engaging in what Piaget calls secondary circular reactions.

Secondary circular reactions are schemes regarding repeated actions meant to bring about a desirable consequence. The major difference between primary circular reactions and secondary circular reactions is whether the infant's activity is focused on the infant and his or her own body (primary circular reactions) or involves actions relating to the world outside (secondary circular reactions).

During the third substage, the degree of vocalization increases substantially as infants come to notice that if they make noises, other people around them will respond with noises of their own. Similarly, infants begin to imitate the sounds made by others. Vocalization becomes a secondary circular reaction that ultimately helps lead to the development of language and the formation of social relationships.

Substage 4: Coordination of Secondary Circular Reactions. One of the major leaps forward in cognitive development comes as infants move through the next substage, *Substage 4: Coordination of secondary circular reactions*, which lasts from around 8 months to 12 months. Before this stage, behavior involved direct action on objects. When something caught an infant's interest, she attempted to repeat the event using a single scheme. However, in Substage 4, infants begin to use more calculated approaches to producing events. They employ **goal-directed behavior**, in which several schemes are combined and coordinated to generate a single act to solve a problem. For instance, they will push one toy out of the way to reach another toy that is lying, partially exposed, under it. They also begin to anticipate upcoming events. For instance, Piaget tells of his son Laurent, who at 8 months "recognizes by a certain noise caused by air that he is nearing the end of his feeding and, instead of insisting on drinking to the last drop, he rejects his bottle . . ." (Piaget, 1952, pp. 248–249).

Infants' newfound purposefulness, their ability to use means to attain particular ends, and their skill in anticipating future circumstances owe their appearance in part to the developmental achievement of object permanence that emerges in Substage 4. **Object permanence** is the realization that people and objects exist even when they cannot be seen. It is a simple principle, but its mastery has profound consequences.

Consider, for instance, how a 7-month-old infant named Chu, who has yet to learn the idea of object permanence, reacts when his father, who has been shaking a rattle in front of him, takes the rattle and places it under a blanket. To Chu, who has not mastered the concept of object permanence, the rattle no longer exists, and he will make no effort to look for it.

Several months later, when he is in Substage 4, the story is quite different (see Figure 5-2). This time, as soon as his father places the rattle under the blanket, Chu tries to toss the cover aside, eagerly searching for the rattle. Chu clearly has learned that the object continues to exist even when it cannot be seen. For the infant who achieves an understanding of object permanence, then, out of sight is decidedly not out of mind.

The attainment of object permanence extends not only to inanimate objects, but to people, too. It gives Chu the security that his father and mother still exist even when they have left the room. This awareness is likely a key element in the development of social attachments, which we consider in Chapter 6. The recognition of object permanence also feeds infants' growing assertiveness: As they realize that an object taken away from them doesn't just cease to exist, but is merely somewhere else, their only-too-human reaction may be to want it back—and quickly.

Although the understanding of object permanence emerges in Substage 4, it is only a rudimentary understanding. It takes several months for the concept to be fully comprehended, and infants continue for several months to make certain kinds of errors relating to object permanence. For instance, they often are fooled when they watch as a toy is first

goal-directed behavior *behavior in which several schemes are combined and coordinated to generate a single act to solve a problem*

object permanence *the realization that people and objects exist even when they cannot be seen*

FIGURE 5-2

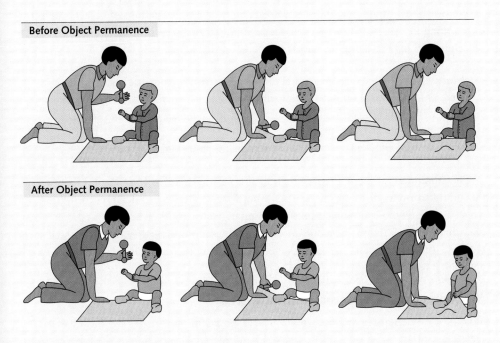

Before Object Permanence

After Object Permanence

Before an infant has understood the idea of object permanence, he will not search for an object that has been hidden right before his eyes. But several months later, he will search for it, illustrating that he has attained object permanence.

hidden under one blanket and then under a second blanket. In seeking out the toy, Substage 4 infants most often turn to the first hiding place, ignoring the blanket under which the toy is currently located—even though the hiding was done in plain view.

Substage 5: Tertiary Circular Reactions. *Substage 5: Tertiary circular reactions* is reached at around the age of 12 months and extends to 18 months. As the name of the stage indicates, during this period infants develop what Piaget labeled *tertiary circular reactions*, schemes regarding the deliberate variation of actions that bring desirable consequences. Rather than just repeating enjoyable activities, as they do with secondary circular reactions, infants appear to carry out miniature experiments to observe the consequences.

For example, Piaget observed his son Laurent dropping a toy swan repeatedly, varying the position from which he dropped it, carefully observing each time to see where it fell. Instead of just repeating the action each time (as in a secondary circular reaction), Laurent made modifications in the situation to learn about their consequences. As you may recall from our discussion of research methods in Chapter 1, this behavior represents the essence of the scientific method: An experimenter varies a situation in a laboratory to learn the effects of the variation. To infants in Substage 5, the world is their laboratory, and they spend their days leisurely carrying out one miniature experiment after another.

What is most striking about infants' behavior during Substage 5 is their interest in the unexpected. Unanticipated events are treated not only as interesting, but also as something to be explained and understood. Infants' discoveries can lead to newfound skills, some of which may cause a certain amount of chaos. For instance, an infant may pull at a tablecloth in order to reach a plate of cookies or throw a water toy into the tub with increasing vigor to see how high the water splashes.

Substage 6: Beginnings of Thought. The final stage of the sensorimotor period is *Substage 6: Beginnings of thought*, which lasts from around 18 months to 2 years. The major achievement of Substage 6 is the capacity for mental representation, or symbolic thought. A **mental representation** is an internal image of a past event or object. Piaget argued that by this stage infants can imagine where objects might be that they cannot see. They can

mental representation *an internal image of a past event or object*

deferred imitation *an act in which a person who is no longer present is imitated by children who have witnessed a similar act*

even plot in their heads unseen trajectories of objects, so if a ball rolls under a piece of furniture, they can figure out where it is likely to emerge on the other side.

Because of children's new abilities to create internal representations of objects, their understanding of causality also becomes more sophisticated. For instance, consider Piaget's description of his son Laurent's efforts to open a garden gate:

> Laurent tries to open a garden gate but cannot push it forward because it is held back by a piece of furniture. He cannot account either visually or by any sound for the cause that prevents the gate from opening, but after having tried to force it he suddenly seems to understand; he goes around the wall, arrives at the other side of the gate, moves the armchair which holds it firm, and opens it with a triumphant expression. (Piaget, 1954, p. 296)

The attainment of mental representation also permits another important development: the ability to pretend. Using the skill of what Piaget refers to as **deferred imitation**, in which a person who is no longer present is imitated later, children are able to pretend that they are driving a car, feeding a doll, or cooking dinner long after they have witnessed such scenes played out in reality. To Piaget, deferred imitation provided clear evidence for internal mental representation.

Appraising Piaget: Support and Challenges

Most developmental researchers would probably agree that in many significant ways, Piaget's descriptions of how cognitive development proceeds during infancy are quite accurate (Harris, 1983, 1987). Yet, when many of the specifics of Piagetian theory are considered, there is substantial disagreement over the validity of the theory and its predictions.

Let's start with what is clearly correct about the Piagetian approach. Piaget was a masterful reporter of children's behavior, and his descriptions of their growth during infancy remain a monument to his powers of observation. Furthermore, literally thousands of studies have supported Piaget's view that children learn much about the world by acting on objects in their environment. Finally, the broad outlines sketched out by Piaget of the sequence of cognitive development and the increasing cognitive accomplishments that occur during infancy are generally accurate (Gratch & Schatz, 1987).

On the other hand, specific aspects of the theory have come under increasing scrutiny—and criticism—in the decades since Piaget carried out his pioneering work. For example, some researchers question the stage conception that forms the basis of Piaget's theory. To critics, development proceeds in a much more continuous fashion than Piaget's

With the attainment of the cognitive skill of deferred imitation, children are able to imitate people and scenes they have witnessed in the past.

stage theory suggests. Rather than showing major leaps of competence at the end of one stage and the beginning of the next, improvement comes in more gradual increments, growing step-by-step in a skill-by-skill manner.

For instance, developmental researcher Robert Siegler suggests that cognitive development proceeds not in stages but in "waves." According to him, children don't one day drop a mode of thinking and the next take up a new form. Instead, there is an ebb and flow of cognitive approaches that children use to understand the world. One day children may use one form of cognitive strategy, whereas another day they may choose a less advanced strategy—moving back and forth over a period of time. Although one strategy may be used most frequently at a given age, children still may have access to alternative ways of thinking. Siegler thus sees cognitive development as in constant flux (Siegler, 1995).

Other critics dispute Piaget's notion that cognitive development is grounded in motor activities. Some developmental specialists charge that such a view ignores the importance of the sophisticated sensory and perceptual systems that are present from a very early age in infancy—systems about which Piaget knew little, because so much of the research illustrating their sophistication was done relatively recently (Butterworth, 1994). Critics also point to studies involving children born without arms and legs (due to their mothers' use of drugs during pregnancy that, unbeknown to them at the time, could cause birth defects.) These studies show that such children display normal cognitive development, despite their lack of practice with motor activities (Decarrie, 1969).

To bolster their views, Piaget's critics also point to recent studies that cast doubt on Piaget's view that infants are incapable of mastering the concept of object permanence until they are close to a year old. For instance, some work suggests that younger infants may not appear to understand object permanence because the techniques used to test their abilities are too insensitive (Baillargeon & DeVos, 1991; Munakata et al., 1997).

It may be that a 4-month-old doesn't search for a rattle hidden under a blanket because she hasn't learned the motor skills necessary to do the searching—not because she doesn't understand that the rattle still exists. Similarly, the apparent inability of young infants to comprehend object permanence may reflect more about their memory deficits than their lack of understanding of the concept: The memories of young infants may be poor enough that they simply do not recall the earlier concealment of the toy (Diamond, 1991). In fact, when more age-appropriate tasks were employed, some researchers found indications of object permanence in children as young as 3 1/2 months (Baillargeon, 1987; Mandler, 1990; Spelke, 1991).

Other types of behavior likewise seem to emerge earlier than Piaget suggested. For instance, recall the ability of neonates to imitate basic facial expressions of adults just hours after birth, as we discussed in Chapter 3. The presence of such skill at such an early age contradicts Piaget's view that initially infants are able to imitate only behavior that they see in others, using parts of their own body that they can plainly view—such as their hands and feet. In fact, facial imitation suggests that humans are born with a basic, innate capability for imitating others' actions, a capability that depends on certain kinds of environmental experiences (Meltzoff & Moore, 1989), but one that Piaget believed develops later in infancy.

Some of the most powerful evidence against Piaget's views emerges from work with children in non-Western cultures. For instance, some evidence suggests that the timing of the emergence of various cognitive skills among children in non-Western cultures differs from the timing observed in children living in Europe and the United States. Infants raised in the Ivory Coast of Africa, for example, reach the various substages of the sensorimotor period at an earlier age than infants reared in France (Dasen et al., 1978). This is not altogether surprising, because parents in the Ivory Coast tend to emphasize motor skills more heavily than parents in Western societies, thereby providing greater opportunity for practice of those skills (Dasen et al., 1978; Rogoff & Chavajay, 1995).

Despite these problems regarding Piaget's view of the sensorimotor period, even his most passionate critics concede that he has provided us with a masterful description of the broad outlines of sensorimotor development during infancy. His failings seem to be in underestimating the capabilities of younger infants and in his claims that sensorimotor skills develop in a consistent, fixed pattern. Still, his influence has been enormous, and although the focus of many contemporary developmental researchers has shifted to newer information-processing approaches that we discuss next, Piaget remains a towering and pioneering figure in the field of development (Beilin & Pufall, 1992; Demetriou, Shayer, & Efklides, 1993; Siegler, 1994; Fischer & Hencke, 1996).

REVIEW AND RETHINK

REVIEW

■ Jean Piaget's theory of human cognitive development involves a succession of stages through which children progress from birth to adolescence.

■ As humans move from one stage to another, the way they understand the world changes as a function of their maturation and their experiences.

■ The sensorimotor stage, from birth to about 2 years, involves a gradual progression through simple reflexes, single coordinated activities, interest in the outside world, purposeful combinations of activities, manipulation of actions to produce desired outcomes, and symbolic thought.

■ Piaget, whose influence has been substantial, is respected as a careful observer of children's behavior and a generally accurate interpreter of the way human cognitive development proceeds.

■ Critics of Piaget fault him for underestimating infants' capabilities and for regarding as universal some aspects of human development that appear to be subject to cultural and individual variations.

RETHINK

■ In this chapter, an individual's approach to a book is used as an example of a difference in scheme between children and adults. Name some other examples of different ways that adults and children understand and interpret objects or events in their worlds.

■ Name some examples of the principles of assimilation and accommodation at work in child development. Do these principles function in adult human learning?

■ In what ways do you think the concept of object permanence might foster the infant's social and emotional development?

■ Why is the emergence of a capacity for mental representation essential for the development of thought? In what ways do you think the mental representations of a blind infant differ from those of a sighted infant? In what ways might they be the same?

■ In general, what are some implications for childrearing practices of Piaget's observations about the ways children gain an understanding of the world?

INFORMATION-PROCESSING APPROACHES TO COGNITIVE DEVELOPMENT

At the age of 3 months, Amber Nordstrom breaks into a smile as her brother Marcus stands over her crib, picks up a doll, and makes a whistling noise through his teeth. In fact, Amber never seems to tire of Marcus's efforts at making her smile, and soon whenever Marcus appears and simply picks up the doll, her lips begin to curl into a smile.

Clearly, Amber remembers Marcus and his humorous ways. But how did she learn this? What is it that makes Marcus distinctive to her? How does she come to associate Marcus's presence with previous entertaining encounters?

To answer questions such as these, we need to diverge from the road that Piaget laid out for us. Rather than seeking to identify the universal milestones in cognitive development through which all infants pass, as Piaget tried to do, we must consider the processes by which individuals acquire and use the information to which they are exposed. We need, then, to focus less on the qualitative changes in infants' mental lives and consider more closely their quantitative capabilities.

Information-processing approaches to cognitive development seek to identify the way that individuals take in, use, and store information (Siegler, 1998). According to this approach, the quantitative changes in infants' abilities to organize and manipulate information represent the hallmarks of cognitive development.

Taking this perspective, cognitive growth is characterized by increasing sophistication in information processing, similar to the way a computer program becomes more sophisticated and useful as the programmer modifies it and as the size of the computer's memory and its computational sophistication increase. Information-processing approaches, then, focus on the types of "mental programs" that people use when they seek to solve problems (Mehler & DuPoux, 1994; Reyna, 1997).

information-processing approaches
the model that seeks to identify the way that individuals take in, use, and store information

Encoding, Storage, and Retrieval: The Foundations of Information Processing

Information processing has three basic aspects: encoding, storage, and retrieval (see Figure 5-3). *Encoding* is the process by which information is initially recorded in a form usable to memory. Infants and children—indeed, all people—are exposed to a massive amount of information; if they tried to process it all, they would be overwhelmed. Consequently, they encode selectively, picking and choosing the information to which they will pay attention.

Even if someone has been exposed to the information initially, and has encoded it in an appropriate way, there is still no guarantee that he or she will be able to use it in the future. Information must also have been stored in memory adequately. *Storage* refers to the maintenance of material saved in memory. Finally, success in using the material in the future depends on retrieval processes. *Retrieval* is the process by which material in memory storage is located, brought into awareness, and used.

Information-processing approaches suggest that the processes of encoding, storage, and retrieval are analogous to different parts of a computer. Encoding can be thought of as a computer's keyboard, through which one inputs information; storage is the computer's hard drive, where information is stored; and retrieval is analogous to a computer's screen, where information is displayed. Only when all three processes are operating—encoding, storage, and retrieval—can information be processed.

Automatization.   In some cases, encoding, storage, and retrieval are relatively automatic, but in other cases they are deliberate. *Automatization* is the degree to which an activity requires attention. Processes that require relatively little attention are automatic; processes that require relatively large amounts of attention are controlled.

FIGURE 5-3

Encoding (initial recording of information)	Storage (information saved for future use)	Retrieval (recovery of stored information)

INFORMATION PROCESSING

The process by which information is encoded, stored, and retrieved.

memory *the process by which information is initially recorded, stored, and retrieved*

Automatic processes help children in their initial encounters with the world by "automatically" priming them to process information in particular ways. For instance, by the age of 5, children automatically encode information in terms of frequency. For instance, they automatically become aware of how often they have encountered various people, permitting them to differentiate familiar from unfamiliar people (Hasher & Zacks, 1984).

Furthermore, without intending to and without being aware of it, infants and children develop a sense of how often different stimuli are found together simultaneously. This permits them to develop an understanding of *concepts*, categorizations of objects, events, or people that share common properties. For example, by encoding the information that four legs, a wagging tail, and barking are often found together, we learn very early in life to understand the concept of "dog." Children—as well as adults—are rarely aware of how they learn such concepts, and they are often unable to articulate the features that distinguish one concept (such as a dog) from another (such as cat). Instead, learning tends to occur automatically. (And sometimes such learning is unexpectedly sophisticated, as we consider in the "Directions in Development" box.)

Automatization also provides the benefit of permitting more efficient information processing, allowing children to concentrate on other mental problems. On the other hand, automatization can backfire: In some situations a nonautomatic response is required, but an automatic response, which occurs readily, is employed instead. For instance, a young child who encounters a cat for the first time, but who automatically categorizes it as a dog because it has four legs and a tail, is a victim of automaticity.

Cognitive Architecture. Although the ability to encode, store, and retrieve material is central to information processing, these processes are not the whole story. In fact, they don't provide an explanation of how information actually moves through the cognitive architecture. *Cognitive architecture* refers to the basic, enduring structures and features of information processing that are relatively constant over the course of development.

Cognitive architecture determines the specific steps through which material is processed as it travels through the human mind. Information-processing theorists assume that the basic architecture of information-processing systems is constant over the course of development, although the speed and capacity of the system are thought to grow. In short, developmental change is reflected not in changes in cognitive architecture, but in the efficiency and capacity of information processing over time (Rose & Feldman, 1997; Siegler, 1998).

We turn now to several aspects of information processing, focusing on memory and individual differences in intelligence.

Memory During Infancy: They Must Remember This . . .

Think back to the story of Simona, the Romanian orphan described at the beginning of the chapter. How likely is it that Simona truly remembers nothing of her infancy? And if she ever does recall her first 2 years of life, how accurate will her memories be? To answer these questions, we need to consider the qualities of memory that exist during infancy.

Memory Capabilities in Infancy. Certainly, infants have **memory** capabilities, defined as the process by which information is initially recorded, stored, and retrieved. As we've seen, the ability of infants to distinguish new stimuli from old, as illustrated by habituation, implies that some memory of the old must be present. Unless the infants had some memory of an original stimulus, it would be impossible for them to recognize that a new stimulus differed from the earlier one (Newcombe, Drummey, & Lie, 1995).

However, infants' capability to habituate and show other basic forms of learning tells us little about how age brings about changes in the capacities of memory and in its fundamental nature. Consider the question of capacity: Do infants' memory capabilities increase as they get older? The answer is clearly affirmative. In one study, infants were taught that they could move a mobile hanging over the crib by kicking (see Figure 5-4). It took only a

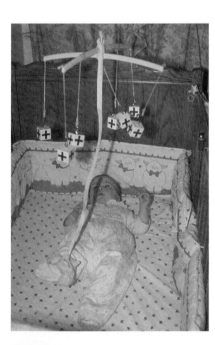

FIGURE 5-4 EARLY SIGNS OF MEMORY

Infants who had learned the association between a moving mobile and kicking showed surprising recall ability if they were exposed to a reminder.

Directions in Development

Running the Numbers: The Surprising Ability of Infants to Learn Statistical and Mathematical Relationships

Suppose you listened to a series of three-syllable nonsense words, spoken sequentially with no pauses between the words. After listening for 2 minutes, would you be able to tell where one nonsense word stopped and the next word started, and which of the nonsense words you'd heard most frequently?

It wouldn't be easy, but surprising evidence from a recent study finds that even 8-month-old infants can manage to do surprisingly well at the task. In the study, infants heard a series of three-syllable words strung together with no pauses between syllables. Some of the three-syllable sequences were repeated as a unit several times, whereas other sequences occurred less frequently (Saffran, Aslin, & Newport, 1996).

The idea behind the study was to determine whether infants could learn to pick out specific three-syllable words based on variations in the probability of which sound would follow another. More specifically, over the 2-minute period, infants heard a stream of syllables repeated without any interruption, such as *bidakupadotigolabubidaku*. . . . There were no pauses and the syllables did not vary in speed or pitch. The only clues as to where a nonsense word began or stopped was variation in the statistical probability that certain sounds would be followed by another.

In the later test phase of the study, the 8-month-old infants were able to discriminate words that contained syllable patterns that they had heard earlier from syllable patterns that they had not heard earlier. In short, the infants had learned, and remembered, the syllable patterns following a 2-minute, one-time exposure, based only on the statistical probabilities relating to what syllables were most likely to be close together.

The results of the study demonstrate that infants have the ability to learn subtle statistical patterns and relationships; these results are consistent with a growing body of research showing that the mathematical skills of infants are surprisingly sophisticated. For instance, another experiment showed that infants as young as 5 months are able to calculate the outcome of simple addition and subtraction problems (Wynn, 1992, 1995). In a study by developmental psychologist Karen Wynn, infants first were shown an object—a 4-inch-high Mickey Mouse statuette (see Figure 5-5). A screen then came

FIGURE 5-5 MICKEY MOUSE MATH

Research conducted by Dr. Karen Wynn found that 5-month-olds like Michelle Follet, pictured here, reacted differently according to whether the number of Mickey Mouse statuettes they saw represented correct or incorrect addition.

up, hiding the statuette. Next, the experimenter showed the infants a second, identical Mickey Mouse, and then placed it behind the same screen.

Finally, depending on the experimental condition, one of two outcomes occurred. In the "correct addition" condition, the screen dropped, revealing the two statuettes (analogous to 1 + 1 = 2). But in the "incorrect addition" condition, the screen dropped to reveal just one statuette (analogous to the incorrect 1 + 1 = 1).

Because infants look longer at unexpected occurrences than at expected ones, the researchers examined the pattern of infants' gazes in the different conditions. In support of the notion that infants can distinguish between correct and incorrect addition, the infants in the experiment gazed longer at the incorrect result than at the correct one. In a similar procedure, infants looked longer at incorrect subtraction problems than at correct ones. The conclusion: Infants have rudimentary mathematical skills.

The results of this research suggest that infants have an innate ability to comprehend certain basic mathematical functions and statistical patterns. This inborn proficiency is likely to form the basis for learning more complex mathematics and statistical relationships later in life, as well as paving the way for language acquisition (Sansavini, Bertoncini, & Giovanelli, 1997).

few days for 2-month-old infants to forget their training, but 6-month-old infants still remembered for as long as 3 weeks (Rovee-Collier, 1984, 1993).

Furthermore, infants who were later prompted to recall the association between kicking and moving the mobile showed evidence that the memory continued to exist even longer.

Infants who had received just two training sessions lasting 9 minutes each still recalled about a week later, as illustrated by the fact that they began to kick when placed in the crib with the mobile. Two weeks later, however, they made no effort to kick, suggesting that they had forgotten entirely.

But they hadn't: When a reminder was given—a look at a moving mobile—the memory was apparently reactivated. In fact, the infants could remember the association, following prompting, for as long as an additional month (Sullivan, Rovee-Collier, & Tynes, 1979). Other evidence confirms these results, suggesting that hints can reactivate memories that at first seem lost, and that the older the infant, the more effective such prompting is (Rovee-Collier & Hayne, 1987; Hayne & Rovee-Collier, 1995; Rovee-Collier & Gerhardstein, 1997).

Is memory in infants different from that in older children and adults? Some researchers suggest that memory during infancy depends on particular neurological systems in the brain—specifically, the hippocampus—and that memory in later life involves additional structures of the brain (Nelson, 1995).

On the other hand, although information and the parts of the brain involved in memory may differ during infancy, other researchers suggest that information is processed similarly throughout the life span. According to memory expert Carolyn Rovee-Collier, people, regardless of their age, gradually lose memories, although they may regain them if reminders are provided. Moreover, the more times a memory is retrieved, the more enduring the memory becomes (Rovee-Collier, 1993).

The Duration of Memories.   Although the processes that underlie memory retention and recall seem similar throughout the life span, the quantity of information stored and recalled does differ markedly as infants develop. Older infants can remember information longer, and they can retrieve it more rapidly.

Researchers disagree on the age from which memories can be retrieved. Some research supports the notion of **infantile amnesia**, the lack of memory for experiences that occurred prior to 3 years of age. For instance, consider whether you can recall the birth of a younger brother or sister. For most college students, if the birth happened before they reached the age of 3, they can remember virtually nothing about the event (Sheingold & Tenney, 1982).

However, other research shows surprising retention in infants (Mandler & McDonough, 1994; Jusczyk & Hohne, 1997). For example, Nancy Myers and her colleagues exposed a group of 6-month-old children to an unusual series of events in a laboratory, such as intermittent periods of light and dark and unusual sounds. When the children were later tested at the age of 1 1/2 years or 2 1/2 years, they demonstrated clear evidence that they had some memory of their participation in the earlier experience. Not only did particular behaviors, such as reaching, reflect their earlier participation, but they seemed more familiar with the testing situation itself, showing more willingness to remain in the situation than a control group of same-age children (Myers, Clifton, & Clarkson, 1987; Perris, Myers, & Clifton, 1990).

Such findings are consistent with evidence that the physical record of a memory in the brain appears to be relatively permanent, suggesting that memories, even from infancy, may be enduring (Newcombe & Fox, 1994). However, because memories may be stored somewhere in the recesses of the brain, they may not be easily, or accurately, retrieved. Memories are susceptible to interference from other, newer information, which may displace or block out the older information, thereby preventing its recall (Potter, 1990). Furthermore, recall of memories is sensitive to the environmental context in which the memories were initially formed. If changes have occurred in the context relating to the initial memories, then recall may be difficult, if not impossible (Ceci & Hembrooke, 1993; Rovee-Collier, 1993).

infantile amnesia   *the lack of memory for experiences that occurred prior to 3 years of age*

Ultimately, the issue of whether memories formed during infancy are retained into adulthood remains an open—and controversial—issue (Bauer, 1996). Although infants' memories may be highly detailed and can be enduring if the infants experience repeated reminders, it is still not clear how accurate those memories remain over the course of the life span. In fact, research shows that early memories are susceptible to misrecollection if people are exposed to related, and contradictory, information following the initial formation of the memory. Not only does such new information potentially impair recall of the original material, but the new material may be inadvertently incorporated into the original memory, thereby corrupting its accuracy (Rovee-Collier et al., 1993; Fivush, 1995).

In sum, the data suggest that, at least theoretically, it is possible for memories to remain intact from a very young age—if subsequent information does not interfere with them. This is a big "if" because most memories are likely to involve experiences that are somehow related to subsequent experiences and therefore susceptible to interference. Ultimately, it may be that the validity of recollections of memories from infancy needs to be evaluated on a case-by-case basis.

Individual Differences in Intelligence: Is One Infant Smarter Than Another?

Maddy Rodriguez is a bundle of curiosity and energy. At 6 months of age, she cries heartily if she can't reach a toy, and when she sees a reflection of herself in a mirror, she gurgles and seems, in general, to find the situation quite amusing.

***

Jared Lynch, at 6 months, is a good deal more inhibited than Maddy. He doesn't seem to care much when a ball rolls out of his reach, losing interest in it rapidly. And, unlike Maddy, when he sees himself in a mirror, he pretty much ignores the reflection.

As anyone who has spent any time at all observing more than one baby can tell you, not all infants are alike. Some are full of energy and life, apparently displaying a natural-born curiosity, whereas others seem, by comparison, somewhat less interested in the world around them. Does this mean that such infants differ in intelligence?

Answering questions about how and to what degree infants vary in their underlying intelligence is not easy. Although it is clear that different infants show significant variations in their behavior, the issue of just what types of behavior may be related to cognitive ability is complicated. Interestingly, the examination of individual differences among infants was the initial approach taken by developmental specialists to understand cognitive development, and such issues still represent an important focus within the field.

What Is Infant Intelligence?   Before we can address whether and how infants may differ in intelligence, we need to consider what is meant by the term *intelligence*. Educators, psychologists, and other experts on development have yet to agree on a general definition of intelligent behavior, even among adults. Is it the ability to do well in scholastic endeavors? Competence in navigating across treacherous seas, such as that shown by peoples of the South Pacific, who have no knowledge of Western navigational techniques? Proficiency in business negotiations?

Defining intelligence in infants is even more problematic than with adults. Is it the speed with which a new task is learned through classical or operant conditioning? The rapidity of habituation? The age at which an infant learns to crawl or walk? Furthermore, even if we are able to identify particular behaviors that seem validly to differentiate one infant from another in terms of intelligence during infancy, we need to address a further, and probably more important, issue: How well do measures of infant intelligence relate to eventual adult intelligence?

Determining what is meant by intelligence in infants represents a major challenge for developmentalists.

developmental quotient an overall developmental score that relates to performance in four domains: motor skills, language use, adaptive behavior, and personal-social

Bayley Scales of Infant Development a measure that evaluates an infant's development from 2 to 30 months

Clearly such questions are not simple, and no simple answers have been found. However, developmental specialists have devised several approaches (summarized in Table 5-2) to illuminate individual differences in intelligence during infancy.

Developmental Scales. Developmental psychologist Arnold Gesell formulated the earliest measure of infant development, which was designed to screen out normally developing babies from those with atypical development (Gesell, 1946). Gesell based his scale on examinations of hundreds of babies. He compared their performance at different ages to learn what behaviors were most common at a particular age. If an infant varied significantly from the norms of a given age, he or she was considered to be developmentally delayed or advanced.

Gesell's primary motivation in developing his norms was to screen out abnormally developing infants for adoption. Following the lead of researchers who sought to quantify intelligence through a specific score (known as an intelligence quotient, or IQ, score), Gesell developed a developmental quotient, or DQ. The **developmental quotient** is an overall developmental score that relates to performance in four domains: motor skills (for example, balance and sitting), language use, adaptive behavior (such as alertness and exploration), and personal-social (for example, feeding and dressing).

Later researchers were motivated by different goals. For instance, Nancy Bayley developed one of the most widely used measures for infants. The **Bayley Scales of Infant Development** evaluate an infant's development from 2 to 30 months (Bayley, 1969). The Bayley Scales focus on two areas: mental and motor abilities. The mental scale focuses on the senses, perception, memory, learning, problem solving, and language, whereas the motor scale evaluates fine and gross motor skills (see Table 5-3). Like Gesell's approach, the Bayley yields a developmental quotient (DQ). A child who scores at an average level—meaning average performance for other children at the same age—receives a score of 100.

The virtue of approaches such as those taken by Gesell and Bayley is that they provide a good snapshot of an infant's current developmental level. Using these scales, we can tell in an objective manner whether a particular infant falls behind or is ahead of his or her

TABLE 5-2

APPROACHES USED TO DETECT DIFFERENCES IN INTELLIGENCE DURING INFANCY

Development quotient	Formulated by Arnold Gesell, the developmental quotient is an overall developmental score that relates to performance in four domains: motor skills (balance and sitting), language use, adaptive behavior (alertness and exploration), and personal-social (feeding and dressing).
Bayley Scales of Infant Development	Developed by Nancy Bayley, the Bayley Scales of Infant Development evaluate an infant's development from 2 to 30 months. The Bayley Scales focus on two areas: mental (senses, perception, memory, learning, problem solving, and language) and motor abilities (fine and gross motor skills).
Visual-recognition memory measurement	Measures of visual-recognition memory, the memory of and recognition of a stimulus that has been previously seen, also relate to intelligence. The more quickly an infant can retrieve a representation of a stimulus from memory, the more efficient, presumably, is that infant's information processing.

TABLE 5-3

SAMPLE ITEMS FROM THE BAYLEY SCALES OF INFANT DEVELOPMENT

MENTAL SCALE		MOTOR SCALE	
Age (in Months)	Item	Age (in Months)	Item
0.1	Responds to sound of rattle	0.1	Lifts head when held at shoulder
1.5	Social smile	1.8	Turns: side to back
2.0	Visually recognizes mother	2.3	Sits with support
3.8	Turns head to sound of cube	3.2	Turns: back to side
4.1	Reaches for cube	5.3	Pulls to sitting
4.8	Discriminates stranger	6.4	Rolls: back to stomach
6.0	Looks for fallen spoon	6.6	Sits alone steadily
7.0	Vocalizes four different syllables	8.1	Pulls to standing
9.1	Responds to verbal request	9.6	Walks with help
13.4	Removes pellet from bottle	11.7	Walks alone
14.2	Says two words	14.6	Walks backward
18.8	Uses words to make wants known	16.1	Walks upstairs with help
19.3	Names one picture (e.g., dog)	23.4	Jumps off floor

(*Source*: Adapted from the *Bayley Scales of Infant Development*. Copyright © 1969 by The Psychological Corporation. Reproduced by permission. All rights reserved. "Bayley Scales of Infant Development" is a registered trademark of the Psychological Corporations.

same-age peers. They are particularly useful in identifying infants who are substantially behind their peers, and who therefore need immediate special attention (Culbertson & Gyurke, 1990).

On the other hand, except in extreme cases, such scales are not very good at all in predicting a child's future course of development. A child whose development at the age of 1 year is relatively slow, as identified by these measures, does not necessarily display slow development at age 5, or 12, or 25. The association between most measures of behavior during infancy and adult intelligence, then, is minimal (Bornstein & Sigman, 1986; Siegel, 1989; DiLalla et al., 1990; Milfese & Acheson, 1997).

Because it is difficult with these global measures to obtain measures of infant intelligence that are related to later intelligence, investigators have turned in the last decade to other techniques that may help assess intelligence in a meaningful way. Some have proven to be quite useful.

Information-processing Approaches to Individual Differences in Intelligence.   When we speak of intelligence in everyday parlance, we often differentiate between "quick" individuals and those who are "slow." Actually, according to research on the speed of information processing, such terms hold some truth. Contemporary approaches to infant intelligence suggest that the speed with which infants process information may correlate most strongly with later intelligence, as measured by IQ tests administered during adulthood (Rose & Feldman, 1997).

For instance, infants who process information efficiently ought to be able to learn about stimuli more quickly, and thus we would expect that they would turn their attention away from a given stimulus more rapidly than those who are less efficient at information processing. Similarly, measures of **visual-recognition memory**, the memory and recognition of a stimulus that has been previously seen, also relate to IQ. The more quickly an infant can retrieve a representation of a stimulus from memory, the more efficient, presumably, is that infant's information processing (Tamis-LeMonda & Bornstein, 1993; Canfield et al., 1997).

visual-recognition memory   *the memory and recognition of a stimulus that has been previously seen*

What Can You Do to Promote Infants' Cognitive Development?

All parents want their children to reach their full cognitive potential, but sometimes efforts to reach this goal take a bizarre path. For instance, some parents pay hundreds of dollars to enroll in workshops with titles such as "How to Multiply Your Baby's Intelligence" and to buy books with titles such as *How to Teach Your Baby to Read* (Sharpe, 1994).

Do such efforts ever succeed? Although some parents swear they do, there is no scientific support for the efficacy of such programs. For example, despite the many cognitive skills of infants, no infant has the capability to actually read. Furthermore, "multiplying" a baby's intelligence is impossible, and such organizations as the American Academy of Pediatrics and the American Academy of Neurology have denounced programs that claim to do so.

On the other hand, certain things can be done to promote cognitive development in infants. The following suggestions, based on findings of developmental researchers, offer a starting point (Meyerhoff & White, 1986; Schwebel, Maher, & Fagley, 1990; Schulman, 1991):

- *Provide infants the opportunity to explore the world.* As Piaget suggests, children learn by doing, and they need the opportunity to explore and probe their environment. Make sure that environment contains a variety of toys, books, and other sources of stimulation. (Also see the "Speaking of Development" box.)

- *Be responsive to infants, on both a verbal and a nonverbal level.* Try to speak *with* babies, as opposed to *at* them. Ask questions, listen to their responses, and provide further communication.

- *Read to your infants.* Although they may not understand the meaning of your words, they will respond to your tone of

Even if they don't understand the meaning of the words, infants still benefit from being read to.

voice and the intimacy provided by the activity. Reading together also begins to create a lifelong reading habit.

- *Keep in mind that you don't have to be with an infant 24 hours a day.* Just as infants need time to explore their world on their own, parents and other caregivers need time off from child-care activities.

- *Don't push infants and don't expect too much too soon.* Your goal should not be to create a genius; it should be to provide a warm, nurturing environment that will allow an infant to reach his or her potential.

Research using an information-processing framework is clear in suggesting a relationship between information processing and cognitive abilities: Measures of how quickly infants lose interest in stimuli that they have previously seen, as well as their responsiveness to new stimuli, correlate moderately well with later measures of intelligence. Infants who are more efficient information processors during the 6 months following birth tend to have higher intelligence scores between 2 and 12 years of age, as well as higher scores on other measures of cognitive competence (Thompson, Fagen, & Fulker, 1991; Rose, Feldman, & Wallace, 1992; Perleth, Lehwald, & Browder, 1993; Rolfe, 1994; Rose & Feldman, 1995; Slater, 1995; Sigman et al., in press).

SPEAKING OF DEVELOPMENT

Ellen Sackoff, Toy Designer

Education: . . . . Hood College, B.A. in art
City University of New York, M.A. in developmental psychology

Position: . . . . Managing partner for the Discover Group

Home: . . . . New York, New York

How would you like to blend your educational background and personal interests and end up in a job developing, evaluating, and marketing kids' toys? That's exactly what Ellen Sackoff did.

Armed with an art degree, Sackoff started her work life as a textile designer. But she wanted something more. She was determined to combine her art background with her interest in human behavior. So she started a company that designs and develops toys for infants.

As a managing partner of the Discovery Group, Sackoff uses her background in child development to alert parents about the best toys of the year and tests toys for the Children's Television Workshop.

"One might wonder why the field of child development would be involved in making toys for infants," she observes. "The reason is that play has long been a major area of research in psychology. Psychologists look at the play of animals and humans, and they think about what constitutes play and what its role is in development.

"For infants, play serves an important function in their exploration of the world. It is all they do. Through their explorations, infants learn about their world."

Involving child development experts in the design of toys for infants is a relatively new phenomenon, but already there appears to be considerable demand for it.

"Play contributes to all aspects of development," Sackoff explains. "People now are focusing more and more on making toys that tune into children's developmental stages. We make use of the fact that the development of a child follows a fairly universal course.

"In the first few months, we know that infants rely on their eyes and ears, but particularly their eyes. Babies focus more on objects that have sharp contrasts, and that is why there has been a proliferation of black-and-white toys. A lot of bold primary colors are used as well, but pastels are not used much because infants do not see their lack of contrast well."

Another development fact used by toy developers in the creation of new products is that babies like to look at faces, largely because faces are in constant movement.

"Things that move are fascinating to infants. The constant movement and changing of a face are what keep a baby's attention," Sackoff notes. "Many toys incorporate images of faces even though the image is static."

A toy with high play value, according to Sackoff, is one that will sustain infants' interest over time. Children tend to get bored playing with the same toy all the time.

"We test toys largely through observation of kids. We try to see which features are used, and which are not," she adds. "This is the basis for removing weak features and emphasizing strong ones.

"Play is important, and good toys are therefore important," she says. "If toys are truly tools for play, then let's give babies tools that work well, tools that keep their attention."

"People now are focusing more and more on making toys that tune into children's developmental stages."

"If toys are truly tools for play, then let's give babies tools that work well, tools that keep their attention."

cross-modal transference *the ability to identify a stimulus that previously has been experienced only through one sense by using another sense*

Other research suggests that abilities related to the *multimodal approach to perception,* which we considered in Chapter 4, may offer clues about later intelligence. For instance, the information-processing skill of cross-modal transference is associated with intelligence. **Cross-modal transference** is the ability to identify a stimulus that previously has been experienced through only one sense by using another sense. For instance, a baby who is able to recognize by sight a screwdriver that she has only previously touched, but not seen, is displaying cross-modal transference. Research has found that the degree of cross-modal transference displayed by an infant at age 1—which requires a high level of abstract thinking—is associated with intelligence scores several years later (Rose & Ruff, 1987; Spelke, 1987; Rose et al., 1991).

Although information-processing efficiency and cross-modal transference abilities during infancy relate moderately well to later IQ scores, we need to keep in mind two qualifications. First, even though there is an association between early information-processing capabilities and later measures of IQ, the correlation is only moderate in strength. Other factors, such as the degree of environmental stimulation, also play a crucial role in helping to determine adult intelligence. Consequently, we should not assume that intelligence is somehow permanently fixed in infancy.

Second, and perhaps even more important, intelligence measured by traditional IQ tests relates to a particular type of intelligence, one that emphasizes abilities that lead to academic, and certainly not artistic or professional, success. Consequently, predicting that a child may do well on IQ tests later in life is not the same as predicting that the child will be successful later in life.

Still, the relatively recent finding that an association exists between efficiency of information processing and later IQ scores has changed how we view the consistency of cognitive development across the life span. Whereas the earlier reliance on scales such as the Bayley led to the misconception that little continuity existed, the more recent information-processing approaches suggest that cognitive development unfolds in a more orderly, continuous manner from infancy to the later stages of life.

REVIEW AND RETHINK

REVIEW

■ Information-processing approaches to the study of cognitive development consider quantitative changes in children's abilities to organize and use information. Cognitive growth is regarded simply as the increasing sophistication of the three aspects of information processing—encoding, storage, and retrieval.

■ Recently, researchers have found evidence that infants have an innate ability to comprehend basic mathematical functions and statistical patterns—an ability that may form the basis of certain types of learning later in life.

■ Infants clearly have memory capabilities from a very early age, although the duration and accuracy of such memories over the long term are unresolved questions.

■ Traditional measures of infant intelligence focus on behavioral attainments, which can help identify developmental delays or advances. However, these measures are not strongly related to measures of adult intelligence.

■ Information-processing approaches to assessing intelligence rely on variations in the speed and quality with which infants process information in such areas as visual-recognition memory and cross-modal transference. Infants' information-processing abilities correlate moderately with adult measures of IQ.

RETHINK

■ What information from this chapter could you use to refute the claims of books or educational programs that promise to help parents multiply their babies' intelligence or instill advanced intellectual skills in infants?

■ Why might the statistical ability uncovered in the "three-syllable nonsense word" study described in this chapter form the basis of language acquisition?

■ This chapter refers to the issue of the duration and accuracy of early childhood memories as "controversial." What sorts of controversies arise out of this issue? Can such controversies be resolved? How?

■ In what ways is the use of such developmental scales as Gesell's or Bayley's helpful? In what ways is it dangerous? How would you maximize the helpfulness and minimize the danger?

■ Information-processing speed in infants correlates moderately well with one sort of adult intelligence. Might there be other indicators in infants that correlate with other adult skills or intelligences? Of what use would such indicators be? What would be their limitations?

THE ROOTS OF LANGUAGE

Mama. No. Cookie. Dad. Jo. When an infant utters his or her first word, no matter what it is, it marks the start of a transformation: from an entity seemingly not so different from animals of many other species to an entity with skills that are, arguably, unique to human beings.

But those initial words are just the first and most obvious manifestations of language. Many months earlier, infants began using language to comprehend the world around them. How does this linguistic ability develop? What is the pattern and sequence of language development? And how does the use of language mark a transformation in the cognitive world of infants and their parents? We consider these questions, and others, as we address the development of language during the first years of life.

The Fundamentals of Language: From Sounds to Symbols

Language, the systematic, meaningful arrangement of symbols, provides the basis for communication. But it does more than this: It is closely tied to the way infants think and understand the world. It enables them to reflect on people and objects, and to convey their thoughts to others.

Language has several formal characteristics that must be mastered as linguistic competence is developed. They include:

■ *Phonology*. Phonology refers to the basic sounds of language, called *phonemes*, that can be combined to produce words and sentences. For instance, the "a" in "mat" and the "a" in "mate" represent two different phonemes in English. Although English employs just 40 phonemes to create every word in the language, other languages have as many as 85 phonemes—and some as few as 15 (Akmajian, Demers, & Harnish, 1984).

■ *Morphemes*. A morpheme is the smallest language unit that has meaning. Some morphemes are complete words, whereas others add information necessary for interpreting a word, such as the endings "-s" for plural and "-ed" for past tense.

■ *Semantics*. Semantics are the rules that govern the meaning of words and sentences. As their knowledge of semantics develops, children are able to understand the distinction between "Ellie was hit by a car" (an answer to the question of why Ellie has not been in school for the last week) and "A car hit Ellie" (used to announce an emergency situation).

language *the systematic, meaningful arrangement of symbols, which provides the basis for communication*

In considering the development of language, we need to distinguish between linguistic *comprehension*, the understanding of speech, and linguistic *production*, the use of language to communicate. One principle underlies the relationship between the two: Comprehension precedes production. An 18-month-old may be able to understand a complex series of directions ("pick up your coat from the floor and put it on the chair by the fireplace") but may not yet have strung more than two words together. Comprehension, then, begins earlier than production, and throughout infancy comprehension increases at a faster rate than production (Jusczyk, 1997). For instance, during infancy comprehension of words expands at a rate of 22 new words a month, whereas production of words increases at a rate of about 9 new words a month (Benedict, 1979). Other forms of language ability show the same pattern, with comprehension consistently preceding production (see Figure 5-6).

FIGURE 5-6

COMPREHENSION PRECEDES PRODUCTION

Throughout infancy, the comprehension of speech precedes the production of speech.

(*Source:* Adapted from Bornstein & Lamb, 1992a).

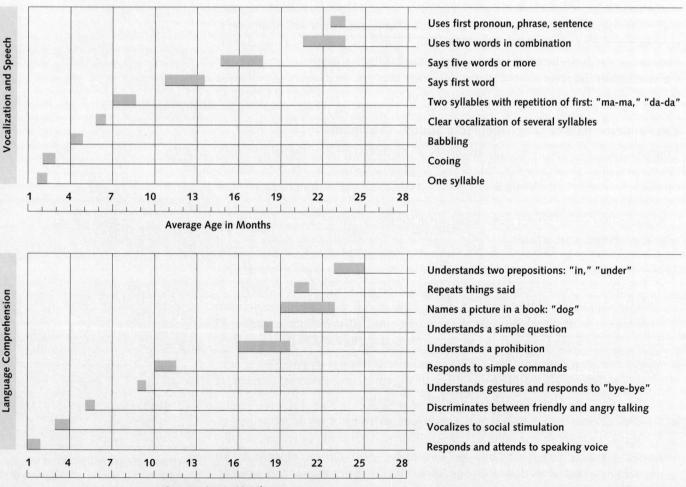

Prelinguistic Communication. Consider the following "dialogue" between a mother and her 3-month-old child (Snow, 1977b):

Mother	Infant
	[Smiles]
Oh, what a nice little smile!	
Yes, isn't that pretty?	
There now.	
There's a nice little smile.	
	[Burps]
What a nice wind as well!	
Yes, that's better, isn't it?	
Yes.	
Yes.	
	[Vocalizes]
Yes!	
There's a nice noise.	

Although we tend to think of language in terms of the production first of words and then of groups of words, infants actually begin to communicate linguistically well before they say their first word. Spend 24 hours with even a very young infant and you will hear a variety of sounds: cooing, crying, gurgling, murmuring, and various types of other noises. These sounds, although not meaningful in themselves, play an important role in linguistic development, paving the way for true language (Bloom, 1993).

Prelinguistic communication is communication through sounds, facial expressions, gestures, imitation, and other nonlinguistic means. When a father responds to his daughter's "ah" with an "ah" of his own, and then the daughter repeats the sound, and the father responds once again, they are engaged in prelinguistic communication. Clearly, the "ah" sound has no particular meaning. However, its repetition, which mimics the give-and-take of conversation, teaches the infant something about turn-taking (Dromi, 1993).

The most obvious manifestation of prelinguistic communication is babbling. **Babbling**, making speechlike but meaningless sounds, starts at the age of 2 or 3 months and continues until around the age of 1 year. When they begin to babble, infants repeat the same vowel sound over and over, changing the pitch from high to low (as in "ee-ee-ee," repeated at different pitches). After the age of 5 months, the sounds of babbling begin to expand, reflecting the addition of consonants (such as "bee-bee-bee-bee").

Babbling is a universal phenomenon, accomplished in the same way throughout all cultures. While they are babbling, infants spontaneously produce all of the sounds found in every language, not just the language they hear people around them speaking. In fact, even deaf children display their own form of babbling: Infants who cannot hear and who are exposed to sign language babble with their hands instead of their voices (Jakobson, 1971; Petitto & Marentette, 1991; Locke, 1993, 1994).

The form of babbling follows a progression from sounds that are the simplest to make to more complex sounds. Furthermore, although initially exposure to a particular language does not seem to influence babbling, experience eventually does make a difference. By the age of 6 months, babbling differs according to the language to which infants are exposed (Blake & Boysson-Bardies, 1992). The difference is so noticeable that even untrained listeners can distinguish between babbling infants who have been raised in cultures in which French, Arabic, or Cantonese languages are spoken (Locke, 1983; Boysson-Bardies, Sagart, & Durand, 1984; Boysson-Bardies & Vihman, 1991; Vihman, 1991; Oller et al., 1997).

Babbling may be the most obviously language-like achievement of early infancy, but there are other indications of prelinguistic speech. For instance, consider 5-month-old Marta, who spies her red ball just beyond her reach. After reaching for it and finding

prelinguistic communication *communication through sounds, facial expressions, gestures, imitation, and other nonlinguistic means*

babbling *making speechlike but meaningless sounds*

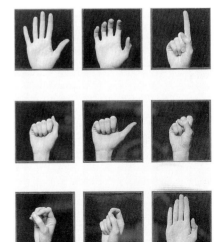

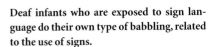
Deaf infants who are exposed to sign language do their own type of babbling, related to the use of signs.

that she is unable to get to it, she makes a cry of anger that alerts her parents that something is amiss, and her mother hands it to her. Communication, albeit prelinguistic, has occurred.

Four months later, when Marta faces the same situation, she no longer bothers to reach for the ball and doesn't respond in anger. Instead, she holds out her arm in the direction of the ball, but now, with great purpose, seeks to catch her mother's eye. When her mother sees the behavior, she knows just what Marta wants. Clearly, Marta's communicative skills—although still prelinguistic—have taken a leap forward.

Even these prelinguistic skills are supplanted in just a few months, when the gesture gives way to a new communicative skill: producing an actual word. Marta's parents clearly hear her say "ball."

First Words.   When a mother and father first hear their child say "Mama" or "Dada," which may occur as early as 9 months, it is hard to be anything but delighted. But their initial enthusiasm may be dampened a bit when they find that the same sound is used to ask for a cookie, a doll, and a ratty old blanket.

First words generally are spoken somewhere around the age of 10 to 14 months. Linguists differ on just how to recognize that a first word has actually been uttered. Some say it is when an infant clearly understands words and can produce a sound that is close to a word spoken by adults, such as a child who uses "mama" for any request she may have. Other linguists use a stricter criterion for the first word; they restrict "first word" to cases in which children give a clear, consistent name to a person, event, or object. In this view, "mama" counts as a first word only if it is consistently applied to the same person, seen in a variety of situations and doing a variety of things, and is not used to label other people (Kamhi, 1986; Bornstein & Tamis-LeMonda, 1989).

Although there is disagreement over when we can say a first word has been uttered, there is no disputing the fact that once an infant starts to produce words, the rate of increase in vocabulary is rapid. By the age of 15 months, the average child has a vocabulary of 10 words. The child's vocabulary methodically expands until the one-word stage of language development ends at around 18 months. Around that time, a sudden spurt in vocabulary occurs. In just a short period—a few weeks somewhere between 16 and 24 months of age—a child's vocabulary typically increases from 50 to 400 words (Bates, Bretherton, & Snyder, 1988; Gleitman & Landau, 1994; Pine, Lieven, & Rowland, 1997; Thal et al., 1997).

As you can see from the list in Table 5-4, the first words in children's early vocabularies typically regard objects and things, both animate and inanimate. Most often they refer to people or objects who constantly appear and disappear ("Mama"), to animals ("kitty"), or to temporary states ("wet"). These first words are often **holophrases**, one-word utterances whose meaning depends on the particular context in which they are used. For instance, a youngster may use the phrase "ma" to refer to his mother's coming in and out or to ask for something to eat (Nelson, 1981; Clark, 1983; Dromi, 1987).

First Sentences.   When Aaron was 19 months old, he heard his mother coming up the back steps, as she did every day just before dinner. Aaron turned to his father and distinctly said, "Ma come." In stringing those two words together, Aaron took a giant step in his language development.

The increase in vocabulary that comes at around 18 months is accompanied by another accomplishment: the linking together of individual words into sentences that convey a single thought. Although there is a good deal of variability in the time at which children first create two-word phrases, it is generally around 8 to 12 months after they say their first word.

---

holophrases   *one-word utterances whose meaning depends on the particular context in which they are used*

TABLE 5-4

COMPREHENSION AND PRODUCTION OF WORDS

	Comprehension Percentage	Production Percentage
1. *Nominals (Words referring to "things")*	56	61
Specific (people, animals, objects)	17	11
General (words referring to all members of a category)	39	50
Animate (objects)	9	13
Inanimate (objects)	30	37
Pronouns (e.g., this, that, they)	1	2
2. *Action words*	36	19
Social action games (e.g., peek-a-boo)	15	11
Events (e.g., "eat")	1	NA
Locatives (locating or putting something in specific location)	5	1
General action and inhibitors (e.g., "don't touch")	15	6
3. *Modifiers*	3	10
Status (e.g., "all gone")	2	4
Attributes (e.g., "big")	1	3
Locatives (e.g., "outside")	0	2
Possessives (e.g., "mine")	1	1
4. *Personal-social*	5	10
Assertions (e.g., "yes")	2	9
Social expressive (e.g., "bye-bye")	4	1

Note: Percentage refers to percentage of children who include this type of word among their first 50 words.
(*Source:* Adapted from Benedict, 1979.)

The linguistic advance represented by two-word combinations is important because the linkage not only provides labels for things in the world but also indicates the relations between them. For instance, the combination may declare something about possession ("Mama key") or recurrent events ("Dog bark"). Interestingly, most early sentences don't represent demands or even necessarily require a response. Instead, they are often merely comments and observations about events occurring in the child's world (Slobin, 1970; Halliday, 1975).

Two-year-olds using two-word combinations tend to employ particular sequences that are similar to the ways in which adults construct sentences. For instance, sentences in English typically follow a pattern in which the subject of the sentence comes first, followed by the verb, and then the object ("Josh threw the ball"). Children's speech most often uses a similar order, although not all the words are initially included. Consequently, a child might say "Josh threw" or "Josh ball" to indicate the same thought. What is significant is that the order is typically not "threw Josh" or "ball Josh," but rather the usual order of English, which makes the utterance much easier for an English speaker to comprehend (Brown, 1973; Maratsos, 1983; Hirsh-Pasek & Michnick-Golinkoff, 1995).

telegraphic speech   *speech in which words not critical to the message are left out*

underextension   *the overly restrictive use of words, common among children just mastering spoken language*

overextension   *the overly broad use of words, overgeneralizing their meaning*

learning theory approach   *the theory that language acquisition follows the basic laws of reinforcement and conditioning*

Although the creation of two-word sentences represents an advance, the language used by children still is by no means adultlike. For instance, 2-year-olds produce **telegraphic speech**, in which words not critical to the message are left out, similar to the way we might write a telegram for which we were paying by the word. Rather than saying, "I showed you the book," a child using telegraphic speech might say, "I show book." "I am drawing a dog" might become "Drawing dog" (see Table 5-5).

Early language has other characteristics that differentiate it from the language used by adults. For instance, consider Sarah, who refers to each of the blankets she sleeps with as a "blankie." However, when her Aunt Ethel gives her a new blanket, Sarah refuses to call the new one a "blankie," restricting the word to her original blankets.

Sarah's inability to generalize the label of "blankie" to blankets in general is an example of **underextension**, using words too restrictively, which is common among children just mastering spoken language. Underextension occurs when language novices think that a word refers to a specific concept, instead of to all examples of the concept (Caplan & Barr, 1989).

As infants grow more adept with language, the opposite phenomenon sometimes occurs. In **overextension**, words are used too broadly, overgeneralizing their meaning. For example, when Sarah refers to buses, trucks, and tractors as "cars," she is guilty of overextension, making the assumption that any object with wheels must be a car. Although overextension reflects speech errors, it also shows that advances are occurring in the child's thought processes: The child is beginning to develop general mental categories and concepts (Behrend, 1988).

The Origins of Language Development.   The immense strides in language development during the preschool years raise a fundamental question: How does proficiency in language come about? Linguists are deeply divided on how to answer this question.

One response comes from the basic principles of learning. According to the **learning theory approach**, language acquisition follows the basic laws of reinforcement and conditioning discussed earlier. For instance, a child who articulates the word "da" may be hugged and praised by her father, who jumps to the conclusion that she is referring to him. This reaction reinforces the child, who is more likely to repeat the word. In sum, the learning theory perspective on language acquisition suggests that children learn to speak by being rewarded for making sounds that approximate speech. Through the process of *shaping*, language becomes more and more similar to adult speech (Skinner, 1957).

TABLE 5-5

CHILDREN'S IMITATION OF SENTENCES SHOWING DECLINE OF TELEGRAPHIC SPEECH

	Eve, 25.5 Months	Adam, 28.5 Months	Helen, 30 Months	Ian, 31.5 Months	Jimmy, 32 Months	June, 35.5 Months
I showed you the book.	I show book.	(I show) book.	C	I show you the book.	C	Show you the book.
I am very tall.	(My) tall.	I (very) tall.	I very tall.	I'm very tall.	Very tall.	I very tall.
It goes in a big box.	Big box.	Big box.	In big box.	It goes in the box.	C	C
I am drawing a dog.	Drawing dog.	I draw dog.	I drawing dog.	Dog.	C	C
I will read the book.	Read book.	I will read book.	I read the book.	I read the book.	C	C
I can see a cow.	See cow.	I want see cow.	C	Cow.	C	C
I will not do that again.	Do–again.	I will that again.	I do that.	I again.	C	C

C = correct imitation.
(*Source:* Adapted from R. Brown & C. Fraser, 1963.)

There's a problem, though, with the learning theory approach. It doesn't seem to explain adequately how readily children acquire the rules of language. For instance, novice users of language are reinforced not only when they use grammatically impeccable language, but also when they make errors. Parents are apt to be just as responsive if their child says, "Why the dog won't eat?" as they are if the child phrases the question more correctly ("Why won't the dog eat?"). Both forms of the question are understood correctly, and both elicit the same response; reinforcement is provided for both correct and incorrect language usage. Under such circumstances, learning theory is hard-put to explain how children learn to speak properly.

Still other problems exist with learning theory explanations. For instance, research shows that children are able to move beyond specific utterances they have heard, and produce novel phrases, sentences, and constructions. Furthermore, children can apply rules to nonsense words. In one study, 4-year-old children heard the nonsense verb "to pilk" in the sentence "the bear is pilking the horse." Later, when asked what was happening to the horse, they responded by placing the nonsense verb in the correct tense and voice: "He's getting pilked by the bear."

Such conceptual difficulties with the learning theory approach have led to the development of an alternative approach, championed by the linguist Noam Chomsky (1968, 1978, 1991). Chomsky argues that there is a genetically determined, innate mechanism that directs the development of language. He suggests that people are born with an innate capacity to use language that emerges, more or less automatically, due to maturation.

Chomsky's analysis of different languages suggests that all the world's languages share a similar underlying structure, which he calls **universal grammar**. In this view, the human brain is wired with a neural system called the **language-acquisition device**, or **LAD**, that both permits the understanding of language structure and provides a set of strategies and techniques for learning the particular characteristics of the language to which a child is exposed. In this view, language is uniquely human, made possible by a genetic predisposition to both comprehend and produce words and sentences (Lust, Hermon, & Kornfilt, 1994; Lust, Suner, & Whitman, 1995).

Like the learning theory approach, the view that language represents an innate ability unique to humans has its critics. For instance, some researchers argue that certain primates are able to learn at least the basics of language, an ability that calls into question the uniqueness of the human linguistic capacity. Other critics suggest that we must identify mechanisms other than either a language-acquisition device or learning theory principles if we are to understand fully the processes that underlie language development. In short, the origins of language remain hotly contested (MacWhinney, 1991; Savage-Rumbaugh et al., 1993).

Speaking to Children: The Language of Infant-directed Speech

Say the following sentence aloud: Do you like the apple dumpling?

Now pretend that you are going to ask the same question of an infant, and speak it as you would for the child's ears.

Chances are several things happened when you translated the phrase for the infant. First, the wording probably changed, and you may have said something like, "Does baby like the apple dumpling?" At the same time, the pitch of your voice probably rose, your general intonation most likely had a singsong quality, and you probably separated your words carefully.

Infant-directed Speech.   The shift in your language was due to an attempt to use what has been called **infant-directed speech**, a style of speech directed toward infants. This type of speech pattern was previously called *motherese*, because it was assumed that it applied only to mothers. However, that assumption was wrong, and the gender-neutral term *infant-directed speech* is now used more frequently.

Infant-directed speech is characterized by short, simple sentences, and it typically refers to concrete objects in the baby's environment. Pitch becomes higher, the range of frequencies increases, and intonation is more varied. There is also repetition of words, and topics are restricted to items that are assumed to be comprehensible to infants.

universal grammar   *Noam Chomsky's theory that all the world's languages share a similar underlying structure*

language-acquisition device (LAD)   *a neural system of the brain hypothesized to permit understanding of language*

infant-directed speech   *a type of speech directed toward infants, characterized by short, simple sentences*

Motherese, or, more precisely, infant-directed speech, includes the use of short, simple sentences and is said in a pitch that is higher than that used with older children and adults.

Sometimes infant-directed speech includes amusing sounds that are not even words, imitating the prelinguistic speech of infants. In other cases, it has little formal structure, but is similar to the kind of telegraphic speech that infants use as they develop their own language skills. Even deaf mothers use a form of infant-directed speech: When communicating with their infants, deaf mothers use signed language at a significantly slower tempo than when communicating with adults, and they frequently repeat the signs (Swanson, Leonard, & Grandour, 1992; Masataka, 1993, 1996).

Infant-directed speech changes as children become older. Around the end of the first year, infant-directed speech takes on more adultlike qualities. Sentences become longer and more complex, although individual words are still spoken slowly and deliberately. Pitch is also used to focus attention on particularly important words.

Infant-directed speech plays an important role in infants' acquisition of language. Newborns prefer such speech to regular language, a fact that suggests that they may be particularly receptive to it (Fernald, 1991; Hepper, Scott, & Shahidullah, 1993). Furthermore, some research suggests that unusually extensive exposure to infant-directed speech early in life is related to the comparatively early appearance of first words and earlier linguistic competence in other areas (Bornstein & Ruddy, 1984; Hoff-Ginsberg, 1986; Hampson & Nelson, 1993; Cooper & Aslin, 1990, 1994).

Gender Differences.   To a girl, a bird is a birdie, a blanket a blankie, and a dog a doggy. To a boy, a bird is a bird, a blanket a blanket, and a dog a dog.

At least that's what parents of boys and girls appear to think, as illustrated by the language they use toward their sons and daughters. Virtually from the time of birth, the language parents employ with their children differs depending on the child's sex, according to research conducted by developmental psychologist Jean Berko Gleason (Gleason, 1987; Gleason et al., 1991).

Gleason found that, by the age of 32 months, girls hear twice as many diminutives (words such as "kitty" or "dolly" instead of "cat" or "doll") as boys hear. Although the use of diminutives declines with increasing age, their use consistently remains higher in speech directed at girls than in that directed at boys (see Figure 5-7).

Parents also are more apt to respond differently to children's requests depending on the child's gender. For instance, when turning down a child's request, mothers are likely to respond with a firm "no" to a male child, but to soften the blow to a female child by providing a diversionary response ("Why don't you do this instead?") or by somehow making the refusal less direct. Consequently, boys tend to hear firmer, clearer language,

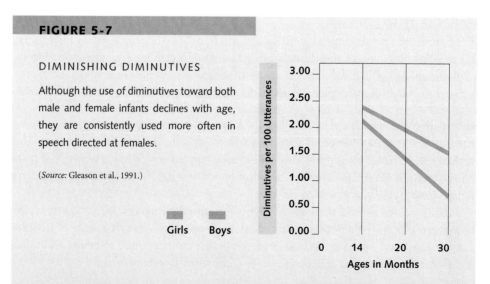

FIGURE 5-7

DIMINISHING DIMINUTIVES

Although the use of diminutives toward both male and female infants declines with age, they are consistently used more often in speech directed at females.

(*Source:* Gleason et al., 1991.)

whereas girls are exposed to warmer phrases, often referring to inner emotional states (Perlmann & Gleason, 1990).

Do such differences in language directed at boys and girls during infancy affect their behavior as adults? Although there is no direct evidence that plainly supports such an association, it is clear that men and women use different sorts of language as adults. For instance, as adults, women tend to use more tentative, less assertive language than men. Although we don't know whether these differences are a reflection of early linguistic experiences, such findings are certainly intriguing (Matlin, 1987; Tannen, 1991; Leaper, Anderson, & Sanders, 1998).

Developmental Diversity

Is Infant-directed Speech Similar Across All Cultures?

Do mothers in the United States, Sweden, and Russia speak the same way to their infants?

In some respects, they clearly do. Although the words themselves differ across languages, the way the words are spoken is quite similar. According to a growing body of research, infant-directed speech has basic similarities across cultures (Grieser & Kuhl, 1988; Papousek & Papousek, 1991; Rabain-Jamin & Sabeau-Jouannet, 1997).

Consider, for instance, the comparison in Table 5-6 of the major characteristics of speech directed at infants used by native speakers of English and Spanish. Of the 10 most frequent features, 6 are common to both: exaggerated intonation, high pitch, lengthened vowels, repetition, lower volume, and instructional emphasis (that is, heavy stress on certain key words, such as emphasizing the word *ball* in the sentence, "No, that's a *ball*") (Blount, 1982). Similarly, mothers in the United States, Sweden, and Russia all exaggerate and elongate the pronunciation of the three vowel sounds of "ee," "ah," and "oh" when speaking to infants in similar ways, despite the differences in language in which the sounds are used (Kuhl et al., 1997).

The cross-cultural similarities in infant-directed speech are so great, in fact, that they appear in some facets of language specific to particular types of interactions. For instance, evidence comparing American English,

German, and Mandarin Chinese speakers shows that in each of the languages, pitch rises when a mother is attempting to get an infant's attention or produce a response, whereas pitch falls when she is trying to calm an infant (Papousek & Papousek, 1991).

Why do we find such similarities across very different languages? One hypothesis is that the characteristics of infant-directed speech activate innate responses in infants. As we have noted, infants seem to prefer infant-directed speech over adult-directed speech, suggesting that their perceptual systems may be more responsive to such characteristics. Another explanation is that infant-directed speech facilitates language development, providing cues as to the meaning of speech before infants have developed the capacity to understand the meaning of words (Fernald & Kuhl, 1987; Fernald, 1989; Fisher & Tokura, 1996; Kuhl et al., 1997).

TABLE 5-6

RANKING 10 MOST COMMON FEATURES IN ENGLISH AND SPANISH

English	Spanish
1. Exaggerated intonation	1. Exaggerated intonation
2. Breathiness	2. Repetition
3. High pitch	3. High pitch
4. Repetition	4. Instructional
5. Lowered volume	5. Attentionals
6. Lengthened vowel	6. Lowered volume
7. Creaky voice	7. Raised volume
8. Instructional	8. Lengthened vowel
9. Tenseness	9. Fast tempo
10. Falsetto	10. Personal pronoun substitution

(*Source:* Adapted from B.G. Blount, 1982.)

The Informed Consumer of Development

Assessing Language Development

Given the critical role that language plays in cognitive development, parents often are concerned that their infant's language development proceeds on schedule. Although there are no hard-and-fast rules, given the wide variability in the timing of children's first words and the ways their vocabularies develop (Shore, 1994), there are several guidelines that indicate whether language development is normal. An infant who shows the following abilities is probably developing normally, according to psycholinguist Anne Dunlea (Yarrow, 1990; Fowler, 1990):

- *Understanding at least some things that are heard.* This means that, at a minimum, the child has some receptive language and is capable of hearing. For instance, most children can discriminate between friendly and angry speech by the age of 6 months.

- *Producing sounds, such as a raspberry noise, at around 6 or 7 months of age.* Children who are deaf may end prelinguistic speech at this point, even if they produced it earlier, because they cannot hear themselves.

- *Using gestures to communicate.* Pointing and reaching are often forerunners of language. Most children look toward an object pointed to by an adult by the age of 9 months, and most use pointing themselves before the end of their first year.

- *Pretending to use language.* Even if the words make no sense, children may pretend to use language before they actually begin to speak, indicating that they at least know how language functions.

What if you cannot answer any of these questions affirmatively? It would be reasonable to have a pediatrician evaluate your child. Keep in mind, however, the wide range of variations in language development among different children, and the fact that the vast majority of children develop quite normally.

REVIEW AND RETHINK

REVIEW

- Before they speak their first word, infants understand many adult utterances and engage in several forms of prelinguistic communication, including the use of facial expressions, gestures, and babbling.

- Children typically produce their first words between 10 and 14 months, and rapidly increase their vocabularies from that point on, especially during a spurt at about 18 months.

- Children's language development proceeds through a pattern of holophrases, two-word combinations, and telegraphic speech. Their linguistic development reflects their growing sense of the relations between objects in the world, and their acquisition of general mental categories and concepts.

- Learning theorists believe that basic learning processes adequately account for language development, whereas Noam Chomsky and his followers argue that humans have an innate language capacity that naturally facilitates language development.

- When talking to infants, adults of all cultures tend to use infant-directed speech. This type of speech seems to appeal to infants and to facilitate their linguistic development.

- According to some research, adults tend to speak less directly to girls than to boys, which may contribute to behavioral differences later in life.

RETHINK

- What are some ways in which children's linguistic development reflects their acquisition of new ways of interpreting and dealing with their world?

■ If Chomsky is correct about the language-acquisition device, why do children raised in isolation not develop language naturally? Why do adults have such difficulty learning a second language?

■ American Sign Language (ASL) is generally regarded as a true language. What characteristics must ASL have to fit Chomsky's conception of a language? Do you think humans are genetically predisposed to acquire a language such as ASL?

■ What are some implications of differences in the ways adults speak to boys and girls? How might such speech differences contribute to later differences not only in speech, but in attitudes?

LOOKING BACK

■ **What are the fundamental features of Piaget's theories of cognitive development?**

• Jean Piaget's stage theory asserts that children pass through stages of cognitive development in a fixed order. The stages represent changes not only in the quantity of knowledge infants gain, but in the quality of that knowledge as well.

• According to Piaget, all children pass gradually through the four major stages of cognitive development (sensorimotor, preoperational, concrete operational, and formal operational) and their various substages when the children are at an appropriate level of maturation and are exposed to relevant types of experiences.

• In the Piagetian view, children's understanding grows through assimilation of their experiences into their current way of thinking or through accommodation of their current way of thinking to their experiences.

• During the sensorimotor period (birth to about 2 years) with its six substages, infants progress from the use of simple reflexes, through the development of repeated and integrated actions that gradually increase in complexity, to the ability to generate purposeful effects from their actions. By the end of the sixth substage of the sensorimotor period, infants are beginning to engage in symbolic thought.

■ **How do infants process information?**

• Information-processing approaches to the study of cognitive development seek to learn how individuals receive, organize, store, and retrieve information. Such approaches differ from Piaget's by considering quantitative changes in children's abilities to process information.

• Infants have memory capabilities from their earliest days, although the accuracy of infant memories is a matter of debate.

■ **How is infant intelligence measured?**

• Traditional measures of infant intelligence, such as Gesell's developmental quotient and the Bayley Scales of Infant Development, focus on average behavior observed at particular ages in large numbers of children.

• Information-processing approaches to assessing intelligence rely on variations in the speed and quality with which infants process information.

■   **By what processes do children learn to use language?**

- Prelinguistic communication involves the use of sounds, gestures, facial expressions, imitation, and other nonlinguistic means to express thoughts and states. Prelinguistic communication prepares the infant for speech.

- Infants typically produce their first words between the ages of 10 and 14 months. At around 18 months, children typically begin to link words together into primitive sentences that express single thoughts. Beginning speech is characterized by the use of holophrases, telegraphic speech, underextension, and overextension, in which an overly generalized meaning is assigned to a word.

- The learning theory approach to language acquisition assumes that adults and children use basic behavioral processes—such as conditioning, reinforcement, and shaping—in language learning. A different approach proposed by Chomsky holds that humans are genetically endowed with a language-acquisition device, which permits them to detect and use the principles of universal grammar that underlie all languages.

■   **How do children influence the language that adults use to address them?**

- Adult language is influenced by the children to whom it is addressed. Infant-directed speech takes on characteristics, surprisingly invariant across cultures, that make it appealing to infants and that probably encourage language development.

- Adult language also exhibits differences based on the gender of the child to whom it is directed, which may have effects that emerge later in life.

EPILOGUE: THE FORGOTTEN MEMORIES OF SIMONA YOUNG

In this chapter we looked at infants' cognitive development from the perspective of Jean Piaget, focusing on the substages of the sensorimotor stage through which infants pass in the first 2 years of life. We also looked at a different perspective on infant development based on information-processing theory. We examined infant learning, memory, and to adult intelligence, and concluded the chapter with a look at language.

Turn to the prologue of this chapter, about Simona Young, and answer the following questions.

1. Taking a Piagetian perspective, how do you think these circumstances of Simona's infancy might have affected her cognitive development? Did she pass through the substages of the sensorimotor stage?

2. How do you think Simona's linguistic development may have been affected by her 2 years in the Romanian orphanage? Discuss your answer in terms of both learning theory and Chomsky's theory of linguistic development.

3. Do you think Simona easily acquired the language of her adoptive parents when she was brought to Canada at 2 years of age? Do you think her linguistic abilities at age six are on the same level as those of a 6-year-old raised from infancy in Canada? Why?

4. Do you think Simona really remembers nothing of her years in the orphanage? How does the concept of infantile amnesia apply to her case? Suppose a therapist were to stimulate her memory of her infancy. Do you think her recollections would be accurate?

5. If a developmental scale had been administered to Simona soon after she arrived in Canada, do you think the results would have been accurate? Why or why not?

KEY TERMS AND CONCEPTS

scheme (p. 151)

assimilation (p. 151)

accommodation (p. 151)

sensorimotor stage (of cognitive development) (p. 152)

circular reaction (p. 153)

goal-directed behavior (p. 154)

object permanence (p. 154)

mental representation (p. 155)

deferred imitation (p. 156)

information-processing approaches (p. 159)

memory (p. 160)

infantile amnesia (p. 162)

developmental quotient (p. 164)

Bayley Scales of Infant Development (p. 164)

visual-recognition memory (p. 165)

cross-modal transference (p. 167)

language (p. 169)

prelinguistic communication (p. 171)

babbling (p. 171)

holophrases (p. 172)

telegraphic speech (p. 174)

underextension (p. 174)

overextension (p. 174)

learning theory approach (p. 174)

universal grammar (p. 175)

language-acquisition device (LAD) (p. 175)

infant-directed speech (p. 175)

INFANCY

Social and Personality Development

PROLOGUE: FIRST ENCOUNTERS

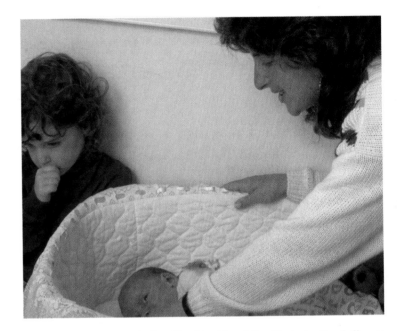

The lack of enthusiasm displayed by this older sibling illustrates the challenges posed by the arrival of a new member of the family.

Louis became the center of attention on the way home [from the hospital]. His father brought Martha, aged five, and Tom, aged three, to the hospital with him when Louis and his mother was discharged. Martha rushed to see "her" new baby and ignored her mother. Tom clung to his mother's knees in the reception hall of the hospital.

A hospital nurse carried Louis to the car, placing him in Mrs. Moore's arms for the ride home. The two older children immediately climbed over the seat and swamped mother and baby with their attention. Both children stuck their faces into his, smacked at him, and talked to him. They soon began to fight over him with loud voices. The loud argument and the jostling of his mother upset Louis and he started to cry. He let out a wail that came like a shotgun blast into the noisy car. The children quieted immediately and looked with awe at this new infant. His insistent wails drowned out their bickering. He had already asserted himself in their eyes. Martha's lip quivered as she watched her mother attempt to comfort Louis, and she added her own soft cooing in imitation of her mother. Tom squeezed even closer to his mother, put his thumb in his mouth, and closed his eyes to shut out the commotion. (Brazelton, 1983, p. 48)

LOOKING AHEAD   The arrival of a newborn brings a dramatic change to a family's dynamics. No matter how welcome a baby's birth, it causes a fundamental shift in the roles that people play within the family. Mothers and fathers must start to build a relationship with their infant, and older children must adjust to the presence of a new member of the family and build their own alliance with their infant brother or sister.

Although the process of social development during infancy is neither simple nor automatic, it is crucial: The bonds that grow between infants and their parents, family, and others provide the foundation a lifetime worth of social relationships.

In this chapter we consider social and personality development in infancy. We begin by examining the emotional lives of infants, considering which emotions they feel and how well they can decode others' emotions. We also consider how infants use others to shape their own reactions and how they view their own and others' mental lives.

We then turn to a consideration of infants' social relationships. We look at how they forge bonds of attachment and the ways they interact with family members and peers.

Finally, we cover the characteristics that differentiate one infant from another. We'll discuss differences in the way children are treated depending on their gender. We'll consider the nature of family life as the 21st century begins and discuss how it differs from earlier eras. The chapter closes with a look at the advantages and disadvantages of infant day care outside the home, a child-care option that today's families increasingly employ.

In sum, after reading this chapter, you will be able to answer these questions:

- What sort of emotional lives do infants have?
- What sort of mental lives do infants have?
- What is attachment in infancy? How does it relate to the future social competence of individuals?
- What roles do other people play in infants' social development?
- What sorts of individual differences do infants display?
- Is day care beneficial or harmful for infants?

FORMING THE ROOTS OF SOCIABILITY

Germaine smiles when he catches a glimpse of his mother. Tawanda looks angry when her mother takes away the spoon that she is playing with. Sydney scowls when a loud plane flies overhead.

A smile. A look of anger. A scowl. The emotions of infancy are written all over a baby's face. Yet do infants experience emotions in the same way that adults do? When do they become capable of understanding what others are experiencing emotionally? And how do they use others' emotional states to make sense of their environment? We consider some of these questions as we seek to understand how infants develop emotionally and socially.

Emotions in Infancy: Do Infants Experience Emotional Highs and Lows?

Anyone who spends any time at all around infants knows they display facial expressions that seem indicative of their emotional states. In situations in which we expect them to be happy, they seem to smile; when we might assume they are frustrated, they show anger; and when we might expect them to be unhappy, they look sad.

In fact, these basic facial expressions are remarkably similar across the most diverse cultures. Whether we look at babies in India, the United States, or the jungles of New Guinea, the expression of basic emotions is the same (see Figure 6-1). Furthermore, the nonverbal expression of emotion, called *nonverbal encoding*, is fairly consistent throughout the life span. These consistencies have led researchers to conclude that the capacity to display basic emotions is innate (Feldman, 1982; Camras, Malatesta, & Izard, 1991; Ekman & O'Sullivan, 1991; Izard et al., 1995).

Infants appear to display a fairly wide range of emotional expressions. According to research on what mothers see in their children's nonverbal behavior, almost all think that by the age of one month, their babies have expressed interest and joy. In addition, 84 percent of mothers think their infants have expressed anger, 75 percent surprise, 58 percent fear, and 34 percent sadness (Johnson et al.,1982; Sroufe, 1996).

Experiencing Emotions.   Yet does the capability of infants to encode emotions nonverbally in a consistent, reliable manner mean that they actually *experience* emotions, and—if they do—is the experience similar to that of adults? These questions are not easy to answer.

The fact that children display nonverbal expressions in a manner similar to that of adults does not necessarily mean that the actual experience is identical. In fact, if such displays are innate, facial expressions may occur without any accompanying emotional experience. Nonverbal expressions, then, might be emotionless in young infants, in much the same way that your knee reflexively jerks forward when a physician taps it, without the involvement of emotions (Soussignan et al., 1997).

However, most developmental researchers think otherwise: They argue that the nonverbal expressions of infants represent emotional experiences. In fact, developmental psychologist Carroll Izard suggests in his **differential emotions theory** that emotional expressions not only reflect emotional experiences, but also help regulate the emotion itself. Izard suggests that infants are born with an innate repertoire of emotional expressions, reflecting basic emotional states. As infants and children grow older, they expand and modify these basic expressions and become more adept at controlling their nonverbal

differential emotions theory *Izard's theory that emotional expressions reflect emotional experiences and help in the regulation of emotion itself*

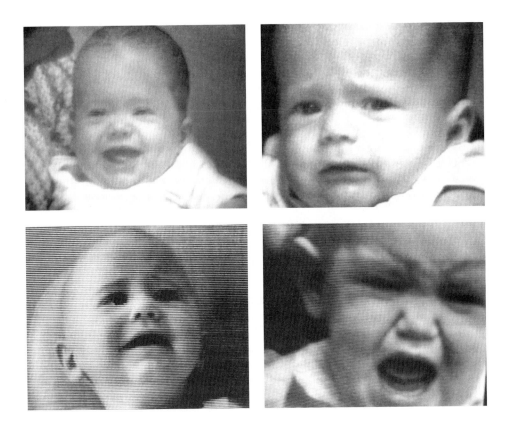

FIGURE 6-1 UNIVERSAL FACIAL EXPRESSIONS

Infants show these types of facial expressions relating to basic emotions, regardless of the culture in which they are raised.

behavioral expressions and more sophisticated in their ability to experience a wider array of emotions (Izard, 1977; Izard & Malatesta, 1987; Camras, Malatesta, & Izard, 1991).

In sum, infants do appear to experience emotions, although the range of emotions at birth is fairly restricted. However, as they get older, infants both display and experience a wider range of increasingly complex emotions (Fox, 1994).

Stranger Anxiety and Separation Anxiety. "She used to be such a friendly baby," thought Erika's mother. "No matter who she encountered, she had a big smile. But now, I don't know what's happened. Almost the day she turned 7 months old, she began to react to strangers as if she were seeing a ghost. Her face crinkles up with a frown, and she either turns away or stares at them with suspicion. And she doesn't want to be left with anyone she doesn't already know. It's as if she has undergone a personality transplant."

What happened to Erika is, in fact, quite typical. By the end of the first year, infants often develop both stranger anxiety and separation anxiety. **Stranger anxiety** is the caution and wariness displayed by infants when encountering an unfamiliar person, which sometimes appears in the second half of the first year.

What brings on stranger anxiety? One basic cause is the increased cognitive abilities of infants, allowing them to separate the people they know from the people they don't. The same cognitive advances that allow them to respond so positively to those people with whom they are familiar also means that they are able to recognize people who are unfamiliar. Furthermore, between 6 and 9 months, infants begin to try to make sense of their world. When they can't—such as with the appearance of an unknown person—they experience fear. It's as if an infant has a question but is unable to answer it (Ainsworth, 1973; Kagan, Kearsley, & Zelazo, 1978).

Although stranger anxiety is common after the age of 6 months, significant differences exist between children. Some infants, particularly those who have a lot of experience with strangers, tend to show less anxiety than those whose experience with strangers is limited. Furthermore, not all strangers evoke the same reaction. For instance, infants tend to show less anxiety with strangers who are female than those who are male. In addition, they react more positively to strangers who are children than to strangers who are adults, perhaps because their size is less intimidating (Lenssen, 1973; Brooks & Lewis, 1976; Thompson & Limber, 1990).

Separation anxiety is the distress displayed by infants when a customary care provider departs. Separation anxiety starts a little later than stranger anxiety, usually beginning at about 8 or 9 months. It peaks around 14 months, and then slowly decreases. Separation anxiety is largely attributable to the same reasons as stranger anxiety. Infants' growing cognitive skills allow them to ask questions with no readily apparent answers: "Why is my mother leaving?" "Where is she going?" and "Will she come back?"

Stranger anxiety and separation anxiety represent important social progress. They reflect both cognitive advances and the growing emotional and social bond between infants and their caregivers—bonds that we'll consider later in the chapter when we discuss infants' social relationships.

Smiling. As Luz lay sleeping in her crib, her mother and father caught a glimpse of the most beautiful smile crossing her face. Her parents were sure that Luz was having a pleasant dream. Were they right?

Probably not. The earliest smiles expressed during sleep probably have little meaning, although no one can be absolutely sure. However, by 6 to 9 weeks babies begin to smile reliably at the sight of stimuli that please them, including toys, mobiles, and—to the delight of parents—people. Smiling in response to other individuals is considered a **social smile**, in comparison to smiling at nonhuman stimuli.

Actually, the first smiles tend to be relatively indiscriminate, as infants first begin to smile at the sight of almost anything they find amusing. However, as they get older, they

---

stranger anxiety *the caution and wariness displayed by infants when encountering an unfamiliar person*

separation anxiety *the distress displayed by infants when a customary care provider departs*

social smile *smiling in response to other individuals*

True social smiles emerge by the age of 6 to 9 weeks.

become more selective in their smiles, and their social smiles become directed toward particular individuals, not just anyone (Wolff, 1963).

Furthermore, by the age of 18 months, social smiling, directed more toward mothers and other caregivers, becomes more frequent than smiling directed toward nonhuman objects. Moreover, if an adult is unresponsive to a child, the amount of smiling decreases. In sum, by the end of the second year children are quite purposefully using smiling to communicate their positive emotions, and they are sensitive to the emotional expressions of others (Jones & Raag, 1989; Jones, Collins, & Hong, 1991; Toda & Fogel, 1993; Dickson, Walker, & Fogel, 1997).

Decoding Others' Facial and Vocal Expressions. You may recall from Chapter 3 that neonates are able to imitate adults' facial expressions, a capability that is apparent even minutes after birth (Kaitz et al., 1988; Reissland, 1988). Although their imitative abilities certainly do not imply that they can understand the meaning of others' facial expressions, such imitation does pave the way for future *nonverbal decoding* abilities, which begin to emerge fairly soon. Using these abilities, infants can interpret others' facial and vocal expressions that carry emotional meaning (Mumme, Fernald, & Herrera, 1996; Slater & Butterworth, 1997; Walker-Andrews, 1997).

Although relatively little attention has been given to infants' perception of vocal expressions, it does appear that they are able to discriminate happy and sad vocal expressions at the age of 5 months. Infants also seem to be able to discriminate vocal expressions of emotion at a slightly earlier age than they discriminate facial expressions (Walker-Andrews & Grolnick, 1983; Walker-Andrews & Lennon, 1991).

Scientists know more about the *sequence* in which nonverbal facial decoding ability progresses. In the first 6 to 8 weeks, infants' visual precision is sufficiently limited that they cannot pay much attention to others' facial expressions. But they soon begin to discriminate among different facial expressions of emotion and even seem to be able to respond to differences in emotional intensity conveyed by facial expressions. They also respond to unusual facial expressions. For instance, they show distress when their mothers pose bland, unresponsive, neutral facial expressions (Klinnert et al., 1983; Kuchuk et al., 1986; Nelson, 1987; Kogan & Carter, 1996).

By the time they reach the age of 4 months, infants may already have begun to understand the emotions that lie behind the facial and vocal expressions of others (Walker-Andrews, 1997). How do we know this? One important clue comes from a study in which

social referencing   *the intentional search for information from others to help explain the meaning of uncertain circumstances and events*

7-month-old infants were shown a pair of facial expressions relating to joy and sadness and, simultaneously, heard a vocalization representing either joy (a rising tone of voice) or sadness (a falling tone of voice). The infants paid more attention to the face that matched the tone, suggesting that they had at least a rudimentary understanding of the emotional meaning of facial expressions and voice tones (Phillips et al., 1990).

In sum, infants learn early both to encode and to decode emotions. Such abilities play an important role not only in helping them experience their own emotions, but—as we see next—in using others' emotions to understand the meaning of ambiguous social situations.

Social Referencing: Feeling What Others Feel

> When 23-month-old Stephania watches as her mother and father loudly argue with one another, she glances at her older brother. He appears unperturbed by the scene, having witnessed it all too often in the past, and he wears a small smile of embarrassment on his face. On seeing this, Stephania smiles slightly, too, mimicking her brother's facial expression.

Like Stephania, most of us have been in situations in which we feel uncertain. In such cases, we sometimes turn to others to see how they are reacting. This reliance on others, known as social referencing, helps us decide what an appropriate response ought to be.

Social referencing is the intentional search for information from others to help explain the meaning of uncertain circumstances and events. Social referencing is used to clarify the meaning of a situation by reducing our uncertainty about what is occurring (Campos & Stenberg, 1981; Klinnert, 1984).

Social referencing first tends to occur around the age of 8 or 9 months (Walden & Ogan, 1988). It is a fairly sophisticated social ability: Infants need it not only to understand the significance of others' behavior, such as their facial expressions, but also to realize that others' behavior has meaning with reference to specific circumstances (Rosen, Adamson, & Bakeman, 1992).

Infants make particular use of facial expressions in their social referencing. For instance, in one study infants were given an unusual toy to play with. The amount of time they played with it depended on their mothers' facial expressions. When their mothers displayed disgust,

Social referencing is used by children to help explain the meaning of circumstances and events that they find puzzling.

they played with it significantly less than when their mothers appeared pleased. Furthermore, when given the opportunity to play with the same toy later, the infants revealed lasting consequences of their mothers' earlier behavior, despite the mothers' now neutral- appearing facial reactions (Hornik, Risenhoover, & Gunner, 1987; Hornik & Gunner, 1988).

Although social referencing begins fairly early in life, researchers are still not certain *how* it operates. Consider, for instance, one possibility: It may be that observing someone else's facial expression brings about the emotion the expression represents. That is, an infant who views someone looking sad may come to feel sad herself, and her behavior may be affected. On the other hand, it may be the case that viewing another's facial expression simply provides information. In this case, the infant does not experience the particular emotion represented by another's facial expression; she simply uses the display as data to guide her own behavior.

Both explanations for social referencing have received support, and so we still don't know which is correct. What we do know is that social referencing is most likely to occur when a situation breeds uncertainty and ambiguity. Furthermore, infants who reach the age when they are able to use social referencing become quite upset if they receive conflicting nonverbal messages from their mothers and fathers. Mixed messages, then, are a real source of stress for an infant (Walden & Baxter, 1989; Hirshberg, 1990; Hirshberg & Svejda, 1990; Camras & Sachs, 1991).

The Development of Self: Do Infants Know Who They Are?

> Elysa, 8 months old, crawls past the full-length mirror that hangs on a door in her parents' bedroom. She barely pays any attention to her reflection as she moves by. On the other hand, her cousin Brianna, who is almost 2 years old, stares at herself in the mirror as she passes and laughs as she touches her forehead with her fingers.

Perhaps you have had the experience of catching a glimpse of yourself in a mirror and noticing a hair out of place. You probably reacted by attempting to push the unruly hair back into place. Your reaction shows more than that you care about how you look. It implies that you have a sense of yourself, the awareness and knowledge that you are an independent social entity to which others react, and which you attempt to present to the world in ways that reflect favorably on you.

However, we are not born with the knowledge that we exist independently from others and the larger world. Although it is difficult to demonstrate, the youngest infants—other than some apes—do not seem to have a sense of themselves as individuals. They do not recognize likenesses of themselves, whether in photos or in mirrors, and they show no evidence of being able to distinguish themselves from other people (Gallup, 1977).

The roots of **self-awareness**, knowledge of oneself, begin to grow at around the age of 12 months. We know this from a simple but ingenious experimental technique known as the *mirror-and-rouge task*. In it, an infant's nose is secretly colored with a dab of red rouge, and the infant is seated in front of a mirror. If infants touch their noses or attempt to wipe off the rouge, we have evidence that they have at least some knowledge of their physical characteristics. For them, this awareness is one step in developing an understanding of themselves as independent objects.

Although some infants as young as 12 months seem startled on seeing the rouge spot, for most a reaction does not occur until between 17 and 24 months of age. It is also around this age that children begin to show awareness of their own capabilities. For instance, infants between the ages of 23 and 25 months sometimes begin to cry when asked in experiments to imitate a complicated sequence of behaviors involving toys, although they readily accomplish simpler ones. According to developmental psychologist Jerome Kagan, their reaction suggests that they are conscious that they lack the capability to carry out difficult tasks, and are unhappy about it—a reaction that provides a clear indication of self-awareness (Lewis &

self-awareness *knowledge of oneself*

Research suggests that this 18-month-old is exhibiting a clearly developed sense of self.

theory of mind *children's knowledge and beliefs about their mental world*

empathy *an emotional response that corresponds to the feelings of another person*

Brooks-Gunn, 1979; Kagan, 1981; Lipka & Brinthaupt, 1992; Asendorpf & Baudonniere, 1993; Asendorpf, Warkentin, & Baudonniere, 1996).

In sum, by the age of 18 to 24 months, infants have developed at least the rudiments of awareness of their own physical characteristics, and they understand that their appearance is stable over time. Although it is not clear how far this awareness extends, it is becoming increasingly evident that, as we discuss next, infants have not only a basic understanding of themselves, but also the beginnings of an understanding of how the mind operates—what has come to be called a "theory of mind" (Damon & Hart, 1992; Moore, 1996; Legerstee, Anderson, & Schaffer, 1998).

Theory of Mind: Infants' Perspectives on the Mental Lives of Others—and Themselves

What are infants' thoughts about thinking? According to developmental psychologist John Flavell, infants begin to understand certain things about the mental processes of themselves and others at quite an early age. Flavell has investigated children's **theory of mind**, their knowledge and beliefs about the mental world. Theories of mind are the explanations that children use to explain how others think. For instance, cognitive advances during infancy permit older infants to come to see people in ways that are very different from other objects. They learn to see others as *compliant agents*, beings similar to themselves who behave under their own power and who have the capacity to respond to infants' requests (Flavell, 1993; Lewis & Mitchell, 1994; Flavell, Green, & Flavell, 1995; Shwe & Markman, 1997).

In addition, children's capacity to understand intentionality and causality grows during infancy. They begin to understand that others' behaviors have some meaning and that the behaviors they see people enacting are designed to accomplish particular goals, in contrast to the "behaviors" of inanimate objects (Parritz, Mangelsdorf, & Gunnar, 1992; Gelman & Kalish, 1993; Golinkoff, 1993).

By the age of 2, infants begin to demonstrate the rudiments of empathy. **Empathy** is an emotional response that corresponds to the feelings of another person. At 24 months of age, infants sometimes comfort others or show concern for them (Zahn-Waxler, Robinson, & Emde, 1992). To do this, they need to be aware of others' emotional states. Further, during their second year infants begin to use deception, both in games of "pretend" and in outright attempts to fool others. A child who plays "pretend" and who uses falsehoods must be aware that others hold beliefs about the world—beliefs that can be manipulated (Leslie, 1987; Dunn, 1991). In short, by the end of infancy children have developed the rudiments of their own personal theory of mind. It helps them understand the actions of others and it affects their own behavior (Wellman, 1990; Moses & Chandler, 1992).

By the age of 2, children demonstrate the foundations of empathy, an emotional response that corresponds to the feelings of another person.

REVIEW AND RETHINK

REVIEW

■ Infants appear both to express and to experience emotions, at first displaying a limited range, and then a wider range reflecting increasingly complex emotional states.

■ Infants begin to experience stranger anxiety at about 6 months, and separation anxiety at around 8 months of age.

■ Infants from different cultures use similar facial expressions to express basic emotional states. As the infant matures, the meaning of an expression such as the smile grows increasingly specific, with a more limited range of applicability.

■ The ability to decode the nonverbal facial and vocal expressions of others develops early in infants. By 8 or 9 months, infants begin to use such nonverbal decoding to clarify situations of uncertainty and determine appropriate responses, an ability termed *social referencing*.

■ At first infants are not aware that they exist separately from the rest of the world. They develop self-awareness gradually, starting after 12 months of age.

■ By the age of 2, children have developed the rudiments of a theory of mind, including a realization that people are essentially different from inanimate objects, a growing sense of intentionality and causality, fundamental feelings of empathy, and the ability to pretend and to deceive.

RETHINK

■ If the facial expressions that convey basic emotions are similar across cultures, how do such expressions arise? Can you think of facial expressions that are culture specific? How do they arise?

■ Why might the ability to discriminate vocal expressions emerge earlier than the ability to discriminate facial expressions?

■ In what situations do adults rely on social referencing to work out appropriate responses? How might social referencing be used to manipulate individuals' responses?

■ How might a child's developing sense of empathy be fostered by parents and other caregivers?

■ How do Flavell's ideas about a growing sense of causality, pretense, and deception in children compare to Piaget's notions of experimentation and deferred imitation by children?

FORGING RELATIONSHIPS

The problem in the day-care center first arose during the windy days of March. Its source: 10-month-old Russell Ruud. Otherwise a model of decorum, Russell had somehow learned how to unzip the Velcro chin strap to his winter hat. He would remove the hat whenever he got the urge, seemingly oblivious to the potential health problems that might follow.

But that was just the start of the real difficulty. To the chagrin of the teachers in the day-care center, not to speak of the children's parents, soon other children were following his lead, removing their own caps at will.

Russell's mother, made aware of the anarchy at the day-care center—and the other parents' distress over Russell's behavior—pleaded innocent. "I never showed Russell how to unzip the Velcro," claimed his mother, Judith Ruud, an economist with the

attachment *the positive emotional bond that develops between a child and a particular individual*

Congressional Budget Office in Washington, D.C. "He learned by trial and error, and the other kids saw him do it one day when they were getting dressed for an outing" (Goleman,1993, p. C10).

By then, however, it was too late for excuses: Russell, it seems, was an excellent teacher. Keeping the children's hats on their heads proved to be no easy task. Even more ominous was the thought that if the infants could master the Velcro straps on their hats, would they soon be opening the Velcro fasteners on their shoes and removing *them*?

Russell's behavior exemplifies an unexpected outcome of infants' participation in day care: the acquisition of new skills and abilities from more "expert" peers. But it also exemplifies the importance of social interactions that are a significant part of infancy. During the first years of life, children become genuinely social creatures as they develop socially.

Attachment: Forming Social Bonds

The most important form of social development that takes place during infancy is attachment. **Attachment** is the positive emotional bond that develops between a child and a particular individual. The nature of our attachment during infancy affects how we relate to others throughout the rest of our lives (Greeberg, Cicchetti, & Cummings, 1990; Kochanska, 1995; Colin, 1996; Bretherton, Golby, & Cho, 1997).

To understand attachment, the earliest researchers turned to the bonds that form between parents and children in the nonhuman animal kingdom. For instance, ethologist Konrad Lorenz (1965) observed newborn goslings, who have an innate tendency to follow their mother, the first moving object to which they typically are exposed after birth. Lorenz found that goslings whose eggs were raised in an incubator and who viewed *him* just after hatching would follow *his* every movement, as if he were their mother. He labeled this process *imprinting*: behavior that takes place during a critical period and involves attachment to the first moving object that is observed.

Lorenz's findings suggested that attachment was based on biologically determined factors, and other theorists agreed. For instance, Freud suggested that attachment grew out of a mother's ability to satisfy a child's oral needs.

On the other hand, the ability to provide food and other physiological needs is not as crucial as Freud and other theorists first thought. In a classic study, psychologist Harry Harlow gave infant monkeys the choice of cuddling a wire "monkey" that provided food or a soft, terry cloth "monkey" that was warm but did not provide food (see Figure 6-2). Their preference was clear: They would spend most of their time clinging to the cloth "monkey," although they made occasional expeditions to the wire monkey to nurse. Harlow suggested that the preference for the warm cloth "monkey" provided *contact comfort* (Harlow & Zimmerman, 1959).

Harlow's work clearly illustrates that food alone is insufficient to bring about attachment. Furthermore, these findings are congruent with the research we discussed in Chapter 3 showing no evidence for the existence of a critical bonding period between human mothers and infants immediately after birth.

The earliest work on human attachment, which is still highly influential, was carried out by John Bowlby (1951). Bowlby's theorizing about attachment had a biological basis, although it was supplemented by observations of emotionally disturbed children with whom he worked in a London clinic.

In Bowlby's view, attachment is based primarily on infants' needs for safety and security—their genetically determined motivation to avoid predators. As they develop, infants come to learn that their safety is best provided by a particular individual, a realization that ultimately leads to the development of a special relationship, typically with the mother. He suggests that this single relationship is qualitatively different from the bonds formed with

FIGURE 6-2 HARLOW'S MONKEYS.

Despite the food provided by the wire "monkey," the infant monkeys spent most of their time clinging to the warm, terry cloth monkey.

Mary Ainsworth, who devised the "strange situation" to measure infant attachment.

others, including the father—a suggestion that, as we'll see later, has been a source of some subsequent dispute.

Bowlby also suggests, somewhat ironically, that attachment—which has its roots in the desire to seek the protective security of the mother—is critical in allowing an infant to explore the world. According to his view, having strong, firm attachment provides a kind of home base away from which growing children can progressively roam as they become more independent.

Using Bowlby's theorizing as a base, developmental psychologist Mary Ainsworth developed a widely used experimental technique to measure attachment (Ainsworth et al., 1978). The **Ainsworth Strange Situation** consists of a sequence of staged episodes that illustrates the strength of attachment between a child and (typically) his or her mother. The "strange situation" follows this general eight-step pattern: (1) The mother and baby enter an unfamiliar room; (2) the mother sits down, leaving the baby free to explore; (3) an adult stranger enters the room and converses first with the mother and then with the baby; (4) the mother exits the room, leaving the baby alone with the stranger; (5) the mother returns, greeting and comforting the baby, and the stranger leaves; (6) the mother departs again, leaving the baby alone; (7) the stranger returns; and (8) the mother returns and the stranger leaves (Ainsworth et al., 1978).

Infants' reactions to the various aspects of the Strange Situation vary considerably, depending on the nature of their attachment to their mothers. One-year-olds show three major patterns—securely attached, avoidant, and ambivalent (summarized in Table 6-1). **Securely attached children** use the mother as a kind of home base, at ease in the Strange Situation as long as she is present. They explore independently, returning to her occasionally. When she leaves, though, they act upset, and they go to her as soon as she returns. Most children—about two-thirds—fall into the securely attached category.

In contrast, **avoidant children** do not seek proximity to the mother, and after the mother has left, they seem to avoid her when she returns. It is as if they are angered by her behavior. Some 20 percent of 1-year-old children are in the avoidant category.

Finally, the last group, labeled **ambivalent children**, display a combination of positive and negative reactions to their mothers. Ambivalent children are in such close contact with the mother that they may not explore their environment much. They may be anxious even before the mother leaves, and when she does they show great distress. On her return, however, they show ambivalent reactions, simultaneously seeking close contact but also hitting and kicking her. About 12 percent of 1-year-olds fall into the ambivalent classification (Cassidy & Berlin, 1994).

Ainsworth Strange Situation *a sequence of staged episodes that illustrates the strength of attachment between a child and (typically) his or her mother*

securely attached children *children who use the mother as a kind of home base and are at ease when she is present; when she leaves, they become upset and go to her as soon as she returns*

avoidant children *children who do not seek proximity to the mother; after the mother has left, they seem to avoid her when she returns as if they are angered by her behavior*

ambivalent children *children who display a combination of positive and negative reactions to their mothers; they show great distress when the mother leaves, but upon her return they may simultaneously seek close contact but also hit and kick her*

TABLE 6-1

CLASSIFICATIONS OF INFANT ATTACHMENT

Label	Proximity Seeking	Contact Maintaining	Proximity Avoiding	Contact Resisting	Crying
		CLASSIFICATION CRITERIA			
Avoidant	Low	Low	High	Low	Low (pre-separation), high or low (separation), low (reunion)
Secure	High	High (if distressed)	Low	Low	Low (pre-separation), high or low (separation), low (reunion)
Ambivalent	High	High (often pre-separation)	Low	High	Occasionally (pre-separation), high (separation), moderate to high (reunion)

(*Source:* Waters, 1978.)

In this illustration of the strange situation, the infant first explores the playroom on his own, as long as his mother is present. But when she leaves, he begins to cry. On her return, however, he is immediately comforted and stops crying. The conclusion: he is securely attached.

disorganized-disoriented children   *children who show inconsistent, often contradictory behavior, such as approaching the mother when she returns but not looking at her; they may be the least securely attached children of all*

Although Ainsworth identified only three categories, a more recent expansion of her work suggests that there is a fourth category: disorganized-disoriented. **Disorganized-disoriented children** show inconsistent, often contradictory behavior, such as approaching the mother when she returns but not looking at her. Their confusion suggests that they may be the least securely attached children of all (Egeland & Farber, 1984; O'Connor, Sigman, & Brill, 1987; Mayseless, 1996).

A child's attachment style would be of only minor consequence were it not for the fact that the nature of attachment between infants and their mothers has significant consequences for relationships at later stages of life. For example, boys who are securely attached at the age of 1 year show fewer psychological difficulties at older ages than do avoidant or ambivalent children. Similarly, children who are securely attached as infants tend to be more socially and emotionally competent later, and others view them more positively. Adult romantic relationships are associated with the kind of attachment style developed during infancy. In fact, as we discuss in the "Directions in Development" box, attachment styles are related to how effectively children react to stress (Ainsworth & Bowlby, 1991; Shaw & Vondra, 1995; van Ijzendoorn, 1995; Belsky et al., 1996; Belsky, Spritz, & Crnic, 1996; Seifer et al., 1996; Tidwell, Reiss, & Shaver, 1996).

On the other hand, we cannot say that children who do not have a secure attachment style during infancy invariably experience difficulties later in life, nor that those with a secure attachment at age 1 always have good adjustment later on. In fact, some evidence suggests that children with avoidant and ambivalent attachment—as measured by the Strange Situation—do quite well (Lamb et al., 1984; Fox, 1995).

Producing Attachment: The Roles of the Mother and Father

As 5-month-old Annie cries passionately, her mother comes into the room and gently lifts her from her crib. After just a few moments, as her mother rocks Annie and speaks softly, Annie's cries cease, and she cuddles in her mother's arms. But the moment her mother places her back in the crib, Annie begins to wail again, leading her mother to pick her up once again.

The pattern is familiar to most parents. The infant cries, the parent reacts, and the child responds in turn. Yet such seemingly insignificant sequences as these, repeatedly occurring in the lives of infants and parents, help pave the way for the development of relationships between children, their parents, and the rest of the social world. We'll consider how each of the major caregivers and the infant play a role in the development of attachment.

Mothers and Attachment.   Sensitivity to their infants' needs and desires is the hallmark of mothers of securely attached infants. Such a mother tends to be aware of her child's moods, and she takes into account her child's feelings as they interact. She is also responsive during face-to-face interactions, provides feeding "on demand," and is warm and affectionate to her infant (Field, 1987; Pederson et al, 1990; Ainsworth, 1993; Isabella, 1993; DeWolff & van Ijzendoorn, 1997).

Attachment styles are stable from one generation to the next.

Directions in Development

How Secure Attachment Helps Reduce Stress

Although attachment is usually thought of in terms of the psychological bonds between caregivers and children, good attachment may also help reduce the harmful consequences of stress.

At least that is the conclusion that can be drawn from work done by developmental psychologist Megan Gunnar and her colleagues at the Institute of Child Development at the University of Minnesota. In recent studies, Gunnar has been examining how children react to mildly stressful events. To test the children's reactions, researchers measure the hormone cortisol, which is an indicator of stress, by taking samples of children's saliva (Gunnar, Brodersen, Nachmias, & Buss, 1996; Gunnar, Brodersen, Krueger, & Rigatuso, 1996).

In one study, for example, 18-month-old children were exposed to a live clown, a robot clown, and a puppet show, three stimuli that were designed to evoke a mild level of anxiety. The children were free to approach, ignore, or avoid the stimuli. Although the children's mothers were always present, they were told not to intervene in the situation for the first 3 minutes. For the second 3 minutes, mothers were told to comfort their children (Nachmias et al., 1996).

Following the children's exposure to the stimulus, the researchers took samples of the children's saliva to measure cortisol levels. Later they assessed children's attachment styles, using the Ainsworth Strange Situation.

The results were clear in showing that the cortisol levels of children who were fearful of approaching the stimuli varied according to their attachment level. For the children with secure attachment, no rise in cortisol levels was detected. However, children with avoidant or ambivalent styles showed a rise in cortisol levels, indicating higher levels of stress.

There were also differences in how successful mothers were in calming their children. Mothers of securely attached children were easily able to calm their children, but mothers of less securely attached children needed significantly more time to quiet their children.

These findings are congruent with work on stress levels found in children who spent most of their lives in Romanian orphanages. As described in the case of Simona Young, discussed in the Chapter 5 prologue, Romanian orphanages were squalid, and infants rarely received either emotional or physical stimulation. The average caretaker-to-child ratio was 1 to 20. In such cases, there was no one with whom the infants could form secure attachment. Not surprisingly, the orphans demonstrated abnormal patterns of cortisol secretion (Carlson & Earls, 1997; Marcovitch et al., 1997).

The accumulating results suggest that secure attachment acts as a buffer against stress, moderating children's physiological reactions. However, poor attachment may produce children who react badly to stressful stimuli, making them more vulnerable to the stress that is part of every child's life.

It is not only a matter of responding in *any* fashion to their infants' signals that separates mothers of securely attached and insecurely attached children. Mothers of secure infants tend to provide the appropriate level of response. For instance, research has shown that overly responsive mothers are just as likely to have insecurely attached children as underresponsive mothers (Belsky, Rovine, & Taylor, 1984).

The research showing the correspondence between mothers' sensitivity to their infants and the security of the infants' attachment is consistent with Ainsworth's arguments that attachment depends on how mothers react to their infants' social overtures. Ainsworth suggests that mothers of securely attached infants respond rapidly and positively to their infants. In contrast, the way for mothers to produce insecurely attached infants, according to Ainsworth, is to ignore their behavioral cues, to behave inconsistently with them, and to ignore or reject their social efforts.

But how do mothers know how to respond to their infants' cues? One answer is that they learn from their own mothers. For instance, mothers tend to have attachment styles that are similar to those developed by their infants. In fact, some research finds substantial stability in attachment patterns from one generation to the next (Boit & Parker, 1994).

In part, mothers' (and others') behavior toward infants is a reaction to the children's ability to provide effective cues. A mother may not be able to respond effectively to a child whose own behavior is unrevealing, misleading, or ambiguous. The kind of signals an infant sends may in part determine how successful the mother will be in responding.

Fathers and Attachment.   Up to now, we've barely touched on one of the key players involved in the upbringing of a child: the father. In fact, if you looked at the early theorizing and research on attachment, you'd find little mention of the father and his potential contributions to the life of the infant (Russell & Radojevic, 1992).

There are at least two reasons for this absence. First, John Bowlby, who provided the initial theory of attachment, suggested that there was something unique about the mother–child relationship. He believed the mother as uniquely equipped, biologically, to provide sustenance for the child, and he concluded that this capability led to the development of a special relationship between mothers and children. Second, the early work on attachment was influenced by the traditional social views of the time, which considered it "natural" for the mother to be the primary caregiver, whereas the father's role was to work outside the home to provide a living for his family.

Several factors led to the demise of this view. One was that societal norms changed, and fathers began to take a more active role in childrearing activities. More important, it became increasingly clear from research findings that—despite societal norms that relegated fathers to secondary childrearing roles—some infants formed their primary initial relationship with their fathers. Moreover, many infants had strong attachment relationships with more than one individual (Lamb, 1982b; Goossens & van Ijzendoorn, 1990; Volling & Belsky, 1992).

For example, one study found that although most infants formed their first primary relationship with one person, around one-third had multiple relationships, and it was difficult to determine which attachment was primary (Schaffer & Emerson, 1964). Furthermore, by the time the infants were 18 months old, most had formed multiple relationships. In sum, infants may develop attachments not only to their mothers, but to a variety of others as well (Parke & Tinsley, 1987; Fox, Kimmerly, & Schafer, 1991).

Still, the nature of attachment between infants and mothers, on the one hand, and infants and fathers, on the other hand, is not identical (Cox et al., 1992; Pipp, Easterbrooks, & Brown, 1993). For example, when they are in unusually stressful circumstances, they prefer to be soothed by their mothers, rather than by their fathers (Lamb, 1977).

One reason for qualitative differences in attachment involves the differences in what fathers and mothers do with their children. Mothers spend a greater proportion of their time feeding and directly nurturing their children. In contrast, fathers spend more time, proportionally, playing with infants. Nevertheless, almost all fathers do contribute to child care: Surveys show that 95 percent say they do some child-care chores every day. But on average they still do less than mothers. For instance, 30 percent of fathers with wives who work do 3 or more hours of daily child care, in comparison with 74 percent of employed married

Some children form their primary initial relationship with their fathers, and some have more than one strong attachment relationship.

mothers who spend that amount of time in child-care activities (see Figure 6-3; Parke, 1981; NSFH, 1988; Jacobsen & Edmondson, 1993; Bailey, 1994).

Furthermore, the nature of fathers' play with their infants is often quite different from that of mothers. Fathers engage in more physical, rough-and-tumble activities with their children. In contrast, mothers play traditional games such as peek-a-boo and games with more verbal elements (Lamb, 1986; Parke, 1990, 1996).

These differences in the ways that fathers and mothers play with their children occur even in the minority of families in the United States in which the father is the primary caregiver. Moreover, the differences occur in very diverse cultures: Fathers in Australia, Israel, India, Japan, and even in the Aka Pygmy tribe in central Africa all engage more in play than in caregiving (Lamb, 1987; Roopnarine, 1992). These similarities raise an important question: Are there similarities in attachment styles across cultures, or do diverse cultural practices result in differences in attachment?

mutual regulation model   *the model in which infants and parents learn to communicate emotional states to one another and to respond appropriately*

Infant Interactions: Developing a Working Relationship

Research on attachment is clear in showing that infants may develop multiple attachment relationships, and that over time the specific individuals with whom the infant is primarily attached may change. These variations in attachment highlight the fact that the development of relationships is an ongoing process, not only during infancy, but throughout childhood.

Which processes underlie the development of relationships during infancy? One answer comes from studies that examine how parents interact with their children. For instance, across almost all cultures, mothers behave in typical ways with their infants. They tend to exaggerate their facial and vocal expressions—the nonverbal equivalent of the infant-directed speech that they use when they speak to infants (as we discussed in Chapter 5). Similarly, they often imitate their infants' behavior, responding to distinctive sounds and movements by repeating them. There are even types of games, such as peek-a-boo, itsy-bitsy spider, and pat-a-cake, that are nearly universal (Field, 1979, 1990; Kochanska, 1997).

According to the **mutual regulation model**, infants and parents learn to communicate emotional states to one another and to respond appropriately. For instance, both infant and parent act jointly to regulate turn-taking behavior, with one individual waiting until the other completes a behavioral act before starting another. Consequently, at

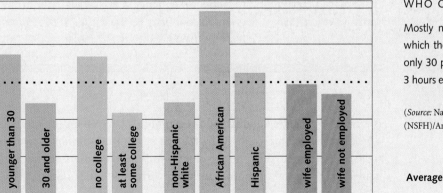

FIGURE 6-3

WHO CARES FOR THE KIDS?

Mostly not the fathers: Even in families in which the mother works outside the home, only 30 percent of fathers put in more than 3 hours each day caring for their preschooler.

(*Source:* National Survey of Families and Households (NSFH)/American Demographics.)

· · · · ·
Average for all married fathers with a preschooler

Fathers Who Spend 3 or More Hours a Day Caring for a Preschooler

Developmental Diversity

Does Attachment Differ Across Cultures?

Recall that the work on attachment was initially inspired by John Bowlby's observations of the biologically motivated efforts of the young of other species to seek safety and security. From these observations, Bowlby suggested that seeking attachment was a biological universal, one that we should not only find in other species, but among humans as well. Such reasoning suggests that we should see attachment strivings in all humans, regardless of their culture.

However, research has brought this contention into question. For example, one study of German infants showed that most fell into the avoidant category (Grossmann et al., 1982). Other studies, conducted in Israel and Japan, have found a smaller proportion of infants who were securely attached than in the United States (Sagi et al., 1985; Takahashi, 1986; Sagi, 1990).

Other cross-cultural analyses confirm not only that there are differences in the proportions of infants who fall into the various attachment categories, but also that subcultural differences exist even within particular societies (van Ijzendoorn & Kroonenberg, 1988; Sagi, van Ijzendoorn, & Koren-Karie, 1991; Sagi et al., 1994, 1995). Do such findings suggest that we should abandon the notion that attachment is a universal biological tendency?

Not necessarily. Most of the data on attachment have been obtained by using the Ainsworth Strange Situation, which may not be the most appropriate measure in non-Western cultures. For example, Japanese parents seek to avoid separation and stress during infancy, and they don't strive to foster independence to the same degree as parents in many Western societies. Because of their relative lack of prior experience in separation, then, infants placed in the Strange Situation may experience unusual stress—producing the appearance of less secure attachment in Japanese children. If a different measure of attachment were used, one that might be administered later in infancy, more Japanese infants could likely be classified as secure (Nakagawa, Lamb, & Miyaki, 1992; Posada et al., 1995; Mizuta et al., 1996; Vereijken et al., 1997).

Japanese parents seek to avoid separation and stress during infancy and do not foster independence. As a result, Japanese children often have the appearance of being less securely attached according to the Strange Situation, but using other measurement techniques they may well score higher in attachment.

In sum, on the one hand, cross-cultural and within-cultural differences in attachment reflect the nature of the measure employed. On the other hand, it is possible that Bowlby's claim that the desire for attachment is universal was too strongly stated. In fact, more recent approaches view attachment as not entirely biologically determined, but rather as susceptible to cultural norms and expectations.

Specifically, some developmental specialists suggest that attachment should be viewed as a general tendency, but one that is modifiable according to how actively caregivers in a society seek to instill independence in their children. Consequently, secure attachment may be seen earliest in cultures that promote independence, but may be delayed in societies in which independence is a less important cultural value (van Ijzendoorn & Taveccio, 1987; Harwood, Miller, & Irizarry, 1995).

the age of 3 months, infants and their mothers have about the same influence on each other's behavior. Interestingly, by the age of 6 months, infants have more control over turn-taking, although by the age of 9 months both partners once again become roughly equivalent in terms of mutual influence (Tronick & Gianino, 1986; Cohn & Tronick, 1989; Nwokah & Fogel, 1993).

One of the ways infants and parents signal each other when they interact is through facial expressions. Even quite young infants are able to read, or decode, the facial expressions of their caregivers, and they react to those expressions (Lelwica & Haviland, 1983; Camras, Malatesta, & Izard, 1991; Anisfeld, 1996).

For example, an infant whose mother, during an experiment, displays a stony, immobile facial expression reacts by making a variety of sounds, gestures, and facial expressions of her own in response to such a puzzling situation—and possibly to elicit some new response from her mother. Infants also show more happiness themselves when their mothers appear happy, and they look at their mothers longer. On the other hand, infants are apt to respond with sad looks and to turn away when their mothers display unhappy expressions (Termin & Izard, 1988).

In sum, the development of attachment in infants does not merely represent a reaction to the behavior of the people around them. Instead, there is a process of **reciprocal socialization**, in which infants' behaviors invite further responses from parents and other caregivers. In turn, the caregivers' behaviors bring about a reaction from the child, continuing the cycle. Ultimately, these actions and reactions lead to an increase in attachment, forging and strengthening bonds between infants and caregivers. Figure 6-4 summarizes the sequence of infant-caregiver interaction (Bell & Ainsworth, 1972; Ainsworth & Bowlby, 1991; Egeland, Pianta, & O'Brien, 1993; Bradley & Caldwell, 1995).

reciprocal socialization *a process in which infants' behaviors invite further responses from parents and other caregivers, which in turn bring about further responses from the infants*

Infants' Sociability with Their Peers: Infant–Infant Interaction

How sociable are infants with other children? Although it is clear that they do not form "friendships" in the traditional sense, they do react positively to the presence of peers from early in life, and they engage in rudimentary forms of social interaction (Field, 1990).

Infants' sociability is expressed in several ways. From the earliest months of life they smile, laugh, and vocalize while looking at their peers. They show more interest in peers than in inanimate objects, and they pay greater attention to other infants than they do to a mirror image of themselves (Fogel, 1980; Field, 1981; Field & Roopnarine, 1982).

FIGURE 6-4

SEQUENCE OF INFANT–CAREGIVER INTERACTION

The actions and reactions of caregivers and infants influence each other in complex ways.

(*Source:* Adapted from Bell & Ainsworth, 1972, and Tomlinson-Keasey, 1985.)

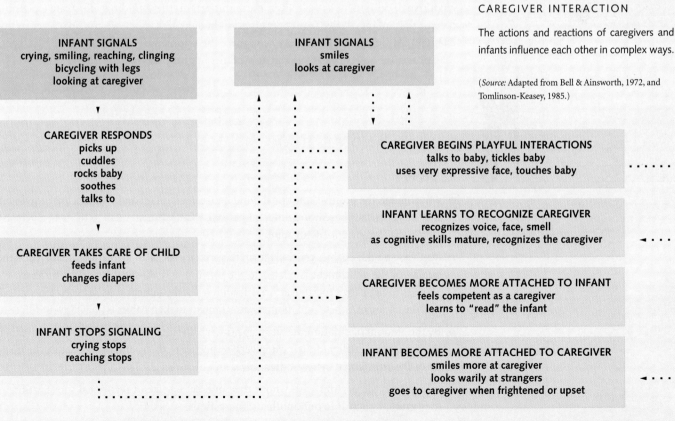

On the other hand, infants are not consistently sociable. For one thing, by the end of the first year they start to show more interest in inanimate toys as they become better able to manipulate objects and to move around in the world. Furthermore, they begin to show preferences for people with whom they are familiar compared with those they do not know. For example, studies of identical twins show that twins exhibit a higher level of social behavior toward each other than toward an unfamiliar infant (Field & Roopnarine, 1982; Field, 1990).

Still, an infant's level of sociability generally rises with age. Nine- to twelve-month-olds mutually present and accept toys, particularly if they know each other. They also play social games, such as peek-a-boo or crawl-and-chase (Vincze, 1971; Endo, 1992). Such behavior is important, as it serves as a foundation for future social exchanges involving the elicitation of responses from others and the offering of reactions to those responses (Brownell, 1986; Howes, 1987).

Finally, as infants age, they begin to imitate each other (Russon & Waite, 1991). For instance, 14-month-old infants who are familiar with one another sometimes reproduce each other's behavior (Mueller & Vandell, 1979). Such imitation serves a social function and can also be a powerful teaching tool. For example, recall the story of 10-month-old Russell Ruud, who showed the other children in his day-care center how he could remove his hat by unfastening its Velcro straps, and soon had others following his lead.

According to Andrew Meltzoff, a developmental psychologist at the University of Washington, Russell's ability to impart this information is only one example of how so-called expert babies are able to teach skills and information to other infants. According to the research of Meltzoff and his colleagues, the abilities learned from the "experts" are retained and later utilized to a remarkable degree. Moreover, learning by exposure starts early in life. For example, recent evidence shows that even 6-week-old infants perform delayed imitation of a novel stimulus to which they have earlier been exposed, such as an adult sticking the tongue out the side of the mouth (Hanna & Meltzoff, 1993; Meltzoff & Moore, 1994).

Finding that infants learn new behaviors, skills, and abilities due to exposure to other children has several implications. For one thing, it suggests that interactions between infants provide more than social benefits; they may have an impact on children's future cognitive development as well. Even more important, these findings illustrate a possible benefit that infants derive from participation in day care (which we consider later in this chapter). Although we don't know for sure, the opportunity to learn from their peers may prove to be a lasting advantage for infants in group day-care settings.

REVIEW AND RETHINK

REVIEW

- Attachment, the positive emotional bond between an infant and a significant individual, may be genetically based, and different patterns of attachment seem to relate to a person's later social competence as an adult.

- Mothers and their babies generally form the primary social attachment in infancy, and the quality of the attachment is related to the warmth and effectiveness of the mother's responses to her baby's social overtures. Traditionally, the father's role has been less central, and the nature of fathers' and mothers' attachments to their babies is qualitatively different.

- By the amount of emotion they display nonverbally, infants to some extent may mediate the nature and quality of their caregivers' responses to them, and consequently the quality of the attachment between themselves and their caregivers.

- Infants and the persons with whom they interact engage in reciprocal socialization as they mutually adjust to one another's interactions.

■ Infants react differently to other children than to inanimate objects, and gradually they engage in increasing amounts of peer social interaction, even participating in reciprocal teaching and learning.

RETHINK

■ In what sort of society might the attachment style labeled "avoidant" be encouraged by cultural attitudes toward childrearing? In such a society, would characterizing the infant's consistent avoidance of its mother as anger be an accurate interpretation?

■ In what ways might overly responsive and underresponsive caregivers equally contribute to insecure attachment in their infants?

■ Does the importance of infants' early attachment to primary caregivers have social policy implications relating to working parents? Do current policies reveal societal assumptions pertaining to the different roles of mothers and fathers?

■ Can you discern a relationship between reciprocal socialization and operant conditioning? Explain.

■ Why do you think that learning from peers is so effective for young children? Does this finding have implications for educational practices? Explain.

DIFFERENCES AMONG INFANTS

"It's a boy." "It's a girl."

One of these two statements, or some variant, is probably the first announcement made in the delivery room after the birth of a child. Why does this differentiation occur, and what are the implications of dividing children so rigorously according to their gender?

We turn now to such questions as we consider some of the differences among infants and the lives they lead—differences not only in gender, but also in overall personality, temperament, the nature of infants' families, and the ways in which infants are cared for.

Personality Development: The Characteristics That Make Infants Unique

The origins of **personality**, the sum total of the enduring characteristics that differentiate one individual from another, stem from infancy. From birth onward, infants begin to show unique, stable traits and behaviors that ultimately lead to their development as distinct, special individuals (Halverson, Kohnstamm, & Martin, 1994; Pipp-Siegel & Foltz, 1997).

According to psychologist Erik Erikson, whose approach to personality development we first discussed in Chapter 1, infants' early experiences are responsible for shaping one of the key aspects of their personalities: whether they will be basically trusting or mistrustful.

Erikson's theory of psychosocial development considers how individuals come to understand themselves and the meaning of others'—and their own—behavior (Erikson, 1963). The theory suggests that developmental change occurs throughout people's lives in eight distinct stages, the first of which occurs in infancy.

According to Erikson, infancy marks the time of the **trust-versus-mistrust stage**, encompassing birth to 18 months. During this period, infants develop a sense of trust or mistrust, largely depending on how well their needs are met by their caregivers. Erikson suggests that if infants are able to develop trust, they experience a sense of hope, which permits them to feel as if they can fulfill their needs successfully. On the other hand, feelings of mistrust lead infants to see the world as harsh and unfriendly, and they may have later difficulties in forming close bonds with others.

During the end of infancy, children enter the **autonomy-versus-shame-and-doubt stage**, which lasts from around 18 months to 3 years. During this period, children develop independence and autonomy if parents encourage exploration and freedom. However, if children are restricted and overly protected, they feel shame, self-doubt, and unhappiness.

personality the sum total of the enduring characteristics that differentiate one individual from another

Erikson's theory of psychosocial development the theory that considers how individuals come to understand themselves and the meaning of others'—and their own—behavior

trust-versus-mistrust stage according to Erikson, the period during which infants develop a sense of trust or mistrust, largely depending on how well their needs are met by their caregivers

autonomy-versus-shame-and-doubt stage the period during which, according to Erikson, toddlers (aged 18 months to 3 years) develop either independence and autonomy if they are allowed the freedom to explore or shame and self-doubt if they are restricted and overprotected

temperament *patterns of arousal and emotionality that are consistent and enduring characteristics of an individual*

Erikson argues that personality is primarily shaped by infants' experiences. However, as we discuss next, other developmentalists concentrate on consistencies of behavior that are present at birth. These consistencies are viewed as largely genetically determined and as providing the raw material of personality.

Temperament: Stabilities in Infant Behavior

Sarah's parents thought there must be something wrong. Unlike her older brother, Josh, who had been so active as an infant that he seemed never to be still, Sarah was much more placid. She took long naps and was easily soothed on those relatively rare occasions when she became agitated. What could be producing her extreme calmness?

The most likely answer: The difference between Sarah and Josh reflected differences in temperament. As we first discussed in Chapter 2, **temperament** encompasses patterns of arousal and emotionality that are consistent and enduring characteristics of an individual.

Temperament refers to *how* children behave, as opposed to *what* they do or *why* they do it (Thomas & Chess, 1984). Infants show temperamental differences in general disposition from the time of birth. These differences appear to be largely determined by genetic factors, although evidence also suggests that the prenatal environment and the nature of a child's birth may also have some influence. Regardless of cause, temperament is quite consistent, with longitudinal studies showing stability from infancy well into adolescence (Guerin & Gottfried, 1994; Caspi et al., 1995; Gunnar et al., 1995; Goldsmith, Buss, & Lemery, 1997; Newman et al., 1997).

Several dimensions of behavior reflect temperament. One central dimension is *activity level*, which reflects the degree of overall movement. Some babies (like Sarah) are relatively placid, and their movements are slow and almost leisurely. In contrast, the activity level of other infants (like Josh) is quite high, with strong, restless movements of the arms and legs.

Another important dimension of temperament is the nature and quality of an infant's mood, and in particular a child's *irritability*. Some infants are easily disturbed and cry easily, whereas others are relatively easygoing. Irritable infants fuss a great deal, and they are easily upset. They are also difficult to soothe when they do begin to cry. Such irritability is relatively stable: Researchers find that infants who are irritable at birth remain irritable at the age of 1, and even at age 2 they are still more easily upset than infants who were not irritable just after birth (Worobey & Bajda, 1989). (Other aspects of temperament are listed in Table 6-2).

 Categorizing Temperament: Easy, Difficult, and Slow-to-warm Babies.   Because temperament can be viewed along so many dimensions, some researchers have asked whether there are broader categories that can be used to describe children's overall behavior. According to

---

TABLE 6-2

DIMENSIONS OF TEMPERAMENT

Dimension	Temperament
Activity level	Proportion of active time periods to inactive time periods
Approach-withdrawal	The response to a new person or object, based on whether the child accepts the new situation or withdraws from it
Adaptability	How easily the child is able to adapt to changes in his or her environment
Quality of mood	The contrast of the amount of friendly, joyful, and pleasant behavior with unpleasant, unfriendly behavior
Attention span and persistence	The amount of time the child devotes to an activity and the effect of distraction on that activity
Distractibility	The degree to which stimuli in the environment alter behavior
Rhythmicity (regularity)	The regularity of basic functions such as hunger, excretion, sleep, and wakefulness
Intensity of reaction	The energy level or reaction of the child's response
Threshold of responsiveness	The intensity of stimulation needed to elicit a response

(*Source:* Thomas, Chess & Birch, 1968.)

Alexander Thomas and Stella Chess, who carried out a large-scale study of a group of infants that has come to be known as the *New York Longitudinal Study*, babies can be described according to one of several profiles:

- Easy babies. **Easy babies** have a positive disposition. Their body functions operate regularly, and they are adaptable. They are generally positive, showing curiosity about new situations, and their emotions are moderate or low in intensity. This category applies to about 40 percent (the largest number) of infants.
- Difficult babies. **Difficult babies** have more negative moods and are slow to adapt to new situations. When confronted with a new situation, they tend to withdraw. About 10 percent of infants belong in this category.
- Slow-to-warm babies. **Slow-to-warm babies** are inactive, showing relatively calm reactions to their environment. Their moods are generally negative, and they withdraw from new situations, adapting slowly. Approximately 15 percent of infants are slow-to-warm.

As for the remaining 35 percent, they cannot be consistently categorized. These children show a variety of combinations of characteristics. For instance, one infant may have relatively sunny moods, but react negatively to new situations, or another may show little stability of any sort in terms of general temperament.

The Consequences of Temperament: Does Temperament Matter? The obvious question to emerge from the findings of the relative stability of temperament is whether a particular kind of temperament is beneficial. The answer seems to be that no single type of temperament is invariably good or bad. Instead, children's long-term adjustment depends on the **goodness of fit** of their particular temperament and the nature and demands of the environment in which they find themselves. For instance, children with a low activity level and low irritability may do particularly well in an environment in which they are left to explore on their own and are allowed largely to direct their own behavior. In contrast, high activity level, highly irritable children may do best with greater direction, which permits them to channel their energy in particular directions (Thomas & Chess, 1977, 1980; Mangelsdorf et al., 1990; Bornstein & Lamb, 1992b).

Some research does suggest that certain temperaments are, in general, more adaptive than others. For instance, Thomas and Chess found that difficult children, in general, were more likely to show behavior problems by school age than those who were classified in infancy as easy children (Thomas, Chess, & Birch, 1968). But not all difficult children experience problems. The key determinant seems to be the way parents react to their infants' difficult behavior. If they react by showing anger and inconsistency—responses that their child's difficult, demanding behavior readily evokes—then the child is ultimately more likely to experience behavior problems. On the other hand, parents who display more warmth and consistency in their responses are more likely to have children who avoid later problems (Crockenberg, 1986; Belsky, Fish, & Isabella, 1991).

Furthermore, temperament seems to be at least weakly related to infants' attachment to their adult caregivers. For example, infants vary considerably in how much emotion they display nonverbally. Some are "poker-faced," showing little expressivity, whereas others' reactions tend to be much more easily decoded (Field et al., 1982; Feldman & Rimé, 1991). More expressive infants may provide more easily discernible cues to others, thereby easing the way for caregivers to be more successful in responding to their needs and facilitating attachment (Belsky & Rovine, 1987; Calkins & Fox, 1992; Vaughn et al., 1992; Goldsmith & Harman, 1994; Seifer et al., 1996).

Cultural differences also have a major influence on the consequences of a particular temperament. For instance, children who would be described as "difficult" in Western cultures actually seem to have an advantage in the East African Masai culture. The reason? Mothers offer their breast to their infants only when they fuss and cry; therefore, the irritable, more

easy babies *babies who have a positive disposition; their body functions operate regularly, and they are adaptable*

difficult babies *babies who have negative moods and are slow to adapt to new situations; when confronted with a new situation, they tend to withdraw*

slow-to-warm babies *babies who are inactive, showing relatively calm reactions to their environment; their moods are generally negative, and they withdraw from new situations, adapting slowly*

goodness of fit *the notion that development is dependent on the degree of match between children's temperament and the nature and demands of the environment in which they are being raised*

gender *the sense of being male or female*

difficult infants are apt to receive more nourishment than the more placid, easy infants. Particularly when environmental conditions are bad, such as during a drought, difficult babies are apt to have an advantage (deVries, 1984).

Recent approaches to temperament grow out of the framework of behavioral genetics that we discussed in Chapter 2. For instance, David Buss and Robert Plomin (1984) argue that temperamental characteristics represent inherited traits that are fairly stable during childhood and across the entire life span. These traits are seen as making up the core of personality and playing a substantial role in future development.

Gender: Why Do Boys Wear Blue and Girls Wear Pink?

From the moment of birth, girls and boys are treated differently. Their parents send out different kinds of birth announcements. They are given different clothes to wear and different-colored blankets. The toys that are chosen for them differ (Bridges, 1993; Coltrane & Adams, 1997).

Parents play with them differently: From birth on, fathers tend to interact more with sons than daughters, and mothers interact more with daughters (Parke & Sawin, 1980). Because, as we noted earlier in the chapter, mothers and fathers play in different ways (with fathers typically engaging in more physical, rough-and-tumble activities and mothers in traditional games such as peek-a-boo), male and female infants are clearly exposed to different styles of activity and interaction from their parents (Power & Parke, 1982; Lamb, 1986; Parke, 1990; Grant, 1994).

The behavior exhibited by girls and boys is interpreted in very different ways by adults. For instance, in one experiment researchers showed adults a video of an infant whose name was given as either "John" or "Mary" (Condry & Condry, 1976). Although it was the same baby performing a single set of behaviors, adults perceived "John" as adventurous and inquisitive, whereas "Mary" was fearful and anxious. Clearly adults view the behavior of children through the lens of **gender**, the sense of being male or female. ("Gender" and "sex" are not the same: Sex typically refers to sexual anatomy and sexual behavior, whereas gender refers to the perception of maleness or femaleness related to membership in a particular society; Stern & Karraker, 1989; Pomerleau et al., 1990; Burnham & Harris, 1992.)

Although to some extent boys and girls live in different worlds due to gender, there is a considerable amount of argument over both the extent and causes of such gender differences. Some gender differences are fairly clear from the time of birth. For example, male infants tend to be more active and fussier than female infants. Boys grimace more, although no gender difference exists in the overall amount of crying, and boys' sleep tends to be more disturbed than that of girls. There is also some evidence that male newborns are more irritable than female newborns, although the findings are inconsistent (Moss, 1974; Phillips, King, & DuBois, 1978; Eaton & Enns, 1986).

Furthermore, the differences among male and female infants are generally minor. In fact, in most ways infants seem so similar that usually adults cannot discern whether a baby is a boy or girl. Furthermore, it is important to keep in mind that the differences among individual boys, and the differences among individual girls, are much more extensive than the average differences found when boys and girls are compared (Langlois et al., 1991; Unger & Crawford, 1992; Beal, 1994).

Gender differences emerge more clearly as children age—and become increasingly influenced by the gender roles that society sets out for them. For instance, by the age of one year, infants are able to distinguish between males and females. Furthermore, girls prefer to play with dolls or stuffed animals, whereas boys seek out blocks and trucks. Often, of course, these are the only options available to them, due to the choices their parents and other adults have made in the toys they provide (Jacklin, Maccoby, & Dick, 1973; Poulin-Dubois et al., 1994).

Children's preferences for certain kinds of toys are reinforced by their parents, although parents of boys are more apt to be concerned

Parents of girls who play with toys related to activities associated with boys are apt to be less concerned than parents of boys who play with toys associated with girls.

about their child's choices than are parents of girls. For example, 1-year-old boys receive more positive reactions for playing with transportation and building toys than do girls. Moreover, the amount of reinforcement boys receive for playing with toys that society deems appropriate increases with age, and boys receive increasing discouragement for playing with toys that society views as more acceptable for girls. On the other hand, girls who play with toys seen by society as "masculine" are less discouraged for their behavior than boys who play with toys seen as "feminine" (Eisenberg et al., 1985; Fagot & Hagan, 1991).

By the time they reach the age of 2, boys behave more independently and less compliantly than girls. Much of this behavior can be traced to parental reactions to earlier behavior. For instance, when a child takes his or her first steps, parents tend to react differently, depending on the child's gender: Boys are encouraged more to go off and explore the world, whereas girls are hugged and kept close. In general, exploratory behavior tends to be encouraged more in boys than in girls. It is hardly surprising, then, that by the age of 2, girls tend to show less independence and greater compliance (Fagot, 1978; Brooks-Gunn & Matthews, 1979; Kuczynski, & Kochanska, 1990).

In sum, differences in behavior between boys and girls begin in infancy, and—as we will see in future chapters—continue throughout childhood (and beyond). Although gender differences have complex causes, representing some combination of innate, biologically related factors and environmental factors, they play a profound role in the social and emotional development of infants. Beginning at birth, boys and girls are treated differently on the basis of gender, and this differential treatment produces dissimilar worlds for members of the two sexes, even during infancy.

Family Life at the Dawn of the New Century: Ozzie and Harriet Go the Way of the Dinosaurs

A look back at television shows of the 1950s (such as *Ozzie and Harriet* and *Leave It to Beaver*) finds a world of families portrayed in a way that today seems oddly old-fashioned and quaint: mothers and fathers, married for years, and their good-looking children making their way in a world that seems to have few, if any, serious problems.

As we discussed in Chapter 1, even in the 1950s such a view of family life was overly romantic and unrealistic. Today, however, it is broadly inaccurate, representing only a minority of families in the United States. A quick review of statistics collected by the U.S. Census Bureau tells the story (Bird & Melville, 1994; Carnegie Task Force, 1994; Gelles, 1994):

The view of the family, as reflected in media depictions ranging from *Ozzie and Harriet* to *The Simpsons*, has changed radically from the 1950s to the present.

- The number of single-parent families has increased dramatically in the last two decades, as the number of two-parent households has declined. Around 56 percent of white children live with both parents, whereas just one-quarter of African American children and one-third of Hispanic children live with both parents. If current trends continue, 60 percent of all children will live at some time during their lives with a single parent (Demo & Acock, 1991; U.S. Bureau of the Census, 1991b).

- The average size of families is shrinking. Today, on average, there are 2.6 persons per household, compared to 2.8 in 1980. The number of people living in nonfamily households (without any relatives) is close to 30 million.

- In 1960, 5 percent of all births in the United States were to unmarried mothers. By the 1990s, more than 25 percent of births were to unmarried mothers.

- Every minute, an adolescent in the United States gives birth.

- More than 5 million children under the age of 3 are cared for by other adults while their parents work, and more than half of mothers of infants work outside the home.

- In 1990, one-quarter of families with children under 3 years of age lived in poverty in the United States. The rates are even higher for African American and Hispanic families, and for single-parent families of young children. More children under 3 live in poverty than do older children, adults, or the elderly (Einbinder, 1992).

Such statistics are disheartening. At the very least, they suggest that infants are being raised in environments in which substantial stressors are present, factors that make an unusually difficult task of raising children—never easy even under the best circumstances.

On the other hand, society is adapting to the new realities of family life in the 1990s. Several kinds of social support exist for the parents of infants, and society is evolving new institutions to help in their care. One example is the growing array of child-care arrangements available to help working parents.

Infant Day Care: Assessing the Consequences

Should infants be placed in day care? For many parents, there is little choice: Economic realities, or the desire to maintain a career, require that their children be left in the care of others for a portion of the day, typically in infant day-care settings. In fact, recent figures indicate that almost 25 percent of preschool children whose mothers work outside the home spend their days in day-care centers (see Figure 6-5). Do such arrangements have any discernible effects on infant development?

FIGURE 6-5

WHERE ARE CHILDREN CARED FOR?

Most children spend their days at home, but almost one-quarter of children younger than 5 years of age whose mothers work outside the home spend their days in day-care centers.

(*Source:* U.S. Bureau of the Census; Child Health USA, 1993).

Child's home ▮
Day care or preschool ▮
Nonrelative's home ▮
Relative's home ▮
Other ▮

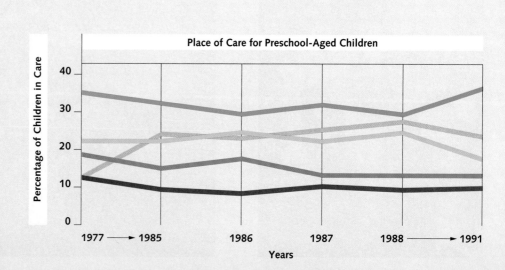

The answer, although not definitive, is reassuring. According to the initial findings of a large study supported by the U.S. National Institute of Child Health and Development, high-quality day care seems to produce only minor differences from home care in most respects and may even enhance certain aspects of development. For example, most research finds little or no difference in the strength or nature of parental attachment bonds of infants who have been in day care compared with infants raised solely by their parents. However, the research suggests that infants were less likely to be secure when they had been placed in low-quality child care and had mothers with relatively low sensitivity and responsiveness. The same was true if they had more than one child-care arrangement. Furthermore, there was a gender difference: Boys who experienced high levels of care and girls who had minimal amounts of care were somewhat less apt to be securely attached—although the meaning of this finding is unclear (NICHD Early Child Care Research Network, 1997).

In fact, various studies have found clear benefits from participation in day care. For instance, compared with children not in day care, children who participated in day care during their first year showed higher levels of play, laughing, and touching; they kicked and pushed less; and they were found to be more sociable and cooperative (Field et al., 1988; Howes, Phillips, & Whitebook, 1992; Fein, Gariboldi, & Boni, 1993; Volling & Feagans, 1995; Howes, 1997).

In addition, the beneficial effects of infant day care may be lasting. For instance, a study of children from low-income families who had participated in day care from infancy through 3 years of age found that at age 12 the children experienced advantages in terms of cognitive and academic achievement (Campbell & Ramey, 1994).

On the other hand, some research on the outcomes of infant day care has yielded mixed, or even negative, results (Matlock & Green, 1990). For example, one study found that high-risk, poor children who had secure attachment to their mothers showed negative, avoidant, and more aggressive behavior several years after participating in infant day care. However, the results were not uniformly negative: For insecurely attached infants, participation in infant day care was associated with more positive outcomes. Apparently, involvement in day care acted as a protective factor for the children who had come from insecurely attached backgrounds (Egeland & Hiester, 1995).

Other research finds that participation in infant day care may actually produce less secure attachment. For instance, one study found that infants involved in care outside the home for more than 20 hours a week during their first year showed less secure attachment to their mothers than those who had not been in day care. Moreover, boys in day care for 35 or more hours a week showed some evidence of less secure attachment to their fathers (Chase-Lansdale & Owen, 1987; Belsky & Rovine, 1988).

High quality infant day care seems to produce only minor differences from home care in most respects, and some aspects of development may even be enhanced.

Other research points to further potential drawbacks of day care—at least in extensive quantities—during infancy. For instance, infants who spend their first year in full-time day care have sometimes been found to exhibit more aggression, less obedience, and more negative reactions to frustration than those who were cared for at home. Furthermore, some studies suggest that children who spend more time in day care may adjust less successfully when they get to kindergarten (Rubenstein, Howes, & Boyule, 1981; Haskins, 1985; Bates et al., 1994).

Although such findings are troubling, their implications may be less far-reaching than we might at first assume. For instance, not all of the children in the studies were enrolled in high-quality day-care settings; many were in less-than-optimal situations. Furthermore, some of the findings may not be entirely negative: The greater aggression and lower compliance found in some studies may simply reflect increased assertiveness among children who have more experience in the company of groups of other children (Howes, Phillips, & Whitebook, 1992; Aviezer et al., 1994).

Finally, there is no assurance that the personalities and socioeconomic status of children who are in day care are similar to those of children who are raised in the home by parents. Although the use of day care is prevalent throughout all segments of society, it is likely that certain groups are overrepresented in day care centers. Consequently, until more research is done on just who makes use of day care and how it is used by members of different segments of society, we will be unable to understand fully the consequences of participation. Furthermore, research must take into account the quality of day care centers and the specific activities they engage in to optimize the potential benefits and minimize the negative consequences of care outside the home (Clarke-Stewart, Gruber, & Fitzgerald, 1994; Appelbaum, 1995).

The Informed Consumer of Development

Choosing the Right Infant Care Provider

If there is one finding that emerges with crystal clarity from research conducted on the consequences of infant day care, it is that benefits occur only when day care is of high quality (Zigler & Styfco, 1994; Volling & Feagans, 1995). But what distinguishes high-quality day care from low-caliber programs?

The American Psychological Association suggests that parents consider these questions in choosing a program (Committee on Children, Youth and Families, 1994):

■ Are there enough providers? A desirable ratio is one adult for every three to four infants.

■ Are group sizes manageable? Even with several providers, a group of infants should not be larger than eight.

■ Do the individuals providing the care seem to like what they are doing? What is their motivation? Is day care just a temporary job, or is it a career? Are they experienced? Do they seem happy in the job, or is offering day care just a way to earn money?

■ What do the caregivers do during the day? Do they spend their time playing with, listening and talking to, and paying attention to the children? Do they seem genuinely interested in the children, rather than merely going through the motions of caring for them?

■ Are the children safe and clean? Does the environment allow infants to move around safely? Is the equipment and furniture in good repair? Do the providers adhere to the highest levels of cleanliness? After changing a baby's diaper, do providers wash their hands?

■ What training do the providers have in caring for children? Do they demonstrate a knowledge of the basics of infant development and an understanding of how normal children develop? Do they seem alert to signs that development may depart from normal patterns?

■ Finally, is the environment happy and cheerful? Day care is not just a babysitting service: For the time an infant is there, it is the child's whole world. You should feel fully comfortable and confident that the day care center is a place where your infant will be treated as an individual.

In addition to following these guidelines, you may contact the National Association for the Education of Young Children, from which you may be able to get the name of a resource and referral agency in your area. Write (enclosing a self-addressed, stamped envelope) to NAEYC Information Service, 1834 Connecticut Avenue NW, Washington, DC 20009; or call (800) 424-2460.

Melinda Rauch, Child-Care Provider

Education: . . . . University of Colorado at Denver, B.A. in psychology

Position: . . . . Infant/toddler teacher for HeartsHome Early
Learning Center in Houston, Texas

Home: . . . . Spring, Texas

Upon graduation from college, Melinda Rauch answered an ad for a preschool teacher, expecting that it would be just a temporary job. As it turned out, her love of children had guided her to her current vocation.

For the past 4½ years, Rauch has worked with infants and toddlers at HeartsHome, providing far more than basic day-care services.

"We meet our children's basic needs by making sure they're happy, clean, dry, and fed, but we also meet their developmental needs by teaching them to take turns, get along with others, and accept that they don't alway get their own way," Rauch says.

Activities that include teaching are an integral part of an infant's day at HeartsHome, according to Rauch. "We work with infants from 6 weeks to 3 years old, and we vary the activities by age group. We do a lot of sensory play with different substances, such as rice, cornmeal, and water. When we do artwork, we don't focus on the products that the child creates so much as on the process the child uses in creating.

"Everything is a hands-on experience," she explains. "Basically, I take a crayon and model what to do with it. Then I put the crayon in their hands and help them make the same motions. Often they'll stick it in their mouths, and so we'll have a learning experience that crayons aren't food. We can go through several learning experiences just using crayons."

Getting along with others is an important socialization task, and Rauch says she works with children as young as 18 months on the concept of sharing.

"We don't expect them to learn the concept completely at 18 months, but we will use a popular toy like mini-basketballs to teach sharing. There may be more than one of a particular item, but it's still a problem when all the children want to do the same thing at the same time. I try to explain turn-taking, and then I might take the child who doesn't have the item and guide him or her to read a book or play with another toy. It's important to give them a sense that there are alternatives."

"We also meet their developmental needs by teaching them to take turns, get along with others."

"When we do artwork, we don't focus on the products that the child creates so much as on the process the child uses in creating."

REVIEW AND RETHINK

REVIEW

■ Personality is the sum total of the enduring characteristics that differentiate one individual from another. According to Erikson, during infancy individuals move from the first stage of psychosocial development, the trust-versus-mistrust stage, to the second, the autonomy-versus-shame-and-guilt stage.

■ Temperament encompasses enduring levels of arousal and emotionality that are characteristic of an individual.

■ Gender differences become more pronounced as infants age, due mostly to environmental influences, especially the different expectations, attitudes, and actions displayed by parents and other adults toward boys and girls.

■ Substantial changes in the nature of the family have brought about corresponding adjustments in the ways children are nurtured and reared.

■ Day care can have neutral, positive, or negative effects on the social development of children, depending largely on its quality.

■ Research on the effects of day-care must take into account the varying quality of different day care settings and the social characteristics of the parents who tend to use day care.

RETHINK

■ Does the concept of social referencing help explain the development of gender-based behavioral differences in young children? How?

■ The "John" and "Mary" video experiment described in this chapter demonstrates how identical actions of boys and girls can be interpreted differently. Can you think of examples of the same phenomenon occurring in adulthood?

■ What are some social implications of the changes in family life described in this chapter? What sorts of family policies might be instituted to address these changes?

■ Can you relate the issue of day care to the phenomenon of attachment studied earlier in this chapter? What factors complicate the relationship between day-care and attachment?

■ How might social attitudes toward such issues as women's careers and alternative lifestyles influence studies of the effects of day care and the interpretation of their findings?

LOOKING BACK

■ **What sort of emotional lives do infants have?**

• Infants display a variety of facial expressions, which are similar across cultures, that appear to reflect their basic emotional states.

• By the end of the first year, infants often develop both stranger anxiety, wariness around an unknown person, and separation anxiety, distress when a customary care provider departs.

• Early in life infants develop the capability of nonverbal decoding: determining the emotional states of others based on their facial and vocal expressions.

- Through social referencing, infants from the age of 8 or 9 months use the expressions of others to clarify ambiguous situations and learn appropriate reactions to them.

■ **What sort of mental lives do infants have?**

- Infants begin to develop self-awareness at about the age of 12 months.

- They also begin to develop a theory of mind at this time: knowledge and beliefs about how they and others think.

■ **What is attachment in infancy? How does it relate to the future social competence of individuals?**

- Attachment, a strong, positive emotional bond that forms between an infant and one or more significant persons, is a crucial factor in enabling individuals to develop social relationships.

- Infants display one of four major attachment patterns: securely attached, avoidant, ambivalent, and disorganized-disoriented. Research suggests an association between an infant's attachment pattern and his or her adult social and emotional competence.

■ **What roles do other people play in infants' social development?**

- Mothers' interactions with their babies are particularly important for social development. Mothers who respond effectively to their babies' social overtures appear to contribute to the babies' ability to become securely attached.

- Through a process of reciprocal socialization, infants and caregivers interact and affect one another's behavior, which strengthens their mutual relationship.

- From an early age, infants engage in rudimentary forms of social interaction with other children, and their level of sociability rises as they age.

■ **What sorts of individual differences do infants display?**

- The origins of personality, the sum total of the enduring characteristics that differentiate one individual from another, arise during infancy.

- Temperament encompasses enduring levels of arousal and emotionality that are characteristic of an individual. Temperamental differences underlie the broad classification of infants into easy, difficult, and slow-to-warm categories.

- As infants age, gender differences become more pronounced, mostly due to the influence of environmental factors. Differences are accentuated by parental expectations and behavior.

■ **Is day care beneficial or harmful for infants?**

- Day care, a societal response to the changing nature of the family, can be beneficial to the social development of children, fostering social interaction and cooperation, if it is of high quality.

EPILOGUE: FIRST ENCOUNTERS

In this chapter, we looked at the ways infants develop as social individuals, decoding and encoding emotions using social referencing, and a "theory of mind." We considered the attachment patterns that infants display and their potential long-range effects. We examined personality, taking a close look at Erik Erikson's theory of psychosocial development. We also discussed temperament, and we explored the nature and causes of gender differences. We concluded with a discussion of infant day care.

Return to the prologue of this chapter, about Louis Moore's homecoming from the hospital, and answer the following questions.

1. What kind of emotional life does Louis have as he is being driven home from the hospital? How does this differ from the emotional life he will develop within a year?

2. In what ways do the actions of Martha, Tom, and Mrs. Moore in the car exemplify social referencing?

3. Could Louis have decoded and imitated Martha's and Tom's facial expressions as they crowded around him and looked at him? Why or why not?

4. What should Mrs. Moore do in response to Louis's crying if she wants to start off the process of forming a secure attachment correctly? Does Louis's wailing indicate that he will be a "difficult baby"?

5. Is there evidence of gender differences in Martha's and Tom's reactions to Louis and their actions in the car?

KEY TERMS AND CONCEPTS

CHAPTER 7

Physical and Cognitive Development

PROLOGUE: THE LONG GOODBYE

The first day of school can prove to be a stressful experience.

Samantha Sterman doesn't know it yet, but she has just taken a giant stride on the road to independence. The curly haired tot is mixing well with the other three-year-olds kneading Play-Doh and bathing dolls at West Village Nursery School in Greenwich Village.

For her father, Bruce Sterman, the first day of nursery school is a bit more stressful. Squirming in his tiny chair in a corner of the classroom, . . . he is going to spend his mornings here in the classroom, easing Samantha's oh-so-gradual transition into school.

This is an autumn ritual known as "separation," the weaning of child from parent—and vice versa—that transpires at the beginning of preschool. For countless parents whose children attend developmentally sensitive nursery schools, it is a time of high anxiety and disrupted work schedules. The protracted parting sometimes can go on for weeks—a far cry from the kiss-and-run approach of years gone by. . . .

At West Village Nursery, the day of reckoning dawns the third week of September. Paint pots and crayons at the ready, the teachers throw the door open to welcome the first shift. The coatroom, a boisterous tumble of denim and plaid, is ablaze with flashbulbs, as parents capture for a lifetime the first meeting of teacher and child. Jack Kamine clings to his mother's leg. Nina Boyd clutches a well-worn doll.

But the classroom beckons, and as the children scamper off, their parents give each other meaningful, misty glances. "I feel like chopped liver," Mr. Sterman jokes—both proud and rueful—as he takes up his station in the corner. (Graham, 1994, p. A1)

215

LOOKING AHEAD   For both preschoolers and their parents, the experience of attending school for the first time produces a combination of apprehension, exhilaration, and anticipation. It marks the start of an intellectual, as well as social, journey that will continue for many years and shape the development of children in significant ways.

Traditionally, the preschool years are a time of preparation: a period spent anticipating and getting ready for the start of a child's formal education, through which society will begin the process of passing on its intellectual tools to a new generation.

But it is a mistake to take the label "preschool" too literally. The years between 3 and 6 are hardly a mere way-station in life, an interval spent waiting for the next, more important period to start. Instead, the preschool years are a time of tremendous change and growth, in which physical, intellectual, and social development proceeds at a rapid pace.

In this chapter, we focus on the physical, cognitive, and linguistic growth that occurs during the preschool years. We begin by considering the physical changes during those years. We discuss weight and height, nutrition, and health and wellness. We consider changes in the brain and its neural byways, and touch on some intriguing findings relating to gender differences in the way that the brain functions. We also look at how both gross and fine motor skills change over the preschool years.

Intellectual development is the focus of much of the remainder of the chapter. We examine the major approaches to cognitive development, including Piaget's theory, information-processing approaches, and Vygotsky's view of cognitive development, which takes culture into account.

Finally, the chapter considers the important advances in language development that occur during the preschool years. We end with a discussion of several factors that influence cognitive development, including exposure to television and participation in child-care and preschool programs.

After reading this chapter, then, you will be able to answer the following questions:

Q

- What is the state of children's bodies and overall health during the preschool years?
- How do preschool children's brains and physical skills develop?
- How does Piaget interpret cognitive development during the preschool years?
- How do other views of cognitive development differ from Piaget's?
- How does children's language develop in the preschool years?
- What effects does television have on preschoolers?
- What kinds of preschool educational programs are available?

PHYSICAL GROWTH

It is an unseasonably warm spring day at the Cushman Hill Preschool, one of the first after a long winter. The children in Mary Scott's class have happily left their winter coats in the classroom for the first time this spring, and they are excitedly playing outside. Jessie plays a game of catch with Germaine, and Sarah and Molly climb on the jungle gym. Craig and Marta chase one another; Jesse and Bernstein try, with gales of giggles, to play leap-frog. Virginia and Ollie sit across from each other on the teeter-totter, successively bumping it so hard into the ground that they both are in danger of being knocked off. Erik, Jim, Scott, and Paul race around the perimeter of the playground, running for the sheer joy of it.

These same children, now so active and mobile, were unable even to crawl or walk just a few years earlier. The advances in their physical abilities that have occurred in such a short time are nothing short of astounding. Just how far they have developed is apparent when we look at the specific changes they have undergone in their size, shape, and physical abilities.

The Growing Body

Two years after birth, the average child in the United States weighs in at around 25 to 30 pounds and is close to 34 inches tall—around half the height of the average adult. Children grow steadily during the preschool period, and by the time they are 6 years old they weigh, on average, about 46 pounds and stand 46 inches tall (see Figure 7-1).

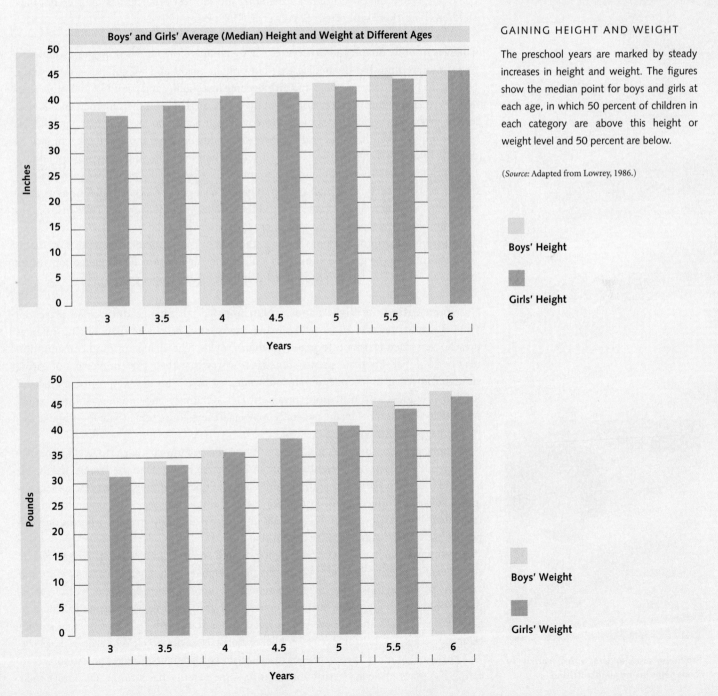

FIGURE 7-1

GAINING HEIGHT AND WEIGHT

The preschool years are marked by steady increases in height and weight. The figures show the median point for boys and girls at each age, in which 50 percent of children in each category are above this height or weight level and 50 percent are below.

(*Source:* Adapted from Lowrey, 1986.)

Boys' Height

Girls' Height

Boys' Weight

Girls' Weight

obesity   *body weight more than 20 percent higher that the average weight for a person of a given age and height*

Individual Differences in Height and Weight.   These averages mask great individual differences in height and weight. For instance, 10 percent of 6-year-olds weigh 55 pounds or more, and 10 percent weigh 36 pounds or less. Furthermore, average differences in height and weight between boys and girls increase during the preschool years. Although at age 2 the differences are relatively small, by the age of 6 boys begin to be taller and heavier, on average, than girls.

Furthermore, profound differences in height and weight exist between children in economically developed countries and those in developing countries. The better nutrition and health care received by children in developed countries translates into significant differences in growth. For instance, the average Swedish 4-year-old is as tall as the average 6-year-old in Bangladesh (United Nations, 1990).

Differences in height and weight reflect economic factors within the United States, as well. For instance, more than 10 percent of children in the United States whose family incomes are below the poverty level are among the shortest 5 percent of all preschool-age children (Barrett & Frank, 1987; Sherry et al., 1992; Egan, 1994).

Changes in Body Shape and Structure.   If we compare the bodies of a 2-year-old and a 6-year-old, we find that the bodies vary not only in height and weight, but also in shape. During the preschool years, boys and girls become less chubby and roundish and more slender. They begin to burn off some of the fat they have carried from their infancy, and they no longer have a pot-bellied appearance. Moreover, their arms and legs lengthen, and the size relationship between the head and the rest of the body becomes more adultlike. In fact, by the time children reach 6 years of age, their proportions are quite similar to those of adults.

The changes in size, weight, and appearance we see during the preschool years are only the tip of the iceberg. Internally, other physical changes are occurring. Children grow stronger as their muscle size increases and their bones become sturdier. The sense organs continue their development. For instance, the *eustachian tube* in the ear, which carries sounds from the external part of the ear to the internal part, moves from a position that is almost parallel to the ground at birth to a more angular position. This change sometimes leads to an increase in frequency of earaches during the preschool years.

Nutrition: Eating the Right Foods.   Nutritional needs change during the preschool years. Because the rate of growth during this period is slower than during infancy, preschoolers need less food to maintain their growth. The change in food consumption may be so noticeable that parents sometimes worry that their preschooler is not eating enough. However, children tend to be quite adept at maintaining an appropriate intake of food, if provided with nutritious meals. In fact, anxiously encouraging children to eat more than they seem to want naturally may lead them to increase their food intake beyond an appropriate level.

Ultimately, some children's food consumption can become so high as to lead to **obesity**, which is defined as a body weight more than 20 percent higher than the average weight for a person of a given age and height. The prevalence of obesity among older preschoolers has increased significantly over the last 20 years. For example, one series of surveys found that more than 10 percent of 4- and 5-year-old girls were overweight in 1994, whereas only 5.8 percent were overweight in 1974 (Ogden et al., 1997).

Obesity is brought about by both biological and social factors. There is a clear genetic component of obesity, illustrated by the fact that adopted children tend to have weights that are more similar to those of their birth parents than those of their adoptive parents. In addition, children who are obese during the preschool years tend to have responded more to sweet tastes at birth and to have been more responsive at birth to environmental stimuli (Unger, Kreeger, & Christoffel, 1990; Schlicker, Borra, & Regan, 1994; Whitaker et al., 1997).

The degree of encouragement—or discouragement—parents provide on the subject of eating also plays a role in obesity. For instance, some parents may strongly encourage their

Providing preschoolers with a variety of foods helps insure good nutrition.

preschoolers to eat, in the mistaken belief that their children are not eating enough. Conversely, other parents may place strong restraints on children's food intake in order to prevent obesity.

In either case, such behavior may prevent children from developing their own internal controls over eating. Without such controls, children may become less aware of their internal hunger cues—and may ultimately become obese. For instance, a recent study of a group of children aged 3 to 5 found that those with the highest proportion of body fat had mothers who exerted the greatest level of control over the amount of food their children ate (Johnson & Birch, 1994). Furthermore, the more control the mothers in the study reported exerting, the less self-regulation of food intake their children exhibited. In sum, strong parental involvement in what children eat may suppress the children's natural ability to monitor and control their food intake, and may lead to obesity and even to more severe eating problems in the future (Rodin & Hall, 1987; Brownell & Rodin, 1994).

How do parents ensure that their children have good nutrition without turning mealtimes into a tense, adversarial situation? In most cases, the best strategy is to make sure that a variety of foods, low in fat and high in nutritional content, is available. Foods that have a relatively high iron content are particularly important: Iron deficiency anemia, which causes chronic fatigue, is one of the prevalent nutritional problems in developed countries such as the United States. High-iron foods include dark green vegetables (such as broccoli), whole grains, and some kinds of meat (Ranade, 1993).

On the other hand, preschool children, like adults, will not find all foods equally appealing, and children should be given the opportunity to develop their own natural preferences. As long as their overall diet is adequate, no single food is indispensable (Shapiro, 1997).

Health and Illness.   For the average child in the United States, a runny nose due to the common cold is the most frequent—and happily, the most severe—kind of health problem during the preschool years. In fact, the majority of children in the United States are reasonably healthy during this period (Kalb, 1997).

This was not always the case. Before the discovery of vaccines and the routine immunization of children, the preschool period was a dangerous time. Even today, this period is risky in certain lower socioeconomic segments of the U.S. population, as well as in many parts of the world. In fact, probably because of the lack of a national health care policy in the United States and the complacency on the part of government officials, the proportion of children immunized in the United States has fallen during some portions of the last two decades—at the same time it has been rising in many third-world countries (Williams, 1990).

Injuries During the Preschool Years: Playing It Safe.   Consider the following situation:

> Aaron, an energetic 3-year-old, was trying to stretch far enough to reach the bowl of cookies on the kitchen counter. Because the bowl was just beyond his grasp, he pushed a chair from the kitchen table over to the counter and was able to pick out a cookie. As he tried to get down, however, the chair slid away from the counter, and he fell to the floor, twisting, and fracturing, his arm. His wails brought his father on the run from the next room.

In some ways, Aaron was lucky, for some injuries sustained by preschoolers are far more serious, resulting in permanent disfigurement or even death. In fact, statistically speaking, the greatest risk that preschoolers face comes from neither illness nor nutritional problems but from accidents: Before the age of 10, children have twice the likelihood of dying from an injury than from an illness. In fact, children in the United States have a 1 in 3 likelihood every year of receiving an injury that requires medical attention (National Safety Council, 1989).

The danger of injuries during the preschool years is in part a result of the children's high levels of physical activity. A 3-year-old might think that it is perfectly reasonable to climb on a chair to get something that is out of reach, and a 4-year-old might enjoy holding on to a low tree branch and swinging her legs up and down. At the same time, children lack the judgment to know that their activities may hold some danger, and they are less likely than older children to be careful.

Furthermore, some children are more apt to take risks than others, and such preschoolers are more likely to be injured than their more cautious peers. Boys, who are both more active than girls and tend to take more risks, have a higher rate of injuries (Morrongiello, 1997). Ethnic differences, probably due to differences in cultural norms about how closely children need to be supervised, can also be seen in accident rates. Asian American children in the United States, who tend to be supervised particularly strictly by their parents, have one of the lowest accident rates for children. Economic factors also play a role. Children raised under conditions of poverty in urban areas, whose inner-city neighborhoods may contain more hazards than more affluent areas, are two times more likely to die of injuries than children living in affluence.

The range of dangers that preschoolers face is wide. Injuries come from falls, burns from stoves and fires, drowning in bathtubs indoors and standing water outdoors, and suffocation in places such as abandoned refrigerators. Auto accidents also account for a large number of injuries. Finally, children face injuries from poisonous substances such as household cleaners, or as we discuss in the "Directions in Development" box, long-term exposure to poisons such as lead.

The Growing Brain

The brain grows at a faster rate than any other part of the body. Two-year-olds have brains that are about three-quarters the size and weight of an adult brain. By age 5, children's brains weigh 90 percent of average adult brain weight. In comparison, the average 5-year-old's total body weight is just 30 percent of average adult body weight (Lowrey, 1986; Schuster & Ashburn, 1986; Nihart, 1993).

Why does the brain grow so rapidly? One reason is an increase in the number of interconnections among cells. These interconnections allow for more complex communication between neurons, and they permit the rapid growth of cognitive skills that we'll discuss later in the chapter. In addition, the amount of myelin—protective insulation that surrounds parts of neurons—increases, which speeds the transmission of electrical impulses along brain cells but also adds to brain weight.

The two halves of the brain also begin to become increasingly differentiated and specialized. **Lateralization**, the process in which certain functions are located more in one hemisphere than the other, becomes more pronounced during the preschool years.

For most people, the left hemisphere concentrates on tasks that necessitate verbal competence, such as speaking, reading, thinking, and reasoning. The right hemisphere develops its own strengths, especially in nonverbal areas such as comprehension of spatial relationships, recognition of patterns and drawings, music, and emotional expression (Kitterle, 1991; Hellige, 1994; Zaidel, 1994; Fiore & Schooler, 1998; see Figure 7-2).

Each of the two hemispheres begins to process information in a slightly different manner. Whereas the left hemisphere considers information sequentially, one piece of data at a time, the right hemisphere processes information in a more global manner, reflecting on it as a whole (Gazzaniga, 1983; Springer & Deutsch, 1989; Leonard et al., 1996).

Despite the specialization of the hemispheres, we need to keep in mind that in most respects the two hemispheres of the brain act in tandem. They are interdependent, and the differences between the two are minor. Furthermore, there are many individual differences in lateralization. For example, many of the 10 percent of people who are left-handed or ambidextrous (able to use both hands interchangeably) have language centered in their right hemispheres or have no specific language center (Banich & Nicholas, 1998).

Even more intriguing are differences in lateralization related to gender and culture. For instance, starting during the first year of life and continuing in the preschool years, boys

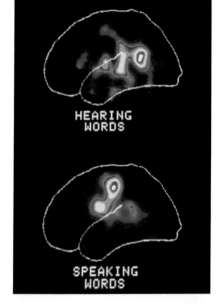

FIGURE 7-2 LOOKING INTO THE BRAIN

These scans show how different parts of the brain are activated during particular tasks, illustrating the increasing specialization of the brain.

lateralization   *the process in which certain cognitive functions are located more in one hemisphere of the brain than the other*

Directions in Development

The Silent Danger: Lead Poisoning in Young Children

At the age of 3, Tory couldn't sit still. He was unable to watch a television show for more than 5 minutes, and sitting still while his mother read to him seemed to be an impossibility. He was often irritable, and he impulsively took risks when he was playing with other children.

When his behavior reached a point at which his parents thought there was something seriously wrong with him, they took him to a pediatrician for a thorough physical examination. After testing Tory's blood, the pediatrician found that his parents were right: Tory was suffering from lead poisoning.

Some 14 million children are at risk for lead poisoning due to exposure to potentially toxic levels of lead, according to the Centers for Disease Control. Although there are now stringent legal restrictions on the amount of lead in paint and gasoline, lead is still found on painted walls and window frames—particularly in older homes, and in gasoline, ceramics, lead-soldered pipes, and even dust and water. People who live in areas of substantial air pollution due to automobile and truck traffic may also be exposed to high levels of lead. The U.S. Department of Health and Human Services has called lead poisoning the most hazardous health threat to children under the age of 6 (Centers for Disease Control, 1991; Tesman & Hills, 1994).

Even tiny amounts of lead can permanently harm children. Exposure to lead has been linked to lower intelligence, problems in verbal and auditory processing, and—as in the case of Tory—hyperactivity and distractibility. High lead levels have also been linked to higher levels of antisocial behavior, including aggression and delinquency in school-age children (see Figure 7-3). At yet higher levels of exposure, lead poisoning results in illness and death (Leviton et al., 1993; Needleman et al., 1996).

Poor children are particularly susceptible to lead poisoning, and the results of poisoning tend to be worse for them than for children from more affluent families. Children living in poverty are more apt to reside in housing that contains peeling and chipping lead paint, or to live near heavily trafficked urban areas with high levels of air pollution. At the same time, many families living in poverty may be less stable and unable to provide consistent opportunities for intellectual stimulation that might serve to offset some of the cognitive problems caused by the poisoning. Consequently, lead poisoning is especially harmful to poorer children (Harvey et al., 1984; Tesman & Hills, 1994).

Efforts to reduce the incidence of lead poisoning have taken many forms. One approach is through legislation that mandates the removal of paint that contains lead in dwellings in which children reside. Another is through parent education (Porter, 1997).

In one program, for example, parents who lived near a previously functioning lead smelter, and whose pre-1920s homes still contained high levels of lead, were trained to take several preventive measures. For instance, they were taught to wash their children's hands before mealtime and bedtime, to clip their children's fingernails short, and to furnish their children with a good diet. In addition, they were taught to take precautions in the home, such as removing peeling paint and cordoning off high-lead areas. The program was effective: Over a 4-month period, the lead levels in the bodies of the children in the study, who ranged in age from 6 months to 6 years, declined significantly (Kimbrough, LeVois, & Webb, 1994; Tesman & Hills, 1994).

Still, the problem of potentially dangerous levels of lead in many children's surroundings persists. The question that must be addressed is how to remove such dangers, and what the costs will be. Clearly, there is no easy solution to the problem.

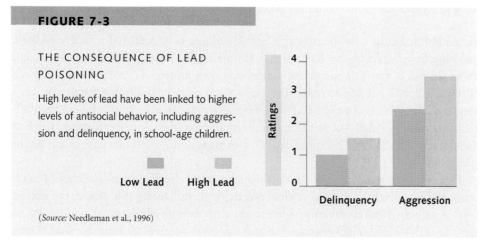

FIGURE 7-3

THE CONSEQUENCE OF LEAD POISONING

High levels of lead have been linked to higher levels of antisocial behavior, including aggression and delinquency, in school-age children.

(*Source:* Needleman et al., 1996)

and girls show some hemispheric differences associated with lower body reflexes and the processing of auditory information (Shucard et al., 1981; Grattan et al., 1992). Furthermore, males clearly tend to show greater lateralization of language in the left hemisphere; among females, however, language is more evenly divided between the two hemispheres

(Gur et al., 1982). Such differences may help explain why—as we'll see later in the chapter—females' language development proceeds at a more rapid pace during the preschool years than males' language development.

We still don't know the source of the difference in lateralization between females and males. One explanation is genetic: that female and male brains are predisposed to function in slightly different ways. Such a view is supported by data suggesting that there are minor structural differences between males' and females' brains. For instance, a section of the *corpus callosum,* a bundle of fibers that connects the hemispheres of the brain, is proportionally larger in women than in men. Furthermore, studies conducted among other species, such as primates, rats, and hamsters, have found size and structural differences in the brains of males and females (Hammer, 1984; Allen et al., 1989; Whitelson, 1989).

Before we accept a genetic explanation for the differences between female and male brains, we need to consider an equally plausible alternative: It may be that verbal abilities emerge earlier in girls because girls receive greater encouragement for verbal skills than boys do. For instance, some evidence suggests that, even as infants, girls are spoken to more than boys. Such higher levels of verbal stimulation may produce growth in particular areas of the brain that does not occur in boys. Consequently, environmental factors rather than genetic ones may lead to the gender differences we find in brain lateralization. Once again, we find that teasing out the relative impact of heredity and environment is a challenging task.

Motor Development

As their parents watched from the edge of the summer school playground, 3-year-old Jorge tore after Henry, with Cary in hot pursuit. Eleanor and Heidi threw a ball to each other. Mick and Satra sat at a bench, painstakingly cutting out paper flowers with a scissors for a party. It was hard for their parents to recall that just a few years earlier, these same children were not even able to lift up their heads or roll over, let alone walk.

In their motor development, preschool children have come a long way since birth. Both their gross and fine motor skills have become increasingly fine-tuned.

 Gross Motor Skills.   By the time they are 3, children have mastered a variety of skills: jumping, hopping on one foot, skipping, and running. By 4 and 5, their skills have become more refined, as they gain increasing control over their muscles. For instance, at 4 they can throw a ball with enough accuracy that a friend can catch it, and by age 5 they can toss a ring and have it land on a peg 5 feet away. Five-year-olds can learn to ride bikes, climb ladders, and ski downhill—activities that all require considerable coordination (Clark & Humphrey, 1985). (Table 7-1 summarizes major gross motor skills that emerge during the preschool years.)

One reason that motor skills develop at such a rapid clip during the preschool years is that children spend a great deal of time practicing them. During this period, the general level of activity is extraordinarily high: Preschoolers seem to be perpetually in motion. In fact, the activity level is higher at age 3 than at any other point in the entire life span (Eaton & Yu, 1989; Poest et al., 1990).

Girls and boys differ in certain aspects of gross motor coordination, in part because of differences in muscle strength, which is somewhat greater in boys than in girls. For instance, boys can typically throw a ball better and jump higher. Furthermore, a boy's overall activity level tends to be greater than a girl's (Eaton & Yu, 1989). On the other hand, girls generally surpass boys in tasks that involve the coordination of limbs. For instance, at the age of 5, girls are better than boys at jumping jacks and balancing on one foot (Cratty, 1979).

TABLE 7-1

MAJOR GROSS MOTOR SKILLS IN EARLY CHILDHOOD

3-Year-Olds	4-Year-Olds	5-Year-Olds
Cannot turn or stop suddenly or quickly	Have more effective control of stopping, starting, and turning	Start, turn, and stop effectively in games
Jump a distance of 15 to 24 inches	Jump a distance of 24 to 33 inches	Can make a running jump of 28 to 36 inches
Ascend a stairway unaided, alternating the feet	Descend a long stairway alternating the feet, if supported	Descend a long stairway alternating the feet, if supported
Can hop, using largely an irregular series of jumps with some variations added	Hop 4 to 6 steps on one foot	Easily hop a distance of 16 feet

(*Source:* C. Corbin, 1973.)

Fine Motor Skills.   At the same time gross motor skills are developing, children are progressing in their ability to use fine motor skills, which involve more delicate, smaller body movements. These skills encompass such varied activities as using a fork and spoon, cutting with scissors, tying one's shoelaces, and playing the piano.

The skills involved in fine motor movements require a good deal of practice, as anyone knows who has watched a 4-year-old struggling painstakingly to copy letters of the alphabet. Yet fine motor skills show clear developmental patterns. At the age of 3, children are already able to draw a circle and square with a crayon, and they can undo their clothes when they go to the bathroom. They can put a simple jigsaw puzzle together, and they can fit blocks of different shapes into matching holes. However, they do not show much polish in accomplishing such tasks: For instance, they may try to force puzzle pieces into place.

By the age of 4, their fine motor skills are considerably better. They can draw a person that looks like a person, and they can fold paper into triangular designs. And by the time they are 5, they are able to hold and manipulate a thin pencil properly.

Handedness.   Beginning in early infancy, many children begin to show signs of a preference for the use of one hand over another—the development of **handedness**. For instance, young infants may show a preference for one side of their bodies over another. By the age of 7 months, some infants seem to favor one hand by grabbing more with it than the other (Ramsay, 1980; Michel, 1981).

handedness *the preference of using one hand over another*

During the preschool years, children grow in both gross and fine motor skills.

The Informed Consumer of Development

Keeping Preschoolers Healthy

There is no way around it: Even the healthiest preschooler occasionally gets sick. Social interaction with others ensures that illnesses will be passed from one child to another. However, some diseases are preventable, and others can be minimized if simple precautions are taken:

■ Preschoolers should eat a well-balanced diet containing the proper nutrients, particularly foods containing sufficient protein. (The recommended energy intake for children at age 24 months is about 1,300 calories a day, and for those aged 4 to 6 it is around 1,700 calories a day.) Because preschoolers' stomachs are small, they may need to eat as often as five to seven times a day.

■ Children should get as much sleep as they wish. Being run-down, from lack of either nutrition or sleep, makes children more susceptible to illness.

■ Children should avoid contact with others who are ill. Parents should make sure that children wash their hands after playing with other kids who are obviously sick. Cold germs are often carried from one person to another via the hands.

■ Children should follow an appropriate schedule of immunizations. As illustrated in Table 7-2, current recommendations state that a child should have received nine different vaccines and other preventive medicines in five to seven separate visits to the doctor.

■ Finally, if a child does get ill, remember this: Minor illnesses during childhood sometimes provide immunity to more serious illnesses later on.

TABLE 7-2

RECOMMENDED IMMUNIZATION SCHEDULE FOR INFANTS AND CHILDREN

| | | | | | | AGE | | | | | |
Vaccine	Birth	1 Month	2 Months	4 Months	6 Months	12 Months	15 Months	18 Months	4–6 Years	11–12 Years	14–16 Years
Hepatitis B†	Hep B										
			Hep B		Hep B					Hep B	
Diphtheria and tetanus toxoids and pertussis*			DTaP	DTaP	DTaP		DTaP		DTaP	Td	
H. influenzae type b			Hib	Hib	Hib	Hib					
Poliovirus			IPV	IPV		Polio			Polio		
Rotavirus††			Rv	Rv	Rv						
Measles-mumps-rubella						MMR			MMR	MMR	
Varicella**							Var			Var	

    Range of acceptable ages for vaccination
    Vaccines to be assessed and administered if necessary
    Incorporation of this new vaccine into clinical practice may require additional time and resources from health-care providers.
*DTP is also acceptable
**If not given earlier and no history of chicken pox
(*Source:* Kaiser Permanente Northeast Division)

Most children display a clear-cut tendency to use one hand over the other by the end of the preschool years. Some 90 percent are right-handed and 10 percent are left-handed. Furthermore, there is a gender difference: More boys than girls are left-handed.

Much speculation has been devoted to the meaning of handedness, fueled in part by long-standing myths about the sinister nature of left-handedness. (In fact, the word *sinister* itself is derived from the Latin word meaning "on the left.") In Islamic cultures, for instance, the left hand is generally used in going to the toilet, and it is considered uncivilized to serve food with that hand. Many artistic portrayals of the devil show him as left-handed.

However, there is no scientific basis for myths that suggest that there is something wrong with being left-handed. In fact, some evidence exists that left-handedness may be associated with certain advantages. For example, a study of 100,000 students who took the Scholastic Aptitude Test (SAT) showed that 20 percent in the highest-scoring category were left-handed, double the proportion of left-handed people in the general population. Moreover, such individuals as Michelangelo, Leonardo da Vinci, Benjamin Franklin, and Pablo Picasso were left-handed (Bower, 1985).

Although some educators of the past tried to force left-handed children to use the right hand, particularly when learning to write, thinking has changed. Most teachers now encourage children to use the hand they prefer. Still, most left-handed people will agree that the design of desks, scissors, and most other everyday objects favors those who are right-handed. In fact, the world is so "right-biased" that it may prove to be a dangerous place for those who are left-handed: Left-handed people have more accidents and are at greater risk of dying younger than right-handed people (Coren, 1989; Coren & Halpern, 1991).

REVIEW AND RETHINK

REVIEW

- The preschool period is marked by steady physical growth. Children's bodies increase in height and weight, and change in shape and structure.

- Nutrition significantly affects physical growth. Preschoolers tend to eat less than they did as babies, but generally regulate their food intake appropriately, given nutritious options and the freedom to develop their own choices and controls.

- The preschool period is generally the healthiest time of life, with only minor illnesses threatening children. In the developed countries, most diseases to which preschoolers are susceptible have been controlled by immunization. The risk of accidents and the danger of environmental hazards, such as lead poisoning, are the greatest threats to preschoolers' health.

- Brain growth is rapid during the preschool years. In addition, the brain develops lateralization, a tendency of the two hemispheres to adopt specialized tasks within the context of a unified brain.

- Gross and fine motor development also advances rapidly during the preschool years. During this period, boys' and girls' gross motor skills begin to diverge, and children develop handedness.

RETHINK

- How might biology and environment combine to affect the physical growth of a child adopted as an infant from a developing country and taken to a more industrialized country to live?

■ Aside from obesity, to what other sorts of eating problems might overly controlling parents contribute? How?

■ If the left hemisphere of the brain tends to process information more sequentially, and the right hemisphere more globally, how might the union of the two hemispheres be beneficial for processing different kinds of inputs from sight, hearing, touch, taste, and smell?

■ How do genetics and culture interact to enable boys, in general, to play baseball more proficiently than girls? Can a girl overcome these factors to become a proficient baseball player? Why or why not?

■ Assuming it can be shown that left-handers perform disproportionately well on tests of scholastic aptitude, should parents train their children to become left-handed? Why or why not?

INTELLECTUAL DEVELOPMENT

Three-year-old Sam was talking to himself. As his parents listened with amusement from another room, they could hear him using two very different voices. "Find your shoes," he said in a low voice. "Not today. I'm not going. I hate the shoes," he said in a higher-pitched voice. The lower voice answered, "You are a bad boy. Find the shoes, bad boy." The higher-voiced response was "No, no, no."

Sam's parents realized that he was playing a game with his imaginary friend, Gill. Gill was a bad boy who often disobeyed his mother, at least in Sam's imagination. In fact, according to Sam's musings, Gill often was guilty of misdeeds for which his parents blamed Sam.

In some ways, the intellectual sophistication of 3-year-olds is astounding. Their creativity and imagination leap to new heights, their language is increasingly sophisticated, and they reason and think about the world in ways that would have been impossible even a few months earlier. But what underlies the dramatic advances in intellectual development that start in the preschool years and continue throughout that period? We can consider several approaches, starting with a look at Piaget's findings on the cognitive changes that occur during the preschool years.

Piaget's Stage of Preoperational Thinking

The Swiss psychologist Jean Piaget, whose stage approach to cognitive development we discussed in Chapter 5, saw the preschool years as a time of both stability and great change. He suggests that the preschool years fit entirely into a single stage of cognitive development—the preoperational stage—which lasts from the age of 2 years until around 7 years.

During the **preoperational stage**, children's use of symbolic thinking grows, mental reasoning emerges, and the use of concepts increases. Children become better at representing events internally, and they grow less dependent on the use of direct sensorimotor activity to understand the world around them. Yet they are still not capable of **operations**: organized, formal, logical mental processes. It is only at the end of the preoperational stage that the ability to carry out operations comes into play.

According to Piaget, a key aspect of preoperational thought is *symbolic function*, the ability to use a mental symbol, a word, or an object to stand for or represent something that is not physically present. For example, during this stage, preschoolers can use a mental symbol for a car (the word *car*), and they likewise understand that a small toy car is representative of the real thing. Because of their ability to use symbolic function,

preoperational stage   *according to Piaget, the stage from approximately age 2 to age 7 in which children's use of symbolic thinking grows, mental reasoning emerges, and the use of concepts increases*

operations   *organized, formal, logical mental processes*

children have no need to get behind the wheel of an actual car to understand its basic purpose and use.

Symbolic function is at the heart of one of the major advances that occurs in the preoperational period: the increasingly sophisticated use of language. As we discuss later in this chapter, children make substantial progress in language skills during the preschool period.

It is important to consider Piaget's approach to cognitive development within the appropriate historical context and in the light of more recent research findings. Recall, as we discussed in Chapter 5, that his theory is based on extensive observations of relatively few children. Despite his insightful and ground-breaking observations, recent experimental investigations suggest that, in certain regards, Piaget underestimated children's capabilities. Nevertheless, the broad outlines of his approach, which we consider here, provide a useful means of thinking about the advances in cognitive ability that occur during the preschool years (Siegal, 1997).

The Relation Between Language and Thought.   Piaget suggests that language and thinking are inextricably intertwined, and that the advances in language that occur during the preschool years offer several improvements over the type of thinking that is possible during the earlier sensorimotor period. For instance, thinking embedded in sensorimotor activities is relatively slow, because it depends on actual movements of the body that are bound by human physical limitations. In contrast, the use of symbolic thought allows preschoolers to represent actions symbolically, permitting much greater speed.

Even more important, the use of language allows children to think beyond the present to the future. Consequently, rather than being grounded in the immediate here-and-now, preschoolers can imagine future possibilities through language.

Do the increased language abilities of preschoolers lead to increased thinking proficiency, or do the improvements in thinking during the preoperational period lead to enhancements in language ability? This question—whether thought determines language, or language determines thought—is one of the enduring and most controversial questions within the field of psychology. Piaget's answer is that language grows out of cognitive advances, rather than the other way around. He argues that improvements during the earlier sensorimotor period are necessary for language development, and that continuing growth in cognitive ability during the preoperational period provides the foundation for language ability. Consequently, Piaget suggests that language development is based on the development of more sophisticated modes of thinking—and not the other way around.

Centration: What You See Is What You Think.   Place a dog mask on a cat and what do you get? According to 3- and 4-year-old preschoolers, a dog. To them, a cat with a dog mask ought to bark like a dog, wag its tail like a dog, and eat dog food. In every respect, the cat has been transformed into a dog (deVries, 1969).

Piaget suggests that the root of this belief is centration, a key element, and limitation, of the thinking of children in the preoperational period. **Centration** is the process of concentrating on one limited aspect of a stimulus and ignoring other aspects.

Preschoolers are unable to consider all available information about a stimulus. Instead, they focus on superficial, obvious elements that are within their sight. These external elements come to dominate preschoolers' thinking, leading to inaccuracy in thought.

For example, consider what preschoolers say when they are shown two rows of buttons, one with 10 buttons that are closely spaced together, and the other with 8 buttons spread

centration the process of concentrating on one limited aspect of a stimulus and ignoring other aspects

FIGURE 7-4

WHICH ROW CONTAINS MORE BUTTONS?

When preschoolers are shown these two rows and asked the question of which row has more buttons, they usually respond that the lower row of buttons contains more, because it looks longer. They answer in this way even though they know quite well that 10 is greater than 8.

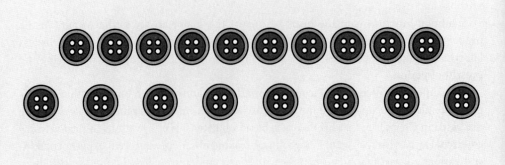

out to form a longer row (see Figure 7-4). If asked which of the rows contains more buttons, children who are 4 or 5 usually choose the row that looks longer, rather than the one that actually contains more buttons. This occurs in spite of the fact that children this age know quite well that 10 is more than 8.

The cause of the children's mistake is that the visual image dominates their thinking. Rather than taking into account their understanding of quantity, they focus on appearance. To a preschooler, appearance is everything.

Egocentrism: The Inability to Take Others' Perspectives.   One hallmark of the preoperational period is egocentric thinking. **Egocentric thought** is thinking that does not take into account the viewpoints of others. Preschoolers do not understand that others have different perspectives from their own. Egocentric thought takes two forms: the lack of awareness that others see things from a different physical perspective, and the failure to realize that others may hold thoughts, feelings, and viewpoints that differ from theirs. (Note what egocentric thought does *not* imply: that preoperational children intentionally think in a selfish or inconsiderate manner.)

Egocentric thinking underlies children's lack of concern over their nonverbal behavior and the impact it has on others. For instance, a 4-year-old who is given an unwanted gift of socks when he was expecting something more desirable may frown and scowl as he opens the package, unaware that his face can be seen by others and may reveal his true feelings about the gift (Feldman, 1992).

Egocentrism lies at the heart of several types of behavior during the preoperational period. For instance, preschoolers may talk to themselves, even in the presence of others, and at times they simply ignore what others are telling them. Rather than being a sign of eccentricity, such behavior illustrates the egocentric nature of preoperational children's thinking: the lack of awareness that their behavior acts as a trigger to others' reactions and responses. Consequently, a considerable amount of verbal behavior on the part of preschoolers has no social motivation behind it but is meant for the preschoolers' own consumption.

Similarly, egocentrism can be seen in hiding games with children during the preoperational stage. In a game of hide-and-seek, 3-year-olds may attempt to hide by covering their faces with a pillow—even though they remain in plain view. Their reasoning: If they cannot see others, others cannot see them. They assume that others share their view.

Incomplete Understanding of Transformation.   Children in the preoperational period are unable to understand the notion of transformation. **Transformation** is the process in which one state is changed into another. For instance, adults know that if a pencil that is held upright and allowed to fall down, it passes through a series of successive stages until it reaches its final, horizontal resting spot (see Figure 7-5). In contrast, children in the preoperational period are unable to envision or recall the successive transformations that

egocentric thought   *thinking that does not take into account the viewpoints of others*

transformation   *the process in which one state is changed into another*

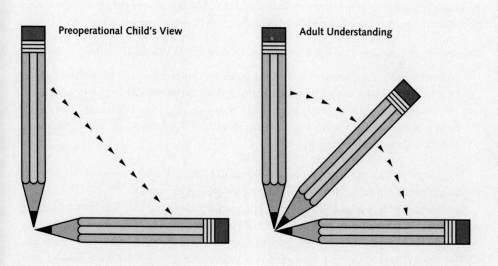

FIGURE 7-5

THE FALLING PENCIL

Children in Piaget's preoperational stage do not understand that as a pencil falls from the upright to the horizontal position it moves through a series of intermediary steps. Instead, they think that there are no intermediate steps in the change from the upright to horizontal position.

the pencil followed in moving from the upright to the horizontal position. If asked to reproduce the sequence in a drawing, they draw the pencil upright and lying down, with nothing in between. Basically, they ignore the intermediate steps.

Similarly, a preoperational child who sees several slugs during a walk in the woods may believe that they are all the same slug. The reason: She views each sighting in isolation and is unable to reconstruct the transformation from one sighting to the next.

The Emergence of Intuitive Thought. Because Piaget labeled the preschool years as the "*pre*operational period," it is easy to assume that this is a period of marking time, waiting for the more formal emergence of operations. As if to support this view, many of the characteristics of the preoperational period highlight cognitive skills that the preschooler has yet to master. However, the preoperational period is far from idle. Cognitive development proceeds steadily, and in fact several new types of ability emerge. A case in point: the development of intuitive thought.

Intuitive thought refers to preschoolers' use of primitive reasoning and their avid acquisition of knowledge about the world. From about age 4 through 7, children's curiosity blossoms. They constantly seek out the answers to a wide variety of questions.

At the same time, children may act as if they are authorities on particular topics, feeling certain that they have the correct—and final—word on an issue. If pressed, they are unable to back up their reasoning, and they are inattentive to how they know what they know. In other words, their intuitive thought leads them to believe that they know answers to all kinds of questions, but there is little or no logical basis for this confidence in their understanding of the way the world operates.

On the other hand, the intuitive thinking that children display in the late stages of the preoperational period has certain qualities that prepare them for more sophisticated forms of reasoning. For example, by the end of the preoperational stage, preschoolers begin to understand the notion of functionality. *Functionality* refers to the concept that actions, events, and outcomes are related to one another in fixed patterns. For instance, preschoolers come to understand that pushing harder on the pedals makes a bicycle move faster, or that pressing a button on a remote control makes the television change channels.

Furthermore, children begin to show an awareness of the concept of identity in the later stages of the preoperational period. *Identity* is the understanding that certain things stay the same, regardless of changes in shape, size, and appearance. For instance, knowledge of identity allows one to understand that a lump of clay contains the same amount of clay regardless of whether it is clumped into a ball or stretched out like a snake. Comprehension of identity is

intuitive thought thinking that reflects preschoolers' use of primitive reasoning and their avid acquisition of knowledge about the world necessary for children to develop a cognitive skill that, according to Piaget, marks the transition from the preoperational period to the next one: an understanding of conservation.

conservation *the knowledge that quantity is unrelated to the arrangement and physical appearance of objects*

Conservation: Learning That Appearances Are Deceiving. Consider the following scenario:

> Four-year-old Jaime is shown two drinking glasses of different shapes. One is short and broad, the other tall and thin. A teacher half-fills the short, broad glass with apple juice. The teacher then pours the juice into the tall, thin glass. The juice fills the tall glass almost to the brim. The teacher asks Jaime a question: Is there more juice in the second glass than there was in the first?

If you view this as an easy task, so do children like Jaime. They have no trouble answering the question. However, they almost always get the answer wrong.

Most 4-year-olds respond that there is more apple juice in the tall, thin glass than there was in the short, broad one. In fact, if the juice is poured back into the shorter glass, they are quick to say that there is now less juice than there was in the taller glass (see Figure 7-6).

The reason for the error in judgment is that children of this age have not mastered conservation. **Conservation** is the knowledge that quantity is unrelated to the arrangement and physical appearance of objects. During the preoperational period, preschoolers are unable to understand that changes in one dimension (such as appearance) do not necessarily mean that other dimensions (such as quantity) are changed.

Children who do not yet understand the principle of conservation feel quite comfortable in asserting that the amount of liquid changes as it is poured between glasses of different sizes. They simply are unable to realize that the transformation in appearance does not imply a transformation in quantity.

The inability to conserve manifests itself in several ways during the preoperational period. For example, if 5-year-olds are shown a row of checkers and asked to build a row that is "the same," the row they typically build will be identical in length—but it may vary in the number of checkers. Similarly, if shown two rows of checkers, each with the same number of checkers, but one with the checkers more spread out, children in the preoperational stage will reason that the two rows are not equal.

The lack of conservation also manifests itself in children's understanding of area, as illustrated by Piaget's cow-in-the-field problem (Piaget, Inhelder, & Szenubsjam, 1960). In the problem, two sheets of green paper, equal in size, are shown to a child, and a toy cow is placed in each field. Next, a toy barn is placed in each field, and children are asked which cow has more to eat. The typical—and, so far, correct—response is that the cows have the same amount.

In the next step, a second toy barn is placed in each field. But in one field, the barns are placed adjacent to one another, whereas in the second field, they are separated from one another. Children who have not mastered conservation usually say that the cow in the field with the adjacent barns has more grass to eat than the cow in the field with the separated barns. In contrast, children who can conserve answer, correctly, that the amount available is identical. (Some other conservation tasks are shown in Figure 7-7).

FIGURE 7-6 WHICH CONTAINER CONTAINS MORE?

Even after seeing that the amount of liquid in the two cups is identical (left), and watching while the liquid is poured into the glass, most 4-year-olds believe that the glass contains more liquid than the cup (right).

FIGURE 7-7

COMMON TESTS OF CHILDREN'S UNDERSTANDING OF THE PRINCIPLE OF CONSERVATION

Type of Conservation	Modality	Change in Physical Appearance	Average Age Invariance is Grasped
Number	Number of elements in a collection 	Rearranging or dislocating elements 	6–7 years
Substance (mass)	Amount of a malleable substance (e.g., clay or liquid) 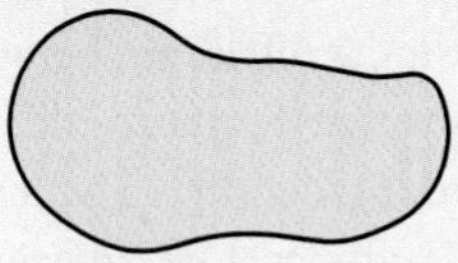	Altering shape 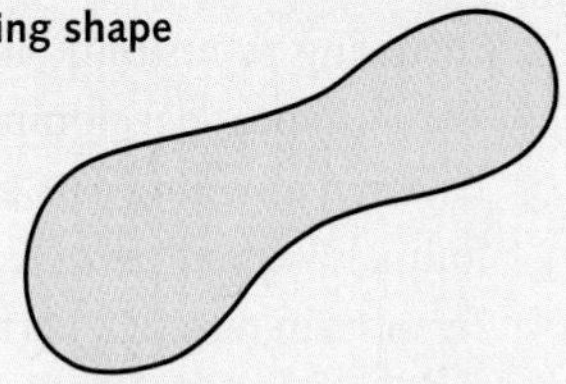	7–8 years
Length	Length of a line or object 	Altering shape or configuration 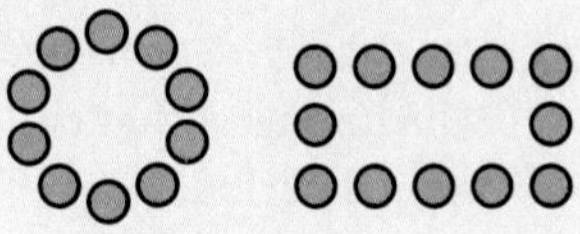	7–8 years
Area	Amount of surface covered by a set of plane figures 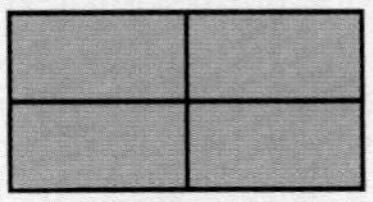	Rearranging the figures 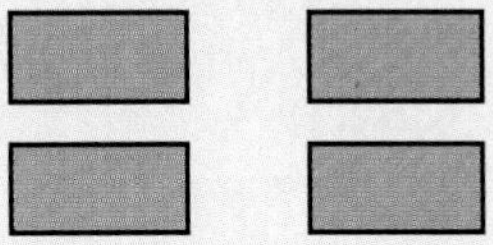	8–9 years
Weight	Weight of an object 	Altering shape 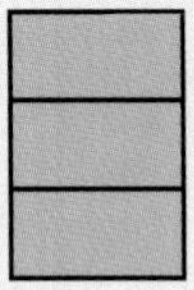	9–10 years
Volume	Volume of an object (in terms of water displacement) 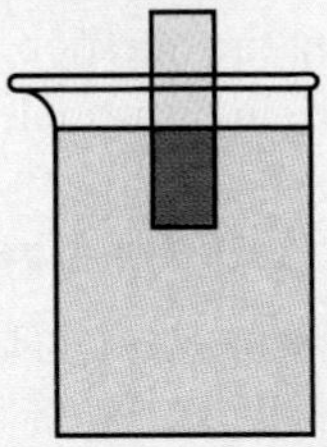	Altering shape 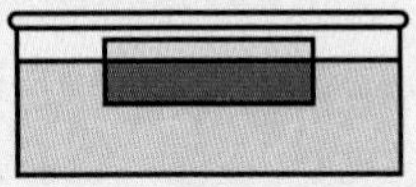	14–15 years

Why do children in the preoperational stage make errors on tasks that require conservation? Piaget suggests that the main reason is that their tendency toward centration prevents them from focusing on the relevant features of the situation. Furthermore, they cannot follow the sequence of transformations that accompanies changes in the appearance of a situation.

Evaluating Piaget's Approach to Cognitive Development.   Piaget, a masterful observer of children's behavior, provides a detailed portrait of preschoolers' cognitive abilities. His rich description of how children view the world is simply unmatched by most other accounts of cognitive development.

However, Piaget's portrait is both incomplete and, in certain respects, flawed. Several aspects of his theory seriously underestimate children's capabilities. Take, for instance, Piaget's views of how children in the preoperational period understand number. He contends that preschoolers' thinking is seriously handicapped, as evidenced by their performance on tasks involving reversibility and conservation. Yet recent experimental work suggests otherwise. For instance, developmental psychologist Rochel Gelman has found in her research that children as young as 3 can readily discern the difference between rows of two and three toy animals, regardless of the animals' spacing. Furthermore, older children are able to note differences in number, performing tasks such as identifying which of two numbers is larger and indicating that they understand some rudiments of addition and subtraction (Gelman, 1972; Wynn, 1992; Sophian, Garyantes, & Chang, 1997).

Based on such evidence, Gelman concludes that children have an innate ability to count, one akin to the ability to use language that some theorists see as universal and genetically determined. Such a conclusion is clearly at odds with Piagetian notions, which suggest that children's numerical abilities do not blossom until after the preoperational period.

Some developmental psychologists also believe that cognitive skills develop in a more continuous manner than Piaget's stage theory implies. Rather than thought changing in quality, as Piaget argues, critics of Piaget suggest that developmental changes are more quantitative in nature. The underlying processes that produce cognitive skill are regarded by such critics as undergoing only minor changes with age (Gelman & Baillargeon, 1983; Case, 1991).

There are further difficulties with Piaget's view of cognitive development. His contention that conservation does not emerge until the end of the preoperational period and, in some cases, even later, has not stood up to careful experimental scrutiny. For instance, performance on conservation tasks can be improved by providing preoperational children with certain kinds of training and experiences. The mere possibility of enhancing performance argues against the Piagetian view that children in the preoperational period have not reached a level of cognitive maturity that would permit them to understand conservation (Field, 1987).

Clearly, children are more capable at an earlier age than Piaget's account would lead us to believe. Why did Piaget underestimate children's cognitive abilities? One answer is that he tended to concentrate on preschoolers' *deficiencies* in thinking, focusing his observations on children's lack of logical thought. In contrast, more recent theorists have focused more on children's competence. By shifting the question, they have found increasing evidence for a surprising degree of competence in preschoolers.

Information-processing Approaches to Cognitive Development

Even as an adult, Paco has clear recollections of his first trip to a farm, which he took when he was 3 years old. He was visiting his godfather, who lived in Puerto Rico, and the two of them went to a nearby farm. Paco recounts seeing what seemed like hundreds of chickens, and he clearly recalls his fear of the pigs, who seemed huge, smelly, and frightening. Most of all he recalls the thrill of riding on a horse with his godfather.

That Paco has a clear memory of his farm trip is not surprising: Most people have unambiguous, and seemingly accurate, memories dating as far back as the age of 3. But are the processes used to form memories during the preschool years similar to those that operate later in life? More broadly, what general changes in the processing of information occur during the preschool years? To answer these questions, we will focus on two domains that highlight the approach taken by information-processing theorists: understanding of numbers and memory development during the preschool years.

Preschoolers' Understanding of Numbers.   Researchers using information-processing approaches to cognitive development have found increasing evidence for the sophistication of preschoolers' understanding of numbers. The average preschooler is able not only to count, but to do so in a fairly systematic, consistent manner (Siegler, 1991).

For instance, developmental psychologist Rochel Gelman suggests that preschoolers follow a number of principles in their counting. When shown a group of several items, they know they should assign just one number to each item, and that each item should be counted only once. Moreover, even when they get the *names* of numbers wrong, they are consistent in their usage. For instance, a 4-year-old who counts three items as "1, 3, 7" will say "1, 3, 7" when counting another group of different items. And she will probably say that there are 7 items in the group, if asked how many there are (Gelman & Gallistel, 1978; Gelman, 1972).

In short, preschoolers may demonstrate a surprisingly sophisticated understanding of numbers, although their understanding is not totally firm. Still, by the age of 4, most are able to carry out simple addition and subtraction problems by counting, and they are able to compare different quantities quite successfully.

Memory: Recalling the Past.   Think back to your own earliest memory. If you are like most people, it probably is of an event that occurred after the age of 3. According to Katherine Nelson (1989), **autobiographical memory**, memory of particular events from one's own life, achieves little accuracy until after 3 years of age. Accuracy then increases gradually and slowly throughout the preschool years (Nelson, 1989, 1992).

Preschool children's recollections of events that happened to them are sometimes, but not always, accurate. For instance, 3-year-olds can remember fairly well central features of routine occurrences, such as the sequence of events involved in eating at a restaurant. In addition, preschoolers are typically accurate in their responses to open-ended questions, such as "What rides did you like best at the amusement park?" (Goodman & Reed, 1986; Nelson, 1986; Price & Goodman, 1990).

One important determinant of the accuracy of preschoolers' autobiographical memories is how soon they are assessed. Unless an event is particularly vivid or meaningful, it is not likely to be remembered at all. Moreover, not all autobiographical memories last into later life. For instance, a 3-year-old may remember the first day of preschool 6 months later, but the event may not be recalled at all later in life.

Preschoolers' autobiographical memories not only fade, but the ones that are remembered may not be wholly accurate. For instance, preschoolers have difficulty describing certain kinds of information, such as complex causal relationships, and may oversimplify recollections. And, as we consider next, their memories are also susceptible to the suggestions of others.

Children's Eyewitness Testimony: Memory on Trial.

I was looking and then I didn't see what I was doing and it got in there somehow. . . . The mousetrap was in our house because there's a mouse in our house. . . . The mousetrap is down in the basement, next to the firewood. . . . I was playing a game called "Operation" and then I went downstairs and said to Dad, "I want to eat lunch," and then it got stuck in the mousetrap. . . . My daddy was down in the basement collecting firewood. . . . [My

How specific and accurate will this preschooler's memory be of this event in the future?

autobiographical memory *memory of particular events from one's own life*

brother] pushed me [into the mousetrap]. . . . It happened yesterday. The mouse was in my house yesterday. I caught my finger in it yesterday. I went to the hospital yesterday. (Coleman, 1993, p. A23)

Despite the detailed account by this 4-year-old boy of his encounter with a mousetrap and subsequent trip to the hospital, there's a problem: The incident never happened, and the memory is entirely false.

The 4-year-old's explicit recounting of a mousetrap incident that had not actually occurred was the product of a study on children's memory. Each week for 11 weeks, the 4-year-old boy was told, "You went to the hospital because your finger got caught in a mousetrap. Did this ever happen to you?"

The first week, the child quite accurately said, "No. I've never been to the hospital." But by the second week, the answer changed to, "Yes, I cried." In the third week, the boy said, "Yes. My mom went to the hospital with me." By the eleventh week, the answer had expanded to the quote above (Coleman, 1993).

The embellishment of a completely false incident is characteristic of the fragility and inaccuracy of memory in young children. Young children may recall things quite mistakenly, but with great conviction, contending that events occurred that never really happened, and forgetting events that did occur.

Furthermore, children's memories are susceptible to the suggestions of adults asking them questions. This is particularly true of preschoolers, who are considerably more vulnerable to suggestion than either adults or school-age children. Preschoolers are also more prone to make inaccurate inferences about the reasons behind others' behavior, and less able to draw appropriate conclusions based on their knowledge of a situation (Ceci et al., Bruck, 1994; Ceci & Huffman, 1997; Loftus, 1997; Thompson, Clark-Stewart, & Lepore, 1997).

Of course, preschoolers recall many things accurately; as we discussed earlier in the chapter, children as young as 3 recall some events in their lives without distortion. However, not all recollections are accurate, and some events that are recalled with seeming accuracy never actually occurred.

The error rate for children is further heightened when the same question is asked repeatedly (Cassel, Roebers, & Bjorklund, 1996). Furthermore, false memories—of the type reported by the 4-year-old who "remembered" going to the hospital after his finger was caught in a mousetrap—in fact may be more persistent than actual memories (Brainerd, Reyna, & Brandse, 1995).

In addition, when questions are highly suggestive (that is, when questioners attempt to lead a person to particular conclusions), children are more apt to make mistakes in recall (Ceci & Huffman, 1997). For instance, consider the following excerpt, which presents an extreme example of a preschool child being questioned. It comes from an actual case involving a teacher, Kelly Michaels, who was accused of sexually molesting children in a preschool.

Preschool techer Kelly Michaels was convicted of sexually molesting several preschool children as the result of highly suggestive questions posed to the children.

Social worker: Don't be so unfriendly. I thought we were buddies last time.
Child: Nope, not any more.
Social worker: We have gotten a lot of other kids to help us since I last saw you. . . . Did we tell you that Kelly is in jail?
Child: Yes. My mother already told me.
Social worker: Did I tell you that this is the guy (pointing to the detective) that arrested her?. . . Well, we can get out of here real quick if you just tell me what you told me the last time, when we met.
Child: I forgot.
Social worker: No you didn't. I know you didn't.
Child: I did! I did!
Social worker: I thought we were friends last time.
Child: I'm not your friend any more!
Social worker: How come?

such broad concepts as the zone of proximal development are not terribly precise, and they do not always lend themselves to experimental tests.

Furthermore, Vygotsky was largely silent on how basic cognitive processes such as attention and memory develop, and how children's natural cognitive capabilities unfold. Because of his emphasis on broad cultural influences, he did not focus on how individual bits of information are processed and synthesized. These processes, which must be taken into account if we are to have a complete understanding of cognitive development, are more directly addressed by information-processing theories.

Still, Vygotsky's melding of the cognitive and social worlds of children has been an important advance in our understanding of cognitive development. One can only imagine what his impact would have been if he had lived a longer life.

REVIEW AND RETHINK

REVIEW

- According to Piaget, children in the preoperational stage develop symbolic function, a qualitative change in their thinking that is the foundation of further cognitive advances, including the development of language and intuitive thought.

- Preoperational children use intuitive thought to explore and draw conclusions about the world, and their thinking begins to encompass the important notions of functionality and identity.

- Recent developmental psychologists, while acknowledging Piaget's gifts and contributions, take issue with his emphasis on children's limitations and his underestimation of their capabilities.

- Proponents of information-processing approaches argue that quantitative changes in children's processing skills, such as memory and attention, largely account for their cognitive development.

- Vygotsky believed that children develop cognitively within a context of culture and society that influences the path and sequence of their development. He suggested that children learn most effectively from tasks that are within their zone of proximal development—the level at which a child can *almost*, but not fully, perform a task independently, but can do so with the assistance of someone more competent.

- Scaffolding is the temporary support that children need to help them frame and complete tasks. Scaffolding involves the use of cultural tools—specific materials used within a given society and a conceptual framework based on cultural thinking and understanding—that define how tasks are addressed and solved within a particular culture.

RETHINK

- Do you agree with Piaget that symbolic thought does not emerge until children leave the sensorimotor period? How might you design a study to investigate the presence or absence of symbolic thought in very young children?

- In your view, how do thought and language interact in preschoolers' development? Is it possible to think without language? How do prelingually deaf children think?

- Are there cultural aspects to intuitive thought? Do you think children in all cultures develop logical thinking identically, or are there cultural differences? Why?

- If children's cognitive development is dependent on interactions with others, what obligations does the broader society have regarding such social settings as preschools, schools, and neighborhoods?

THE GROWTH OF LANGUAGE AND LEARNING

I tried it out and it was very great!

This is a picture of when I was running through the water with Mommy.

Where you are going when I go to the fireworks with Mommy and Daddy?

We can always pretend we have another one.

And the teacher put it up on the counter so no one could reach it.

You need to get your own ball if you want to play "hit the tree."

When I grow up and I'm a baseball player, I'll have my baseball hat, and I'll put it on, and I'll play baseball. (Schatz, 1994, p. 179)

Listen to Ricky, at the age of 3. In addition to recognizing most letters of the alphabet, printing the first letter of his name, and writing the word "HI," he is readily capable of producing the complex sentences quoted above.

TABLE 7-3

GROWING SPEECH CAPABILITIES

Over the course of just a year, the sophistication of the language of a boy named Adam increases amazingly, as these speech samples show:

2 years, 3 months:	Play checkers. Big drum. I got horn. A bunny-rabbit walk.
2 years, 4 months:	See marching bear go? Screw part machine. That busy bulldozer truck.
2 years, 5 months:	Now put boots on. Where wrench go? Mommy talking bout lady. What that paper clip doing?
2 years, 6 months:	Write a piece of paper. What that egg doing? I lost a shoe. No, I don't want to sit seat.
2 years, 7 months:	Where piece a paper go? Ursula has a boot on. Going to see kitten. Put the cigarette down. Dropped a rubber band. Shadow has hat just like that. Rintintin don't fly, Mommy.
2 years, 8 months:	Let me get down with the boots on. Don't be afraid a horses. How tiger be so healthy and fly like kite? Joshua throw like a penguin.
2 years, 9 months:	Where Mommy keep her pocket book? Show you something funny. Just like turtle make mud pie.
2 years, 10 months:	Look at that train Ursula brought. I simply don't want put in chair. You don't have paper. Do you want little bit, Cromer? I can't wear it tomorrow.
2 years, 11 months:	That birdie hopping by Missouri in bag. Do want some pie on your face? Why you mixing baby chocolate? I finish drinking all up down my throat. I said why not you coming in? Look at that piece of paper and tell it. Do you want me tie that round? We going turn light on so you can't see.
3 years, 0 months:	I going come in fourteen minutes. I going wear that to wedding. I see what happens. I have to save them now. Those are not strong mens. They are going sleep in wintertime. You dress me up like a baby elephant.
3 years, 1 month:	I like to play with something else. You know how to put it back together. I gon' make it like a rocket to blast off with. I put another one on the floor. You went to Boston University? You want to give me some carrots and some beans? Press the button and catch it, sir. I want some other peanuts. Why you put the pacifier in his mouth? Doggies like to climb up.
3 years, 2 months:	So it can't be cleaned? I broke my racing car. Do you know the light wents off? What happened to the bridge? When it's got a flat tire it's need a go to the station. I dream sometimes. I'm going to mail this so the letter can't come off. I want to have some espresso. The sun is not too bright. Can I have some sugar? Can I put my head in the mailbox so the mailman can know where I are and put me in the mailbox? Can I keep the screwdriver just like a carpenter keep the screwdriver?

(Source: Pinker, 1994.)

During the preschool years, children's language skills reach new heights of sophistication. They begin the period with reasonable linguistic capabilities, although with significant gaps in both comprehension and production. In fact, no one would mistake the language used by a 3-year-old for that of an adult. However, by the end of the preschool years, they can hold their own with adults, both comprehending and producing language that has many of the qualities of adults' language. How does this transformation occur?

syntax   *the way in which an individual combines words and phrases to form sentences*

Language Development

The two-word utterances of the 2-year-old soon increase in both number of words and scope. Indeed, language blooms so rapidly between the late twos and the mid-threes that researchers have yet to understand the exact pattern. What is clear is that sentence length increases at a steady pace, and the ways in which children at this age combine words and phrases to form sentences—known as **syntax**—doubles each month. By the time a preschooler is 3, the various combinations reach into the thousands (see Table 7-3 for an example of one child's growth in the use of language; Pinker, 1994).

In addition to the increasing complexity of sentences, there are enormous leaps in the number of words children use. By age 6 the average child has a vocabulary of around 14,000 words. To reach this number, preschoolers acquire vocabulary at a rate of nearly one new word every 2½ hours, 24 hours a day (Clark, 1983).

By the age of 3, preschoolers routinely use plurals and possessive forms of nouns (such as "boys" and "boy's"), employ the past tense (adding "-ed" at the end of words), and use articles ("the" and "a"). They can ask, and answer, complex questions ("Where did you say my book is?" and "Those are trucks, aren't they?").

Preschoolers' skills extend to the appropriate formation of words that they have never before encountered. For example, in one classic experiment, preschool children were shown cards with drawings of a cartoon-like bird, such as those shown in Figure 7-9 (Berko, 1958). The experimenter told the children that the figure was a "wug," and then showed them a card with two of the cartoon figures. "Now there are two of them," the children were told, and they were then asked to supply the missing word in the sentence, "There are two ____" (the answer to which, as *you* no doubt know, is "wugs").

Children showed that they not only knew rules about the plural forms of nouns, they understood possessive forms of nouns and the third-person singular and past-tense forms of verbs—all for words that they never had previously encountered, because they were nonsense words with no real meaning.

FIGURE 7-9

APPROPRIATE FORMATION
OF WORDS

Even though no preschooler—like the rest of us—is likely to have ever before encountered a wug, they are able to produce the appropriate word to fill in the blank (which, for the record, is *wugs*).

(*Source:* Adapted from Berko, 1958.)

This is a wug.

Now there is another one.
There are two of them.
There are two _____ .

The preschool years mark the growth of social speech.

Preschoolers also learn what *cannot* be said as they acquire the principles of grammar. **Grammar** is the system of rules that determine how our thoughts can be expressed. For instance, preschoolers come to learn that "I am sitting" is correct, whereas the similarly structured "I am knowing [that]" is incorrect. Although they still make frequent mistakes of one sort or another, 3-year-olds follow the principles of grammar most of the time. Some errors are very noticeable—such as the use of "mens" and "catched"—but these errors are actually quite rare, occurring between one-tenth of a percent and eight percent of the time. Put another way, more than 90 percent of the time young preschoolers are correct in their grammatical constructions (de Villiers & de Villiers, 1992; Pinker, 1994).

Private Speech and Social Speech. In even a short visit to a preschool, you're likely to notice some children talking to themselves during play periods. A child might be reminding a doll that the two of them are going to the grocery store later, or another child, while playing with a toy racing car, might speak of an upcoming race. In some cases, the talk is sustained, as when a child, working on a puzzle, says things like, "This piece goes here. . . . Uh-oh, this one doesn't fit. . . . Where can I put this piece? . . . This can't be right."

To Vygotsky, such musings play an important role in cognitive development. He suggests that **private speech**, speech by children that is spoken and directed to themselves, is used as a guide to behavior and thought. By communicating with themselves through private speech, children are able to try out ideas, acting as their own sounding boards.

Over the course of the preschool years, the use of private speech is common. As much as 20 to 60 percent of what children say is private speech, and such speech is a normal practice during even later stages of childhood. In fact, some research suggests that its use grows over the preschool years, peaking between the ages of 4 and 7. On the other hand, private speech becomes more secretive as children grow older and realize that talking to oneself is discouraged. Consequently, older children tend to whisper private speech or silently move their lips, rather than speaking out loud (Berk & Landau, 1993; Berk, 1994; Berk & Spuhl, 1995; Flavell et al., 1997).

Some developmentalists suggest that private speech performs an important function. For instance, Vygotsky suggests that it facilitates children's thinking and that they use it to help them control their behavior. In his view, private speech ultimately serves an important social function, allowing children to solve problems and reflect on difficulties they encounter (Winsler, Diaz, & Montero, 1997). He suggests further that private speech is a forerunner to the internal dialogues that we use when we reason with ourselves during thinking. Clearly, Vygotsky's views are at odds with those of Piaget, who suggests that private speech is egocentric and a sign of immature thought and ultimately a failure to communicate effectively (Vygotsky, 1962, 1986).

The preschool years also mark the growth of social speech. **Social speech** is speech directed toward another person and meant to be understood by that person. Before the age of 3, children may seem to be speaking only for their own entertainment, apparently uncaring whether anyone else can understand. However, during the preschool years, children begin to direct their speech to others, wanting others to listen and becoming frustrated when they cannot make themselves understood. As a result, they begin to adapt their speech to others. Recall that Piaget contended that most speech during the preoperational period was egocentric: Preschoolers were seen as taking little account of the effect their speech was having on others. However, more recent experimental evidence suggests that children are somewhat more adept in taking others into account than Piaget initially suggested.

Poverty and Language Development. The language that preschoolers hear at home has profound consequences for future cognitive success, according to results of a landmark study by psychologists Betty Hart and Todd Risley (1995). The researchers studied the language used by a group of parents of varying levels of affluence as they interacted with their

grammar the system of rules that determine how our thoughts can be expressed

private speech speech by children that is spoken and directed to themselves

social speech speech directed toward another person and meant to be understood by that person

children over a 2-year period. Coding some 1,300 hours of everyday interactions between parents and children produced several major findings:

- The rate at which language was addressed to children varied significantly according to the economic level of the family. As shown in Figure 7-10, the greater the affluence of the parents, the more they spoke to their children.

- In a typical hour, professional parents spent almost two times as much time interacting with their children as did welfare parents.

- By the age of 4, children in welfare families were likely to have been exposed to some 13 million fewer words than those in families classified as professionals.

- The kind of language used in the home differed among the various types of families. Children in welfare families were apt to hear prohibitions ("no" or "stop," for example) twice as frequently than those in professional families.

Ultimately, the study found that the type of language to which children were exposed was associated with their performance on tests of intelligence. The greater the number and variety of words a child heard, for instance, the better the performance of the children at age 3 on a variety of measures of intellectual achievement.

Clearly, such findings argue for the importance of early exposure to language, in terms of both quantity and variety. The findings also suggest that intervention programs that teach parents to use more language and more varied language may be useful in alleviating some of the damaging consequences of poverty.

The research is also consistent with an increasing body of evidence demonstrating that family income and poverty have powerful consequences on general cognitive development and children's behavior. By the age of 5, children raised in poorer homes tend to have lower IQ scores and do worse on other measures of cognitive development. Furthermore, the longer children live in poverty, the more severe are the consequences. Poverty not only reduces the educational resources available to children; it also has such negative effects on *parents* that it limits the psychological support that they can give to their children. In short,

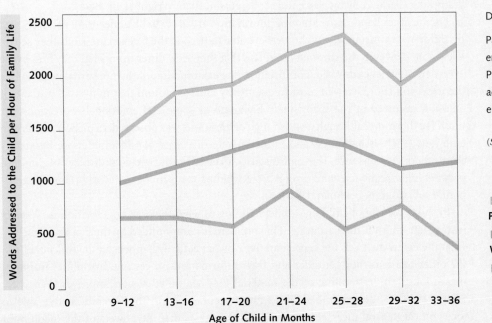

FIGURE 7-10

DIFFERENT LANGUAGE EXPOSURE

Parents at differing levels of economic affluence provide different language experiences. Professional parents and working parents address more words to their children, on average, than parents on welfare.

(*Source:* Hart & Risley, 1995, p. 239.)

Professional Parents

Working Parents

Welfare Parents

the consequences of poverty are severe, and they linger (Bolger et al., 1995; Duncan & Brooks-Gunn, 1997; Stipek & Ryan, 1997; McLoyd, 1998; Ramey & Ramey, 1998).

Television: Learning from the Media

It's a Thursday afternoon at Unitel Studio on Ninth Avenue, where *Sesame Street* is taping its nineteenth season. Hanging back in the wings is a newcomer on the set, a compact young woman with short blonde hair named Judy Sladky. Today is her screen test. Other performers come to New York aspiring to be actresses, dancers, singers, comedians. But Sladky's burning ambition is to be Alice, a shaggy mini-mastodon who will make her debut later this season as the devoted baby sister of Aloysius Snuffle-upagus, the biggest creature on the show. (Hellman, 1987, p. 50)

Ask almost any preschooler, and she or he will be able to identify Snuffle-upagus, as well as Big Bird, Bert, Ernie, and a host of other characters: the members of the cast of *Sesame Street*. *Sesame Street* is the most successful television show in history targeted at preschoolers; its audience is in the millions.

But *Sesame Street* is not all that preschoolers are watching, for television plays a central role in many U.S. households. In fact, it is one of the most potent and widespread stimuli to which children are exposed, with the average preschooler watching some 20 to 30 hours of TV a week. In contrast, preschoolers spend less than an hour per week with books (Rosemond, 1988; Robinson & Bianchi, 1997).

Television: Ubiquitous Presence, Uncertain Consequences.   Almost every home in the United States has a television, and more than half of all households own more than one. Statistics show there are more televisions than toilets in this country. These televisions do not sit idle: It has been estimated that the average American child spends more time watching television than talking to adults, playing with siblings, or attending school (Singer & Singer, 1983; Liebert & Sprafkin, 1988; Van Evra, 1997).

Despite television's ubiquitous presence, the consequences of watching so much television are not entirely clear. For instance, research suggests that children do not fully understand the plots of the stories they are viewing, particularly in longer programs. They are unable to recall significant story details after viewing a program, and the inferences they make about the motivations of characters are limited and often erroneous. Moreover, preschool children may have difficulty separating fantasy from reality in television programming (Parke & Slaby, 1983; Rule & Ferguson, 1986; Wright et al., 1994).

On the other hand, some kinds of information are likely to be understood relatively well by children. For instance, preschoolers are able to decode the facial expressions they see on television. However, the emotional displays that they view differ from what they find in the everyday, nontelevised world. For instance, one examination of the nonverbal behavior on the television shows viewed most frequently by children found that nonverbal displays of emotion occurred at the surprisingly high rate of some 200 emotional expressions per hour. Furthermore, although a wide range of emotions was observed, depictions of certain emotions (such as happiness and sadness) were displayed considerably more frequently than others (for instance, fear and disgust). Consequently, televised displays of emotion occur at high frequencies and diverge from what happens in the real world (Houle & Feldman, 1991; Coats & Feldman, 1995).

In short, preschool children's understanding of what they see on television is typically incomplete and not fully accurate. This problem is compounded by the fact that much of what they view on TV is not representative of what actually happens in the real world. On the other hand, as they get older and their information-processing capabilities improve, preschoolers' understanding of the material they see on television improves (Wilson & Smith, 1998). They remember things more accurately, and they become better able to focus on the central message of a show. This suggests that the powers of the medium of television may be harnessed to bring about cognitive gains—exactly what the producers of *Sesame Street* set out to do (Van Evra, 1990; Wright et al., 1995; Cornachio, 1998; Weisinger, 1998).

Sesame Street: A Teacher in Every Home?   *Sesame Street* is, without a doubt, the most popular educational program for children in the United States. Almost half of all preschoolers in the United States watch the show, and it is broadcast in almost 100 different countries and in 13 foreign languages. Characters like Big Bird and Kermit the Frog have become familiar throughout the world, to both adults and preschoolers (Liebert & Sprafkin, 1988).

Sesame Street was devised with the express purpose of providing an educational experience for preschoolers. Its specific goals include teaching letters and numbers, increasing vocabulary, and teaching preliteracy skills. Has *Sesame Street* achieved its goals? Most evidence suggests that it has.

For example, a 2-year longitudinal study compared three groups of 3- and 5-year-olds: those who watched cartoons or other programs, those who watched the same amount of *Sesame Street,* and those who watched little or no TV. Children who watched *Sesame Street* had significantly larger vocabularies than those who watched other programs or those who watched little television. These findings held regardless of the children's gender, family size, and parent education and attitudes. Such findings are consistent with earlier evaluations of the program, which concluded that viewers showed dramatic improvements in skills that were directly taught, such as alphabet recitation, and improvements in other areas that were not directly taught, such as reading words (Bogatz & Ball, 1972; Rice et al., 1990).

Formal evaluations of the show find that preschoolers living in lower income households who watch the show are better prepared for school, and they perform significantly higher on several measures of verbal and mathematics ability at ages 6 and 7 than those who do not watch it. Furthermore, viewers of *Sesame Street* spend more time reading than nonviewers. And by the time they are 6 and 7, viewers of *Sesame Street* and other educational programs tend to be better readers and judged more positively by their teachers (Wright, et al. 1995).

On the other hand, *Sesame Street* has not been without its critics. For instance, some educators claim the frenetic pace at which different scenes are shown makes viewers less receptive to the traditional forms of teaching that they will experience when they begin school. Traditional teaching moves at a slower pace and the lessons are typically less visually appealing than those presented on *Sesame Street.* However, careful evaluations of the program find no evidence that viewing *Sesame Street* leads to declines in enjoyment of traditional schooling (Van Evra, 1990).

In sum, the results of research on the consequences of watching *Sesame Street* are largely positive. Still, it is important to keep in mind the difficulties of carrying out evaluations of the effects of viewing. For instance, parents who encourage their children to watch a show reputed to improve academic performance may also encourage their children's academic performance in other spheres. Consequently, it may be the parents' high level of encouragement, and not the program itself, that leads to the children's improved cognitive performance. Without the use of true experiments—which are difficult, if not impossible, to carry out because it is hard to maintain experimental control of what children watch in their homes—conclusions about the consequences of TV viewing remain uncertain. (We will discuss this issue more in Chapter 8, when we consider the consequences of viewing violence in the media.)

Careful research suggests that *Sesame Street* has met its goal of teaching letters and numbers, increasing vocabulary, and teaching preliteracy skills.

Early Childhood Education: Taking the "Pre" Out of the Preschool Period

The term *preschool period* is something of a misnomer: Almost three-quarters of children in the United States are enrolled in some form of care outside the home, much of which is designed either explicitly or implicitly to teach skills that will enhance intellectual, as well as social, abilities

day-care centers *places that typically provide care for children all day, while their parents are at work*

preschools (or **nursery schools**) *child-care facilities designed to provide intellectual and social experiences for children*

(see Figure 7-11). There are several reasons for this increase, but one major factor is the rise in the number of families in which both parents work outside the home. For instance, a high proportion of fathers work outside the home, and close to 60 percent of women with children under 6 are employed, most of them full-time (Gilbert, 1994; Borden, 1998).

However, there is another reason, one less tied to the practical considerations of child care: Developmental psychologists have found increasing evidence that children can benefit substantially from involvement in some form of educational activity before they enroll in formal schooling, which typically takes place at age 5 or 6 in the United States. When compared with children who stay at home and have no formal educational involvement, those children enrolled in *good* preschools experience clear cognitive and social benefits (McCartney, 1984; Haskins, 1989; Clarke-Stewart, 1993).

The Varieties of Early Education.   The variety of early education alternatives is vast. Some outside-the-home care for children is little more than babysitting, whereas other options are designed to promote intellectual and social advances. Among the major choices of the latter type are the following:

- Day-care centers. **Day-care centers** typically provide care for children all day, while their parents are at work. Although many day-care centers were first established as safe, warm environments where children could be cared for and could interact with other children, today their purpose tends to be broader, aimed at providing some form of intellectual stimulation. Still, their primary purpose tends to be more social and emotional than cognitive.

  Some day care is provided in family day-care centers, small operations run in private homes. Because such centers are often unlicensed, the quality of care can be uneven, and parents should investigate carefully before enrolling their children. In contrast, providers of center-based care, which is offered in institutions such as school classrooms, community centers, and churches and synagogues, are licensed and regulated by governmental authorities. Because teachers in such programs are more often trained professionals than those who provide family day care, the quality of care is often higher and more stable.

- Preschools or nursery schools. **Preschools** (or **nursery schools**) are more explicitly designed to provide intellectual and social experiences for children. Because they tend to be more limited in their schedules, typically providing care for only 3 to 5 hours per day, preschools mainly serve children from middle and higher socioeconomic levels.

  Like day-care centers, preschools vary enormously in the activities they provide. Some emphasize social skills, whereas others focus on intellectual development. Some

FIGURE 7-11

CARE OUTSIDE THE HOME

Approximately 75 percent of children in the United States are enrolled in some form of care outside the home—a trend that is the result of more parents employed full time. Evidence suggests that children can benefit from early childhood education.

(*Sources:* U.S. Department of Education, National Center for Education Statistics.)

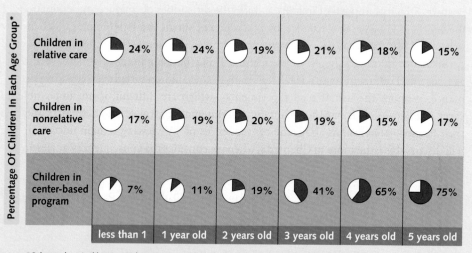

*Columns do not add up to 100 because some children participated in more than one type of day care.

do both. For instance, Montessori preschools, which use a method developed by Italian educator Maria Montessori, employ a carefully designed set of materials to create an environment that fosters sensory, motor, and language development.

■ School day care. **School day care** is provided by some local school systems in the United States. Almost half the states in the United States fund prekindergarten programs for 4-year-olds, often targeted at disadvantaged children. Because they typically are staffed by better-trained teachers than less-regulated day-care centers, school day-care programs are often of higher quality than other early education alternatives.

school day care   *child-care facility provided by some local school systems in the United States*

How effective are such programs? According to developmental psychologist Alison Clarke-Stewart, who has studied the issue extensively, preschoolers enrolled in day-care centers show intellectual development that at least matches that of children at home, and often is better. For instance, some studies find that day-care preschoolers are more verbally fluent, show memory and comprehension advantages, and even achieve higher IQ scores than at-home children (Clarke-Stewart, 1993). Other studies find that early and long-term participation in day care is particularly helpful for children from impoverished home environments or otherwise at risk (Guralnick, 1996; Broberg et al., 1997; Burchinal et al., 1997; Reynolds & Temple, 1998).

Analogous advantages are found in social development. Children in high-quality programs tend to be more self-confident, independent, and knowledgeable about the social world in which they live than those who do not participate. On the other hand, not all the outcomes of outside-the-home care are positive: Children in day care have been found to be less polite, less compliant, less respectful of adults, and sometimes more competitive and aggressive than their peers (Belsky, Steinberg, & Walker, 1982; Thornburg et al., 1990; Bates et al., 1991).

It is important to keep in mind that not all early childhood care programs are equally effective. As we observed of infant day care in Chapter 6, one key factor is program *quality:* High-quality care provides intellectual and social benefits, whereas low-quality care not only is unlikely to furnish benefits, but also may actually harm children (Phillips et al., 1994).

How can we define "high quality"? Several characteristics are important; they are analogous to those that pertain to infant day care (see Chapter 6). For example, high-quality facilities have well-trained care providers. Furthermore, both the overall size of the group and the ratio of care providers to children are critical. Single groups should not have many more than 14 to 20 children, and there should be no more than 5 to ten 3-year-olds per caregiver, or seven to ten 4- or 5-year-olds per caregiver. Finally, the curriculum of a child-care facility should not be left to chance, but should be carefully planned out and coordinated among the teachers (National Research Council, 1991; Cromwell, 1994).

*"I didn't realize how much I needed to get
away from that day-care grind."*

Developmental Diversity

Preschools Around the World: Why Does the United States Lag Behind?

In France and Belgium, accessibility to preschool is a legal right. In Sweden and Finland, preschoolers whose parents work have day care provided, if it is wanted. Russia has an extensive system of state-run *yasli-sads*, nursery schools and kindergartens, attended by 75 percent of children age 3 to 7 in urban areas.

In contrast, the United States has no coordinated national policy on preschool education—or on the care of children in general. There are several reasons for this. For one, decisions about education have traditionally been left to the states and local school districts. For another, the United States has no tradition of teaching preschoolers, unlike other countries in which preschool-age children have been enrolled in formal programs for decades. Finally, the status of preschools in the United States has been traditionally low. Consider, for instance, that preschool and nursery school teachers are the lowest paid of all teachers. (Teacher salaries increase as the age of students rises. Thus, college and high school teachers are paid most, and preschool and elementary school teachers are paid least.)

Finally, the quantity and nature of preschools may differ from one country to another according to the views that different societies hold of the purpose of early childhood education (Lamb et al., 1992). For instance, in a cross-country comparison of preschools in China, Japan, and the United States, researchers

In many industrialized countries other than the United States, preschool education receives significantly more national support.

found that parents in the three countries view the purpose of preschools very differently. Whereas parents in China tend to see preschools primarily as a way of giving children a good start academically, Japanese parents view them primarily as a way of giving children the opportunity to be members of a group. In the United States, in comparison, parents regard the primary purpose of preschools as making children more independent and self-reliant, although obtaining a good academic start and having group experience are also important (see Figure 7-12; Tobin, Wu, & Davidson, 1989; Huntsinger et al., 1997).

FIGURE 7-12

THE PURPOSE OF PRESCHOOL

To parents in China, Japan, and the United States, the main purpose of preschools is very different. Whereas parents in China see preschools mainly as a way of giving children a good start academically, parents in Japan see them primarily as a means of giving children the experience of being a member of a group. In contrast, parents in the United States view preschools as a way of making children more independent, although obtaining a good academic start and group experience are also important.

China ▪
United States ▪
Japan ▪

(*Source:* Based on Tobin, Wu, & Davidson, 1989.)

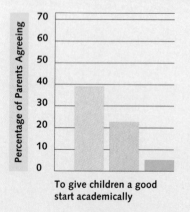

No one knows how many programs in the United States can be considered "high quality," but there are many fewer than desirable. In fact, the United States lags behind almost every other industrialized country in the quality of its day care, as well as in its quantity and affordability (Zigler & Finn-Stevenson, 1995; Scarr, 1998).

Preparing Preschoolers for Academic Pursuits: Does Head Start Truly Provide a Head Start?   Although many programs designed for preschoolers focus primarily on social and emotional factors, some programs are geared primarily toward promoting cognitive gains and preparing preschoolers for the more formal instruction they will experience when they start kindergarten. In the United States, the best-known program designed to promote future academic success is Head Start. Born in the 1960s when the United States declared a War on Poverty, the program has served over 13 million children and their families. Although it was designed to serve the "whole child," including children's physical health, self-confidence, social responsibility, and social and emotional development, the program has been scrutinized most closely in relation to the goal of improving cognitive processes (U.S. Department of Education, 1992; Zigler, Styfco, & Gilman, 1993; Zigler & Styfco, 1994).

Whether Head Start is seen as successful or not depends on the lens through which one is looking. If, for instance, the program is expected to provide long-term increases in IQ scores, it is a disappointment. Although graduates of Head Start programs tend to show immediate IQ gains, these increases do not last. On the other hand, preschoolers who participate in Head Start are more ready for future schooling than those who do not. Furthermore, graduates of Head Start programs have better future school adjustment than their peers, and they are less likely to be in special education classes or to be retained in grade. Finally, some research suggests that ultimately Head Start graduates show higher academic performance at the end of high school, although the gains are modest (Lee et al., 1990; Currie & Thomas, 1995; Galper, Wigfield, & Seefeldt, 1997).

In addition, results from other types of preschool readiness programs indicate that those who participate and graduate are less likely to repeat grades, and they complete school more frequently than those who are not in the program. Moreover, according to a cost-benefit analysis of one preschool readiness program, for every one dollar spent on the program, taxpayers saved seven dollars by the time the graduates reached the age of 27 (Schweinhart, Barnes, & Weikart, 1993).

The most recent comprehensive evaluation of early intervention programs suggests that, taken as a group, they can provide significant benefits, and that government funds invested early in life may ultimately lead to a reduction in future costs. For instance, compared with children who did not participate in early intervention programs, participants in various programs showed gains in emotional or cognitive development, better educational outcomes, increased economic self-sufficiency, reduced levels of criminal activity, and improved health-related behaviors. Of course, not every program produced all these benefits, and not every child benefited to the same extent. Still, the results of the evaluation were promising, suggesting that the potential benefits of early intervention can be substantial (Karoly et al., 1998).

Despite evidence supporting the effectiveness of early interventions in general, Head Start remains controversial. Some researchers suggest that the cost of Head Start—which, because of its intensity, is a relatively expensive form of child care—could be better spent on other forms of child care. For instance, developmentalist Sandra Scarr suggests that low-income preschool children may be better off spending more time in less costly programs than part-time in Head Start programs (Scarr, 1996, 1998). (For more on Head Start from the perspective of a caregiver, see the "Speaking of Development" interview.)

Should We Seek to Improve Cognitive Skills During the Preschool Years?   Not everyone agrees that programs that seek to enhance academic skills during the preschool years are a good thing. In fact, according to developmental psychologist David Elkind, U.S. society tends to push children so rapidly that they begin to feel stress and pressure at a young age (Elkind, 1984, 1988).

SPEAKING OF DEVELOPMENT

Yolanda Garcia

Education: . . . . University of California at Santa Barbara, B.A., combined social sciences, history, sociology, and political science; University of Chicago School of Social Services, M.A., administration, child welfare, and public policy; San Jose State University, California, M.A., education administration

Position: . . . . Head Start Director

Home: . . . . San Jose, California

"The children learn by doing, with the teacher helping the children develop cognitive skills and reinforcing their interest areas."

As an undergraduate student, Yolanda Garcia had to work to put herself through school, and as a result found a job working with preschoolers. That, coupled with a desire to work in the field of social services, prepared her for her life's vocation as part of one of the federal government's most well-known programs: Head Start.

As the Director of the Children Services Department, a branch of the Santa Clara County Office of Education, Garcia is responsible for the Head Start program that serves 1,799 children at 56 facilities in two counties.

"In Head Start classes, the children learn by doing," she explains, "with the teacher helping the children develop cognitive skills and reinforcing their interest areas. The teacher guides the children based on their interest and sets up an environment that is conducive to the child's interest."

Much of the teaching and planning is done through a variety of learning activities, according to Garcia. The children themselves play an active role in their education.

"We utilize an open framework of learning where teachers plan with the children. The teacher becomes the observer, recorder, and the guide from one step in the learning process to the next," she explains. "Teachers will guide the child through the processes that build on their level of cognitive development."

"Teachers will guide the child through the processes that build on their level of cognitive development."

The goal of each Head Start program, according to Garcia, is to have a ratio of one teacher to seven students. This ratio, she says, allows for quality interaction.

"It also allows the teacher to individualize the teaching, permitting group activities to be based on what the teacher knows about the individuals making up the specific group of children."

"Say, Dad, think you could wrap it up? I have a long day tomorrow."

The Informed Consumer of Development

Promoting Cognitive Development in Preschoolers: From Theory to the Classroom

We have considered the notion that one focus of the preschool period should be on promoting future academic success, and we have also discussed the alternative view that pushing children too hard academically may be hazardous to their well-being.

There is, however, a middle ground. Drawing on research conducted by developmental psychologists who examine cognitive development during the preschool years, we can make several suggestions for parents and preschool teachers who wish to improve the academic readiness of children without creating undue stress. Among them are the following:

■ Both parents and teachers should be aware of the stage of cognitive development, with its capabilities and limitations, that each individual child has reached. Unless they are aware of a child's current level of development, it will be impossible to provide appropriate materials and experiences.

■ Instruction should be at a level that reflects—but is just slightly higher than—each student's current level of cognitive development. Piaget, for instance, suggests that cognitive growth is more likely to occur when information and material are of moderate novelty. With too little novelty, children will be bored; with too much, they will be confused.

■ Instruction should be individualized as much as possible. Because children of the same age may hover around different levels of cognitive development, curriculum materials that are prepared individually stand a better chance of success.

■ Students should be kept actively engaged in learning, and they should be allowed to pace themselves as they move through new material.

■ Opportunities for social interaction—both with other students and with adults—should be provided. By receiving feedback from others and observing how others react in given situations, preschoolers learn new approaches and ways of thinking about the world.

■ Students should be allowed to make mistakes. Cognitive growth often flows from confronting errors.

■ Because cognitive development can occur only when children have achieved the appropriate level of maturation, preschoolers should not be pushed too far ahead of their current state of cognitive development. For instance, although it may be possible through intensive training to get preoperational children to recite, in a rote manner, the correct response to a conservation problem, this does not mean that they will have true comprehension of what they are verbalizing.

Ultimately, keep in mind that children require **developmentally appropriate educational practice**, which is education that is based on both typical development and the unique characteristics of a given child (Bredekamp, 1989; Cromwell, 1994).

Elkind argues that academic success largely depends on factors out of parents' control, such as inherited abilities and a child's rate of maturation. Consequently, children of a particular age cannot be expected to master educational material without taking into account their current level of cognitive development.

Rather than arbitrarily expecting children to master material at a particular age, Elkind suggests that a better strategy is to provide an environment in which learning is encouraged, but not pushed. By creating an atmosphere in which learning is facilitated—for instance, by reading to preschoolers or taking them on visits to museums—parents will allow children to proceed at their own pace, rather than one that pushes them beyond their limits.

Although Elkind's suggestions are appealing—it is certainly hard to argue that increases in children's anxiety levels and stress should be avoided—they are not without their detractors. For instance, some educators have argued that pushing children is largely a phenomenon of the middle and higher socioeconomic levels, possible only if parents are relatively affluent. For poorer children, whose parents may not have substantial resources available to push their children nor the easy ability to create an environment that promotes learning, the benefits of formal programs that promote learning are likely to outweigh their drawbacks.

developmentally appropriate educational practice *education that is based on both typical development and the unique characteristics of a given child*

REVIEW AND RETHINK

REVIEW

- In the preschool years, children rapidly increase in linguistic ability, developing an improved sense of grammar and shifting gradually from private to social speech. There is evidence that poverty can affect children's language development by limiting the opportunities for parents and other caregivers to interact linguistically with children.

- The effects of television on preschoolers are unclear. Some people are concerned about the emotional messages children are receiving, whereas others are hopeful about the use of television as an educational tool.

- Preschool educational programs are beneficial if they are of high quality, with trained staff, good curriculum, proper group sizes, and small staff-student ratios. With the exception of Head Start, the U.S. government pays comparatively little attention to early childhood education.

- Although some contend that attempting to improve preschoolers' cognitive skills causes undue stress, most researchers would agree that preschool children benefit from a developmentally appropriate, individualized, and supportive environment for learning.

RETHINK

- Is private speech egocentric or useful? Do adults ever use private speech? What functions does it serve?

- Why is it difficult to set up an experiment on the effects of children's television viewing? Why are results from TV viewing experiments so inconclusive?

- In this chapter, a number of negative outcomes of child care outside the home were mentioned, such as a lack of politeness and compliance. Do you think such outcomes are inherent in outside child care, or are they related to cultural views of the purpose of preschool programs?

- Do you think the United States should formulate a national educational policy, like many other countries, or should continue to leave most educational issues to the states? Why?

- Do you accept the view that children in U.S. society are "pushed" academically to the extent that they feel too much stress and pressure at a young age? Why?

LOOKING BACK

- **What is the state of children's bodies and overall health during the preschool years?**

  - In addition to gaining height and weight, the bodies of the preschool children undergo changes in shape and structure. Children grow more slender and their bones and muscles strengthen.

  - Children in the preschool years are generally quite healthy. Obesity in these years is caused by genetic and environmental factors. The greatest health threats are accidents and environmental factors.

■ **How do preschool children's brains and physical skills develop?**

- Brain growth is particularly rapid during the preschool years, with the number of interconnections among cells and the amount of myelin around neurons increasing greatly. The halves of the brain begin to specialize in somewhat different tasks—a process called lateralization.

- Both gross and fine motor skills advance rapidly during the preschool years. Gender differences begin to emerge, fine motor skills are honed, and handedness begins to assert itself.

■ **How does Piaget interpret cognitive development during the preschool years?**

- During the stage that Piaget has described as *preoperational*, children are not yet able to engage in organized, formal, logical thinking. However, their development of symbolic function permits quicker and more effective thinking as they are freed from the limitations of sensorimotor learning.

- According to Piaget, children in the preoperational stage engage in intuitive thought for the first time, actively applying rudimentary reasoning skills to the acquisition of world knowledge.

■ **How do other views of cognitive development differ from Piaget's?**

- A different approach to cognitive development is taken by proponents of information-processing theories, who focus on preschoolers, storage and recall of information and on quantitative changes in information-processing abilities (such as attention).

- Lev Vygotsky proposed that the nature and progress of children's cognitive development are dependent on the children's social and cultural context.

■ **How does children's language develop in the preschool years?**

- Children rapidly progress from two-word utterances to longer, more sophisticated expressions that reflect their growing vocabularies and emerging grasp of grammar.

- The development of linguistic abilities is affected by socioeconomic status. The result can be lowered linguistic—and ultimately academic—performance by poorer children.

■ **What effects does television have on preschoolers?**

- The effects of television are mixed. Preschoolers' sustained exposure to emotions and situations that are not representative of the real world have raised concerns. On the other hand, preschoolers can derive meaning from such targeted programs as *Sesame Street* which are designed to bring about cognitive gains in children.

■ **What kinds of preschool educational programs are available?**

- Early childhood educational programs, offered as center-based or school-based daycare or as preschool, can lead to cognitive and social advances.

- The United States lacks a coordinated national policy on preschool education. The major federal initiative in U.S. preschool education has been the Head Start program, which has yielded mixed results.

EPILOGUE: THE LONG GOODBYE

In this chapter, we looked at children in the preschool years, focusing on their physical development, growth, nutritional needs, overall health, brain growth, and advances in gross and fine motor skills. We discussed cognitive development from the Piagetian perspective, with its description of the characteristics of thought in the preoperational stage, and from the perspective information-processing theorists and Lev Vygotsky. We then discussed the burst in linguistic ability that occurs during the preschool years and the influence of television on preschoolers' development. We concluded with a discussion of preschool education and its effects.

Return to the prologue, which describes Samantha Sterman's first day at preschool, and answer these questions.

1. Can you explain the gradual "separation" ritual at Samantha's preschool in terms of attachment?

2. According to Piaget, what sorts of understandings and limitations will Samantha have as she plays with her Play-Doh and dolls?

3. From a broad developmental perspective (including physical and cognitive development), what is Samantha now able to do that she couldn't do a year or two ago?

4. Can you discuss from an information-processing perspective the likely course of Samantha's cognitive development during her preschool years? What is likely to change as she progresses toward kindergarten, and why?

5. To what aspects of the preschool "culture" that Samantha is joining do Vygotsky's theories apply? What features of the preschool program would a follower of Vygotsky emphasize?

KEY TERMS AND CONCEPTS

obesity (p. 218)

lateralization (p. 220)

handedness (p. 223)

preoperational stage (p. 226)

operations (p. 226)

centration (p. 227)

egocentric thought (p. 228)

transformation (p. 228)

intuitive thought (p. 229)

conservation (p. 230)

autobiographical memory (p. 233)

zone of proximal development (ZPD) (p. 237)

scaffolding (p. 238)

syntax (p. 241)

grammar (p. 242)

private speech (p. 242)

social speech (p. 242)

day-care centers (p. 246)

preschools (or nursery schools) (p. 246)

school day care (p. 247)

developmentally appropriate educational practice (p. 251)

Social and Personality Development

PROLOGUE: THE GATHERING

A preschooler's development of individualism can be expressed in many ways.

Sandy Rossoff was cooking for a family get-together and was delighted that her 3-year-old daughter, Sarah, was happily playing in the living room. Ten minutes later, Sandy peeked in. The room had been transformed from order into chaos. Sarah had up-ended her play table, draped a blanket over it to make a tent, and strewn toys and crayons all over the floor. She had also removed all the cushions from the sofa and chairs, making them into a mountain perfect for a headlong jump.

"Oh, no, Sarah! Guests are coming. We need to clean up," Sandy said as she frantically started picking up debris. But when she put the table back on its legs and began to heap toys onto it, Sarah tipped it over again. "Noooo, Mommy," she implored. "I *need* to mess." (Greenspan, 1997, p. 96)

LOOKING AHEAD

Sarah Rossoff's assertion that she needed to make a mess, whether literally true or not, does clearly signify something quite important: her growing sense of who she is. During the preschool years, children's sense of themselves as distinct individuals begins to grow, and it colors their relationships with others.

In this chapter, we address social and personality development during the preschool period, a time of enormous growth and change. We begin by examining how preschool-age children continue to form a sense of self, focusing on how they develop their self-concepts. We especially examine issues of self relating to gender, a central aspect of children's views of themselves and others.

Preschoolers' social lives are the focus of the next part of the chapter. We look at how children play with one another, examining the various types of play. We consider how parents and other authority figures use discipline to shape children's behavior. We also look at a grimmer side of family interaction: child abuse and psychological maltreatment.

Finally, we examine two key aspects of preschool-age children's social behavior: moral development and aggression. We consider how children develop a notion of right and wrong, and how that development can lead them to be helpful to others. We also look at the other side of the coin—aggression—and examine the factors that lead preschool-age children to behave in a way that hurts others. We end on an optimistic note: considering how we may help preschool-age children to be more moral, and less aggressive, individuals.

In sum, after reading this chapter, you will be able to answer these questions:

Q

- How do preschool-age children develop a concept of themselves?
- How do children develop a sense of racial identity and gender?
- In what sorts of social relationships do preschool-age children engage?
- What sorts of disciplinary styles do parents employ, and what effects do they have?
- What factors contribute to child abuse and neglect?
- How do children develop a moral sense?
- How does aggression develop in preschool-age children?

FORMING A SENSE OF SELF

Although the question "Who am I?" is not explicitly posed by most preschool-age children, it underlies a considerable amount of development during the preschool years. During this period, children wonder about the nature of the self, and the way they answer the "Who am I?" question may affect them for the rest of their lives.

Self-concept in the Preschool Years: Thinking About the Self

If you ask preschool-age children to specify what makes them different from other kids, they readily respond with such answers as "I'm a good runner" or "I like to color" or "I'm a big girl." Such answers relate to **self-concept**—their identity, or their set of beliefs about what they are like as individuals (Breakwell, 1992; Hattie, 1992; Byrne, 1996; Brown, 1998).

The statements that describe children's self-concepts are not necessarily accurate. In fact, preschool children typically overestimate their skills and knowledge across all domains of expertise. Consequently, their view of the future is quite rosy: They expect to win the next game they play, to beat all opponents in an upcoming race, and even to write great stories when they grow up. Even when they have just experienced failure at a task, they are likely to expect to do well in the future (Stipek & Hoffman, 1980; Ruble, 1983; Damon & Hart, 1988).

self-concept *a person's identity, or set of beliefs about what one is like as an individual*

Preschool-age children also begin to develop a view of self that reflects the way their particular culture considers the self. Such views pervade a culture, sometimes in subtle ways. For instance, one well-known saying in Western cultures states that "the squeaky wheel gets the grease." Children in Asian cultures are exposed to a different perspective; they are told that "the nail that stands out gets pounded down." Such adages represent two very different views of the world. In the view that predominates in Western cultures, one should seek to get the attention of others by standing out and making one's needs known. In contrast, the predominant Asian perspective suggests that individuals should attempt to blend in and refrain from making themselves distinctive (Markus & Kitayama, 1991; Triandis, 1995).

Such varying philosophies may lead to differences in how children begin to view the self during the preschool years. Asian societies tend to have a **collectivistic orientation**, promoting the notion of interdependence. People in such cultures tend to regard themselves as parts of a larger social network in which they are interconnected with others.

In contrast, children in Western cultures are more likely to develop an independent view of the self, reflecting an **individualistic orientation** that emphasizes personal identity and the uniqueness of the individual. They are more apt to see themselves as self-contained and autonomous, in competition with others for scarce resources. Consequently, children in Western cultures are more likely to focus on their uniqueness and what sets them apart from others—what makes them special.

Of course, even within a culture there is great heterogeneity in orientation. Furthermore, members of subcultural minority groups may sometimes reflect their ethnicity and family backgrounds, rather than the culture at large. For example, cross-cultural psychologist Harry Triandis suggests that Asian Americans are more collectivistic than European Americans (Triandis, 1994).

In short, preschoolers' self-concepts are a result not only of how their parents treat them, but also of their society and their exposure to the philosophy of the culture in which they are being reared (Marjoribanks, 1994).

Psychosocial Development: Resolving the Conflicts

According to psychoanalyst Erik Erikson (1963), by the time they reach the preschool years, children have already passed through several stages of psychosocial development. As we discussed in Chapter 6, **psychosocial development** encompasses changes both in the understandings individuals have of themselves as members of society and in their comprehension of the meaning of others' behavior.

Erikson suggests that throughout life, society and culture present particular challenges, which shift as people age. As we noted in Chapter 6, Erikson suggests that people pass through eight distinct stages, each of which necessitates resolution of a crisis or conflict.

In the early part of the preschool period, children are ending the autonomy-versus-shame-and-doubt stage, which lasts from around 18 months to 3 years. In this period, children either become more independent and autonomous if their parents encourage exploration and freedom, or experience shame and self-doubt if they are restricted and overprotected.

The preschool years largely encompass the **initiative-versus-guilt stage**, which lasts from around age 3 to age 6. During this period, children's views of themselves undergo major change as preschool-age children face conflicts between, on the one hand, the desire to act independently of their parents and, on the other hand, the guilt that comes from the unintended consequences of their actions. In essence, preschool-age children come to realize that they are persons in their own right, and they begin to make decisions and to shape the kind of persons that they will become.

Parents who react positively to this transformation toward independence can help their children resolve the opposing forces of taking initiative versus experiencing guilt that is characteristic of this period. By providing their children with opportunities to act

collectivistic orientation *a philosophy that promotes the notion of interdependence*

individualistic orientation *a philosophy that emphasizes personal identity and the uniqueness of the individual*

psychosocial development *the approach that encompasses changes in our interactions with and understandings of one another, as well as in our knowledge and understanding of ourselves as members of society*

initiative-versus-guilt stage *according to Erikson, the period during which children aged 3 to 6 years experience conflict between independence of action and the sometimes negative results of that action*

self-reliantly, while still giving them direction and guidance, they can support and encourage their children's initiative. On the other hand, parents who discourage their children's efforts to seek independence may contribute to a sense of guilt that persists throughout their lives.

Developmental Diversity

Developing Racial and Ethnic Awareness

The preschool years mark an important turning point for children. Their answer to the question of who they are begins to take into account their racial and ethnic identity.

For most preschool-age children, racial awareness comes relatively early. Certainly, even infants are able to distinguish different skin colors; their perceptual abilities allow for such color distinctions quite early in life. However, it is only later that children begin to attribute meaning to different racial characteristics. By the time they are 3 or 4 years of age, preschool-age children distinguish between African Americans and whites and begin to understand the significance that society places on racial membership.

At the same time, some preschool-age children start to experience ambivalence over the meaning of their racial and ethnic identity. Some preschool-age children experience **race dissonance**, the phenomenon in which minority children indicate preferences for majority values or people. For instance, some studies find that as many as 90 percent of African American children, when asked about their reactions to drawings of black and white children, react more negatively to the drawings of black children than to those of white children. However, these negative reactions did not translate into lower self-esteem for the African American subjects. Instead, their preferences appear to be a result of the powerful influence of the dominant white culture, rather than a disparagement of their own racial characteristics (Holland, 1994).

By the time they are 3 or 4 years of age, preschoolers distinguish between members of different races and begin to understand the significance of race in society.

Ethnic identity emerges somewhat later. For instance, in one study of Mexican American ethnic awareness, preschool-age children displayed only a limited knowledge of their ethnic identity. However, as they became older, their understanding of their racial background grew in both magnitude and complexity. In addition, those preschool-age children who were bilingual, speaking both Spanish and English, were most apt to be aware of their racial identity (Bernal, 1994).

Gender Identity: Developing Femaleness and Maleness

Boys' awards: Very Best Thinker, Most Eager Learner, Most Imaginative, Most Enthusiastic, Most Scientific, Best Friend, Mr. Personality, Hardest Worker, Best Sense of Humor.

Girls' awards: All-Around Sweetheart, Sweetest Personality, Cutest Personality, Best Sharer, Best Artist, Biggest Heart, Best Manners, Best Helper, Most Creative.

What's wrong with this picture? To one parent, whose daughter received one of the girls' awards during a kindergarten graduation ceremony, quite a bit. Although the girls were getting pats on the back for their pleasing personalities, the boys were receiving awards for their intellectual and analytic skills (Deveny, 1994).

Such a situation is not rare: Girls and boys often live in very different worlds. Differences in the ways males and females are treated begin at birth (as we noted in Chapter 6), con-

race dissonance *the phenomenon in which minority children indicate preferences for majority values or people*

During the preschool period, differences in play, relating to gender, become more pronounced. In addition, boys tend to play with boys, and girls with girls.

tinue during the preschool years, and—as we will see later—extend into adolescence and beyond (Coltrane & Adams, 1997).

Gender, the sense of being male or female, is well established by the time children reach the preschool years. (As we first noted in Chapter 6, "gender" and "sex" do not mean the same thing. *Sex* typically refers to sexual anatomy and sexual behavior, whereas *gender* refers to the perception of maleness or femaleness related to membership in a given society.) By the age of 2, children consistently label themselves and those around them as male or female (Fagot & Leinbach, 1993; Signorella, Bigler, & Liben, 1993; Poulin-Dubois et al., 1994.)

One way gender is manifested is in play. During the preschool years, boys spend more time than girls in rough-and-tumble play, whereas girls spend more time than boys in organized games and role-playing. Furthermore, boys begin to play more with boys, and girls play more with girls, a trend that increases during middle childhood. Actually, girls begin preferring same-sex playmates a little earlier than boys. Girls first have a clear preference for interacting with other girls at age 2, whereas boys don't show much preference for same-sex partners until age 3 (Fagot, 1991; Lloyd & Duveen, 1991; Benenson, 1994; Ramsey, 1995).

Such same-sex preferences appear in many cultures. For instance, studies of kindergartners in mainland China show no examples of mixed-gender play. Similarly, gender "outweighs" ethnic variables when it comes to play: A Hispanic boy would rather play with a white boy than with a Hispanic girl (Whiting & Edwards, 1988; Shepard, 1991; Fishbein & Imai, 1993; Martin, 1993; Turner, Gervai, & Hinde, 1993).

Preschool-age children also begin to hold expectations about appropriate behavior for girls and boys. In fact, their expectations about gender-appropriate behavior are even more rigid and gender-stereotyped than those of adults, and may be less flexible during the preschool years than at any other point in the life span. For instance, beliefs in gender stereotypes become more pronounced up to age 5, and have already started to become somewhat less rigid by age 7. On the other hand, gender expectations do not disappear, and the content of gender stereotypes held by preschool-age children is similar to that held traditionally by adults in society (Urberg, 1982; Golombok & Fivush, 1994).

And what are preschoolers' gender expectations? Like adults, preschool-age children expect that males are more apt to have traits involving competence, independence, forcefulness, and competitiveness. In contrast, females are viewed as more likely to have traits such as warmth, expressiveness, nurturance, and submissiveness. Although these are *expectations*, and say nothing about the way that men and women actually behave, such expectations both provide the lens through which preschool-age children view the world and affect their own behavior and the way they interact with their peers and with adults (Signorella, Bigler, & Liben, 1993).

The prevalence and strength of preschoolers' gender expectations, and differences in behavior between boys and girls, have proven puzzling. Why should gender play such a powerful role during the preschool years (as well as during the rest of the life span)? Developmentalists have proposed several explanations.

Biological Perspectives on Gender.   Recall that gender relates to the sense of being male or female, whereas sex refers to the physical characteristics that differentiate males and females. It would hardly be surprising to find that the physical characteristics associated with sex might themselves lead to gender differences, and this in fact has been shown to be true.

For example, some research has focused on girls whose mothers had, prior to being aware that they were pregnant, inadvertently taken drugs that contained high levels of *androgens* (male hormones) due to certain medical problems. These androgen-exposed girls are more likely to display behaviors associated with male stereotypes than are their sisters who were not exposed to androgens (Money & Ehrhardt, 1972). Androgen-exposed girls preferred boys as playmates and spent more time than other girls playing with toys associated with the male role, such as cars and trucks. Similarly, boys prenatally exposed to unusually high levels of female hormones are apt to display more behaviors that are stereotypically female than is typical (Berenbaum & Hines, 1992; Hines & Kaufman, 1994).

Moreover, as we first noted in Chapter 7, some research suggests that biological differences exist in the structure of female and male brains. For instance, part of the *corpus callosum*, the bundle of nerves that connects the hemispheres of the brain, is proportionally larger in women than in men. To some theoreticians, evidence such as this suggests that gender differences may be produced by biological factors (Benbow, Lubinski, & Hyde, 1997).

Before accepting such contentions, however, it is important to note that alternative explanations abound. For example, it may be that the *corpus callosum* is proportionally larger in women as a result of certain kinds of experiences that influence brain growth in particular ways. If this is true, environmental experience produces biological change—and not the other way around.

In sum, as in many other domains that involve the interaction of inherited, biological characteristics and environmental influences, it is difficult to attribute behavioral characteristics unambiguously to biological factors. Because of this difficulty, we must consider other explanations for gender differences.

Psychoanalytic Perspectives.   You may recall from Chapter 1 that Freud's psychoanalytic theory suggests that we move through a series of stages related to biological urges. To Freud, the preschool years encompass the *phallic stage*, in which the focus of a child's pleasure relates to genital sexuality.

Freud argued that the end of the phallic stage is marked by an important turning point in development: the Oedipal conflict. According to Freud, the *Oedipal conflict* occurs at around the age of 5, when the anatomical differences between males and females become particularly evident. Boys begin to develop sexual interests in their mothers, viewing their fathers as rivals. As a consequence, boys conceive a desire to kill their fathers—just as Oedipus did in the ancient Greek tragedy. However, because they view their fathers as all-powerful, boys develop a fear of retaliation, which takes the form of *castration anxiety.* To overcome this fear, boys repress their desires for their mothers and instead begin to identify with their fathers, attempting to be as similar to them as possible. **Identification** is the process in which children attempt to be similar to their same-sex parent, incorporating the parent's attitudes and values.

identification   *the process in which children attempt to be similar to their same-sex parent, incorporating the parent's attitudes and values*

Girls, according to Freud, go through a different process. They begin to feel sexual attraction toward their fathers and experience *penis envy*—a view that not unexpectedly has led to accusations that Freud viewed women as inferior to men. To resolve their penis envy, girls ultimately identify with their mothers, attempting to be as similar to them as possible.

In both boys and girls, the ultimate result of identifying with the same-sex parent is that the children adopt their parents' gender attitudes and values. In this way, says Freud, society's expectations about the ways females and males "ought" to behave are perpetuated into new generations.

If you are like many people, you may find it difficult to accept Freud's elaborate explanation of gender differences. So do most developmentalists, who believe that gender development is best explained by other mechanisms. In part, they base their criticisms of Freud on the lack of scientific support for his theories. For example, children learn gender stereotypes much earlier than the age of 5. Furthermore, this learning occurs even in single-parent households. However, some aspects of psychoanalytic theory have been supported, such as findings indicating that preschool-age children whose same-sex parents support sex-stereotyped behavior tend to demonstrate that behavior also. Still, far simpler processes can account for this phenomenon, and many developmentalists have searched for explanations of gender differences other than Freud's (Mussen, 1969; Maccoby, 1980).

Social Learning Approaches.   According to social learning approaches, children learn gender-related behavior and expectations from their observation of others. In this view, children watch the behavior of their parents, teachers, and even peers. Their observation of the rewards that these others attain for acting in a gender-appropriate manner leads them to conform to such behavior themselves.

Books and the media, and in particular television, also play a role in perpetuating traditional views of gender-related behavior from which preschool-age children may learn. For instance, television shows typically define female characters in terms of their relationships with males. Furthermore, females are more apt to appear with males, whereas female–female relationships are relatively uncommon. Also, females appear as victims far more often than do males (Signorelli, 1987; Condry, 1989; Turner-Bowker, 1996).

According to social learning approaches, children observe the behavior of same-sex adults and come to imitate it.

Television also presents men and women in traditional gender roles. Although such shows as *ER* and *Murphy Brown* portray women in atypical, counter-stereotypical roles, preschool-age children generally do not watch these shows. Instead, preschool-age children are often exposed to repeats of older shows such as *Leave It to Beaver* and *The Brady Bunch*, which portray women and men in highly traditional roles. And contemporary programming is, by and large, little better. For instance, analyses of the most popular television shows find that male characters outnumber female characters by 2 to 1. Furthermore, women are much less likely to be illustrated as decision makers or productive individuals, and more likely to be portrayed as characters interested in romance, their homes, and their families. Such models, according to social learning theory, are apt to have a powerful influence on preschoolers' definitions of appropriate behavior (Signorelli, 1990).

In some cases, learning of social roles does not involve models, but occurs more directly. For example, most of us have heard preschool-age children being told by their parents to act like a "little girl" or "little man." What this generally means is that girls should behave politely and courteously, or that boys should be tough and stoic—traits associated with society's traditional stereotypes of men and women. Such direct training sends a clear message about the behavior expected of a preschool-age child (Witt, 1997).

Cognitive Approaches.   In the view of some theorists, the desire to form a clear sense of identity leads children to establish a **gender identity**, a perception of themselves as male or female. To do this, they develop a **gender schema**, a cognitive framework that organizes information relevant to gender (Bem, 1987; Stangor et al., 1992).

gender identity   *the perception of one-self as male or female*

gender schema   *a cognitive framework that organizes information relevant to gender*

gender constancy *the belief that people are permanently males or females, depending on fixed, unchangeable biological factors*

androgynous *a state in which gender roles encompass characteristics thought typical of both sexes*

Gender schemas are developed early in life, forming a lens through which preschool-age children view the world. For instance, preschool-age children use their increasing cognitive abilities to develop "rules" about what is right, and what is inappropriate, for males and females. Thus, some girls decide that wearing pants is inappropriate for a female, and apply the rule so rigidly that they refuse to wear anything but dresses. Or a preschool boy may reason that because makeup is typically worn by females, it is inappropriate for him to wear makeup even when he is in a preschool play and all the other boys and girls are wearing it.

According to *cognitive-developmental theory*, proposed by Lawrence Kohlberg, this rigidity is in part an outcome of changes in preschoolers' understanding of gender (Kohlberg, 1966). Initially, gender schemas are influenced by erroneous beliefs about sex differences. Specifically, young preschool-age children believe that sex differences are based not on biological factors but on differences in appearance or behavior. Employing this view of the world, a girl may reason that she can be a father when she grows up, or a boy may think he could turn into a girl if he put on a dress and tied his hair in a ponytail. However, by the time they reach the age of 4 or 5, children develop an understanding of **gender constancy**, the belief that people are permanently males or females, depending on fixed, unchangeable biological factors.

Although research has supported the notion that the understanding of gender constancy changes during the preschool period, it has been less supportive of the idea that this understanding is the cause of gender-related behavior. In fact, the appearance of gender schemas occurs well before children understand gender constancy. Even young preschool-age children assume that certain behaviors are appropriate—and others are not—on the basis of stereotypic views of gender (Bussey & Bandura, 1992).

Can we reduce the objectionable consequences of viewing the world in terms of gender schemas? According to Sandra Bem, one way is to encourage children to be **androgynous**, a state in which gender roles encompass characteristics thought typical of both sexes. For instance, androgynous males may be encouraged to be assertive (typically viewed as a male-appropriate trait) but at the same time to be warm and tender (usually viewed as female-appropriate traits). Similarly, girls might be encouraged to be both empathetic and tender (typically seen as female-appropriate traits) and competitive, assertive, and independent (typical male-appropriate traits).

Like the other approaches to gender development (summarized in Table 8-1), the cognitive perspective does not imply that differences between the two sexes are in any way improper or inappropriate. Instead, it suggests that preschool-age children should be taught to treat others as individuals. Furthermore, preschool-age children need to learn the importance of fulfilling their own talents, acting as individuals and not as representatives of a particular gender.

TABLE 8-1

FOUR APPROACHES TO GENDER DEVELOPMENT

Perspective	Key Concepts
Biological	Inborn, genetic factors produce gender differences.
Psychoanalytic	Gender development is the result of moving through a series of stages related to biological urges.
Social learning	Children learn gender-related behavior and expectations from their observation of others' behavior.
Cognitive	Through the use of gender schemas, developed early in life, preschoolers form a lens through which they view the world. They use their increasing cognitive abilities to develop "rules" about what is appropriate for males and females.

REVIEW AND RETHINK

REVIEW

- During the preschool years, children develop their self-concepts, beliefs about themselves that they derive from their own perceptions, their parents' behaviors, and society.

- According to Erikson's psychosocial development theory, preschool children move from the autonomy-versus-shame-and-doubt stage to the initiative-versus-guilt stage.

- Racial and ethnic awareness begins to form in the preschool years. Members of minority groups may experience race dissonance before establishing a sense of identity regarding their race and ethnicity.

- Gender awareness also develops in the preschool years. Explanations of this phenomenon that emphasize the action of universal factors within the individual include purely biological explanations and psychoanalytical explanations such as Freud's.

- Whereas the social learning approach to explaining gender expectations focuses on the influence of society, the cognitive approach focuses on the individual's formation of a cognitively based gender schema.

RETHINK

- Is an individual's self-concept fully formed by the time he or she reaches adulthood? What processes might influence an adult's self-concept?

- How does the issue of secure attachment discussed in an earlier chapter relate to Erikson's stages of trust versus mistrust, autonomy versus shame and doubt, and initiative versus guilt?

- How might the Black Power and Black Pride movements of the 1960s and 1970s have addressed issues of self-concept for African Americans? In what ways might these movements have affected white Americans' self-concepts?

- What are the distinctions among gender differences, gender expectations, and gender stereotypes? How are they related?

- Why do cognitive approaches to gender differences appear to offer the most hope of causing changes in gender expectations? What is a gender schema, what are its contents, and how might a schema change over time?

PRESCHOOLERS' SOCIAL LIVES

To Nicole and Diana Schoo, the movie *Home Alone* probably didn't seem too funny. For them, the tale of a child mistakenly left behind by his vacationing parents was all too similar to their own experience. In their case, though, their abandonment was no comic error: Their parents intentionally left them behind.

Diana, age 4, and her older sister Nicole, age 9, were found at home—alone—while their parents were on a nine-day vacation in Acapulco, Mexico. It was not the first time the girls had been left unattended; their parents had left them unaccompanied while they went off on a four-day visit to Massachusetts the previous summer.

Local authorities who learned of the girls' plight arrested the Schoo parents on their return from Acapulco. The Schoos faced charges on two felony counts of child abandonment and cruelty to children, and a misdemeanor charge of child endangerment.

For an increasing number of preschool-age children, life does not mirror what we see in reruns of *The Cosby Show* or *Leave it to Beaver*. Many face the realities of an increasingly complicated world. For instance, as we noted in Chapter 6 and will discuss in greater detail in Chapter 10, children are increasingly likely to live with only one parent. In 1960, less than 10 percent of all children under the age of 18 lived with one parent; by 1989, almost a quarter lived in a single-parent household. In fact, in 1993, almost 50 percent of all children experienced their parents' divorce and lived with one parent for an average of 5 years (Carnegie Task Force, 1994).

Still, for most children the preschool years are not a time of upheaval and turmoil. Instead, the period encompasses a growing interaction with the world at large. For instance, preschool-age children begin to develop genuine friendships with other children, in which close ties emerge.

Preschool Social Life: The Development of Friendships

When Juan was 3, he had his first best friend, Emilio. Juan and Emilio, who lived in the same apartment building in San Jose, were inseparable. They played incessantly with toy cars, racing them up and down the apartment hallways until some of the neighbors began to complain about the noise. They pretended to read to one another, and sometimes they slept over at each other's home—a big step for a 3-year-old. Neither boy seemed more joyful than when he was with his "best friend"—the term each used of the other.

At around the age of 3, children develop real friendships. Although they play together earlier, much of their activity involves simply being in the same place at the same time, without real social interaction.

Something changes around age 3. Peers come to be seen not as miniature, less powerful adults, but as individuals who hold some special qualities and rewards. Preschoolers' relations with adults reflect children's needs for care, protection, and direction, but their relations with peers are based more on the desire for companionship, play, and entertainment.

Furthermore, as they get older, preschoolers' conception of friendship gradually evolves. With age, they come to view friendship as a continuing state, a stable relationship that has meaning beyond the immediate moment, and that bears implications for future activity (Furman & Bierman, 1983; Snyder, Horsch, & Childs, 1997).

The quality of interactions that children have with friends changes during the preschool period. The focus of friendship in 3-year-olds is the enjoyment of carrying out shared activities—doing things together and playing jointly. Older preschool-age children, however, pay more attention to abstract concepts such as trust, support, and shared interests (Park, Lay, & Ramsay, 1993).

Even at the age of 3, preschool-age children are interested in maintaining smooth social relations with their friends. They try to create a sense of agreement with one another and attempt to avoid disagreement. In fact, they are more concerned with avoiding disagreement than older preschool-age children, who more readily accept dissension as the occasional outcome of a social relationship (Gottman & Parkhurst, 1980).

Why Are Some Children More Popular Than Others? Not all preschool-age children form close friendships with others in the way that Juan and Emilio did. In fact, some children have relatively few friends, experiencing difficulty in interacting with others and forming stable relationships.

Several qualities are associated with popularity during the preschool years, an association that in many cases persists throughout much of the life span. For instance, one unfortunate by-product of society's emphasis on physical attractiveness is the "beautiful is good" stereotype, which suggests that physical attractiveness is linked to other positive qualities. Physically attractive preschool-age children are judged more likable, by both peers and adults, than less attractive preschool-age children, and their behavior is interpreted in the light of their attractive-

The Schoos faced charges of child abandonment, cruelty to children, and child endangerment for leaving their children Diana, 4, and Nicole, 9, home alone while they vacationed.

ness. As a result, physically attractive children who misbehave are judged more leniently than those who are less attractive. In sum, beginning as early as infancy and continuing into old age those who are physically attractive are responded to more favorably than those who are unattractive (Dion, 1972; Hatfield & Sprecher, 1986; Langlois et al., 1995).

But it is not only physical attractiveness that determines popularity. Preschoolers' social skills and behavior play an even more important role. For instance, disliked children are more likely to display aggressive behavior, to be disruptive, and to impose themselves on their peers. They are less cooperative, and they do not take turns (Newcomb, Bukowski, & Pattee, 1993; Mendelson, Aboud, & Lanthier, 1994).

In contrast, children who are more popular are more outgoing and sociable. They speak more, and nonverbally they are more positive, smiling more often than those who are less popular. In general, they have a greater understanding of others' emotions and are more sensitive to the meaning of others' nonverbal behavior (Philippot, Feldman, & McGee, 1990; Garner, Jones, & Miner, 1994; Dunn, 1995; Sroufe, 1996).

Improving Children's Social Skills.   Are unpopular preschool-age children destined for a life with few friends? Not necessarily. The social skills that make some children more popular than others can be promoted by parents and preschool teachers.

For instance, children can be taught to be more cooperative, to share with others, and to play with others in appropriate ways. At the same time, they can be encouraged to decrease the incidence of aggressive behaviors that put others off and to avoid taking things from others (Roopnarine & Honig, 1985; Bierman, Miller, & Stabb, 1987; Ogilvy, 1994).

In addition, parents can promote positive peer relations by providing a warm, supportive home environment. A good deal of research evidence shows that children with parents who were rejecting or authoritarian tend to be less socially skilled than those with more parental support. The evidence suggests that strong, positive relationships between parents and children facilitate children's relationships with others (Hartup, 1989; Hinde, Tamplin, & Barrett, 1993; Sroufe, 1994).

Playing by the Rules: The Work of Play

In Minka Arafat's class of 3-year-olds, Minnie bounces her doll's feet on the table as she sings softly to herself. Ben pushes his toy car across the floor, making motor noises. Sarah chases Abdul around and around the perimeter of the room.

Categorizing Play.   These children are engaged in **functional play**—simple, repetitive activities typical of 3-year-olds. Functional play may involve objects, such as dolls or cars, or repetitive muscular movements such as skipping, jumping, or rolling and unrolling a piece of clay. Functional play, then, involves doing something for the sake of being active, rather than with the aim of creating some end product (Rubin et al., 1983).

As children get older, functional play declines. By the time they are 4, children become involved in a more sophisticated form of play. In **constructive play** children manipulate objects to produce or build something. A child who builds a house out of Legos or puts a puzzle together is involved in constructive play: He or she has an ultimate goal—to produce something. Such play is not necessarily aimed at creating something novel, because children may repeatedly build a house of blocks, let it fall into disarray, and then rebuild it.

Constructive play permits children to test their developing physical and cognitive skills and to practice their fine muscle movements. They gain experience in solving problems about the ways and the sequences in which things fit together (Tegano et al., 1991). They also learn to cooperate with others—a development we observe as the social nature of play shifts during the preschool period.

The Social Aspects of Play.   If two preschool-age children are sitting at a table side by side, each putting a different puzzle together, are they engaged jointly in play?

functional play   *play that involves simple, repetitive activities typical of 3-year-olds*

constructive play   *play in which children manipulate objects to produce or build something*

In parallel play, children play with similar toys, in a similar manner, but don't necessarily interact with one another.

According to pioneering work done by Mildred Parten (1932), the answer is yes. She suggests that these preschool-age children are engaged in **parallel play**, in which children play with similar toys, in a similar manner, but do not interact with each other. Parallel play is typical for children during the early preschool years. Preschool-age children also engage in another form of play, a highly passive one: onlooker play. In **onlooker play**, children simply watch others at play, but do not actually participate themselves. They may look on silently, or they may make comments of encouragement or advice.

As they get older, however, preschool-age children engage in more sophisticated forms of social play that involve a greater degree of interaction. In **associative play** two or more children actually interact with one another by sharing or borrowing toys or materials, although they do not do the same thing. In **cooperative play**, children genuinely play with one another, taking turns, playing games, or devising contests. (The various types of play are summarized in Table 8-2).

Although associative and cooperative play do not typically become prevalent until children reach the end of the preschool years, the amount and kind of social experience children have had significantly influences the nature of play. For instance, children who have had substantial preschool experience are apt to engage in more social forms of behavior, such as associative and cooperative play, fairly early in the preschool years than those with less experience (Roopnarine, Johnson, & Hooper, 1994).

Furthermore, solitary and onlooker play continue in the later stages of the preschool period. There are simply times when children prefer to play by themselves. And when newcomers join a group, one strategy for becoming part of the group—often successful—is to engage in onlooker play, waiting for an opportunity to join the play more actively (Smith, 1978; Howes, Unger, & Seidner, 1989; Hughes, 1995).

Pretend or make-believe play also changes during the preschool period. In some ways, pretend play becomes increasingly *un*realistic, as preschool-age children change from using only realistic objects to using less concrete ones. Thus, at the start of the preschool period, children may pretend to listen to a radio only if they actually have a plastic radio that looks realistic. Later, however, they are more likely to use an entirely different object, such as a large cardboard box, as a pretend radio (Bornstein et al., 1996).

parallel play *action in which children play with similar toys, in a similar manner, but do not interact with each other*

onlooker play *action in which children simply watch others at play, but do not actually participate themselves*

associative play *play in which two or more children actually interact with one another by sharing or borrowing toys or materials, although they do not do the same thing*

cooperative play *play in which children genuinely interact with one another, taking turns, playing games, or devising contests*

TABLE 8-2

PRESCHOOLERS' PLAY

Type of Play	Definition of Type of Play
Functional play	Functional play involves simple, repetitive activities typical of 3-year-olds. It may involve objects, such as dolls or cars, or repetitive muscular movements such as skipping, jumping, or rolling and unrolling a piece of clay.
Constructive play	By the time they are 4, children become involved in more sophisticated play in which they manipulate objects to produce or build something. A child who builds a house out of Legos or puts together a puzzle is involved in constructive play. This type of play permits children to test their developing physical and cognitive skills as well as practice their fine muscle movements.
Parallel play	Children who engage in parallel play use similar toys, in a similar manner, but do not interact with each other. This form of play is typical of children during the early preschool years.
Onlooker play	In onlooker play, children simply watch others at play, but do not actually participate themselves. They may look on silently, or they may make comments of encouragement or advice. This type of play is common among preschoolers.
Associative play	As they get older, preschoolers are involved in the greater degree of interaction of associative play. Here, two or more children actually interact with one another by sharing or borrowing toys or materials, although they do not do the same thing.
Cooperative play	In cooperative play, children genuinely play with one another, taking turns, playing games, or devising contests.

Russian developmentalist Lev Vygotsky argued that pretend play, particularly if it involves social play, is an important means for expanding preschool-age children's cognitive skills. Through make-believe play, children are able to "practice" activities that are a part of their particular culture and broaden their understanding of the way the world functions (Vygotsky, 1930/1978).

Children's cultural backgrounds also result in different styles of play. For example, comparisons of Korean Americans and Anglo-Americans find that Korean American children engage in a higher proportion of parallel play than their Anglo-American counterparts, and Anglo-American preschool-age children are involved in more pretend play (Farver, Kim, & Lee, 1995; see Figure 8-1).

FIGURE 8-1

COMPARING PLAY COMPLEXITY

An examination of Korean American and Anglo-American preschoolers' play complexity finds clear differences in patterns of play.

(*Source*: Adapted from Farver, Kim, & Lee, 1995).

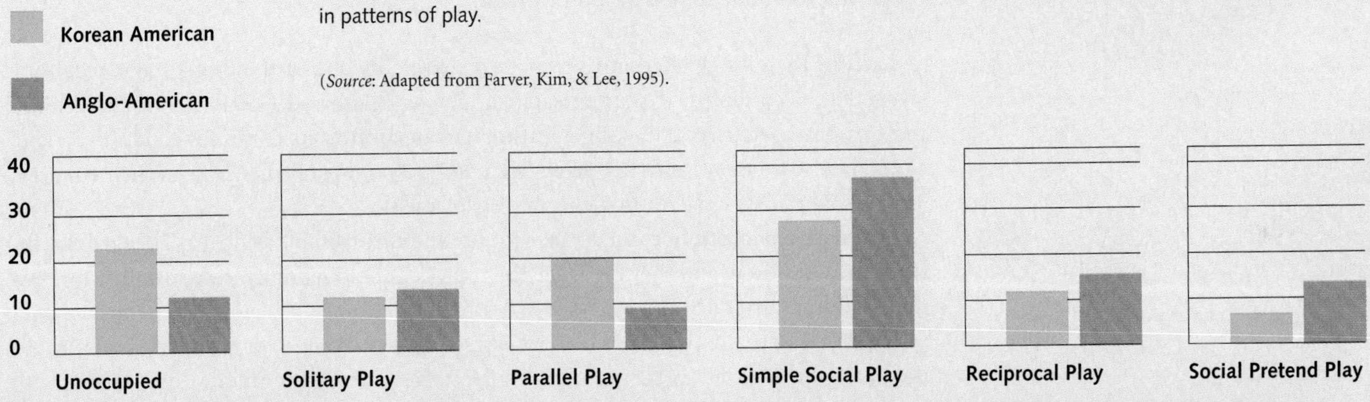

authoritarian parents *parents who are controlling, punitive, rigid, and cold, and whose word is law; they value strict, unquestioning obedience from their children and do not tolerate expressions of disagreement*

permissive parents *parents who provide lax and inconsistent feedback and require little of their children*

Theory of Mind

One reason behind the developmental changes in children's play is the continuing development of preschoolers' theory of mind. As we first discussed in Chapter 6, *theory of mind* refers to knowledge and beliefs about the mental world. Using their theory of mind, children are able to come up with explanations for how others think and the reasons for their behaving in the way they do.

During the preschool years, children increasingly can see the world from others' perspectives. Even children as young as 2 are able to understand that others have emotions and that these emotions can affect others' behavior. By the age of 3 or 4, they can distinguish between mental phenomena and physical actuality. For instance, 3-year-olds know that they can imagine something that is not physically present, such as a pretend animal, and that others can do the same. They can also pretend that something has happened, and react as if it really had occurred. And they know that others have the same capability (Hickling, Wellman, & Gottfried, 1997).

Preschool-age children also understand that people have motives and reasons for their behavior. A child at this age can understand that his mother is angry because she was late for an appointment, even if the child himself hasn't seen her be late. Furthermore, by the age of 4, preschool-age children's understanding that people can be fooled and that they can be mistaken by physical reality becomes surprisingly sophisticated (Fischer & Rose, 1994).

Not surprisingly, there are significant cultural variations in children's theory of mind. For example, children in more industrialized Western cultures may be more likely to regard others' behavior as due to the kind of people they are, seeing it as a function of their personal traits and characteristics. In contrast, children in non-Western cultures may see others' behavior as produced by forces that are less under their personal control, such as unhappy gods or bad fortune (Lillard, 1998).

Discipline: Teaching Desired Behavior

> While no one is looking—she thinks—Maria goes into her brother Alejandro's bedroom, where he has been saving the last of his Halloween candy. Just as Maria takes Alejandro's last Reese's Peanut Butter Cup, the children's mother walks into the room and immediately takes in the situation.

If you were Maria's mother, which of the following reactions seems most reasonable?

1. Tell Maria that she must go to her room and stay there for the rest of the day, and that she is going to lose access to her favorite blanket, the one she sleeps with every night and during naps.

2. Mildly tell Maria that what she did was not such a good idea, and she shouldn't do it in the future.

3. Explain why her brother Alejandro was going to be upset, and tell her that she must go to her room for an hour as punishment.

Each of these three alternative responses represents one of the three major parenting styles that, according to classic research by Diana Baumrind (1971, 1980), characterize most parents' patterns of discipline. **Authoritarian parents** are controlling, punitive, rigid, cold. Their word is law, and they value strict, unquestioning obedience from their children. They also do not tolerate expressions of disagreement.

Permissive parents, in contrast, provide lax and inconsistent feedback. They require little of their children, and they don't see themselves as holding much responsibility for how their children turn out.

There are actually two types of permissive parents. *Permissive-indifferent* parents are unusually uninvolved in their children's lives; they show little interest or concern with

EPILOGUE: THE GATHERING

In this chapter, we examined the social and personality development of preschool-age children, including their development of self-concept. We looked at the social relationships of preschool-age children and the changing nature of play. We considered styles of parental discipline typically and their effects of later in life and we examined the factors that lead to child abuse. We discussed the development of a moral sense, from several developmental perspectives, and we concluded with a discussion of aggression.

Reread the prologue to this chapter, about Sarah Rossoff's living room "tent," and answer the following questions.

1. How does Sarah "need to mess" relate to Erikson's autonomy-versus-shame-and-doubt stage of moral development?

2. Can you think of a response to this situation that a parent might make that would reinforce Sarah's emerging cultural stereotypes about gender? Can you think of a different response that would reinforce a more androgynous identity?

3. Can you analyze Sarah's activity in terms of "play," as it is discussed by developmentalists? If Sarah were playing with a friend, what characteristics do you think their play would have?

4. How would parents react to this situation using each of the three disciplinary styles typical in the United States (i.e., authoritarian, permissive, and authoritative)? Which response do you think is most appropriate? Why?

5. How might you design an experiment around a situation like this one, focusing on the effects of social models on a child's compliance with his or her mother's instructions to clean up a room? What would be your hypothesis? What variable would you manipulate (i.e., your independent variable)? What variable would you measure (i.e., your dependent variable)?

KEY TERMS AND CONCEPTS

self-concept (p. 258)
collectivistic orientation (p. 259)
individualistic orientation (p. 259)
psychosocial development (p. 259)
initiative-versus-guilt stage (p. 259)
race dissonance (p. 260)
identification (p. 262)
gender identity (p. 263)
gender schema (p. 263)
gender constancy (p. 264)
androgynous (p. 264)
functional play (p. 266)
constructive play (p. 266)
parallel play (p. 268)
onlooker play (p. 268)

associative play (p. 268)
cooperative play (p. 268)
authoritarian parents (p. 270)
permissive parents (p. 270)
authoritative parents (p. 271)
cycle-of-violence hypothesis (p. 274)
psychological maltreatment (p. 275)
resilience (p. 276)
moral development (p. 278)
heteronomous morality (p. 278)
immanent justice (p. 279)
prosocial behavior (p. 279)
abstract modeling (p. 280)
empathy (p. 280)
aggression (p. 281)

CHAPTER 9

Physical and Cognitive Development

P R O L O G U E : LA-TOYA PANKEY AND *THE WITCHES*

La-Toya Pankey

There are few books in La-Toya Pankey's apartment on 102nd Street near Amsterdam Avenue in Manhattan, and even fewer places for an 8-year-old girl to steal away to read them.

There is no desk, no bookshelf, no reading lamp or even a bureau in La-Toya's small room, one of only two bedrooms in the apartment she shares with seven other people: her mother, her five sisters and her infant brother.

At night, there is little light, save a couple of bare bulbs mounted on the peeling, beige walls. And there are few places to sit, except a lone, wooden chair at a battered kitchen table, which La-Toya must wait her turn to occupy.

Yet there was La-Toya, on a rainy evening earlier this month, leaning against that table and reading aloud, flawlessly, to her mother from the Roald Dahl classic *The Witches*, which she had borrowed from the makeshift library in her third-grade classroom. (Steinberg, 1997, p. B1)

293

LOOKING AHEAD

It was a significant moment for La-Toya. It marked a shift from the first-grade-level books that she had previously chosen to read to a far more challenging one, written at a grade level 2 years higher than her own.

Middle childhood is characterized by a procession of moments such as these, as children's physical, cognitive, and social skills ascend to new heights. Beginning at age 6 and continuing to the start of adolescence at around age 12, the period of middle childhood is often referred to as the "school years" because it marks the beginning of formal education for most children. Sometimes the physical and cognitive growth that occurs during middle childhood is gradual; other times it is sudden; but always it is remarkable.

We begin our consideration of middle childhood by examining physical development. We discuss how children's bodies change, and the twin problems of malnutrition and—the other side of the coin—childhood obesity. We also consider both typical development and some of the special needs that affect exceptional children's sensory and physical abilities.

Next, we turn to cognitive development in middle childhood. We examine several approaches, including Piagetian and information-processing theories and the important ideas of Lev Vygotsky. We look at language development and the critical questions revolving around bilingualism—an increasingly pressing social issue in the United States due to the growing diversity of the school-age population.

Finally, we consider several issues involving schooling. After discussing the scope of education throughout the world, we examine the critical skill of reading and the nature of multicultural education. The chapter ends with a discussion of intelligence, a characteristic closely tied to school success. We look at IQ tests and at the education of children who are either significantly below or above the intellectual norm.

In short, after reading this chapter, you will be able to answer these questions:

Q

- In what ways do children grow during the school years, and what factors influence their growth?
- What are the main health concerns of school-age children?
- What sorts of special needs manifest themselves in the middle childhood years, and how can they be met?
- In what ways do children develop cognitively during these years, according to major theoretical approaches?
- How does language develop during the middle childhood period?
- What are some trends in schooling today?
- How can intelligence be measured, and how are children with exceptionalities educated?

PHYSICAL DEVELOPMENT

Dusty Nash, an angelic-looking blond child of 7, awoke at five one recent morning in his Chicago home and proceeded to throw a fit. He wailed. He kicked. Every muscle in his 50-pound body flew in furious motion. Finally, after about 30 minutes, Dusty pulled himself together sufficiently to head downstairs for breakfast. While his mother bustled about the kitchen, the hyperkinetic child pulled a box of Kix cereal from the cupboard and sat on a chair.

Seven-year-old Dusty Nash's high energy and low attention span is due to attention-deficit hyperactivity disorder, which occurs in 3 to 5 percent of the school-age population.

But sitting still was not in the cards this morning. After grabbing some cereal with his hands, he began kicking the box, scattering little round corn puffs across the room. Next he turned his attention to the TV set, or rather, the table supporting it. The table was covered with checkerboard Con-Tact paper, and Dusty began peeling it off. Then he became intrigued with the spilled cereal and started stomping it to bits. At this point his mother interceded. In a firm but calm voice she told her son to get the stand-up dust pan and broom and clean up the mess. Dusty got out the dust pan but forgot the rest of the order. Within seconds he was dismantling the plastic dust pan, piece by piece. His next project: grabbing three rolls of toilet paper from the bathroom and unraveling them around the house. (Wallis, 1994, p. 43)

It was only 7:30 a.m.

Dusty suffers from a disorder that no one had heard of just a few decades ago—attention-deficit hyperactivity disorder. Although not common, occurring in only 3 to 5 percent of the school-age population, the disorder represents one of several challenges that children may face as they pass through middle childhood. Yet even in children without identifiable difficulties, the range of skills and abilities encompassed by typical development is enormous. We'll first consider typical physical growth during middle childhood, and then return to look at exceptional children, such as Dusty, whose development does not conform to typical patterns.

The Growing Body

Slow but steady. If three words could characterize growth during middle childhood, it would be these. Especially when compared with the swift growth during the first 5 years of life and the remarkable growth spurt characteristic of adolescence, middle childhood is relatively tranquil.

The body has not shifted into neutral, however. Physical growth continues, although at a more stately pace. For instance, while they are in elementary school, children in the United States grow, on average, 2 to 3 inches a year. By the age of 11, the average height for girls is 4 feet, 10 inches tall and the average height for boys is slightly shorter at 4 feet, 9½ inches tall. This is the only time during the life span when girls are, on average, taller than boys. This height difference reflects the slightly more rapid physical development of girls, who start their adolescent growth spurt around the age of 10.

Weight gain follows a similar pattern. During middle childhood, both boys and girls gain around 5 to 7 pounds a year. Weight also becomes redistributed. As the rounded look of "baby fat" disappears, children's bodies become more muscular and their strength increases.

Average height and weight increases disguise significant individual differences, as anyone who has seen a line of fourth-graders walking down a school corridor has doubtless noticed. Variations of a half-foot between children of the same age are not unusual, and well within normal ranges.

Cultural Patterns of Growth. Because most children in North America receive sufficient nutrients to reach their full potential, most height and weight differences among North American children are due to genetically determined variability. In other parts of the world, inadequate nutrition and disease take their toll, producing children who are shorter and who weigh less than they would if they had sufficient nutrients. The discrepancies can be dramatic: Children in poorer areas of cities such as Calcutta, Hong Kong, and Rio de Janeiro are smaller than their counterparts in affluent areas of the same cities.

Other variations in height and weight are the result of genetic factors relating to racial and ethnic background. For instance, children from Asian and Oceanic Pacific backgrounds tend to be shorter, on average, than those with northern and central European heritages (Meredith, 1971). However, even within particular racial and ethnic groups there is significant variation. Furthermore, we cannot attribute racial and ethnic differences solely to inherited factors, because dietary customs, as well as possible variations in levels of affluence, also may contribute to the differences.

Promoting Growth with Hormones: Should Short Children Be Made to Grow? The manufacturers of Protropin, an artificial human growth hormone that can make short children taller, had a problem: They needed to find short children in order to promote the use of their drug. One of the ways they solved their problem was by paying for surveys to identify short children in schools.

Although such practices are legal, they are on the fringe of ethical conduct, at least according to some developmentalists. The problem is not so much whether the drug is effective in increasing the growth of unusually short children—it is—but whether drug manufacturers are being overly aggressive in their quest to market the drug to potential patients (Kolata, 1994).

The problem is a new one: Artificial hormones to promote growth have become available only in the last decade. Although some 20,000 children who have insufficient natural growth hormone are taking such drugs, some observers question whether shortness is a serious enough problem to warrant the use of the drug. Certainly one can function well in society without being tall. Furthermore, the drug is costly and has potentially dangerous side effects. In some cases, the drug may lead to the premature onset of puberty, which may—ironically—restrict later growth.

On the other hand, there is no denying that artificial growth hormones are effective in increasing children's height. In fact, for those children whose height is projected to be well below normal, the effect of such drugs can be dramatic. In some cases the drug has added well over a foot in height to extremely short children, placing them within normal height ranges.

Severe malnutrition, like that experienced by this child in Somalia, not only has profound physical consequences, but also ultimately can slow cognitive development substantially.

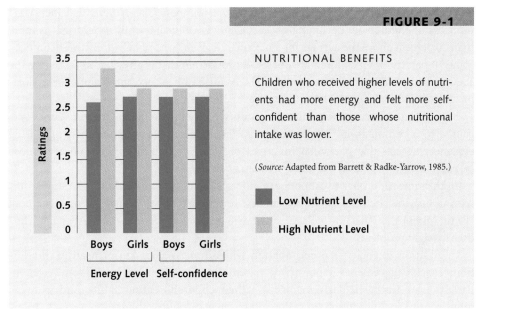

FIGURE 9-1

NUTRITIONAL BENEFITS

Children who received higher levels of nutrients had more energy and felt more self-confident than those whose nutritional intake was lower.

(*Source:* Adapted from Barrett & Radke-Yarrow, 1985.)

■ Low Nutrient Level

▫ High Nutrient Level

Nutrition.   The level of nutrition children experience during their lives significantly affects many aspects of their behavior. For instance, longitudinal studies over many years in Guatemalan villages show that children's nutritional backgrounds are related to several dimensions of social and emotional functioning at school age. Children who had received more nutrients were more involved with their peers, showed more positive emotion, had less anxiety, and had more moderate activity levels than their peers who had received less adequate nutrition. Furthermore, the children with a better nutritional history were more eager to explore new environments, showed more persistence in frustrating situations, were more alert on some types of activities, and generally displayed higher energy levels and more self-confidence (Barrett & Frank, 1987; see Figure 9-1).

Nutrition is also linked to cognitive performance. For instance, in one study, well-nourished children in Kenya performed better on a test of verbal abilities and on other cognitive measures than those who had mild to moderate undernutrition. Other research suggests that malnutrition may influence cognitive development by dampening children's curiosity, responsiveness, and motivation to learn (Sigman et al., 1989; Ricciuti, 1993; Brown & Pollitt, 1996).

Although undernutrition and malnutrition clearly lead to physical, social, and cognitive difficulties, in some cases *over*nutrition—the intake by a child of too many calories—presents problems of its own, particularly when it leads to childhood obesity.

Childhood Obesity.   When Ruthellen's mother asks if she would like a piece of bread with her meal, Ruthellen replies that she better not—she thinks that she may be getting fat. Ruthellen, who is of normal weight and height, is 6 years old.

Height can be of concern to both children and parents during middle childhood, but a greater worry for many is maintaining the appropriate weight. In fact, concern about weight can border on an obsession, particularly among girls. For instance, many 6-year-old girls worry about becoming "fat," and some 40 percent of 9- and 10-year-olds are trying to lose weight. Why? Their concern is most often the result of the U.S. preoccupation with being slim, which permeates every sector of society (Schreiber et al., 1996).

What is ironic about the widely held view that thinness is a virtue is that increasing numbers of children are becoming obese. *Obesity* is defined as body weight that is more than 20 percent above the average for a person of a given age and height. By this definition, some 10 percent of all children are obese—a proportion that is growing. In fact, since the 1960s, obesity among children aged 6 to 11 has risen by 54 percent (Lamb, 1984; Gortmaker et al., 1987; Ungrady, 1992; Troiano et al., 1995).

Several factors account for childhood obesity. As we first noted in Chapter 7, obesity is caused by a combination of genetic and social characteristics. For instance, increasing evidence suggests that particular inherited genes are related to obesity and predispose certain children to be overweight (Friedman et al., 1994).

At the same time, obesity cannot be attributable solely to inherited factors, because it is hard to link the rise in obesity over the past several decades to changes in the gene pool (Faith, Johnson, & Allison, 1997). Clearly, various social factors must also enter into children's weight problems.

In addition to society's preoccupation with slimness as a sign of beauty, an additional social ingredient in obesity is parental worry about their children's weight. Parents who are particularly involved in their children's eating habits, and who exhibit controlling behavior regarding them, may produce children who lack internal controls to regulate their own food intake (Brownell & Rodin, 1994; Johnson & Birch, 1994).

Another important social factor that determines obesity is exercise—or rather, the lack of exercise (Epstein, 1992). School-age children, by and large, tend to engage in relatively little exercise and are not particularly fit (Wolf et al., 1993). For instance, around 40 percent of boys 6 to 12 are unable to do more than one pull-up, and a quarter can't do any. Furthermore, school fitness surveys reveal that children in the United States have shown little or no improvement in the amount of exercise they get, despite national efforts to increase the level of fitness of school-age children. From the ages of 6 to 18, boys decrease their physical activity by 24 percent and girls by 36 percent (Ungrady, 1992; Murray, 1996).

Why, when our visions of childhood include children running happily on school playgrounds, playing sports, and chasing one another in games of tag, is the actual level of exercise relatively low? One answer is that many kids are closeted in their homes, watching television.

The correlation between television viewing and obesity is significant: The more television children watch, the more likely they are to be overweight. There are several reasons for

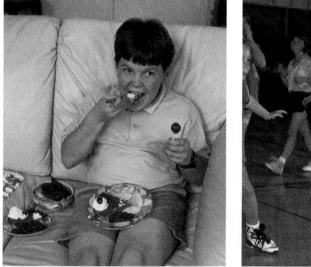

Television viewing is associated with obesity, in part because watching TV replaces more social activities that involve physical exercise.

this pattern. For one thing, television viewing is a sedentary activity; few people engage in vigorous exercise while watching TV. Another factor is that children tend to snack while watching television, thereby increasing their caloric intake beyond nutritional need. It is even possible that frequent exposure to commercials for food products entices habitual television viewers to be overly interested in food and eating (Dietz, 1987; Gortmaker et al, 1996; Harrell et al., 1997).

Health During Middle Childhood

Imani was miserable. Her nose was running, her lips were chapped, and her throat was sore. Although she had been able to stay home from school and spend the day watching old reruns on TV, she still felt that she was suffering mightily.

Despite her misery, Imani's situation is not so bad. She'll get over the cold in a few days and be no worse for having experienced it. In fact, she may be a little *better* off, for she is now immune to the specific cold germs that made her ill in the first place.

For Imani, as well as most children, a cold or other type of upper respiratory infection is just about the most serious illness that occurs during middle childhood. For most children, this is a period of robust health, and most of the ailments they do contract tend to be mild and brief.

On the other hand, illness is not uncommon. For instance, more than 90 percent of children are likely to have at least one serious medical condition over the 6-year period of middle childhood, according to the results of one large survey. And, although most children have short-term illnesses, about one in nine has a chronic, persistent condition, such as repeated migraine headaches (Starfield, 1991).

Routine immunizations during childhood have produced a considerably lower incidence of the life-threatening illnesses that 50 years ago claimed the lives of a significant number of children. Despite these gains, however, some illnesses are becoming more prevalent.

Asthma.   Asthma is among the diseases that have shown a significant increase in prevalence over the last several decades. **Asthma** is a chronic condition characterized by periodic attacks of wheezing, coughing, and shortness of breath. More than 5 million U.S. children suffer from the disorder—a rate that has almost doubled over the last decade (see Figure 9-2 ; Cowley & Underwood, 1997).

Asthma occurs when the airways leading to the lungs constrict, partially blocking the passage of oxygen. Because the airways are obstructed, more effort is needed to push air through them, making breathing more difficult. Furthermore, as air is forced through the obstructed airways, it makes the whistling sound called wheezing.

Not surprisingly, children are often exceedingly frightened by asthma attacks, and the anxiety and agitation produced by their breathing difficulties may actually make the attack

asthma *a chronic condition characterized by periodic attacks of wheezing, coughing, and shortness of breath*

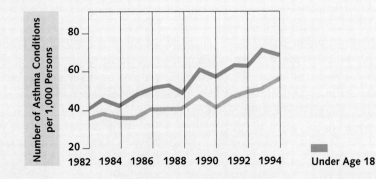

FIGURE 9-2

RISING RATES OF ASTHMA

Since the early 1980s the rate of asthma among children has almost doubled. A number of factors explain the rise, including increased air pollution and better means of detecting the disease.

(*Source:* National Center for Health Statistics, 1997.)

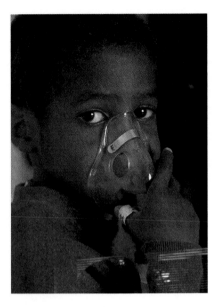

The incidence of asthma, a chronic respiratory condition, has increased dramatically over the last several decades.

worse. In some cases, breathing becomes so difficult that further physical symptoms develop, including sweating, an increased heart rate, and—in the most severe cases—a blueness in the face and lips due to a lack of oxygen.

Asthma attacks are triggered by a variety of factors. Among the most common are respiratory infections (such as colds or flu), allergic reactions to airborne irritants (such as pollution, cigarette smoke, dust mites, and animal dander and excretions), stress, and exercise. Sometimes even a sudden change in air temperature or humidity is enough to bring on an attack.

Although asthma can be serious, treatment is increasingly effective for those who suffer from the disorder. Some children who experience frequent asthma attacks use a small aerosol container with a special mouthpiece to spray drugs into the lungs. Other patients take tablets or receive injections (Klinnert, McQuaid, & Gavin, 1997).

One of the most puzzling questions about asthma is why the incidence has increased over the last two decades. Some researchers suggest that increasing air pollution has led to the rise; others believe that cases of asthma that might have been missed in the past are simply being identified more accurately. Still others have suggested that exposure to "asthma triggers," such as dust, may be increasing, because new buildings are more weatherproof—and therefore less drafty—than old ones, and consequently the flow of air within them is more restricted.

Finally, poverty may play an indirect role. Children living in poverty have a higher incidence of asthma than other children, probably due to poorer medical care and less sanitary living conditions. For instance, poor youngsters are more likely than more affluent ones to be exposed to triggering factors that are associated with asthma, such as dust mites, cockroach feces and body parts, and rodent feces and urine (Nossiter, 1995).

Psychological Disorders.   Jackson had always been a quiet child, and had, since his days as a toddler, seemed less exuberant than most other children. But when his third-grade teacher called his parents to report that Jackson seemed increasingly withdrawn from his classmates and had to be coaxed into going out to the playground, the parents thought they might have a serious problem on their hands. They took Jackson to a psychologist, who diagnosed Jackson as suffering from *childhood depression*.

For years most people neglected the symptoms of childhood depression, and even today parents and teachers may overlook its presence. In part, their neglect is due to the fact that its symptoms are not entirely consistent with the ways adults express depression. Rather than being manifested in a profound sadness or hopelessness, a negative outlook on life, and, in extreme cases, suicidal thoughts, as adult depression is, childhood depression may instead be characterized by the expression of exaggerated fears, clinginess, or avoidance of everyday activities. In older children, childhood depression may produce sulking, school problems, and even acts of delinquency. (Wenar, 1994)

The incidence of childhood depression is surprisingly high. Experts suggest that between 2 and 5 percent of school-age children suffer from the disorder, and in around 1 percent the depression is so acute that it leads to suicidal thoughts (Cohen et al., 1993).

It is important to keep in mind that all children are occasionally sad, and short periods of unhappiness should not be mistaken for childhood depression. The distinguishing characteristics of childhood depression are its depth, which can be truly profound, and its duration, which can extend for days or even weeks (Besseghini, 1997).

Like adult depression, childhood depression can be treated effectively through a variety of approaches. In addition to psychological counseling, drugs are sometimes prescribed, although their use is controversial, as we discuss in the "Directions in Development" box. Whatever treatment is chosen, it is important that childhood depression not be ignored, particularly because children who are depressed are at risk for mood disorders during adulthood (Harrington et al., 1990; Alloy, Acocella, & Bootzin, 1996).

Directions in Development

Orange-Flavored Prozac: The Growing Use of Antidepressants to Treat Childhood Psychological Problems

Andrew Crittendon was only 7 when an inexplicable bleakness descended on him. "I lost interest in everything," he recalls. "I just sat in my room and thought about how horrible life was." Andrew's mother, Beverly, started to worry when a trip to Six Flags Great Adventure didn't lift his spirits, and her concern turned to terror when the child started talking about suicide. Dr. Graham Emslie, the Dallas-based psychiatrist who diagnosed Andrew's depression, offered to enroll him in a study of Prozac. "I didn't care what they did," Andrew says, "as long as there was a chance it would make me feel better." It did—and he stayed on the drug for four years. At 11, he discovered he no longer needed it. Andrew is now a six-foot-tall ninth grader with his sights set on a career in filmmaking. "I'm really one of the happiest people I know," he says. (Crowley, 1997, p. 73)

The use of Prozac has become a popular—if highly controversial—treatment for a variety of childhood psychological disorders. In 1996 alone, some 200,000 prescriptions were written for children between the ages of 6 to 12, an increase of close to 300 percent over the previous year (Strauch, 1997).

Surprisingly, though, the drug has never been approved by governmental regulators for use with children. In fact, no antidepressant drug has ever received approval for use by children or adolescents. Still, because the drug has received approval for adult use, it is perfectly legal for physicians to write prescriptions for children.

Proponents of the increased use of Prozac, as well as other antidepressants such as Zoloft and Paxil, for children suggest that depression and other psychological disorders can be treated quite successfully using drug therapies. In many cases, more traditional nondrug therapies that largely employ verbal methods simply are ineffective. In such cases, drugs can provide the only form of relief. Furthermore, at least one clinical test has shown that the drugs are effective with children (Emslie et al., 1997).

Critics, on the other hand, contend that there is little evidence for the long-term effectiveness of depressants with children. Even worse, no one knows what are the consequences of the use of antidepressants on the developing brains of children, nor the long-term consequences more generally. Little is known about the correct dosages for children of given ages. Finally, some observers suggest that the use of special children's versions of the drugs, in orange- or mint-flavored syrups, might lead to overdoses or perhaps eventually encourage the use of illegal drugs (Strauch, 1997).

Although the use of antidepressant drugs to treat children is controversial, what is clear is that childhood depression and other psychological disorders remain a significant problem for many children. For instance, experts suggest that between 2 and 5 percent of school-age children suffer from childhood depression. In some children it is particularly severe: About 1 percent are so depressed that they express unmistakable suicidal ideas (Larsson & Melin, 1992). Furthermore, some 8 to 9 percent of children suffer from *anxiety disorders*, in which they experience intense, uncontrollable anxiety about situations that most people would not find bothersome. For instance, some children have strong fears about specific stimuli—such as germs or school—whereas others have bouts of generalized anxiety, the source of which they cannot pinpoint (Wenner, 1994; Ollendick et al., 1996).

It is important that childhood psychological disorders not be ignored. Not only are the disorders disruptive during childhood, but those who suffer from psychological problems as children are at risk for future disorders during adulthood (Kazdin, 1990; Alloy, Acocella, & Bootzin, 1996).

Motor Development

The fact that the fitness level of school-age children is not as high as we would desire does not mean that such children are physically incapable. In fact, even without regular exercise, children's gross and fine motor skills develop substantially over the course of the school years.

Gross Motor Skills.   One important improvement in gross motor skills is in the realm of muscle coordination. Watching a softball player pitch a ball past a batter to her catcher, or a runner reach the finish line in a race, we are struck by the huge strides that these children have made since the more awkward days of preschool.

During middle childhood, children master many types of skills that earlier they could not perform well. For instance, riding a bike, ice skating, swimming, and skipping rope are readily mastered by most school-age children (Cratty, 1986; see Figure 9-3).

Do boys and girls differ in their motor skills? Traditionally, developmentalists have concluded that gender differences in gross motor skills become increasingly pronounced during these years, with boys outperforming girls (Espenschade, 1960). However, more recent research casts some doubt on this conclusion. When comparisons are made between boys and girls who regularly take part in similar activities—such as softball—gender variations in gross motor skills are minimized (Hall & Lee, 1984).

Why? Performance differences were probably found in the first place because of differences in motivation and expectations. Society told girls that they would do worse than boys in sports, and the girls' performance reflected that message.

Today, however, society's message has changed, at least officially. For instance, the American Academy of Pediatrics suggests that boys and girls should engage in the same sports and games, and that they can do so together in mixed-gender groups. There is no reason to separate the sexes in physical exercise and sports until puberty, when the smaller size of females begins to make them more susceptible to injury in contact sports (American Academy of Pediatrics, 1989).

Fine Motor Skills.   Typing at a computer keyboard. Writing in cursive with pen and pencil. Drawing detailed pictures.

FIGURE 9-3

GROSS MOTOR SKILLS

Gross motor skills developed by children between the ages of 6 and 12 years.

(*Source:* Adapted from Cratty, 1979, p. 222.)

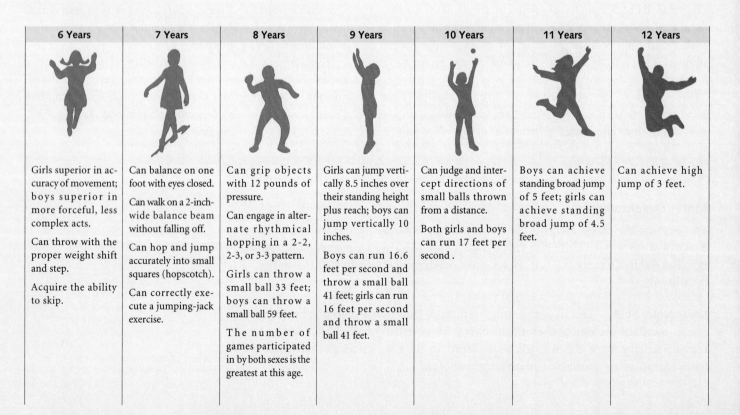

6 Years	7 Years	8 Years	9 Years	10 Years	11 Years	12 Years
Girls superior in accuracy of movement; boys superior in more forceful, less complex acts.	Can balance on one foot with eyes closed.	Can grip objects with 12 pounds of pressure.	Girls can jump vertically 8.5 inches over their standing height plus reach; boys can jump vertically 10 inches.	Can judge and intercept directions of small balls thrown from a distance.	Boys can achieve standing broad jump of 5 feet; girls can achieve standing broad jump of 4.5 feet.	Can achieve high jump of 3 feet.
Can throw with the proper weight shift and step.	Can walk on a 2-inch-wide balance beam without falling off.	Can engage in alternate rhythmical hopping in a 2-2, 2-3, or 3-3 pattern.	Boys can run 16.6 feet per second and throw a small ball 41 feet; girls can run 16 feet per second and throw a small ball 41 feet.	Both girls and boys can run 17 feet per second.		
Acquire the ability to skip.	Can hop and jump accurately into small squares (hopscotch).	Girls can throw a small ball 33 feet; boys can throw a small ball 59 feet.				
	Can correctly execute a jumping-jack exercise.	The number of games participated in by both sexes is the greatest at this age.				

These are just some of the accomplishments that depend on improvements in fine motor coordination that occur during early and middle childhood. Six- and 7-year-olds are able to tie their shoes and fasten buttons; by age 8, they can use each hand independently; and by 11 and 12, they can manipulate objects with almost as much capability as they will show in adulthood.

One of the reasons for advances in fine motor skills is that the amount of myelin in the brain increases significantly between the ages of 6 and 8 (Lecours, 1982). *Myelin* provides protective insulation that surrounds parts of nerve cells. Because increased levels of myelin raise the speed at which electrical impulses travel between neurons, messages can reach muscles more rapidly and control them better.

Children with Special Needs

> Andrew Mertz was a very unhappy little boy. . . . Third grade was a disaster, the culmination of a crisis that had been building since he entered kindergarten in suburban Maryland. He couldn't learn to read, and he hated school. "He would throw temper tantrums in the morning because he didn't want to go," recalls his mother, Suzanne. The year before, with much prodding from Suzanne, the school had authorized diagnostic tests for Andrew. The results revealed a host of brain processing problems that explained why he kept mixing up letters and sounds. Andrew's problem now had a label—he was officially classified as learning disabled—and he was legally entitled to help. (Wingert & Kantrowitz, 1997)

Andrew joined millions of other children who are classified as learning disabled, one of several types of special needs that children can have. Although every child has different specific capabilities, children with *special needs* differ significantly from typical children in terms of physical attributes or learning abilities. Furthermore, their needs present major challenges for both care providers and teachers.

We turn now to the most prevalent exceptionalities that affect children of normal intelligence: sensory difficulties, learning disabilities, and attention deficit disorders. (We will consider the special needs of children who are significantly below and above average in intelligence later in the chapter.)

Sensory Difficulties: Visual, Auditory, and Speech Problems.   Anyone who has temporarily lost his or her eyeglasses or a contact lens has had a glimpse of how difficult even rudimentary, everyday tasks must be for those with sensory impairments. To function with less than typical vision, hearing, or speech can be a tremendous challenge.

Visual impairment can be considered in both a legal and an educational sense. The definition of legal impairment is quite straightforward: *Blindness* is visual acuity of less than 20/200 after correction (meaning the inability to see even at 20 feet what a typical person can see at 200 feet), whereas *partial sightedness* is visual acuity of less than 20/70 after correction.

Even when the legal limits of impairment are not reached, however, visual impairment in an educational sense can be present. For one thing, the legal criterion pertains solely to distance vision, whereas most educational tasks require close-up vision. In addition, the legal definition does not consider abilities in the perception of color, depth, and light—all of which might influence a student's educational success. About one student in a thousand requires special education services relating to a visual impairment.

Although most severe visual problems are identified fairly early, it sometimes happens that an impairment goes undetected. Furthermore, visual problems can emerge gradually as children develop physiologically and changes occur in the visual apparatus of the eye. Parents must be aware of the signals of visual problems in their children. Frequent eye irritation (redness, sties, or infection), continual blinking and facial contortions when reading,

CW

visual impairment   *a difficulty in seeing that may include blindness or partial sightedness*

Auditory impairments can produce both academic and social difficulties, and they may lead to speech difficulties.

holding reading material unusually close to the face, difficulty in writing, and frequent headaches, dizziness, or burning eyes are some of the signs of visual problems.

Another relatively frequent special need relates to **auditory impairment**. Auditory impairments can cause academic problems, and they can produce social difficulties as well, because considerable peer interaction takes place through informal conversation. Hearing loss, which affects some 1 to 2 percent of the school-age population, is not simply a matter of not hearing enough. Rather, auditory problems can vary along a number of dimensions (U.S. Department of Education, 1987; Harris, Van-Zandt, & Rees, 1997).

In some cases of hearing loss, only a limited range of frequencies, or pitches, is affected. For example, the loss may be great at pitches in the normal speech range yet quite minor in other frequencies, such as those of very high or low sounds. In addition, a child may require different levels of amplification at different frequencies. For this reason, a hearing aid that indiscriminately amplifies all frequencies equally may be ineffective.

The age of onset of a hearing loss is critical in determining the degree to which a child can adapt to the impairment. If the loss of hearing occurs in infancy, the effects will probably be much more severe than if it occurs after the age of 3. The reason relates to the critical role that hearing plays in the development of language. Children who have had little or no exposure to the sound of language are unable to understand or produce oral language themselves. On the other hand, loss of hearing after a child has learned language will not have serious consequences on subsequent linguistic development.

Severe and early loss of hearing is also associated with difficulties in abstract thinking. Because hearing-impaired children may have limited exposure to language, abstract concepts that can be understood fully only through the use of language may be less well understood than concrete concepts that can be illustrated visually (Hewett & Forness, 1974).

Auditory difficulties are sometimes accompanied by speech impairments. A speech impairment is one of the most public types of exceptionality: Every time the child speaks aloud, the impairment is obvious to listeners. In fact, the definition of **speech impairment** suggests that speech is impaired when it deviates so much from the speech of others that it calls attention to itself, interferes with communication, or produces maladjustment in the speaker (Van Riper, 1972). In other words, if a child's speech sounds impaired, it probably is. Speech impairments are present in around 3 to 5 percent of the school-age population (U.S. Department of Education, 1987).

Stuttering, which entails substantial disruption in the rhythm and fluency of speech, is the most common speech impairment. Despite a great deal of research on the topic, no single cause has been identified. Although the disfluencies of stuttering are relatively normal in young children—and occasionally occur in normal adults—chronic stuttering can be a severe problem. Not only does stuttering hinder communication, but it can produce embarrassment and stress in children, who may become inhibited from conversing with others and speaking aloud in class.

Parents and teachers can adopt several strategies for dealing with stuttering. For starters, attention should not be drawn to the stuttering, and children should be given sufficient time to finish what they begin to say, no matter how protracted the statement becomes. It does not help stutterers to finish their sentences for them or otherwise correct their speech (Onslow, 1992).

auditory impairment   *a special need that involves the loss of hearing or some aspect of hearing*

speech impairment   *speech that deviates so much from the speech of others that it calls attention to itself, interferes with communication, or produces maladjustment in the speaker*

stuttering   *substantial disruption in the rhythm and fluency of speech; the most common speech impairment*

Learning Disabilities: Discrepancies Between Achievement and Capacity to Learn.
Some 2.6 million school-age children in the United States are officially labeled as having
learning disabilities. **Learning disabilities** are characterized by difficulties in the acquisition and use of listening, speaking, reading, writing, reasoning, or mathematical abilities. A
somewhat ill-defined, grab-bag category, learning disabilities are diagnosed when there is a
discrepancy between children's actual academic performance and their apparent potential
to learn (Roush, 1995; Wong, 1996).

Such a broad definition encompasses a wide and heterogeneous variety of difficulties.
For instance, some children suffer from *dyslexia*, a reading disability that can result in the
misperception of letters during reading and writing, unusual difficulty in sounding out letters, confusion between left and right, and difficulties in spelling. Although the causes of
dyslexia are not fully understood, one likely explanation is a problem in the part of the
brain responsible for breaking words into the sound elements that make up language
(Shaywitz, 1996).

The causes of learning disabilities are not well understood. Although they are generally
attributed to some form of brain dysfunction, probably due to genetic factors, some experts suggest that they are produced by such environmental causes as poor early nutrition
or allergies (Mercer, 1992).

Attention-deficit Hyperactivity Disorder.   **Attention-deficit hyperactivity disorder**, or
ADHD, is marked by inattention, impulsiveness, a low tolerance for frustration, and generally a great deal of inappropriate activity. Although all children show such traits some of
the time, for those diagnosed with ADHD (like Dusty Nash, whose case was discussed earlier) such behavior is common and interferes with their home and school functioning
(Sandberg, 1996; Barkley, 1995, 1997b).

Although it is hard to know how many children have the disorder, most estimates put
the number at from 3 to 5 percent of the school-age population, or some 3.5 million Americans under the age of 18. What is clear is that a child with ADHD is physically active, has
limited self-control, is easily distracted, and is likely to have difficulty staying on task and
working toward goals. An ADHD child can be a whirlwind of activity, exhausting the energy and patience of parents, teachers, and even peers (Baker, 1994; Barkley, 1997a; Hin-
shaw et al., 1997).

The treatment of children with ADHD has been a source of considerable controversy.
Because it has been found that doses of Ritalin or Dexadrine (which, paradoxically, are
stimulants) reduce activity levels in hyperactive children, many physicians routinely pre-
scribe drug treatment (Rief, 1995).

Although in many cases such drugs are effective in increasing attention span and compliance, in some cases the side effects are considerable, and the long-term health consequences of this treatment are unclear. Furthermore, although in the short run drugs often
help scholastic performance (Weber, Frankenberger, & Heilman, 1992), the long-term evidence for continuing improvement is mixed. In fact, some studies suggest that after a few
years, children treated with drugs do not perform academically any better than untreated
children (McDaniel, 1986).

What are the most common signs of ADHD? Although it is often difficult to distinguish
between children who simply have a high level of activity and those with ADHD, some of
the most common symptoms include persistent difficulty in finishing tasks, following instructions, and organizing work; inability to watch an entire television program; frequent
interruption of others; and a tendency to jump into a task before hearing all the instructions. If a child is suspected of having ADHD, he or she should be evaluated by a specialist.
(Parents can receive support from the Center for Hyperactive Child Information, P.O. Box
66272, Washington, DC 20035.)

learning disabilities   *difficulties in the
acquisition and use of listening, speaking,
reading, writing, reasoning, or mathematical abilities*

*attention-deficit hyperactivity disorder
(ADHD)*   *a learning disability marked by
inattention, impulsiveness, a low tolerance for
frustration, and generally a great deal of inappropriate activity*

The Informed Consumer of Development

Keeping Children Fit

Here is a brief portrait of a contemporary American: Sam works all week at a desk and gets no regular physical exercise. On weekends he spends many hours sitting in front of the TV, often snacking on sodas and sweets. Both at home and at restaurants, his meals feature high-calorie, fat-saturated foods. (Segal & Segal, 1992, p. 235)

Although this sketch could apply to many adult men and women, Sam is actually a 6-year-old. He is one of many school-age children in the United States who get little or no regular exercise, and who consequently are physically unfit and at risk for obesity and other health problems.

However, several approaches can be taken to encourage children to become more physically active (Squires, 1991; O'Neill, 1994):

- Make exercise fun. For children to build the habit of exercising, they need to find it enjoyable. Activities that keep children on the sidelines or that are overly competitive may give children with inferior skills a lifelong distaste for exercise.

- Gear activities to the child's physical level and motor skills. For instance, use child-size equipment that can make participants feel successful.

- Encourage the child to find a partner. It could be a friend, a sibling, or a parent. Exercising can involve a variety of activities, such as roller skating or hiking, but almost all activities are carried out more readily if someone else is doing them too.

- Start slowly. Sedentary children—those who haven't habitually engaged in physical activity—should start off gradually. For instance, they could start with 5 minutes of exercise a day, 7 days a week. Over 10 weeks, they could move toward a goal of 30 minutes of exercise 3 to 5 days a week.

- Urge participation in organized sports activities, but do not push too hard. Not every child is athletically inclined, and pushing too hard for involvement in organized sports may backfire. Make participation and enjoyment the goals of such activities, not winning.

- Don't make physical activity, such as jumping jacks or push-ups, a punishment for unwanted behavior.

- Schools and parents should encourage children to participate in an organized physical fitness program. For instance, the Cooper Institute for Aerobics Research has designed a program called the "Fitnessgram," which is used by two million children in three thousand schools around the United States. (For more information, write Cooper Institute for Aerobics Research, 12330 Preston Road, Dallas, Texas 75230.)

REVIEW AND RETHINK

REVIEW

- During the middle childhood years, the body grows at a slow but steady pace that is influenced by both genetic and social factors.

- Adequate nutrition is important for physical, social, and cognitive development in the middle childhood years, but avoid overnutrition, which may lead to obesity.

- The incidence of asthma and childhood depression has increased significantly over the last several decades. Both can interfere with normal functioning and should be treated actively.

- Children substantially improve their gross and fine motor skills during the school years, with muscular coordination and manipulative skills advancing to near-adult levels.

- Many school-age children have special needs, particularly in the areas of vision, hearing, and speech. Some also have learning disabilities.

- Attention-deficit hyperactivity disorder, marked by attention, organization, and activity problems, affects between 3 and 5 percent of the school-age population. Treatment through the use of drugs is highly controversial.

RETHINK

- Under what circumstances would you recommend the use of a growth hormone such as Protropin? Is shortness primarily a physical or a cultural problem?

- Do proven links among affluence, nutrition, and the development of cognitive and social skills provide insight into the notion of "the cycle of poverty"? How might the cycle be broken?

- In general, are social attitudes toward people with speech impairments supportive? How would you advise parents to treat a child with a noticeable speech impairment?

- Before accepting the treatment of ADHD with drugs, what questions would you want answered about the child and the drugs?

INTELLECTUAL DEVELOPMENT

Jared's parents were delighted when he came home from kindergarten one day and explained that he had learned why the sky was blue. He talked about the earth's atmosphere—although he didn't pronounce the word correctly—and how tiny bits of moisture in the air reflected the sunlight. Although his explanation had rough edges (he couldn't quite grasp what the "atmosphere" was), he still had the general idea, and that, his parents felt, was quite an achievement for their 5-year-old.

***

Fast-forward six years. Jared, now 11, had already spent an hour laboring over his evening's homework. After completing a two-page worksheet on multiplying and dividing fractions, he had begun work on his U.S. Constitution project. He was taking notes for his report, which would explain what political factions had been involved in the writing of the document and how the Constitution had been amended since its creation.

Jared, of course, is not alone in having made vast intellectual advances during his middle childhood. In this period, cognitive abilities broaden, and children become increasingly able to understand and master complex skills. At the same time, though, their thinking is still not fully adultlike.

What are the advances, and the limitations, in thinking during childhood? Several perspectives explain what goes on cognitively during middle childhood.

Piagetian Approaches to Cognitive Development

Let's return for a moment to Jean Piaget's view of the preschooler, which we considered in Chapter 7. From Piaget's perspective, the preschooler thinks *preoperationally*. This type of thinking is largely egocentric, and preoperational children lack the ability to use *operations*—organized, formal, logical mental processes.

The Rise of Concrete Operational Thought.   All this changes, according to Piaget, during the concrete operational period, which coincides with the school years. The **concrete operational stage**, which occurs between 7 and 12 years of age, is characterized by the active, and appropriate, use of logic. Concrete operational thought involves applying *logical operations* to concrete problems. For instance, when children in the concrete operational stage are confronted with a conservation problem (such as determining whether the amount of liquid poured from one container to another container of a different shape stays the same), they use cognitive and logical processes to answer, no longer being influenced solely by appearance. Consequently, they easily—and correctly—solve conservation problems. Because they are less egocentric, they can take multiple aspects of a situation into account, an ability known as **decentering**.

concrete operational stage   *the period of cognitive development between 7 and 12 years of age, which is characterized by the active, and appropriate, use of logic*

decentering   *the ability to take multiple aspects of a situation into account*

Cognitive development makes substantial advances in middle childhood.

The shift from preoperational thought to concrete operational thought does not happen overnight, of course. During the 2 years before children move firmly into the concrete operational period, they shift back and forth between preoperational and concrete operational thinking. For instance, they typically pass through a period when they can answer conservation problems correctly but can't articulate why they did so. When asked to explain the reasoning behind their answers, they may respond with an unenlightening "Because."

However, once concrete operational thinking is fully engaged, children show several cognitive advances. For instance, they attain the concept of *reversibility*, which is the notion that processes that transform a stimulus can be reversed, returning it to its original form. Grasping reversibility permits children to understand that a ball of clay that has been squeezed into a long, snakelike rope can be returned to its original state. More abstractly, it allows school-age children to understand that if 3 + 5 equals 8, then 5 + 3 also equals 8—and, later during the period, that 8 − 3 equals 5.

Concrete operational thinking also permits children to understand such concepts as the relationship between time and speed. For instance, consider the problem shown in Figure 9-4, in which two cars start and finish at the same points in the same amount of time, but travel different routes. Children who are just entering the concrete operational period reason that the cars are traveling at the same speed. However, between the ages of 8 and 10, children begin to draw the right conclusion: that the car traveling the longer route must be moving faster if it arrives at the finish point at the same time as the car traveling the shorter route.

Despite the advances that occur during the concrete operational stage, children still experience one critical limitation in their thinking. They remain tied to concrete, physical reality. Furthermore, they are unable to understand truly abstract or hypothetical questions, or ones that involve formal logic.

Piaget in Perspective: Piaget Was Right, Piaget Was Wrong.   As we learned in our prior consideration of Piaget's views in Chapters 5 and 7, researchers following in Piaget's footsteps have found much to cheer about—as well as much to criticize.

Piaget was a virtuoso observer of children, and his many books contain pages of brilliant, careful observations of children at work and play. Furthermore, his theories have powerful educational implications, and many schools employ principles derived from his views to guide the nature and presentation of instructional materials (Flavell, 1985, 1996; Ravitch, 1985; Siegler & Ellis, 1996).

In some ways, then, Piaget's approach was quite successful in describing cognitive development (Lourenco & Machado, 1996). At the same time, though, critics have raised

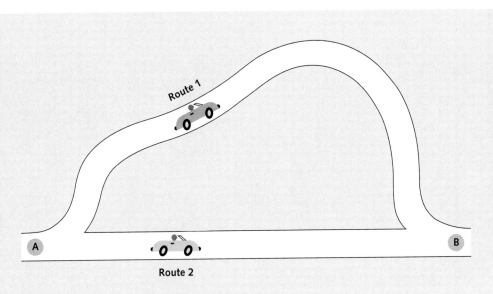

FIGURE 9-4

ROUTES TO CONSERVATION

After being told that the two cars traveling the Routes 1 and 2 start and end their journeys in the same amount of time, children who are just entering the concrete operational period still reason that the cars are traveling at the same speed. Later, however, they reach the correct conclusion: that the car traveling the longer route must be moving at a higher speed if it starts and ends its journey at the same time as the car traveling the shorter route.

compelling, and seemingly legitimate, grievances about his approach. As we have noted before, many researchers argue that Piaget underestimated children's capabilities, in part because of the limited nature of the mini-experiments he conducted. When a broader array of experimental tasks is used, children show less consistency within stages than Piaget would predict (Siegler, 1994; Bjorklund, 1997).

Furthermore, Piaget seems to have misjudged the age at which children's cognitive abilities emerge. As might be expected from our earlier discussions of Piaget's stages, increasing evidence suggests that children's capabilities emerge earlier than Piaget envisioned. Some children show evidence of a form of concrete operational thinking before the age of 7, the time at which Piaget suggested these abilities first appear.

Still, we cannot dismiss the Piagetian approach. Although some early cross-cultural research seemed to imply that children in certain cultures never left the preoperational stage, failing to master conservation and to develop concrete operations, more recent research suggests otherwise. For instance, with proper training in conservation, children in non-Western cultures who do not conserve can readily learn to do so. For instance, in

Research conducted in such places as remote areas of Australia shows that, contrary to Piaget's assertion, not everyone reaches the concrete operational stage.

FIGURE 9-5

CONSERVATION TRAINING

Rural Australian Aborigine children trail their urban counterparts in the development of their understanding of conservation; with training they later catch up. Without training, around half of 14-year-old Aborigines do not have an understanding of conservation.

(*Source:* Adapted from Dasen, Ngini, & Lavallee, 1979.)

Urban Australians

Rural Australian Aborigines

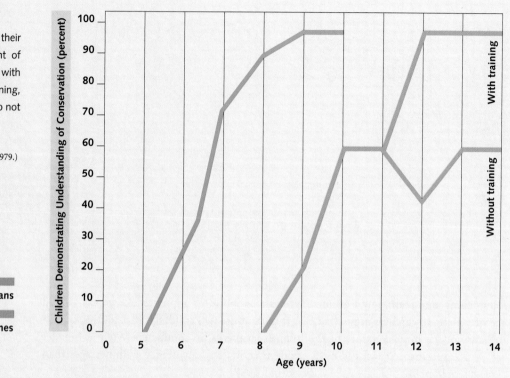

one study urban Australian children—who develop concrete operations on the same timetable as Piaget suggested—were compared to rural Aborigine children, who typically do not demonstrate an understanding of conservation at the age of 14 (Dasen, Ngini, & Lavallee, 1979). When the rural Aborigine children were given training, they began to conserve as adequately as their urban counterparts, although with a time lag of around 3 years (see Figure 9-5).

Furthermore, when children are interviewed by researchers from their own culture, who know the language and customs of the culture well and who use reasoning tasks that are related to domains important to the culture, the children are considerably more likely to display concrete operational thinking (Nyiti, 1982; Jahoda, 1983). Ultimately, such research suggests that Piaget was right when he argued that concrete operations were universally achieved during middle childhood. Although school-age children in some cultures may differ from Westerners in the demonstration of certain cognitive skills, the most probable explanation of the difference is that the non-Western children have had different sorts of experiences from those that permit children in Western societies to perform well on Piagetian measures of conservation and concrete operations. The progress of cognitive development, then, cannot be understood without looking at the nature of a child's culture (Jahoda & Lewis, 1988; Beilin & Pufall, 1992; Berry et al., 1992; Mishra, 1997).

Information Processing in Middle Childhood

It is a significant achievement for first-graders to learn basic math tasks, such as addition and subtraction of single-digit numbers, as well as the spelling of simple words such as *dog* and *run*. But by the time they reach the sixth grade, children are able to work with fractions and decimals, and *exhibit* and *residence* are typical spelling words.

According to *information-processing approaches*, children become increasingly sophisticated in their handling of information. Like computers, they can process more data as the

Furthermore, school-age children's mastery of grammar improves. For instance, the use of the passive voice is rare during the early school-age years (as in "The dog was walked by Jon," compared with the active voice "Jon walked the dog"). Six- and 7-year-olds only infrequently use conditional sentences, such as "If Sarah will set the table, I will wash the dishes." However, over the course of middle childhood, the use of both passive voice and conditional sentences increases. In addition, children's understanding of *syntax*, the rules that indicate how words and phrases can be combined to form sentences, grows during middle childhood.

By the time they reach first grade, most children pronounce words quite accurately. However, certain *phonemes*, units of sound, remain troublesome. For instance, the ability to pronounce *j, v, th,* and *zh* sounds develops later than the ability to pronounce other phonemes.

School-age children also may have difficulty decoding sentences when the meaning depends on *intonation*, or tone of voice. For example, consider the sentence, "George gave a book to David and he gave one to Bill." If the word *he* is emphasized, the meaning is "George gave a book to David and David gave a different book to Bill." But if the intonation emphasizes the word *and*, then the meaning changes to "George gave a book to David and George also gave a book to Bill." School-age children cannot easily sort out subtleties such as these (Moshman, Glover, & Bruning, 1987; Woolfolk, 1993).

Children also become more competent during the school years in their use of *pragmatics*, the rules governing the use of language to communicate in a social context. Pragmatics concern children's ability to use appropriate and effective language in a given social setting.

For example, although children are aware of the rules of conversational turn-taking at the start of the early childhood period, their use of these rules is sometimes primitive. Consider the following conversation between 6-year-olds Yonnie and Max:

Yonnie: My dad drives a FedEx truck.
Max: My sister's name is Molly.
Yonnie: He gets up really early in the morning.
Max: She wet her bed last night.

Later, however, conversations show more give-and-take, with the second child actually responding to the comments of the first. For instance, this conversation between 11-year-olds Mia and Josh reflects a more sophisticated mastery of pragmatics:

Mia: I don't know what to get Claire for her birthday.
Josh: I'm getting her earrings.
Mia: She already has a lot of jewelry.
Josh: I don't think she has that much.

How Language Promotes Self-control.   The growing sophistication of their language helps school-age children control their behavior. For instance, in one experiment, children were told that they could have one marshmallow treat if they chose to eat one immediately, but two treats if they waited. Most of the children, who ranged in age from 4 to 8, chose to wait, but the strategies they used while waiting differed significantly.

The 4-year-olds often chose to look at the marshmallows while waiting, a strategy that was not terribly effective. In contrast, 6- and 8-year-olds used language to help them overcome temptation, although in different ways. The 6-year-olds spoke and sang to themselves, reminding themselves that if they waited they would get more treats in the end. The 8-year-olds focused on aspects of the marshmallows that were not related to taste, such as their appearance, which helped them to wait.

Metalinguistic Awareness.   One of the most significant developments in middle childhood is the increasing metalinguistic awareness of children. **Metalinguistic awareness** is an understanding of one's own use of language. By the time children are 5 or 6, they under-

metalinguistic awareness *an understanding of one's own use of language*

The increasing diversity of the United States is illustrated by this Girl Scout troop, sponsored by a Buddhist church.

bilingualism *the use of more than one language*

stand that language is governed by a set of rules. Whereas in the early years they learn and comprehended these rules implicitly, during middle childhood children come to understand them more explicitly (Kemper & Vernooy, 1993).

Metalinguistic awareness helps children achieve comprehension when information is fuzzy or incomplete. For instance, when preschoolers are given ambiguous or unclear information, they rarely ask for clarification, and they tend to blame themselves if they do not understand. By the time they reach the age of 7 or 8, children realize that miscommunication may be due to factors attributable not only to themselves, but to the person communicating with them as well. Consequently, school-age children are more likely to ask for clarifications of information that is unclear to them (Beal & Belgrad, 1990; Kemper & Vernooy, 1993).

Bilingualism: Speaking in Many Tongues

> For picture day at New York's P.S. 217, a neighborhood elementary school in Brooklyn, the notice to parents was translated into five languages. That was a nice gesture, but insufficient: More than 40 percent of the children are immigrants whose families speak any one of twenty-six languages, ranging from Armenian to Urdu. (Leslie, 1991, p. 56)

From the smallest towns to the biggest cities, the voices with which children speak are changing. In seven states, including Texas, New York, and Colorado, more than a quarter of the students are not native English speakers. In fact, English is the second language for more than 32 million Americans. **Bilingualism**—the use of more than one language—is growing increasingly common (U.S. Bureau of the Census, 1993; see Figure 9-6).

FIGURE 9-6

THE VOICES OF AMERICA

The number of U.S. residents over the age of 5 who speak at home a language other than English is substantial.

(*Source:* U.S. Bureau of the Census, 1993.)

The Top 20 Languages

Spanish	
French	
German	
Italian	
Chinese	
Tagalog	
Polish	
Korean	
Vietnamese	
Portuguese	
Japanese	
Greek	
Arabic	
Hindu, Urdu	
Russian	
Yiddish	
Thai	
Persian	
French Creole	
Armenian	

Number of Speakers (in millions): 0 2 4 6 8 10 12 14 16 18 20

Developmental Diversity

The Benefits of Bilingualism: Children Do Swimmingly in Language-Immersion Programs

One by one, the first graders recite the characters the teacher has drawn on the board. Only it's not the ABCs that these six- and seven-year-olds are rattling off but the hiragana characters of the Japanese language.

The students in this inner-city public-school classroom have no Japanese heritage. In fact, almost all of them are African American. But all day long, they hear only Japanese from their teachers. They recite their math problems in Japanese. Their language readers open from left to right as in Japan. When the teacher asks in Japanese, "Do you understand?" the children chirp, "Hai." (Reitman, 1994, B1)

These students, enrolled in Detroit's Foreign Language Immersion and Cultural Studies School, are participating in a program designed to capitalize on younger children's ability to learn second languages with relative ease. The school represents a sharp departure from traditional language instruction. In what is called a *language-immersion program*, the school teaches all of its subjects in a foreign language.

Children in language-immersion programs make rapid advances with the foreign language in which they are being taught, for several reasons. One is that, unlike older children, they have not learned to be frightened by the task of learning a language. Furthermore, they feel relatively little embarrassment if they mispronounce words or make grammatical errors.

For those enrolled in language-immersion programs, learning a second language provides several benefits beyond command of the language. It can also raise self-esteem due to the sense of mastery that comes from achieving proficiency in a difficult subject. Moreover, it can make students more sensitive to other cultures. Furthermore, although parents sometimes worry that their children's progress in English will be limited by their concentration on a foreign language, such concerns seem misplaced. Research suggests that children in immersion programs perform as well as their peers, and sometimes even better, in English grammar, reading comprehension, and tests of English vocabulary (Larsen-Freeman & Long, 1991).

On the other hand, not all language-immersion programs are successful. The most positive results have come from programs in which majority group children are learning languages that are not spoken by the dominant culture. In contrast, when minority group children who enter school knowing only a language other than English are immersed in English-only programs, the results are less positive. In fact, children from minority language backgrounds enrolled in English-only programs sometimes perform worse in both English *and* their native languages than same-age peers (Genesee, 1994).

Clearly, the effectiveness of language-immersion programs varies widely. Furthermore, such programs are difficult to operate administratively. Finding an adequate number of bilingual teachers can be difficult, and teacher and student attrition can be a problem. Still, the results of participation in immersion programs can be impressive, particularly as knowledge of multiple languages becomes less of a luxury and more of a necessity in today's multicultural world. (See also the "Speaking of Development" interview).

Children who speak English either haltingly or, initially, not at all present a challenge to educators. One approach to educating non-English speakers is *bilingual education*, in which children are initially taught in their native language, while at the same time learning English. With bilingual instruction, students are able to develop a strong foundation in basic subject areas using their native language. The ultimate goal of most bilingual education programs is to shift instruction into English.

An alternative approach is to immerse students in English, teaching solely in that language. To proponents of this approach, initially teaching students in a language other than English hinders students' efforts to learn English and slows their integration into society.

The two quite different approaches have been highly politicized, with some politicians arguing in favor of "English only" laws. Still, the psychological research is clear in suggesting that knowing more than one language offers several cognitive advantages. For instance, speakers of two languages show greater cognitive flexibility. Because they have a wider range of linguistic possibilities to choose from as they assess a situation, they can solve problems with greater creativity and versatility. Furthermore, some research suggests that learning in one's native tongue is associated with higher self-esteem in minority students (Romaine, 1994; Wright & Taylor, 1995).

Bilingual students often have greater metalinguistic awareness, understanding the rules of language more explicitly. They even may score higher on tests of intelligence, according to some research. For example, one survey of French- and English-speaking schoolchildren in Canada found that bilingual students scored significantly higher on both verbal and nonverbal tests of intelligence than those who spoke only one language (Lambert & Peal, 1972; Ricciardelli, 1992; Genesee, 1994; Bochner, 1996).

Finally, because many linguists contend that universal processes underlie language acquisition, as we noted in Chapter 5, instruction in a native language may enhance instruction in a second language. In fact, as we discuss next, many educators believe that second-language learning should be a regular part of elementary schooling (Lindholm, 1991; Perozzi & Sanchez, 1992; Yelland, Pollard, & Mercuri, 1993).

The Ebonics Controversy: Is Black English a Separate Language from Standard English?

Although the word *Ebonics* had been in use since the 1970s, few people had heard of it before the Oakland, California, school board declared it a distinctive language. Their decision affirmed that Ebonics—a word derived from a combination of the words *ebony* and *phonics*—was a language separate from English. According to the school board's declaration, Ebonics was a distinct language with roots in Africa, one spoken by many African Americans in inner cities. The school board ordered that students who spoke Ebonics should receive their initial classroom instruction using Ebonics and not standard English (Applebome, 1997).

The school board's decision provoked a national controversy, and within a month the board had reversed its decision. Members of the board said that they had never meant for students to learn anything other than standard English, and that they had merely wanted recognition for the fact that many African American students needed instruction to make the leap from the Ebonics they spoke at home to standard English.

The controversy raised several issues, none of which have had definitive resolutions. For instance, linguists vary in their views of the legitimacy of Ebonics as a language. According to linguist Dennis Baron, most linguists consider what they call African American Vernacular English, or sometimes Black English, to be a dialect or variety of standard English. Although it has some characteristics that are derived from African languages, it can be understood fairly well by speakers of standard English. Furthermore, certain features of Ebonics, such as the use of different conjugations of the verb "to be" (as in "I be going") are evidence that it is not a separate language, but a dialect of English.

On the other hand, it is also clear that Black English operates according to a set of consistent rules and conventions. Although in the past African American Vernacular English has been treated as a form of speech disability, one that required the intervention of speech pathologists or special education teachers, today educators have become more accepting. Probably most educators would argue that any such nonstandard English is not an *inferior* form of language, but one that is *different*—an important distinction. Furthermore, they point out that many words that have their origins in Black English have entered the mainstream of standard English, including "hip," "cool," "chill out," "slick," and "rip-off" (Sanchez, 1997).

Still, the issues revolving around Ebonics or Black English or African American Vernacular English—or whatever else it may be called—are not likely to go away soon. The controversy raises important issues that are social as well as linguistic.

Lauro Cavazos, Former Secretary of Education

Education: .... **B.A., M.A., Texas Tech University; Ph.D., Iowa State University; numerous honorary degrees**

Position: .... **United States Secretary of Education, 1988–1990**

Home: .... **Concord, MA**

As the 21st century dawns, many facets of society in America will change, and much of that change will be the result of education, according to Lauro F. Cavazos, Secretary of Education (1988–90) in the administration of President George Bush.

In his cabinet position Cavazos worked toward three main goals: raising the expectations of students, teachers, and parents; providing access to quality education for all students, especially those most at risk of failing; and promoting the notion that quality education is the responsibility of every member of society. This was a tremendous task, considering the growing diversity of the student population.

"First of all, we're finally starting to recognize that there is cultural diversity and acknowledge it in a serious fashion," says the sixth-generation Texan. "Already some 30 percent of the students in elementary and secondary public education are Hispanic or African American, and these numbers are going to continue to grow."

Noting the increase in bilingual students, Cavazos points out that the trend will have an impact on the areas of literature, history, geography, and economics, among others—all contributing to the changing of American society.

"We need to recognize that diversity is a bonus in America," he notes. "I'm a strong supporter of bilingual education, but certain conditions need to be met in order for it to work. First, I think non-English-speaking students need to learn English as quickly as possible, hopefully within a year, but at most three years. Second, they should retain their original language, whatever that language is—Cambodian, Spanish, or whatever. And third, each group should be expected to add to the culture of America, because America is an amalgamation of many different cultures. We need to recognize that America is already a pluralistic society."

Maintaining that one of America's biggest problems is an education deficit, Cavazos stresses the importance of the educational development of children.

"Some 27 million Americans are illiterate, and 40 to 50 million Americans read at the fourth-grade level," he says. "We have 600,000 to 700,000 youngsters who drop out of school each year, and we haven't had a significant increase in SAT scores in years. I call that the education deficit.

"Our first major goal is to help those students who are in need—the minorities, handicapped, students in special education, and so forth. Our second central goal is to support good research. I've had tremendous resistance to some of the things I've said, and some people really take offense," Cavazos states. "But if we don't change things, in one or two generations this nation is going to be in serious trouble."

"We're finally starting to recognize that there is cultural diversity and acknowledge it in a serious fashion."

"We need to recognize that diversity is a bonus in America."

REVIEW AND RETHINK

REVIEW

- According to Piaget, school-age children are in the concrete operational stage of cognitive development, characterized by the application of logical processes to concrete problems.

- Information-processing approaches attribute cognitive development during the school years to quantitative improvements in memory and in the sophistication of the mental programs that the school-age child can handle.

- Vygotsky's approach, which has influenced instruction significantly, holds that children in the school years should have the opportunity to experiment and participate actively with their colleagues in their educational experiences.

- The three processes of memory—encoding, storage, and retrieval—come under increasing control during the school years, and the development of meta-memory permits the use of control strategies to improve cognitive processing and memorization.

- Language development in middle childhood is characterized by improvements in vocabulary, syntax, and pragmatics; by the use of language as a self-control device; and by the growth of metalinguistic awareness.

- Bilingualism, the ability to speak more than one language, can produce improvements in cognitive flexibility, metalinguistic awareness, and even IQ test performance.

RETHINK

- Do you think a non-Western Piaget working in a different culture might have developed a theory of stages involving cognitive tasks that Western children would have difficulty performing without explicit instruction? Why?

- Why do control strategies such as grouping into patterns and using keywords work? What do they tell us about memory?

- We can infer that two rules of pragmatics, which govern the social uses of language, are (1) speakers should take turns, and (2) speakers should address the same topic. Name other rules of pragmatics.

- Why might instruction in one's first language enhance instruction in another language, such as English? Do the notions of metalinguistic awareness and universal grammar relate to this phenomenon?

SCHOOLING: THE THREE RS (AND MORE) OF MIDDLE CHILDHOOD

As the eyes of the six other children in his reading group turned to him, Glenn shifted uneasily in his chair. Reading had never come easily to him, and he always felt anxious when it was his turn to read aloud. But as his teacher nodded in encouragement, he plunged in, hesitantly at first, then gaining momentum as he read the story about a mother's first day on a new job. He found that he could read the passage quite nicely, and he felt a surge of happiness and pride at his accomplishment. When he was done, he broke into a broad smile as his teacher said simply, "Well done, Glenn."

Small moments such as these, repeated over and over, make—or break—a child's educational experience. Schooling marks a time when society formally attempts to transfer to new generations its accumulated body of knowledge, beliefs, values, and wisdom. The success with which this transfer is managed determines, in a very real sense, the future fortunes of the world.

The 1990s have seen a return to the basic fundamentals of education that include emphasis on the traditional three *R*s of reading, writing, and arithmetic.

Schooling Around the World: Who Gets Educated?

In the United States, as in most developed countries, a primary school education is both a universal right and a legal requirement. Virtually all children are provided with a free education through the 12th grade.

Children in other parts of the world are not so fortunate. In 1990, more than 100 million children, 60 percent of them female, did not have access to even a primary school education. An additional 100 million children did not complete a basic education, and overall more than 960 million individuals (two-thirds of them women) were illiterate throughout their lives (see Figure 9-7). Projections suggest that by the year 2000 more than 160 million of the world's children will not have access to even a primary school education (World Conference on Education for All, 1990).

In almost all developing countries, fewer females than males receive formal education, a discrepancy found at every level of schooling. Even in developed countries, women lag behind men in their exposure to science and technological topics. These differences reflect widespread and deeply held cultural and parental biases that favor males over females.

FIGURE 9-7

THE PLAGUE OF ILLITERACY

Illiteracy remains a significant problem worldwide, particularly for women. Across the world, close to a billion people were illiterate throughout their lives.

(*Source:* UNESCO, 1990.)

■ Male

■ Female

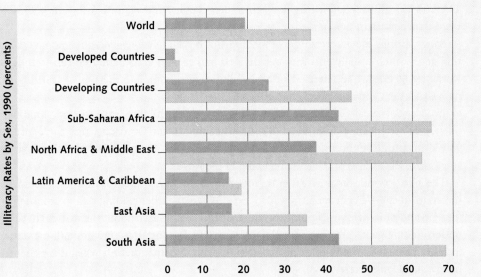

What Makes Children Ready for School?

Do children who are younger than most of the other children in their grade suffer as a result? According to traditional wisdom, the answer is yes. Because younger children are assumed to be slightly less advanced developmentally than their peers, it has been assumed that such children would be at a competitive disadvantage. In some cases, teachers have recommended that students delay entry into kindergarten in order to cope better academically and emotionally.

However, recent research has begun to dispel this view. According to a massive study conducted by developmental psychologist Frederick Morrison, children who are among the youngest in first grade progress at the same rate as the oldest. Although they were slightly behind older first-graders in reading, the difference was negligible. It was also clear that parents who chose to hold their children back in kindergarten, thereby ensuring that they would be among the oldest in first grade and after, were not doing their children a favor. These older children did no better than their younger classmates (Morrison, 1993; DeAngelis, 1994).

Other research even has identified some delayed negative reaction to delayed entry. For example, one longitudinal study examined adolescents whose entrance into kindergarten was delayed by a year. Even though many seemed to show no ill effects from the delay during elementary school, during adolescence a surprising number of these children had emotional and behavioral problems (Byrd, Weitzman, & Auinger, 1997).

In short, delaying children's entry into school does not necessarily provide an advantage, and in some cases may actually be harmful. Ultimately age, per se, is not a critical indicator of when children should begin school. Instead, the start of formal schooling is more reasonably tied to overall developmental readiness, the product of a complex combination of several factors.

Reading: Learning to Decode the Meaning Behind Words

The efforts of La-Toya Pankey (described in the chapter prologue) to improve her reading are no small matter, for there is no other task that it is more fundamental to schooling than learning to read. Reading involves a significant number of skills, from low-level cognitive skills (the identification of single letters and associating letters with sounds) to higher-level skills (matching written words with meanings located in long-term memory and using context and background knowledge to determine the meaning of a sentence).

Development of reading skill generally occurs in several broad, frequently overlapping, stages (see Table 9-1; Chall, 1979). In *Stage 0*, which lasts from birth to the start of first grade, children learn the essential prerequisites for reading, including identification of the letters in the alphabet, sometimes writing their names, and reading a few very familiar words (such as their own names or "stop" on a stop sign).

Stage 1 brings the first real type of reading, but it is largely *phonological recoding skill*. At this stage, which usually encompasses the first and second grade, children can sound out words by blending the letters together. Children also complete the job of learning the names of letters and the sounds that go with them.

In *Stage 2*, typically around second and third grades, children learn to read aloud with fluency. However, they do not attach much meaning to the words, because the effort involved in simply sounding out words is usually so great that relatively few cognitive resources are left over to process the meaning of the words.

The next period, *Stage 3*, extends from fourth to eighth grades. Reading becomes a means to an end—in particular, a way to learn. Whereas earlier reading was an accomplishment in and of itself, by this point children use reading to learn about the world. However, understanding gained from reading is not complete. For instance, one limitation children have at this stage is that they are able to comprehend information only when it is presented from a single perspective.

TABLE 9-1

DEVELOPMENT OF READING SKILLS

Stage	Age	Key Characteristics
Stage 0	Birth to start of first grade	learns prerequisites for reading, such as identification of the letters
Stage 1	First and second grades	learns phonological recoding skills; starts reading
Stage 2	Second and third grades	reads aloud fluently, but without much meaning
Stage 3	Fourth to eighth grades	uses reading as a means for learning
Stage 4	Eighth grade and beyond	understands reading in terms of reflecting multiple points of view

(*Source:* Based on Chall, 1979.)

In the final period, *Stage 4*, children are able to read and process information that reflects multiple points of view. This ability, which begins during the transition into high school, permits children to develop a far more sophisticated understanding of material. This explains why great works of literature are not read at an earlier stage of education. It is not so much that younger children do not have the vocabulary to understand such works (although this is partially true); it is that they lack the ability to understand the multiple points of view that sophisticated literature invariably presents.

The mechanisms by which information is processed during reading lies at the heart of an ongoing debate among educators regarding the most effective means of teaching reading. According to proponents of *code-based approaches to reading*, reading should be taught by presenting the basic skills that underlie reading. Code-based approaches emphasize the components of reading, such as the sounds of letters and their combinations—phonics—and how letters and sounds are combined to make words. They suggest that reading consists of processing the individual components of words, combining them into words, and then using the words to derive the meaning of written sentences and passages (Rayner & Pollatsek, 1989; Vellutino, 1991).

In contrast, some educators argue that reading is taught most successfully by using a whole-language approach. In *whole-language approaches to reading*, reading is viewed as a natural process, similar to the acquisition of oral language. According to this view, children should learn to read through exposure to complete writing—sentences, stories, poems, lists, charts, and other examples of actual uses of writing. Instead of being taught to painstakingly sound out words, children are encouraged to make guesses about the meaning of words based on the total context in which they appear. Through such a trial-and-error approach, children come to learn whole words and phrases at a time, gradually becoming proficient readers. To encourage this process, children are immersed in literature and encouraged to take informed guesses as they work through it. As their skill increases, they are better able to quickly look at a word and automatically retrieve its meaning from long-term memory (Smith, 1992; Graham & Harris, 1997).

Research has not been able to ascertain whether the whole-language or code-based approach to reading instruction is better. Both seem to be effective not only in developing proficient readers, but also in producing the same level of positive attitudes toward reading. In fact, the National Research Council, in a landmark 1998 report, argued that the optimum approach was to use a combination of elements of code-based and whole-language approaches. Still, the debate continues to rage (Pressley, 1994; Stahl, McKenna, & Pagnucco, 1994; McKenna et al., 1995; Steinberg, 1998).

Educational Trends: Beyond the Three Rs

Schooling in the late 1990s is very different from what it was as recently as a decade ago. U.S. schools are experiencing a definite return to the educational fundamentals embodied in the traditional three Rs (reading, writing, and arithmetic). As can be seen in the model curriculum promoted by the U.S. Department of Education (Table 9-2), the emphasis on educational basics is strong. This trend marks a departure from the 1970s and 1980s, when the emphasis was on socioemotional issues and on allowing students to choose study topics on the basis of their interests, instead of in accordance with a set curriculum (Short & Talley, 1997).

Elementary classrooms in the late 1990s also stress issues of individual accountability. Teachers are more likely to be held responsible for their students' learning, and both students and teachers are more likely to be required to take tests, developed at the state or national level, to assess their competence (Woolfolk, 1993).

TABLE 9-2

JAMES MADISON ELEMENTARY SCHOOL: A MODEL CURRICULUM FOR KINDERGARTEN THROUGH GRADE 6

Subject	Kindergarten Through Grade 3	Grades 4 Through 6
ENGLISH	INTRODUCTION TO READING AND WRITING (phonics, silent and oral reading, basic rules of grammar and spelling, vocabulary, writing and penmanship, elementary composition, and library skills)	INTRODUCTION TO CRITICAL READING (children's literature, independent reading and book reports, more advanced grammar, spelling and vocabulary, and composition skills)
SOCIAL STUDIES	INTRODUCTION TO HISTORY, GEOGRAPHY AND CIVICS (significant Americans, explorers, Native Americans; American holidays, customs, and symbols; citizenship; and landscape, climate, and mapwork)	Grade 4: U.S. HISTORY TO CIVIL WAR Grade 5: U.S. HISTORY SINCE 1865 Grade 6: WORLD HISTORY TO THE MIDDLE AGES
MATHEMATICS	INTRODUCTION TO MATHEMATICS (numbers, basic operations, fractions and decimals, rounding, geometric shapes, measurement of length, area, and volume, bar graphs, and estimation and elementary statistics)	INTERMEDIATE ARITHMETIC AND GEOMETRY (number theory, negative numbers, percentages, and exponents, line graphs, the Pythagorean theorem, and basic probability)
SCIENCE	INTRODUCTION TO SCIENCE (plants and animals, the food chain, the solar system, rocks and minerals, weather, magnets, energy and motion, properties of matter, and simple experiments)	Grade 4: EARTH SCIENCE AND OTHER TOPICS Grade 5: LIFE SCIENCE AND OTHER TOPICS Grade 6: PHYSICAL SCIENCE AND OTHER TOPICS
FOREIGN LANGUAGE	(OPTIONAL)	INTRODUCTION TO FOREIGN LANGUAGE (basic vocabulary, grammar, reading, writing, conversation, and cultural material)
FINE ARTS	MUSIC AND VISUAL ART (songs, recordings, musical sounds and instruments, painting, craftmaking, and visual effects)	MUSIC AND VISUAL ART (great composers, musical styles and forms, elementary music theory, great painters, interpretation of art, and creative projects)
PHYSICAL EDUCATION AND HEALTH	PHYSICAL EDUCATION AND HEALTH (body control, fitness, sports, games, and exercises, sportsmanship, safety, hygiene, nutrition, and drug prevention education)	PHYSICAL EDUCATION AND HEALTH (team and individual sports, first aid, drug prevention education, and appropriate sex education)

(*Source:* U.S. Department of Education, 1988.)

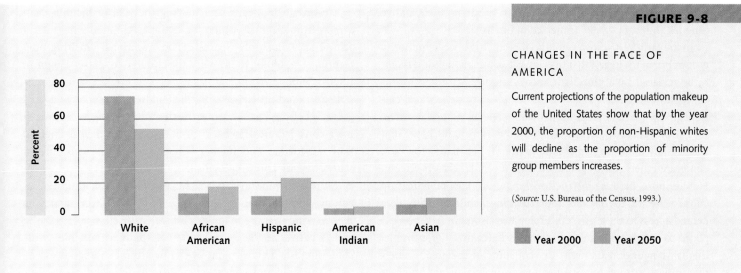

FIGURE 9-8

CHANGES IN THE FACE OF AMERICA

Current projections of the population makeup of the United States show that by the year 2000, the proportion of non-Hispanic whites will decline as the proportion of minority group members increases.

(*Source:* U.S. Bureau of the Census, 1993.)

■ Year 2000   ■ Year 2050

Furthermore, education in the late 1990s pays increased attention to issues involving student diversity and multiculturalism. And with good reason: The demographic makeup of students in the United States is undergoing an extraordinary shift. For instance, the proportion of Hispanics will in all likelihood more than double in the next 50 years. Moreover, by the year 2050, Caucasians will make up just over half of the total population of the United States (U.S. Bureau of Census, 1993; see Figure 9-8). Consequently, educators have been increasingly serious about multicultural concerns.

multicultural education   *a form of education in which the goal is to help minority students develop competence in the culture of the majority group while maintaining positive group identities that build on their original cultures*

cultural assimilation model   *the model that fostered the view of American society as the proverbial melting pot*

Developmental Diversity

Multicultural Education

Since the earliest period of formal education in the United States, classrooms have been populated by individuals from a broad range of backgrounds and experiences. Yet it is only relatively recently that variations in student backgrounds have been viewed as one of the major challenges—and opportunities—that educators face.

In fact, the diversity of background and experience in the classroom relates to a fundamental objective of education, which is to provide a formal mechanism to transmit the information a society holds important. As the famous anthropologist Margaret Mead once said, "In its broadest sense, education is the cultural process, the way in which each newborn human infant, born with a potentiality for learning greater than that of any other mammal, is transformed into a full member of a specific human society, sharing with the other members of a specific human culture" (Mead, 1942, p. 633).

Culture, then, can be thought of as a set of behaviors, beliefs, values, and expectations shared by members of a particular society. But although culture is often thought of in a relatively broad

context (as in "Western culture" or "Asian culture"), it is also possible to focus on particular *subcultural* groups within a larger, more encompassing culture. For example, we can consider particular racial, ethnic, religious, socioeconomic, or even gender groups within the United States as manifesting characteristics of a subculture.

Membership in a cultural or subcultural group might be of only passing interest to educators were it not for the fact that students' cultural backgrounds have a substantial impact on the way that they—and their peers—are educated. In fact, in recent years a considerable amount of thought has gone into establishing **multicultural education**, a form of education in which the goal is to help minority students develop competence in the culture of the majority group while maintaining positive group identities that build on their original cultures (Grant & Sleeter, 1986).

Cultural Assimilation or Pluralistic Society?   Multicultural education developed in part as a reaction to a **cultural assimilation model**, which fostered the view of American society as the proverbial melting pot. According to this view, the goal of education was to assimilate individual cultural identities into a unique, unified American culture. In practical terms this meant that students were discouraged from speaking their native tongues and were totally immersed in English.

In the early 1970s, however, educators and members of minority groups began to suggest that the cultural assimilation model ought to be replaced by a **pluralistic society model**. According to this conception, American society is made up of diverse, coequal cultural groups that should preserve their individual cultural features.

The pluralistic society model grew in part from the belief that teachers, by discouraging children's use of their native tongues, denigrated their cultural heritages and lowered their self-esteem. Furthermore, because instructional materials inevitably feature culture-specific events and understandings, children who were denied access to their own cultural materials might never be exposed to important aspects of their backgrounds. For example, English-language texts rarely present some of the great themes that appear throughout Spanish literature and history (such as the search for the Fountain of Youth and the Don Juan legend). Hispanic students immersed in such texts might never come to understand important components of their own heritage.

Ultimately, educators began to argue that the presence of students representing diverse cultures enriched and broadened the educational experience of all students. Pupils and teachers exposed to people from different backgrounds could better understand the world and gain greater sensitivity to the values and needs of others.

Fostering a Bicultural Identity. Today, most educators agree that the pluralistic society model is the most valid one for schooling, and that minority children should be encouraged to develop a **bicultural identity**. They recommend that children be supported in maintaining their original cultural identities while they integrate themselves into the dominant culture. This view suggests that an individual can live as a member of two cultures, with two cultural identities, without having to choose one over the other (LaFromboise, Coleman, & Gerton, 1993).

However, the means of achieving the goal of biculturalism are far from clear. Consider, for example, children who enter a school speaking only Spanish. The traditional "melting-pot" technique would be to immerse the children in classes taught in English while providing a crash course in English-language instruction (and little else) until the children demonstrate a suitable level of proficiency. Unfortunately, the traditional approach has a considerable drawback: Until the children master English, they fall further and further behind their peers who entered school already knowing English.

More contemporary approaches emphasize a bicultural strategy, in which children are encouraged to maintain simultaneous membership in more than one culture. Instruction begins in the child's native language and shifts as rapidly as possible to include English. This element of the bicultural strategy is essentially the bilingual education approach discussed above; but there is more to bicultural education.

Even after the children have mastered English, some instruction in the native language continues. At the same time, the school conducts a program of multicultural education for all students, in which teachers present material on the cultural backgrounds and traditions of speakers of all the languages spoken in the school. Such instruction is designed to enhance the self-image of speakers from both majority and minority cultures (Grant & Sleeter, 1986).

Successful bicultural programs also attempt to bring multiple languages into the context of everyday social interactions. Children are encouraged to use a variety of languages in their social relationships and to become equally adept at several languages.

Although most educational experts favor bicultural approaches, the general public does not always agree. For instance, a national "English-only" movement has as one of its goals the prohibition of school instruction in any language other than English. Whether such a perspective will prevail remains to be seen.

Intelligence: Determining Individual Strengths

"Why should you tell the truth?" "How far is Los Angeles from New York?" "A table is made of wood; a window of _____."

As 10-year-old Hyacinth sat hunched over her desk, trying to answer a long series of questions like these, she tried to guess the point of the test she was taking in her fifth-grade classroom. Clearly, the test didn't cover material that her teacher, Ms. White-Johnston, had talked about in class.

"What number comes next in this series: 1, 3, 7, 15, 31, ____?"

As she continued to work her way through the questions, she gave up trying to guess the rationale for the test. She'd leave that to her teacher, she sighed to herself. Rather than attempting to figure out what it all meant, she simply tried to do her best on the individual test items.

pluralistic society model   the concept that American society is made up of diverse, coequal cultural groups that should preserve their individual cultural features

bicultural identity   maintaining one's original cultural identity while integrating oneself into the dominant culture

Hyacinth might be surprised to learn that she was not alone in questioning the meaning and import of the items on the test she was taking. For although the test items were painstakingly developed, many developmental psychologists would admit to harboring their own doubts as to whether questions such as these are appropriate to the task of assessing what they are designed to measure: intelligence.

Understanding just what is meant by the concept of intelligence has proven to be a major challenge for educational psychologists and other authorities interested in delineating what separates intelligent from unintelligent behavior. Nonexperts have their own concepts of intelligence: One survey found, for instance, that lay persons believe intelligence consists of three components—problem-solving ability, verbal ability, and social competence. It has been more difficult for experts to concur (Sternberg et al., 1981; Weinberg, 1989; Howe, 1997). Still, a general definition of intelligence is possible: **Intelligence** is the capacity to understand the world, think with rationality, and use resources effectively when faced with challenges (Wechsler, 1975).

Part of the difficulty in defining intelligence stems from the many—and sometimes unsatisfactory—paths that have been followed over the years in the quest to distinguish more intelligent people from less intelligent ones. To understand how educational psychologists have approached the task of devising batteries of assessments, called *intelligence tests*, we need to consider some of the historical milestones in the area of intelligence.

Intelligence Benchmarks: Differentiating the Intelligent from the Unintelligent.

The Paris school system was faced with a problem at the dawning of the 20th century: A significant number of children were not benefiting from regular instruction. Unfortunately, these children—many of whom we would now call mentally retarded—were generally not identified early enough to shift them to special classes. The French minister of instruction approached psychologist Alfred Binet with the problem of devising a technique for the early identification of students who might benefit from instruction outside the regular classroom.

Binet tackled his task in a thoroughly practical manner. His years of observing school-aged children suggested that previous efforts to distinguish intelligent from unintelligent students—some of which were based on reaction time or keenness of sight—were off the mark. Instead, he launched a trial-and-error process in which items and tasks were administered to students who had been previously identified by teachers as being either "bright" or "dull." He retained for the tests tasks that the bright students completed correctly and the dull students failed to complete correctly. He discarded tasks that did not discriminate between the two groups. The end result of this process was a test that reliably distinguished students who had previously been identified as fast or slow learners.

Binet's pioneering efforts in intelligence testing left three important legacies. The first was his pragmatic approach to the construction of intelligence tests. Binet did not have theoretical preconceptions about what intelligence was. Instead, he used a trial-and-error approach to psychological measurement that continues to serve as the predominant approach to test construction today. His definition of intelligence as *that which his test measured* has been adopted by many modern psychologists, and it is particularly popular among test developers who respect the widespread utility of intelligence tests but wish to avoid arguments about the underlying nature of intelligence.

Our second inheritance from Binet stems from his focus on linking intelligence and school success. Binet's procedure for constructing an intelligence test ensured that intelligence—defined as performance on the test—and school success would be virtually one and the same. Binet's intelligence test and its current successors, then, have become reasonable indicators of the degree to which students possess attributes that contribute to successful school performance. Unfortunately, they do not provide particularly useful information regarding a vast number of other attributes that are largely unrelated to academic proficiency.

Finally, Binet developed a procedure of assigning each intelligence test score to a **mental age**, the age of the children taking the test who, on average, achieved that score. For example, if a 6-year-old girl received a score of 30 on the test, and this was the average score

The French educator Alfred Binet originated the intelligence test.

intelligence the capacity to understand the world, think with rationality, and use resources effectively when faced with challenges

mental age the typical intelligence level found for people at a given chronological age

received by 10-year-olds, her mental age would be considered 10 years. Similarly, a 15-year-old boy who scored a 90 on the test—thereby matching the mean score for 15-year-olds—would be assigned a mental age of 15 years.

Although assigning a mental age to students provides an indication of whether or not they are performing at the same level as their peers, it does not permit adequate comparisons between students of different **chronological**, or **physical, ages**. By using mental age alone, for instance, it would be assumed that a 15-year-old responding with a mental age of 17 years would be as bright as a 6-year-old responding with a mental age of 8 years, when actually the 6-year-old would be showing a much greater *relative* degree of brightness.

A solution to this problem comes in the form of the **intelligence quotient**, or **IQ score**, a measure of intelligence that takes into account a student's mental *and* chronological age. The traditional method of calculating an IQ score uses the following formula, in which MA stands for mental age and CA for chronological age:

$$\text{IQ SCORE} = \frac{\text{MA}}{\text{CA}} \times 100$$

As a bit of trial-and-error with this formula demonstrates, people whose mental age (MA) is equal to their chronological age (CA) will always have an IQ of 100. Furthermore, if the chronological age exceeds the mental age—implying below-average intelligence—the score will be below 100; and if the chronological age is lower than the mental age—suggesting above-average intelligence—the score will be above 100.

Using this formula, we can return to our earlier example of a 15-year-old who scores at a 17-year-old mental age. This student's IQ is 17/15 × 100, or 113. In comparison, the IQ of a 6-year-old scoring at a mental age of 8 is 8/6 × 100, or 133—a higher IQ score than the 15-year-old's.

Although the basic principles behind the calculation of an IQ score still hold, scores today are calculated in a more mathematically sophisticated manner and are known as *deviation IQ scores*. Rather than comparing performance to children who are younger and older, deviation IQ scores are computed by comparing other children of the same age. The average deviation IQ score remains set at 100, and tests are now statistically constructed so that approximately two-thirds of children of a given age fall within 15 points of the average score of 100, achieving scores between 85 and 115. As scores rise or fall beyond this range, the percentage of children in the same score category drops significantly.

Measuring IQ: Present-day Approaches to Intelligence. Since the time of Binet, tests of intelligence have become increasingly accurate in their measure of IQ. However, most of them can still trace their roots to his original work in one way or another. For example, one of the most widely used tests—the **Stanford-Binet Intelligence Scale**—began as an American revision of Binet's original test. The test consists of a series of items that vary according to the age of the person being tested. For instance, young children are asked to answer questions about everyday activities or to copy complex figures. Older people are asked to explain proverbs, solve analogies, and describe similarities between groups of words. The test is administered orally and test-takers are given progressively more difficult problems until they are unable to proceed.

The **Wechsler Intelligence Scale for Children (WISC-III)** and its adult version, the **Wechsler Adult Intelligence Scale (WAIS-III)**, are two other widely used intelligence tests. The tests provide separate measures of verbal and performance (or nonverbal) skills, as well as a total score. As you can see from the sample items in Figure 9-9, the verbal tasks are traditional word problems testing skills such as understanding a passage, whereas typical nonverbal tasks are copying a complex design, arranging pictures in a logical order, and assembling objects. The separate portions of the test allow for easier identification of any specific problems a test-taker may have. For example, significantly higher scores on the performance part of the test than on the verbal part may indicate difficulties in linguistic development.

chronological (or physical) age the actual age of the child taking the intelligence test

intelligence quotient (or IQ score) a measure of intelligence that takes into account a student's mental and chronological age

Stanford-Binet Intelligence Scale a test that consists of a series of items that vary according to the age of the person being tested

Wechsler Intelligence Scale for Children (WISC-III) a test for children that provides separate measures of verbal and performance (or nonverbal) skills, as well as a total score

Wechsler Adult Intelligence Scale (WAIS-III) a test for adults that provides separate measures of verbal and performance (or nonverbal) skills, as well as a total score

FIGURE 9-9

MEASURING INTELLIGENCE

The Wechsler Intelligence Scales for Children (WISC-III) includes items such as these.

NAME	GOAL OF ITEM	EXAMPLE
VERBAL SCALE		
Information	Assess general information	Where does honey come from?
Comprehension	Assess understanding and evaluation of social norms and past experience	Why do we use an umbrella when it rains?
Arithmetic	Assess math reasoning through verbal problems	Alice found three baseballs in a field. She gives two to her friend Jocelyn. How many baseballs does Alice have left?
Similarities	Test understanding of how objects or concepts are alike, tapping abstract reasoning	In what way are birds and airplanes alike?
PERFORMANCE SCALE		
Digit symbol	Assess speed of learning	Match symbols to numbers using key. 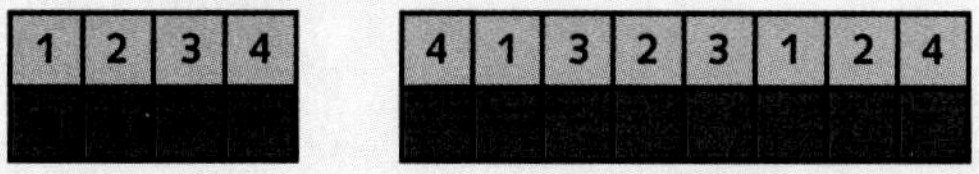
Picture completion	Visual memory and attention	Identify what is missing. 
Object assembly	Test understanding of relationship of parts to wholes	Put pieces together to form a whole. 

What IQ Tests Don't Tell: Alternative Conceptions of Intelligence. The intelligence tests used most frequently in school settings today share an underlying premise: Intelligence is composed of a single, unitary mental ability factor, commonly called *g* (Spearman, 1927). The *g* factor is assumed to underlie performance on every aspect of intelligence, and it is the *g* factor that intelligence tests presumably measure (Brody, 1997).

However, many theorists dispute the notion that intelligence is unidimensional (Weinberg, 1989). For example, some psychologists suggest that in fact two kinds of intelligence exist: fluid intelligence and crystallized intelligence (Cattell, 1967; 1987). **Fluid intelligence** is the ability to deal with new problems and situations. For example, a student asked to group a series of letters according to some criterion or to remember a set of numbers would be using fluid intelligence. In contrast, **crystallized intelligence** is the store of information, skills, and strategies that people have acquired through their use of fluid intelligence. A student would likely be relying on crystallized intelligence to solve a puzzle or deduce the solution to a mystery, in which it was necessary to draw on past experience.

Other theorists divide intelligence into an even greater number of parts. For example, psychologist Howard Gardner suggests that we have seven distinct intelligences, each relatively independent (see Table 9-3). Gardner suggests that these separate intelligences operate not in isolation, but together, depending on the type of activity in which we are engaged (Gardner & Hatch, 1989; Kronhaber, Krechevsky, & Gardner, 1991).

Taking another tack, psychologist Robert Sternberg suggests that intelligence is best thought of in terms of information processing. In this view, the way people store material in memory and later use it to solve intellectual tasks provides the most precise conception of intelligence. Rather than focusing on the structure of intelligence in the form of its various subcomponents, then, information-processing approaches examine the processes that underlie intelligent behavior (Sternberg, 1987, 1990, 1997).

Researchers who have divided tasks and problems into their component parts have noted critical differences in the nature and speed of problem-solving processes between those who score high and those who score low on traditional IQ tests (Sternberg, 1982). For instance, when verbal problems such as analogies are broken into their component parts, it becomes clear that people with higher intelligence levels differ from others not only in the number of problems they ultimately are able to solve, but in their method of solving the problems as well. People with high IQ scores spend more time on the initial stages of problem solving, retrieving relevant information from memory. In contrast, those who score lower on traditional IQ tests tend to spend less time on the initial stages, instead skipping ahead and making less informed guesses. The processes used in solving problems, then, may reflect important differences in intelligence.

Sternberg's work on information-processing approaches to intelligence has led him to develop the **triarchic theory of intelligence**. According to this model, intelligence consists of three aspects of information processing: the componential element, the experiential element, and the contextual element. The componential aspect of intelligence reflects how efficiently people can process and analyze information. Efficiency in these areas allows people to infer relationships among different parts of a problem, solve the problem, and then evaluate their solution. People who are strong on the componential element score highest on traditional tests of intelligence (Sternberg, 1997a).

The experiential element is the insightful component of intelligence. People who have a strong experiential element can easily compare new material with what they already know, and can combine and relate facts that they already know in novel and creative ways. Finally, the contextual element of intelligence concerns practical intelligence, or ways of dealing with the demands of the everyday environment.

In Sternberg's view, people vary in the degree to which each of these three elements is present, and a person's success on a given task reflects the match between the task and the person's specific pattern of strength on the three components of intelligence (Sternberg, 1985b, 1991, 1996, 1997a).

fluid intelligence *the ability to deal with new problems and situations*

crystallized intelligence *the store of information, skills, and strategies that people have acquired through education and prior experiences, and through their previous use of fluid intelligence*

triarchic theory of intelligence *a model that states that intelligence consists of three aspects of information processing: the componential element, the experiential element, and the contextual element*

TABLE 9-3

GARDNER'S SEVEN INTELLIGENCES

1. *Musical intelligence* (skills in tasks involving music). Case example:
When he was 3, Yehudi Menuhin was smuggled into the San Francisco Orchestra concerts by his parents. The sound of Louis Persinger's violin so entranced the youngster that he insisted on a violin for his birthday and Louis Persinger as his teacher. He got both. By the time he was 10 years old, Menuhin was an international performer.

2. *Bodily kinesthetic intelligence* (skills in using the whole body or various portions of it in the solution of problems or in the construction of products or displays, exemplified by dancers, athletes, actors, and surgeons). Case example:
Fifteen-year-old Babe Ruth played third base. During one game, his team's pitcher was doing poorly and Babe loudly criticized him from third base. Brother Mathias, the coach, called out, "Ruth, if you know so much about it, *you* pitch!" Babe was surprised and embarrassed because he had never pitched before, but Brother Mathias insisted. Ruth said later that at the very moment he took the pitcher's mound, he *knew* he was supposed to be a pitcher.

3. *Logical mathematical intelligence* (skills in problem solving and scientific thinking). Case example:
Barbara McClintock won the Nobel Prize in medicine for her work in microbiology. She describes one of her breakthroughs, which came after thinking about a problem for half an hour. . . : "Suddenly I jumped and ran back to the {corn} field. At the top of the field (the others were still at the bottom) I shouted, "Eureka, I have it!'"

4. *Linguistic intelligence* (skills involved in the production and use of language). Case example:
At the age of 10, T.S. Elliot created a magazine called *Fireside*, to which he was the sole contributor. In a three-day period during his winter vacation, he created eight complete issues.

5. *Spatial intelligence* (skills involving spatial configurations, such as those used by artists and architects). Case example:
Navigation around the Caroline Islands . . . is accomplished without instruments. . . . During the actual trip, the navigator must envision mentally a reference island as it passes under a particular star and from that he computes the number of segments completed, the proportion of the trip remaining, and any corrections in heading.

6. *Interpersonal intelligence* (skills in interacting with others, such as sensitivity to the moods, temperaments, motivations, and intentions of others). Case example:
When Anne Sullivan began instructing the deaf and blind Helen Keller, her task was one that had eluded others for years. Yet, just two weeks after beginning her work with Keller, Sullivan achieved a great success. In her words, "My heart is singing with joy this morning. A miracle has happened! The wild little creature of two weeks ago has been transformed into a gentle child."

7. *Intrapersonal intelligence* (knowledge of the internal aspects of oneself; access to one's own feelings and emotions). Case example:
In her essay "A Sketch of the Past," Virginia Woolf displays deep insight into her own inner life through these lines, describing her reaction to several specific memories from her childhood that still, in adulthood, shock her: "Though I still have the peculiarity that I receive these sudden shocks, they are now always welcome; after the first surprise, I always feel instantly that they are particularly valuable. And so I go on to suppose that the shock-receiving capacity is what makes me a writer."

(*Source:* Adapted from Walters & Gardner, 1986.)

Racial Differences in IQ.   Consider the following test item:

A "jontry" is an example of a
  (a) rulpow
  (b) flink
  (c) spudge
  (d) bakwoe

If you were to find an item such as this on an intelligence test that you were taking, your immediate—and quite legitimate—reaction would likely be to complain. How could a test that purports to measure intelligence include test items that incorporate meaningless terminology?

But suppose, instead, that you found the following item, which at first may appear to be equally inappropriate:

A "handkerchief head" is
  (a) a cool cat
  (b) a porter
  (c) an "Uncle Tom"
  (d) a hoddi

Although this example may seem equally improper to you, you might feel otherwise if you were familiar with the language used in predominately African American areas of certain cities and rural sections of the United States. For unlike the first example, which was made up of nonsense syllables, the second example uses meaningful words that a small but significant minority of English speakers would have little trouble understanding. In fact, one might argue that an intelligence test using the language of the second example would be more appropriate to administer to people who spoke that language than a traditional intelligence test using standard English.

The second item (the correct answer to which is "c," by the way) is drawn from a series of questions devised by sociologist Adrian Dove, as part of a pseudo-intelligence test designed to make a point (Dove, 1968). Dove contended that cultural experience played a crucial role in determining intelligence test scores, and he suggested that traditional measures of intelligence were biased in favor of white, upper- and middle-class students and against groups with different cultural experiences.

Dove created his "test" in reaction to a long-standing debate among developmentalists regarding the finding that members of certain racial groups consistently score lower on IQ tests than members of other groups. For example, the mean score of African Americans tends to be about 15 IQ points lower than the mean score of whites—although the measured difference varies a great deal depending on the particular IQ test employed (e.g., Samuda, 1998; Vance, Hankins, & Brown, 1988).

The question that emerges from such results, of course, is whether they reflect actual differences in intelligence, or, instead, are caused by bias in the intelligence tests themselves in favor of majority groups and against minorities. For example, if whites perform better than African Americans because of their greater familiarity with the language used in the test items, the test hardly can be said to provide a fair measure of the intelligence of African Americans. Similarly an intelligence test that used language such as that used in Dove's test could not be considered an impartial measure of intelligence for whites (Greenfield, 1997).

The question of how to interpret differences between intelligence scores of different cultural groups lies at the heart of one of the major controversies in developmental psychology: To what degree is an individual's intelligence determined by heredity and to what degree by environment? The issue is crucial because of its social implications. For instance, if intelligence is primarily determined by heredity and is therefore largely fixed at birth, attempts to alter intelligence later in life will meet with limited success. On the other hand, if intelligence is largely determined by environment, modifying social conditions is a more promising strategy for bringing about increases in intelligence (Sternberg & Grigorenko, 1996; Suzuki & Valencia, 1997).

***The Bell Curve* Controversy.**   Although investigations into the relative contributions of heredity and environment to intelligence have been conducted for decades, the smoldering debate became a raging fire with the publication in 1994 of a book by Richard J. Herrnstein and Charles Murray, titled *The Bell Curve*. In the book, Herrnstein and Murray argue that the average 15-point IQ difference between whites and African Americans is due primarily to heredity rather than environment. Furthermore, they argue that this IQ difference accounts for the higher rates of poverty, lower employment, and higher use of welfare among minority groups, as compared with majority groups (Herrnstein & Murray, 1994).

"I don't know anything about the bell curve, but I say heredity is everything."

Herrnstein and Murray contend that whites score higher than African Americans on traditional IQ tests even when socioeconomic status (SES) is taken into account. Specifically, middle- and upper-SES African Americans tend to score lower than middle- and upper-SES whites, just as lower-SES African Americans score lower on average than lower-SES whites. Herrnstein and Murray use this evidence to argue that the IQ score difference between whites and African Americans is primarily due to genetic factors.

The conclusions reached by Herrnstein and Murray raised a storm of protest, and many psychologists who examined the data reported in the book came to conclusions that were quite different. Most developmentalists and psychologists responded by arguing that the differences between races in measured IQ can be explained by environmental differences between the races. Furthermore, critics maintain that there is little evidence to suggest that IQ is related to poverty and other social ills. Indeed, some researchers go further, suggesting that IQ scores are unrelated in meaningful ways to later success in life (e.g., McClelland, 1993; Sternberg & Wagner, 1993; Nisbett, 1994; Jacoby & Glauberman, 1995; Sternberg, 1995, 1997a).

Herrnstein and Murray's critics base their conclusions on several pieces of evidence. For one thing, even when socioeconomic conditions are supposedly held constant, wide variations remain in the home environments among different households. Thus, living conditions of African Americans and whites are hardly identical, even when their socioeconomic status seems to be similar. Consequently, we cannot rule out the possibility that significant environmental differences exist between white and African American families. In fact, a recent study found that when a variety of indicators of economic and social factors (and not just socioeconomic status) are statistically taken into account simultaneously, mean IQ scores of black and white children turn out to be actually quite similar (Brooks-Gunn, Klebanov, & Duncan, 1996).

Finally, members of cultural and social minority groups may score lower than members of the majority group due to the intelligence tests themselves. As we discussed earlier, traditional intelligence tests may discriminate against minority groups who have not had exposure to the same environment as majority group members have had (Miller-Jones, 1989).

In sum, most members of the psychological community believe that Herrnstein and Murray came to a conclusion about the source of racial IQ differences that is not supported by evidence. Still, the view set forth in *The Bell Curve* remains noteworthy, and it is likely to continue to influence both political and the developmental agendas.

Below and Above Intelligence Norms: Mental Retardation and the Intellectually Gifted

Although Connie kept pace with her classmates in kindergarten, by the time she reached first grade she was academically the slowest in almost every subject. It was not that she didn't try, but rather that it took her longer than other students to catch on to new material, and she regularly required special attention to keep up with the rest of the class.

On the other hand, in some areas she excelled: When asked to draw or produce something with her hands, she not only matched her classmates' performance but exceeded it, producing beautiful work that was much admired by her classmates. Although the other students in the class felt that there was something different about Connie, they were hard-pressed to identify the source of the difference, and in fact they didn't spend much time pondering the issue.

Connie's parents and teacher knew what made her special. Extensive testing in kindergarten had shown that Connie's intelligence was well below normal, and she was officially classified as a special-needs student.

If Connie had been attending school before 1975, she would most likely have been removed from her regular class as soon as her low IQ was identified, and placed in a class taught by a special-needs teacher. Often consisting of students with a hodgepodge of afflictions, including emotional difficulties, severe reading problems, and physical disabilities such as multiple sclerosis, such classes were traditionally kept separate and apart from the regular educational process.

However, all that changed in 1975 when Congress passed Public Law 94-142, the Education for All Handicapped Children Act. The intent of the law—an intent that has been largely realized—was to ensure that children with special needs received a full education in the **least restrictive environment**, the setting most similar to that of children without special needs (Yell, 1995).

In practice, the law has meant that children with special needs must be integrated into regular classrooms and regular activities to the greatest extent possible, as long as doing so is educationally beneficial. Children are to be isolated from the regular classroom only for those subjects that are specifically affected by their exceptionality; for all other subjects they are to be taught with nonexceptional children in regular classrooms. Of course, some children with severe handicaps still need a mostly or entirely separate education, depending on the extent of their condition. But the goal of the law is to integrate exceptional children and typical children to the fullest extent possible (Yell, 1995).

This educational approach to special education, designed to end the segregation of exceptional students as much as possible, has come to be called mainstreaming. In **mainstreaming**, exceptional children are integrated as much as possible into the traditional educational system and are provided with a broad range of educational alternatives (Hocutt, 1996).

Ending Segregation by Intelligence Levels: The Benefits of Mainstreaming.   In many respects, the introduction of mainstreaming—although clearly increasing the complexity of classroom teaching—was a reaction to failures of traditional special education. For one thing, there was little research support for the advisability of special education for exceptional students. Research that examined such factors as academic achievement, self-concept, social adjustment, and personality development generally failed to discern any advantages for special-needs children placed in special, as opposed to regular, education classes (Dunn, 1968; Wang, Peverly, & Catalano, 1987). Furthermore, systems that compel minorities to be educated separately from majorities historically tend to be less effective—as an examination of schools that were once segregated on the basis of race clearly demonstrates (Wang, Reynolds, & Walberg, 1996).

least restrictive environment   *the setting that is most similar to that of children without special-needs*

mainstreaming   *an educational approach in which exceptional children are integrated to the extent possible into the traditional educational system and are provided with a broad range of educational alternatives*

An additional important argument in favor of mainstreaming concerns the issue of labeling students into such categories as "mentally deficient," "emotionally disturbed," or a host of other classifications. Labeling students, which is frequently done with little precision, often produces negative expectations regarding the students' capabilities, which in turn can lead to behavior in themselves and others that actually causes the expectations to be fulfilled. Furthermore, being labeled negatively can lead to a decrease in peer acceptance and self-concept. For example, research has found that a behavior is viewed more negatively when it is carried out by a student labeled "mentally retarded" than when the same behavior is performed by a presumably "normal" student (Archibald, 1974; Cook & Wollersheim, 1976; Singer et al., 1989).

Ultimately, though, the most compelling argument in favor of mainstreaming is philosophical: Because special-needs students must ultimately function in a normal environment, greater experience with their peers ought to enhance their integration into society, as well as positively affecting their learning. Mainstreaming, then, provides a mechanism to equalize the opportunities available to all children. The ultimate objective of mainstreaming is to ensure that all persons, regardless of ability or disability, will have—to the greatest extent possible—opportunities to choose their goals on the basis of a full education, enabling them to obtain a fair share of life's rewards (Fuchs & Fuchs, 1994).

Does the reality of mainstreaming live up to its promise? To some extent the benefits extolled by proponents have been realized, at least where mainstreaming is done with care and classroom teachers receive substantial support. Furthermore, mainstreaming provides important benefits not only for exceptional children, but for typical children as well. For instance, typical children in mainstreamed classes come to understand better the nature of others' disabilities and, at least potentially, come to hold more positive attitudes toward persons with disabilities. In short, everyone—typical and exceptional children alike—can potentially benefit from mainstreaming (Kauffman, 1993; Daly & Feldman, 1994; Scruggs & Mastropieri, 1994).

The proven benefits of mainstreaming have led some professionals to promote an alternative educational model known as full inclusion. *Full inclusion* is the integration of all students, even those with the most severe disabilities, into regular classes. In such a system, separate special-education programs would cease to operate. Full inclusion is controversial, and it remains to be seen how widespread such a practice will become (Hocutt, 1996; Siegel, 1996).

This boy, who has been identified as mentally retarded, is mainstreamed into this fifth grade class.

Below the Norm: Mental Retardation. Approximately 1 to 3 percent of the school-age population is considered to be mentally retarded (U.S. Department of Education, 1987). The wide variation in these incidence estimates stems from the breadth of the most widely accepted definition of mental retardation, which leaves ample room for interpretation. According to the American Association on Mental Retardation (AAMR), **mental retardation** refers to "substantial limitations in present functioning" characterized by "significantly subaverage intellectual functioning, existing concurrently with related limitations in two or more of the following applicable adaptive skill areas: communication, self-care, home living, social skills, community use, self direction, health and safety, functional academics, leisure and work. Mental retardation manifests before age 18" (AAMR, 1992).

Although "subaverage intellectual functioning" can be measured in a relatively straightforward manner—using standard IQ tests—it is more difficult to determine how to gauge limitations in "applicable adaptive skills." Ultimately, this imprecision leads to a lack of uniformity in the ways experts apply the label of "mental retardation." Furthermore, it has resulted in significant variation in the abilities of people who are categorized as mentally retarded. Accordingly, mentally retarded people range from those who can be taught to work and function with little special attention to those who are virtually untrainable and who never develop speech or such basic motor skills as crawling or walking (Matson & Mulick, 1991).

In addition, even when objective measures such as IQ tests are used to identify mentally retarded individuals, discrimination may occur against children from ethnically diverse backgrounds. Most traditional intelligence tests are standardized using white, English-speaking, middle-class populations. As a result, children from different cultural backgrounds may perform poorly on the tests—not because they are retarded, but because the tests use questions that are culturally biased in favor of majority group members. In fact, one classic study found that in one California school district, Mexican American students were ten times more likely than whites to be placed in special-education classes (Mercer, 1973).

The vast majority of the mentally retarded—some 90 percent—have relatively low levels of deficits. Classified with **mild retardation**, they score in the range of 50 or 55 to 70 on IQ tests. Typically their retardation is not even identified before they reach school, although their early development often is slower than average. Once they enter elementary school, their retardation and their need for special attention usually become apparent. With appropriate training, these students can reach a third- to sixth-grade educational level, and although they cannot carry out complex intellectual tasks, they are able to hold jobs and function quite independently and successfully.

Intellectual and adaptive limitations become more apparent, however, at higher levels of mental retardation. People whose IQ scores range from around 35 or 40 to 50 or 55 are classified with **moderate retardation**. Composing between 5 and 10 percent of those classified as mentally retarded, the moderately retarded display distinctive behavior early in their lives. They are slow to develop language skills, and their motor development is also affected. Regular schooling is usually not effective in training the moderately retarded to acquire academic skills, because generally they are unable to progress beyond the second-grade level. Still, they are capable of learning occupational and social skills, and they can learn to travel independently to familiar places. Typically, they require moderate levels of supervision.

At the most significant levels of retardation—those who are classified with **severe retardation** (IQs ranging from around 20 or 25 to 35 or 40) and **profound retardation** (IQs below 20 or 25)—the ability to function is severely limited. Usually, such people have little or no speech, show poor motor control, and need 24-hour nursing care. At the same time, though, some people with severe retardation are capable of learning basic self-care skills, such as dressing and eating, and they may even develop the potential to become partially independent as adults. Still, the need for relatively high levels of care continues throughout

---

mental retardation *a significantly subaverage level of intellectual functioning that occurs with related limitations in two or more skill areas*

mild retardation *retardation in which IQ scores fall in the range of 50 or 55 to 70*

moderate retardation *retardation in which IQ scores range from around 35 or 40 to 50 or 55*

severe retardation *retardation in which IQ scores range from around 20 or 25 to 35 or 40*

profound retardation *retardation in which IQ scores fall below 20 or 25*

the life span, and most severely and profoundly retarded people are institutionalized for the majority of their lives.

Above the Norm: The Gifted and Talented.   Consider this situation:

> I was standing at the front of the room explaining how the earth revolves and how, because of its huge size, it is difficult for us to realize that it is actually round. All of a sudden, Spencer blurted out, "The earth isn't round." I curtly replied, "Ha, do you think it's flat?" He matter-of-factly said, "No, it's a truncated sphere." I quickly changed the subject. Spencer said the darndest things. (Payne et al., 1974, p. 94)

It sometimes strikes people as curious that the gifted and talented are considered to have a form of exceptionality. Yet—as the above quote suggests—the 3 to 5 percent of school-age children who are gifted and talented present special challenges of their own.

Which students are considered to be **gifted and talented**? Because of the breadth of the term, researchers do not agree on a single definition. However, the federal government considers the term *gifted* to include "children who give evidence of high performance capability in areas such as intellectual, creative, artistic, leadership capacity, or specific academic fields, and who require services or activities not ordinarily provided by the school in order to fully develop such capabilities" (Sec 582, P.L. 97-35). Intellectual capabilities, then, represent only one type of exceptionality; unusual potential in areas outside the academic realm are also included in the concept. Gifted and talented children have so much potential that they, no less than students with low IQs, warrant special concern (Azar, 1995; Winner, 1997).

Although the stereotypic description of the gifted—particularly those with exceptionally high intelligence—would probably include adjectives such as "unsociable," "poorly adjusted," and "neurotic," such a view is far off the mark. In fact, most research suggests that highly intelligent people also tend to be outgoing, well adjusted, and popular (Stanley, 1980; Southern, Jones, & Stanley, 1993; Gottfried et al., 1994).

For instance, one landmark, long-term study of 1,500 gifted students, which began in the 1920s, found that the gifted did better in virtually every dimension studied. Not only were they smarter than average, but they were healthier, better coordinated, and psychologically better adjusted than their less intelligent classmates. Furthermore, their lives played out in ways that most people would envy. The subjects received more awards and distinctions, earned more money, and made many more contributions in art and literature than the average person. For instance, by the time they had reached the age of 40, they had collectively produced more than 90 books, 375 plays and short stories, and 2,000 articles, and they had registered more than 200 patents. Perhaps not surprisingly, they reported greater satisfaction with their lives than the nongifted (Terman & Oden, 1947; Sears, 1977; Shurkin, 1992).

Yet being gifted and talented is no guarantee of success in school, as we can see if we consider the particular components of the category. For example, the verbal abilities that allow the eloquent expression of ideas and feelings can equally permit the expression of glib and persuasive statements that happen to be inaccurate. Furthermore, teachers may sometimes misinterpret the humor, novelty, and creativity of unusually gifted children, considering their intellectual fervor to be disruptive or inappropriate. And peers are not always sympathetic: Some very bright children try to hide their intelligence in an effort to fit in better with other students (Feldman, 1982).

Two main approaches to educating the gifted and talented have been devised: acceleration and enrichment (Feldhusen, Haeger, & Pellegrino, 1989). **Acceleration** allows gifted students to move ahead at their own pace, even if this means skipping to higher grade levels. The materials that students receive under acceleration programs are not necessarily different from what other students receive; they simply are provided at a faster pace than for the average student.

gifted and talented children who show evidence of high performance capability in areas such as intellectual, creative, artistic, leadership capacity, or specific academic fields

acceleration special programs that allow gifted students to move ahead at their own pace, even if this means skipping to higher grade levels

enrichment   *an approach through which students are kept at grade level but are enrolled in special programs and given individual activities to allow greater depth of study on a given topic*

An alternative approach is **enrichment**, through which students are kept at grade level but are enrolled in special programs and given individual activities to allow greater depth of study on a given topic. In enrichment, the material provided to gifted students differs not only in the timing of its presentation, but in its sophistication as well. Thus, enrichment materials are designed to provide an intellectual challenge to the gifted student, encouraging higher-order thinking.

Acceleration programs can be remarkably effective. Most studies have shown that gifted students who begin school even considerably earlier than their age-mates do as well as or better than those who begin at the traditional age (Rimm & Lovance, 1992). One of the best illustrations of the benefits of acceleration is the "Study of Mathematically Precocious Youth," an ongoing program at Johns Hopkins University in Baltimore. In this program, seventh and eighth graders who have unusual abilities in mathematics participate in a variety of special classes and workshops. The results have been nothing short of sensational, with students successfully completing college courses and sometimes even enrolling in college early. Some students have even graduated from college before the age of 18 (Stanley & Benbow, 1983; Brody & Benbow, 1987).

The Informed Consumer of Development

Creating an Atmosphere That Promotes School Success

What makes children succeed in school? Although there are many factors, some of which we will discuss in the next chapter, there are several practical steps that can be taken to maximize children's chances of success. Among them:

■ Promote a "literacy environment." Parents should read to their children and familiarize them with books and reading. Adults should provide reading models: Children should see that reading is an important activity in the lives of the adults with whom they interact.

■ Talk to children. Discuss events in the news, talk about their friends, and share hobbies. Getting children to think about and discuss the world around them is one of the best preparations for school.

■ Provide a place for children to work. This can be a desk, a corner of a table, or an area of a room. What's important is that it be a separate, designated area.

■ Encourage children's problem-solving skills. To solve a problem, they should learn to identify their goal, what they know, and what they don't know; to design and carry out a strategy; and finally to evaluate their result.

REVIEW AND RETHINK

REVIEW

■ Schooling in the United States, which is nearly universally available, has recently focused on the basic academic skills, student and teacher accountability, and multiculturalism.

■ The development of reading skill, which is fundamental to schooling, generally occurs in several stages. Generally, a combination of elements from the two opposing approaches to reading instruction—code-based (i.e., phonics) approaches versus whole-language approaches—appears to offer the most promise.

■ Multicultural education is in transition from a melting pot model of cultural assimilation to a pluralistic society model, in which coexisting cultures make unique contributions to the whole.

■ The measurement of intelligence has traditionally been a matter of testing skills that promote academic success, and calculating the ratio of mental age (measured in relation to average test performance by age group) to chronological age.

■ Recent theories of intelligence suggest that the concept of academic intelligence may be insufficient, and that there may be several distinct intelligences or several components of intelligence that reflect different ways of processing information.

■ U.S. educators are attempting to deal with substantial numbers of exceptional persons, whose intellectual and other skills are significantly lower or higher than normal.

RETHINK

■ Is an educational focus on the basic academic skills appropriate? How does the theory that there are multiple intelligences relate to this issue?

■ Should instruction be provided to children in the United States in their home languages or only in English? Why?

■ What are the advantages of mainstreaming? What challenges does it present? Are there situations in which you would not support mainstreaming?

■ Some people argue that expending additional resources on gifted and talented children is wasteful, because these children will succeed anyway. What is your opinion of this suggestion, and why?

LOOKING BACK

■ **In what ways do children grow during the school years, and what factors influence their growth?**

• The middle childhood years are characterized by slow and steady growth. Weight is redistributed as baby fat disappears. In part, growth is genetically determined, but societal factors such as affluence, dietary habits, nutrition, and disease also contribute significantly.

• During the middle childhood years, great improvements occur in gross motor skills. Cultural expectations appear to underlie most gross motor skill differences between boys and girls.

■ **What are the main health concerns of school-age children?**

• Adequate nutrition is important because of its contributions to growth, health, social and emotional functioning, and cognitive performance.

• Obesity is partially influenced by genetic factors, but is also associated with children's failure to develop internal controls over eating, overindulgence in sedentary activities such as television viewing, and lack of physical exercise.

• Asthma and childhood depression are fairly prevalent among children of school age.

■ **What sorts of special-needs manifest themselves in the middle childhood years, and how can they be met?**

• Visual, auditory, and speech impairments, as well as other learning disabilities, can lead to academic and social problems and must be handled with sensitivity and appropriate assistance.

• Children with attention-deficit hyperactivity disorder exhibit another form of special need. ADHD is characterized by inattention, impulsiveness, failure to complete tasks, lack of organization, and excessive amounts of uncontrollable activity. Treatment of ADHD by drugs is controversial because of unwanted side effects and doubts about long-term consequences.

■   **In what ways do children develop cognitively during these years, according to major theoretical approaches?**

- According to Piaget, school-age children enter the concrete operational period and for the first time become capable of applying logical thought processes to concrete problems.

- According to information-processing approaches, children's intellectual development in the school years can be attributed to substantial increases in memory capacity and the sophistication of the "programs" children can handle.

- Vygotsky recommends that students focus on active learning through child–adult and child–child interactions that fall within each child's zone of proximal development.

■   **How does language develop during the middle childhood period?**

- The language development of children in the school years is substantial, with improvements in vocabulary, syntax, and pragmatics. Children learn to control their behavior through linguistic strategies and they learn more effectively by seeking clarification when they need it.

- Bilingualism can be beneficial in the school years. Children who are taught all subjects in the first language, with simultaneous instruction in English, appear to experience few deficits and several linguistic and cognitive advantages.

■   **What are some trends in schooling today?**

- Schooling, which is available to nearly all children in most developed countries, is not as accessible to children, especially girls, in many less developed countries.

- The development of reading skill, which is fundamental to schooling, generally occurs in several stages: identifying letters, reading highly familiar words, sounding out letters and blending sounds into words, reading words with fluency but with little comprehension, reading with comprehension and for practical purposes, and reading material that reflects multiple points of view.

- Multiculturalism and diversity are significant issues in U.S. schools, where the melting pot society, in which minority cultures were assimilated to the majority culture, is being replaced by the pluralistic society, in which individual cultures maintain their own identities while participating in the definition of a larger culture.

■   **How can intelligence be measured, and how are children with exceptionalities educated?**

- Intelligence testing has traditionally focused on factors that differentiate successful academic performers from unsuccessful ones. The intelligence quotient, or IQ, reflects the ratio of a person's mental age to his or her chronological age. Other conceptualizations of intelligence focus on different types of intelligence or on different aspects of the information-processing task.

- In today's schools children with exceptionalities—including intellectual deficits—are to be educated in the least restrictive environment, typically the regular classroom. If done properly, this strategy can benefit all students and permit the exceptional student to focus on strengths rather than weaknesses.

- Gifted and talented children can benefit from special educational programs including acceleration programs and enrichment programs.

EPILOGUE: LA-TOYA PANKEY AND *THE WITCHES*

In this chapter, we discussed children's physical and cognitive development during the middle childhood years. We considered physical growth, nutrition, and health concerns, as well as intellectual growth as interpreted by Piaget, information-processing approaches, and Lev Vygotsky. We noted children's increased capabilities in memory and language, which facilitate and support gains in many other areas. We looked at some aspects of schooling worldwide and, especially, in the United States concluding with an examination of intelligence: how it is defined, how it is tested, and how children who fall significantly below or above the intellectual norm are educated and treated.

Look back to the prologue of this chapter, about La-Toya Pankey's development of reading skills, and answer the following questions.

1. Judging from the cues provided in the Prologue, how would you have estimated La Toya's chances for academic success before you learned about her ability to read? Why?

2. If you wished to isolate the factors in La-Toya's genetic or environmental background that contributed to her interest and ability in reading, how would you proceed? Which factors would you examine? Which questions would you ask?

3. Given her circumstances, what threats to academic accomplishment does La-Toya still face? What advantages does she seem to have?

4. Discuss La-Toya's situation in the light of the premises of the authors of *The Bell Curve*. If La-Toya succeeds academically, outperforming students of higher socioeconomic status, how would the authors explain this phenomenon? How do you explain it?

KEY TERMS AND CONCEPTS

asthma (p. 299)
visual impairment (p. 303)
auditory impairment (p. 304)
speech impairment (p. 304)
stuttering (p. 304)
learning disabilities (p. 305)
attention-deficit hyperactivity disorder (ADHD) (p. 305)
concrete operational stage (p. 307)
decentering (p. 307)
memory (p. 311)
meta-memory (p. 311)
metalinguistic awareness (p. 313)
bilingualism (p. 314)
multicultural education (p. 323)
cultural assimilation model (p. 323)
pluralistic society model (p. 324)
bicultural identity (p. 324)
intelligence (p. 325)
mental age (p. 325)

chronological (or physical) age (p. 326)
intelligence quotient (or IQ score) (p. 326)
Stanford-Binet Intelligence Scale (p. 326)
Wechsler Intelligence Scale for Children-Revised (WISC-III) (p. 326)
Wechsler Adult Intelligence Scale-Revised (WAIS-III) (p. 326)
fluid intelligence (p. 328)
crystallized intelligence (p. 328)
triarchic theory of intelligence (p. 328)
least restrictive environment (p. 332)
mainstreaming (p. 332)
mental retardation (p. 334)
mild retardation (p. 334)
moderate retardation (p. 334)
severe retardation (p. 334)
profound retardation (p. 334)
gifted and talented (p. 335)
acceleration (p. 335)
enrichment (p. 336)

CHAPTER 10

MIDDLE CHILDHOOD

Social and Personality Development

PROLOGUE: BALANCING CULTURES

Regardless of cultural background, middle childhood is a period of significant social and personality development.

If someone had told Lirong Wen that she would bring up children with a penchant for brand-name clothes, "please knock before entering" signs on their bedroom doors, and the nerve to ask "why?" when she prods them to study, she might never have come to the United States. After all, that summer in 1989, she was merely coming to see her husband, a visiting scholar at the University of Massachusetts, their twin 8-year-olds in tow, to see what the land of democracy and Dunkin' Donuts was like.

Eight years later, she sits at the small round kitchen table in the Amherst apartment her children have long called home, recalling her first impressions of the third-grade class she enrolled her children in when their visit was extended.

"In China, the two hands had to be like this, their feet flat like this"—she clasps her hands and puts her feet square on the linoleum floor to demonstrate. "They can only watch the teacher talking, they can't speak until spoken to. Here, some sat, some lay down. They could do anything. They say they're thirsty, the teacher lets them go."

When her children came home from school, Wen would be waiting to sit down with them to help them with their homework, as any good mother in China was expected to do and as she had done with them since their earliest days in school. But what little homework there was they would breeze through in 20 or 30 minutes, then go play with friends. Coming from a country where schoolchildren wore uniforms, they quickly became attuned to the dress code—and social index—of the grammar school: clothing labels that reflect an impressive price tag. It was a life of informality, and values she did not want her children to get too comfortable with. . . .

"I always told them 'don't compare who is rich, who spends more; compare who studies hard and catch up with them,'" said Wen. . . . "They ask me 'Why do you ask me to do more homework than American parents ask?' They think they are doing enough. I want them to be over the top." (Crolius, 1997, pp. 8–9)

LOOKING AHEAD   For Lirong Wen, raising children in the United States, with a culture very different from that of her native China, was hardly an easy venture. Yet in some ways the challenges faced by the Wen children were no greater than those encountered by many others who did not have a major cultural change to navigate, for the time of middle childhood is a period of significant social and personality development. It is a period when children's views of themselves undergo significant changes, they form new bonds with friends and family, and they become increasingly attached to social institutions outside the home.

We start our consideration of personality and social development during middle childhood by examining the changes that occur in the ways children see themselves, including their views of their personal characteristics and their self-esteem. We also discuss several approaches to moral development.

Next, the chapter turns to relationships during middle childhood. We discuss the stages of friendship and the ways gender and race affect how and with whom children interact. We also look at how to improve children's social competence.

The last part of the chapter examines two major societal institutions in children's lives: family and school. We consider the consequences of divorce, self-care children, and the phenomenon of group care. Finally, we look at schooling, considering such topics as how children explain their academic performance and how teachers' expectations can affect student performance.

In sum, after reading this chapter, you will be able to answer the following questions:

Q

- In what ways do children's views of themselves change during the middle childhood years?

- Why is self-esteem important during these years?

- Through what stages does moral development proceed as children age?

- What sorts of relationships and friendships do children have in the middle childhood years?

- How do gender and race affect friendships?

- How do today's diverse family arrangements affect children?

- How do social and emotional factors contribute to school outcomes?

THE DEVELOPING SELF

Nine-year-old Karl Haglund is perched in his eagle's nest, a treehouse built high in the willow that grows in his backyard. Sometimes he sits there alone among the tree's spreading branches, his face turned toward the sky, a boy clearly enjoying his solitude. Sometimes he's with his friend, engrossed in the kind of talk that boys find fascinating.

This morning Karl is busy sawing and hammering. "It's fun to build," he says. "I started the house when I was 4 years old. Then when I was about 7, my dad built me this platform. 'Cause all my places were falling apart and they were crawling with carpenter ants. So we destroyed them and then built me a deck. And I built on top of it. It's stronger now. You can have privacy here, but it's a bad place to go when it's windy 'cause you almost get blown off." (Kotre & Hall, 1990, p. 116)

Karl's growing sense of competence is reflected in the passage above, as he describes how he and his father built his treehouse. Conveying what psychologist Erik Erikson calls "industriousness," Karl's quiet pride in his accomplishment illustrates one of the ways in which children's views of themselves evolve.

Understanding One's Self: A New Response to "Who Am I?"

During middle childhood, children continue their efforts to answer the question "Who am I" as they seek to understand the nature of the self. Although the question does not yet have the urgency it will assume in adolescence, elementary-school-age children still seek to pin down their place in the world.

The Shift in Self-understanding from the Physical to the Psychological. Several changes in children's views of themselves during middle childhood illustrate the quest for self-understanding. For one thing, they begin to view themselves less in terms of external, physical attributes and more in terms of psychological traits (Aboud & Skerry, 1983).

For instance, 6-year-old Carey describes herself as "a fast runner and good at drawing"— both characteristics dependent on skill in external, motoric activities. In contrast, 11-year-old Trisha characterizes herself as "pretty smart, friendly, and helpful to my friends." Trisha's portrayal is based on psychological characteristics, inner traits that are more abstract than the younger child's descriptions. The use of inner traits to determine self-concept results from the child's increasing cognitive skills, a development that we discussed in Chapter 9.

In addition to shifting focus from external characteristics to internal, psychological traits, children's views of self become more differentiated. As they get older, children discover that they may be good at some things, and not so good at others. Ten-year-old Ginny, for instance, comes to understand that she is good at arithmetic but not very good at spelling; 11-year-old Malcolm determines that he is good at softball but doesn't have the stamina to play soccer very well.

Furthermore, children's self-concepts become divided into personal and academic spheres. In fact, research on students' self-concepts in English, mathematics, and

Children's view of who they are shifts with age.

social comparison   *the desire to evaluate one's own behavior, abilities, expertise, and opinions by comparing them to those of others*

nonacademic realms has found that the separate self-concepts are not always correlated, although there is overlap among them.

Furthermore, as can be seen in Figure 10-1, self-concept in each of the three domains can be further broken down. For instance, the nonacademic self-concept includes the components of physical appearance, peer relations, and physical ability. In sum, self-concept becomes increasingly differentiated as children mature (Marsh, 1990; Marsh & Holmes, 1990; Burnett, 1996).

Social Comparison.   If someone asks you how good you are at math, how would you respond? Most of us would compare our performance to others who are roughly of the same age and educational level. It is unlikely that we would answer the question by comparing ourselves either to Albert Einstein or to a kindergartner just learning about numbers. Elementary-school-age children begin to follow the same sort of reasoning when they seek to understand how able they are. Whereas earlier they tended to consider their abilities in terms of absolutes, now they begin to use social comparison processes to determine their levels of accomplishment during middle childhood (Weiss, Ebbeck, & Horn, 1997).

Social comparison is the desire to evaluate one's own behavior, abilities, expertise, and opinions by comparing them to those of others. According to a theory first suggested by psychologist Leon Festinger (1954), when concrete, objective measures of ability are lacking, people turn to *social reality* to evaluate themselves. Social reality refers to understanding that is derived from how others act, think, feel, and view the world.

But who provides the most adequate comparison? Generally, children compare themselves to persons who are similar along relevant dimensions. Consequently, when they cannot objectively evaluate their ability, children during middle childhood increasingly look to others who are similar to themselves (Ruble et al., 1989; Wood, 1989; Suls & Wills, 1991).

Although children typically compare themselves to similar others, in some cases—particularly when their self-esteem is at stake—students choose to make *downward social comparisons* with others who are obviously less competent or successful (Pyszczynski, Greenberg, & LaPrelle, 1985).

Downward social comparison protects self-image. By comparing themselves to those who are less able, children ensure that they will come out on top and thereby preserve an image of themselves as successful.

Downward social comparison helps explain why some students in elementary schools with low achievement levels are found to have stronger academic self-esteem than very

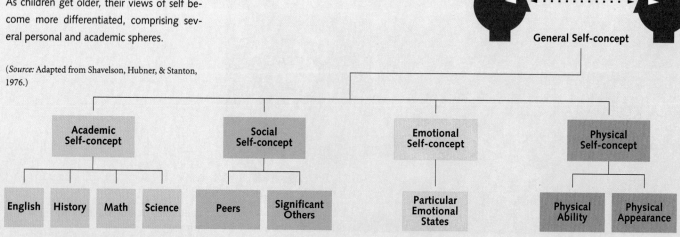

FIGURE 10-1

LOOKING INWARD

As children get older, their views of self become more differentiated, comprising several personal and academic spheres.

(*Source:* Adapted from Shavelson, Hubner, & Stanton, 1976.)

According to Erik Erikson, middle childhood encompasses the industry-versus-inferiority stage, characterized by a focus on meeting the challenges presented by the world.

capable students in schools with high achievement levels. The reason seems to be that students in the low-achievement schools observe others who are not doing terribly well academically, and they feel relatively good by comparison. In contrast, students in the high-achievement schools may find themselves competing with a more academically proficient group of students, and their perception of their performance may suffer in comparison. In some ways, then, it is better to be a big fish in a small pond than a small fish in a big one (Marsh & Parker, 1984).

Psychosocial Development: Industry Versus Inferiority

According to Erik Erikson, whose approach to psychosocial development we last discussed in Chapter 8, middle childhood encompasses the **industry-versus-inferiority stage**. Lasting from roughly age 6 to age 12, the industry-versus-inferiority stage is characterized by a focus on efforts to attain competence in meeting the challenges presented by parents, peers, school, and the other complexities of the modern world.

Success in this stage brings with it feelings of mastery and proficiency and a growing sense of competence. On the other hand, difficulties in this stage lead to feelings of failure and inadequacy. As a result, children may withdraw both from academic pursuits, showing less interest and motivation to excel, and from interactions with peers.

Attaining a sense of industry during the middle childhood years has lasting consequences. For example, one study examined how childhood industriousness and hard work were related to adult behavior by following a group of 450 men over a 35-year period, starting in early childhood. The men who were most industrious and hardworking during childhood were most successful as adults, both in occupational attainment and in their personal lives. In fact, childhood industriousness was more closely associated with adult success than was intelligence or family background (Vaillant & Vaillant, 1981).

Self-esteem: Evaluating the Self

Children don't dispassionately view themselves just in terms of an itemization of physical and psychological characteristics. Instead, they think of themselves as being good, or bad, in particular ways. **Self-esteem** is an individual's overall and specific positive and negative self-evaluation. Whereas self-concept reflects beliefs and cognitions about the self, self-esteem is more emotionally oriented (Baumeister, 1993).

industry-versus-inferiority stage *the period from age 6 to 12 characterized by a focus on efforts to attain competence in meeting the challenges presented by parents, peers, school, and the other complexities of the modern world*

self-esteem *an individual's overall and specific positive and negative self-evaluation*

Self-esteem develops in important ways during middle childhood. Children increasingly compare themselves to others, and as they do, they assess how well they measure up to society's standards. In addition, they increasingly develop their own, internal standards of success, and they can see how well they compare to those.

One of the advances that occurs during middle childhood is an increasing differentiation of self-esteem. At the age of 7, most children have self-esteem that reflects a global, undifferentiated view of themselves. If their overall self-esteem is positive, they assume that they are relatively good at all things. Conversely, if their overall self-esteem is negative, they assume that they are inadequate at most things (Marsh & Shavelson, 1985; Harter, 1990a). As children progress into the middle childhood years, however, their self-esteem becomes differentiated: higher for some areas that they evaluate and lower for others.

 Change and Stability in Self-esteem.   Generally, the self-esteem of most children tends to increase during middle childhood, with a brief decline around the age of 12. Although there are probably several reasons for the decline, the main one appears to be the school transition that typically occurs around this age: Students leaving elementary school and entering either middle school or junior high school show a decline in self-esteem, which then gradually rises again (Eccles et al., 1989).

Children with chronically low self-esteem face a tough road, in part because their self-esteem becomes enmeshed in a cycle of failure that grows increasingly difficult to break. Assume, for instance, that Harry, a student with chronically low self-esteem, is facing an important test. Because of his low self-esteem, he expects to do poorly. As a consequence, he is quite anxious—so anxious that he is unable to concentrate well and study effectively. Furthermore, he may decide not to study much, because he figures that if he's going to do badly anyway, why bother studying?

Ultimately, of course, Harry's high anxiety and lack of effort bring about the result he expected: He does poorly on the test. This failure, which confirms Harry's expectation, reinforces his low self-esteem, and the cycle of failure continues (see Figure 10-2).

Race and Self-esteem.   If you were a member of a minority group whose members routinely experienced prejudice and discrimination, how might your self-esteem be affected? For many decades, developmentalists hypothesized—and found supportive evidence for

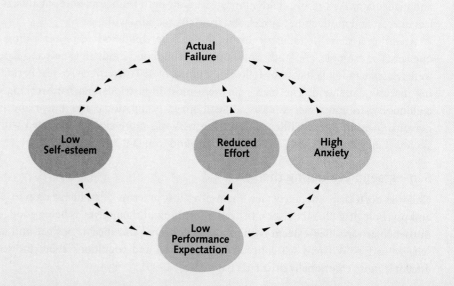

FIGURE 10-2

A CYCLE OF LOW SELF-ESTEEM

Because children with low self-esteem may expect to do poorly on a test, they may experience high anxiety and not work as hard as those with higher self-esteem. As a result, they actually do perform badly on the test, which in turn confirms their negative view of themselves.

In pioneering research conducted several decades ago, African American girls' preference for white dolls was viewed as an indication of low self-esteem. More recent evidence, however, suggest that whites and African American children show little difference in self-esteem.

the notion—that members of minority groups would feel lower self-esteem than members of majority groups. In particular, the evidence seemed clear that African Americans had lower self-esteem than whites (Deutsch, 1967).

Some of the first evidence was found in a set of pioneering studies a generation ago, in which African American children were shown a black doll and a white doll (Clark & Clark, 1947). In the study, the children received a series of requests, including "Give me the doll that looks bad" and "Give me the doll that is a nice color." In every case, the African American children preferred white dolls over black ones. The interpretation that was drawn from the study: The self-esteem of the African American children was low.

Subsequent research in the 1950s and 1960s supported the notion that children showed lower self-esteem as a consequence of being members of minority groups that were discriminated against. In fact, some research even suggested that members of minority groups preferred members of majority groups to members of their own groups, and that they rejected membership in their own groups, showing a form of self-hatred due to minority group status (Milner, 1983).

More recent theorizing, however, sheds a different light on the issue of self-esteem and racial group membership. According to French psychologist Henri Tajfel (1982), members of a minority group are likely to accept the negative views held by a majority group only if they perceive that there is little realistic possibility of changing the power and status differences between the groups.

On the other hand, if the existing differences between majority and minority group members are viewed as illegitimate, unstable, and potentially changeable, then minority group members will place the blame for the prejudice and discrimination they experience on societal forces and bias, and not on themselves. In this case, African Americans and whites should experience equivalent levels of self-esteem.

In fact, societal attitudes favoring group pride and ethnic awareness for minority group members, as well as increased sensitivity to the importance of multiculturalism in general, have become considerably more widespread in the last several decades. Such attitudes have resulted in a narrowing of measured differences in self-esteem between members of different ethnic groups (Garbarino, 1985; Harter, 1990b; Duckitt, 1994; Goodstein & Ponerotto, 1997).

Self-efficacy: Building Expectations of the Self

"Will I do well in arithmetic?" "How will I be able to complete this project?" "Can I make the after-school basketball team?"

These questions are typical of those that children ask themselves during the elementary school years. How each is answered depends in large measure on a child's self-efficacy. **Self-efficacy** refers to learned expectations that one is capable of carrying out a behavior or producing a desired outcome in a particular situation (Bandura, 1986, 1993; Schunk, 1991).

Self-efficacy is critical to children's success because it motivates greater effort and persistence in the face of a challenging task. As a result, children with high self-efficacy are more likely to be successful, whether the realm is academics or athletics (Bandura & Schunk, 1981; Taylor et al., 1984; Scheier & Carver, 1992).

Self-efficacy develops over the course of middle childhood. By observing their prior successes and failures on particular tasks, children begin to develop a sense of how well they can expect to do within a particular domain. For instance, a child who has even moderate success roller-blading for the first time is on the road to developing self-efficacy in that domain and is more likely to try it in the future. In contrast, a child who has little initial success is less likely to try it in the future.

There are other sources of children's self-efficacy. For instance, observation of others' success (or failure) in an activity can affect a child's sense of self-efficacy. Direct reinforcement from others, in the form of praise or encouragement, is also an important determinant (Bandura, 1988).

Moral Development

> Your wife is near death from an unusual kind of cancer. One drug exists that the physicians think might save her—a form of radium that a scientist in a nearby city has recently developed. The drug, though, is expensive to manufacture, and the scientist is charging ten times what the drug costs him to make. He pays $1,000 for the radium and charges $10,000 for a small dose. You have gone to everyone you know to borrow money, but you can get together only $2,500—one-quarter of what you need. You've told the scientist that your wife is dying and asked him to sell it more cheaply or let you pay later. But the scientist has said, "No, I discovered the drug and I'm going to make money from it." In desperation, you consider breaking into the scientist's laboratory to steal the drug for your wife. Should you do it?

According to developmental psychologist Lawrence Kohlberg and his colleagues, the answer that children give to this question reveals central aspects of their sense of morality and justice. He suggests that people's responses to moral dilemmas such as this one reveal the stage of moral development they have attained—as well as yielding information about their general level of cognitive development (Kohlberg, 1984; Colby & Kohlberg, 1987).

Kohlberg contends that people pass through a series of stages in the evolution of their sense of justice and in the kind of reasoning they use to make moral judgments. Primarily due to cognitive characteristics that we discussed earlier, school-age children tend to think either in terms of concrete, unvarying rules ("It is always wrong to steal" or "I'll be punished if I steal") or in terms of the rules of society ("Good people don't steal" or "What if everyone stole?").

By the time they reach adolescence, however, individuals are able to reason on a higher plane, typically having reached Piaget's stage of formal operations. They are capable of comprehending abstract, formal principles of morality, and they consider cases such as the one presented above in terms of broader issues of morality and of right and wrong ("Stealing may be justifiable if you are following your own standards of conscience.")

Kohlberg suggests that moral development can best be understood within the context of a three-level sequence, which is further subdivided into six stages (see Table 10-1). At the lowest level, *preconventional morality* (Stages 1 and 2), people follow unvarying rules based

---

self-efficacy   *learned expectations that one is capable of carrying out a behavior or producing a desired outcome in a particular situation*

TABLE 10-1

KOHLBERG'S SEQUENCE OF MORAL REASONING

		SAMPLE MORAL REASONING	
Level	Stage	In Favor of Stealing	Against Stealing
LEVEL 1 Preconventional morality: At this level, the concrete interests of the individual are considered in terms of rewards and punishments.	STAGE 1 Obedience and punishment orientation: At this stage, people stick to rules in order to avoid punishment, and obedience occurs for its own sake.	"If you let your wife die, you will get in trouble. You'll be blamed for not spending the money to save her, and there'll be an investigation of you and the druggist for your wife's death."	"You shouldn't steal the drug because you'll get caught and sent to jail if you do. If you do get away, your conscience will bother you thinking how the police will catch up with you at any minute."
	STAGE 2 Reward orientation: At this stage, rules are followed only for a person's own benefit. Obedience occurs because of rewards that are received.	"If you do happen to get caught, you could give the drug back and you wouldn't get much of a sentence. It wouldn't bother you much to serve a little jail term, if you have your wife when you get out."	"You may not get much of a jail term if you steal the drug, but your wife will probably die before you get out, so it won't do much good. If your wife dies, you shouldn't blame yourself; it isn't your fault she has cancer."
LEVEL 2 Conventional morality: At this level, people approach moral problems as members of society. They are interested in pleasing others by acting as good members of society.	STAGE 3 "Good boy" morality: Individuals at this stage show an interest in maintaining the respect of others and doing what is expected of them.	"No one will think you're bad if you steal the drug, but your family will think you're an inhuman husband if you don't. If you let your wife die, you'll never be able to look anybody in the face again."	"It isn't just the druggist who will think you're a criminal; everyone else will, too. After you steal the drug, you'll feel bad thinking how you've brought dishonor on your family and yourself; you won't be able to face anyone again."
	STAGE 4 Authority and social-order-maintaining morality: People at this stage conform to society's rules and consider that "right" is what society defines as right.	"If you have any sense of honor, you won't let your wife die just because you're afraid to do the only thing that will save her. You'll always feel guilty that you caused her death if you don't do your duty to her."	"You're desperate and you may not know you're doing wrong when you steal the drug. But you'll know you did wrong after you're sent to jail. You'll always feel guilty for your dishonesty and law-breaking."
LEVEL 3 Postconventional morality: At this level, people use moral principles which are seen as broader than those of any particular society.	STAGE 5 Morality of contract, individual rights and democratically accepted law: People at this stage do what is right because of a sense of obligation to laws which are agreed upon within society. They perceive that laws can be modified as part of changes in an implicit social contract.	"You'll lose other people's respect, not gain it, if you don't steal. If you let your wife die, it will be out of fear, not out of reasoning. So you'll just lose self-respect and probably the respect of others, too."	"You'll lose your standing and respect in the community and violate the law. You'll lose respect for yourself if you're carried away by emotion and forget the long-range point of view."
	STAGE 6 Morality of individual principles and conscience: At this final stage, a person follows laws because they are based on universal ethical principles. Laws that violate the principles are disobeyed.	"If you don't steal the drug, and if you let your wife die, you'll always condemn yourself for it afterward. You won't be blamed and you'll have lived up to the outside rule of the law but you won't have lived up to your own standards of conscience."	"If you steal the drug, you won't be blamed by other people, but you'll condemn yourself because you won't have lived up to your own conscience and standards of honesty."

(*Source:* Adapted from Kohlberg, 1969.)

on rewards and punishments. For example, a student at the preconventional level might evaluate the moral dilemma posed in the story above by saying that it was not worth stealing the drug because if you were caught, you would go to jail.

In the next level, that of *conventional morality* (Stages 3 and 4), people approach moral problems in terms of their own position as good, responsible members of society. Thus, students who decide *against* stealing the drug because they think they would feel guilty or dishonest, and students who decide *in favor of* stealing the drug because if they did nothing in this situation they would be unable to face others, would be reasoning at the conventional level of morality.

Finally, individuals using *postconventional morality* (Level 3; Stages 5 and 6) invoke universal moral principles that are considered broader than the rules of the particular society in which they live. Students who feel that they would condemn themselves if they did not steal the drug because they would not be living up to their own moral principles would be reasoning at the postconventional level.

Kohlberg's theory proposes that people move through the periods of moral development in a fixed order and that they are unable to reach the highest stage until adolescence, due to deficits in cognitive development that are not overcome until then (Kurtines & Gewirtz, 1987). However, not everyone is presumed to reach the highest stages: Kohlberg found that postconventional reasoning is relatively rare.

Unfortunately, although Kohlberg's theory provides a good account of the development of moral *judgments*, it is less adequate in predicting moral *behavior* (Malinowski & Smith, 1985; Snarey, 1985). For example, one experiment found that 15 percent of students who reasoned at the postconventional level of morality—the highest category—cheated on a task, although they were not as prone to cheating as those at lower levels: Some 55 percent of those at the conventional level and 70 percent of those at the preconventional level also cheated (Kohlberg, 1975; Wonderly & Kupfermid, 1980). Clearly, though, knowing what is morally right does not always mean acting that way (Killen & Hart, 1995).

Still, a good deal of research suggests that aspects of moral conduct are clearly related to Kohlberg's levels of moral reasoning, although the results are often complex and not easy to interpret. For instance, children who reason at Stage 1 and Stage 3 tend to be the best behaved in school, whereas those who reason at Stage 2 are more apt to exhibit poor social behavior in school settings. Such findings suggest that we have not heard the last word on Kohlberg's stages (Richards et al., 1992; Bear & Rys, 1994; Langford, 1995).

Moral Development in Girls. An aspect of Kohlberg's theory that has proved particularly problematic is the difficulty it has explaining *girls'* moral judgments. Because the theory initially was based largely on data from males, some researchers have argued that it does a better job describing boys' moral development than girls'.

In fact, psychologist Carol Gilligan (1982, 1987) has suggested an alternative account of the development of moral behavior in girls. She suggests that differences in the ways boys and girls are raised in our society lead to basic distinctions in how men and women view moral behavior. According to her, boys view morality primarily in terms of broad principles such as justice or fairness, whereas girls see it in terms of responsibility toward individuals and willingness to sacrifice themselves to help specific individuals within the context of particular relationships. Compassion for individuals, then, is a more prominent factor in moral behavior for women than it is for men (Gilligan, Ward, & Taylor, 1988; Gilligan, Lyons, & Hammer, 1990).

Because Kohlberg's theory considers moral behavior largely in terms of principles of justice, it is inadequate in describing the moral development of females. This accounts for the surprising finding that women typically score at a lower level than males on tests of moral judgments using Kohlberg's stage sequence. In Gilligan's view, a female's morality is centered more on individual well-being than on moral abstractions, and the highest levels of morality are represented by compassionate concern for the welfare of others.

TABLE 10-2

GILLIGAN'S THREE STAGES OF MORAL DEVELOPMENT FOR WOMEN

STAGE 1 Orientation toward individual survival	In this first stage a female initially concentrates on what is practical and best for her, gradually making a transition from selfishness to responsibility, in which she thinks about what would be best for others.
STAGE 2 Goodness as self-sacrifice	In the second stage she begins to think that she must sacrifice her own wishes to what other people want, ultimately making the transition from "goodness" to "truth" in which she takes into account her own needs and those of others.
STAGE 3 Morality of nonviolence	In the final stage, she comes to see that hurting anyone—including herself—is immoral. This realization establishes a moral equivalence between herself and others, and, according to Gilligan, represents the most sophisticated level of moral reasoning.

(*Source:* Gilligan, 1982.)

Gilligan views morality as developing among females in a three-stage process (summarized in Table 10-2). In the first stage, *orientation toward individual survival*, females first concentrate on what is practical and best for them, gradually making a transition from selfishness to responsibility, in which they think about what would be best for others. In the second stage, *goodness as self-sacrifice*, females begin to think that they must sacrifice their own wishes to what other people want, ultimately making the transition from "goodness" to "truth," in which they take into account their own needs plus those of others. Finally, in the third stage, *morality of nonviolence*, women come to see that hurting anyone is immoral—including hurting themselves. This realization establishes a moral equivalence between themselves and others and represents, according to Gilligan, the most sophisticated level of moral reasoning.

It is obvious that Gilligan's sequence of stages is quite different from that of Kohlberg, and some developmentalists have suggested that her rejection of Kohlberg's work is too sweeping and that gender differences are not as pronounced as first thought (Colby & Damon, 1987). For instance, some research has found that both males and females use similar "justice" and "care" orientations in making moral judgments. Clearly, the question of how boys and girls differ in their moral orientations, as well as the nature of moral development in general, is far from settled (Cassidy, Chu, & Dahlsgaard, 1997; Chiu et al., 1997; Wygant, 1997).

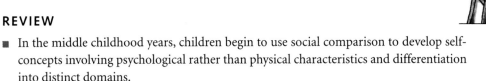

REVIEW AND RETHINK

REVIEW

■ In the middle childhood years, children begin to use social comparison to develop self-concepts involving psychological rather than physical characteristics and differentiation into distinct domains.

■ According to Erikson, children at this time are in the industry-versus-inferiority stage, focusing on efforts to achieve competence and to meet increasingly complex challenges.

■ During the middle childhood years, self-esteem develops significantly through comparisons with others and the formation of internal standards of success; if self-esteem is low, the result can be a cycle of failure.

- Self-efficacy—a sense of one's own capabilities—develops over the course of middle childhood through reflections on one's own performance, observations of others, and feedback.

- According to Kohlberg, moral development proceeds from an early concern with rewards and punishments, through a focus on social conventions and rules, toward a sense of universal moral principles.

RETHINK

- Does the fact that students in low-achievement schools often have higher academic self-esteem than students in high-achievement schools argue against high-achievement schools? Why or why not?

- If industriousness is a more accurate predictor of future success than IQ, how might industriousness be measured? How might an individual's industriousness be improved? Should this be a focus of schooling?

- What is an example of the relationship between low self-esteem and the cycle of failure in an area other than academics? How might the cycle of failure be broken?

- Are there cultural differences in the stages of moral development that might cast doubt on the universality of either Kohlberg's or Gilligan's theories?

RELATIONSHIPS: BUILDING FRIENDSHIP

In Lunch Room Number Two, Jamillah and her new classmates chew slowly on sandwiches and sip quietly on straws from cartons of milk. They huddle into their seats, staring blankly ahead, in awe of what's happening. The school principal moves among them with a microphone. "We eat quietly and we eat in our seats. No one gets up." On this day, no one seems inclined to test him. Boys and girls look timidly at the strange faces across the table from them, looking for someone who might play with them in the schoolyard, someone who might become a friend.

For these children, what happens in the schoolyard will be just as important as what happens in the school. And when they're out on the playground, there will be no one to protect them. No child will hold back to keep from beating them at a game, humiliating them in a test of skill, or harming them in a fight. No one will run interference or guarantee membership in a group. Out on the playground, it's sink or swim. No one automatically becomes your friend. (Kotre & Hall, 1990, pp. 112-113)

As Jamillah and her classmates demonstrate, friendship comes to play an increasingly important role during middle childhood. Children grow progressively more sensitive to the importance of friends, and building and maintaining friendships becomes a large part of children's social lives.

The formation of friendships influences children's development in several ways. For instance, friendships provide children with information about the world and other people, as well as about themselves. Friends provide emotional support that allows children to respond more effectively to stress. Friends can teach children how to manage and control their emotions, and help them to interpret their own emotional experiences. Friendships also provide a training ground for communicating and interacting with others, and they can foster intellectual growth. Finally, friendships allow children to practice their skills in forming close relationships with others—skills that will become increasingly important in their future lives (Asher & Parker, 1991; Hartup, 1992; Bukowski, Newcomb, & Hartup, 1996; Hartup & Stevens, 1997).

Status among School-age Children: Establishing One's Position

Who's on top? Although school-age children are not likely to articulate such a question, the reality of children's friendships is that they exhibit clear hierarchies in terms of status. **Status** is the evaluation of a role or person by other relevant members of a group. Children

status *the evaluation of a role or person by other relevant members of a group*

who have higher status have greater access to available resources, such as games, toys, books, and information. In contrast, lower-status children are more likely to follow the lead of children of higher status.

Status is an important determinant of children's friendships. High-status children tend to form friendships with higher-status individuals, whereas lower-status children are more likely to have friends of lower status. The number of friends a child has is also related to status: Higher-status children are more apt to have a greater number of friends than those of lower status.

But the separation of higher-status children from lower-status children occurs not only in the quantity of social interactions, but also in the nature of their interactions. Higher-status children are more likely to be viewed as friends by other children. They are more likely to form cliques, groups that are viewed as exclusive and desirable, and they tend to interact with a greater number of other children. In contrast, children of lower status are more likely to play with younger or less popular children (Ladd, 1983).

Popularity, then, is a reflection of children's status. School-age children who are mid to high in status are more likely to initiate and coordinate joint social behavior, making their general level of social activity higher than that of children low in social status (Erwin, 1993).

Stages of Friendship

During middle childhood, a child's conception of friendship undergoes some profound changes. According to developmental psychologist William Damon, a child's view of friendship passes through three distinct stages (Damon, 1977; Damon & Hart, 1988).

In the first stage, which ranges from around 4 to 7 years of age, children see friends as others who like them and with whom they share toys and other activities. They view the children with whom they spend the most time as their friends. For instance, a kindergartner who was asked, "How do you know that someone is your best friend?" responded in this way:

> I sleep over at his house sometimes. When he's playing ball with his friends he'll let me play. When I slept over, he let me get in front of him in 4-squares. He likes me. (Damon, 1983, p. 140)

What children in this first stage don't do much of, however, is to take others' personal qualities into consideration. For instance, they don't see their friendships as being based on their peers' unique positive personal traits. Instead, they use a very concrete approach to deciding who is a friend, primarily dependent on others' behavior. They like those who share and with whom they can share, and they don't like those who don't share, who hit, or who don't play with them. In sum, in the first stage, friends are viewed largely in terms of presenting opportunities for pleasant interactions.

In the next stage, however, children's view of friendship becomes more complicated. Lasting from around age 8 to age 10, this stage covers a period in which children take others' personal qualities and traits into consideration. In addition, friends are viewed in terms of the kinds of rewards they provide. For instance, consider how an 8-year-old girl explains why another girl is her "best friend":

> She never disagrees, she never eats in front of me, she never walks away when I'm crying, and she helps me on my homework. (Damon, 1988, pp. 80–81)

Clearly, this girl's view of friendship is based on the responsivity of her "best friend" to her needs, not just on how often they engage in shared activities. In fact, the centerpiece of friendship in this second stage is mutual trust. Friends are seen as those who can be counted on to help out when they are needed. This means that violations of trust are taken very seriously, and friends cannot make amends for such violations just by engaging in positive play, as they might at earlier ages. Instead, the expectation is that

Friendships provide children with emotional support as well as information about others and themselves.

formal explanations and formal apologies must be provided before a friendship can be reestablished.

The third stage of friendship begins toward the end of middle childhood, from 11 to 15 years of age. During this period, children begin to develop the view of friendship that they hold during adolescence. As we'll see when we discuss this perspective in detail in Chapter 12, the main criteria for friendship shift toward intimacy and loyalty. Friendship is characterized by psychological closeness, mutual disclosure, and exclusivity. By the time they reach the end of middle childhood, children seek out friends who will be loyal (Newcomb & Bagwell, 1995).

Consider, for instance, the following sixth-grader's response to the question "How do you know that someone is your best friend?":

> If you can tell each other things that you don't like about each other. If you get in a fight with someone else, they'd stick up for you. If you can tell them your phone number and they don't give you crank calls. If they don't act mean to you when other kids are around. (Damon, 1983, p. 140)

The twin themes of intimacy and loyal support are clearly sounded in this child's response. By the end of middle childhood, then, children come to view friendship not so much in terms of shared activities as in terms of the psychological benefits that friendship brings.

Children also develop clear ideas about which behaviors they seek in their friends—and which they dislike. As can be seen in Table 10-3, fifth- and sixth-graders most enjoy others who invite them to participate in activities and who are helpful, both physically and psychologically. In contrast, displays of physical or verbal aggression, among other behaviors, are disliked.

Individual Differences in Friendship: What Makes a Child Popular?

Why is it that some children are the schoolyard equivalent of the life of the party, and others are social isolates, whose overtures to others are dismissed or disdained?

TABLE 10-3

THE MOST-LIKED AND LEAST-LIKED BEHAVIORS THAT CHILDREN NOTE IN THEIR FRIENDS, IN ORDER OF IMPORTANCE

Most-Liked Behaviors	Least-Liked Behaviors
Having a sense of humor	Verbal aggression
Being nice or friendly	Expressions of anger
Being helpful	Dishonesty
Being complimentary	Being critical or criticizing
Inviting one to participate in games, etc.	Being greedy or bossy
Sharing	Physical aggression
Avoiding unpleasant behavior	Being annoying or bothersome
Giving one permission or control	Teasing
Providing instructions	Interfering with achievements
Loyalty	Unfaithfulness
Performing admirably	Violating of rules
Facilitating achievements	Ignoring others

(*Source:* Adapted from Zarbatany, Hartmann, & Rankin, 1990.)

Developmentalists have attempted to answer this question by examining individual differences in popularity, seeking to identify the reasons some children climb the ladder of popularity and others remain firmly on the ground.

What Personal Characteristics Lead to Popularity? Popular children share several personality characteristics. They are usually helpful, cooperating with others on joint projects. They are also funny, tending to have good senses of humor and to appreciate others' attempts at humor. Compared with children who are less popular, they are better able to understand others' emotional experiences by more accurately reading their nonverbal behavior. In sum, popular children are high in **social competence**, the collection of social skills that permit individuals to perform successfully in social settings (Feldman, Philippot, & Custrini, 1991; Erwin, 1993; Hubbard & Coie, 1994).

Popular children are not totally self-sufficient. They show interest in others, and they are not afraid to ask for others' help when necessary. At the same time, though, they are not overly reliant on others. Consequently, popular children maintain a balance between independence and dependence (Hartup, 1970; Rubin, Daniels-Beirness, & Hayvren, 1982).

When they enter a new social situation, popular children have a sense of what is occurring and learn to adapt their behavior to the situation. They are aware that it takes time to build relationships and that they may only gradually become a full member of a new group (Asher, 1983; Putallaz, 1983).

Children who are unpopular, in contrast, can be sad figures, for school-age children can be particularly unwelcoming to social outcasts. Unpopular children may be the last chosen to participate in activities with other children, or they may be actively discriminated against in classroom activities (Oldenburg & Kerns, 1997).

On the other hand, unpopular children are not always unhappy children, and they often have at least some friends. For example, one study showed that only a moderate association existed between unpopularity in school and children's reports of how lonely they were. One explanation may be that the children who are unpopular in school compensate by playing with neighborhood friends or siblings (Asher, Hymel, & Renshaw, 1984; Vandell & Hembree, 1994).

What makes some children unpopular? Some are unliked because they are immature, acting silly or in ways that are more appropriate to younger children. Others are overly aggressive, showing hostility to their peers or acting in an overbearing manner, whereas still others are so withdrawn that they permit little interaction. Some children are unpopular because they are far from society's stereotypes of physical attractiveness. Consequently, children who are unusually obese or thin, who "look funny," or who are extremely slow academically may find themselves in the unenviable role of class outcast (Dodge & Crick, 1990; Rys & Bear, 1997).

Lack of popularity may take one of two forms (Asher & Parker, 1991). **Neglected children** are those who receive relatively little attention from their peers. They are not necessarily disliked; they just do not receive much attention in the form of either positive or negative interactions. It turns out, however, that neglected children do not fare all that badly. Although they see themselves as less socially competent than other children, they often do not feel less happy or accepted than their more popular peers (Erwin, 1993).

On the other hand, a second form of unpopularity—active rejection—is more harmful. **Rejected children** are actively disliked, and their peers may react to them in an obviously negative manner. Rejected children are disruptive, aggressive, uncooperative, short-tempered, and unfriendly. In general, they lack social competence. Moreover, their behavior is often seen as a problem not only by other children, but by adults as well

social competence the collection of social skills that permit individuals to perform successfully in social settings

neglected children children who receive relatively little attention from their peers in the form of either positive or negative interactions

rejected children children who are actively disliked, and whose peers may react to them in an obviously negative manner

A variety of factors lead some children to be unpopular and socially isolated from their peers.

social problem-solving *The use of strategies for solving social conflicts in ways that are satisfactory both to oneself and to others*

(Volling et al., 1993; DeRosier, Kupersmidt, & Patterson, 1994; Boivin, Dodge, & Coie, 1995).

The long-term outcomes for rejected children can be quite negative. Rejected children are more likely to be poorly adjusted and to show delinquency in their later lives than popular or neglected children. Of course, it is not clear whether these difficulties are caused by their rejection by their peers, or by behavior problems that may have led them to become rejected in the first place (Bagwell, Newcomb, & Bukowski, 1998; Eron, 1998). (Also see the accompanying "Directions in Development" box.)

Social Problem-solving Abilities. Another factor that relates to children's popularity is their skill at social problem-solving. **Social problem-solving** refers to the use of strategies for solving social conflicts in ways that are satisfactory both to oneself and to others. Because social conflicts among school-age children are a not infrequent occurrence—even among the best of friends—successful strategies for dealing with them are an important element of social success (Hay, 1984; Laursen, Hartup, & Koplas, 1996).

According to developmental psychologist Kenneth Dodge, successful social problem-solving proceeds through a series of steps that correspond to children's information-

Directions in Development

Stopping the Torment: Dealing with Schoolyard Bullies

Sitting around the dinner table with his family three years ago, Raul Ugarte found himself hungering only for justice. His daughter Tianna, a sixth-grade cheerleader at Bidwell Elementary School in Antioch, California, near Sacramento, had mentioned that one of her classmates was verbally harassing her. And these were not ordinary schoolyard toughs. Tianna said the boy had used degrading sexual epithets and had even threatened to kill her. Aghast, Ugarte said he would ask school officials to put a stop to it. But Tianna, then 11, begged him not to; it would only make the situation worse, she told him. "When I looked at her face, I saw total fear," says Ugarte, who owns a shipping supply company. "It was the first time I'd ever seen that in her eyes. And then I knew something very serious was happening to her." (Hewitt, 1996, p. 53)

Unfortunately, many children have had experiences similar to this one. According to the National Association of School Psychologists, 160,000 U.S. schoolchildren stay home from school each day because they are afraid of being bullied.

The victims of bullies typically share several characteristics. Most often they are loners who are fairly passive. They often cry easily, and they tend to lack the social skills that might otherwise defuse a bullying situation with humor. But even children without these characteristics are bullied at some point in their school careers: Some 90 percent of middle-school students report being bullied at some point in their time at school (Bernstein & Watson, 1997; Egan & Perry, 1998).

About 15 percent of students bully others at one time or another. About half of all bullies come from abusive homes—meaning, of course, that half do not come from such homes. They tend to watch more television containing violence, and they misbehave more at home and at school than nonbullies. When their bullying gets them into trouble, they may try to lie their way out of the situation, and they show little remorse for their victimization of others. Furthermore, bullies, compared with their peers, are more likely to break the law as adults. Ironically, bullies are often relatively popular among their peers (Olweus, 1993, 1995; Franklin, 1996).

Despite the prevalence of bullying, it is possible to stop the behavior by "bully-proofing" schools. According to psychologists Carla Garrity, Kathryn Jens, and William Porter (1996), victims of bullying can be taught skills that help them defuse difficult circumstances that might otherwise lead to being victimized. They can be taught to protect themselves by leaving situations in which bullying can occur. They also need to increase their tolerance, understanding that they should not get upset by a bully's taunts and realizing that they are not responsible for the bully's behavior.

Of course, changing the behavior of the bully is also a good way to address the problem of bullying. For instance, bullies and their classmates need to be taught the importance of creating a caring, warm environment. By attempting to change the norms of the school to ones in which bullying is not tolerable, social pressures on bullies can help to keep their bullying in check.

Bullying is a real problem for many children. Without sustained intervention, it is unlikely to go away on its own. Consequently, programs designed to reduce the incidence of bullying are increasingly being adopted by school systems (Seppa, 1996).

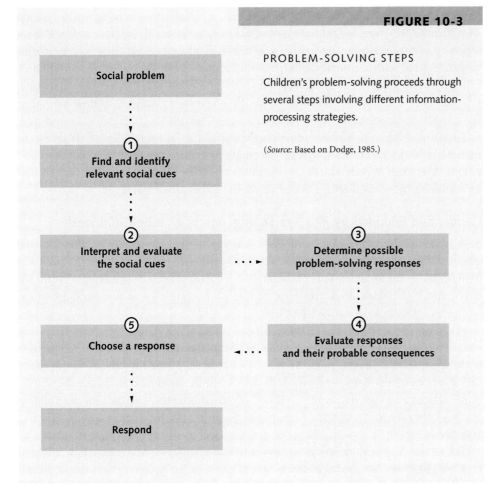

FIGURE 10-3

PROBLEM-SOLVING STEPS

Children's problem-solving proceeds through several steps involving different information-processing strategies.

(*Source:* Based on Dodge, 1985.)

processing strategies (see Figure 10-3). Dodge argues that the manner in which children solve social problems is a consequence of the decisions that they make at each point in the sequence (Dodge, 1985; Dodge et al., 1986; Dodge & Crick, 1990; Dodge & Price, 1994).

By carefully delineating each of the stages, Dodge provides a means by which interventions can be targeted toward a specific child's deficits. For instance, some children routinely misinterpret the meaning of other children's behavior (Step 2), and then respond according to their misinterpretation.

Consider, for example, Frank, a fourth-grader, who is playing a game with Bill. While playing the game, Bill begins to get angry because he is losing. If Frank mistakenly assumes that Bill is angry not because he is losing but because of something that Frank has done, Frank's misunderstanding may lead *him* to react with anger, making the situation more volatile. If Frank had interpreted the source of Bill's anger more accurately, Frank might have been able to behave in a more effective manner, thereby defusing the situation.

Generally, children who are popular are better at interpreting the meaning of others' behavior. Furthermore, they possess a wider inventory of techniques for dealing with social problems. In contrast, less popular children tend to be less effective at understanding the causes of others' behavior, and their strategies for dealing with social problems are more limited (Vitaro & Pelletier, 1991).

Teaching Social Competence. Can anything be done to help unpopular children learn social competence? Happily, the answer appears to be yes. Several programs have been developed to teach children a set of social skills that seem to underlie general social competence. For example, in one experimental program, a group of unpopular fifth- and

dominance hierarchy *rankings that represent the relative social power of those in a group*

sixth-graders were taught the skills that underlie such abilities as holding a conversation with friends. They were taught ways to disclose material about themselves, to learn about others by asking questions, and to offer help and suggestions to others in a nonthreatening way. Compared with a group of children who did not receive such training, the children who were in the experiment interacted more with their peers, held more conversations, developed higher self-esteem, and—most critically—were more accepted by their peers than before training (Bierman & Furman, 1984; Asher & Rose, 1997).

Similarly, children in another program were taught to be more adept at decoding the meaning of facial expressions, thereby becoming more sensitive to others' emotions and moods. As a result of their training, some children in the program became noticeably better at making friends and getting along with their teachers (Nowicki, 1989).

Gender and Friendships: The Sex Segregation of Middle Childhood

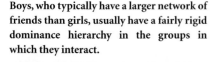

Boys are idiots. Girls have cooties. At least those are the typical views offered by boys and girls regarding members of the opposite sex during the elementary school years. Avoidance of the opposite sex becomes quite pronounced during those years, to the degree that the social networks of most boys and girls consist almost entirely of same-sex groupings (Gottman, 1986; Adler, Kless, & Adler, 1992).

When boys and girls make occasional forays into the other gender's territory, the action often has romantic overtones. For instance, girls may threaten to kiss a boy, or boys might try to lure girls into chasing them. Such behavior, termed *border work*, helps to emphasize the clear boundaries that exist between the two sexes. In addition, it may pave the way for future interactions that do involve romantic or sexual interests when school-age children reach adolescence and cross-sex interactions become more socially endorsed (Thorne, 1986; Beal, 1994).

The lack of cross-gender interaction in the middle childhood years means that boys' and girls' friendships are restricted to members of their own gender. However, the nature of friendships within the two genders is quite different.

Boys typically have larger networks of friends than girls, and they tend to play in groups, rather than pairing off. The status hierarchy is usually fairly blatant, with an acknowledged leader and members falling into particular levels of status. Because of this fairly rigid **dominance hierarchy**, rankings that represent the relative social power of those in the group, members of higher status can safely question and oppose children lower in the hierarchy (Beal, 1994).

Boys tend to be concerned with their place in the status hierarchy, and they attempt to maintain their status and improve it. This makes for a style of play known as *restrictive*. In restrictive play, interactions are interrupted when a child feels that his status is challenged.

Boys, who typically have a larger network of friends than girls, usually have a fairly rigid dominance hierarchy in the groups in which they interact.

Thus, a boy who feels that he is unjustly challenged by a peer of lower status may attempt to end the interaction by scuffling over a toy or otherwise behaving assertively. Consequently, boys' play tends to come in bursts, rather than in more extended, tranquil episodes (Boulton & Smith, 1990; Benenson & Apostoleris, 1993).

The language of friendship used among boys reflects their concern over status and challenge. For instance, consider this conversation between two African American boys who were good friends:

Child 1: Why don't you get out of my yard.
Child 2: Why don't you *make* me get out the yard.
Child 1: I *know* you don't want that.
Child 2: You're not gonna make me get out the yard cuz you can't.
Child 1: Don't force me.
Child 2: You can't. Don't force me to hurt you (*snickers*). (Goodwin, 1990, p. 37)

Friendship patterns among girls are quite different. Rather than having a wide network of friends, school-age girls focus on one or two "best friends" who are of relatively equal status. In contrast to boys, who seek out status differences, girls profess to avoid differences in status, preferring to maintain friendships at equal-status levels.

Conflicts among school-age girls are solved through compromise, by ignoring the situation, or by giving in, rather than by seeking to make one's own point of view prevail. In sum, the goal is to smooth over disagreements, making social interaction easy and nonconfrontational (Goodwin, 1990).

According to developmental psychologist Carole Beal, the motivation of girls to solve social conflict indirectly does not stem from a lack of self-confidence or from apprehension over the use of more direct approaches. In fact, when school-age girls interact with other girls who are not considered friends or with boys, they can be quite confrontational. However, among friends their goal is to maintain equal-status relationships—ones lacking a dominance hierarchy (Beal, 1994).

The language used by girls tends to reflect their view of relationships. Rather than blatant demands ("Give me the pencil"), girls are more apt to use language that is less confrontational and directive. Girls tend to use indirect forms of verbs, such as "Let's go to the movies" or "Would you want to trade books with me?" rather than "I want to go to the movies" or "Let me have these books" (Goodwin, 1980, 1990).

Interestingly, the segregation of friendships according to gender occurs in almost all societies. Why should this be? In nonindustrialized societies, same-gender segregation may be the result of the types of activities that children engage in. For instance, in many cultures, boys are assigned one type of chore and girls another. Segregation in activities leads to the development of same-gender friendships (Harkness & Super, 1985; Whiting & Edwards, 1988).

Promoting Cross-race Friendships: Integration In and Out of the Classroom

Are friendships color-blind? For the most part, the answer is no. Children's closest friendships tend largely to be with others of the same race. In fact, as children age there is a decline in the number and depth of friendships outside their own racial group. By the time they are 11 or 12, it appears that African American children become particularly aware of and sensitive to the prejudice and discrimination directed toward members of their race, and they are more apt to make ingroup–outgroup distinctions (Singleton & Asher, 1979; Hartup, 1983; Bigler, Jones, & Lobliner, 1997).

Although closest friendships tend to be with others of the same race, members of different racial and ethnic groups can show a high degree of mutual acceptance, particularly in schools with ongoing integration efforts.

For instance, when third-graders from one long-time integrated school were asked to name a best friend, around one-quarter of white children and two-thirds of African American children chose a child of the other race. In contrast, by the time they reached tenth grade, less than 10 percent of whites and 5 percent of African Americans named a different-race best friend (Singleton & Asher, 1979; Asher, Singleton, & Taylor, 1982).

On the other hand, although they may not choose each other as best friends, whites and African Americans—as well as members of other minority groups—can show a high degree of mutual acceptance. This pattern is particularly true in schools with ongoing integration efforts. This makes sense: A good deal of research supports the notion that contact between majority and minority group members can reduce prejudice and discrimination (Gaertner et al., 1990; Desforges et al., 1991; Wells & Crain, 1994).

The Informed Consumer of Development

Increasing Children's Social Competence

It is clear that building and maintaining friendships is critical in children's lives. Is there anything that parents and teachers can do to increase children's social competence?

The answer is a clear yes. Among the strategies that can work are the following:

- Encourage social interaction. Teachers can devise ways in which children are led to take part in group activities, and parents can encourage membership in such groups as Brownies and Cub Scouts or participation in team sports.

- Teach listening skills to children. Show them how to listen carefully and respond to the underlying meaning of a communication as well as its overt content.

- Make children aware that people display emotions and moods nonverbally and that consequently they should pay attention to others' nonverbal behavior, not only to what they are saying on a verbal level.

- Teach conversational skills, including the importance of asking questions and self-disclosure. Encourage students to use "I" statements in which they clarify their own feelings or opinions, and avoid making generalizations about others.

- Don't ask children to choose teams or groups publicly. Instead, assign children randomly: It works just as well in ensuring a distribution of abilities across groups and avoids the public embarrassment of a situation in which some children are chosen last.

REVIEW AND RETHINK

REVIEW

- Children pass through three stages in their understanding of friendship, from the sharing of enjoyable activities, through the consideration of personal traits that can meet their needs, to a focus on intimacy and loyalty.

- Friendships in childhood display status hierarchies, with popular, high-status children manifesting social competence and engaging in more relationships; low-status children becoming followers; and unpopular children being either neglected or rejected by their peers.

- Because social competence affects popularity, improvements in such abilities as social problem-solving and social information-processing can lead to better interpersonal skills and greater popularity.

- Boys and girls engage increasingly in same-sex friendships, with boys' friendships involving group relationships, dominance hierarchies, and restrictive play, and girls' friendships characterized by equal-status pairings, cooperation, compromise, and the avoidance of confrontation.

■ Interracial friendships decrease in frequency as children age, but equal-status contacts among members of different races can promote mutual acceptance and appreciation.

RETHINK

■ Do you think the stages of friendship are a childhood phenomenon, or do adults' friendships display similar stages?

■ Is there a "cycle of success" in the relationship between social competence and popularity? A cycle of failure in their opposites? Explain.

■ Do you think boys' and girls' different approaches to friendship are primarily genetic or environmental? In what ways might they be influenced by cultural factors?

■ Is it possible to decrease the segregation of friendships along racial lines? What factors would have to change in individuals or in society?

FAMILY AND SCHOOL: SHAPING CHILDREN'S BEHAVIOR IN MIDDLE CHILDHOOD

The routine is similar every day. Five days a week, after school gets out, 10-year-old Marlene O'Connor gets off the school bus and trudges up the hill to her home. She takes the house key, which she keeps on a string around her neck to avoid losing it, and opens the front door to her empty home. Locking the door behind her, she turns on the television and calls her mother, who is at work as a service representative for an Ohio electric utility. After chatting briefly with her mother, assuring her that she is well, Marlene turns her attention to the television as she eats a snack she has found in the kitchen. She watches TV until her mother and father return home a few hours later.

Is Marlene paying a price because both her parents work outside the home? This question is one of several that we need to address as we consider how children's schooling and home life profoundly affect their lives during middle childhood.

Family: The Changing Home Environment

The original plot goes like this: first comes love. Then comes marriage. Then comes Mary with a baby carriage. But now there's a sequel: John and Mary break up. John moves in with Sally and her two boys. Mary takes the baby Paul. A year later Mary meets Jack, who is divorced with three children. They get married. Paul, barely 2 years old, now has a mother, a father, a stepmother, a stepfather, and five stepbrothers and stepsisters— as well as four sets of grandparents (biological and step) and countless aunts and uncles. And guess what? Mary's pregnant again. (Katrowitz & Wingert, 1990, p. 24)

We've already noted in earlier chapters the changes that have occurred in the structure of the family over the last few decades. With a soaring divorce rate, an increase in the number of parents who both work outside of the home, and a rise in single-parent families, the environment faced by children passing through middle childhood in the 1990s is very different from the one prior generations faced.

The Consequences of Divorce.   Having divorced parents is no longer very distinctive. Only around half of children in the United States will pass through childhood living with both of their parents, each of whom has been married only one time. Thirty years ago, about three quarters of children lived in these circumstances (Jacobson, 1987). The rest will live in single-parent homes; or with stepparents, grandparents, or other nonparental relatives; and some will end up in foster care. Minority groups have been hit particularly hard by these trends: More than half of all black children and almost one-third of all Hispanic children live in homes with only one parent.

How do children react to divorce? The answer depends on how soon you ask the question following a divorce, as well as how old the children are at the time. Immediately after a divorce, the results can be quite devastating. Both children and parents may show several types of psychological maladjustment for a period that may last from 6 months to 2 years. For instance, children may be anxious, experience depression, or show sleep disturbances and phobias. Even though children most often live with their mothers following a divorce, the quality of the mother–child relationship declines in the majority of cases (Gottman, 1993; Guttman, 1993; Holroyd & Sheppard, 1997).

During the early stage of middle childhood, children whose parents are divorcing often tend to blame themselves for the breakup. By the age of 10, children feel pressure to choose sides, taking the position of either the mother or the father. They thereby experience some degree of divided loyalty (Wallerstein & Blakeslee, 1989).

On the other hand, the consequences of divorce become less devastating from 18 months to 2 years later. After reaching a low point approximately a year after the divorce, most children begin to return to their predivorce state of psychological adjustment. Still, twice as many children of divorced parents require psychological counseling as children from intact families, and the effects may linger. For example, people who have experienced parental divorce are more at risk for experiencing divorce themselves later in life (Zill, 1983; Hetherington, Stanley-Hagan, & Anderson, 1989; Tucker et al., 1997).

Several factors relate to how children react to divorce. One is the economic standing of the family the child is living with. In many cases, divorce brings a decline in both parents' standards of living. When this occurs, children may be thrown into poverty, which can have a negative effect on many aspects of their upbringing.

In other cases, the negative consequences of divorce are less severe than they might otherwise be because the divorce reduces the hostility and anger in the home. Because the predivorce household was overflowing with parental strife, in some cases the relative lack of conflict of a postdivorce household may be beneficial to children. This is particularly true for children who maintain a close, positive relationship with the parent with whom they do not live. Consequently, for some children, living with parents who have an intact but unhappy marriage, high in conflict, has more and stronger negative consequences than experiencing a parental divorce (Booth & Edwards, 1989; Cherlin, 1993; Davies & Cummings, 1994; Gelles, 1994; Gottfried & Gottfried, 1994).

Living in Blended Families.   For many children, the aftermath of divorce includes the subsequent remarriage of one or both parents. In fact, more than 10 million households in the United States contain at least one spouse who has remarried. More than 5 million remarried couples have at least one stepchild living with them in what has come to be called **blended families**. Experts predict that by the year 2000, over 50 percent of children born in the last decade will be stepdaughters and stepsons (Glick, 1989; U.S. Bureau of the Census, 1991b).

Living in a blended family is challenging for the children involved. There often is a fair amount of *role ambiguity*, in which roles and expectations are unclear. Children may be uncertain about their responsibilities, how to behave to stepparents and stepsiblings, and how to make a host of decisions that have wide-ranging implications for their role

blended families   *a remarried couple that has at least one stepchild living with them*

"Blended" families occur when previously married husbands and wives with children remarry.

in the family. For instance, a child in a blended family may have to choose which parent to spend each vacation and holiday with, or to decide between the conflicting suggestions they have received from biological parent and stepparent (Cherlin, 1993; Dainton, 1993).

How do school-age children in blended families fare? In many cases, surprisingly well. In comparison to adolescents, who have more difficulties, school-age children often adjust relatively smoothly to blended arrangements, for several reasons. For one thing, the family's financial situation is often improved after a parent remarries. In addition, in a blended family more people are available to share the burden of household chores. Finally, the fact that the family contains more individuals can increase the opportunities for social interaction (Hetherington & Clingempeel, 1992; Hetherington, Stanley-Hagan, & Anderson, 1989).

On the other hand, not all children adjust well. Some find the disruption of routine and of established networks of family relationships difficult. For instance, a child who is used to having her mother's complete attention may find it difficult to observe her mother showing interest and affection to a stepchild. The blending of families does not always proceed smoothly.

When Both Parents Work: How Do Children Fare?   In most cases, children whose parents both work full-time outside of the home fare quite well. Most research suggests that children whose parents are loving, are sensitive to their children's needs, and provide appropriate substitute care develop no differently from children in families in which one of the parents does not work (Kamerman & Hayes, 1982; Hoffman, 1989).

One reason that children whose mothers and fathers both work develop no differently relates to the psychological adjustment of the parents. In general, women who are satisfied with their lives tend to be more nurturing with their children. When work provides a high level of satisfaction, then, mothers who work outside of the home may be more psychologically supportive of their children. Thus, it is not so much a question of whether a mother chooses to work full-time, to stay at home, or to arrange some combination of the two. What matters is how satisfied she is with the choices she has made (Scarr, Phillips, & McCartney, 1989; Barnett & Rivers, 1992; Gilbert, 1994).

Although we might expect that children whose parents both work would spend comparatively less time with their parents than children with one parent at home full-time, research suggests otherwise. Children with mothers and fathers who work full-time spend essentially the same amount of time with family, in class, with friends, and alone as children in families where one parent stays at home (Galambos & Dixon, 1984; Richards & Duckett, 1991, 1994).

Furthermore, as much time is spent on family meals and evening activities for children in families in which mothers are employed as in families in which mothers are not employed. In fact, some evidence suggests that working parents try to compensate for time that they are away from home, spending even more time in the evenings with their children than parents who do not both work.

On the other hand, the parent with whom children spend their time may be different. For instance, one survey of 10- to 13-year-olds found that children whose mothers were employed full-time spent more time alone with their fathers than children whose mothers were not so employed (Richards & Duckett, 1994).

Self-care Children.   Although children in families in which both parents work typically fare well, their success is due in part to the availability of adequate substitute care. For many children, however, no care is available, and they return after school to empty houses. These are **self-care children**, children who let themselves into their homes after school and wait alone until their parents return from work.

Concern about self-care children has centered on their lack of supervision and the emotional costs of being alone. In fact, such children were previously called *latchkey children*, raising connotations of sad, pathetic, and neglected children. However, research has not identified many differences between self-care children and children who return to homes with parents. Although many children report negative experiences while at home

The consequences of being a so-called latchkey child are not necessarily harmful, and may even lead to a greater sense of independence and competence.

self-care children   children who let themselves into their homes after school and wait alone until their caretakers return from work; previously known as latchkey children

by themselves (such as loneliness), they seem emotionally undamaged by the experience. In addition, if they stay at home by themselves rather than "hanging out" unsupervised with friends, they may avoid involvement in activities that can lead to difficulties (Long & Long, 1983; Steinberg, 1986; Belle, 1997).

In sum, the consequences of being a self-care child are not necessarily harmful. In fact, children may develop an enhanced sense of independence and competence. Furthermore, the time spent alone provides an opportunity to work uninterrupted on homework or school projects. Some findings even suggest that children with employed parents can have higher self-esteem because they feel they are contributing to the household in significant ways (Hoffman, 1989).

 Single-parent Families.   Almost one-quarter of all children under the age of 18 in the United States live with only one parent. If present trends continue, almost three-quarters of American children will spend some portion of their lives in a single-parent family before they are 18 years old. For minority children, the numbers are even higher: Some 60 percent of African American children and 35 percent of Hispanic children under the age of 18 live in single-parent homes (Demo & Acock, 1991; U.S. Bureau of the Census, 1990b, 1994; see Figure 10-4).

In most cases of single-parent households, no spouse was ever present (that is, the mother never married), the spouses have divorced, or the spouse is absent. In the vast majority of cases, the single parent who is present is the mother.

What consequences are there for children living in homes with just one parent? This is a difficult question to answer. Much depends on whether a second parent was present earlier and, if so, whether the two parents got along with each other or were constantly fighting. In cases of high parental strife, the decrease in overall tension and anxiety in a

FIGURE 10-4

INCREASE OF SINGLE MOTHERS, 1940–1993

The number of mothers without spouses has increased significantly over the last five decades.

(*Source:* National Center for Health Statistics, 1995.)

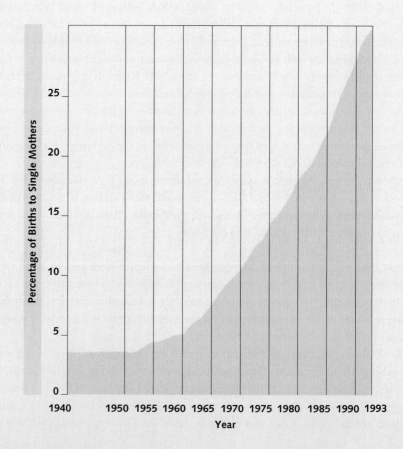

household reduced to a single parent may actually enhance a child's adjustment (Gongla & Thompson, 1987; Gottman & Katz, 1989).

Furthermore, the economic status of the single-parent family plays a role in determining the consequences on children. Living in relative poverty—and single-parent families are often less well-off financially than two-parent families—has a negative impact on children.

In sum, the impact of living in a single-parent family is not, by itself, invariably negative or positive. Given the large number of single-parent households, the stigma that once existed toward such families has largely declined. The ultimate consequences for children depend on a variety of factors that accompany single parenthood, such as the economic status of the family, the amount of time that the parent is able to spend with the child, and the degree of stress in the household.

The Consequences of Group Care: Orphanages in the 1990s.   The term *orphanage* evokes images of pitiful youngsters clothed in rags, eating porridge out of tin cups and housed in huge, prisonlike institutions. The reality today is different. Even the term *orphanage* is rarely used, having been replaced by *group home* or *residential treatment center*. Typically housing a relatively small number of children, group homes are used for children whose parents are no longer able to care for them adequately.

Group care has grown significantly in the last decade. In fact, in just the 4-year period from 1987 to 1991, the number of children in foster care increased by more than 50 percent. Today, close to one-half million children in the United States live in foster care (Carnegie Task Force on Meeting the Needs of Young Children, 1994).

About three-quarters of children in group care are victims of neglect and abuse. Most of them can be returned to their homes following intervention with their families by social service agencies. But the remaining one-quarter are so psychologically damaged due to abuse or other causes that, once they are placed in group care, they are likely to remain there throughout childhood. With severe problems, such as high levels of aggression or anger, they are largely unadoptable. No family even wants to house them temporarily in a foster home (Fanshel, Finch, & Grundy, 1990; Sugden, 1995; Rosenfeld et al., 1997).

Although some politicians have suggested that an increase in group care is a solution to complex social problems associated with unwed mothers who become dependent on welfare, experts in providing social services and psychological treatment are not so sure. For one thing, group homes cannot always consistently provide the support and love potentially available in a family setting. Moreover, group care is hardly cheap: It can cost some $40,000 per year to support a child in group care—about ten times the cost of

Although the orphanages of the early 1900s were crowded and institutional (left), today the equivalent, called group homes or residential treatment centers (right), are much more pleasant.

maintaining a child in foster care or on welfare (Cox & Cox, 1985; Fanshel, Finch, & Grundy, 1990, 1992).

Other experts argue that group care is inherently neither good nor bad. Instead, the consequences of living away from one's family may be quite positive, depending on the particular characteristics of the staff of the group home and whether child and youth care workers are able to develop an effective, stable, and strong emotional bond with a specific child. (Table 10-4 shows the personal characteristics of the best—and worst—child and youth care workers.) On the other hand, if a worker is unable to form a meaningful relationship with a child in a group home, the results may well be unfavorable (Shealy, 1995; McKenzie, 1997; Reddy & Pfeiffer, 1997). (For another view of group care, see the "Speaking of Development" box.)

School: The Academic Environment

Where do children spend most of their time? During the school year, at least, more of the day is spent in the classroom than anywhere else. It is not surprising, then, that schools have a profound impact on children's lives, shaping and molding not only their ways of thinking but the ways they view the world. We turn now to a number of critical aspects of schooling in middle childhood.

How Children Explain Academic Success and Failure.   Most of us, at one time or another, have done poorly on a test. Think back to how you felt when you received a bad grade. Did you feel shame? Anger at the teacher? Fear of the consequences? According to psychologist Bernard Weiner (1994), your response in such situations is determined largely by the particular causes to which you attribute your failure. And the kinds of attributions you make ultimately determine how hard you strive to do well on future tests.

TABLE 10-4

PERSONAL CHARACTERISTICS OF THE BEST AND WORST CHILD
AND YOUTH CARE WORKERS

The best workers:	The worst workers:
Flexible	Exhibit pathology
Mature	Selfish
Integrity	Defensive
Good judgment	Dishonest
Common sense	Abusive
Appropriate values	Abuse drugs/alcohol
Responsible	Uncooperative
Good self-image	Poor self-esteem
Self-control	Rigid
Responsive to authority	Irresponsible
Interpersonally adept	Critical
Stable	Passive-aggressive
Unpretentious	Inappropriate boundaries
Predictable/consistent	Unethical
Nondefensive	Authoritarian/coercive
Nurturant/firm	Inconsistent/unpredictable
Self-aware	Avoidant
Empowering	Don't learn from experience
Cooperative	Poor role model
Good role model	Angry/explosive

(*Source:* Adapted from Shealy, 1995.)

Sam Schmidt, Family Teacher

Education: .... University of Nebraska at Lincoln, B.A. in business administration

Position: .... Family teacher at Boys Town

Home: .... Boys Town, Nebraska

Following graduation from college 4½ years ago, Sam and Kristin Schmidt became house parents, or as they are called at Boys Town, family teachers, to four youths in one of the 74 individual homes at Boys Town.

"Many of the kids who come to Boys Town have been physically or sexually abused, and almost all of them have been emotionally abused," Schmidt says. "They have a strange perception of such things as how to treat other children and adults. We try to teach them boundaries and gradually to build a relationship with them to the point where they are comfortable when others are around.

"The major problem Boys Town deals with is behavior, and the philosophy here is very behavior-oriented. Instead of trying to change the kids themselves from the inside out, we try to change their behavior through behavior modification," says Schmidt. "We teach them a lot of different skills, such as how to follow instructions, accept criticism, and agree and disagree appropriately with adults."

Boys Town has its own elementary school and high school, and the same techniques are applied there as are used in the home, according to Schmidt. One of the basic approaches is called SODAS, or Situation, Options, Disadvantages, Advantages, and Solution.

"We start by asking the individuals to write down what the situation is—say, taking out the trash," Schmidt explains. "They then think of two or three options, such as 'I will do it' and 'I won't do it.' Then they write down the advantages and disadvantages of each option and think about them. This process usually helps them arrive at a solution."

Another motivational program used at Boys Town is a point system. Positive points are awarded for good behavior and point fines for negative behavior.

"Once a day the point cards are totaled, and if the kids have enough points they get privileges like watching television, going to the gym, or using the telephone," Schmidt says. "If they don't make the point total, they are assigned academic work or other work, or they may have to write on a problem-solving situation.

"When they come here they learn the basic skills, and usually they respond to them very well," he adds. "Many of them do it over time, until, gradually, appropriate behavior becomes internalized and they do it without thinking about it."

"Instead of trying to change the kids themselves from the inside out, we try to change their behavior through behavior modification."

"Gradually, appropriate behavior becomes internalized and they do it without thinking about it."

attributions *people's understanding of the reasons behind their behavior*

Weiner has proposed a theory of motivation based on people's **attributions**, their understanding of the reasons behind their behavior. He suggests that people attempt to determine the causes of their academic success or failure by considering three basic dimensions: (1) whether the cause is internal (dispositional) or external (situational); (2) whether the cause is stable or unstable; and (3) whether the cause is controllable or uncontrollable.

Consider, for instance, a student named Henry who gets a 98, the highest score in the class, on an exam. To what can he attribute his success? He might think it is a result of his ability, his effort in studying for the test, or the fact that he was rested and relaxed when he took the test. Because each of these factors is related to what Henry is or has done, they are internal attributions. But note how they differ on the other dimensions: Ability is a stable, enduring factors, whereas study effort and degree of relaxation are both unstable and can fluctuate from one test to another. Finally, study effort and degree of relaxation differ from each other in terms of controllability: Although amount of effort is controllable, degree of relaxation may not be.

The attributions people make have important implications for their perceptions of their performance. For example, the internal–external dimension is related to esteem-related emotions. When a success is attributed to internal factors, students tend to feel pride; but failure attributed to internal factors causes shame. On the other hand, the stability dimension determines future expectations about success and failure. Specifically, when students attribute success or failure to factors that are relatively stable and invariant, they are apt to expect similar performance in the future. In contrast, when they attribute performance to unstable factors such as effort or luck, their expectations about future performance are relatively unaffected.

Finally, the controllability dimension affects emotions that are directed toward others. If children feel that failure was due to factors within their control—e.g., lack of effort—they are apt to experience anger; but if the failure was uncontrollable, they are likely to feel sadness or pity.

Cultural Comparisons: Individual Differences in Attribution. Not everyone comes to the same conclusions about the sources of success and failure. In fact, among the strongest influences on people's attributions are their race, ethnicity, and socioeconomic status. Because different experiences give us different perceptions about the ways things in the world fit together, it is not surprising that there are subcultural differences in how achievement-related behaviors are understood and explained.

One important difference is related to racial factors: African Americans are less likely than whites to attribute success to internal rather than external causes. Specifically,

Doonesbury

BY GARRY TRUDEAU

African American children sometimes feel that task difficulty and luck (external causes) are the major determinants of their performance outcomes, and even if they put in maximum effort, prejudice and discrimination will prevent them from succeeding (Friend & Neale, 1972; Ogbu, 1988; Graham, 1990, 1994).

An attributional pattern that overemphasizes the importance of external causes is maladaptive. Attributions to external factors reduce a student's sense of personal responsibility for success or failure. But when attributions are based on internal factors, they suggest that a change in behavior—such as increased effort—can bring about a change in success (Graham, 1990; Glasgow et al., 1997).

African Americans are not the only group susceptible to maladaptive attributional patterns. Women, for example, often attribute their unsuccessful performance to low ability, an uncontrollable factor. Ironically, though, they do not attribute successful performance to high ability, but to factors outside their control. A belief in this pattern suggests the conclusion that even with future effort, success will be unattainable. Females who hold these views may be less inclined to expend the effort necessary to improve their rate of success (Dweck & Bush, 1976; Phillips & Zimmerman, 1990; Dweck, 1991; Nelson & Cooper, 1997).

Expectation Effects: How Others' Expectancies Influence Children's Behavior.   Suppose you were told at the beginning of a new school year that the children in your class had taken a test described in this way:

> All children show hills, plateaus, and valleys in their scholastic progress. A study being conducted at Harvard with the support of the National Science Foundation is interested in those children who show an unusual forward spurt of academic progress. These spurts can and do occur at any level of academic and intellectual functioning. When these spurts occur in children who have not been functioning too well academically, the result is familiarly referred to as "late blooming."
>
> As part of our study we are further validating a test which predicts the likelihood that a child will show an inflection point or "spurt" within the near future. This test which will be administered in your school will allow us to predict which youngsters are most likely to show an academic spurt. . . . The development of the test for predicting inflections or "spurts" is not yet such that *every* one of the top 20 percent will show the spurt or "blooming" effect. But the top 20 percent of the children *will* show a more significant inflection or spurt within the next year or less than will the remaining 80 percent of the children. (Rosenthal & Jacobson, 1968, p. 66)

Consider your reaction to the children on the list of "bloomers" identified by the test. Would you treat them differently from the children who were not so designated?

If the results of a classic, but controversial, study are any guide, your answer should be affirmative: Teachers do, in fact, seem to treat children for whom they have expectations of improvement differently from those for whom they have no such expectations (Rosenthal & Jacobson, 1968). In the experiment, elementary school teachers were told at the beginning of a new school year that five children in their classes would be likely to "bloom" in the upcoming year, based on the test described above. In reality, however, the information was bogus: The names of the children had simply been picked at random, although the teachers didn't know that. The teachers received no further details from the experimenters for the rest of the year.

At the end of the year, the children completed an intelligence test that was identical to one taken a year earlier. According to the experimenters, the results showed that clear differences existed in the intellectual growth of the so-called bloomers compared with that of the other members of their classes. Those randomly designated as likely to make significant gains did, in fact, improve more than the other children. However, the results were

Developmental Diversity

Cultural Differences in Attributions for Academic Performance: Explaining Asian Academic Success

Consider two students, Ben and Hannah, each performing poorly in school. Suppose you thought that Ben's poor performance was due to unalterable, stable causes, such as a lack of intelligence, whereas Hannah's was produced by temporary causes, such as a lack of hard work. Who would you think would ultimately do better in school?

If you are like most people, you'd probably predict that the outlook was better for Hannah. After all, Hannah could always work harder, but it is hard for someone like Ben to develop higher intelligence.

According to psychologist Harold Stevenson, this reasoning lies at the heart of the superior school performance of Asian students, compared with students in the United States. Stevenson's research suggests that teachers, parents, and students in the United States are likely to attribute school performance to stable, internal causes, whereas people in Japan, China, and other

East Asian countries are more likely to see temporary, situational factors as the cause of their performance. The Asian view, which stems in part from ancient Confucian writings, tends to accentuate the necessity of hard work and perseverance.

This cultural difference in attributional styles is displayed in several ways. For instance, surveys show that mothers, teachers, and students in Japan and Taiwan all believe strongly that students in a typical class tend to have the same amount of ability. In contrast, mothers, teachers, and students in the United States are apt to disagree, arguing that there are significant differences in ability among the various students (see Figure 10-5).

It is easy to imagine how such different attributional styles can influence teaching approaches. If, as in the United States, students and teachers seem to believe that ability is fixed and locked in, poor academic performance will be greeted with a sense of failure and reduced motivation to work harder to overcome it. In contrast, Japanese teachers and students are apt to see failure as a temporary setback, due to their lack of hard work. After making such an attribution, they are more apt to expend increased effort on future academic activities.

Some developmentalists have suggested that these different attributional orientations may explain the fact that Asian students frequently outperform American students in international comparisons of student achievement (Linn, 1997; Wheeler, 1998). Because Asian students tend to assume that academic success results from hard work, they may put greater effort into their schoolwork than American students, who believe that their inherent ability determines their performance. These arguments suggest that the attributional style of students and teachers in the United States might well be maladaptive. They also argue that the attributional styles taught to children by their parents may have a significant effect on their future success (Chen & Stevenson, 1995; Geary, 1996; Little & Lopez, 1997).

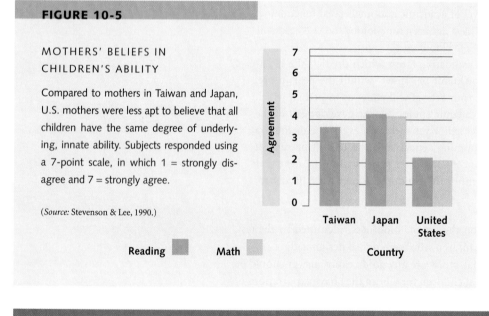

FIGURE 10-5

MOTHERS' BELIEFS IN CHILDREN'S ABILITY

Compared to mothers in Taiwan and Japan, U.S. mothers were less apt to believe that all children have the same degree of underlying, innate ability. Subjects responded using a 7-point scale, in which 1 = strongly disagree and 7 = strongly agree.

(*Source:* Stevenson & Lee, 1990.)

Reading   Math

Country

not uniform: The greatest differences were found for children in first and second grades, with smaller differences for children in grades three through six.

When the findings of the experiment, reported in a book dubbed *Pygmalion in the Classroom*, were published, they caused an immediate stir among educators—and among the public at large. The reason for this furor was the implication of the results: If merely holding high expectations is sufficient to bring about gains in achievement, wouldn't holding low expectations lead to slowed achievement? And because teachers sometimes may hold low expectations about children from lower socioeconomic and minority backgrounds, did this mean that children from such backgrounds were destined to show low achievement throughout their educational careers?

Although the original experiment has been criticized on methodological and statistical grounds (Snow, 1969; Wineburg, 1987), enough new evidence has been amassed to make it clear that the expectations of teachers are communicated to their students and can in fact bring about the expected performance. The phenomenon has come to be called the **teacher expectancy effect**—the cycle of behavior in which a teacher transmits an expectation about a child and actually brings about the expected behavior (Babad, 1992).

The teacher expectancy effect can be viewed as a special case of a broader concept known as the *self-fulfilling prophecy*, in which a person's expectation is capable of bringing about an outcome. For instance, physicians have long known that providing patients with placebos (fake, inactive drugs) can sometimes "cure" them, simply because the patients expect the medicine to work.

In the case of teacher expectancy effects, the basic explanation seems to be that teachers, after forming an initial expectation about a child's ability, transmit it to the child through a complex series of verbal and nonverbal cues. These communicated expectations in turn indicate to the child what behavior is appropriate, and the child behaves accordingly (Harris & Rosenthal, 1986; Rosenthal, 1987, 1994).

Once teachers have developed expectations about a child, by what method do they transmit them? Generally, four major factors relate to the transmission of expectations (Harris & Rosenthal, 1986; Rosenthal, 1994):

- *Classroom social-emotional climate.* Teachers create a warmer, more accepting environment for children for whom they hold high expectations than for those they expect less from. They convey more positive attitudes by smiling and nodding more often, and they look at high-expectation children more frequently.

- *Feedback.* When teachers hold high expectations for a child, they provide more positive evaluations of the child's work and they are more accepting of the child's ideas. In contrast, low-expectation children receive more criticism and little or no feedback in some situations. Even when low-expectation children do well, the kind of feedback teachers offer is less positive than when a high-expectation child does well.

- *Input to children.* Children who are expected to do well receive greater quantities of material from their teachers, and they are asked to complete more difficult material. Consequently, they are given more opportunities to perform well.

- *Output from teachers.* Teachers initiate more contacts with high-expectation children, and the overall number of contacts between teachers and high-expectation children is higher than with low-expectation children. As a result, high-expectation children have more opportunities to respond in class.

The final link in the chain of events that encompasses the teacher expectation effect is the child. And given the range of teacher behaviors brought about by teacher expectations, it is hardly surprising that children's performance would be significantly affected. Clearly, children who encounter a warm social-emotional climate, who are the recipients of more feedback from their teachers, who are given more material to complete, and who have more contact with teachers are going to develop more positive self-concepts, be more motivated, and work harder than those who receive negative treatment or neglect. Ultimately, the high-expectation children are likely to perform better in class.

The cycle, then, is complete: A teacher who expects a child to do better treats that child more positively. The child responds to such treatment and eventually performs in accord with the teacher's expectations. But note that the cycle does not stop there: Once children behave congruently with the teacher's expectations, the expectations are reinforced. As a

teacher expectancy effect *the cycle of behavior in which a teacher transmits an expectation about a child and thereby actually brings about the expected behavior*

FIGURE 10-6

TEACHER EXPECTATIONS AND STUDENT PERFORMANCE

Teachers' expectations about their students—positive or negative—can actually bring about positive or negative performance from their students.

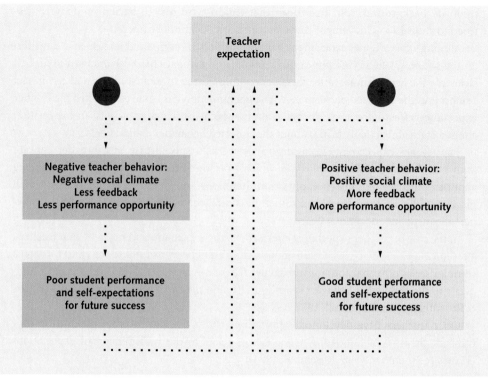

consequence, a child's behavior ultimately may cement the expectation initially held by the teacher (see Figure 10-6).

Expectations are an omnipresent phenomenon in classrooms and are not the province of teachers alone. For instance, children develop their own expectations about their teacher's competence, based on rumors and other bits of information, and they communicate their expectations to those teachers. In the end, a teacher's behavior may be brought about in significant measure by children's expectations (Feldman & Prohaska, 1979; Feldman & Theiss, 1982; Jamieson et al., 1987).

Finally, remember that the classroom is not the only place in which expectations operate. *Any* setting in which one person holds an expectation about a child, and vice versa, may produce analogous expectancy effects. Clearly, children's views of themselves and of their behavior are in part a consequence of what others expect of them (Eden, 1990; Harris et al., 1992).

Beyond the 3Rs: Should Schools Teach Emotional Intelligence?   In many elementary schools, the hottest topic in the curriculum has little to do with the traditional 3Rs. Instead of seeking to improve students' intellectual skills, it is meant to improve their emotional abilities.

Exemplifying a significant educational trend, educators in many elementary schools throughout the United States are being taught techniques to increase students' **emotional intelligence**, the set of skills that underlies the accurate assessment, evaluation, expression, and regulation of emotions (Goleman, 1995; Mayer & Salovey, 1997; Salovey & Sluyter, 1997).

Psychologist Daniel Goleman (1995), who wrote a best-seller entitled *Emotional Intelligence*, argues that emotional literacy should be a standard part of the school curriculum. He points to several programs that are effective in teaching students to manage their emotions more effectively. For instance, in one program, children are provided with lessons in empathy, self-awareness, and social skills. In another, children are taught about caring and friendship as early as first grade through exposure to stories.

However, programs meant to increase emotional intelligence have not been met with universal acceptance. Critics suggest that the nurturance of emotional intelligence is best left to students' families and that schools ought to concentrate on more traditional curriculum matters. Others suggest that adding emotional intelligence to an already crowded

emotional intelligence   *the set of skills that underlie the accurate assessment, evaluation, expression, and regulation of emotions*

curriculum may reduce time spent on academics. Finally, some critics argue that there is no well-specified set of criteria for what constitutes emotional intelligence, and consequently it is difficult to develop appropriate, effective curriculum materials.

Still, most people consider emotional intelligence to be something that is worthy of nurturance. Certainly, emotional intelligence is quite different from traditional conceptions of intelligence. For example, most of us can think of individuals who, although quite intelligent in a traditional sense, are also insensitive and socially unskilled. The goal of emotional intelligence training is to produce people who are not only cognitively sophisticated but also able to manage their emotions effectively (Schulman & Mekler, 1994; Sleek, 1997).

REVIEW AND RETHINK

REVIEW

- Divorce can cause psychological difficulties in children during the middle childhood years, but the consequences depend on such factors as financial circumstances and the comparative levels of tension in the family before and after the divorce.

- Children whose parents work outside the home usually receive about the same amount of parental attention and care as children with an at-home parent, and self-care children may develop independence and enhanced self-esteem from their experience.

- Being raised in a single-parent household may have either positive or negative effects, depending on financial circumstances, the amount of parent–child interaction, and the level of tension in the family.

- People attribute successes and failures to factors according to their attributional patterns, which seem to differ along individual, cultural, and gender dimensions.

- Expectancies can affect the behavior of both the person holding and the person receiving them, eventually producing outcomes that reflect and confirm the expectancies.

- Emotional intelligence—which refers to skills related to the management of emotions—is becoming accepted as an important aspect of social intelligence.

RETHINK

- How might the development of self-esteem in middle childhood be affected by a divorce? By a family situation characterized by constant hostility and tension between parents?

- Politicians often speak of "family values." How does this term relate to the diverse family situations covered in this chapter, including divorced parents, single parents, blended families, working parents, self-care children, abusive families, and group care?

- Identify ways in which the attributions people apply to others may work to confirm stereotypes along racial or gender lines.

- How might the negative expectancies of a teacher work to produce results that confirm those expectancies? Are expectancies related to attributions?

- Do expectancies operate outside the classroom, among adults? How?

LOOKING BACK

- **In what ways do children's views of themselves change during the middle childhood years?**

  - Children in the middle childhood years begin to view themselves in terms of psychological characteristics and to differentiate their self-concepts into separate areas. They use social comparison to evaluate their behavior, abilities, expertise, and opinions.

- According to Erikson, children in the middle childhood years are in the industry-versus-inferiority stage, focusing on achieving competence and responding to a wide range of personal challenges.

■ **Why is self-esteem important during these years?**

- Children in these years are developing self-esteem; those with chronically low self-esteem can become trapped in a cycle of failure in which low self-esteem feeds on itself by producing low expectations and poor performance. Children also develop a sense of self-efficacy during these years.

■ **Through what stages does moral development proceed as children age?**

- According to Kohlberg, people pass from preconventional morality (motivated by rewards and punishments), through conventional morality (motivated by social reference), to postconventional morality (motivated by a sense of universal moral principles). Gilligan has sketched out an alternative progression for girls, from an orientation toward individual survival, through goodness as self-sacrifice, to the morality of nonviolence.

■ **What sorts of relationships and friendships do children have in the middle childhood years?**

- Children's friendships display status hierarchies their understanding of friendship passes through stages, from a focus on mutual liking and time spent together, through the consideration of personal traits and the rewards that friendship provides, to an appreciation of intimacy and loyalty.

- Popularity in children is related to traits that underlie social competence, while unpopularity can result from socially unacceptable behavior, physical unattractiveness, or "differentness."

- Popular children engage in activities that promote social development and skill. Unpopular children may be either neglected or rejected by their peers. Neglect is less perious than rejection, which can endanger children's social adjustment.

■ **How do gender and race affect friendships?**

- Boys and girls in middle childhood increasingly prefer same-gender friendships. Male friendships are characterized by groups, status hierarchies, and restrictive play. Female friendships tend to involve one or two close relationships, equal status, and a reliance on cooperation.

- Cross-race friendships diminish in frequency as children age. Equal-status interactions among members of different racial groups can lead to improved understanding, mutual respect and acceptance, and a decreased tendency to stereotype.

■ **How do today's diverse family arrangements affect children?**

- Immediately after a divorce, the effects on children in the middle childhood years can be serious, depending on the financial condition of the family and the hostility level between spouses before the divorce. Blended families present challenges to the child, but can also offer opportunities for increased social interaction.

- Children in families in which both parents work outside the home generally fare well; having fend for themselves after school can lead to independence and a sense of competence and contribution.

- The consequences of living in a single-parent family depend on the financial condition of the family and, if there had been two parents, the level of hostility that existed between them.

- Children in group care tend to have been victims of neglect and abuse. Many can be helped and placed with their own or other families, but about 25 percent of them will spend their childhood years in group care.

■ **How do social and emotional factors contribute to school outcomes?**

- People attach attributions to their academic successes and failures. Differences in attributional patterns are not only individual, but appear to be influenced by culture and gender as well.

- The expectancies of others, particularly teachers, can produce outcomes that conform to those expectancies by leading students to modify their behavior.

- Emotional intelligence is the set of skills that permit people to manage their emotions effectively.

EPILOGUE: BALANCING CULTURES

In this chapter, we considered social and personality development in middle childhood, looking at self-esteem, self-efficacy, and moral development. We discussed relationships, friendships, and popularity, and we looked at the ways gender and race affect friendships. We considered family arrangements and their effects on social and personality development and on schooling. We concluded with a discussion of social and emotional factors that can affect school outcomes, including people's attributions for success and failure, the expectancies of others, and emotional intelligence.

Return to the prologue—about Lirong Wen's Americanized children—and answer the following questions.

1. How might the differences that Wen reports between U.S. and Chinese classroom etiquette relate to individualistic versus collectivistic cultural orientations?

2. How does social comparison apply to the social and personality development of Lirong Wen's children? Why does Wen herself seem less affected than her children by U.S. culture?

3. Do you think the stages of moral development identified by Kohlberg apply equally to U.S. and Chinese culture? Is the moral development of Wen's children likely to be different from her own and her husband's sense of morality?

4. What accounts for the different attitudes of Wen and her children regarding the value and importance of effort in school? Do you think Wen and her children share similar attributions for academic success and failure?

5. What sorts of expectancies are the teachers of Wen's children likely to hold for them, given their Asian origin and their father's academic interests? How might these expectancies affect the children's schooling and academic performance?

KEY TERMS AND CONCEPTS

social comparison (p. 344)
industry-versus-inferiority stage (p. 345)
self-esteem (p. 345)
self-efficacy (p. 348)
status (p. 352)
social competence (p. 355)
neglected children (p. 355)
rejected children (p. 355)

social problem-solving (p. 356)
dominance hierarchy (p. 358)
blended families (p. 362)
self-care children (p. 363)
attributions (p. 368)
teacher expectancy effect (p. 371)
emotional intelligence (p. 372)

CHAPTER 11

ADOLESCENCE

Physical and Cognitive Development

PROLOGUE: ALEKSANDR KHAZANOV

Aleksandr Khazanov

The bedtime stories Aleksandr Khazanov's father told him were multiplication tables and long division.

When Aleksandr was 14—a little over a year after his family immigrated to Brooklyn as refugees from Russia—his math teacher at Stuyvesant High School watched him whiz through differential equations and felt the boy was so advanced that he could learn more studying on his own.

At age 15, long before he was old enough to get his driver's license, Aleksandr took qualifying exams for Pennsylvania State University's doctoral program in math. He passed all three tests on the first try.

So when Aleksandr submitted a paper to the Westinghouse Science Talent Search competition, the most prestigious science contest for high school students, the Stuyvesant coordinator for contest entries, Stan Teitel, took an extraordinary step.

"I had the audacity to call up Westinghouse and question them as to whether they had someone advanced enough to understand his paper," Mr. Teitel said. "I'm telling you, this kid is way above the rest of us" (Belluck, 1995, p. A1). The people at Westinghouse must have agreed: Khazanov was named a finalist in the contest.

LOOKING AHEAD

Although most adolescents do not reach the heights of mathematical sophistication that Aleksandr attained—nor do most adults, for that matter—we all make significant gains during adolescence. In fact, by the end of the period, adolescents' cognitive proficiencies match those of adults in major respects.

In this chapter and the next, we consider the basic issues and questions that underlie adolescence. **Adolescence** is the developmental stage that lies between childhood and adulthood. It begins and ends imprecisely, starting just before the teenage years and ending just after them. This imprecision reflects society's treatment of the period: Adolescents are considered no longer children, but not yet adults. Clearly, though, adolescence is a time of considerable physical and psychological growth and change.

This chapter focuses on physical and cognitive growth during adolescence. We begin by considering the extraordinary physical maturation that occurs during adolescence, triggered by the onset of puberty. We discuss the consequences of early and late maturation, as well as nutrition and eating disorders.

Next we turn to a consideration of cognitive development during adolescence. After reviewing several approaches to understanding changes in cognitive capabilities, we examine school performance, focusing on the ways that socioeconomic status, ethnicity, and race affect scholastic achievement.

The chapter concludes with a discussion of several of the major threats to adolescents' well-being. We will focus on drug, alcohol, and tobacco use, as well as sexually transmitted diseases.

After reading this chapter, then, you will be able to answer the following questions:

- What physical changes do adolescents experience?
- What are the consequences of early and late maturation?
- What nutritional needs and concerns do adolescents have?
- In what ways does cognitive development proceed during adolescence?
- What factors affect adolescent school performance?
- What dangerous substances do adolescents use and why?
- What dangers do adolescent sexual practices present, and how can these dangers be avoided?

PHYSICAL MATURATION

For the male members of the Awa tribe, the beginning of adolescence is signaled by an elaborate and—to Western eyes—gruesome ceremony marking the transition from childhood to adulthood. First the boys are whipped for two or three days with sticks and prickly branches. Through the whipping, the boys atone for their previous infractions and honor tribesmen who were killed in warfare.

But that's just for starters. In the next phase of the ritual, sharpened sticks are punched into the boys' nostrils, producing a considerable amount of blood. Then, adults force a five-foot length of vine into the boys' throats, causing them to choke and vomit. Finally, deep cuts are made in the boys' genitals. Jeering onlookers poke at the cuts to make them bleed even more.

Most of us probably feel gratitude that we did not have to endure such physical trials when we entered adolescence. But members of Western cultures do have their own rites of passage into adolescence, admittedly less fearsome, such as bar mitzvahs and bat mitzvahs at

adolescence   *the developmental stage between childhood and adulthood*

age 13 for Jewish boys and girls, and confirmation ceremonies in many Christian denominations (Myerhoff, 1982; Dunham, Kidwell, & Wilson, 1986; Delaney, 1995).

Regardless of the nature of the ceremonies celebrated by various cultures, their underlying purpose tends to be similar from one culture to the next: symbolically celebrating the onset of the physical changes that take a child to the doorstep of adulthood.

Growth During Adolescence: The Rapid Pace of Physical and Sexual Maturation

The growth in height and weight during adolescence can be breathtaking. In only a few months, an adolescent can grow several inches and require a virtually new wardrobe. In fact, in a period of only 4 years, boys and girls undergo a transformation, at least in physical appearance, from children to young adults.

The dramatic changes during adolescence constitute the adolescent growth spurt, a period of very rapid growth in height and weight. During the adolescent growth spurt, height and weight increase as quickly as they did during infancy. On average, boys grow 4.1 inches a year and girls 3.5 inches a year. Some adolescents grow as much as 5 inches in a single year (Tanner, 1972).

Boys' and girls' adolescent growth spurts begin at different times. On average, girls start their spurts 2 years earlier than boys, and they complete them earlier as well. As you can see in Figure 11-1, girls begin their spurts around age 10, whereas boys start at about age 12. For the 2-year period starting at age 11, girls tend to be a bit taller than boys. This soon changes, however: By the age of 13, boys, on average, are taller than girls—a state of affairs that persists for the remainder of the life span.

FIGURE 11-1

GROWTH PATTERNS

Patterns of growth are depicted in two ways. The first figure shows height at a given age, whereas the second shows the height *increase* that occurs from birth through the end of adolescence. Notice that girls begin their growth spurt around age 10, whereas boys begin the growth spurt at about age 12. However, by the age of 13, boys tend to be taller than girls.

■ Boy

■ Girl

(*Source:* Adapted from Cratty, 1986.)

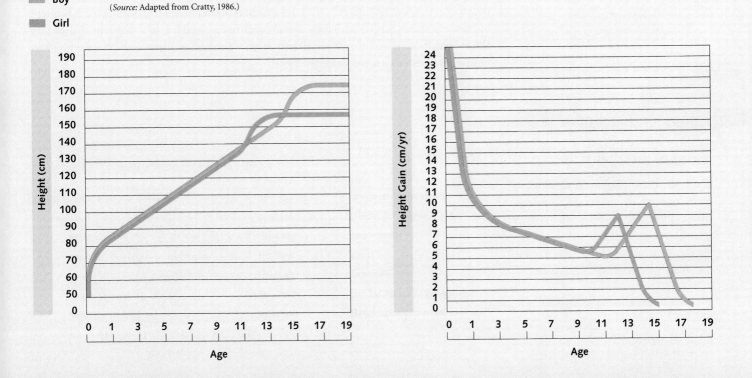

puberty   *the period during which the sexual organs mature, beginning earlier for girls than for boys*

menarche   *the onset of menstruation*

Puberty: The Start of Sexual Maturation

Like the growth spurt, **puberty**, the period during which the sexual organs mature, begins earlier for girls than for boys. Girls start puberty at around age 11 or 12, and boys begin at around age 13 or 14. However, there are wide variations among individuals. For example, some girls begin puberty as early as 8 or 9 or as late as 16 years of age.

Puberty begins when children's bodies begin to produce androgens (male hormones) or estrogens (female hormones) at adult levels. This surge in the production of hormones leads to the growth spurt and puberty.

What triggers the start of puberty? Although we know what happens when it begins, no one has yet identified the reason that it begins at a particular time. However, it is clear that environmental and cultural factors play a role. For example, **menarche**, the onset of menstruation, and probably the most conspicuous signal of puberty in girls, varies greatly in different parts of the world. In poorer, developing countries, menstruation begins later than in more economically advantaged countries. Even within wealthier countries, girls in more affluent groups begin to menstruate earlier than less affluent girls (see Figure 11-2). Consequently, it appears that girls who are better nourished and healthier are more apt to start menstruation at an earlier age than those who suffer from malnutrition or chronic disease.

Other factors can affect the timing of menarche. For instance, environmental stress can bring about an early onset (Kim, Smith, & Palermiti, 1997). To illustrate, one recent study found that girls from divorced families or families high in interparental conflict tended to begin menstruation earlier than girls from families with lower levels of stress (Wierson, Long, & Forehand, 1993; Graber, Brooks-Gunn, & Warren, 1995).

Within the United States, historical patterns of menarche are congruent with that in other cultures. Near the end of the 19th century, menstruation began, on average, around age 14 or 15, compared with today's 11 or 12. The earlier onset today is likely the result of reduced disease and improved nutrition.

Does this mean that the age at which puberty starts will continue to decline? Probably not. It is likely that there is a genetically determined limit on how early menstruation can occur. In fact, we may have reached it already: For the last few decades, despite generally rising health and affluence, there has been no further decline in the age at which puberty begins. Furthermore, although it was once widely thought that there were racial and ethnic differences in onset of puberty (with, for example, individuals of African descent thought to mature earlier than Caucasians), more recent research comes to a different conclusion. When nutrition is sufficient, racial and ethnic differences disappear (Bullough, 1981; Dreyer, 1982; Brooks-Gunn & Reiter, 1990).

FIGURE 11-2

ONSET OF MENSTRUATION

The onset of menstruation occurs earlier in more economically advantaged countries than in those that are poorer. But even in wealthier countries, girls living in more affluent circumstances begin to menstruate earlier than those living in less affluent situations.

(*Source:* Adapted from Eveleth & Tanner, 1976.)

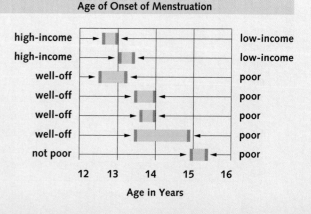

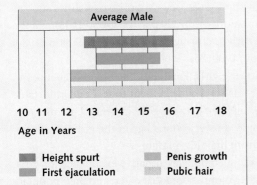

Both males and females undergo significant bodily changes during adolescence, and they show increased interest in their physical appearance.

Menstruation is just one of several changes in puberty that are related to the development of primary and secondary sex characteristics. **Primary sex characteristics** are associated with the development of the organs and structures of the body that directly relate to reproduction. In contrast, **secondary sex characteristics** are the visible signs of sexual maturity that do not involve the sex organs directly.

For instance, girls experience the development of primary sex characteristics through changes in the vagina and uterus as a result of maturation. Secondary sex characteristics include the development of breasts and pubic hair. Breasts begin to grow at around the age of 10, and pubic hair begins to appear at about age 11. Underarm hair appears about 2 years later.

Boys' sexual maturation follows a somewhat different course. In terms of primary sex characteristics, the penis and scrotum begin to grow at an accelerated rate around the age of 12, and they reach adult size about 3 or 4 years later. By the age of about 14, a boy is usually able to have his first ejaculation, although his body has already been producing sperm for a few years. At the same time, there is development in secondary sex characteristics. Pubic hair begins to grow around the age of 12, followed by the growth of underarm and facial hair. Finally, boys' voices deepen as the vocal cords become longer and the larynx larger. (Figure 11-3 summarizes the changes that occur in sexual maturation during early adolescence.)

primary sex characteristics *characteristics associated with the development of the organs and structures of the body that directly relate to reproduction*

secondary sex characteristics *the visible signs of sexual maturity that do not directly involve the sex organs*

FIGURE 11-3

SEXUAL MATURATION

Sexual maturation occurs for males and females during early adolescence.

(*Source:* Adapted from Tanner, 1978.)

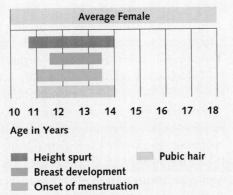

Average Male

| 10 | 11 | 12 | 13 | 14 | 15 | 16 | 17 | 18 |

Age in Years

- Height spurt
- First ejaculation
- Penis growth
- Pubic hair

Average Female

| 10 | 11 | 12 | 13 | 14 | 15 | 16 | 17 | 18 |

Age in Years

- Height spurt
- Breast development
- Onset of menstruation
- Pubic hair

Body Image: Reactions to Physical Changes in Adolescence

Unlike infants, who also undergo extraordinarily rapid growth, adolescents are well aware of what is happening to their bodies, and they may react with horror or joy. Few, though, are neutral about the changes they are witnessing (Mehran, 1997).

For instance, menarche produces several psychological consequences. In the past, Western society has emphasized the more negative aspects of menstruation, such as the potential of cramps and messiness, and girls tended to react to menarche with anxiety (Ruble & Brooks-Gunn, 1982). Today, however, society's view of menstruation tends to be more positive, in part because menstruation has been demystified and discussed more openly. (For instance, television commercials for tampons are commonplace.) As a consequence, menarche is typically accompanied by an increase in self-esteem, a rise in status, and greater self-awareness (Brooks-Gunn & Reiter, 1990).

In some ways, a boy's first ejaculation is roughly equivalent to menarche in a girl. However, while girls generally tell their mothers about the onset of menstruation, boys rarely mention their first ejaculation to either their parents or their friends (Stein & Reiser, 1994). Moreover, there is little evidence that the first ejaculation causes boys much anxiety or worry (Gaddis & Brooks-Gunn, 1985). Several factors may explain this: It may be that the event is actually of little concern or interest to boys, and therefore not worthy of mention. However, it seems more likely that boys see the first ejaculation as part of their sexuality, an area about which they are quite uncertain and which they are therefore reluctant to discuss with others.

How children react to the onset of puberty depends, in part, on when it happens. Girls and boys who mature either earlier or later than most of their peers are especially affected by the timing of puberty.

The Timing of Puberty: The Consequences of Early and Late Maturation

What are the social consequences of early or late maturation? One of the most persistent questions addressed by developmental psychologists who specialize in adolescence is whether early and late maturation bring with them any particular advantages or disadvantages. The answer, it turns out, differs for boys and girls.

For boys, early maturation is largely a plus. Early-maturing boys tend to be more successful at athletics, presumably because of their larger size. Furthermore, they tend to be more popular and to have a more positive self-concept.

On the other hand, early maturation in boys does have a downside. Boys who mature early are more apt to have difficulties in school, and they are more likely to become involved in delinquency and substance abuse. The reason: Their larger size makes it more likely that they will seek out the company of older boys who may involve them in activities that are inappropriate for their age. Furthermore, although early maturers are more responsible and cooperative in later life, they are also more conforming and lacking in humor. In contrast, late-maturing boys grow up to have several positive qualities such as assertiveness and insightfulness, and they are more creatively playful. Overall, though, the pluses seem to outweigh the minuses for early-maturing boys (Livson & Peskin, 1980; Duncan et al., 1985; Andersson & Magnusson, 1990).

The story is a bit different for early-maturing girls. For them, the obvious changes in their bodies—such as the development of breasts—may lead them to feel uncomfortable and different from their peers (Lee, 1997). Moreover, because girls, in general, mature earlier than boys, early maturation tends to come at a very young age in the girl's life. Early-maturing girls may have to endure ridicule from their less mature classmates.

On the other hand, early maturation is not a completely negative experience for girls. Girls who mature earlier tend to be sought after more as potential dates, and their popularity may enhance their self-concepts. Still, they may not be socially ready to participate in the kind of dating situations that most girls deal with at a later age, and such situations may be psychologically challenging for early-maturing girls. Moreover, the conspicuousness of their deviance from their later-maturing classmates may have a negative effect on them (Simmons & Blyth, 1987).

Whether girls face difficulties with early maturation depends in part on cultural norms and standards. For instance, in the United States, the notion of female sexuality is looked on with adegree of ambivalence. Consequently, the outcome of early maturation may be negative. On the other hand, in countries in which attitudes about sexuality are more liberal, the results of early maturation may be more positive. For example, in Germany, which has a more open view of sex, early-maturing girls have higher self-esteem than such girls in the United States. Furthermore, the consequences of early maturation vary even within the United States, depending on the views of girls' peer groups and on prevailing community standards regarding sex (Silbereisen et al., 1989; Richards et al., 1990).

As with early maturation, the situation with late maturation is mixed, although in this case boys fare worse than girls. For instance, boys who are smaller and lighter than their more mature peers tend to be viewed as less attractive. Because of their smaller size, they are at a disadvantage when it comes to sports activities. Furthermore, because of the social convention that boys should be taller than their dates, the social lives of late-maturing boys may suffer. Ultimately, these difficulties may lead to a decline in self-concept. In fact, the disadvantages of late maturation for boys may extend well into adulthood (Mussen & Jones, 1957; Livson & Peskin, 1980).

The picture for late-maturing girls, on the other hand, is a bit more complicated. Girls who mature later may be overlooked in dating and other mixed-sex activities during junior high school and middle school, and they may have relatively low social status (Apter et al., 1981; Clarke-Stewart & Friedman, 1987). However, by the time they are in 10th grade and have begun to mature visibly, late-maturing-girls' satisfaction with themselves and their bodies may be greater than that of early maturers. In fact, late-maturing girls may end up with fewer emotional problems. The reason? Late-maturing girls are more apt to fit the societal ideal of a slender, "leggy" body type than early maturers, who tend to look heavier in comparison (Simmons & Blythe, 1987; Petersen, 1988).

In sum, the reactions to early and late maturation present a complex picture. Some developmental psychologists suggest that the concern over early and later maturation, and over the effects of puberty in general, may have been overemphasized in the past (Petersen & Crockett, 1985; Paikoff & Brooks-Gunn, 1990). Rather than focusing on the growth spurt and sexual maturation that occur during adolescence, they suggest that other factors, such as changes in peer groups, family dynamics, and particularly schools and other societal institutions, may be more pertinent in determining an adolescent's behavior. As we have seen repeatedly, we need to take into consideration the complete constellation of factors affecting individuals in order to understand their development.

Nutrition, Food, and Eating Disorders: Fueling the Growth of Adolescence

A rice cake in the afternoon, an apple for dinner. That was Heather Rhodes's typical diet her freshman year at St. Joseph's College in Rensselaer, Indiana, when she began to nurture a fear (exacerbated, she says, by the sudden death of a friend) that she was gaining weight. But when Rhodes, now 20, returned home to Joliet, Illinois, for summer vacation a year and a half ago, her family thought she was melting away. "I could see the outline of her pelvis in her clothes . . ." says Heather's mother . . . , so she and the rest of the family confronted Heather one evening, placing a bathroom scale in the middle of the family room. "I told them they were attacking me and to go to hell," recalls Heather, who nevertheless reluctantly weighed herself. Her 5'7" frame held a mere 85 pounds—down 22 pounds from her senior year in high school. "I told them they rigged the scale," she says. It simply didn't compute with her self-image. "When I looked in the mirror," she says, "I thought my stomach was still huge and my face was fat." (Sandler, 1994, p. 56)

This girl suffers from anorexia nervosa, a sever eating disorder in which people refuse to eat, while denying that their behavior and appearance are out of the ordinary.

Heather's problem: a severe eating disorder, anorexia nervosa.

The rapid physical growth of adolescence is fueled by an increase in food consumption. Particularly during the growth spurt, adolescents eat substantial quantities of food, increasing their intake of calories rather dramatically. During the teenage years, the average girl requires some 2,200 calories a day, and the average boy 2,800.

Of course, not just any calories help nourish adolescents' growth. Several key nutrients are essential, including in particular calcium and iron. The calcium provided by milk helps bone growth, which may prevent the later development of osteoporosis—the thinning of bones—that affects 25 percent of women later in their lives. Similarly, iron is necessary to prevent iron-deficiency anemia, an ailment that is not uncommon among teenagers.

For most adolescents, the major nutritional issue is ensuring the consumption of a sufficient balance of appropriate foods. But for a substantial minority, nutrition can be a major concern and can create a real threat to health. Among the most prevalent problems: obesity and more severe eating disorders like the one afflicting Heather Rhodes.

Obesity. The most common nutritional concern during adolescence is obesity (Brook & Tepper, 1997). As we discussed in earlier chapters (see Chapters 4, 7, and 9), *obesity* is defined as body weight that is more than 20 percent above the average for a given age and height. Under this definition, some 5 percent of adolescents are formally classified as obese, and an additional 15 percent are overweight to some degree (Gans, 1990).

Although adolescents are obese for the same reasons as younger children, the psychological consequences may be particularly severe during a time of life when body image is of special concern. Furthermore, the potential health consequences of obesity during adolescence are also problematic. For instance, obesity taxes the circulatory system, increasing the likelihood of high blood pressure and diabetes. Finally, obese adolescents stand an 80 percent chance of becoming obese adults.

Anorexia Nervosa and Bulimia. The desire to avoid obesity sometimes becomes so strong that it turns into a problem. For instance, Heather Rhodes suffered from anorexia nervosa. **Anorexia nervosa** is a severe eating disorder in which individuals refuse to eat, while denying that their behavior and appearance, which may become skeletal, are out of the ordinary.

Anorexia is a severe psychological disorder; some 15 to 20 percent of its victims literally starve themselves to death. It primarily afflicts women between the ages of 12 and 40; those most susceptible are intelligent, successful, and attractive white adolescent girls from affluent homes (Hsu, 1990; Button, 1993).

In the early stages, anorexics' lives become centered on food. Even though they eat little, they may go shopping often, collect cookbooks, talk about food, or cook huge meals for others. Although they may be incredibly thin, their body images are so distorted that they see their reflections in mirrors as disgustingly fat, and try to lose more and more weight. Even when they look like skeletons, they are unable to see what they have become.

Bulimia, another eating disorder, is characterized by binges on large quantities of food, followed by purges of the food through vomiting or the use of laxatives. Bulimics may eat an entire gallon of ice cream or a whole package of tortilla chips. But after such a binge, sufferers experience powerful feelings of guilt and depression, and they intentionally rid themselves of the food.

Although the weight of a person with bulimia remains fairly normal, the disorder is quite hazardous. The constant vomiting and diarrhea of the binge-and-purge cycles may produce a chemical imbalance that can lead to heart failure.

The exact reasons for the occurrence of eating disorders are not clear, although several factors appear to be implicated (Striegel-Moore, 1997). For one thing, girls who mature earlier than their peers and who have a higher level of body fat are more susceptible to eating disorders during later adolescence. In addition, several psychological problems are also associated

anorexia nervosa *a severe eating disorder in which individuals refuse to eat, while denying that their behavior and appearance, which may become skeletal, are out of the ordinary*

bulimia *an eating disorder characterized by binges on large quantities of food, followed by purges of the food through vomiting or the use of laxatives*

with subsequent eating disorders. Girls who show clinical levels of depression are more likely to develop eating disorders later (Graber et al., 1994; Cauffman & Steinberg, 1996).

Some theorists suggest that a biological cause lies at the root of both anorexia nervosa and bulimia. In fact, there appear to be genetic components to the disorders, and in some cases doctors have found hormonal imbalances in sufferers (Holland, Sicotte, & Treasure, 1988; Condit, 1990; Irwin, 1993; Treasure & Tiller, 1993).

Other attempts to explain the eating disorders emphasize psychological and social factors. For instance, some experts suggest that the disorders are a result of overdemanding parents or byproducts of other family difficulties (Miller, McCluskey-Fawcett, & Irving, 1993). In addition, the societal preference for slender bodies and disapproval of obesity may contribute to the disorder (Crandall & Biernat, 1990; Rothblum, 1990; Logue, 1991; Sohlberg & Strober, 1994).

There are also clear cultural causes. Anorexia nervosa, for instance, is found only in cultures that idealize slender female bodies. Because in most places such a standard does not hold, anorexia is not prevalent outside the United States. For instance, there is no anorexia in all of Asia, with two interesting exceptions: the upper classes of Japan and of Hong Kong, where Western influence is greatest. Furthermore, anorexia nervosa is a fairly recent disorder. It was not seen in the 17th and 18th centuries, when the ideal of the female body was a plump corpulence (Kleinman, 1991; Carson, Butcher, & Coleman, 1992).

Because anorexia nervosa and bulimia are products of both biological and environmental causes, treatment typically involves multiple approaches. For instance, both psychological therapy and dietary modifications are likely to be needed for successful treatment (Fairburn et al., 1993; Lask & Bryant-Waugh, 1993; Schmidt & Treasure, 1993; Theander, 1996).

REVIEW AND RETHINK

REVIEW

- Adolescence is a period of rapid physical growth, including the hormonal and bodily changes associated with puberty. Girls typically begin their growth spurts and puberty about 2 years earlier than boys.

- Puberty, whose timing is the result of biological, cultural, and environmental factors, can cause reactions in adolescents ranging from confusion to increased self-esteem.

- Early or late maturation can bring advantages and disadvantages. The disadvantages are largely due to dissonance between physical maturity and emotional and psychological maturity.

- Adequate nutrition is essential in adolescence because of the need to fuel physical growth. Changing physical needs and environmental pressures can induce obesity or an obsession with avoiding obesity that can manifest itself as an eating disorder.

- The two most common eating disorders among adolescents are anorexia nervosa and bulimia.

RETHINK

- Why do you think the passage to adolescence is regarded in many cultures as such a significant transition that it calls for unique ceremonies?

- What are some of the educational implications of the variations in maturation rate that adolescents experience? How can a teacher help students deal with the wide variety of changes they are witnessing and experiencing?

■ In what ways might the popularity of early-developing boys and girls offer both benefits and threats?

■ How can societal and environmental influences contribute to the emergence of an eating disorder?

COGNITIVE DEVELOPMENT AND SCHOOLING

What distinguishes adolescents' thinking from that of younger children? One of the major changes is the ability to think beyond the concrete, current situation to what *might* or *could* be. Adolescents are able to keep in their heads a variety of abstract possibilities, and they can understand issues in relative, as opposed to absolute, terms. Instead of viewing problems as having black-and-white solutions, they are capable of perceiving shades of gray (Keating, 1980, 1990).

As with other stages of life, we can use several approaches to explain adolescents' cognitive development. We begin by returning to Piaget's theory, which has had a significant influence on how developmental psychologists think about thinking during adolescence.

Piagetian Approaches to Cognitive Development

Fourteen-year-old Siena is asked to solve a problem that anyone may have pondered who has seen a grandfather's clock: What determines the speed at which a pendulum moves back and forth? In the version of the problem that she is asked to solve, Siena is given a weight hanging from a string. She is told that she can vary several things: the length of the string, the weight of the object at the end of the string, the amount of force used to push the string, and the height to which the weight is raised in an arc before it is released.

Siena does not remember, but she was asked to solve the same problem when she was 8 years old. At that time, she was in the concrete operational period, and her efforts to solve the problem were not very successful. For instance, she approached the problem haphazardly, with no systematic plan of action. She simultaneously tried to push the pendulum harder *and* shorten the length of the string *and* increase the weight on the string. Because she was varying so many factors at once, when the speed of the pendulum changed she had no way of knowing which factor or factors made a difference.

Now, however, Siena is much more systematic. Rather than immediately beginning to push and pull at the pendulum, she stops a moment and thinks. Then, just like a scientist conducting an experiment, she varies only one factor at a time. By examining each variable separately and systematically, she is able to come to the correct solution: The length of the string determines the speed of the pendulum.

Using Formal Operations to Solve Problems.   Siena's approach to the pendulum question, a problem devised by Piaget, illustrates that she has moved into the formal operations period (Piaget & Inhelder, 1958). The **formal operations period** is the stage at which people develop the ability to think abstractly. Most people reach it at the start of adolescence, around the age of 12.

By bringing formal principles of logic to bear on problems they encounter, adolescents in the formal operations period are able to consider problems in the abstract rather than in concrete terms. They are able to test their understanding by systematically carrying out rudimentary experiments on problems and situations, and observing what their experimental "interventions" bring about.

Although Piaget proposed that children enter the formal operational stage at the beginning of adolescence, you may recall that he also hypothesized that—as with all the stages of cognitive development—full capabilities do not emerge suddenly, at one stroke. Instead,

formal operations period *the stage at which people develop the ability to think abstractly*

they gradually unfold through a combination of physical maturation and environmental experiences. According to Piaget, adolescents are not fully settled in the formal operations state until about age 15.

In fact, some evidence suggests that a sizable proportion of people hone their formal operational skills at a later age, and in some cases, never fully employ formal operational thinking. For instance, most studies show that only 40 to 60 percent of college students and adults fully achieve formal operational thinking, and some estimates run as low as 25 percent (Keating & Clark, 1980; Sugarman, 1988).

Adolescents' use of formal operations also differs for cultural reasons. For instance, people who live in isolated, scientifically unsophisticated societies and who have little formal education are less likely to perform at the formal operations level than formally educated persons living in more technologically sophisticated societies (Jahoda, 1980; Segall et al., 1990).

Does this mean that adolescents (and adults) from cultures in which formal operations tend not to emerge are incapable of attaining them? Not at all. A more probable conclusion is that the scientific reasoning that characterizes formal operations is not equally valued in all societies. If everyday life does not require or promote a certain type of reasoning, it is irrational to expect people to employ that type of reasoning when confronted with a problem (Greenfield, 1976; Shea, 1985).

Evaluating Piaget's Approach.   Each time we have considered Piaget's theory in previous chapters, several concerns have cropped up. To summarize some of the issues:

■ Piaget suggests that cognitive development proceeds in universal, steplike advances that occur at particular stages. Yet we find significant differences in cognitive abilities from one person to the next, especially when we compare individuals from different cultures. Furthermore, we find inconsistencies in the performance of tasks even within the same individual—tasks that, if Piaget was correct, the person ought to perform uniformly well once she or he reaches a given stage (Siegler, 1994).

■ The notion of stages proposed by Piaget suggests that cognitive abilities do not grow gradually or smoothly. Instead, the stage viewpoint implies that cognitive growth is typified by relatively rapid shifts from one stage to the next. In contrast, many developmental psychologists argue that cognitive development proceeds in a more continuous fashion, increasing not so much in qualitative leaps forward as in quantitative accumulations (Gelman & Baillargeon, 1983; Case, 1991).

■ Because of the tasks Piaget employed to measure cognitive abilities, critics suggest that he miscalculated the age at which certain capabilities emerge. It is now widely accepted that infants and children are more sophisticated at an earlier age than Piaget asserted (Bornstein & Sigman, 1986).

■ Piaget had a relatively narrow view of what is meant by *thinking* and *knowing*. To Piaget knowledge consists primarily of the kind of understanding displayed in the pendulum problem. However, as we discussed in Chapter 9, developmental psychologists such as Howard Gardner suggest that we have many kinds of intelligence, separate from and independent of one another (Gardner & Hatch, 1989).

These criticisms of Piaget's approach to cognitive development have considerable merit. On the other hand, Piaget made momentous contributions to our understanding of cognitive development, and his work remains highly influential. He was a brilliant observer of children's and adolescents' behavior, although his focus on particular aspects of their cognitive lives may have been too narrow. His theory was the impetus for an enormous number of studies on the development of thinking capacities and processes, and it also spurred a good deal of classroom reform. Finally, his bold statements about cognitive development

information-processing perspective a *perspective that sees changes in cognitive abilities as gradual transformations in the capacity to take in, use, and store information*

metacognition the knowledge that people have about their own thinking processes, and their ability to monitor their cognition

provided a springboard from which many opposing positions on cognitive development bloomed, such as the information-processing perspective, to which we turn next (Demetriou, Shayer, & Efklides, 1993; Elkind, 1996).

Information-processing Perspectives

Proponents of information-processing approaches to cognitive development argue that growth in mental abilities proceeds gradually and continuously. Unlike Piaget's view that the increasing cognitive sophistication of the adolescent is a reflection of stagelike spurts, the **information-processing perspective** sees changes in cognitive abilities as gradual transformations in the capacity to take in, use, and store information.

In this view, increases in information-processing capabilities lie at the heart of the advances in mental ability that take place during adolescence. Developmental advances are brought about by progressive changes in the ways people organize their thinking about the world, develop strategies for dealing with new situations, sort facts, and achieve advances in memory capacity and perceptual abilities (Keating & Clark, 1980; Gagne, 1985; Burbules & Lin, 1988; Wellman & Gelman, 1992).

And the cognitive strides made during adolescence are considerable. Although general intelligence—as measured by traditional IQ tests—remains stable, dramatic improvements evolve in the specific mental abilities that underlie intelligence. Verbal, mathematical, and spatial abilities increase. Memory capacity grows, and adolescents become more adept at effectively dividing their attention between more than one stimulus at a time—such as simultaneously studying for a biology test and listening to an Aerosmith CD.

Furthermore, adolescents grow increasingly sophisticated in their understanding of problems, their ability to grasp abstract concepts and to think hypothetically, and their comprehension of the possibilities inherent in situations. They know more about the world, too; their store of knowledge increases as the amount of material to which they are exposed grows and their memory capacity enlarges (Pressley et al., 1988). Taken as a whole, the mental abilities that underlie intelligence show a marked improvement during adolescence, peaking at around age 20 (see Figure 11-4).

The Growth of Metacognition. According to information-processing explanations of cognitive development during adolescence, one of the most important reasons for advances in mental abilities is the growth of metacognition (Schommer et al., 1997). **Metacognition** is the knowledge that people have about their own thinking processes, and their ability to monitor their cognition.

For example, as adolescents improve their understanding of their memory capacity, they get better at gauging how long they need to study a particular kind of material to learn

FIGURE 11-4

MENTAL ABILITIES

The mental abilities that underlie intelligence show a marked improvement during adolescence, peaking at around age 20.

(*Source:* Adapted from Bayley, 1949.)

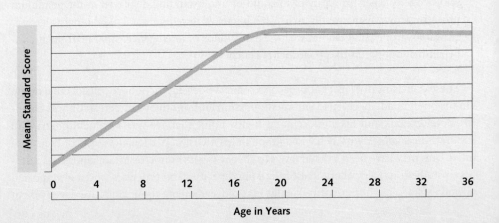

it for a test. Furthermore, they can judge when they have fully memorized the material considerably more accurately than when they were younger. These improvements in metacognitive abilities permit adolescents to comprehend and master school material more effectively (Flavell, 1979; Garner & Alexander, 1989; Nelson, 1990, 1994).

Egocentrism in Adolescents' Thinking

Carlos is furious at his parents. He sees them as totally unfair because, when he borrows their car, they insist that he call home and let them know where he is. Eleanor is angry at Molly because Molly inadvertently bought earrings just like hers and sometimes wears them to school. Josh is upset with his biology teacher, Ms. Sebastian, for giving a long, difficult midterm exam on which he did poorly.

Each of these adolescents is furious, angry, or upset over what may seem like not-so-unreasonable behavior on the part of others. Why? It is quite possible that the cause lies in the egocentrism that may sometimes dominate adolescents' thinking.

According to developmental psychologist David Elkind, this period of life fosters **adolescent egocentrism**, a state of self-absorption in which the world is viewed from one's own point of view (Elkind, 1967, 1985). Egocentrism makes adolescents highly critical of authority figures such as parents and teachers, unwilling to accept criticism, and quick to find fault with others' behavior.

Adolescent egocentrism helps explain why adolescents sometimes perceive that they are the focus of everyone else's attention. In fact, an adolescent may develop what has been called an **imaginary audience**, the belief that his or her own behavior is a primary focus of others' attentions and concerns.

Because of adolescents' newly sophisticated metacognitive abilities, they readily imagine that others are thinking about them, and they may construct elaborate scenarios about others' thoughts. Unfortunately, these scenarios may suffer from the same kind of egocentrism as the rest of their thinking. The imaginary audience is usually perceived as focusing on the one thing that adolescents think most about: themselves. For instance, a student sitting in a class may be sure a teacher is focusing on her, and a teenager at a basketball game may just know that everyone around is focusing on the pimple on his chin.

Egocentrism leads to a second distortion in thinking: the notion that one's experiences are unique. Adolescents develop **personal fables**, the view that what happens to them is unique, exceptional, and shared by no one else. For instance, teenagers whose romantic relationships have ended may feel that no one has ever experienced the hurt they feel, that no one has ever been treated so badly, that no one can understand what they are going through.

Personal fables also may make adolescents feel invulnerable to the risks that threaten others (Klacynski, 1997). They may think that there is no need to use condoms during sex, because the personal fables they construct make them immune to pregnancy and to sexually transmitted diseases such as AIDS. They may drive after drinking, because their personal fables paint them as careful drivers, always in control. Much of adolescents' risk-taking behavior may well be traced to the personal fables they construct for themselves (Dolcini et al., 1989; Arnett, 1995; Lightfoot, 1997).

School Performance

Do the advances that occur in cognitive abilities in adolescence translate into improvements in school performance? If we use students' grades as the measure of school performance, the answer is no. On average, students' grades *decline* during the course of schooling (Schulenberg, Asp, & Peterson, 1984; Simmons & Blyth, 1987).

The reasons for this decline are not entirely clear. Obviously, the material to which students are exposed becomes increasingly complex and sophisticated over the course of adolescence. But the growing cognitive abilities of adolescents might be expected to compensate

adolescent egocentrism   *a state of self-absorption in which the world is viewed from one's own point of view*

imaginary audience   *an adolescent's belief that his or her own behavior is a primary focus of others' attentions and concerns*

personal fables   *the view held by some adolescents that what happens to them is unique, exceptional, and shared by no one else*

for the increased sophistication of the material. Thus, we need to look to other explanations to account for the grade decline.

A better explanation seems to relate not to student performance but to teachers' grading practices. It turns out that teachers grade older adolescents more stringently than younger ones. Even though the level of sophistication of student performance, in an absolute sense, may be improving, then, their grades do not necessarily reflect the improvement (Simmons & Blyth, 1987).

Socioeconomic Status and School Performance: Individual Differences in Achievement. Despite the ideal that all students are entitled to the same opportunity in the classroom, certain groups clearly have more educational advantages than others. One of the most telling indicators of this reality is the relationship between educational achievement and socioeconomic status (SES).

Middle- and high-SES students earn higher grades, score higher on standardized tests of achievement, and complete more years of schooling than students from lower-SES homes. Of course, this disparity does not start in adolescence; the same findings hold for children in lower grades. However, by the time students are in high school, the effects of socioeconomic status become even more pronounced (Garbarino & Asp, 1981).

Why do students from middle- and high-SES homes show, in general, greater academic success? There are several explanations, most involving environmental factors. For one thing, children living in poverty lack many of the advantages enjoyed by other children. Their nutrition and health may be less adequate. Often living in crowded conditions, they may have few places to do homework. Their homes may lack the books and computers commonplace in more economically advantaged households.

Furthermore, parents living in poverty are less likely to be involved in their children's schooling—a factor that is related to school success. Poorer adolescents, who may live in impoverished areas of cities with high levels of violence, may also attend older and generally inadequate schools with run-down facilities and a higher incidence of violence. Taken together, these factors clearly result in a less-than-optimal learning environment (Garbarino et al., 1992; Grolnick & Slowiaczek, 1994; Caldas & Bankston, 1997).

Although most developmental psychologists reject the approach, some researchers point to genetic factors as a source of SES differences in educational attainment. According to the controversial argument put forward by the authors of *The Bell Curve* (discussed in Chapter 9), lower school performance of children living in poverty may be due to inherited differences in intelligence levels. According to this argument, the parents' lower IQ scores lead them into poorer-paying professions and a life of poverty. The children, inheriting their parents' low IQ and subject to the harsh conditions of poverty, are unlikely to do well in school. So goes the argument (Herrnstein & Murray, 1994).

There are several reasons to reject this reasoning. For one thing, there is substantial variation in school performance *within* a particular SES level—often, in fact, more than the variation *between* students of different SES. Put another way, many low-SES students perform far better than the average performance of higher-SES students. Likewise, many higher-SES students perform well below the average performance of lower-SES students.

More important, the consequences of environment are particularly potent. Students from impoverished backgrounds may be at a disadvantage from the day they begin their schooling. Consequently, they may perform less well initially than their more affluent peers. As they grow older, their school performance may continue to lag, and in fact their disadvantage may snowball. Because later school success builds heavily on basic skills presumably learned early in school, children who experience problems early may find themselves falling increasingly behind the academic eight ball as adolescents (Huston, 1991; Phillips et al., 1994).

There are significant differences in school achievement between members of different racial and ethnic groups.

Ethnic and Racial Differences in School Achievement. Do various ethnic groups and races perform differently in school? Although the answer is fairly simple—it is "yes, they do"—reasons for the differences are as hard to come by as they were when we examined socioeconomic differences in school performance (Dornbusch, Ritter, & Steinberg, 1992).

Achievement differences between ethnic and racial groups are significant, and they paint a troubling picture of American education. For instance, data on school achievement indicate that, on average, African American and Hispanic students tend to perform at lower levels, receive lower grades, and score lower on standardized tests of achievement than Caucasian students (see Table 11-1). In contrast, Asian American students tend to receive higher grades than Caucasian students.

TABLE 11-1

PERFORMANCE ON TESTS OF ACHIEVEMENT

Reading, 1987–88	9-Year-Olds	13-Year-Olds	17-Year-Olds
National average	211.8	257.5	290.1
White	217.7	261.3	294.7
Black	188.5	242.9	274.4
Hispanic	193.7	240.1	270.8

Writing, 1988	4th Graders	9th Graders	11th Graders
National average	173.3	208.2	220.7
White	180.0	213.1	225.3
Black	150.7	190.1	206.9
Hispanic	162.2	197.2	202.0

Mathematics, 1985–86	9-Year-Olds	13-Year-Olds	17-Year-Olds
National average	222.0	269.0	302.0
White	227.0	274.0	308.0
Black	202.0	249.0	279.0
Hispanic	205.0	254.0	283.0

National Assessment of Educational Progress scales in reading, writing, and mathematics range from 0 to 500.
(*Source:* National Center for Education Statistics, 1991.)

FIGURE 11-5

RACIAL AND ETHNIC HIGH
SCHOOL ENROLLMENT

The proportion of individuals enrolled in high
school differs according to racial and ethnic
background.

(*Source:* U.S. Bureau of the Census, 1994.)

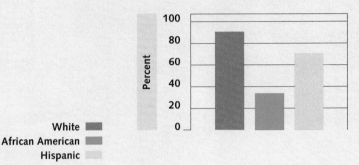

Moreover, as shown in Figure 11-5, even continuing enrollment in school differs according to race. For instance, by the time minority students reach high school age, the proportion of them still enrolled in school is lower than the proportion of Caucasian students (U.S. Bureau of the Census, 1994).

What is the source of such ethnic and racial differences in academic achievement? Clearly, much of the difference is due to socioeconomic factors: Because more African American and Hispanic families live in poverty, their economic disadvantage may be reflected in their school performance. In fact, when we take socioeconomic levels into account by comparing different ethnic and racial groups at the same socioeconomic level, achievement differences diminish (Woolfolk, 1993; Steinberg, Dornbusch, & Brown, 1992; Luster & McAdoo, 1994).

But socioeconomic factors are not the full story. For instance, anthropologist John Ogbu (1992) argues that members of certain minority groups may perceive school success as relatively unimportant. They may believe that societal prejudice in the workplace will dictate that they will not succeed, no matter how much effort they expend. The conclusion is that hard work in school will have no eventual payoff.

Furthermore, Ogbu suggests that members of minority groups who enter a new culture voluntarily are more likely to be successful in school than those who are brought into a new culture against their will. For instance, he notes that Korean children who are the sons and daughters of voluntary immigrants to the United States tend to be, on average, quite successful in school. On the other hand, Korean children in Japan, whose parents were forced to immigrate during World War II and work as forced laborers, tend to do relatively poorly in school. The reason for the disparity? The children of parents who were forced to immigrate are less likely to succeed than those whose parents immigrated voluntarily (Ogbu, 1992; Gallagher, 1994).

Another factor in the differential success of various ethnic and racial group members has to do with attributions for academic success. As we discussed in Chapter 10, students from many Asian cultures tend to view achievement as the consequence of temporary situational factors, such as how hard they work. In contrast, African American students are more apt to view success as the result of external causes over which they have no control, such as luck. Students who subscribe to the belief that effort will lead to success, and then expend that effort, are more likely to do better in school than students who believe that effort makes less of a difference (Stevenson, 1992; Stevenson & Stigler, 1992; Graham, 1986, 1990; Fuligni, 1997).

Another explanation for ethnic differences in adolescent performance comes from developmental psychologist Laurence Steinberg. He and his colleagues suggest that differ-

Directions in Development

Cyberspace: Adolescents Online

Students at McClymonds High School in Oakland, California, have a mission: In conjunction with local entomologists, they are creating an online collection of insects in the neighborhood. By placing their "collection" on the World Wide Web, they expect to provide a long-term resource for local residents (Harmon, 1997)

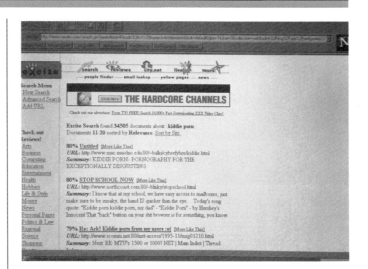

A new threat to children's well being may come from the World Wide Web, where material can be found that many parents would find objectionable.

The widespread availability of the Internet and World Wide Web is likely to produce significant changes in many adolescents' lives. Accessibility to far-flung information and contacts is likely to bring benefits and, at the same time, both real and virtual dangers.

By 1997, close to three quarters of U.S. schools had at least one connection to the Internet, and the stated goal of the federal government is to have all schools connected by the turn of the century. In addition, home usage of the Internet by adolescents is expected to increase substantially (Harmon, 1997; Cravatta, 1997).

The educational promise of the Internet is significant. Through the Internet, students can tap into a vast array of information, ranging from library catalogs to government statistics to views of the landscape of Mars transmitted by cameras actually sitting on that planet.

Although the Internet clearly is having an impact on education, how it will change education or whether the impact will be uniformly positive is not yet obvious. For instance, schools must change their curricula to include specific instruction in a key skill for deriving value from the Internet: learning to sort through huge bodies of information to identify what is most useful and discard what is not. Without some basic curricular changes, the Web may remain a largely untapped resource. To obtain the full benefits of the Internet, then, students must obtain the ability to search, choose, and integrate information in order to create new knowledge.

Despite the substantial benefits of the Internet and World Wide Web, its use also has a downside. Claims that cyberspace is overrun with pornography and child molesters may be exaggerated, but it is true that cyberspace makes available material that many parents and other adults find highly objectionable (Lohr, 1995).

Computer software programs are available that permit parents to block particular computer sites, but they are not always completely successful. Consequently, most experts believe that the most reliable safeguard is close supervision by parents. According to the National Center for Missing and Exploited Children, a nonprofit organization that works with the U.S. Department of Justice, parents should warn their children never to provide personal information, such as home addresses or telephone numbers, to people on public computer "bulletin boards" or in "chat rooms." In addition, younger adolescents should not be allowed to hold face-to-face meetings with people they "meet" via computer, not unless a parent is present.

It is too early to have clear statistics that provide a true sense of the risk presented by exposure to cyberspace. But certainly a potential hazard exists. Clearly it would be erroneous to think that, just because adolescents are in the supposed safety of their own rooms logged on to home computers, they are completely safe.

Finally, the growing use of computers presents a challenge involving race. Specifically, whites are significantly more likely than African Americans to have a home computer in their households. For instance, one survey found that whereas 22 percent of whites reported using the World Wide Web in the past 6 months, only 17 percent of African Americans had done so. For lower income individuals, these disparities were even greater. Of those people earning less than $40,000 a year, more than twice as many whites as African Americans report owing computers. These are wide disparities, and they suggest that African Americans may be at a disadvantage in terms of their access to computers. How society reduces these discrepancies is a matter of considerable importance (Hoffman & Novak, 1998).

ences in adolescents' beliefs about the consequences of not doing well in school may account for ethnic and racial differences in school performance.

Specifically, Steinberg argues that African American and Hispanic students tend to believe that they can succeed *despite* poor school performance. This belief may cause them to put less effort into their studies. In contrast, Asian American students tend to believe that if they do not do well in school, they are unlikely to get good jobs and be successful. Asian Americans, then, are motivated to work hard in school by a fear of the consequences of poor academic performance (Steinberg, Dornbusch, & Brown, 1992).

The research on ethnic and racial differences in achievement suggests a strategy for improving the performance of groups that do less well in school. If, in fact, the root of the problem is the belief that poor school performance brings few negative consequences, society needs to provide a clearer message about the value of education and to make the point that school failure clearly has negative consequences. More broadly, adolescent minority group members need to believe that their future success depends, in part, on their academic performance, and that—despite the societal hurdles faced by minority group members—they can overcome such barriers and succeed.

For another aspect of adolescent behavior related to schooling, see the "Directions in Development" box.

REVIEW AND RETHINK

REVIEW

■ Adolescence, with its substantial cognitive advances, corresponds to Piaget's formal operations period, a stage characterized by abstract reasoning and an experimental approach to problems.

■ According to the information-processing perspective, the cognitive advances of adolescence are quantitative and gradual, involving improvements in many aspects of thinking and memory.

■ Improved metacognition is one of the cognitive advances of adolescence, enabling the monitoring of thought processes and of mental capacities.

■ Adolescents are susceptible to adolescent egocentrism, which can cause social problems, and to the perception that their behavior is constantly observed by an imaginary audience. They also construct personal fables that stress their uniqueness and immunity to harm.

■ Declines in school performance during adolescence have been attributed to teachers' grading practices.

RETHINK

■ When faced with complex problems, do you think most adults spontaneously apply formal operations like those used to solve the pendulum problem? Why or why not?

■ If a gifted observer had focused on one or more of Gardner's *other* intelligences (i.e., not academic intelligence), do you think he or she would have observed stages of development like Piaget's cognitive stages?

■ In what ways does adolescent egocentrism complicate adolescents' social and family relationships? Do adults entirely outgrow egocentrism and personal fables?

■ Is socioeconomic status destiny? How would you examine and critique *The Bell Curve* contention that low IQ ultimately leads to low SES, rather than the other way around?

THREATS TO ADOLESCENTS' WELL-BEING

Like most parents, I had thought of drug use as something you worried about when your kids got to high school. Now I know that, on the average, kids begin using drugs at 11 or 12, but at the time that never crossed our minds. Ryan had just begun attending mixed parties. He was playing Little League. In the eighth grade, Ryan started getting into a little trouble—one time he and another fellow stole a fire extinguisher, but we thought it was just a prank. Then his grades began to deteriorate. He began sneaking out at night. He would become belligerent at the drop of a hat, then sunny and nice again. By then he was pretty heavy into drugs, but we were denying what we saw. You build up this trust with your child, and the last thing you want to do is break it. But looking back, there were signs everywhere. His room was filled with bottles of eye drops, to cover the redness from smoking marijuana. Money was missing from around the house, and he began burning incense in his room.

It wasn't until Ryan fell apart at 14 that we started thinking about drugs. He had just begun McLean High School, and to him, it was like going to drug camp every day. Back then, everything was so available. He began cutting classes, a common tip-off, but we didn't hear from the school until he was flunking everything. It turned out that he was going to school for the first period, getting checked in, then leaving and smoking marijuana all day. (Shafer, 1990, p. 82)

Ryan's parents learned all too soon that marijuana was not the only drug Ryan was using. As his friends later admitted, Ryan was what they called a "garbage head." He would try anything. Despite efforts to curb his use of drugs, he never succeeded in stopping. He died at the age of 16, hit by a passing car after wandering into the street during an episode of drug use.

Although most cases of adolescent drug use produce far less extreme results, the use of drugs, as well as other kinds of substance use and abuse, represents the primary threat to health during adolescence, which is usually one of the healthiest periods of life. Consider some of these preventable problems, such as drug, alcohol, and tobacco use, as well as sexually transmitted diseases.

Illegal Drugs

How common is illegal drug use during adolescence? Very prevalent. For instance, the most recent annual survey of nearly 50,000 U.S. students showed that almost 20 percent of eighth graders and close to 40 percent of seniors said they had smoked marijuana at least

The use of marijuana among high school students has increased significantly since the early 1990s.

FIGURE 11-6

GOING TO POT

According to the most recent annual survey, marijuana use over the last 12 months has increased since 1994 for 10th and 12th graders, but dropped slightly for 8th graders.

(*Source:* Johnston, Bachman, & O'Malley, 1997.)

12th Graders

10th Graders

8th Graders

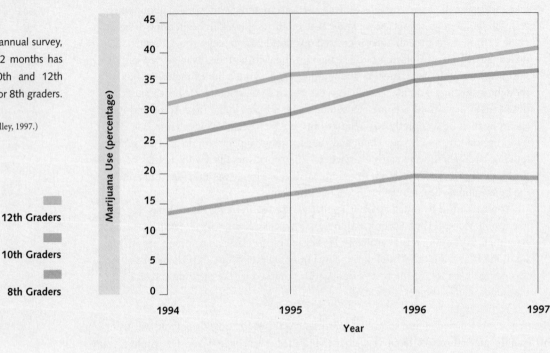

once within the last year (see Figure 11-6). More than half of high school seniors have used an illegal drug at least once in their lives (Johnston, Bachman, & O'Malley, 1997).

Although the use of drugs by adolescents is less prevalent than it was in the late 1970s and early 1980s, the rate of use is still relatively high. Furthermore, during the early 1990s, drug use began to rise and, although it appears to have leveled off, usage rates for some illegal drugs are two to three times higher than they were in the early 1990s.

Why do adolescents use drugs? There are multiple reasons. Some relate to the perceived pleasurable experience drugs may provide, and others to the escape from the pressures of everyday life that drugs temporarily permit. Some adolescents try drugs simply for the thrill of doing something illegal. Especially in adolescence, the alleged drug use of well-known role models, such as movie star Robert Downey, Jr., or former Washington, D.C., mayor Marion Barry (who served time in prison for the use of cocaine), may also contribute. Finally, peer pressure plays a role: Adolescents, as we'll discuss in greater detail in Chapter 12, are particularly susceptible to the perceived standards of their peer groups (Dinges & Oetting, 1993; Epstein et al., 1995; Petraitis, Flay, & Miller, 1995; Jenkins, 1996).

The use of illegal drugs is dangerous in several respects. For instance, some drugs are addictive. **Addictive drugs** are drugs that produce a biological or psychological dependence in users, leading to increasingly powerful cravings for them. When drugs produce a biological addiction, their presence in the body becomes so common that the body is unable to function in their absence. Drugs can also produce a psychological addiction. In such cases, people grow to depend on drugs to cope with the everyday stress of life.

In addition, if drugs are used as an escape, they may prevent adolescents from confronting—and potentially solving—the problems that led them to drug use in the first place. Finally, drugs may be dangerous because even casual users of less hazardous drugs can escalate to more dangerous forms of substance abuse. For instance, those who smoke marijuana are 85 times more likely to use cocaine than those who do not (Toch, 1995; Segal & Stewart, 1996). (Also see the "Speaking of Development" interview.)

addictive drugs   *drugs that produce a biological or psychological dependence in users, leading to increasingly powerful cravings for them*

SPEAKING OF DEVELOPMENT

Doreen Gail Branch, Substance Abuse Researcher

Education: .... Howard University, Washington, D.C., B.S. and M.A. in psychology

Position: .... Research Associate for the National Public Service Research Institute

Home: .... Greenbelt, Maryland

Abuse of alcohol, tobacco, and drugs cuts across all segments of the population, but one group that is particularly vulnerable to the allure of drugs is adolescents. In an effort to create effective preventive programs, Doreen Branch is working on a project with a community services coalition in Maryland's Prince George's County. The coalition serves adolescents between the ages of 12 and 18.

"We are currently looking at the community and how the different parts can band together to battle alcohol, tobacco, and other drug abuse problems, as well as those associated with their use," says Branch.

After starting college as a premedical student, Branch decided to try her hand at psychology. She was immediately attracted to the discipline, finding that it required more thought and creativity than merely memorizing a text. Her new interest ultimately led her to seek a master's degree in psychology, and shortly after graduating she joined the National Public Service Research Institute.

One major goal of her work is to provide youth with alternatives to using drugs by introducing them to other activities. "Many people are familiar with midnight basketball programs," she says, "but our efforts go beyond them. For instance, one of the things we are developing is a tennis program that not only teaches tennis, but also provides mentoring to at-risk adolescents." She notes that such a program emphasizes that there are other things to do with one's time than use drugs.

"We have to educate students on drugs, and we need to inform them of the dangers of even a little drug use."

"We have to educate students on drugs, and we need to inform them of the dangers of even a little drug use. Many adolescents that we deal with do not believe that marijuana, and sometimes even cocaine, are harmful," Branch adds.

Branch is also studying how tobacco and alcohol manufacturers use advertising to influence teenagers. "One of the things that we are trying to do is to change local policies in terms of billboards that cater to the advertising of cigarettes and alcohol. While many of these advertisements are in the poorest sections of town, all teenagers can be influenced by them," she notes.

"Many adolescents that we deal with do not believe that marijuana, and sometimes even cocaine, are harmful."

One tactic she has used to deter drug use by adolescents has been to ask them to write, produce, and act in their own commercials on the dangers of drug and alcohol abuse. Another has been to provide funding for a large meeting, the "Kiamsha Youth Empowerment Conference." With some help from adult mentors, Maryland adolescents organized the meeting largely by themselves.

"The issues discussed at the conference included drugs, sex, violence, and spirituality," says Branch. "The whole conference was planned and conducted by teenagers. They hit on a lot of issues that kids have to deal with, and—in part because it was planned by the adolescents themselves—it was a great success."

alcoholics   *persons with alcohol problems who have learned to depend on alcohol and are unable to control their drinking*

Alcohol: Use and Abuse

More than 75 percent of college students have something in common: They've consumed at least one alcoholic drink during the last 30 days. More than 40 percent say they have had 5 or more drinks within the past 2 weeks, and some 16 percent drink 16 or more drinks per week. High school students, too, are drinkers: Some 76 percent of high school seniors report having had an alcoholic drink in the last year (Carmody, 1990; NIAAA, 1990; Center on Addiction and Substance Abuse, 1994).

One of the most troubling patterns is the frequency of binge drinking in college students. Binge drinking is defined for men as drinking five or more drinks in one sitting; for women, who tend to weigh less and whose bodies absorb alcohol less efficiently, binge drinking is defined as four drinks in one sitting.

Recent surveys find that some 50 percent of male college students and 39 percent of female college students say they participated in binge drinking during the previous 2 weeks (see Figure 11-7). Even for lighter drinkers and nondrinkers, the high level of drinking among their peers affects their college experience. For instance, two-thirds of lighter drinkers reported that their studying or their sleep had been disturbed by drunk students. Around a third had been insulted or humiliated by a drunk student, and 25 percent of women said they had been the target of an unwanted sexual advance by a drunk classmate (Wechsler, Isaac et al., 1994).

Why do adolescents start to drink? Some believe it is the "adult" thing to do. For some—especially male athletes, whose rate of drinking tends to be higher than that of the adolescent general population—drinking is seen as a way of maintaining a "macho" image (Fromme & Rivet, 1994; Carr, Kennedy, & Dimick, 1996). Others drink for the same reason that they use drugs: It releases inhibitions and tension and reduces stress (Pavis, Cunningham-Burley, & Amos, 1997). Of course, the same chemical reaction that produces these results can also make adolescents feel depressed, cloud their judgment, impair memory, and reduce motor skills necessary for driving. These consequences are the greatest danger of alcohol use.

For some adolescents—perhaps as many as a third—alcohol use becomes a habit that cannot be controlled. **Alcoholics**, those with alcohol problems, learn to depend on alcohol and are unable to control their drinking. They also become increasingly immune to the consequences of drinking, and therefore need to drink ever-larger amounts of liquor to bring about the positive effects they crave. Some drink throughout the day, whereas others go on binges in which they consume huge quantities of alcohol (NIAAA, 1990; Morse & Flavin, 1992).

FIGURE 11-7

BINGE DRINKING AMONG COLLEGE STUDENTS

For men, binge drinking was defined as consuming five or more drinks in one sitting; for women, the total was four or more.

(*Source:* Wechsler, Isaac et al., 1994.)

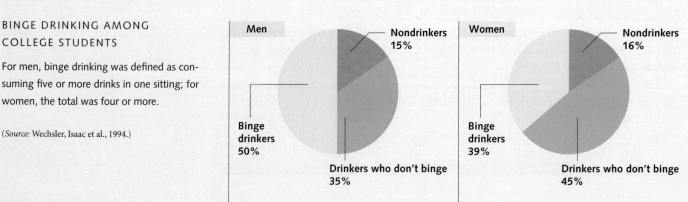

The reasons that some adolescents become alcoholics is not fully known. Genetics plays a role: Alcoholism runs in families. On the other hand, not all alcoholics have others in their family who drink too much. In cases such as these, alcoholism may be triggered by efforts to deal with environmental stress (Bushman, 1993; Boyd, Howard, & Zucker, 1995).

Tobacco

Most adolescents are well aware of the dangers of smoking, but many still indulge in it. Although recent figures show that, overall, a smaller proportion of adolescents smoke than in prior decades, the numbers remain substantial. Furthermore, within certain groups the numbers are increasing. For instance, smoking is more prevalent among girls; and in several countries, including Austria, Norway, and Sweden, the proportion of girls who smoke is higher than the proportion of boys. There are racial differences, as well: Smoking among white males of high school age is significantly greater than among African American males in high school, although the gap has narrowed in recent years (Chollat-Traquet, 1992; Bartecchi, MacKenzie, & Schrier, 1995; Stolberg, 1998).

Adolescents smoke despite growing social sanctions against the habit. As the dangers of secondhand smoke become more apparent, many people look down on smokers. More places, including schools and places of business, have become "smoke-free," a trend that makes it increasingly difficult to find a place to smoke. Furthermore, the health dangers of smoking are hardly in dispute: Every package of cigarettes carries a warning that smoking is linked to a higher mortality rate, and even adolescents who smoke admit that they know the dangers.

Why, then, do adolescents begin to smoke and then maintain the habit? One reason is that smoking is still considered sexy and hip. Advertisements for cigarettes depict

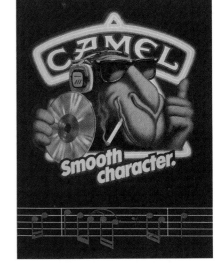

The portrayal of Joe Camel as a hip and smooth character helped to maintain the image of smoking as a "cool" activity.

attractive individuals smoking, and clever ads, such as the highly successful "Joe Camel" series, make an effective pitch to young males. In fact, before Joe Camel commercials were withdrawn from use, children as young as 6 could identify Joe Camel as readily as Mickey Mouse (Lipman, 1992; Bartecchi, MacKenzie, & Schrier, 1995; Ono, 1995; Urberg, Degirmencioglu, & Pilgrim, 1997).

There are other reasons, too. Nicotine, the active chemical ingredient of cigarettes, can produce biological and psychological dependency: Smoking produces a pleasant emotional state that smokers seek to maintain (Pomerleau & Pomerleau, 1989; Nowak, 1994b). Furthermore, exposure to parents and peers who smoke increases the chances that an adolescent will take up the habit (Botvin et al., 1994; Webster, Hunter, & Keats, 1994). Finally, smoking is sometimes seen as an adolescent rite of passage: Trying cigarettes is looked upon as a sign of growing up. Although one or two cigarettes do not usually produce a lifetime smoker, it takes only a little more to start the habit. In fact, people who smoke as few as ten cigarettes early in their lives stand an 80 percent chance of becoming habitual smokers (Bowen et al., 1991; Stacy et al., 1992).

Developmental Diversity

Selling Death: Pushing Smoking to the Less Advantaged

In Dresden, Germany, three women in miniskirts offer passers-by a pack of Lucky Strikes and a leaflet that reads: "You just got hold of a nice piece of America." Says a local doctor, "Adolescents time and again receive cigarettes at such promotions."

A Jeep decorated with the Camel logo pulls up to a high school in Buenos Aires. A woman begins handing out free cigarettes to 15- and 16-year-olds during their lunch recess.

At a video arcade in Taipei, free American cigarettes are strewn atop each game. At a disco filled with high school students, free packs of Salems are on each table. (Ecenbarger, 1993, p. 50)

If you are a cigarette manufacturer and you find that the number of people using your product is declining, what do you do? U.S. companies have sought to carve out new markets by turning to the least advantaged groups of people, both at home and

abroad. For instance, in the early 1990s the R.J. Reynolds tobacco company designed a new brand of cigarettes it named "Uptown." The advertising used to herald its arrival made clear who the target was: African Americans living in urban areas (Quinn, 1990). Because of subsequent protests, the tobacco company withdrew "Uptown" from the market.

In addition to seeking new converts in the United States, tobacco companies aggressively recruit adolescent smokers abroad. In many developing countries the number of smokers is still low. Tobacco companies are seeking to increase this number through marketing strategies designed to hook adolescents on the habit by means of free samples. In addition, in countries where American culture and products are held in high esteem, advertising suggests that the use of cigarettes is an American—and consequently prestigious—habit (Sesser, 1993).

The strategy is effective. For instance, in some Latin American cities as many as 50 percent of teenagers smoke. According to the World Health Organization, smoking will prematurely kill some 200 million of the world's children and adolescents, and overall, 10 percent of the world's population will die because of smoking (Ecenbarger, 1993).

Sexually Transmitted Diseases: One Cost of Sex

In the fall of 1990, Krista Blake was 18 and looking forward to her first year at Youngstown State University in Ohio. She and her boyfriend were talking about getting married. Her life was, she says, "basic, white-bread America." Then she went to the doctor, complaining about a backache, and found out she had the AIDS virus.

Blake had been infected with HIV, the virus that causes AIDS, two years earlier by an older boy, a hemophiliac. "He knew that he was infected, and he didn't tell me," she says. "And he didn't do anything to keep me from getting infected, either." (Becahy, 1992, p. 49)

AIDS. Krista Blake, who later died from the disorder, was not alone: **Acquired immune deficiency syndrome**, or **AIDS**, is one of the leading causes of death among young people. AIDS has no cure and ultimately brings death to those who are infected with the HIV virus that produces the disease.

Because AIDS is spread primarily through sexual contact, it is classified as a **sexually transmitted disease (STD)**. Although it began as a problem that primarily afflicted homosexuals, it has spread to other populations, including heterosexuals and intravenous drug users. Minorities have been particularly hard hit: African Americans and Hispanics account for some 40 percent of AIDS cases, although they make up only 18 percent of the population.

In the United States, experts estimate that by the beginning of 1995, two million people will have been infected with the virus. Worldwide, the figures are mind-boggling: By the year 2000, it is estimated that some 30 million people will be carrying the AIDS virus (HMHL, 1994).

Krista Blake contracted AIDS at the age of 16. She later died from the disease.

AIDS and Adolescent Behavior. It is no secret how AIDS is transmitted—through the exchange of bodily fluids, including semen and blood. However, motivating teenagers to employ safer sex practices that can prevent its spread has proven difficult. On the one hand, the use of condoms during sexual intercourse has increased, and people are less likely to engage in casual sex with new acquaintances (Catania et al., 1992; Kelly, 1995).

On the other hand, the use of safer sex practices is far from universal. Adolescents, who—as we discussed earlier in the chapter—are prone to engage in risky behavior due to feelings of invulnerability, are likely to believe that their chances of contracting AIDS are minimal (Serovich & Greene, 1997). This is particularly true when adolescents perceive that their partner is "safe"—someone they know well and with whom they are involved in a relatively long-term relationship (Moore & Rosenthal, 1991; Rosenthal & Shepherd, 1993; Freiberg, 1998).

Unfortunately, unless an individual knows the complete sexual history and HIV status of a partner, unprotected sex remains risky business. And learning a partner's complete sexual history is difficult. It is often inaccurately communicated because of embarrassment, a sense of privacy, or simply forgetfulness.

Short of celibacy, a solution regarded as improbable for many adolescents involved in relationships, there is no certain way to avoid AIDS. However, health experts suggest several strategies for making sex safer; these are listed in Table 11-2.

acquired immune deficiency syndrome (AIDS) *a sexually transmitted disease, produced by the HIV virus, that has no cure and ultimately causes death*

sexually transmitted disease (STD) *a disease that is spread through sexual contact*

TABLE 11-2

SAFER SEX: PREVENTING THE TRANSMISSION OF AIDS

Health psychologists and educators have devised several guidelines to help prevent the spread of AIDS. Among them are the following:

- **Use condoms.** The use of condoms greatly reduces the risk of transmission of the virus that produces AIDS, which occurs through exposure to bodily fluids such as semen or blood.

- **Avoid high-risk behaviors.** Such practices as unprotected anal intercourse or the exchange of needles used in drug use greatly increase the risk of AIDS.

- **Know your partner's sexual history.** Knowing your sexual partner and his or her sexual history can help you to evaluate the risks of sexual contact.

- **Consider abstinence.** Although not always a practical alternative, the only certain way of avoiding AIDS is to refrain from sexual activity altogether.

FIGURE 11-8

SEXUALLY TRANSMITTED
DISEASES (STDS) AMONG
ADOLESCENTS

(*Source:* Alan Guttmacher Institute, 1993a.)

3 million teenagers, about 1 person in 8 aged 13–19 and about 1 in 4 of those who have had sexual intercourse, acquire an STD every year. Among the most common:

Chlamydia: Chlamydia is more common among teenagers than among older men and women; in some studies, 10 to 29 percent of sexually active adolescent girls and 10 percent of teenage boys have been found to be infected with chlamydia.

Genital herpes: A viral disease that is incurable, often indicated first by small blisters or sores around the genitals. It is periodically contagious.

Trichomoniasis: An infection of the vagina or penis, caused by a parasite.

Gonorrhea: Adolescents aged 15–19 have higher rates of gonorrhea than do sexually active men and women in any 5-year age group between 20–44.

Syphilis: Infectious syphilis rates more than doubled between 1986 and 1990 among women aged 15–19.

The Informed Consumer of Development

Hooked on Drugs or Alcohol?

Although it is not always easy to determine whether an adolescent has a drug or alcohol abuse problem, there are some signals. Among them:

Identification with the drug culture

■ Drug-related magazines or slogans on clothing
■ Conversation and jokes that are preoccupied with drugs
■ Hostility discussing drugs
■ Collection of beer cans

Signs of physical deterioration

■ Memory lapses, short attention span, difficulty concentrating
■ Poor physical coordination, slurred or incoherent speech
■ Unhealthy appearance, indifference to hygiene and grooming
■ Bloodshot eyes, dilated pupils

Dramatic changes in school performance

■ Marked downturn in grades—not just from Cs to Fs, but from As to Bs and Cs; assignments not completed

■ Increased absenteeism or tardiness

Changes in behavior

■ Chronic dishonesty (lying, stealing, cheating); trouble with the police
■ Changes in friends; evasiveness in talking about new ones
■ Possession of large amounts of money
■ Increasing and inappropriate anger, hostility, irritability, secretiveness
■ Reduced motivation, energy, self-discipline, self-esteem
■ Diminished interest in extracurricular activities and hobbies (Adapted from Franck & Brownstone, 1991, pp. 593–594)

If an adolescent—or anyone else, for that matter—fits any of these descriptors, help is probably needed. It is possible to get advice from a national hotline. For alcohol difficulties, call the National Council on Alcoholism at (800) 622-2255; for drug problems, call the National Institute on Drug Abuse at (800) 662-4357. In addition, those who need advice can find a local listing for Alcoholics Anonymous or Narcotics Anonymous in the telephone book. Finally, for help with alcohol and drug problems, contact the National Council on Alcoholism and Drug Dependence at 12 West 21 Street, New York, NY 10010.

Other Sexually Transmitted Diseases.   Although AIDS is the deadliest of sexually transmitted diseases, others are far more common (see Figure 11-8). In fact, one in four adolescents contracts an STD before graduating from high school. Overall, around 2.5 million teenagers contract an STD each year. Contracting an STD is not only an immediate problem during adolescence, but some of these diseases increase the chances of future infertility and cancer (Gans, 1990; Alan Guttmacher Institute, 1993a).

Chlamydia, a disease caused by a parasite, is the most common STD. Initially it has few symptoms, but later it causes burning urination and a discharge from the penis or vagina. It can lead to pelvic inflammation and even to sterility.

Another common STD is **genital herpes**, a virus not unlike the cold sores that sometimes appear around the mouth. The first symptoms of herpes are often small blisters or sores around the genitals, which may break open and become quite painful. Although the sores may heal after a few weeks, the disease often recurs after an interval, and the cycle repeats itself. When the sores reappear, the disease, for which there is no cure, is contagious.

Several other STDs are frequent among adolescents. *Trichomoniasis*, an infection in the vagina or penis, is caused by a parasite. Initially without symptoms, it can eventually cause a painful discharge. *Gonorrhea* and *syphilis* are the STDs that have been recognized for the longest time; cases were recorded by ancient historians. Until the advent of antibiotics, both diseases were deadly; today both can be treated quite effectively.

chlamydia   *the most common sexually transmitted disease, caused by a parasite*

genital herpes   *a common sexually transmitted disease, which is a virus and not unlike cold sores that sometimes appear around the mouth*

REVIEW AND RETHINK

REVIEW

■ Illegal drug use is prevalent among adolescents, who may regard drugs as a way to find pleasure, avoid pressure, or gain the approval of peers. Drug use is dangerous because it can escalate, become addictive, and prevent the confrontation of problems.

■ The use of alcohol is also popular among adolescents, often out of a desire to appear adult or to lessen inhibitions. Impaired judgment and loss of motor control are the main dangers of alcohol use.

■ A third substance that constitutes a serious health hazard to adolescents is tobacco. Despite the well-known dangers of smoking, adolescents often engage in the practice to enhance their images or emulate adults.

■ AIDS is the most serious of the sexually transmitted diseases, ultimately causing death to its victims. Safe sex practices or sexual abstinence can prevent AIDS, although adolescents often ignore these strategies.

RETHINK

■ In what ways do characteristics of adolescent development that have been studied in this chapter contribute to adolescents' tendencies to abuse drugs?

■ How might you address an adolescent's claim that his use of marijuana is harmless and totally under his control?

■ How do adolescents' concerns about self-image and their perception that they are the center of attention contribute to smoking and alcohol use?

■ Why do adolescents' increased cognitive abilities, including the ability to reason and to think experimentally, fail to deter them from irrational behavior such as drug and alcohol abuse, tobacco use, and unsafe sex practices?

LOOKING BACK

■ **What physical changes do adolescents experience?**

- The adolescent years are marked by a physical growth spurt, which for girls begins around age 10, and for boys, around age 12.

- Puberty begins in girls at around 11 and in boys at around 13. The physical changes of puberty often have psychological effects, such as an increase in self-esteem and self-awareness, as well as confusion and uncertainty about sexuality.

■ **What are the consequences of early and late maturation?**

- For boys, early maturation can lead to increased athleticism, greater popularity, and a more positive self-concept. For girls, early maturation can lead to increased popularity and an enhanced social life, but also embarrassment over their bodies. Early maturation can lead boys and girls into situations for which they are not adequately prepared.

- For boys, late maturation can be a physical and social disadvantage that affects self-concept. Girls who mature late may suffer neglect by their peers, but ultimately they appear to suffer no lasting ill effects and may even benefit.

■ **What nutritional needs and concerns do adolescents have?**

- While most adolescents have no greater nutritional worries than fueling their growth with appropriate foods, some are obese or overweight. Excessive concern about obesity can cause some adolescents, especially girls, to contract an eating disorder such as anorexia nervosa or bulimia.

■ **In what ways does cognitive development proceed during adolescence?**

- Cognitive growth during adolescence is rapid, with gains in abstract thinking, reasoning, and the ability to view possibilities in relative rather than absolute terms.

- Adolescence coincides with Piaget's formal operations period of development, when people begin to engage in abstract thought and experimental reasoning.

- According to information-processing approaches, cognitive growth during adolescence is gradual and quantitative, involving improvements in memory capacity, mental strategies, metacognition, and other aspects of cognitive functioning.

- Adolescents may be subject to adolescent egocentrism, imaginary audiences and personal fables.

■ **What factors affect adolescent school performance?**

- School performance declines during the adolescent years. School achievement is linked with socioeconomic status, race, and ethnicity. While many academic achievement differences are due to socioeconomic factors, attributional patterns regarding success factors and belief systems regarding the link between school success and success in life also play a part.

■ **What dangerous substances do adolescents use and why?**

- The use of illicit drugs, alcohol, and tobacco is very prevalent among adolescents, who are motivated by pleasure-seeking, pressure-avoidance, the desire to flout authority, or the imitation of role models.

■ **What dangers do adolescent sexual practices present, and how can these dangers be avoided?**

- AIDS is now the leading cause of death among young people, affecting minority populations with particular severity. Adolescent behavior patterns and attitudes, such as shyness, self-absorption, and a belief in personal invulnerability, work against the use of safe sex practices that can prevent the disease.

- Other sexually transmitted diseases, including chlamydia, genital herpes, trichomoniasis, gonorrhea, and syphilis, occur frequently among the adolescent population and can also be prevented by safe sex practices or abstinence.

EPILOGUE: ALEKSANDR KHAZANOV

In this chapter, we began our examination of adolescence, a period of great change in people's lives. We looked at the significant physical, psychological, and cognitive changes that adolescents undergo, and at some of the consequences of entering and living through adolescence.

Turn back to the prologue of this chapter, about the mathematically gifted Aleksandr Khazanov, and answer the following questions.

1. Can you account for Aleksandr's remarkable cognitive development in terms of Piaget's theory? Can you account for it in terms of information-processing approaches? Which account seems better? Why?

2. Does Aleksandr's accelerated cognitive development imply that his physical maturation has also come early? Why or why not?

3. Does Aleksandr's advanced cognitive development imply that he will escape the usual adolescent quirks of egocentrism, belief in an imaginary audience, and personal fables? Why or why not?

4. Can you speculate on the social consequences for Aleksandr of his cognitive abilities in high school?

5. Would you advise Aleksandr's parents to send him to college or even graduate school far in advance of his peers? What consequences do you anticipate for him if he attends college at a much younger age than typical? What consequences do you anticipate for him if he continues to attend his regular high school?

KEY TERMS AND CONCEPTS

adolescence (p. 378)

puberty (p. 380)

menarche (p. 380)

primary sex characteristics (p. 381)

secondary sex characteristics (p. 381)

anorexia nervosa (p. 384)

bulimia (p. 384)

formal operations period (p. 386)

information-processing perspective (p. 388)

metacognition (p. 388)

adolescent egocentrism (p. 389)

imaginary audience (p. 389)

personal fables (p. 389)

addictive drugs (p. 396)

alcoholics (p. 398)

acquired immune deficiency syndrome (AIDS) (p. 401)

sexually transmitted disease (STD) (p. 401)

chlamydia (p. 403)

genital herpes (p. 403)

CHAPTER 12

ADOLESCENCE

Social and Personality Development

PROLOGUE: THREE ADOLESCENTS

In spite of the rebel stereotype, the majority of adolescents pass through the period in relative tranquility.

Carly, a freshman at Benjamin Franklin High School, a school for gifted kids, says she has no interest in politics or social issues. "It's probably because of my mom—she's racked my brain with statistics and feminism and the environment," she says. "I'm like, 'Well, what do you want me to do?'" Since her parents split when she was 3, Carly has lived mainly in Louisiana with her mother. . . . So what *is* she passionate about? "My friends."

***

"Keep the Hell Out of my Room!" says a sign on Trevor's bedroom wall, just above an unmade bed, a desk littered with dirty T-shirts and candy wrappers, and a floor covered with clothes. Is there a carpet? "Somewhere," he says with a grin. "I think it's gold." Trevor is the third of four sons of Richard Kelson, 56, a retired truck driver, and his wife, JoAnn, 46, a medical tape transcriber. The family lives in a four-bedroom home across from Hunter Junior High School, where Trevor is in ninth grade. He spent the summer volunteering in a leadership-training program at the Sugar House Boys & Girls Club in Salt Lake City. "I guess it gives you a good feeling to help somebody else," he says. In off-hours, he played Nintendo with pal Andy Muhlestein, 15. "When we don't have anything else to do, and we're tired of playing videos," he says, "we sit around and talk about girls."

* * *

A fan of Shakespeare and Kurt Cobain, *Elle* and skateboarding magazines, Abrielle is the youngest of six children of schoolteacher Gail Grissett, 46, and hairdresser Benny Williams, 48, who are separated. She rarely sees some of her siblings, who are in their 20s. Abrielle just started ninth grade at Ramsay Alternative High School. . . . She leads a color-blind social life, which she says occasionally causes trouble with her friends and relatives. "Some black kids have problems with me having white friends," Abielle says. "I'm not bothered by that. I hang out with black kids too." (Fields-Meyer, 1995, pp. 52, 53, 59)

LOOKING AHEAD   Although Carly, Trevor, and Abrielle have never met, the three share remarkably similar concerns focused around friends, parents, and school. None of them is a rebel, and they generally have good relations with their parents—like most of their peers. For despite the reputation of adolescence as a time of confusion and rebellion, research increasingly shows that most people pass through the period without much turmoil. Although they may "try on" different roles and flirt with activities that their parents find objectionable, the majority of adolescents pass through the period in relative tranquillity (Peterson, 1988; Steinberg, 1993).

This is not to say that the transitions adolescents pass through are less than highly challenging. As we shall see in this chapter, in which we examine the personality and social developments of the period, adolescence brings about major changes in the ways in which individuals must deal with the world (Eccles et al., 1993; Crockett & Crouter, 1995; Takanishi, Hamburg, & Jacobs, 1997).

We begin by considering how adolescents form their views of themselves. We look at self-concept, self-esteem, and identity development. We also examine two major psychological difficulties: depression and suicide.

Next, we discuss relationships during adolescence. We consider how adolescents reposition themselves within the family and how the influence of family members declines in some spheres as peers take on new importance. We also examine the ways in which adolescents interact with their friends, and the determinants of popularity and rejection.

Finally, the chapter considers dating and sexual behavior. We look at the role of dating in adolescents' lives, and we consider sexual behavior and the standards that govern adolescents' sex lives. We conclude by looking at the effects of teenage pregnancy and at ways to reduce its incidence.

In sum, after reading this chapter, you will be able to answer these questions:

Q

■ How does the development of self-concept, self-esteem, and identity proceed during adolescence?

■ What dangers do adolescents face as they deal with the stresses of adolescence?

■ How does the quality of relationships with family and peers change during adolescence?

■ What are gender, race, and ethnic relations like in adolescence?

■ What does it mean to be popular and unpopular in adolescence, and how do adolescents respond to peer pressure?

■ What are the functions and characteristics of dating during adolescence?

■ How does sexuality develop in the adolescent years?

■ Why is teenage pregnancy a particular problem in the United States?

IDENTITY: ASKING "WHO AM I?"

Turning 13 was an important period of my life. It was the time when I started to mature physically. It also was the time when more girls started to notice me. My personality changed a lot from a boring nerd to an energetic, funny and athletic kid.

As my year went on as a 13-year-old, as if things couldn't get better, they surprisingly did! My life as a child had ended. I was now a teenager. This just goes to show you that turning 13 meant turning into a new person.

PATRICK BACKER (February 28, 1993, *The New York Times*, p. 2)

As you go to school, things get harder. You sort of realize that you're getting older. Adults treat you like an adult and don't give you the breaks you got when you're a child.

To be 13 you have journeyed only half way to the *real* world. Then you notice that you're going to high school and think of the next four years and then college. Next you vote, a house, job and kids. It seems your life passes right before your eyes.

MIEKO OZEKI (February 28, 1993, *The New York Times*, p. 2)

When I turned 13 it was like starting a new life. It was the year I was finally going to be allowed to do more things. For one thing I was able to hang out later. I wasn't a child anymore. I knew it and my parents knew it, too.

I really can't think of a more important birthday besides your first one.

DMITRI PONOMAREV (February 28, 1993, *The New York Times*, p. 2)

These voices of adolescents resonate with a common theme: a keen awareness and self-consciousness regarding their newly forming place in society and life. During adolescence, questions like "Who am I?" and "Where do I belong in the world?" begin to take a front seat.

Why should issues of identity become so important during adolescence? One reason is that adolescents' intellectual capacities become more adultlike. They can now understand—and appreciate—such abstract issues as the importance of establishing their position in society and the need to form a sense of themselves as individuals. Another reason is that the dramatic physical changes during puberty make adolescents acutely aware of their own bodies—and of the fact that others are reacting to them in ways to which they are unaccustomed.

During adolescence, questions of identity become increasingly crucial.

Whatever the cause, adolescence often brings substantial changes in teenagers' self-concepts and self-esteem—in sum, their notions of their own identity.

Self-concept: Refining Perceptions of the Self

Ask Louella to describe herself, and she says, "Others look at me as laid-back, relaxed, and not worrying too much. But really, I'm often nervous and emotional."

The fact that Louella distinguishes others' views of her from her own perceptions represents a developmental advance of adolescence. In childhood, Louella would have characterized herself according to a list of traits that would not differentiate her view of herself and others' perspectives. However, adolescents are able to make the distinction, and when they try to describe who they are, they take both their own and others' views into account (Harter, 1990b).

This broadening view of themselves is one aspect of adolescents' increasing discernment and perception in their understanding of who they are. The view of the self becomes more organized and coherent, and they can see various aspects of the self simultaneously. Furthermore, they look at the self from a psychological perspective, viewing traits not as concrete entities but as abstractions (Adams, Montemayor, & Gullotta, 1996).

In some ways, however, the increasing differentiation of self-concept is a mixed blessing, especially during the earlier years of adolescence. At that time, adolescents may be troubled by the multiple aspects of their personalities. During the beginning of adolescence, for instance, teenagers may want to view themselves in a certain way ("I'm a sociable person and love to be with people"), and they may become concerned when their behavior is inconsistent with that view ("Even though I want to be sociable, sometimes I can't stand being around my friends and just want to be alone"). By the end of adolescence, however, teenagers accept the fact that different situations elicit different behaviors and feelings (Harter, 1990a; Pyryt & Mendaglio, 1994; Klein, 1995).

Self-esteem: Evaluating Oneself

Knowing who you are and *liking* who you are represent two different things. Although adolescents become increasingly accurate in understanding who they are (their self-concept), this knowledge does not guarantee that they like themselves (their self-esteem) any better. In fact, their increasing accuracy in understanding themselves permits them to see themselves fully—warts and all.

The same cognitive sophistication that allows adolescents to differentiate various aspects of the self also leads them to evaluate those aspects in different ways (Chan, 1997). For instance, an adolescent may have high self-esteem in terms of academic performance, but lower self-esteem in terms of relationships with others. Or it may be just the opposite, as articulated by this adolescent:

> How much do I *like* the kind of person I am? Well, I like some things about me, but I don't like others. I'm glad that I'm popular since it's really important to me to have friends. But in school I don't do as well as the really smart kids. That's OK, because if you're too smart you'll lose your friends. So being smart is just not that important. Except to my parents. I feel like I'm letting them down when I don't do as well as they want. (Harter, 1990a, p. 364)

Gender Differences in Self-esteem.   What determines an adolescent's self-esteem? Several factors make a difference. One is gender: Particularly during early adolescence, girls' self-esteem tends to be lower and more vulnerable than boys' (Simmons & Rosenberg, 1975; Simmons et al., 1978; Cairns et al.,1990; Chubb, Fertman, & Ross, 1997; Watkins, Dong, & Xia, 1997).

One reason is that, compared to boys, girls are more highly concerned about physical appearance and social success—in addition to academic achievement. Although boys are also concerned about these things, their attitudes are often more casual. Moreover,

traditional societal messages may be interpreted as suggesting that female academic achievement is a roadblock to social success. Girls hearing such messages, then, are in a difficult bind: If they do well academically, they jeopardize their social success. No wonder that the self-esteem of adolescent girls is more fragile than that of boys (Hess-Biber, 1996; Mendelson, White, & Mendelson, 1996; Unger & Crawford, 1996).

Socioeconomic Status and Race Differences in Self-esteem. Socioeconomic status (SES) and race also influence self-esteem. Adolescents of higher SES generally have higher self-esteem than those of lower SES, particularly during middle and later adolescence. It may be that the social status factors that especially enhance one's standing and self-esteem—such as having more expensive clothes or a car—become more conspicuous in the later periods of adolescence (Savin-Williams & Demo, 1983; Van Tassel-Baska, Olszewski-Kubilius, & Kulieke, 1994).

Race also plays a role in self-esteem, although the findings are not entirely consistent. Early studies argued that minority status would lead to lower self-esteem. This finding led to the hypothesis—initially supported—that African Americans and Hispanics would have lower self-esteem than Caucasians. Researchers' explanations for this finding were straightforward: Societal prejudice would be incorporated into the self-concepts of the targets of the prejudice, making them feel disliked and rejected.

However, more recent research paints a different picture. Most findings now suggest that African Americans differ little from whites in their levels of self-esteem (Harter, 1990b). Why should this be? One explanation is that social movements within the African

identity-versus-identity-confusion stage
the period during which teenagers seek to determine what is unique and distinctive about themselves

American community that bolster racial pride help support African American adolescents. In fact, research finds that a stronger sense of racial identity is related to a higher level of self-esteem in African Americans and Hispanics (Phinney, Lochner, & Murphy, 1990; Goodstein & Ponterotto, 1997).

Another reason for overall similarity in self-esteem levels between minority and majority adolescents is that teenagers in general focus their preferences and priorities on those aspects of their lives at which they are best. Consequently, African American youths may concentrate on the things that they find most satisfying and gain self-esteem from being successful at them (Hunt & Hunt, 1975; Phinney & Alipura, 1990).

Finally, self-esteem may be influenced not by race alone, but by a complex combination of factors. For instance, some developmental psychologists have considered race and gender simultaneously, coining the term *ethgender* to refer to the joint influence of race and gender. One study that simultaneously took both race and gender into account found that African American and Hispanic males had the highest levels of self-esteem, and Asian and Native American females had the lowest levels (Martinez & Dukes, 1991; Dukes & Martinez, 1994). (For another perspective on self-esteem, see the "Directions in Development" box.)

Identity Formation in Adolescence: Change or Crisis?

According to Erik Erikson, whose theory we last discussed in Chapter 10, the search for identity inevitably leads some adolescents into substantial psychological difficulties as they encounter the adolescent identity crisis (Erikson, 1963). Erikson's theory regarding this stage, which is summarized with his other stages in Table 12-1, suggests that adolescence is the time of the **identity-versus-identity-confusion stage**.

During the identity-versus-identity-confusion stage, teenagers seek to determine what is unique and distinctive about themselves. They strive to discover their particular strengths

TABLE 12-1

A SUMMARY OF ERIKSON'S STAGES

Stage	Approximate Age	Positive Outcomes	Negative Outcomes
1. Trust versus mistrust	Birth–1.5 years	Feelings of trust from environmental support	Fear and concern regarding others
2. Autonomy versus shame and doubt	1.5–3 years	Self-sufficiency if exploration is encouraged	Doubts about self, lack of independence
3. Initiative versus guilt	3–6 years	Discovery of ways to initiate actions	Guilt from actions and thoughts
4. Industry versus inferiority	6–12 years	Development of sense of competence	Feelings of inferiority, no sense of mastery
5. Identity versus identity confusion	Adolescence	Awareness of uniqueness of self, knowledge of role to be followed	Inability to identify appropriate roles in life
6. Intimacy versus isolation	Early adulthood	Development of loving, sexual relationships and close friendships	Fear of relationships with others
7. Generativity versus stagnation	Middle adulthood	Sense of contribution to continuity of life	Trivialization of one's activities
8. Ego-integrity versus despair	Late adulthood	Sense of unity in life's accomplishments	Regret over lost opportunities of life

(*Source:* Erikson, 1963.)

Directions in Development

Self-Esteem, Violence, and Aggression: The Downside of High Self-Esteem

Leigh is on the road to trouble. An eighth grader, he is cutting school, stealing from local stores, and participating in fights. The local police already are well acquainted with him, and his parents have told his teachers that he barely listens to them. The principal of his school, however, thinks she has a solution: Raise Leigh's self-esteem, which, because of his behavior, she is sure must be exceptionally low. Surely, she believes, helping him to feel better about himself will make him less aggressive and hostile.

According to recent findings, high self-esteem may actually be associated with higher levels of aggression than low self-esteem.

If such a solution seems reasonable to you, you are not alone: Many experts believe that bolstering the self-esteem of adolescents can cure a variety of societal ills, most particularly violence and other forms of antisocial behavior (e.g., California Task Force, 1990).

However, according to new research conducted by psychologists Roy Baumeister, Laura Smart, and Joseph Boden, such an approach not only may be wrong, but also may actually make the problem worse. In a comprehensive review of studies of aggression, they found that *high* self-esteem is often associated with violence and aggression (Baumeister, Smart, & Boden, 1996).

In their review of a massive amount of literature from many disciplines, the researchers found that perpetrators of violence frequently not only see themselves in a favorable light, but in fact have an inflated view of themselves. Even in the face of contrary evidence, such as school failure, the inability to get along with peers, and family strife, some individuals hold surprisingly positive views of themselves, and in fact it is these positive views that lead to violence.

According to this argument, when individuals with unusually high self-esteem are challenged, they vigorously seek to maintain their view of themselves as superior, frequently through violent means. In contrast, people with lower self-esteem are less prone to lash out at others when attacked or challenged, because such threats to their self-worth are more in keeping with their more negative view of themselves.

In short, individuals with unusually high self-esteem are motivated to maintain their high level of self-regard. When challenged by others or by various circumstances in which they find themselves, they direct their anger toward others or toward the situation. In turn, this tactic allows them to avoid revising their view of themselves in a negative direction.

Of course, these findings do not mean that every person high in self-esteem is likely to act violently. Nor do they mean that seeking to bolster the self-esteem of perpetrators of violence is necessarily a poor strategy, for many studies have found a relationship between high self-esteem and several types of positive outcome. But they do suggest that raising self-esteem to levels that are incongruent with reality may not be the best approach to dealing with individuals who are violent and aggressive. Unrealistically high self-esteem may, in fact, have a downside.

and weaknesses and the roles they can best play in their future lives. In short, they seek to understand who they are by narrowing and making choices about their personal, occupational, sexual, and political commitments.

In Erikson's view, adolescents who stumble in their efforts to find a suitable identity may follow several dysfunctional courses. They may adopt socially unacceptable roles, such as that of deviant, or they may have difficulty forming and maintaining long-lasting close personal relationships later on in life. In general, their sense of self becomes "diffuse," failing to organize around a central, unified core identity.

On the other hand, those who are successful in forging an appropriate identity set a course that provides a foundation for future psychosocial development. They learn their unique capabilities, and they develop an accurate sense of who they are. They are prepared to set out on a path that takes full advantage of what their unique strengths permit them to do (Kahn et al., 1985; Blustein & Palladino, 1991; Archer & Waterman, 1994).

Societal pressures are high during the identity-versus-identity-confusion stage, as any student knows who has been repeatedly asked by parents and friends "What's your major?" and "What are you going to do when you graduate?" Adolescents feel pressure to decide whether their post-high-school plans include work or college and, if they choose work, which occupational track to follow. These are new choices, because up to this point in their development, U.S. society lays out a universal educational track. However, the track ends at high school, and consequently, adolescents face difficult choices about which of several possible future paths they will follow.

During the identity-versus-identity-confusion period, adolescents increasingly rely on their friends and peers as sources of information. At the same time, their dependence on adults declines. As we discuss later in the chapter, this increasing dependence on the peer group enables adolescents to forge close relationships. It also helps them clarify their own identities as they compare themselves to others.

Erikson suggests that because of the pressures of the identity-versus-identity-confusion period, many adolescents pursue a "psychological moratorium." The *psychological moratorium* is a period during which adolescents take time off from the upcoming responsibilities of adulthood and explore various roles and possibilities.

On the other hand, many adolescents cannot, for practical reasons, pursue a psychological moratorium involving a relatively leisurely exploration of various identities. For instance, some adolescents, for economic reasons, must work part-time after school and then take jobs immediately after graduation from high school. As a result, they have little time to experiment with identities and engage in a psychological moratorium. Does this mean such adolescents will be psychologically damaged in some way? Probably not. In fact, the satisfaction that can come from successfully holding a part-time job while attending school may be a sufficient psychological reward to outweigh the inability to try out various roles.

Marcia's Approach to Identity Development: Updating Erikson

Using Erikson's theory as a springboard, psychologist James Marcia suggests that identity can be seen in terms of four categories, called statuses. The identity statuses depend on whether each of two characteristics—crisis and commitment—is present or absent. *Crisis* is a period of identity development in which an adolescent consciously chooses between various alternatives and makes decisions. *Commitment* is psychological investment in a course of action or an ideology (Marcia, 1966, 1980).

By conducting lengthy interviews with adolescents, Marcia proposed four categories of adolescent identity (see Table 12-2).

1. **Identity achievement.** Following a period of crisis during which they consider various alternatives, adolescents commit to a particular identity. Teenagers within this identity status have successfully explored and thought through who they are and what they want to do. They tend to be the most psychologically healthy, higher in achievement motivation and moral reasoning than adolescents of any other status.

2. **Identity foreclosure.** These are adolescents who have committed to an identity, but who did not do it by passing through a period of crisis in which they explored alternatives. Instead, they accepted others' decisions about what was best for them. Typical adolescents in this category are a son who enters the family business because it is expected of him, and a daughter who decides to become a physician simply because her mother is one. Although foreclosers are not necessarily unhappy, they tend to have what can be called "rigid strength": Happy and self-satisfied, they also have a high need for social approval and tend to be authoritarian.

identity achievement the status of adolescents who commit to a particular identity following a period of crisis during which they consider various alternatives

identity foreclosure the status of adolescents who prematurely commit to an identity without adequately exploring alternatives

TABLE 12-2

MARCIA'S FOUR CATEGORIES OF ADOLESCENT DEVELOPMENT

		COMMITMENT	
		PRESENT	ABSENT
EXPLORATION	PRESENT	Identity achievement	Moratorium
	ABSENT	Identity foreclosure	Identity diffusion

(*Source:* Marcia, 1980.)

3. **Identity diffusion**. Some adolescents in this category consider various alternatives, but never commit to one. Others in this group never even get that far, not even considering their options in any conscious way. They tend to be flighty, shifting from one thing to the next. Although they may seem carefree, their lack of commitment impairs their ability to form close relationships. In fact, they are often socially withdrawn.

4. **Moratorium**. Although adolescents in the moratorium category have explored various alternatives to some degree, they have not yet committed themselves. As a consequence, they show relatively high anxiety and experience psychological conflict. On the other hand, they are often lively and appealing, seeking intimacy with others. Adolescents of this status typically settle on an identity, but only after something of a struggle.

It is important to note that adolescents are not necessarily stuck in one of the four categories. For instance, even though a forecloser may have settled on a career path during early adolescence with little active decision making, he or she may reassess the choice later and move into another category. For some individuals, then, identity formation takes place beyond the period of adolescence. However, identity gels in the late teens and early twenties for most people (Waterman & Waterman, 1981; Waterman, 1982; Kroger, 1995; Meeus, 1996).

Identity, Race and Ethnicity

Although the path to forming an identity is difficult for all adolescents, it presents a particular challenge for members of racial and ethnic minority groups. One part of the problem stems from contradictory societal values. On the one hand, adolescents are told that society should be color blind, that race and ethnic background should not affect opportunities and achievement. Based on a traditional *cultural assimilation model*, this view holds that individual cultural identities should be assimilated into a unified culture in the United States—the proverbial melting pot model.

On the other hand, the *pluralistic society model* suggests that U.S. society is made up of diverse, coequal cultural groups that should preserve their individual cultural features. The pluralistic society model grew in part from the belief that the cultural assimilation model denigrates the cultural heritage of minorities and lowers their self-esteem. According to this view, then, racial and ethnic factors become a central part of adolescents' identity.

There is a middle ground. Some observers suggest that identity in minority adolescents is facilitated by the formation of *bicultural identity* in which adolescents draw from their

identity diffusion *the status of adolescents who consider various identity alternatives, but never commit to one, or never even consider identity options in any conscious way*

moratorium *the status of adolescents who may have explored various identity alternatives to some degree, but have not yet committed themselves*

own cultural identity while integrating themselves into the dominant culture. This view suggests that an individual can live as a member of two cultures, with two cultural identities, without having to choose one over the other (LaFromboise, Coleman & Gerton, 1993).

Regardless of which path to identity a member of a minority group chooses, the process of identity formation is not likely to be simple. Racial and ethnic identity takes time to form, and for some individuals it may occur over a prolonged period. Still, the ultimate result can be the formation of a rich, multifaceted identity (Cross, 1991; Staples & Johnson, 1993; Oyserman, Gant, & Ager, 1995; Tatum, 1997).

Depression and Suicide: Psychological Difficulties in Adolescence

Although by far the majority of teenagers weather the search for identity—as well as the other challenges presented by the period—without major psychological difficulties, some find adolescence particularly stressful. Some, in fact, develop severe psychological problems. Two of the most vexing are adolescent depression and suicide (Besseghini, 1997).

Adolescent Depression.   No one is immune from periods of sadness and bad moods, and adolescents are no exception. The end of a relationship, failure at an important task, the death of a loved one—all may produce profound feelings of sadness, loss, and grief. In situations such as these, depression is a fairly typical reaction.

How common are feelings of depression in adolescence? Although figures are hard to come by, some estimates suggest that 20 to 35 percent of boys and 25 to 40 percent of girls report having experienced depressed moods in the previous 6 months. Reports of feeling "sad and hopeless" are even higher: Almost two-thirds of teenagers say they have experienced such feelings at one time or another (see Figure 12-1). On the other hand, only a small minority of adolescents—some 3 percent—experience *major depression*, a full-blown psychological disorder in which depression is severe and lingers for long periods (Petersen, Compas, & Brooks-Gunn, 1991; Boehm & Campbell, 1995; Culp, Clyman, & Culp, 1995; Cicchetti & Toth, 1998).

Gender, ethnic, and racial differences also are found in depression rates. As is the case among adults, adolescent girls, on average, experience depression more often than boys. Furthermore, some studies have found that African American adolescents have higher rates of depression than white adolescents, although not all research supports this conclusion. Native Americans, too, appear to have higher rates of depression (Fleming & Offord, 1990; Nettles & Pleck, 1990).

Depression has several causes. In cases of severe, long-term depression, biological factors are often involved. Some adolescents, for instance, seem to be genetically predisposed to experience depression (Ehlers, Frank, & Kupfer, 1988; Brooks-Gunn, Petersen, & Compas, 1994).

However, environmental and social factors relating to the extraordinary changes in the social lives of adolescents are also an important cause. Thus, an adolescent who experiences the death of a loved one or grows up with a depressed parent is at a higher risk of depression. In addition, being unpopular, having few close friends, and experiencing rejection are associated with adolescent depression (Hammen, 1991; Aseltine, Gore & Colten, 1994; Hammond & Romney, 1995).

One of the most puzzling questions about depression is why its incidence is higher among girls than boys. Some psychologists speculate that stress is more pronounced for girls than for boys in adolescence, due to the many, sometimes contradictory, aspects of the traditional female gender role. Recall, for instance, the plight of an adolescent girl who, accepting traditional gender roles, is worried both about doing well in school and about being popular. If she feels that academic success undermines her popularity, she is placed in a difficult bind, as we noted earlier in our discussion of self-esteem.

Between 25 and 40 percent of girls, and 20 to 35 percent of boys, experience occasional episodes of depression during adolescence, although the incidence of major depression is far lower.

FIGURE 12-1

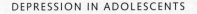

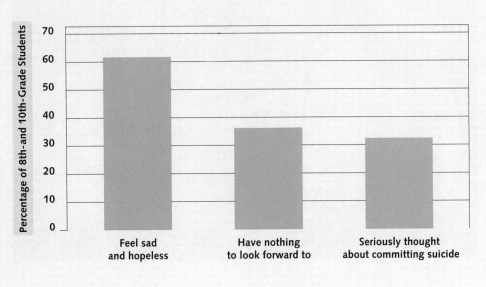

DEPRESSION IN ADOLESCENTS

(*Source*: Adapted from National Adolescent Student Health Survey; cited in Gans, 1990.)

There may also be other causes of girls' generally higher levels of depression during adolescence. They may be more apt than boys to react to stress by turning inward, thereby experiencing a sense of helplessness and hopelessness. In contrast, boys more often react by externalizing the stress and acting more impulsively or aggressively, or by turning to drugs and alcohol. One factor that does not seem to cause the higher incidence of female depression is female hormones: Little evidence links hormonal production in adolescent girls to depression (Rutter & Garmezy, 1983; Gjerde, Block & Block, 1988; Petersen, Sarigiani, & Kennedy, 1991; Nolen-Hoeksema & Girgus, 1994; Lewinsohn et al., 1994).

Adolescent Suicide.   Elyssa Drazin was 16. Although her grades had gone down in the previous 6 months, she was still a pretty good student. Her social life had picked up over the last 2 years, and she had been involved with Hector Segool. In the past month, however, the relationship had cooled considerably, and Hector had told her he wanted to date other girls. Elyssa was devastated, and—as she wrote in a note that was found on her desk—she could not bear the thought of seeing Hector holding hands with another girl. She took a large quantity of sleeping pills and became one of the thousands of adolescents who take their own lives each year.

The rate of adolescent suicide in the United States has tripled in the last 30 years. In fact, one teenage suicide occurs every 90 minutes, for an annual rate of 11.1 suicides per 100,000 adolescents. Moreover, the reported rate may actually understate the true number of suicides; parents and medical personnel are often reluctant to report a death as suicide, preferring to label it an accident. Even with underreporting, suicide is the third most common cause of death in the 15-to-24-year-old age group, after accidents and homicide (Henry et al., 1993).

The rate of suicide is higher for boys than girls, although girls *attempt* suicide more frequently. Suicide attempts among males are more likely to result in death because of the methods they use: Boys tend to use more violent means, such as guns, whereas girls are more apt to choose the more peaceful strategy of drug overdose. Some estimates suggest that there are as many as 200 attempted suicides for every successful one (Hawton, 1986; Berman & Jobes, 1991; Gelman, 1994).

The reasons behind the increase in adolescent suicide over past decades are unclear. The most obvious explanation is that the stress experienced by teenagers has increased, leading those who are most troubled to be more likely to commit suicide (Elkind, 1984). But why should stress have increased only for adolescents? The suicide rate for other segments of

The rate of adolescent suicide has tripled in the last 30 years. These girls console one another following the suicide of a classmate in their New Jersey high school.

the population has remained fairly stable over the same time period. (And it's important to keep in mind that although the rate of suicide for adolescents has risen more than for other age groups, suicide is still more common among adults than it is among younger people.)

Although an explanation for the increase in adolescent suicide has not been found, it is clear that certain factors heighten the risk of suicide. One factor is depression. Depressed teenagers who are experiencing a profound sense of hopelessness are at greater risk of committing suicide (although most depressed individuals do not commit suicide). In addition,

The Informed Consumer of Development

Deterring Adolescent Suicide

If you suspect that an adolescent, or anyone else for that matter, is contemplating suicide, don't stand idly by. Act! The U.S. Public Health Service makes several suggestions for what to do:

■ Talk to the person, listen without judging, and give the person an understanding forum in which to try to talk things through.

■ Talk specifically about suicidal thoughts, such as: Does the person have a plan? Has he or she bought a gun? Where is it? Has he or she stockpiled pills? Where are they? The Public Health Service notes that, "contrary to popular belief, such candor will not give a person dangerous ideas or encourage a suicidal act."

■ Evaluate the situation, trying to distinguish between general upset and more serious danger, as when suicide plans *have* been made. If the crisis is acute, *do not leave the person alone.*

■ Be supportive, let the person know you care, and try to break down his or her feelings of isolation.

■ Take charge of finding help, without concern about invading the person's privacy. Do not try to handle the problem alone; get professional help immediately.

■ Make the environment safe, removing from the premises (not just hiding) weapons such as guns, razors, scissors, medication, and other potentially dangerous household items.

■ Do not keep suicide talk or threats secret; these are calls for help and warrant immediate action.

■ Do not challenge, dare, or use verbal shock treatment. They can have tragic effects.

■ Make a contract with the person, getting a promise or commitment, preferably in writing, not to make any suicidal attempt until you have talked further.

■ Beware of elevated moods and seemingly quick recoveries; sometimes they are illusory, reflecting the relief of finally deciding to commit suicide or the temporary release of talking to someone, though the underlying problems have not been resolved (based on Franck & Brownstone, 1991, pp. 445–446).

For immediate help with a suicide-related problem, call (800) 448-3000, a national hot line staffed with trained counselors.

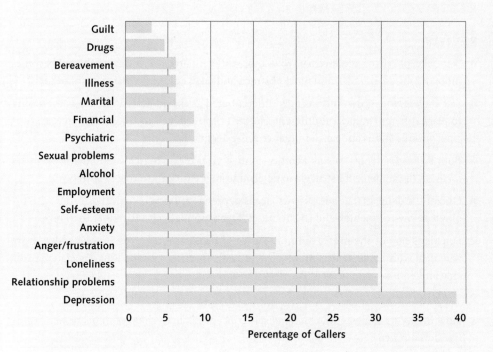

FIGURE 12-2

ADOLESCENT DIFFICULTIES

These problems were the ones most frequently cited by callers to a suicide-prevention hotline who were contemplating suicide.

(*Source*: Boston Samaritans, 1991.)

social inhibition, perfectionism, and a high level of anxiety are related to a greater risk of suicide (Petersen et al., 1993; Lewinsohn, Rohde, & Seeley, 1994; Beautrais, Joyce, & Muilder, 1996).

Some cases of suicide are associated with family conflicts and adjustment difficulties (Pillay & Wassenaar, 1997). Others follow a history of abuse and neglect. The rate of suicide among drug and alcohol abusers is also relatively high. As can be seen in Figure 12-2, those contemplating suicide cite several other factors as well (Garland & Zigler, 1993; Brent et al., 1994).

Some suicides appear to be caused by exposure to the suicide of others. In **cluster suicide**, one suicide leads to attempts by others to kill themselves. For instance, some high schools have experienced a series of suicides following a well-publicized case. As a result, many schools have established crisis intervention teams to counsel students when one student commits suicide (Hazell, 1993).

There are several warning signs that should sound an alarm regarding the possibility of suicide. Among them:

- Direct or indirect talk about suicide, such as "I wish I were dead" or "You won't have me to worry about any longer"

- School difficulties, such as missed classes or a decline in grades

- Making arrangements as if preparing for a long trip, such as giving away prized possessions or arranging for the care of a pet

- Writing a will

- Loss of appetite or excessive eating

- General depression, including a change in sleeping patterns, slowness and lethargy, and uncommunicativeness

- Dramatic changes in behavior, such as a shy person suddenly acting outgoing

- Preoccupation with death in music, art, or literature.

cluster suicide   *a situation in which one suicide leads to attempts by others to kill themselves*

REVIEW AND RETHINK

REVIEW

■ Self-concept during adolescence grows more differentiated as the view of the self becomes more organized, broader, and more abstract, and takes account of the views of others.

■ Self-esteem, too, grows increasingly differentiated as the adolescent develops the ability to place different values on different aspects of the self. Factors of gender, race, and socioeconomic status appear to influence self-esteem.

■ Both Erikson's identity-versus-identity-confusion stage and Marcia's four identity statuses focus on the adolescent's struggle to determine an identity and a role in society.

■ One of the dangers that adolescents face is depression, a psychological disorder with biological, environmental, and social causes. Depression affects girls more than boys.

■ Suicide is one of the most common causes of death among 15 to 24-year-olds. Those who deal with adolescents should familiarize themselves with the warning signs of suicide and with ways to prevent it.

RETHINK

■ How might an adolescent's changing self-concept relate to changes in his or her cognitive development?

■ What are some consequences of the shift from reliance on adults to reliance on peers? Are there advantages? Dangers?

■ Why are females more likely to experience depression than males? How would you design a study to explore the possible effects of biological versus environmental factors?

■ What obligations do you have to a friend who confides in you the intention to commit suicide and asks you to respect confidentiality?

RELATIONSHIPS: FAMILY AND FRIENDS

Slim and dark, with a passing resemblance to actress Demi Moore, Leah is dressed up and ready to go to the first real formal dance of her life. True, the smashing effect of her short beaded black dress is marred slightly by the man's shirt she insists on wearing to cover her bare shoulders. And she is in a sulk. Her boyfriend, Sean Moffitt, is four minutes late, and her mother, Linda, refuses to let her stay out all night at a coed sleep-over party after the dance.

When Sean arrives with his mother, Pam, Leah reluctantly sheds the work shirt. She greets Sean shyly, not sure he'll approve of that afternoon's makeover by hairdresser and manicurist. Sean, an easygoing youth with dimples and rosy cheeks, squirms in his tuxedo. Leah recombs his hair and makes him remove his earring. "None of the guys are wearing them to the dance," she declares. (She's wrong. A few moments later, their friends Melissa and Erik arrive, and Erik is wearing his earring.)

Leah's father, George, suggests a 2 A.M. curfew: Leah hoots incredulously. Sean pitches the all-nighter, stressing that the party will be chaperoned. Leah's mother has already talked to the host's mother, mortifying Leah with her off-hand comment that a coed sleepover seemed "weird." Rolling her eyes, Leah persists: "It's not like anybody's really going to sleep!" Sean asks his mother for another $20. "Why did the amount suddenly jump?" she asks, digging into her purse. (Graham, 1995, p. B1)

This snapshot of the life of 16-year-old Leah Brookner of Norwalk, Connecticut, provides a glimpse of some of the complex, interdependent relationships in which adolescents are involved. As Leah juggles parents, friends, and romantic partners, her life—and those of other adolescents—seems, at times, like an intricate jigsaw puzzle in which not all the pieces fit together perfectly.

The social world of adolescents is considerably wider than that of younger children. As adolescents' relationships with people outside the home grow increasingly important, their interactions with their families evolve and take on a new, and sometimes difficult, character (Montemayor, Adams, & Gulotta,1994; Collins, Gleason, & Sesma, 1997).

autonomy *having independence and a sense of control over one's life*

Family Ties: Reassessing Relations with Relations

When Pepe Lizzagara entered junior high school, his relationship with his parents changed drastically. Although relations were quite good previously, by the middle of seventh grade, tensions grew. In Pepe's view, his parents always seemed to be "on his case." Instead of giving him more freedom, which he felt he deserved at age 13, they actually seemed to be getting more restrictive.

Pepe's parents would probably suggest that they were not the source of the tension in the household—Pepe was. From their point of view, Pepe, with whom they'd established what seemed to be a stable relationship throughout much of his childhood, suddenly seemed transformed. To his parents, Pepe presented novel, and often bewildering, behavior.

The Quest for Autonomy.   Parents are sometimes angered, and even more frequently puzzled, by adolescents' conduct. Children who have previously accepted their parents' judgments, declarations, and guidelines begin to question—and sometimes rebel against—their parents' views of the world.

One reason for these clashes is the shift in the roles that both children and parents must deal with during adolescence. Adolescents increasingly seek **autonomy**, independence and a sense of control over their lives. Most parents intellectually realize that this shift is a normal part of adolescence, representing one of the primary developmental tasks of the period, and in many ways they welcome it as a sign of their children's growth. However, in many cases the day-to-day realities of adolescents' increasing autonomy may prove difficult for them to deal with (Smetana, 1995).

In most families, teenagers' autonomy grows gradually over the course of adolescence. For instance, one study of changes in adolescents' views of their parents found that increasing autonomy led them to perceive parents less in idealized terms and more as persons in their own right. At the same time, adolescents came to depend more on themselves and to feel more like separate individuals (see Figure 12-3).

The increase in adolescent autonomy is reflected in the relationship between parents and teenagers. At the start of adolescence, the relationship tends to be asymmetrical: Parents hold most of the power and influence over the relationship. By the end of adolescence, however, power and influence have become more balanced, and parents and children end up in a more symmetrical, or egalitarian, relationship. Power and influence are shared, although parents typically retain the upper hand.

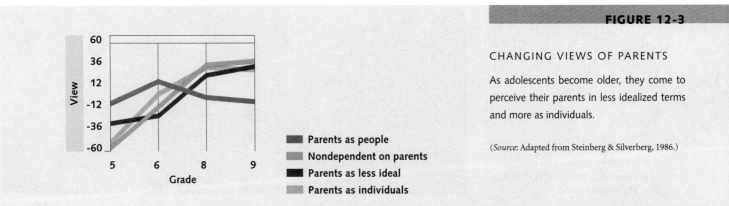

FIGURE 12-3

CHANGING VIEWS OF PARENTS

As adolescents become older, they come to perceive their parents in less idealized terms and more as individuals.

(*Source*: Adapted from Steinberg & Silverberg, 1986.)

Legend:
- Parents as people
- Nondependent on parents
- Parents as less ideal
- Parents as individuals

(y-axis: View — 60, 36, 12, -12, -36, -60; x-axis: Grade — 5, 6, 8, 9)

generation gap *a divide between parents and adolescents in attitudes, values, aspirations, and worldviews*

The degree of autonomy that is eventually achieved varies from one family to the next. Furthermore, cultural factors play an important role. In Western societies, which tend to value individualism, adolescents seek autonomy at a relatively early stage of adolescence. In contrast, Asian societies are *collectivistic*; they promote the idea that the well-being of the group is more important than that of the individual. In such societies, adolescents' aspirations to achieve autonomy are less pronounced (Feldman & Rosenthal, 1990; Kim et al., 1994).

The Myth of the Generation Gap. It might seem that one factor motivating adolescents' efforts to attain autonomy is the discrepancy between parents' and teenagers' views of the world. According to this argument, there is a **generation gap**, a deep divide between parents and children in attitudes, values, aspirations, and worldviews.

The reality, however, is quite different. The generation gap, when it exists, is really quite narrow. Adolescents and their parents tend to see eye-to-eye in a variety of domains. Republican parents generally have Republican children; members of the Christian right have children who espouse similar views; parents who advocate for abortion rights have children who are pro-abortion. On social, political, and religious issues, parents and adolescents tend to be in synch, and children's worries mirror those of their parents. They also have similar career aspirations and attitudes about work. In fact, on most issues of attitudes and values, the differences between one adolescent and another are far greater than the differences between parents and their adolescent children (Conger, 1977; Feather, 1980; Youniss, 1989; Chira, 1994).

Similarly, there is typically no generation gap in the value that parents and adolescents place on the relationship they have with one another. Despite their quest for autonomy and independence, most adolescents have deep love, affection, and respect for their parents—reciprocating the feelings that their parents have for them. Although there are notable exceptions, with some parent–adolescent relationships marked by significant strife, the majority of relationships are more positive than negative. These positive relationships help adolescents avoid peer pressure (Gavin & Furman, 1996; Resnick et al., 1997).

Furthermore, even though adolescents spend decreasing amounts of time with their families in general, the amount of time they spend alone with each parent remains remarkably stable across adolescence (see Figure 12-4). In short, there is no evidence suggesting that family problems are worse during adolescence than at any other stage of development (Steinberg, 1990, 1993; Larson et al., 1996).

On the other hand, parents' and adolescents' relationships are not always sweetness and light. For instance, parents and adolescents often hold different views on matters of personal taste such as music preferences and styles of dress. Significant strife may occur between parents and adolescents, particularly during early adolescence, when conflicts

More conflict between parents and their children occurs during the early stages of adolescence than at later stages of the period.

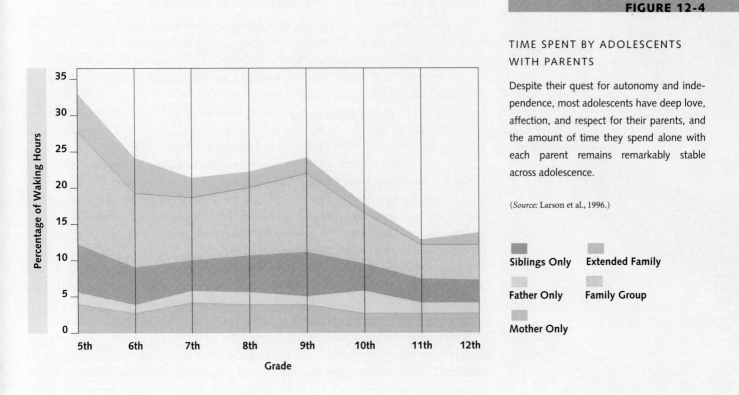

FIGURE 12-4

TIME SPENT BY ADOLESCENTS
WITH PARENTS

Despite their quest for autonomy and independence, most adolescents have deep love,
affection, and respect for their parents, and
the amount of time they spend alone with
each parent remains remarkably stable
across adolescence.

(*Source:* Larson et al., 1996.)

Siblings Only Extended Family

Father Only Family Group

Mother Only

between children's efforts to achieve autonomy and parental reactions are more pronounced than at any other time.

Why should strife be greater during early adolescence than at later stages of the
period? According to developmental psychologist Judith Smetana, the reason involves
differing definitions of, and rationales for, appropriate and inappropriate conduct.
Parents may feel, for instance, that getting one's ear pierced in three places is inappropriate because society traditionally deems it inappropriate. On the other hand, adolescents may view the issue in terms of personal choice (Smetana, 1988, 1989; Smetana,
Yau & Hanson, 1991).

Furthermore, the newly sophisticated reasoning of adolescents (discussed in the previous chapter) leads teenagers to think about parental rules in more complex ways. Consequently, arguments that were convincing to a school-age child ("Do it because I tell you to
do it") are less compelling to an adolescent.

The argumentativeness and assertiveness of early adolescence at first may lead to an increase in conflict, but in many ways they play an important role in the evolution of
parent–child relationships. Although parents may at first react defensively to the challenges
that their children present, and may grow inflexible and rigid, in most cases they eventually
come to realize that their children *are* growing up.

Parents also come to see that their adolescent children's arguments are often compelling
and not so unreasonable, and that their daughters and sons can, in fact, be trusted with
more freedom. Consequently, they become more yielding, allowing and eventually perhaps
even encouraging independence. As this process occurs during the middle stages of adolescence, the combativeness of early adolescence declines.

Of course, this pattern does not apply for all adolescents. Although the majority of
teenagers maintain stable relations with their parents throughout adolescence, as many as
20 percent pass through a fairly rough time (Dryfoos, 1990). We consider some of the factors that place adolescents at risk later in the chapter.

Relationships with Peers: The Importance of Belonging

In the eyes of numerous parents, the most fitting symbol of adolescence is the telephone. For many of their sons and daughters, it appears to be an indispensable lifeline, sustaining ties to friends with whom they may have already spent many hours earlier in the day.

The seemingly compulsive need to communicate with friends is symbolic of the role that peers play in adolescence. Continuing the trend that began in middle childhood, adolescents spend increasing amounts of time with their peers, and the importance of peer relationships grows as well. In fact, there is probably no period of life in which peer relationships are as important as they are in adolescence (Youniss & Haynie, 1992).

There are several reasons for the prominence of peers during adolescence (Coleman, 1980). For one thing, peers provide the opportunity to compare and evaluate opinions, abilities, and even physical changes—a process called *social comparison*. Because physical and cognitive changes are so pronounced, especially during the early stages of puberty, adolescents turn increasingly to others who share, and consequently can shed light on, their own experiences (Weiss, Ebbeck & Horn, 1997).

Parents are unable to provide social comparison. Not only are they well beyond the changes that adolescents undergo, but adolescents' questioning of adult authority and their motivation to become more autonomous make parents, other family members, and adults in general inadequate and invalid sources of knowledge. Who is left to provide such information? Peers.

Finally, adolescence is a time of experimentation, of trying out new roles and conduct. Peers provide information about what roles and behavior are most acceptable by serving as a reference group. **Reference groups** are groups of people with whom one compares oneself.

Reference groups present a set of *norms*, or standards, against which adolescents can judge their social success. An adolescent need not even belong to a group for it to serve as a reference group. For instance, unpopular adolescents may find themselves belittled and rejected by members of a popular group, yet use that more popular group as a reference group.

Cliques and Crowds: Belonging to a Group.   Even if they do not belong to the group they use for reference purposes, adolescents typically are part of some identifiable group. In fact, one of the consequences of the increasing cognitive sophistication of adolescents is the ability to group others in more discriminating ways. Rather than defining people in concrete terms relating to what they do ("football players" or "musicians"), adolescents use more abstract terms packed with greater subtleties ("jocks" or "the artsy-craftsy crowd") (Brown, 1990; Montemayor, Adams & Gullotta, 1994).

What are the typical groups to which adolescence belong? There are actually two types: cliques and crowds. **Cliques** are groups of from 2 to 12 people whose members have frequent social interactions with one another. In contrast, **crowds** are larger, comprising individuals who share particular characteristics but who may not interact with one another. For instance, "toughs," "jocks," and "brains" are separate crowds currently found in the typical high school.

There is a surprisingly high level of agreement among adolescents regarding the characteristics of members of particular groups. For instance, one study found that "jocks" and "normals" were seen as dressing casually, whereas "populars" were viewed as more stylish dressers. "Normals" and "jocks" were perceived as friendly, whereas "populars" and "jocks" were cliquish. "Populars" and "jocks" tried hard in school, whereas "druggies" and "toughs" hated school (Brown, Lohr, & Trujillo, 1983; see Figure 12-5).

Of course, these descriptions are merely stereotypes, and they do not necessarily represent the actual characteristics of individual group members. Still, the stereotypes are powerful and widespread, and the expectation that people in a particular crowd behave in a certain way may constrain members' behavior. In fact, the stereotype may actually bring about the expected behavior—another example of a self-fulfilling prophecy.

Gender Relations.   At the very start of adolescence, groups tend to mirror the makeup of middle childhood groups in that they are composed almost universally of same-sex individuals. Boys hang out with boys; girls hang out with girls. Technically, this sex segregation is called the **sex cleavage**.

---

reference groups   *groups of people with whom one compares oneself*

cliques *groups of from 2 to 12 people whose members have frequent social interactions with one another*

crowds *larger groups than cliques, composed of individuals who share particular characteristics but who may not interact with one another*

sex cleavage   *sex segregation in which boys interact primarily with boys, and girls interact primarily with girls*

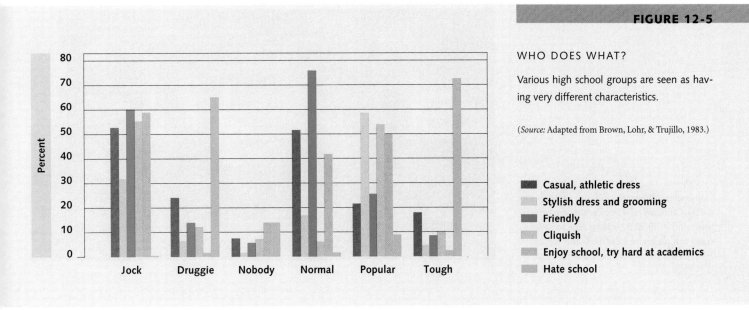

FIGURE 12-5

WHO DOES WHAT?

Various high school groups are seen as having very different characteristics.

(*Source:* Adapted from Brown, Lohr, & Trujillo, 1983.)

■ Casual, athletic dress
■ Stylish dress and grooming
■ Friendly
■ Cliquish
■ Enjoy school, try hard at academics
■ Hate school

However, the situation changes in short order as members of both sexes enter puberty. Both the hormonal surge that marks puberty and causes the maturation of the sex organs and the societal pressures suggesting that the time is appropriate for romantic involvement lead to a change in the ways adolescents view the opposite sex. Rather than seeing every member of the opposite sex as "annoying" and "a pain," boys and girls begin to regard each other with greater interest, in terms of both personality and sexuality.

When this change occurs, boys' and girls' cliques, which previously had moved along parallel but separate tracks, begin to converge. Adolescents begin to attend boy–girl dances or parties, although most of the time the boys still spend their time with boys, and the girls with girls (Csikszentmihalyi & Larson, 1984). (Think back to your own early adolescence, and perhaps you'll recall dances with boys lined up on one side of the room and girls on the other.)

A little later, however, adolescents increasingly spend time with members of the opposite sex (Dunphy, 1963). New cliques emerge, composed of both males and females. Not everyone participates initially: Early on, the teenagers who are leaders of the same-sex cliques and who have the highest status pilot the way. Eventually, however, most adolescents find themselves in cliques that include boys and girls.

The sex segregation of childhood continues during the early stages of adolescence. However, by the time of middle adolescence, this segregation decreases, and boys' and girls' cliques begin to converge.

Unpopular adolescents fall into several categories. Controversial adolescents are liked by some and disliked by others; rejected adolescents are uniformly disliked; and neglected adolescents are neither liked nor disliked.

Cliques and crowds undergo yet another transformation at the end of adolescence: They become less powerful and may, in fact, succumb to the increased pairing off that occurs between males and females. Rather than the clique being the center of adolescents' social lives, then, boy–girl interaction becomes the focus.

Popularity and Rejection: Adolescent Likes and Dislikes

Most adolescents have well-tuned antennae when it comes to determining who is popular and who is not. In fact, for some teenagers, concerns over popularity—or lack of it—may be a central focus of their lives.

Actually, the social world of adolescents is more complex than simply being divided into popular and unpopular individuals (see Figure 12-6). For instance, some adolescents are controversial; in contrast to *popular* adolescents, who are mostly liked, *controversial* adolescents are liked by some and disliked by others. Furthermore, there are *rejected* adolescents, who are uniformly disliked, and *neglected* adolescents, who are neither liked nor disliked. In most cases, however, popular and controversial adolescents tend to be similar in that their overall status is higher, whereas rejected and neglected adolescents share a generally lower status.

FIGURE 12-6

THE SOCIAL WORLD OF ADOLESENCE

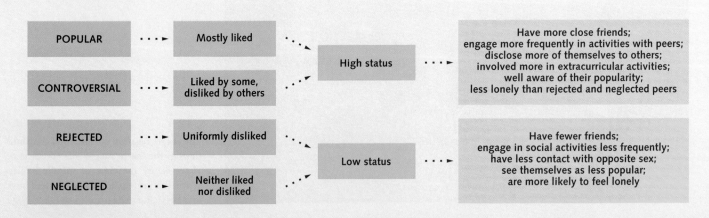

Developmental Diversity

Race Segregation: The Great Divide of Adolescence

When Philip McAdoo, a student at the University of North Carolina, stopped one day to see a friend who worked on his college campus, a receptionist asked if he would autograph a basketball for her son. Because he was African American and tall, "she just assumed that I was on the basketball team," recounted McAdoo.

Jasme Kelly, an African American sophomore at the same college, had a similar story to tell. When she went to see a friend at a fraternity house, the student who answered the door asked if she was there to apply for the job of cook.

White students, too, find racial relations difficult and in some ways forbidding. For instance, Jenny Johnson, a white 20-year-old junior, finds even the most basic conversation with African American classmates difficult. She describes a conversation in which African American friends "jump at my throat because I used the word 'black' instead of African American. There is just such a huge barrier that it's really hard . . . to have a normal discussion." (Sanoff & Minerbrook, 1993, p. 58)

The pattern of race segregation found at the University of North Carolina is repeated over and over in schools and colleges throughout the United States: Even when they attend desegregated schools with a high proportion of minority students, people of different ethnicities and races interact very little. Moreover, even if they have a friend of a different ethnicity within the confines of a school, most adolescents don't interact with that friend outside of school (Dubois & Hirsch, 1990).

It doesn't start out this way. During elementary school and even during early adolescence, there is a fair amount of integration among students of differing ethnicities. However, by middle and late adolescence, the amount of segregation is striking (Shrum, Cheek, & Hunter, 1988; Spencer & Dornbusch, 1990; Spencer, 1991; Ennett & Bauman, 1996).

Why should racial and ethnic segregation be the rule, even in schools that have been desegregated for some time? One reason is that minority students may actively seek support from others who share their minority status. Furthermore, by associating primarily with other members of their own minority group, they are able to affirm their own identity.

Other explanations for campus segregation are less positive. For instance, socioeconomic status (SES) differences between people of different races and ethnicities may keep integration at low levels. Racial and ethnic differences tend to mirror SES differences: People from minority groups are overrepresented in lower SES groups (Coleman, 1961), just as people from the majority group are overrepresented in higher SES groups. Because cliques tend to comprise members who are of similar SES, they also display very little racial integration. It is possible, then, that apparent ethnic differences in interaction patterns are really due to SES characteristics, and not to ethnicity *per se*.

Another explanation for the lack of interaction between members of different racial and ethnic groups relates to differences in academic performance. Because minority group members tend to experience less school success than members of the majority group, as we discussed in Chapter 10, it may be that ethnic and racial segregation is based not on ethnicity itself, but on academic achievement.

Specifically, some students attend schools in which classes are assigned on the basis of students' prior levels of academic success. If minority group members experience less success, they may find themselves in classes with proportionally fewer majority group members. Similarly, majority students may be in classes with few minority students. Such class assignment practices, then, may inadvertently maintain and promote racial and ethnic segregation. This pattern would be particularly prevalent in schools where rigid academic tracking is practiced, with students assigned to "low," "medium," and "high" tracks depending on their prior achievement (Hallinan & Williams, 1989).

Finally, the lack of racial and ethnic interaction in school may reflect negative attitudes held by both majority and minority students. Minority students may feel that the white majority is prejudiced, discriminatory, and hostile, and they may prefer to stick to same-race groups. Conversely, majority students may assume that minority group members are antagonistic and unfriendly. Such mutually destructive attitudes reduce the likelihood that meaningful interaction can take place (Miller & Brewer, 1984; Phinney, Ferguson, & Tate, 1997).

Is the voluntary segregation along racial and ethnic lines found during adolescence inevitable? No. For instance, adolescents who have had extensive interactions with members of different races earlier in their lives are more likely to have friends of different races. Furthermore, schools that actively promote contact between members of different ethnicities in mixed-ability classes may create an environment in which cross-race friendships can flourish (Schofield, 1989).

Still, the task is daunting. Many societal pressures act to keep members of different races from interacting with one another. Furthermore, cliques may actively promote norms that discourage group members from crossing racial and ethnic lines to form new friendships.

For instance, popular and controversial adolescents have more close friends, engage more frequently in activities with their peers, and disclose more about themselves to others than less popular students. They are also more involved in extracurricular school activities. In addition, they are well aware of their popularity, and they are less lonely than their less popular classmates (Franzoi, Davis, & Vasquez-Suson, 1994).

In contrast, the social world of rejected and neglected adolescents is considerably more negative. They have fewer friends, engage in social activities less frequently, and have less contact with the opposite sex. They see themselves—accurately, it turns out—as less popular, and they are more likely to feel lonely.

Conformity: Peer Pressure in Adolescence

Whenever Aldos Henry said he wanted to buy a particular brand of sneakers or a certain style of shirt, his parents complained that he was just giving in to peer pressure and told him to make up his own mind about things.

In arguing with Aldos, his parents were subscribing to a view of adolescence that is quite prevalent in U.S. society: that teenagers are highly susceptible to **peer pressure**, the influence of one's peers to conform to their behavior and attitudes. Were his parents correct?

The research suggests that it all depends. In some cases, adolescents *are* highly susceptible to the influence of their peers. For instance, when considering what to wear, whom to date, and what movies to see, adolescents are apt to follow the lead of their peers. On the other hand, when it comes to many nonsocial matters, such as choosing a career path or trying to solve a problem, they are more likely to turn to an experienced adult (Phelan, Yu, & Davidson, 1994).

In short, particularly in middle and late adolescence, teenagers turn to those they see as experts on a given dimension (Young & Ferguson, 1979). If they have social concerns, they turn to the people most likely to be experts—their peers. If the problem is one about which parents or other adults are most likely to have expertise, teenagers tend to turn to them for advice and are most susceptible to their opinions.

Overall, then, it does not appear that susceptibility to peer pressure suddenly soars during adolescence. Instead, adolescence brings about a change in the people to whom an individual conforms. Whereas children conform fairly consistently to their parents during childhood, in adolescence conformity shifts to include the peer group, in part because pressures to conform increase.

Ultimately, however, adolescents conform less to both peers *and* adults as they develop increasing autonomy over their lives. As they grow in confidence and in the ability to make their own decisions, adolescents are more apt to remain independent and to reject pressures from others, no matter who those others are (Steinberg & Silverberg, 1986; Steinberg, 1993; Crockett & Crouter, 1995.)

Juvenile Delinquency: The Crimes of Adolescence

Although the vast majority of them are law-abiding citizens, adolescents, along with young adults, are more likely to commit crimes than any other age group. Some of the reasons for this state of affairs has to do with the definition of certain behaviors (such as drinking), which are illegal for adolescents but not for older individuals. But even when such crimes are disregarded, adolescents are disproportionately involved in violent crimes, such as murder, assaults, and rape, and property crimes, involving theft, robbery, and arson.

For example, almost 20 percent of serious violent crimes are committed by adolescents, either alone or in groups. Another 8 percent are committed by adolescents in conjunction with older offenders. Overall, a quarter of all serious violent crime involves an adolescent. Furthermore, the numbers are growing. Over the past decade, the arrest rate for violent crimes rose almost 60 percent among adolescents. Experts predict that if present trends continue, by the year 2010 the number of arrests of juveniles for violent crimes will more than double (Juvenile Justice Clearinghouse, 1995).

Why do adolescents become involved in criminal activity? Some offenders are known as **undersocialized delinquents**, adolescents who are raised with little discipline, or with harsh,

---

peer pressure *the influence of one's peers to conform to their behavior and attitudes*

undersocialized delinquents *adolescent delinquents who are raised with little discipline, or with harsh, uncaring parental supervision*

uncaring parental supervision. These children have never been appropriately socialized, and simply have not learned standards of conduct to regulate their own behavior. Undersocialized delinquents typically begin criminal activities at an early age, well before the onset of adolescence.

Undersocialized delinquents share several characteristics. They tend to be relatively aggressive and violent fairly early in life, characteristics that lead them to be rejected by their peers and to fail academically. They also are more likely to have been diagnosed with attention deficit disorder as children and tend to be less intelligent than average (Caspi et al., 1995; Henry et al., 1996).

Undersocialized delinquents often suffer from psychological difficulties, and as adults fit a psychological pattern called antisocial personality disorder. They are relatively unlikely to be successfully rehabilitated, and many undersocialized delinquents live on the margins of society throughout their lives (Lewis et al., 1994; Rönkä & Pulkkinen, 1995; Tate, Reppucci, & Mulvey, 1995; Lynam, 1996).

On the other hand, most adolescent offenders are socialized delinquents. **Socialized delinquents** know and subscribe to the norms of society; they are fairly normal psychologically. For them, transgressions committed during adolescence do not lead to a life of crime. Instead, most socialized delinquents pass through a period during adolescence when they engage in some petty crimes, but they do not continue law-breaking behavior into adulthood.

Socialized delinquents are typically highly influenced by their peers, and their delinquency often occurs in groups (Thornberry & Krohn, 1997). In addition, some research suggests that parents of socialized delinquents supervise their children's behavior less closely than other parents (Miller, 1958; Dornbusch et al., 1985; Windle, 1994; Fletcher et al., 1995).

socialized delinquents *adolescent delinquents who know and subscribe to the norms of society, and who are fairly normal psychologically*

REVIEW AND RETHINK

REVIEW

■ The search for autonomy causes a sometimes painful readjustment in relations between teenagers and their parents, due partly to different definitions of appropriate and inappropriate behavior. However, the gender gap is actually less wide than is generally thought.

■ Belonging becomes a significant issue in adolescence, with cliques and crowds serving as reference groups and offering a ready means of social comparison. Sex cleavage gradually diminishes, until boys and girls begin to pair off.

■ Racial separation increases during adolescence, bolstered by socioeconomic status differences, different academic experiences, and mutually distrustful attitudes.

■ Degrees of popularity in adolescence include popular, controversial, neglected, and rejected adolescents.

■ Adolescents tend to conform to their peers, and to be susceptible to peer pressure, in areas in which they regard their peers as experts, and to conform to adults in areas of perceived adult expertise. In general, conformity to others decreases during adolescence.

■ Adolescents are disproportionately involved in criminal activities, although most do not commit crimes. Juvenile delinquents can be categorized as undersocialized or socialized delinquents.

RETHINK

■ In what ways do you think parents with different styles—authoritarian, authoritative, and permissive—tend to react to attempts to establish autonomy during adolescence?

■ Why does there appear to be no real generation gap in most attitudes, despite adolescents' need to question authority?

■ What school policies do you think would be most effective in decreasing racial segregation?

■ How do the findings about conformity and peer pressure reported in this chapter relate to adolescents' developing cognitive abilities?

DATING, SEXUAL BEHAVIOR, AND TEENAGE PREGNANCY

> It took him almost a month, but Sylvester Chiu finally got up the courage to ask Jackie Durbin to go to the movies. It was hardly a surprise to Jackie, though Sylvester had first told his friend Erik about his resolve to ask Jackie out, and Erik had told Jackie's friend Cynthia about Sylvester's plans. Cynthia, in turn, had told Jackie, who was primed to say yes when Sylvester finally did call.

Welcome to the complex world of dating, an important ritual of adolescence. We'll consider dating, as well as several other aspects of adolescents' relationships with one another, in the remainder of the chapter.

Dating: Boy Meets Girl in the 21st Century

By the time most girls are 12 or 13, and boys 13 or 14, they begin to engage in dating. By the age of 16, more than 90 percent of teenagers have had at least one date, and by the end of high school, some three-quarters of adolescents have dated someone steadily (Dickenson, 1975; McCabe, 1984).

The Functions of Dating.   Although on the surface dating may seem to be simply part of a pattern of courtship that can potentially lead to marriage, it actually serves other functions as well. For instance, dating is a way to learn how to establish intimacy with other individuals. Furthermore, it can provide entertainment and, depending on the status of the person one is dating, prestige. It even can be used to develop a sense of one's own identity (Skipper & Nass, 1966; Savin-Williams & Berndt, 1990; Sanderson & Cantor, 1995).

Just how well dating serves such functions, particularly the development of psychological intimacy, is an open question. What specialists in adolescence do know, however, is surprising: Dating in early and middle adolescence is not terribly successful at facilitating intimacy. On the contrary, dating is often a superficial activity in which the participants so rarely let down their guards that they never become truly close and never expose themselves emotionally to each other. Psychological intimacy may be lacking even when sexual activity is part of the relationship (Douvan & Adelson, 1966; Savin-Williams & Berndt, 1990).

True intimacy becomes more common during later adolescence. At that point, the dating relationship may be taken more seriously by both participants, and it may be seen as a way to select a mate and as a potential prelude to marriage (an institution we consider in Chapter 14).

Dating in Minority Groups.   Cultural influences affect dating patterns among minority adolescents, particularly those whose parents have come to the United States from other countries. Minority parents may try to control their children's dating behavior in an effort to preserve the minority group's traditional values (Spencer & Dornbusch, 1990).

For example, Asian parents may be especially conservative in their attitudes and values, in part because they themselves may have had no experience of dating. (In many cases, the parents' marriage was arranged by others, and the entire concept of dating is unfamiliar.) They may insist that dating be conducted with chaperones, or not at all. As a consequence, they may find themselves involved in substantial conflict with their children (Sung, 1985).

Sexual Relationships: Permissiveness with Affection

The maturation of the sexual organs during the start of adolescence opens a new range of possibilities in relations with others: sexuality. In fact, sexual behavior and thoughts are among the central concerns of adolescents. Almost all adolescents think about sex, and many think about it a good deal of the time (Coles & Stokes, 1985).

Masturbation. For most adolescents, their initiation into sexuality comes from **masturbation**, sexual self-stimulation. Almost half of all adolescent boys and a quarter of adolescent girls report that they have engaged in masturbation. The frequency of masturbation shows a sex difference: Male masturbation is most frequent in the early teens and then begins to decline, whereas females begin more slowly and reach a maximum later (Oliver & Hyde, 1993).

Although masturbation is widespread, it still may produce feelings of shame and guilt. There are several reasons for this. One is that adolescents may believe that masturbation signifies the inability to find a sexual partner—an erroneous assumption, because statistics show that three-quarters of married men and 68 percent of married women report masturbating between 10 and 24 times a year. Another reason is the legacy of shame remaining from misguided past views. For instance, 19th-century physicians and lay persons warned of horrible effects of masturbation, including "dyspepsia, spinal disease, headache, epilepsy, various kinds of fits . . . , impaired eyesight, palpitation of the heart, pain in the side and bleeding at the lungs, spasm of the heart, and sometimes sudden death" (Gregory, 1856). Suggested remedies included bandaging the genitals, covering them with a cage, tying the hands, male circumcision without anesthesia (so that it might better be remembered), and for girls, the administration of carbolic acid to the clitoris. One physician, J.W. Kellogg, believed that certain grains would be less likely to provoke sexual excitation—leading to his invention of corn flakes (Hunt, 1974; Michael et al., 1994).

The reality is different. Today, experts on sexual behavior view masturbation as a normal, healthy, and harmless activity (Leitenberg, Detzer, & Srebnik, 1993). In fact, some suggest that it provides a useful way to learn about one's own sexuality.

Sexual Intercourse. Although it may be preceded by many different types of sexual intimacy, including deep kissing, massaging, petting, and oral sex, sexual intercourse remains a major milestone in the perceptions of most adolescents. Consequently, the focus of researchers investigating sexual behavior has been on the act of intercourse.

The age at which adolescents first have sexual intercourse has been steadily declining over the last 50 years. Overall, around half of adolescents begin having intercourse between the ages of 15 and 18, and at least 80 percent have had sex before the age of 20 (Seidman & Reider, 1994).

There are racial and gender differences in the timing of first intercourse (Leigh et al., 1994). For instance, half of all African American men have intercourse by the time they are 15, and half of all Hispanic men by the time they are around 16½. In comparison, it is not until age 17 that half of white males have had sexual intercourse. The pattern is a little different for women: Although half of black women have intercourse by the time they are around 17, half of white women and half of Hispanic women have intercourse by the time they are just about 18 (Michael et al., 1994; see Figure 12-7).

Clearly, sexual activities are taking place earlier during adolescence than they did in prior eras (Warren et al., 1997). This is in part a result of a change in societal norms

masturbation   sexual self-stimulation

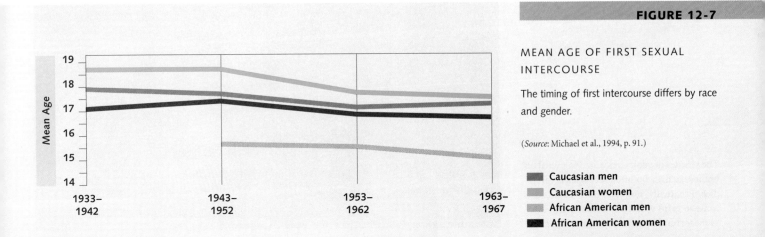

FIGURE 12-7

MEAN AGE OF FIRST SEXUAL INTERCOURSE

The timing of first intercourse differs by race and gender.

(*Source*: Michael et al., 1994, p. 91.)

■ Caucasian men
■ Caucasian women
■ African American men
■ African American women

governing sexual conduct. The prevailing norm several decades ago was the *double standard*, in which premarital sex was considered permissible for males but not for females. Women were told by society that "nice girls don't," whereas men heard that premarital sex was permissible—although they should be sure to marry virgins.

Today, however, the double standard has largely been supplanted by a new norm, called *permissiveness with affection*. According to this standard, premarital intercourse is viewed as permissible for both men and women if it occurs in the context of a long-term, committed, or loving relationship (Reiss, 1960; Hyde, 1994).

On the other hand, the demise of the double standard is far from complete. Attitudes toward sexual conduct are typically more lenient for males than for females, even in relatively socially liberal cultures. And in some cultures, the standards for men and women are quite distinct. For instance, in Mexico, where there are strict standards against premarital sex, males are considerably more likely than females to have premarital sex (Liskin, 1985; Johnson et al., 1992; Spira et al., 1992).

Sexual Orientation: Heterosexuality and Homosexuality

When we consider adolescents' sexual development, the most frequent pattern is *heterosexuality*, sexual attraction and behavior directed to the opposite sex. Yet some teenagers do not follow this path. Instead, some experience *homosexual* feelings, sexual attraction to members of their own sex.

At one time or another, around 20 to 25 percent of adolescent boys, and 10 percent of adolescent girls, have at least one same-sex sexual encounter. However, many fewer adolescents become exclusively homosexual. Although accurate figures are difficult to obtain, estimates range from a low of 1.1 percent to a high of 10 percent. Most experts believe that between 4 and 10 percent of both men and women are exclusively homosexual during extended periods of their lives (Kinsey, Pomeroy, & Martin, 1948; McWhirter, Sanders, & Reinisch, 1990; Alan Guttmacher Institute, 1993b; Michael et al., 1994).

The difficulty in determining the proportion of people who are homosexual is due, in part, to the fact that homosexuality and heterosexuality are not completely distinct sexual orientations. Alfred Kinsey, a pioneer sex researcher, argued that sexual orientation should be viewed as a continuum, in which "exclusively homosexual" is at one end and "exclusively heterosexual" at the other (Kinsey, Pomeroy, & Martin, 1948). In between are people who show both homosexual and heterosexual behavior.

The determination of sexual orientation is further complicated by confusion between sexual orientation and gender identity. Although sexual orientation relates to the object of

The stresses of adolescence are magnified for homosexuals, who often face societal prejudice. Eventually, however, most adolescents come to grips with their sexual orientation, as these students at a symposium exemplify.

one's sexual interests, *gender identity* is the gender a person believes her or she is psychologically. There is no relationship between sexual orientation and gender identity: A man who has a strong masculine gender identity may be attracted to other men. Furthermore, the extent to which men and women enact traditional "masculine" or "feminine" behavior is unrelated to their sexual orientation or gender identity.

The factors that induce people to develop as heterosexual or homosexual are not well understood. Increasing evidence suggests that genetic and biological factors may play an important role. For instance, evidence from studies of twins shows a higher joint incidence of homosexuality in identical twins than in nontwins. Other research finds that various structures of the brain are different in homosexuals and heterosexuals, and hormone production also seems to be linked to sexual orientation (LeVay, 1993; Gladue, 1994; Berenbaum & Snyder, 1995; Meyer-Bahlburg et al., 1995).

On the other hand, evidence of a biological cause is not yet conclusive, given that most findings are based on small samples (Byne & Parsons, 1994). Consequently, some researchers have suggested that family or peer environmental factors play a role. For example, Freud argued that homosexuality was the result of inappropriate identification with the opposite-sex parent (Freud, 1922/1959).

The difficulty with Freud's theoretical perspective and other, similar perspectives that followed is that there simply is no evidence to suggest that any particular family dynamic or childrearing practice is consistently related to sexual orientation. Similarly, explanations based on learning theory, which suggest that homosexuality arises because of rewarding, pleasant homosexual experiences and unsatisfying heterosexual ones, do not appear to be the complete answer (Bell & Weinberg, 1978; Isay, 1990; Golombok & Tasker, 1996).

In short, there is no accepted explanation of why some adolescents develop a heterosexual orientation and others a homosexual orientation. Most experts believe that sexual orientation develops out of a complex interplay of genetic, physiological, and environmental factors (Gladue, 1994).

What is clear is that adolescents who find themselves attracted to members of the same sex face a difficult time (Anderson, 1994). U.S. society still harbors great ignorance and prejudice regarding homosexuality, persisting in the belief that people have a choice in the matter—which they do not. The result is that adolescents who find themselves to be homosexual are at greater risk for depression, and suicide rates are significantly higher for homosexual adolescents than heterosexual adolescents (Henning-Stout, 1996).

Ultimately, though, most adolescents come to grips with their sexual orientation. Once they are past adolescence, homosexuals have the same overall degree of mental and physical health as heterosexuals. Homosexuality is not considered a psychological disorder by any of the major psychological or medical associations, and all of them endorse efforts to eliminate discrimination against homosexuals (Bersoff & Ogden, 1991; Herek, 1993; Patterson, 1994).

Teenage Pregnancy: A Problem of Epidemic Proportions

Night has eased into day, but it is all the same for Tori Michel, 17. Her 5-day-old baby, Caitlin, has been fussing for hours, though she seems finally to have settled into the pink-and-purple car seat on the living-room sofa. "She wore herself out," explains Tori, who lives in a two-bedroom duplex in this St. Louis suburb with her mother, Susan, an aide to handicapped adults. "I think she just had gas."

Motherhood was not in Tori's plans for her senior year at Fort Zumwalt South High School—not until she had a "one-night thing" with James, a 21-year-old she met through friends. She had been taking birth-control pills but says she stopped after breaking up with a long-term boyfriend. "Wrong answer," she now says ruefully.

When she learned she was pregnant last January, Tori decided against having an abortion. "It just doesn't seem right," she says. Her mother, who divorced her husband Robert two years ago, supported her daughter's decision. James is no longer in the picture. . . . Tori cannot help but admit she's a bit shell-shocked. Finishing school, she insists, is her priority.

This 16-year-old mother and her child are representative of a major social problem: teenage pregnancy. Each year, 1 in 10 teenage girls becomes pregnant.

"Ever since I've had Caitlin, I haven't felt like a teenager. I've felt like a mom," she says. "I think it happened too fast." (Gleick, Reed, & Schindehette, 1994, p. 40)

Feedings at 3:00 A.M., diaper changes, and visits to the pediatrician are not part of most people's vision of adolescence. However, millions of teenagers become parents—a problematic trend in the United States, with ramifications for every segment of society.

Every minute of the day, an adolescent in the United States gives birth. Every year, over one million women under the age of 20—one in every 10 teenage girls—become pregnant. Although the birth rates for teenage women aged 15-19 has declined 11 percent since the early 1990s—and even more for African American teenagers, whose rate declined 21 percent—close to 6 percent of teenagers give birth. Around half of all adolescent mothers are unmarried, and in some inner cities, 80 percent of teenagers who have babies are not married. Frequently, a mother must care for her child without the help of the father (Alan Guttmacher Institute, 1994; Coley & Chase-Lansdale, 1998).

The results of an unintended pregnancy can be devastating to both mother and child. Without financial or emotional support, a mother may have to abandon her own education, and consequently she may be relegated to unskilled, poorly paying jobs for the rest of her life. In other cases, she may develop long-term dependency on welfare. An adolescent mother's physical and mental health may suffer as she faces unrelenting stress due to continual demands on her time (Prodromidis et al., 1994; Ambuel, 1995; Trad, 1995; Barratt et al., 1996). (See the "Speaking of Development" box).

The children of teenage mothers also do not fare well when compared with children of older mothers. They are more likely to suffer from poor health and to show poorer school performance. Later, they are more likely to become teenage parents themselves, creating a cycle of pregnancy and poverty from which it is very difficult to extricate themselves (Furstenberg, Brooks-Gunn, & Morgan, 1987; Carnegie Task Force, 1994).

The severity of the problem of teenage pregnancies is peculiarly American. If we look at other industrialized countries, we find much lower rates of teenage pregnancy (see Figure 12-8).

FIGURE 12-8

TEENAGE PREGNANCY RATES

The rate of teenage pregnancy in the United States is significantly greater than in other industrialized countries.

(*Source*: Alan Guttmacher Institute, 1988.)

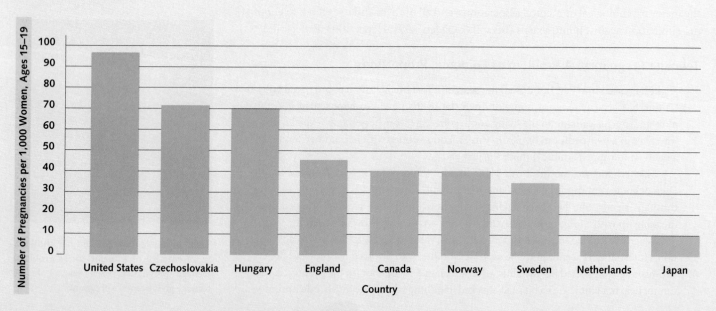

Patricia Canessa, Pregnancy Counselor

Education: .... University of Chile, B.S. in biology; University of Colombia, M.A. in psychology; Northwestern University, Evanston, Illinois, M.A. in psychology; University of Rome, Italy, Ph.D. in family therapy

Position: .... Department director, the Arts of Living Institute

Home: .... Chicago, Illinois

"We need to know what the girl has been doing for prenatal care and to be aware of potential conditions that might affect the pregnancy, such as a sexually transmitted disease or a urinary tract infection—two major contributors to low birth weight."

"The target of the program is comprehensive: to change a pattern of dysfunctional behaviors that cross generations, to break a cycle of behavior."

When a young teenage girl faces pregnancy, it can be a tough world, but for the past 24 years the Arts of Living Institute has helped hundreds of pregnant teenagers, aged 14 to 19, find new lives, raise healthy children, and make the transition from teenager to mother a bit more easily.

Department director Patricia Canessa, who has been with the Institute for the past 10 years, notes that its success rate is attributable to a comprehensive program designed not only for the health of the pregnant teenager and her baby, but for the new mother's social development as well.

Eighty-five to ninety percent of the pregnant teenagers who reach the Institute come from the poorest areas of Chicago and are living below the poverty line, according to Canessa.

"Once the girl comes in with a parent, guardian, or relative who lives in the household, we gather the basic information and a social worker then performs an extensive psychosocial assessment," Canessa explains.

"During the psychosocial assessment we explain the importance of developing the ability to do three things: establish social interactions, develop cognitively through academic accomplishments, and succeed behaviorally in a structured situation such as the school, the family, or the community."

The psychosocial assessment also covers the current living situation, a history of the family, and the precipitating factors that led to the current pregnancy, as perceived by the teenager. A health assessment follows the psychosocial assessment.

"We need to know what the girl has been doing for prenatal care and to be aware of potential conditions that might affect the pregnancy, such as a sexually transmitted disease or a urinary tract infection—two major contributors to low birth weight," Canessa adds.

The teenager's reproductive history and a family health history are also taken. "We follow this with a brief parenting evaluation in which we stress the importance of the father or boyfriend and assess the role he will play in prenatal care, delivery, and parenting. The father can be interviewed either alone or with the girl," Canessa says. "We look at his educational level and his plans in terms of vocation, social development, and engagement in co-parenting activities."

Efforts are also made to reintegrate the girl into school. "The target of the program is comprehensive: to change a pattern of dysfunctional behaviors that cross generations, to break a cycle of behavior," says Canessa. "In working with the families we try to change the mother–daughter relationship so that the daughter–baby relationship is changed as well."

Although it might be suspected that the higher rates of pregnancy in the United States are due to more frequent or earlier sexual activity, that is not the case. For instance, there is little difference among industrialized countries in the age at which adolescents first have sexual intercourse.

What does differ is the use of birth control. Teenage girls in the United States are much less likely to use contraception than teenagers in other countries. And even when they do use birth control, teenagers in the United States are less likely to use effective methods (Musick, 1993).

However, ineffective birth control is only part of the answer. An additional factor is that, despite increasing rates of premarital sexual behavior, people in the United States remain basically intolerant of premarital sex, and they are unwilling to provide the type of sex education that might reduce the rate of teenage pregnancies.

Consequently, sex education is considerably more limited in the United States than in other industrialized countries. And because sex remains a contentious topic, with many political ramifications, effective sex education programs are difficult to develop and implement.

Although adolescent pregnancy and parenthood are difficult problems, some teenagers successfully break the poverty-and-pregnancy cycle. Two key factors for teenage mothers are completing high school and postponing future births. Social programs that help young mothers complete their education and that support them in other basic ways are critically important (Rauch-Elnekone, 1994; Allen et al., 1997).

REVIEW AND RETHINK

REVIEW

- The functions of dating in adolescence include intimacy, entertainment, and prestige. The ability to achieve intimacy develops gradually during the period.

- Masturbation, once viewed very negatively, is now generally regarded as a normal and harmless practice that continues into adulthood.

- The age of first intercourse reflects cultural differences and has been declining over the last 50 years.

- Sexual orientation, which is most accurately viewed as a continuum rather than categorically, develops as the result of a complex combination of factors. Sexual orientation is distinct from gender identity.

- Teenage pregnancy is a major problem in the United States, with negative consequences for adolescent mothers and their children. Effective sex education, stressing among other things the proper use of contraception, can reduce the incidence of teenage pregnancy.

RETHINK

- Which factors in early and middle adolescence work against the achievement of true intimacy in dating?

- Do you think old social attitudes toward masturbation decreased its incidence? Are modern attitudes toward the practice likely to cause an increase? Why or why not?

- Why is the age of first intercourse declining? Which factors contribute to a double standard toward sex for males and females?

- How might the interplay of genetic, physiological, and environmental factors influence sexual orientation?

■ Are social programs that help pregnant teenagers complete high school and postpone future pregnancies beneficial? Do they serve only pregnant teenagers, or are the benefits broader? Explain.

LOOKING BACK

■ **How does the development of self-concept, self-esteem, and identity proceed during adolescence?**

• During adolescence, self-concept differentiates to encompass others' views as well as one's own and to include multiple aspects simultaneously. Differentiation of self-concept can cause confusion as behaviors reflect a complex, definition of the self.

• Adolescents also differentiate their self-esteem, evaluating particular aspects of themselves differently.

• According to Erik Erikson, adolescents are in the identity-versus-identity-confusion stage, seeking to discover their individuality and identity. They may become confused and exhibit dysfunctional reactions, and they may rely for help and information more on friends and peers than on adults.

• James Marcia identifies four identity statuses that individuals may experience in adolescence and in later life: identity achievement, identity foreclosure, identity diffusion, and moratorium.

• The formation of an identity is challenging for members of racial and ethnic minority groups, many of whom appear to be embracing bicultural identity approach.

■ **What dangers do adolescents face as they deal with the stresses of adolescence?**

• Many adolescents have feelings of sadness and hopelessness, and some experience major depression. Biological, environmental, and social factors contribute to depression, and there are gender, ethnic, and racial differences in its occurrence.

• The rate of adolescent suicide is rising, with suicide now the third most common cause of death in the 15-to-24-year-old bracket.

■ **How does the quality of relationships with family and peers change during adolescence?**

• Adolescents' quest for autonomy often brings confusion and tension to their relationships with their parents, but the actual "generation gap" between parents' and teenagers' attitudes is usually small.

• Peers are important during adolescence because they provide a means of social comparison and offer reference groups against which to judge social success. Relationships among adolescents are characterized by the need to belong.

■ **What are gender, race, and ethnic relations like in adolescence?**

• During adolescence, boys and girls begin to spend time together in groups and, toward the end of adolescence, to pair off.

• In general, segregation between people of different races and ethnicities increases in middle and late adolescence, even in schools with a diverse student body.

■ **What does it mean to be popular and unpopular in adolescence, and how do adolescents respond to peer pressure?**

- Degrees of popularity during adolescence include popular and controversial adolescents (on the high end of popularity) and neglected and rejected adolescents (on the low end).

- Peer pressure is not a simple phenomenon. Adolescents conform to their peers in areas of peer expertise, and to adults in areas of adult expertise. As adolescents grow in confidence, their conformity to both peers and adults declines.

- Although most do not commit crimes, adolescents are disproportionately involved in criminal activities. Juvenile delinquents can be categorized as undersocialized or socialized delinquents.

■ **What are the functions and characteristics of dating during adolescence?**

- During adolescence, dating provides intimacy, entertainment, and prestige. Achieving psychological intimacy, difficult at first, becomes easier as adolescents mature, gain confidence, and take relationships more seriously.

■ **How does sexuality develop in the adolescent years?**

- For most adolescents, masturbation serves as the first step into sexuality. The age of first intercourse, which is now in the teens, has declined as the double standard has faded and as the norm of permissiveness with affection has gained ground.

- Most people's sexual orientation is largely or entirely heterosexual, with between 4 and 10 percent being mostly or exclusively homosexual. Sexual orientation apparently develops out of a complex interplay of genetic, physiological, and environmental factors. Sexual orientation is distinct from gender identity, which refers to the gender that a person believes himself or herself to be psychologically.

■ **Why is teenage pregnancy a particular problem in the United States?**

- In the United States, about 10 percent of girls under 20 become pregnant each year. The incidence of both contraception and sex education is comparatively low in the United States, a situation that contributes to the high rate of adolescent pregnancy.

EPILOGUE: THREE ADOLESCENTS

We continued our consideration of adolescence in this chapter, discussing the highly important social and personality issues of self-concept, self-esteem, and identity. We looked at adolescents' relationships with family and peers, and at gender, race, and ethnic relations during adolescence. Our discussion concluded with a look at dating, sexuality, and pregnancy.

Return to the prologue, in which we looked at three adolescents, Carly, Trevor, and Abrielle. Consider the following questions.

1. In what ways does each of these three adolescents appear to be dealing with the issues of self-concept, self-esteem, and identity?

2. How is each one dealing with the issues of belonging and relationships with peers?

3. In what ways is Carly's avoidance of politics an example of the quest for autonomy? Is this evidence of a deep generation gap in Carly's family?

4. Why is Abrielle's "color-blind social life" causing problems for her with her black acquaintances? What sorts of pressures is she probably under? Which model of cultural

identity would Abrielle probably subscribe to: cultural assimilation, pluralistic society, or bicultural identity?

5. Does Trevor show any signs of entering or being in any of Marcia's identity statuses: identity achievement, identity foreclosure, identity diffusion, or moratorium? What evidence is there that he may be exploring his identity?

KEY TERMS AND CONCEPTS

identity-versus-identity-confusion stage (p. 412)

identity achievement (p. 414)

identity foreclosure (p. 414)

identity diffusion (p. 415)

moratorium (p. 415)

cluster suicide (p. 419)

autonomy (p. 421)

generation gap (p. 422)

reference groups (p. 424)

cliques (p. 424)

crowds (p. 424)

sex cleavage (p. 424)

peer pressure (p. 428)

undersocialized delinquents (p. 428)

socialized delinquents (p. 429)

masturbation (p. 431)

EARLY ADULTHOOD

Physical and Cognitive Development

PROLOGUE: A TALE OF TWO STUDENTS

College campuses, like the rest of society, reflect increasing diversity.

The day had started off on a sour note. Crowded with "unnatural triples"—three people stuffed into rooms designed as doubles—Renfield dormitory has a shower shortage. And this morning, when she wakes a little after 9, Miriam Heller has to wait.

"We didn't exactly get our choice of housing," she says as her hair dries. Along with her roommate, Melanie Schatz, she landed in a cinderblock freshman dorm with two identical beds, two desks, two chairs, two bureaus and two open closets. Posters of paintings by Impressionists Renoir, Monet and Van Gogh and one "low-maintenance" plant soften the room's harsh edges. . . .

Having missed study time the night before, Heller squeezes in a five-minute glance at Andre Gide's "The Immoralist" before joining the stream of students heading across campus to classes.

Today's schedule is typical of her heavier class days but is shaped by overriding concern about the physics test tomorrow. In any given week, she spends about 40 hours working on the student newspaper and other extra-curricular activities, 12 hours in class and an average of 15 hours studying, although that triples during midterms and finals so she can keep up her A/A– minus average. This semester, her reading load for four courses is three to four books a week. (Dembner, 1995b, p. 22)

*****

441

By 4:30 this morning, Marion Mealey had checked her son, walked the dogs, and settled back on her bed to study biology for the Graduate Record Exam. . . .

Nearby, on a wall of fame, hang her honorable discharge certificate from the Air Force (1987), an associate's degree from Assassoit Community College (1994) and the Chancellor's Scholarship that makes it possible for her to attend the University of Massachusetts at age 27.

As a clock counts out the seconds, she gathers her breakfast and lunch—prepared the night before—and slips out of her three-decker at 6 A.M. Her son, her mother and most of the neighborhood remain sound asleep.

"She walks him to school and picks him up," says Mealey of her mother Carole, a former switchboard operator. "I don't know how I'd do it without her."

Mealey is among the nearly one-quarter of full-time undergraduates nationally who are 25 years or older. Like many, she must juggle the demands of family and school while also putting food on the table. On this typical day, she will spend four hours in transit (squeezing in some studying), four hours in class and three hours working before returning home to a few precious hours with her family and perhaps another two hours of reading. (Dembner, 1995a, p. 22)

LOOKING AHEAD

Although Miriam Heller and Marion Mealey are following two very different paths, they share the single goal of obtaining a college education. They represent the increasing diversity in family background, socioeconomic status, race, and ethnicity that is coming to characterize college populations today.

For most students, college comes during the period of early adulthood when they are at the height of their cognitive abilities. Physically, too, they are at their peak. The body acts as if it's on automatic pilot: Physical health and fitness are never better.

At the same time, though, considerable development goes on during early adulthood, which starts at the end of adolescence (around age 20) and continues until roughly the start of middle age (around age 40). As we see throughout this and the following chapter, significant changes occur as new opportunities arise and people choose to take on (or to forgo) a new set of roles as spouse, parent, and worker.

This chapter focuses on physical and cognitive development. It begins with a look at the physical changes that extend into early adulthood. We will see not only that growth continues, but that various motor skills change as well. We look at diet and weight, examining the prevalence of obesity. We also consider stress and coping during the early years of adulthood.

The chapter then turns to cognitive development. Although traditional approaches to cognitive development regarded adulthood as an inconsequential plateau, we will examine some new theories that suggest that significant cognitive growth occurs during adulthood. We also consider adult intelligence and how life events are reflected in cognitive development.

Finally, the last part of the chapter considers college, the institution that shapes intellectual growth for those who attend. After considering who goes to college, we will consider how gender and race are related to achievement. We end by looking at why some students drop out of college and examining some of the adjustment problems that college students face.

In short, after reading this chapter, you will be able to answer these questions:

Q

- How does the body develop during early adulthood, and to what risks are young adults exposed?
- What are the effects of stress and what can be done about it?
- Does cognitive development continue in young adulthood?
- How is intelligence defined today, and what causes cognitive growth in young adults?
- Who attends college today, and how is the college population changing?
- What do students learn in college, and what difficulties do they face?

PHYSICAL DEVELOPMENT AND STRESS

It's 5:00 P.M. Rosa Convoy, a 25-year-old single mother, has just finished her work as a receptionist at a dentist's office and is on her way home. She has exactly 2 hours to pick up her daughter, Zoe, from day care, get home, make and eat dinner, pick up and return with a babysitter from down the street, say goodbye to Zoe, and get to her 7 o'clock programming class at a local community college. It's a marathon she runs every Tuesday and Thursday night, and she knows she doesn't have a second to spare if she wants to reach the class on time.

It doesn't take an expert to know what Rosa Convoy is experiencing: stress. Like those of other young adults, Rosa's days pass in a blur of activity, sometimes, it seems, taxing her body—and mind—to the breaking point.

How well Rosa can cope with the multiple demands she faces depends on a complex interplay between physical and psychological factors (Hetherington & Blechman, 1996). As we will see, although most people reach the height of their physical capacities in young adulthood, the stress produced by the challenges of life may sometimes be overwhelming.

Physical Development and the Senses

In most respects, physical development and maturation are complete at early adulthood. Most people are at the peak of their physical capabilities. They have attained their full height, and their limbs are proportional to their size, rendering the gangliness of adolescence a memory. People in their early 20s tend to be healthy, vigorous, and energetic.

On the other hand, not all growth is complete. Some people, particularly late maturers, continue to gain height in their early 20s. Furthermore, certain parts of the body do not fully mature until early adulthood. For instance, the brain continues to grow in both size and weight, reaching its maximum during early adulthood. Brain-wave patterns may also reveal change during early adulthood, although many people in their early 20s show mature patterns (Haug, 1991; Scheibel, 1992; Friedman, Berman, & Hamberger, 1993; Robinson, 1997).

The senses are as sharp as they will ever be. Although there are changes in the elasticity of the eye—a continuation of an aging process that may begin as early as 10—they are so minor that they produce no deterioration in vision. It is not until the 40s that eyesight changes sufficiently to be noticeable—as we will see in Chapter 15.

Hearing, too, is at its peak. However, a gender difference emerges: Women can detect higher tones more readily than men (McGuinness, 1972). In general, though, the hearing of both men and women is quite good. Under quiet conditions the average young adult can hear the ticking of a watch 20 feet away.

The other senses, including taste, smell, and sensitivity to touch and pain, are quite good, and they remain that way throughout early adulthood. These senses do not begin to deteriorate until the 40s or 50s.

Professional athletes, like tennis player Jana Novotna, are at the peak of their psychomotor abilities during early adulthood.

Motor Functioning, Fitness, and Health: Staying Well

If you are a professional athlete, most people probably consider you to be over the hill by the time you leave your 20s. Although there are notable exceptions (think of baseball star Nolan Ryan, who continued playing into his 40s, for instance), even athletes who train constantly tend to lose their physical edge once they reach their 30s. In some sports, the peak passes even earlier. In swimming, for instance, women reach their peak at age 18, and men at age 20 (Schultz & Curnow, 1988).

Most professional athletes—as well as the rest of us—are at the peak of their psychomotor abilities during early adulthood. Reaction time is quicker, muscle strength is greater, and eye-hand coordination is better than at any other period (Salthouse, 1993; Sliwinski et al., 1994).

Physical Fitness. The physical prowess that typically characterizes early adulthood doesn't come naturally, however; nor does it come to everyone. To reach their physical potential, people must exercise and maintain a proper diet.

The benefits of exercise are hardly secret: In the United States, jazzercize and aerobics classes, Nordic Traks and Nautilus workouts, and jogging and swimming are common and seemingly ubiquitous activities. Yet the conspicuousness of exercise activities is misleading. Less than 10 percent of Americans are involved in sufficient regular exercise to keep them in good physical shape, and less than a quarter engage in even moderate regular exercise (MMWR, 1989; Kaplan, Sallis, & Patterson, 1993). Furthermore, the opportunity to exercise is largely an upper- and middle-class phenomenon; people of lower socioeconomic status (SES) often have neither the time nor the money to engage in regular exercise (Atkins et al., 1990).

The amount of exercise required to yield significant health benefits is hardly enormous (Dunn & Blair, 1997). According to recommendations from the American College of Sports Medicine and the Centers for Disease Control and Prevention, people should accumulate at least 30 minutes of moderate physical activity at least 5 days a week. The time spent exercising can be continuous or occur in bouts of at least 10 minutes, as long as it totals 30 minutes each day. Moderate activity includes walking briskly at 3 to 4 mph, biking at speeds up to 10 mph, golfing while carrying or pulling clubs, fishing by casting from shore, playing ping pong, or canoeing at 2 to 4 mph. Even common household chores, such as weeding, vacuuming, and mowing with a power mower provide moderate exercise (American College of Sports Medicine, 1997).

The advantages to those who do become involved in regular exercise programs are many. Exercise increases cardiovascular fitness, meaning that the heart and circulatory system

FIGURE 13-1

THE RESULT OF FITNESS: LONGEVITY

The greater the fitness level, the lower the death rate tends to be for both men and women.

(*Source:* Blair et al., 1989.)

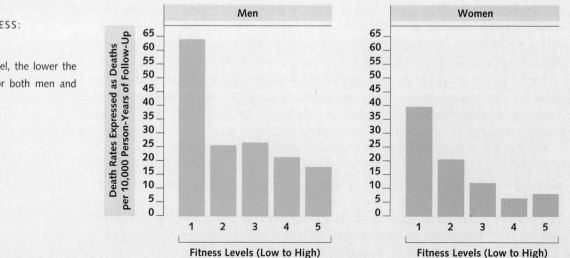

operate more efficiently. Furthermore, lung capacity increases, raising endurance. Muscles become stronger, and the body is more flexible and maneuverable. The range of movement is greater, and the muscles, tendons, and ligaments are more elastic. Moreover, exercise during this period helps reduce *osteoporosis,* the thinning of the bones, in later life.

Exercise also may optimize the immune response of the body, helping it fight off disease. Exercise may even decrease stress and anxiety and reduce depression (Mutrie, 1997). It can provide people with a sense of control over their bodies, as well as impart a feeling of accomplishment (Brown, 1991; Gross, 1991).

Regular exercise provides another, ultimately more important reward: It increases longevity. In brief, the higher the level of fitness, the lower the death rate (see Figure 13-1; Blair et al., 1989).

Health.   Although a lack of exercise may produce poor health (and worse), health risks, in general, are relatively slight during early adulthood. During this period, people are less susceptible to colds and other minor illnesses than they were as children, and when they do come down with illnesses, they usually get over them quickly.

Adults in their 20s and 30s stand a higher risk of dying from accidents, primarily those involving automobiles, than from most other causes. But there are other killers: Among the leading sources of death for people 25 to 34 are AIDS, cancer, heart disease, and suicide. Amid the grim statistics of mortality, the age 35 represents a significant milestone. It is at that point that illness and disease overtake accidents as the leading cause of death—the first time this is true since infancy.

Not all people fare equally well during early adulthood. For instance, men are more apt to die than women, primarily due to their higher involvement in automobile accidents. Furthermore, African Americans have twice the death rate of Caucasians, and minorities in general have a higher likelihood of dying than the Caucasian majority.

Another major cause of death for men is violence, particularly in the United States. The murder rate is significantly higher in the United States than in any other developed country (see Figure 13-2). Compare, for instance, the U.S. murder rate of 21.9 per 100,000 men to Japan's 0.5 murders per 100,000 men—a difference in magnitude of more than 4,000 percent.

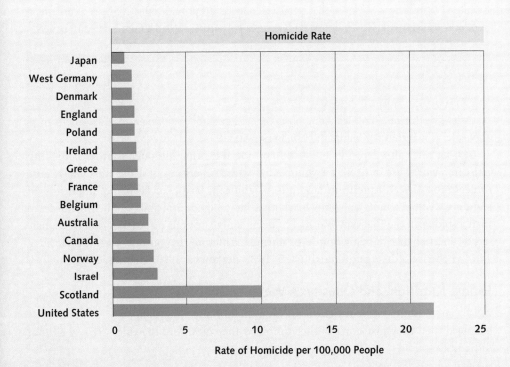

FIGURE 13-2

TRACKING MURDER

The murder rate (per 100,000 men) is far higher in the United States than in any other developed country.

(*Source:* Fingerhut & Kleinman, 1990.)

Developmental Diversity

How Cultural Health Beliefs Influence Use of Health Care

Manolita recently suffered a heart attack. She was advised by her doctor to change her eating and activity habits or face the risk of another life threatening heart attack. During the period that followed, Manolita dramatically changed her eating and activity habits. She also began going to church and praying extensively. After a recent check-up, Manolita is in the best shape of her life. What are some of the reasons for Manolita's amazing recovery? (Murguia, Peterson, & Zea, 1997, p. 16)

After reading the passage above, would you conclude that Manolita recovered her health because (a) she changed her eating and activity habits; (b) she became a better person; (c) God was testing her faith; or (d) her doctor prescribed the correct changes?

In response to a survey asking this question, more than two-thirds of Latino immigrants from Central America, South America, or the Caribbean believed that "God was testing her faith" had a moderate or great effect on her recovery, although most also agreed that a change in eating and activity habits was important (Murguia, Peterson, & Zea, 1997).

The findings are significant, because they help explain why Latinos are the least likely of any Western ethnic group to seek the help of a physician when they are ill. According to psychologists Alejandro Murguia, Rolf Peterson, and Maria Zea (1997), cultural health beliefs, along with demographic and psychological barriers, reduce people's use of physicians and medical care.

Specifically, they suggest that Latinos, as well as members of some other non-Western groups, are more likely to believe in supernatural causes of illness than non-Hispanic whites. For instance, members of these groups may attribute illness to a punishment

Cultural health beliefs, along with demographic and psychological barriers, contribute to people avoiding physicians' help when they are ill.

from God, a lack of faith, or a hex. Such beliefs may reduce the motivation to seek medical care from a physician (Landrine & Klonoff, 1994). Furthermore, demographic barriers, such as lower socioeconomic status, also reduce the ability to rely on traditional medical care, which is expensive. In addition, the lower level of involvement in the mainstream culture that is characteristic of recent immigrants to the United States is associated with a lower likelihood to seek the help of a physician and obtain mainstream medical care (Wells, Golding, & Hough, 1989; Pachter & Weller, 1993).

To ensure that members of every group receive adequate health care, physicians and other health care providers must take cultural health beliefs into account. For example, if a patient believes that the source of his or her illness is a spell cast by a jealous romantic rival, the patient may not comply with medical regimens that ignore that perceived source. To provide effective health care, then, health providers must be sensitive to such cultural health beliefs.

Statistics like this one have led some observers to conclude that violence is "as American as apple pie" (Fingerhut & Kleinman, 1990; Berkowitz, 1993).

Murder rates also depend significantly on racial factors. Although murder is the fifth most frequent cause of death for young adult white Americans, it is *the* most likely cause of death for African Americans, and it is a significant factor for Hispanic Americans. In some areas of the country, a young black male has a higher probability of being murdered than a soldier in the Vietnam War had of being killed. Overall, an African American male has a 1 in 21 chance of being murdered during his lifetime. In contrast, a white male has a 1 in 131 chance of being murdered (CDC, 1991; Berkowitz, 1993; Triandis, 1994).

Eating, Nutrition, and Obesity: A Weighty Concern

Most young adults know which foods are nutritionally sound and how to maintain a balanced diet; they just don't bother to follow the rules. And the rules are not all that difficult to follow.

The murder rate in the United States is significantly higher than in any other developed country.

Good Nutrition. According to guidelines provided by the U.S. Department of Agriculture, people can achieve good nutrition by eating foods that are low in fat, including vegetables, fruits, whole grain foods, fish, poultry, lean meats, and low-fat dairy products. In addition, whole grain foods and cereal products, vegetables (including dried beans and peas), and fruit are beneficial in another way: They help people raise the amount of complex carbohydrates and fiber they ingest. Milk and other sources of calcium are also needed to prevent osteoporosis. Finally, people should reduce salt intake (U.S.D.A., 1992; see Figure 13-3).

During adolescence, a poor diet does not always present a significant problem. For instance, teenagers don't suffer too much from a diet high in junk foods and fat because they are undergoing such tremendous growth. The story changes when they reach young adulthood, however. With growth tapering off, young adults must reduce the caloric intake they were used to during adolescence.

FIGURE 13-3

U.S. GOVERNMENT NUTRITIONAL GUIDELINES

Foods at the base of the pyramid are those that are needed most often, whereas the ones at the top should be eaten infrequently.

(*Source:* Adapted from U.S. Department of Agriculture, 1995.)

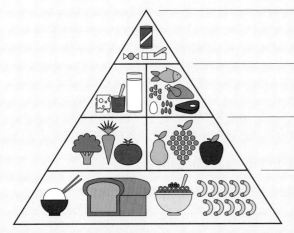

The small tip of the pyramid shows fats, oils, and sweets. These are foods such as salad dressings and oils, cream, butter, margarine, sugars, soft drinks, candies, and sweet desserts. These foods provide calories and little else nutritionally. Most people should use them sparingly.

On this level of the Food Guide Pyramid are two groups of foods that come mostly from animals: milk, yogurt, and cheese; and meat, poultry, fish, dry beans, eggs, and nuts. These foods are important for protein, calcium, iron, and zinc.

This level includes foods that come from plants—vegetables and fruits. Most people need to eat more of these foods for the vitamins, minerals, and fiber they supply.

At the base of the Food Guide Pyramid are breads, cereals, rice, and pasta—all foods from grains. You need the most servings of these foods each day.

Many do not. Although most people enter young adulthood with bodies of average height and weight, they gradually put on weight if their poor dietary habits remain unchanged (Insel & Roth, 1991).

Obesity.   The population of the United States is growing—in more ways than one. Obesity, defined as body weight that is 20 percent or more above the average weight for a person of a given height, is on the rise in the United States: The proportion of the population classified as obese increased by 31 percent from 1980 to 1991 (National Center for Health Statistics, 1994).

Some 7 percent of men and 10 percent of women between the ages of 20 and 25 are classified as obese. The numbers edge up throughout adulthood: At each age increment, a larger percentage of people is classified as obese.

Furthermore, it is not only weight that increases with age; so does the amount of fat in the body. By the age of 18, men's bodies are composed of around 15 to 18 percent body fat, and women's bodies are 20 to 25 percent body fat. However, by the age of 50, body fat in men usually doubles, and body fat in women typically increases by 50 percent (Bray, 1983, 1990).

The exact processes that lead people to become obese remain an unsolved mystery. Some evidence suggests that genetic factors may be at the core of the problem. For instance, researchers have identified specific genes that produce inherited obesity in mice, as well as a gene in humans that appears almost identical. The gene regulates the size of the body's fat stores, apparently by controlling the release of particular types of hormones. It seems plausible, then, that inherited factors play a role in obesity (Zhang et al., 1994).

On the other hand, environmental and social factors may also be at work in producing obesity (Sobal & Devine, 1997). Obese people may be oversensitive to external eating cues based on social standards, such as eating meals at a certain time regardless of whether or not they are hungry. At the same time, they may be less sensitive to the internal hunger cues that, in nonobese people, regulate hunger. For example, when bowls of crackers are placed near people in experiments who have just consumed filling sandwiches, obese people eat more crackers than nonobese people—ignoring internal physiological cues that tell them they are already full (Schachter, Goldman, & Gordon, 1968).

Other research suggests that obese individuals may have higher weight set points than people of normal weight. The **weight set point** is the particular level of weight that the body strives to maintain (Nisbett, 1972; Kupfermann, 1991; Stallone & Stunkard, 1991). The weight set point acts as a type of internal weight thermostat, calling for either more or less food intake, depending on the amount of nutrients required by the body.

According to the weight set point explanation, obese individuals have weight set points that are unusually high, making them particularly vulnerable to external, social cues about foods. Consequently, they are more likely to eat and perpetuate their obesity. Furthermore, as they become obese, their fat cells increase in number and size, which leads to a further rise in weight set point. This cycle obviously makes it very difficult to lower the weight set point—and lose weight permanently (Logue, 1991).

In fact, weight control is a difficult, and often losing, battle for many young adults. Most people who diet ultimately regain the weight they have lost, and they become involved in a see-saw cycle of weight gain and loss (Heatherton, Polivy, & Herman, 1991; Lowe, 1993). In fact, some obesity experts now argue that the rate of dieting failure is so great that people may want to avoid dieting altogether. Instead, if people eat the foods they really want in moderation, they may be able to avoid the binge eating that often occurs when diets fail. Even though obese people may never reach their desired weight, they may, according to this reasoning, ultimately control their weight more effectively (Polivy & Herman, 1985, 1991).

Physical Disabilities: Coping with Physical Challenge

Spotting him as he emerges from beneath a shady tree, the coach goes over and places one arm across the runner's sweaty back. Even though Tony Gorczyca has just claimed an Olympic victory in the 5,000 meters, his coach is not about to let it go to his head.

weight set point   *the particular level of weight that an individual's body strives to maintain*

"It sure got boring watching you run around in circles," the coach, Dave Landau, says as he squints against the blazing sun. "You looked like a gerbil out there."

Gorczyca pauses momentarily, letting Landau's words sink in, then shoots back his reply: "Anytime you want to race, let me know."

It is a warm retort, made of friendship. After a spring of training together, these two Montgomery County [Maryland] residents have established a bond of respect that extends far beyond the white lanes of the track. And while he himself is a marathoner, Landau knows Gorczyca could pose a challenge were they to race—even though Gorczyca is mentally retarded and suffers from a disease that has left him with an under-developed right leg and arm, blind in one eye and prone to violent seizures. (Wisnia, 1994, p. D5)

The physically-challenged face a variety of obstacles, despite the passage of the Americans with Disabilities Act in 1990, which mandates full access to public establishments.

Most young adults do not face the physical challenges—let alone the mental hurdles—that Tony Gorczyca faces. However, some 43 million Americans are physically challenged, according to the official definition of *disability*—a condition that substantially limits a major life activity such as walking or vision. People with disabilities face a difficult, challenging path.

Statistics paint a grim picture of a minority group that is undereducated and underemployed. Fewer than 10 percent of people with major handicaps have finished high school, and fewer than 25 percent of disabled men and 15 percent of disabled women work full time. Overall, between 50 and 75 percent of all adults with handicaps are unemployed (U.S. Commission on Civil Rights, 1983).

Furthermore, even if people with disabilities do find work, the positions they find are often routine and low-paying. For example, 46 percent of workers with disabilities earn less than $15,000 per year, compared with 22 percent of nondisabled workers (*New York Times*, 1989; Schaefer & Lamm, 1992).

Individuals with disabilities face several kinds of barriers to leading full lives that are completely integrated into the broader society. Some barriers are physical. Despite passage in 1990 of the landmark Americans with Disabilities Act (ADA), which mandates full access to public establishments such as stores, office buildings, hotels, and theaters, people in wheel chairs still cannot gain access to many older buildings.

Another barrier—sometimes harder to overcome than a physical one—is prejudice and discrimination. People with disabilities sometimes face pity or avoidance from nondisabled people. Some nondisabled people focus so much on the disability that they overlook other characteristics, reacting to a person with a disability only as a problem category and not as an individual. Others treat people with disabilities as if they were children (Heward & Orlansky, 1988). Ultimately, such treatment can take its toll on the way people with disabilities think about themselves (French & Swain, 1997).

Stress and Coping: Dealing with Life's Challenges

Few of us need much of an introduction to **stress**, the response to events that threaten or challenge us. Stress is a part of nearly everyone's existence, and our lives are crowded with events and circumstances, known as *stressors*, that produce threats to our well-being. Stressors need not be unpleasant events: Even the happiest events, such as starting a long-sought job or planning a wedding, can produce stress (Sarason, Johnson, & Siegel, 1978; Brown & McGill, 1989).

Stress brings several outcomes. The most immediate is typically a biological reaction, as certain hormones, secreted by the adrenal glands, cause a rise in heart rate, blood pressure, respiration rate, and sweating. In some situations, these immediate effects may be beneficial because they produce an "emergency reaction" in the sympathetic nervous system by which people are better able to defend themselves from a sudden, threatening situation (Parkes, 1997).

On the other hand, long-term, continuous exposure to stressors may result in a reduction of the body's ability to deal with stress. As stress-related hormones are constantly secreted, the heart, blood vessels, and other body tissues may deteriorate. As a consequence, people become more susceptible to diseases as their ability to fight off germs declines (Schneiderman, 1983; Kiecolt-Glaser & Glaser, 1986; Cohen, Tyrrell, & Smith, 1993). (See also the "Speaking of Development" box).

stress   *the response to events that threaten or challenge an individual*

"Our main work here focuses on teaching self-regulation, helping people discover their own powers to respond differently—in helpful or unhelpful ways—to all types of things."

"If we think of stress as what is going on in our lives, there isn't much that we can do about it. But if we think of stress as a response, there's a lot we can do."

SPEAKING OF DEVELOPMENT

Patricia Norris, Psychoneuroimmunologist

Education: .... University of California at Santa Barbara, B.A. in psychology; Union Institute, Cincinnati, Ohio, Ph.D. in psychology

Position: .... Director of psychoneuroimmunology at the Life Sciences Institute of Mind–Body Health

Home: .... Topeka, Kansas

After 14 years as director of biofeedback and psychophysiology at the Menninger Clinic in Topeka, Kansas, Patricia Norris went into private practice in 1994.

Today she works at the Life Sciences Institute of Mind–Body health, where she is director of psychoneuroimmunology—the study of the relationship between the body's immune system and psychological factors. Norris works with people who face stress and pain in their everyday lives.

"Just about everyone would agree that any patient who goes to a doctor is experiencing stress on several levels, whether the stress is psychological or physical," she says. "Our main work here focuses on teaching self-regulation, helping people discover their own powers to respond differently—in helpful or unhelpful ways—to all types of things, including panic, anxiety, pain, and life's events. Self-regulation is the bottom line.

"Biofeedback is a technique that people can observe and use. They can watch their hearts actually beat slower," she notes, "and then they can learn to use their knowledge as a tool for self-regulation."

Through biofeedback, Norris teaches patients how to control their muscles and blood flow, a strategy that she has found works well in helping relieve both pain and stress.

"If we think of stress as what is going on in our lives, there isn't much that we can do about it. But if we think of stress as a response, there's a lot we can do. We can actually learn to change the response on a physiological and psychological level," she explains.

"We start with learning to change reactions. It's not your life that is killing you, it's your reactions to it," Norris says. "People aren't capable of dealing with stress until they learn internal strategies for changing their reactions. Once they are able to change their reactions, they can decide to make bigger and more central changes.

"For instance, people with high blood pressure know they should exercise and cut out salt, but because of their tension they don't do it. Once they're able to manage their stress, they can begin to make the changes they need in their lives to treat the high blood pressure itself.

"Many times people's stress patterns come out of their early developmental history. As they start to change some of their stress reactions, they often get in touch with very early life events, beliefs, or 'scripts' they wrote for themselves. Probably all of our stress patterns are developmental in nature."

Although we commonly think of negative events, such as auto mishaps, leading to stress, even welcome events can be stressful.

The Origins of Stress. Not every situation produces stress. What makes some stressful? According to psychologists Arnold Lazarus and Susan Folkman, people move through a series of stages, depicted in Figure 13-4, that determine whether they will experience stress (Lazarus & Folkman, 1984; Lazarus, 1968, 1991).

Primary appraisal is the first step—the individual's assessment of an event to determine whether its implications are positive, negative, or neutral. If the individual sees the event as primarily negative, he or she appraises it in terms of the harm that it has caused in the past, how threatening it is likely to be, and how likely it is that the challenge can be resisted successfully.

primary appraisal *the assessment of an event to determine whether its implications are positive, negative, or neutral*

FIGURE 13-4

STEPS IN THE PERCEPTION OF STRESS

The way an individual appraises a potential stressor determines whether the individual will experience stress.

(*Source:* Adapted from Kaplan, Sallis, & Patterson, 1993.)

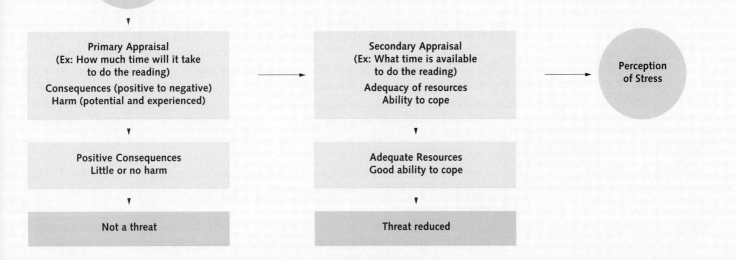

Secondary appraisal follows. **Secondary appraisal** is the individual's assessment of whether one's coping abilities and resources are adequate to overcome the harm, threat, or challenge posed by the potential stressor. At this point, people try to determine whether they will be able to meet the dangers in the situation. If resources are lacking, and the potential threat is great, they will experience stress.

Clearly, stress is a very personal response. For most of us, hang gliding and rock climbing would cause a great deal of stress. However, for some people in early adulthood such activities would be diverting and entertaining.

Still, some general principles help predict when an event will be appraised as stressful. Psychologist Shelley Taylor (1991) suggests the following:

■ Events and circumstances that produce negative emotions are more likely to lead to stress than events that are positive. For example, planning for the adoption of a new baby produces less stress than dealing with the illness of a loved one.

■ Situations that are uncontrollable or unpredictable are more likely to produce stress than those that can be controlled and predicted. Professors who give surprise quizzes in their classes, then, produce more stress than those whose quizzes are scheduled in advance.

■ Events and circumstances that are ambiguous and confusing produce more stress than those that are unambiguous and clear. If people cannot easily understand a situation, they must struggle simply to comprehend it, rather than dealing with it directly.

■ People who must accomplish simultaneously many tasks that strain their capabilities are more likely to experience stress than those who have fewer things to do.

 The Consequences of Stress. If enough stress is experienced in a short time span, it can have formidable costs. Over the long run, the constant wear and tear caused by the physiological arousal that occurs as the body tries to fight off stress produces negative effects. For instance, headaches, backaches, skin rashes, indigestion, chronic fatigue, and even the common cold are stress-related illnesses (Kiecolt-Glaser & Kiecolt-Glaser, 1991; Cohen, Tyrrell, & Smith, 1993, 1997).

Stress may also lead to **psychosomatic disorders**, medical problems caused by the interaction of psychological, emotional, and physical difficulties. For instance, ulcers, asthma, arthritis, and high blood pressure may—although not invariably—be produced by stress (Lepore, Palsane, & Evans, 1991).

Stress may even cause more serious, life-threatening, illnesses. According to some research, the greater the number of stressful events a person experiences over the course of a year, the more likely he or she is to have a major illness (see Table 13-1; Holmes & Rahe, 1967).

Before you start computing whether you are overdue for a major illness, however, keep in mind some important limitations to the research. Not everyone who experiences high stress becomes ill, and the weights given to particular stressors probably vary from one person to the next. Furthermore, there is a kind of circularity to such enumerations of stressors: Because the research is correlational, it is possible that someone who has a major illness to begin with is more likely to experience some of the stressors on the list. For example, a person may have lost a job *because* of the effects of an illness, rather than developing an illness because he or she lost a job. Still, the list of stressors does at least provide a way to consider how most people react to various potentially stressful events in their lives.

Coping with Stress. Some young adults are better than others at **coping**, the effort to control, reduce, or learn to tolerate the threats that lead to stress. What is the key to successful coping?

Some people use *problem-focused coping*, by which they attempt to manage a stressful problem or situation by directly changing the situation to make it less stressful. For example,

secondary appraisal the assessment of whether one's coping abilities and resources are adequate to overcome the harm, threat, or challenge posed by the potential stressor

psychosomatic disorders medical problems caused by the interaction of psychological, emotional, and physical difficulties

coping the effort to control, reduce, or learn to tolerate the threats that lead to stress

TABLE 13-1

WILL STRESS IN YOUR LIFE PRODUCE ILLNESS?

Using the following scale, you can assess the degree of stress in your life (Rahe & Arthur, 1978). To do this, take the stressor value given beside each event you have experienced and multiply it by the number of occurrences over the past year (up to a maximum of four), then add up the scores.

87	Experienced the death of a spouse	50	Changed to a different line of work
77	Getting married	49	Had a major change in amount of independence and responsibility
77	Experienced the death of a close family member	47	Had a major change in responsibilities at work
76	Getting divorced	46	Experienced a major change in use of alcohol
74	Experienced a marital separation from mate	45	Revised personal habits
68	Experienced the death of a close friend	44	Had trouble with school administration
68	Experienced pregnancy or fathered a pregnancy	43	Held a job while attending school
65	Had a major personal injury or illness	43	Had a major change in social activities
62	Were fired from work	42	Had trouble with in-laws
60	Ended a marital engagement or a steady relationship	42	Had a major change in working hours or conditions
58	Had sexual difficulties	42	Changed residence or living conditions
58	Experienced a marital reconciliation with your mate	41	Had your spouse begin or cease work outside the home
57	Had a major change in self-concept or self-awareness	41	Changed your choice of major field of study
56	Experienced a major change in the health or behavior of a family member	41	Changed dating habits
54	Became engaged to be married	40	Had an outstanding personal achievement
53	Had a major change in financial status	38	Had trouble with your boss
52	Took on a mortgage or loan of less than $10,000	38	Had a major change in amount of participation in school activities
52	Had a major change in use of drugs	37	Had a major change in type and/or amount of recreation
50	Had a major conflict or change in values	36	Had a major change in church activities
50	Had a major change in the number of arguments with your spouse	34	Had a major change in sleeping habits
50	Gained a new family member	33	Took a trip or vacation
50	Entered college	30	Had a major change in eating habits
50	Changed to a new school	26	Had a major change in the number of family get-togethers
		22	Were found guilty of minor violations of the law

A total score of 1,435 or higher places you in a high-stress category. According to Marx, Garrity, & Bowers (1975), a high score increases the chances of experiencing a future stress-related illness, although it certainly does not guarantee it.

(*Source:* Adapted from Rahe & Arthur, 1978.)

a man who is having on-the-job difficulties may speak to his boss and ask that his responsibilities be modified.

Other people employ *emotion-focused coping*, which involves the conscious regulation of emotion. For instance, a mother who is having trouble finding appropriate care for her child while she is at work may tell herself that she should look at the bright side: At least she has a job in a difficult economy (Folkman & Lazarus, 1980, 1988).

Coping is also aided by the presence of *social support*, assistance and comfort supplied by others. Turning to others in the face of stress can provide both emotional support (in the form of a shoulder to cry on) and practical, tangible support (such as a temporary loan) (Croyle & Hunt, 1991; Lepore, Palsane, & Evans, 1991; Spiegel, 1993).

Finally, even if people do not consciously cope with stress, some psychologists suggest that they may use unconscious defensive coping mechanisms of which they are unaware and which aid in stress reduction. *Defensive coping* involves unconscious strategies that distort or deny the true nature of a situation. For instance, people may deny the seriousness of a threat, trivializing a life-threatening illness, or they may say to themselves that academic failure on a series of tests is unimportant. If defensive coping becomes a habitual response to stress, it can be problematic. Instead of dealing with the reality of the situation, it merely avoids or ignores the problem.

The Informed Consumer of Development

Coping with Stress

Although no single formula can cover all cases of stress, some general guidelines can help all of us cope with the stress that is part of our lives. Among them are the following (Holahan & Moos, 1987, 1990; Greenglass & Burke, 1991; Kaplan, Sallis, & Patterson, 1993; Sacks, 1993).

■ Seek control over the situation producing the stress. Putting yourself in charge of a situation that is producing stress can take you a long way toward coping with it.

■ Redefine "threat" as "challenge." Changing the definition of a situation can make it seem less threatening. "Look for the silver lining" is not bad advice.

■ Get social support. Almost any difficulty can be faced more easily with the help of others. Friends, family members, and even telephone hot lines staffed by trained counselors can provide significant support. (For help in identifying appropriate hot lines, the U.S. Public Health Service maintains a "master" toll-free number that can provide phone numbers and addresses of many national groups. Call 800-336-4797.)

■ Use relaxation techniques. Procedures that reduce the physiological arousal brought about by stress can be particularly effective. A variety of techniques that produce relaxation, such as transcendental meditation, Zen and yoga, progressive muscle relaxation, and even hypnosis, have been shown to be effective in reducing stress. One that works particularly well was devised by physician Herbert Benson and is illustrated in Table 13-2 (Benson, 1993).

■ If all else fails, keep in mind that a life without any stress at all would be a dull one. Stress is a natural part of life, and successfully coping with it can be a gratifying experience.

TABLE 13-2

HOW TO ELICIT THE RELAXATION RESPONSE

Some general advice on regular practice of the relaxation response:

■ Try to find 10 to 20 minutes in your daily routine; before breakfast is a good time.

■ Sit comfortably.

■ For the period you will practice, try to arrange your life so you won't have distractions. Put the phone on the answering machine, and ask someone else to watch the kids.

■ Time yourself by glancing periodically at a clock or watch (but don't set an alarm). Commit yourself to a specific length of practice, and try to stick to it.

There are several approaches to eliciting the relaxation response. Here is one standard set of instructions:

Step 1. Pick a focus word or short phrase that's firmly rooted in your personal belief system. For example, a nonreligious individual might choose a neutral word like *one* or *peace* or *love*. A Christian person desiring to use a prayer could pick the opening words of Psalm 23, *The Lord is my shepherd*; a Jewish person could choose *Shalom*.
Step 2. Sit quietly in a comfortable position.
Step 3. Close your eyes.
Step 4. Relax your muscles.
Step 5. Breathe slowly and naturally, repeating your focus word or phrase silently as you exhale.
Step 6. Throughout, assume a passive attitude. Don't worry about how well you're doing. When other thoughts come to mind, simply say to yourself, "Oh, well," and gently return to the repetition.
Step 7. Continue for 10 to 20 minutes. You may open your eyes to check the time, but do not use an alarm. When you finish, sit quietly for a minute or so, at first with your eyes closed and later with your eyes open. Then do not stand for one or two minutes.
Step 8. Practice the technique once or twice a day.

(*Source:* Benson, 1993.)

REVIEW AND RETHINK

REVIEW

■ By young adulthood, the body and the senses are generally at their peak, but growth is proceeding, particularly in the brain.

■ Young adults are generally as fit and healthy as they will ever be, and accidents present the greatest risk of death. In the United States, violence is also a significant risk, particularly for nonwhite males.

■ Health must be maintained by proper diet and exercise. Obesity, which is caused by a combination of biological and environmental factors, is increasingly a problem for young adults.

■ Stress, which is a healthy reaction in small doses, can be harmful to body and mind if it is frequent or of long duration.

RETHINK

■ If the advantages of exercise and proper nutrition are evident, why are obesity and poor physical fitness so widespread in the United States? Are these inevitable consequences of a high standard of living?

■ Why is violence so prevalent in the United States, compared with other societies?

■ Why are there individual differences in people's reactions to stress? Do you think there are also cultural differences?

■ The evidence that stress causes disease is called "correlational." What does this mean? Is it possible to design an experiment that would conclusively establish a causal link?

COGNITIVE DEVELOPMENT

John is known to be a heavy drinker, especially when he goes to parties. Mary, John's wife, warns him that if he comes home drunk one more time, she will leave him and take the children. Tonight John is out late at an office party. He comes home drunk. Does Mary leave John?

An adolescent who hears this situation (drawn from research by Adams and Labouvie-Vief, 1986) may find the case to be open-and-shut: Mary leaves John. But in early adulthood, the answer becomes a bit less clear. As people enter adulthood, they become less concerned with the sheer logic of situations and instead take into account real-life concerns that may influence and temper behavior in particular situations.

Intellectual Growth in Early Adulthood

If cognitive development were to follow the same pattern as physical development, we would expect to find little new intellectual growth in early adulthood. In fact, Piaget, whose theory of cognitive development played such a prominent role in our earlier discussions of intellectual change, argued that by the time people left adolescence, their thinking, at least qualitatively, had largely become what it would be for their rest of their lives.

Was Piaget's view correct? Increasing evidence suggests that arguments like his might well be flawed.

Postformal Thought

Developmental psychologist Giesela Labouvie-Vief (1980, 1986) suggests that the nature of thinking changes qualitatively during early adulthood. She asserts that thinking based solely on formal operations (Piaget's final stage, reached during adolescence) is insufficient

According to Giesela Labouvie-Vief, the nature of thought changes qualitatively during early adulthood.

to meet the demands placed on young adults. The complexity of society, which requires specialization, and the increasing challenge of finding one's way through all that complexity require thought that is not necessarily based on pure logic.

Instead, thinking that employs metaphors, confronts society's paradoxes, and involves a more subjective understanding may be especially adaptive, according to Labouvie-Vief. Such thinking is more flexible; it allows for interpretive processes and reflects the fact that reasons behind events in the real world are subtle, painted in shades of gray rather than in black-and-white (Labouvie-Vief, 1990).

To demonstrate how this sort of thinking develops, Labouvie-Vief presented experimental subjects, ranging in age from 10 to 40, with scenarios similar to the John and Mary scenario at the beginning of this section. Each story had a clear, logical conclusion. However, the story could be interpreted differently if real-world demands and pressures were taken into account.

In responding to the scenarios, adolescents relied heavily on the logic inherent in formal operations. For instance, they would predict that Mary would immediately pack up her bags and leave with the children when John came home drunk. After all, that's what she said she would do.

On the other hand, young adults were less prone to use strict logic in determining a character's likely course of action. Instead, they would consider various possibilities that might come into the picture in a real-life situation: Would John be apologetic and beg Mary not to leave? Did Mary really mean it when she said she would leave? Does Mary have some alternative place to go?

In short, young adults exhibited what Labouvie-Vief calls postformal thinking. **Postformal thought** is thinking that goes beyond Piaget's formal operations. Rather than being based on purely logical processes, with absolutely right and wrong answers to problems, postformal thought acknowledges that adult predicaments must sometimes be solved in relativistic terms.

In short, postformal thought acknowledges a world that sometimes lacks clearly right and wrong solutions to problems, a world in which logic may fail to resolve complex human questions. Instead, finding the best resolution to difficulties may involve drawing on and integrating prior experiences.

Schaie's Stages of Development

Developmental psychologist K. Warner Schaie (1977/1978) offers another perspective on postformal thought (Schaie et al., 1989; Schaie & Willis, 1993). Taking up where Piaget left off, Schaie suggests that adults' thinking follows a set pattern of stages (illustrated in Figure 13-5). But Schaie focuses on the ways in which information is *used* during adulthood, rather than on changes in the acquisition and understanding of new information, as in Piaget's approach.

Consequently, Schaie labels the first stage of cognitive development the **acquisitive stage**, which encompasses all of childhood and adolescence. He suggests that before adulthood, the main cognitive developmental task is acquisition of information. But this information is largely squirreled away for future use. In fact, much of the rationale for education during childhood and adolescence is to prepare people for future activities.

The situation changes considerably in early adulthood, however. Instead of targeting the future use of knowledge, the focus shifts to the here-and-now. Schaie suggests that young adults enter the **achieving stage**, in which intelligence is applied to specific situations involving the attainment of long-term goals regarding careers, family, and societal contributions. During the achieving stage, young adults must confront and resolve several major issues, and the decisions they make—such as what job to take and whom to marry—have implications for the rest of their lives.

During the late stages of early adulthood and in middle adulthood, people move into the responsible and executive stages. In the **responsible stage**, the major concerns of

postformal thought thinking that acknowledges that adult predicaments must sometimes be solved in relativistic terms

acquisitive stage according to Schaie, the first stage of cognitive development, encompassing all of childhood and adolescence, in which the main developmental task is to acquire information

achieving stage the point reached by young adults in which intelligence is applied to specific situations involving the attainment of long-term goals regarding careers, family, and societal contributions

responsible stage the stage in which the major concerns of middle-aged adults relate to their personal situations, including protecting and nourishing their spouses, families, and careers

FIGURE 13-5

SCHAIE'S STAGES OF ADULT DEVELOPMENT

(*Source:* Schaie, 1977–1978.)

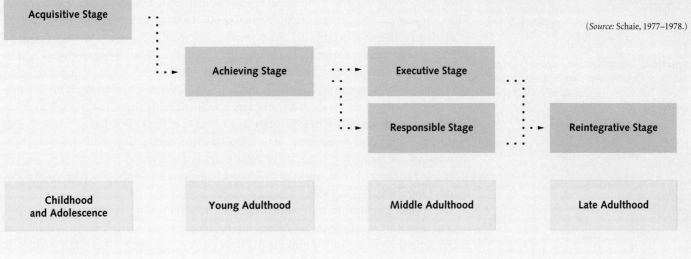

middle-aged adults relate to their personal situations: protecting and nourishing their spouses, families, and careers.

Sometime later during middle adulthood, many people (but not all) enter the executive stage. In the **executive stage**, people take a broader perspective that includes concerns about the world (Sinnott, 1997). Rather than focusing only on their own lives, people in the executive stage also put energy into nourishing and sustaining societal institutions. They may become involved in town government, religious congregations, service clubs, charitable groups, factory unions—organizations that have a larger purpose in society. People in the executive stage, then, look beyond their individual situations.

Old age marks entry into the final period, the reintegrative stage. The **reintegrative stage** is the period of late adulthood during which the focus is on tasks that have personal meaning. In this stage, people no longer focus on acquiring knowledge as a means of solving potential problems that they may encounter. Instead, their information acquisition is directed toward particular issues that specifically interest them. Furthermore, they have less interest in—and patience for—things that they do not see as having some immediate application to their lives. Thus, the abstract issue of whether the federal budget should be balanced may be of less concern to an elderly individual than whether the government should provide universal health care.

Intelligence: What Matters in Early Adulthood?

> Your year on the job has been generally favorable. Performance ratings for your department are at least as good as they were before you took over, and perhaps even a little better. You have two assistants. One is quite capable. The other just seems to go through the motions and is of little real help. Even though you are well liked, you believe that there is little that would distinguish you in the eyes of your superiors from the nine other managers at a comparable level in the company. Your goal is rapid promotion to an executive position. (Based on Wagner & Sternberg, 1985, p. 447)

How do you meet your goal?

The way adults answer this question has a great deal to do with their future success, according to psychologist Robert Sternberg. The question is one of a series designed to assess a particular type of intelligence that may have more of an impact on future

executive stage the period in middle adulthood when people take a broader perspective than earlier, including concerns about the world

reintegrative stage the period of late adulthood during which the focus is on tasks that have personal meaning

triarchic theory of intelligence *Sternberg's theory that intelligence is made up of three major components: componential, experiential, and contextual*

practical intelligence *according to Sternberg, intelligence that is learned primarily by observing others and modeling their behavior*

success than the type of intelligence measured by traditional IQ tests (of the sort we discussed in Chapter 9).

In his **triarchic theory of intelligence**, Sternberg suggests that intelligence is made up of three major components: componential, experiential, and contextual (see Figure 13-6). The *componential* aspect relates to the mental components involved in analyzing data used in solving problems, especially problems involving rational behavior. It relates to people's ability to select and use formulas, to choose appropriate problem-solving strategies, and in general to make use of what they have been taught. The *experiential* component refers to the relationship between intelligence, people's prior experience, and their ability to cope with new situations. This is the insightful aspect of intelligence that allows people to relate what they already know to a new situation and an array of facts never before encountered. Finally, the *contextual* component of intelligence involves the degree of success people demonstrate in facing the demands of their everyday, real-world environments. For instance, the contextual component is involved in adapting to on-the-job professional demands (Sternberg, 1985a; 1991).

Traditional intelligence tests, which yield an IQ score, tend to focus on the componential aspect of intelligence. Yet increasing evidence suggests that a more useful measure, particularly when one is looking for ways to compare and predict adult success, is the contextual component—the aspect of intelligence that has come to be called practical intelligence.

Practical Intelligence: Using Common Sense. According to Robert Sternberg, the IQ score that most traditional tests produce relates quite well to academic success. However, IQ seems to be unrelated to other types of achievement, such as career success. For example, although it is clear that success in business settings requires some minimal level of the sort of intelligence measured by IQ tests, the rate of career advancement and the ultimate success of business executives is only marginally related to IQ scores (Wagner & Sternberg, 1991; Sternberg & Wagner, 1986, 1993; McClelland, 1993).

Sternberg contends that success in a career necessitates a type of intelligence—called **practical intelligence**—that is substantially different from that involved in traditional academic pursuits (Sternberg et al., 1997). Whereas academic success is based on knowledge of particular types of information, obtained largely from reading and listening, practical intelligence is learned primarily by observing others and modeling their behavior. People who are high in practical intelligence can extract and deduce broad principles and norms about appropriate behavior and apply them in particular situations (see Figure 13-7).

FIGURE 13-6

STERNBERG'S TRIARCHIC THEORY OF INTELLIGENCE

(*Source:* Based on Sternberg, 1985a, 1991.)

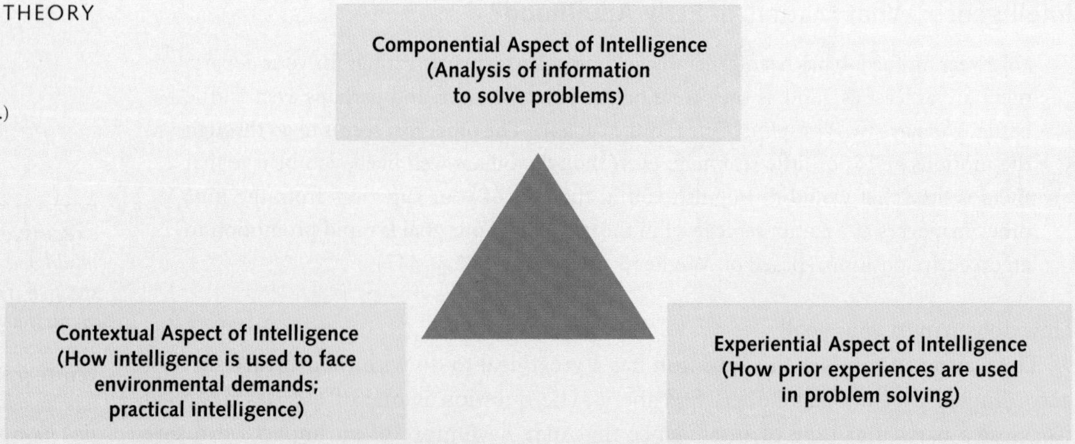

Componential Aspect of Intelligence
(Analysis of information to solve problems)

Contextual Aspect of Intelligence
(How intelligence is used to face environmental demands; practical intelligence)

Experiential Aspect of Intelligence
(How prior experiences are used in problem solving)

FIGURE 13-7

THE FOUR DOMAINS OF PRACTICAL INTELLIGENCE

(*Source:* Sternberg & Wagner, 1993.)

Management

You are responsible for selecting a contractor to renovate several large buildings. You have narrowed the choice to two contractors on the basis of their bids and after further investigation, you are considering awarding the contract to the Wilson & Sons Company. Rate the importance of the following pieces of information in making your decision to award the contract to Wilson & Sons.

_____ The company has provided letters from satisfied former customers.

_____ The Better Business Bureau reports no major complaints about the company.

_____ Wilson & Sons has done good work for your company in the past.

_____ Wilson & Sons' bid was $2000 less than the other contractor's (approximate total cost of the renovation is $325,000).

_____ Former customers whom you have contacted strongly recommended Wilson & Sons for the job.

Sales

You sell a line of photocopy machines. One of your machines has relatively few features and is inexpensive, at $700, although it is not the least expensive model you carry. The $700 photocopy machine is not selling well and it is overstocked. There is a shortage of the more elaborate photocopy machines in your line, so you have been asked to do what you can to improve sales of the $700 machine. Rate the following strategies for maximizing your sales of the slow-moving photocopy machine.

_____ Stress with potential customers that although this model lacks some desirable features, the low price more than makes up for it.

_____ Stress that there are relatively few models left at this price.

_____ Arrange as many demonstrations as possible of the machine.

_____ Stress simplicity of use, since the machine lacks confusing controls that other machines may have.

Academic Psychology

It is your second year as an assistant professor in a prestigious psychology department. This past year you published two unrelated empirical articles in established journals. You don't, however, believe there is yet a research area that can be identified as your own. You believe yourself to be about as productive as others. The feedback about your first year of teaching has been generally good. You have yet to serve on a university committee. There is one graduate student who has chosen to work with you. You have no external source of funding, nor have you applied for any.

Your goals are to become one of the top people in your field and to get tenure in your department. The following is a list of things you are considering doing in the next two months. You obviously cannot do them all. Rate the importance of each by its priority as a means of reaching your goals.

_____ Improve the quality of your teaching.

_____ Write a grant proposal.

_____ Begin a long-term research project that may lead to a major theoretical article.

_____ Concentrate on recruiting more students.

_____ Begin several related short-term research projects, each of which may lead to an empirical article.

_____ Participate in a series of panel discussions to be shown on the local public television station.

College Student Life

You are enrolled in a large introductory lecture course. Requirements consist of 3 exams and a final. Please indicate how characteristic it would be of your behavior to spend time doing each of the following if your goal were to receive an A in the course.

_____ Attend class regularly.

_____ Attend optional weekly review sections with the teaching fellow.

_____ Read assigned text chapters thoroughly.

_____ Take comprehensive class notes.

_____ Speak with the professor after class and during office hours.

Of course, business is not the only sphere in which practical intelligence is important. Psychologist Seymour Epstein argues that *constructive thinking*, a form of practical intelligence, underlies success in such areas as social relationships and physical and emotional health. Constructive thinkers are able to control their emotions effectively and deal with challenges in ways that lead to success. Rather than just complaining about an objectionable situation, for instance, constructive thinkers take action (Epstein & Meier, 1989; Atwater, 1992; Epstein, 1994).

Creativity: Novel Thought. The hundreds of musical compositions of Wolfgang Amadeus Mozart, who died at the age of 35, were largely written during early adulthood. The same is true of many other creative individuals: Their major works were produced during early adulthood (Dennis, 1966a; see Figure 13-8).

One reason for the higher productivity of early adulthood may be what psychologist Sarnoff Mednick (1963) proposed: "Familiarity breeds rigidity." By this he meant that the more people know about a subject, the less likely they are to be creative in that area. According to such reasoning, people in early adulthood may be at the peak of their creativity because many of the problems they encounter on a professional level are novel. As they get older, however, and become more familiar with the problems, their creativity may be stymied.

FIGURE 13-8

CREATIVITY AND AGE

The period of maximum creativity differs depending on the particular field.

(*Source:* Based on Dennis, 1966.)

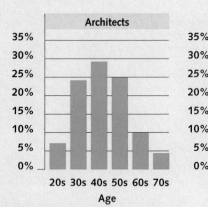

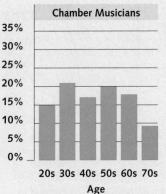

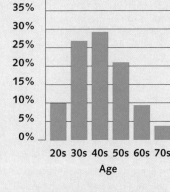

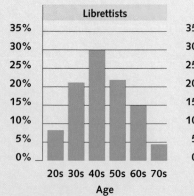

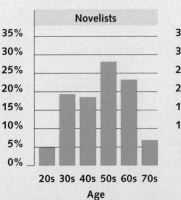

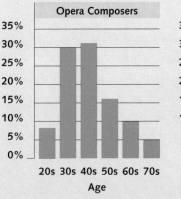

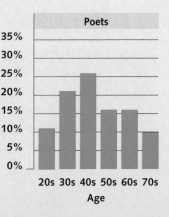

On the other hand, many people do not reach their pinnacle of creativity until much later in life. For instance, Buckminster Fuller did not devise his major contribution, the geodesic dome, until he was in his 50s. Frank Lloyd Wright designed the Guggenheim Museum in New York at age 70. Charles Darwin and Jean Piaget were still writing influential works well into their 70s, and Picasso was painting in his 90s. Furthermore, when we look at overall productivity, as opposed to the period of a person's most important output, we find that productivity remains fairly steady throughout adulthood, particularly in the humanities (Dennis, 1966b; Simonton, 1989).

Overall, the study of creativity reveals few consistent developmental patterns. One reason for this is the difficulty of determining just what constitutes an instance of **creativity**, which is defined as combining responses or ideas in novel ways. Because definitions of what is "novel" may vary from one person to the next, it is hard to identify a particular behavior unambiguously as creative (Glover, Ronning, & Reynolds, 1992; Isaksen & Murdock, 1993; Sasser-Coen, 1993).

That ambiguity hasn't stopped psychologists from trying. For instance, one important component of creativity is a person's willingness to take risks that may result in potentially high payoffs (Sternberg & Lubart, 1992). Creative people are analogous to successful stock market investors, who try to follow the "buy low, sell high" rule. Creative people develop and endorse ideas that are unfashionable or regarded as wrong ("buying low"). They assume that the ideas will eventually come to be viewed more positively, and at that time others will see the value of the ideas and embrace them ("selling high").

Poet Maya Angelou, who spoke at the 1993 presidential inauguration, has maintained a steady pattern of creative productivity throughout adulthood.

creativity   *the combination of responses or ideas in novel ways*

Life Events and Cognitive Development

Marriage. The death of a parent. Starting a first job. The birth of a child. Buying a house.

The course of life comprises many events such as these—important milestones on the path through the life span. Such occurrences, whether they are welcome or unwanted, clearly may bring about stress, as we saw earlier in this chapter. But do they also cause cognitive growth?

Although the research is still spotty, and largely based on case studies, some evidence suggests that major life events may lead to cognitive growth. For instance, the birth of a child—a profound event—may trigger fresh insights into one's relationships with relatives and ancestors, one's broader place in the world, and the role one has in perpetuating humanity. Similarly, the death of a loved one may cause people to reevaluate what is important to them, and to look anew at the manner in which they lead their lives (Feldman, Biringen, & Nash, 1981; Haan, 1985).

In sum, the ups and downs of life events may lead young adults to think about the world in novel, more complex and sophisticated, and often less rigid, ways. Rather than applying formal logic to situations—a strategy of which they are fully capable—they instead apply the broader perspective of postformal thought. Such thinking allows them to deal more effectively with the complex social worlds (discussed in Chapter 14) of which they are a part.

REVIEW AND RETHINK

REVIEW

■ Piaget's view that cognitive development peaks at the end of adolescence is now being reconsidered, as evidence mounts for postformal thought, a kind of thinking that goes beyond logic to encompass interpretive and subjective thinking.

■ According to Schaie, people pass through five stages in the way they use information: acquisitive, achieving, responsible, executive, and reintegrative.

■ New views of intelligence are emerging, including the triarchic theory and a focus on practical intelligence, which is based on experience and observation of others.

■ Creativity seems to peak during early adulthood, which may be a result of the fact that young adults view even long-standing problems as novel situations.

■ Major life events seem to contribute to cognitive growth by providing opportunities and incentives to rethink one's self and one's world.

RETHINK

■ Can you think of situations that you would deal with differently as an adult than as an adolescent? Do the differences reflect postformal thinking?

■ What might be some consequences of Schaie's stages of thought in mixed-age settings, such as the workplace?

■ If practical intelligence depends on the environment and on observations of others, how might practical intelligence differ across cultural and socioeconomic environments?

■ What does "familiarity breeds rigidity" mean? Can you think of examples of this phenomenon from your own experience?

COLLEGE: PURSUING HIGHER EDUCATION

For Enrico Vasquez, there was never any doubt: He was headed for college. Enrico, the son of a wealthy Cuban immigrant who had made a fortune in the medical supply business after fleeing Cuba five years before Enrico's birth, had had the importance of education constantly drummed into him by his family. In fact, the question was never *whether* he would go to college, but what college he would be able to get into. As a consequence, Enrico found high school to be a pressure cooker: Every grade and extracurricular activity was seen as helping—or hindering—his chances of admission to a "good" college.

***

Armando Williams' letter of acceptance to Dallas County Community College is framed on the wall of his mother's apartment. To her, the letter represents nothing short of a miracle, an answer to her prayers. Growing up in a neighborhood saturated with drugs and drive-by shootings, Armando had always been a hard worker and a "good boy," in his mother's view. But when he was growing up she never even entertained the possibility of his making it to college. To see him reach this stage in his education fills her with joy.

Whether a student's enrollment seems almost inevitable or signifies a triumph over the odds, attending college is a significant accomplishment. Although students already enrolled may feel that college attendance is nearly universal, this is not the case at all: Nationwide, only a minority of high school graduates enter college.

The Demographics of Higher Education

What kinds of students enter college? Like the population as a whole, college students are primarily white and middle class. Although nearly 40 percent of white high school graduates enter college, just 29 percent of African American and 31 percent of Hispanic graduates enter college (see Figure 13-9). Even more striking, although the absolute number of

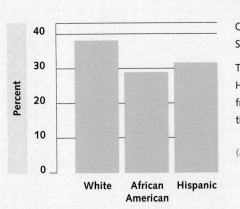

FIGURE 13-9

COLLEGE ENROLLMENT BY HIGH
SCHOOL GRADUATES

The proportion of African Americans and
Hispanics who enter college after graduating
from high school is lower than the proportion of whites.

(*Source:* U.S. Bureau of the Census, 1990a.)

minority students enrolled in college has increased, the *proportion* of the minority population that does enter college has *decreased* over the last decade—a decline that most education experts attribute to changes in the availability of financial aid.

Furthermore, the proportion of students who enter college but ultimately never graduate is substantial. Only around 40 percent of those who start college finish 4 years later with
a degree. Although about half of those who don't receive a degree in 4 years eventually do
finish, the other half never get a college degree. For minorities, the picture is even worse:
The national drop-out rate for African American college students stands at 70 percent (Minorities in Higher Education, 1995).

On the other hand, the sheer number of minority students attending college is rising
dramatically, and minority students make up an increasingly larger proportion of the college population. These trends reflect changes in the racial and ethnic composition of the
United States, and are important, because higher education remains an important way for
families to improve their economic well-being (Kates, 1995).

For instance, by the year 2000, the U.S. Department of Education projects an increase
of 13 percent in African American college attendance and 22 percent in Hispanic college
attendance over levels 10 years earlier. Over the same period, enrollment of whites is projected to rise only 6 percent (U.S. Department of Education, 1992). Already at some colleges, such as the University of California at Berkeley, whites have shifted from the
majority to the minority as what is traditionally called "minority" representation has increased significantly.

In addition to a greater proportion of minorities attending college, the proportion of
women, relative to men, is also increasing. There are now more women than men enrolled in
college, and by the year 2007, women's enrollment is expected to increase 30 percent from
the level reached in 1995, whereas men's enrollment is project to increase only 13 percent.

Why is men's enrollment increasing at a slower pace than women's? It may be that men
have more opportunities to earn money when they graduate from high school. For instance, the military, trade unions, and jobs that require physical strength may be more attractive to men, and consequently more men than women may perceive that good options
other than college are available. Furthermore, as affirmative action has become less a factor
in admissions, women often have better high school academic records than men, and they
may be admitted to college at greater rates (Dortch, 1997).

Of course, college attendance remains an important way to attain economic security for
both men and women. Just 3 percent of adults who have a college education live below the

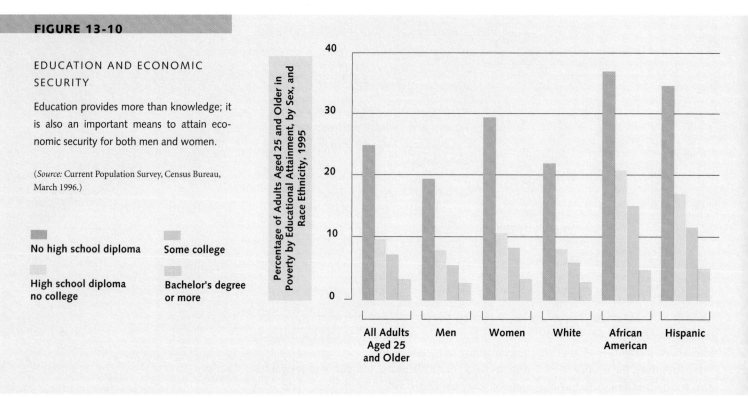

FIGURE 13-10

EDUCATION AND ECONOMIC SECURITY

Education provides more than knowledge; it is also an important means to attain economic security for both men and women.

(*Source:* Current Population Survey, Census Bureau, March 1996.)

■ No high school diploma

■ High school diploma no college

■ Some college

■ Bachelor's degree or more

poverty line. Compare that with high school dropouts: they are 10 times more likely to be living in poverty (see Figure 13-10; O'Hare, 1997).

The Changing College Student: Never Too Late to Go to College?

If the words "average college student" bring to mind an image of a 19-year-old, you should begin to rethink your view. Increasingly, students are older. In fact, more than one-third of students taking college courses for credit in the United States are 25 years old or older. The average age of community college students is 31 (U.S. Bureau of the Census, 1995; Dortch, 1997).

Why are so many older, nontraditional students taking college courses? One reason is economic. As a college degree becomes increasingly important in obtaining a job, some workers feel compelled to get the credential. Furthermore, some employers encourage or

More than one-third of students taking college courses for credit in the United States are 25 years old or older. The average age of community college students is 31.

require workers to undergo training to learn new skills or update their old ones. Finally, older students sometimes enroll in college classes simply for the joy of learning; they appreciate the opportunity for intellectual stimulation.

According to developmental psychologist Sherry Willis (1985), several broad goals underlie adults' participation in learning experiences. First, adults may be seeking to understand their own aging. As they get older, they try to figure out what is happening to them and what to expect in the future. Second, adults seek education to understand more fully the rapid technological and cultural changes that characterize modern life.

Furthermore, adult learners may be seeking a practical edge in combating obsolescence on the job. Some individuals also may be attempting to acquire new vocational skills. Finally, adult educational experiences may be seen as helpful in preparing for future retirement. As adults get older, they become increasingly concerned with shifting from a work orientation to a leisure orientation, and they may see education as a means of broadening their possibilities.

What Do College Students Learn?

The response to this question is not only "math" or "hotel management" or even "lifespan development," although that is part of the answer. Clearly, students gain a body of knowledge that may help them function more effectively in the world. However, college is more than that: It is a period of developmental growth that encompasses mastery not just of particular bodies of knowledge, but of ways of understanding the world.

For example, psychologist William Perry (1970) examined the ways in which students grew intellectually and morally during college. In comprehensive interviews with a group of students at Harvard University, he found that students entering college tended to use *dualistic thinking* in their views of the world. For instance, they reasoned that something was right, or it was wrong; people were good, or they were bad; and others were either for them, or against them.

However, as they encountered new ideas and points of view from other students and their professors, their dualistic thinking declined. Consistent with the increase in postformal thinking that we discussed earlier, students increasingly realized that issues can have more than one plausible side. Furthermore, they understood more clearly that it is possible to hold multiple perspectives on an issue. This *multiple thinking* was characterized by a shift in the way the students viewed authorities: Instead of presupposing that experts had all the answers, they began to assume that their own thinking on an issue had validity if their position was well argued and rational.

In fact, they had entered a stage in which knowledge and values were regarded as *relativistic*. Rather than seeing the world as having absolute standards and values, they argued that different societies, cultures, and individuals could have different standards and values, all of them equally valid.

Gender and College Performance

> I registered for a calculus course my first year at DePauw. Even twenty years ago I was not timid, so on the very first day I raised my hand and asked a question. I still have a vivid memory of the professor rolling his eyes, hitting his head with his hand in frustration, and announcing to everyone, "Why do they expect me to teach calculus to girls?" I never asked another question. Several weeks later I went to a football game, but I had forgotten to bring my ID. My calculus professor was at the gate checking IDs, so I went up to him and said, "I forgot my ID but you know me, I'm in your class." He looked right at me and said, "I don't remember you in my class." I couldn't believe that someone who changed my life and whom I remember to this day didn't even recognize me. (Sadker & Sadker, 1994, p. 162)

Although such incidents of blatant sexism are less likely to occur today, prejudice and discrimination directed at women are still a fact of college life. For instance, the next time you are in class, consider the gender of your classmates—and the subject matter of the class. Although men and women attend college in roughly equal proportions, there is significant variation in the classes they take. Classes in education and the social sciences, for instance, typically have a larger proportion of women than men; and classes in engineering, the physical sciences, and mathematics tend to have more men than women.

Even women who start out in mathematics, engineering, and the physical sciences are more likely than men to drop out. For instance, the attrition rate for women in such fields during the college years is two-and-a-half times greater than the rate for men. Ultimately, although white women make up 43 percent of the U.S. population, they earn just 22 percent of the bachelor of science degrees and 13 percent of the doctorates, and they hold only 10 percent of the jobs in physical science, math, and engineering.

The differences in gender distribution and attrition rates across subject areas are no accident. They reflect the powerful influence of gender stereotypes that operate throughout the world of education—and beyond. For instance, when women in their first year of college are asked to name a likely career choice, they are much less apt to choose careers that have traditionally been dominated by men, such as engineering or computer programming, and more likely to choose professions that have traditionally been populated by women, such as nursing and social work (Glick, Zion, & Nelson, 1988; CIRE, 1990).

These initial expectations about the fields that are of interest to them are reflected in students' anticipation of their entering and peak salaries once they leave college. Women expect to earn less than men, both when they start their careers and when they are at their peaks (Major & Konar, 1984; Martin, 1989; Jackson, Gardner, & Sullivan, 1992; Desmarais & Curtis, 1997). These expectations jibe with reality: On average, women earn 70 cents for every dollar that men earn. Moreover, women who are members of minority groups do even worse: African American women earn 62 cents for every dollar men make, and for Hispanic women the figure is 54 cents (U.S. Bureau of Labor Statistics, 1993).

Male and female college students also have different expectations regarding their areas of competence. For instance, one survey asked first-year college students whether they were above or below average on a variety of traits and abilities. As shown in Figure 13-11, men were more likely than women to think of themselves as above average in overall academic and mathematical ability, competitiveness, and emotional health.

Both male and female college professors treat men and women differently in their classes, even though the different treatment is largely unintentional and the professors are unaware of their actions. For instance, professors call on men in class more frequently than women, and

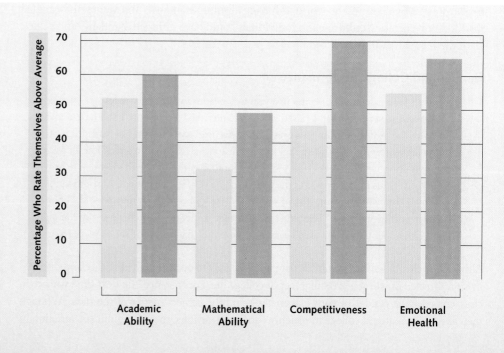

FIGURE 13-11

THE GREAT GENDER DIVIDE

During their first year of college, men, compared to women, are more apt to view themselves as above average on several spheres relevant to academic success.

(*Source:* The American Freshman: National Norms for Fall, 1990; Astin, Korn, & Berz. Higher Education Research Institute, UCLA.)

Women

Men

they make more eye contact with men than with women. Furthermore, male students are more likely than female students to receive extra help from their professors. Finally, the quality of the responses received by male and female students differs, with male students receiving more positive reinforcement for their comments than female students—exemplified by the startling illustration in Table 13-3 (Epperson, 1988; AAUW, 1992; Sadker & Sadker, 1994).

The different treatment of men and women in the college classroom has led some educators to argue in favor of single-sex colleges for women. They point to evidence that the rate of participation and ultimately the success of women in the sciences is greater for graduates of women's colleges than for graduates of coeducational institutions. Furthermore, some research suggests that women who attend same-sex colleges may show higher self-esteem than those attending coeducational colleges (Smith, 1990; Miller-Bernal, 1993).

TABLE 13-3

GENDER BIAS IN THE CLASSROOM

The course on the U.S. Constitution is required for graduation, and more than fifty students, approximately half male and half female, file in. The professor begins by asking if these are questions on next week's midterm. Several hands go up.

BERNIE: Do you have to memorize names and dates in the book? Or will the test be more general?
PROFESSOR: You do have to know those critical dates and people. Not every one but the important ones. If I were you, Bernie, I would spend time learning them. Ellen?
ELLEN: What kind of short-answer questions will there be?
PROFESSOR: All multiple choice.
ELLEN: Will we have the whole class time?
PROFESSOR: Yes, we'll have the whole class time. Anyone else?
BEN (calling out): Will there be an extra-credit question?
PROFESSOR: I hadn't planned on it. What do you think?
BEN: I really like them. They take some of the pressure off. You can also see who is doing extra work.
PROFESSOR: I'll take it under advisement. Charles?
CHARLES: How much of our final grade is this?
PROFESSOR: The midterm is 25 percent. But remember, class participation counts as well. Why don't we begin?

The professor lectures on the Constitution for twenty minutes before he asks a question about the electoral college. The electoral college is not as hot a topic as the midterm, so only four hands are raised. The professor calls on Ben.

BEN: The electoral college was created because there was a lack of faith in the people. Rather than have them vote for the president, they voted for the electors.
PROFESSOR: I like the way you think. (He smiles at Ben, and Ben smiles back.) Who could vote? (Five hands go up, five out of fifty.) Angie?
ANGIE: I don't know if this is right, but I thought only men could vote.
BEN (calling out): That was a great idea. We began going downhill when we let women vote. (Angie looks surprised but says nothing. Some of the students laugh, and so does the professor. He calls on Barbara.)
BARBARA: I think you had to be pretty wealthy, own property—
JOSH (not waiting for Barbara to finish, calls out): That's right. There was a distrust of the poor, who could upset the democracy. But if you had property, if you had something at stake, you could be trusted not to do something wild. Only property owners could be trusted.
PROFESSOR: Nice job, Josh. But why do we still have electors today? Mike?
MIKE: Tradition, I guess.
PROFESSOR: Do you think it's tradition? If you walked down the street and asked people their views of the electoral college, what would they say?
MIKE: Probably they'd be clueless. Maybe they would think that it elects the Pope. People don't know how it works.
PROFESSOR: Good, Mike. Judy, do you want to say something? (Judy's hand is at "half-mast," raised but just barely. When the professor calls her name, she looks a bit startled.)
JUDY (speaking very softly): Maybe we would need a whole new constitutional convention to change it. And once they get together to change that, they could change anything. That frightens people, doesn't it? (As Judy speaks, a number of students fidget, pass notes, and leaf through their books; a few even begin to whisper.)

(*Source:* Sadker & Sadker, 1994.)

According to some research, women who attend same-sex colleges have a higher rate of participation in classes and have higher self-esteem than women who attend coeducational institutions of higher learning.

However, the evidence is not consistent. Although it initially supported single-sex education for women, a more recent report by the American Association of University Women argues that the research evidence does not support single-sex education in terms of learning outcomes. On the other hand, the report did say that single-sex classes may nurture girls' self-esteem and motivation to learn (AAUW, 1998).

Despite the mixed research support for single-sex education, many educators continue to promote the idea that women do better in single-sex colleges, based on several lines of argument. One argument is that they receive more attention than they would in coeducational settings, where professors are affected, however inadvertently, by societal biases. In addition, women's colleges tend to have more female professors than coeducational institutions, and they thereby provide more role models for women. Finally, women attending women's colleges may receive more encouragement for participation in nontraditional subjects such as mathematics and science than those in coeducational colleges. In fact, such an explanation lies at the heart of an innovative program designed to increase women's success in nontraditional areas, as discussed in the accompanying "Directions in Development" box.

Directions in Development

Disidentification with School: How Social Stereotypes Depress the Academic Performance of Women and African Americans

Women lack ability in math and science. African Americans don't do well in academic pursuits.

So say erroneous, damaging, and yet persistent stereotypes about women and African Americans. And in the real world these stereotypes play out in vicious ways. For instance, even though boys and girls perform virtually identically on standardized math tests in elementary school and middle school, this all changes when they reach high school. At that level, and even more in college, men tend to do better in math than women. In fact, when women take college math, science, and engineering courses, they are more likely to do poorly than men who enter college with the same level of preparation and identical SAT scores. Strangely, though, this phenomenon does not hold true for other areas of the curriculum, where men and women perform at similar levels (Hyde, Fennema, & Lamon, 1990).

Analogously, when African Americans start school, their standardized test scores are only slightly lower than those of Caucasian students, and yet a 2-year gap emerges by the sixth grade. And even though more African American high school graduates are enrolling in college, the increase has not been as large as for other groups (American Council on Education, 1995-1996).

According to psychologist Claude Steele, the reason behind the declining levels of performance for both women and African Americans is the same: *academic disidentification*, a lack of personal identification with an academic domain. For women, disidentification is specific to math and science; for African Americans, it is more generalized across academic domains. In both cases, negative societal stereotypes produce a state of "stereotype threat" in which members of the group fear that their behavior will indeed confirm the stereotype (Steele, 1997).

For instance, because of the strength and pervasiveness of society's damaging stereotypes about women's math and science abilities, the performance of women seeking to achieve in nontraditional fields may be hindered as they become distracted by worries about the failure that society predicts for them. In some cases, a woman may decide that failure in a male-dominated field, because it would confirm societal stereotypes, presents such great risks that, paradoxically, the struggle to succeed is not worth the effort. In that instance, the woman may not even try very hard.

Similarly, African Americans may work under the pressure of feeling that they must disconfirm the negative stereotype regarding their academic performance. The pressure can be anxiety-provoking and threatening, and can reduce their performance below their true ability level. Ironically, stereotype threat may be most severe for better, more confident students, who have not internalized the negative stereotype to the extent of questioning their own abilities. It is these unusually good students who may be the most vulnerable to stereotype threat, and whose performance may suffer the most as a consequence (Steele, 1997).

Ultimately, women and African Americans may disidentify with the domain that presents such a threat. Rather than ignoring negative stereotypes, then, they perform less well and eventually disidentify with schooling and academic pursuits relevant to the stereotype.

In support of such reasoning, Steele and colleagues (Spencer, Steele, & Quinn, 1997) devised an experiment using a group of male and female college students and a very difficult math test. Some of the participants were told that the test typically showed gender differences, which implied that, because of their supposed lower math ability, women might experience difficulty in taking the test. However, the other participants were told that the test showed no gender differences. The implication here was that the gender stereotype was irrelevant to participants' performance. The hypothesis was that stereotype threat would be minimized in this condition.

The results fully supported the stereotype threat hypothesis. When women thought the test showed a gender difference, they scored considerably worse than men taking the same test. But when the test was portrayed as being typically gender-neutral, there was no gender difference: Men and women performed virtually the same (see Figure 13-12; Spencer, Quinn, & Steele, 1997).

In short, the evidence from this study, as well as from other experiments, clearly suggests that women are vulnerable to expectations regarding their future success, whether the expectations come from societal stereotypes or from information about the prior performance of women on similar tasks. Other research yields similar results for African Americans: When racial stereotypes are made salient, the performance of African American students is depressed (Steele & Aronson, 1995).

Although stereotype threat is clearly a significant problem, it can be overcome. For instance, Steele and colleagues devised a program for African American students at the University of Michigan who, as a group, had tended to fall further behind similarly qualified white students the further they progressed through their college careers. This held true even for African American students who had entered with stellar standardized test scores. In the program, students were told that their intellectual potential had been recognized by the university and that they would be participating in a special transition-to-college program. The program was explicitly nonremedial; it was presented in the context of providing a challenge to participants. All these characteristics were designed to help minimize the threat of negative group stereotypes.

The program was successful: Participants did not show the typical pattern of underperformance relative to white students and in fact received significantly better grades than their counterparts who did not participate in the program. In short, stereotype threat was reduced, and the students could achieve to their fullest potential.

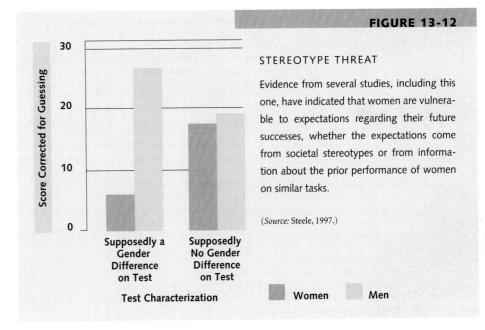

FIGURE 13-12

STEREOTYPE THREAT

Evidence from several studies, including this one, have indicated that women are vulnerable to expectations regarding their future successes, whether the expectations come from societal stereotypes or from information about the prior performance of women on similar tasks.

(*Source:* Steele, 1997.)

Dropping Out of College

Not everyone who enters colleges completes it. In fact, around half of all students who start college never receive a degree. Why is the college dropout rate so high? There are several reasons. One has to do with finances: Given the high cost of college, many students are unable to afford the continued expense. Other people leave college because of changes in their life situations, such as marriage, the birth of a child, or the death of a parent.

first-year adjustment reaction *a cluster of psychological symptoms relating to the college experience suffered by first-year college students*

Academic difficulties also may play a role. Some students simply find that they are not successful in their studies, and they are either forced by academic authorities to drop out or they leave on their own. However, in most cases students who drop out are not in academic jeopardy (Rotenberg & Morrison, 1993).

Dropping out is not always a step backward on a person's life path. In some cases, it gives people breathing room to reassess their goals. For instance, students who view the college experience as simply marking time until they can get on with their "real" lives by earning a living can sometimes benefit from a period of full-time work. During the hiatus from college, they often get a different perspective on the realities of both work and school. Other individuals simply benefit by having some time off from school in which to mature psychologically.

On the other hand, college students who drop out—intending to return one day, but never making it back because they become enmeshed in the nitty-gritty of everyday life—can experience real difficulties. They may become riveted as young adults to undesirable, low-paying jobs for which they are intellectually overqualified. A college education becomes a lost opportunity.

College Adjustment: Reacting to the Demands of College Life

When you began college, did you feel depressed, lonely, anxious, and withdrawn from others? If you did, you weren't alone. Many students, particularly those who are recent high school graduates and who are living away from home for the first time, experience difficulties in adjustment during their first year in college. The **first-year adjustment reaction** is a cluster of psychological symptoms relating to the college experience. Although any first-year student may suffer from one or more of the symptoms of first-year adjustment reaction, it is particularly likely to occur among students who have been unusually successful, either academically or socially, in high school. When they begin college, their sudden change in status may cause them distress.

Most often, first-year adjustment reaction passes as students make friends, experience academic success, and integrate themselves into campus life. in other cases, though, the problems remain and may fester, leading to more serious psychological difficulties.

Several other problems are common to college students (Duke & Nowicki, 1979). As Table 13-4 shows, male students are most likely to be concerned with their grades, social lives, and vocational decisions. In contrast, female students are concerned most with what to do with their lives, relationships, and the strain of too much work.

How prevalent are these concerns? Surveys find that almost half of college students report having at least one significant psychological issue, and certain groups of students show par-

The Informed Consumer of Development

When Do College Students Need Professional Help with Their Problems?

A college friend comes to you and says that she has been feeling depressed and unhappy and can't seem to shake the feeling. She doesn't know what to do and thinks that she may need professional help. How do you answer her?

Although there are no hard-and-fast rules, several signals can be interpreted to determine whether professional help is warranted. Among them (Engler & Goleman, 1992):

- psychological distress that lingers and interferes with a person's sense of well-being and ability to function
- feelings that one is unable to cope effectively with the stress
- hopeless or depressed feelings, with no apparent reason
- the inability to build close relationships with others
- physical symptoms that have no apparent underlying cause

If some of these signals are present, discussions with some kind of help-provider—such as a counseling psychologist, clinical psychologist, or other mental health worker—are warranted. (College students can find an appropriate provider by starting with their campus medical center; others can turn to their personal physicians or to local boards of health for referrals.)

TABLE 13-4

COLLEGE STUDENTS' PROBLEMS

Among the most prevalent problems of college students are the following:

For male students:	*For female students:*
Grades	What to do with their lives
Social life	Developing sexual and emotional relationships
Vocational decisions	Strain from too much work
The future	Grades
Sexual relationships	Adjustment
Peer pressures	Gaining independence
Adjusting to a new environment	Identity
Leaving family for the fist time	Pressure from parents
Competition	Peer pressures
Depression	Morals

(*Source:* Wechsler, Rohman, & Solomon, 1981.)

ticular problems. For example, overweight students report more psychological concerns, and minority women report having a higher frequency of problems relating to motivation than white women (Wechsler, Rohman, & Solomon, 1981; American Council on Education, 1995).

REVIEW AND RETHINK

REVIEW

■ College enrollment differs across racial and ethnic lines, with a larger proportion of white high school graduates attending college than African American or Hispanic American graduates.

■ The average age of college students is steadily increasing as more adults return to college after spending time in the workforce.

■ In college, students learn not only a body of knowledge, but also a way of understanding the world that generally accepts more viewpoints and sees values in relativistic terms.

■ Gender differences in treatment and expectations cause men and women to make different choices and engage in different behaviors in college. A similar situation often confronts minority students and presents barriers to their achievement.

■ The phenomena of academic disidentification and stereotype threat help explain how negative stereotypes work to lower the performance of women and African Americans in certain academic domains.

RETHINK

■ What are some advantages and disadvantages of multiple thinking and a relativistic view of values?

■ Some students are said to "disidentify" with academic success by downgrading its importance. Can you think of other situations in which people manifest this behavior?

■ Why do college professors behave differently toward male and female students? What factors contribute to this phenomenon? Can this situation be changed?

■ Are same-sex colleges the best way to address the problem of stereotyping and low expectations for women students? Why or why not?

LOOKING BACK

■ **How does the body develop during early adulthood, and to what risks are young adults exposed?**

- The body and the senses generally reach their peak in early adulthood. Health risks are minimal, with accidents presenting the greatest risk of death followed by AIDS. In the United States, violence is a significant cause of death, particularly among nonwhite segments of the population.

- Many young adults begin to put on weight because they fail to change poor eating habits developed earlier, and the percentage of obese adults increases with every year of aging. Obesity has both biological and environmental causes, and there is evidence that obese people are overly sensitive to external eating cues and insensitive to internal hunger cues, and that obese people may have higher weight set points than others finding it especially difficult to lose weight and keep it off.

- People with physical disabilities face physical and material difficulties as well as psychological difficulties, including prejudice and stereotyping.

■ **What are the effects of stress and what can be done about it?**

- Moderate, occasional stress is biologically healthy, but long exposure to stressors produces damaging physical and psychosomatic effects. In reacting to potentially stressful situations, people pass through primary appraisal of the situation itself, and secondary appraisal of their own coping abilities.

- People cope with stress in a number of ways, including problem-focused coping, emotion-focused coping, and reliance on social support from others.

■ **Does cognitive development continue in young adulthood?**

- According to Piaget, cognitive development reaches its peak by the end of adolescence with the formal operations stage, and thinking remains qualitatively unchanged throughout adulthood. Other theorists find increasing evidence of postformal thought, which goes beyond formal logic to produce more flexible and subjective thinking that takes account of real-world complexity and yields subtler answers than those found during adolescence.

- Psychologist K. Warner Schaie suggests that the development of thinking follows a set pattern of stages: the acquisitive stage, the achieving stage, the responsible stage, the executive stage, and the reintegrative stage.

■ **How is intelligence defined today, and what causes cognitive growth in young adults?**

- Traditional views that equated IQ with intelligence are being questioned. According to Sternberg's triarchic theory, intelligence is made up of componential, experiential, and contextual components. Practical intelligence seems to be related most closely with career success and to underlie social competence and physical and emotional health.

- Important life events, such as births and deaths, seem to contribute to cognitive growth by generating new insights into the self and revised views of the world.

■ **Who attends college today, and how is the college population changing?**

- The profile of the U.S. college student in the United States has been changing, with many students beyond the traditional 19-to-22-year-old age range. Many older students attend college for personal understanding and improvement, career advance-

TABLE 14-1

THE DEVELOPMENT TASKS OF ADULTHOOD

Adulthood (Ages 20–40)	Middle Adulthood (Ages 40–60)	Late Adulthood (Ages 60+)
1. Psychological separation from parents.	1. Dealing with body changes or illness and altered body image.	1. Maintaining physical health.
2. Accepting responsibility for one's own body.	2. Adjusting to middle-life changes in sexuality.	2. Adapting to physical infirmities or permanent impairment.
3. Becoming aware of one's personal history and time limitation.	3. Accepting the passage of time.	3. Using time in gratifying ways.
4. Integrating sexual experience (homosexual or heterosexual).	4. Adjusting to aging.	4. Adapting to losses of partner and friends.
5. Developing a capacity for intimacy with a partner.	5. Living through illness and death of parents and contemporaries.	5. Remaining oriented to present and future, not preoccupied with the past.
6. Deciding whether to have children.	6. Dealing with realities of death.	6. Forming new emotional ties.
7. Having and relating to children.	7. Redefining relationship to spouse or partner.	7. Reversing roles of children and grandchildren (as caretakers).
8. Establishing adult relationships with parents.	8. Deepening relations with grown children or grandchildren.	8. Seeking and maintaining social contacts: companionship vs. isolation and loneliness.
9. Acquiring marketable skills.	9. Maintaining long-standing friendships and creating new ones.	9. Attending to sexual needs and (changing) expressions.
10. Choosing a career.	10. Consolidating work identity.	10. Continuing meaningful work and play (satisfying use of time).
11. Using money to further development.	11. Transmitting skills and values to the young.	11. Using financial resources wisely, for self and others.
12. Assuming a social role.	12. Allocating financial resources effectively.	12. Integrating retirement into new lifestyle.
13. Adapting ethical and spiritual values.	13. Accepting social responsibility.	
	14. Accepting social change.	

(*Source:* Colarusso & Nemiroff, 1981.)

FORGING RELATIONSHIPS: LIKING AND LOVING

Asia Kaia Linn, whose parents chose her name while looking through a world atlas, met Chris Applebaum about six years ago at Hampshire College in Massachusetts and fell in love with him one Saturday night while they were dancing.

Although many women might swoon over a guy with perfect hair and fluid dance steps, it was his silly haircut and overall lack of coordination that delighted her. "He's definitely a funny dancer, and he spun me around and we were just being goofy," Ms. Linn recalled. "I realized how much fun we were having, and I thought this is ridiculous and fabulous and I love him." (Brady, 1995, p. 47)

Asia followed her first instincts: Ultimately, she and Chris were married in an unconventional wedding ceremony at an art gallery, with guests wearing a psychedelic melange of clothes, and a ring-bearer delivering the wedding ring by steering a remote-control truck down the aisle of the gallery.

Not everyone falls in love quite as easily as Asia. For some, the road to love is tortuous, meandering through soured relationships and fallen dreams; for others, it is a road never taken. For some, love leads to marriage and a life befitting society's storybook view of home, children, and long years together as a couple. For many, it leads to a less happy ending, prematurely concluding in divorce and custody battles.

Intimacy and the formation of relationships are major considerations during early adulthood. In fact, to theorists such as Erik Erikson, the search for intimacy represents *the* crucial issue of the period.

Chris Applebaum and Asia Linn

Seeking Intimacy: Erikson's View of Young Adulthood

Erik Erikson regards young adulthood as the time of the **intimacy-versus-isolation stage** (Douvan, 1997). As we first noted in Chapter 12 (see Table 12-1), the intimacy-versus-isolation stage spans the period of postadolescence into the early 30s. During this period, the focus is on developing close, intimate relationships with others.

To Erikson, intimacy comprises several aspects. One is a degree of selflessness, involving the sacrifice of one's own needs to those of another. A further component involves sexuality, the experience of a kind of joint pleasure from focusing not just on one's own gratification but also on that of one's partner. Finally, there is deep devotion, marked by efforts to fuse one's identity with the identity of a partner.

Erikson suggests that those who experience difficulties during this stage are often lonely and isolated, and fearful of relationships with others. Their difficulties may stem from an earlier failure to develop a strong identity. In contrast, young adults who successfully resolve the crisis of the stage are able to form intimate relationships with others on a physical, intellectual, and emotional level.

Although Erikson's approach has been influential, some aspects of his theory trouble today's developmentalists. For instance, Erikson's view of healthy intimacy was limited to adult heterosexuality, the goal of which was to produce children. Consequently, homosexual partnerships, couples who were childless by choice, and other relationships that deviated from what Erikson saw as the ideal were thought of as less than satisfactory. Furthermore, Erikson focused more on men's development than on women's, greatly limiting the applicability of his theory.

Still, Erikson's work has been influential historically because of its emphasis on examining the continued growth and development of personality throughout the life span. Furthermore, it inspired other developmentalists to consider psychosocial growth during young adulthood.

Falling in Love: When Liking Turns to Loving

intimacy-versus-isolation stage ac-cording to Erikson, the period of postadolescence into the early 30s that focuses on developing close relationships with others

After a few chance encounters at the laundromat where they wash their clothes each week, Shoshana and Jerry begin to talk with one another. They find they have a lot in common, and they begin to look forward to what are now semiplanned meetings. After several weeks, they go out on their first official date and discover that they are well suited to each other.

If such a pattern seems predictable, it is: Most relationships develop in a fairly similar way, following a surprisingly regular progression (Burgess & Huston, 1979; Berscheid, 1985):

■ Two people interact with each other more often and for longer periods of time. Furthermore, the range of settings increases.

■ The two people increasingly seek out each other's company.

■ They open up to each other more and more, disclosing more intimate information about themselves. They begin to share physical intimacies.

■ They are more willing to share both positive and negative feelings, and they may offer criticism in addition to praise.

■ They begin to agree on the goals they hold for the relationship.

■ Their reactions to situations become more similar.

■ They begin to feel that their own psychological well-being is tied to the success of the relationship, viewing it as unique, irreplaceable, and cherished.

■ Finally, their definition of themselves and their behavior changes: They begin to see themselves and act as a couple, rather than as two separate individuals.

The evolution of a relationship can be seen in terms of what psychologist Bernard Murstein calls stimulus-value-role theory (Murstein, 1976, 1986, 1987). According to **stimulus-value-role (SVR) theory**, relationships proceed in a fixed order of three stages.

In the first stage, the *stimulus stage*, relationships are built on surface, physical characteristics such as the way a person looks. Usually, this represents just the initial encounter. The second stage, the *value stage*, usually occurs between the second and the seventh encounter. In the value stage, the relationship is characterized by increasing similarity of values and beliefs. Finally, in the third stage, the *role stage*, the relationship is built on specific roles played by the participants. For instance, the couple may define themselves as boyfriend–girlfriend or husband–wife.

Although stimulus, value, and role factors dominate at particular stages, they are also influential at other junctures in the developing relationship. For instance, consider Figure 14-1, which illustrates the course of a typical relationship.

Of course, not every relationship follows a similar pattern, and this has led to criticism of SVR theory (Gupta & Singh, 1982; Sternberg, 1986). For instance, there seems to be no

stimulus-value-role (SVR) theory   the theory that relationships proceed in a fixed order of three stages: stimulus, value, and role

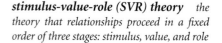

FIGURE 14-1

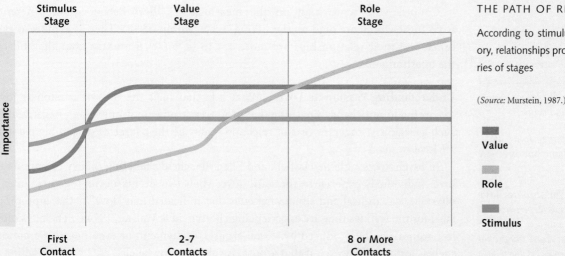

THE PATH OF RELATIONSHIPS

According to stimulus-value-role (SVR) theory, relationships proceed through a fixed series of stages

(*Source*: Murstein, 1987.)

■ Value

■ Role

■ Stimulus

logical reason why value factors could not predominate early in a relationship, rather than stimulus factors. Consequently, additional approaches have been devised to explain the course of relationship development.

Passionate and Companionate Love: The Two Faces of Love

Is "love" just a lot of "liking"? Most developmental psychologists would answer negatively; love differs not only quantitatively from liking, but also qualitatively. For example, love, at least in its early stages, involves relatively intense physiological arousal, an all-encompassing interest in another individual, recurrent fantasies about the other individual, and rapid swings of emotion (Lamm & Wiesman, 1997). As distinct from liking, love includes elements of closeness, passion, and exclusivity (Walster & Walster, 1978; Hendrick & Hendrick, 1989).

Not all love is the same, however. We don't love our mothers the same way we love girlfriends or boyfriends, brothers or sisters, or lifelong friends. What distinguishes these different types of love?

Passionate (or romantic) love is a state of powerful absorption in someone. It includes intense physiological interest and arousal, and caring for another's needs. In comparison, **companionate love** is the strong affection that we have for those with whom our lives are deeply involved (Hatfield, 1988; Hecht, Marston, & Larkey, 1994; Lamm & Wiesman, 1997).

Distinguishing Between Passionate and Companionate Love.   Although passionate and companionate love clearly are different, in practice drawing the distinction is not always easy. One approach to determining when we love someone, as opposed to merely liking her or him, is through the use of questionnaires. For instance, psychologist Zick Rubin devised a series of questions to measure whether someone is liked or loved (Rubin, 1973). The love questionnaire consists of items like these:

- I feel that I can confide in _____ about virtually everything.
- I would do almost anything for _____.
- I feel responsible for _____'s well-being.

On the other hand, the questions designed to measure liking include these:

- I think that _____ is unusually well adjusted.
- I think that _____ is one of those people who quickly wins respect.
- _____ is one of the most likable people I know.

Couples who score high on the measures of "love" behave quite differently from those who score high on the "liking" scale (Rubin, 1973). They gaze more at each other, and their relationships are more apt to be intact 6 months after they fill out the questionnaire.

passionate (or romantic) love   a state of powerful absorption in someone

companionate love   the strong affection for those with whom our lives are deeply involved

labeling theory of passionate love   the theory that individuals experience romantic love when two events occur together: intense physiological arousal and situational cues suggesting that the arousal is due to love

Understanding Passionate Love.   What is it that fuels the fires of passionate love? According to one theory, anything that produces strong emotions—even negative ones such as jealousy, anger, or fear of rejection—may be the source of deepening passionate love.

In psychologists Elaine Hatfield and Ellen Berscheid's **labeling theory of passionate love**, individuals experience romantic love when two events occur together: intense physiological arousal and situational cues that indicated that "love" is the appropriate label for the feelings they are experiencing (Berscheid & Walster, 1974a). The physiological arousal can be produced by sexual arousal, excitement, or even negative emotions such as jealousy. However, if that arousal is subsequently labeled as "I must be falling in love" or "she makes my heart flutter" or "he really turns me on," then the experience is seen as due to passionate love.

The theory is particularly useful in explaining why people may feel deepened love even when they experience continual rejection or hurt from their assumed lover. It suggests that such negative emotions can produce strong physiological arousal. If this arousal is interpreted as being caused by "love," then people may decide that they are even more in love than they were before they experienced such negative emotions.

But why should people label an emotional experience as "love" when there are so many possible alternatives? One answer is that in Western cultures, passionate love is seen as possible, acceptable, desirable—an experience to be sought. The virtues of passion are extolled in love ballads, commercials, television shows, and film. Consequently, young adults are primed and ready to experience love in their lives (Dion & Dion, 1988; Hatfield & Rapson, 1993).

However, this is not the way it is in every culture. For instance, in many cultures passionate, romantic love is a foreign concept. Marriages are arranged in some societies, based on economic and status considerations. Even in Western cultures, the concept of love is of relatively recent origin. For instance, the notion that couples need to be in love was not "invented" until the Middle Ages, when social philosophers first suggested that love ought to be a requirement for marriage. Their goal in making such a proposal: to provide an alternative to the raw sexual desire that had served as the primary basis for marriage (Lewis, 1958; Xiaohe & Whyte, 1990).

Sternberg's Triangular Theory: The Three Faces of Love

To psychologist Robert Sternberg, love is more complex than a simple division into passionate and companionate types. He suggests instead that love is made up of three components: intimacy, passion, and decision/commitment. The **intimacy component** encompasses feelings of closeness, affection, and connectedness. The **passion component** comprises the motivational drives relating to sex, physical closeness, and romance. This component is exemplified by intense, physiologically arousing feelings of attraction. Finally, the third aspect of love, the **decision/commitment component**, embodies both the initial cognition that one loves another person and the longer-term determination to maintain that love (Sternberg, 1986, 1988, 1997b).

By jointly considering whether each of the three components is either present or missing from a relationship, eight unique combinations of love can be formed (see Table 14-2).

intimacy component the component of love that encompasses feelings of closeness, affection, and connectedness

passion component the component of love that comprises the motivational drives relating to sex, physical closeness, and romance

decision/commitment component the third aspect of love that embodies both the initial cognition that one loves another person and the longer-term determination to maintain that love

TABLE 14-2

THE COMBINATIONS OF LOVE

	COMPONENT*		
	Intimacy	Passion	Decision/Commitment
Nonlove	−	−	−
Liking	+	−	−
Infatuated love	−	+	−
Empty love	−	−	+
Romantic love	+	+	−
Companionate love	+	−	+
Fatuous love	−	+	+
Consummate love	+	+	+

*+ = component present; − = component absent.
(*Source:* Sternberg, 1986.)

In part, love involves companionship and mutual enjoyment of various activities.

For instance, *nonlove* refers to people who have only the most casual of relationships; it consists of the absence of the three components of intimacy, passion, and decision/commitment. *Liking* develops when only intimacy is present; *infatuated love* exists when only passion is felt; and *empty love* exists when only decision/commitment is present.

Other types of love are more complex. For instance, *romantic love* occurs when intimacy and passion are present, and *companionate love* when intimacy and decision/commitment occur jointly. When a couple experience romantic love, they are drawn together physically and emotionally, but they do not necessarily view the relationship as lasting. Companionate love, on the other hand, may occur in long-lasting relationships in which physical passion has taken a backseat.

FIGURE 14-2

THE SHAPE OF LOVE

Over the course of a relationship, the three aspects of love—intimacy, passion, and decision/commitment—vary in strength.

(*Source:* Sternberg, 1986.)

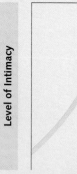
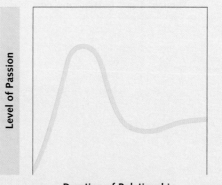
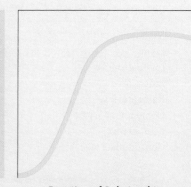

Fatuous love exists when passion and decision/commitment, without intimacy, are present. Fatuous love is a kind of mindless loving, in which there is no emotional bond between the partners.

Finally, the eighth kind of love is *consummate love.* In consummate love, all three components of love are present. Although we might assume that consummate love represents the "ideal" love, such a view may well be mistaken. Many long-lasting and entirely satisfactory relationships are based on types of love other than consummate love. Furthermore, the type of love that predominates in a relationship varies over time. As shown Figure 14-2, in strong, loving relationships the level of decision/commitment peaks and remains fairly stable. By contrast, passion tends to peak early in a relationship, but then declines and levels off. Intimacy also increases fairly rapidly, but can continue to grow over time.

Sternberg's triangular theory of love emphasizes both the complexity of love and its dynamic, evolving quality. As people and relationships develop and change over time, so does their love.

Choosing a Partner: Recognizing Mr. or Ms. Right

For many young adults, the search for a partner is a major pursuit during early adulthood. Certainly society offers a great deal of advice on how to succeed in this endeavor, as a glance at the array of magazines at any supermarket checkout counter confirms. Despite all the counsel, however, the road to identifying an individual to share one's life is not always easy.

Seeking a Partner: Is Love the Only Thing That Matters?   Most people have no hesitation in articulating that the major factor in choosing a spouse is love. Most people in the United States, that is: If we ask people in other societies, love becomes a secondary consideration. For instance, consider the results of a survey, presented in Figure 14-3, in which college students were asked if they would marry someone they did not love. Hardly anyone in the United States, Japan, or Brazil would consider it. On the other hand, a goodly proportion of college students in Pakistan and India would find it acceptable to marry without love (Levine, 1993).

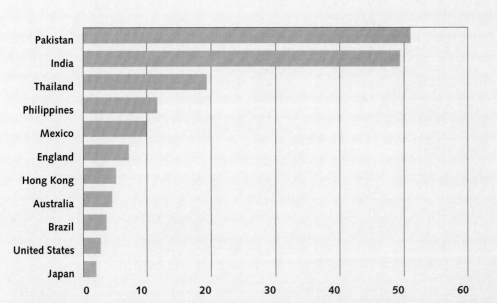

FIGURE 14-3

MARRY WITHOUT LOVE?

The percentage of people saying that they would marry someone even if they did not love that individual varies significantly from one country to another.

(*Source:* Adapted from Levine, 1993.)

If love is not the only important factor, what else matters? The characteristics differ considerably from one culture to another (see Table 14-3). For instance, a survey of nearly 10,000 people from around the world found that although people in the United States believed that love and mutual attraction were the primary characteristics, in China men ranked good health most important and women rated emotional stability and maturity most critical. In contrast, in South Africa men from a Zulu background rated emotional stability first, and women rated dependable character of greatest concern (Buss et al., 1990).

On the other hand, there are commonalities across cultures. For instance, love and mutual attraction, even if not at the top of a specific culture's list, were relatively highly desired across all cultures. Furthermore, traits such as dependability, emotional stability, pleasing disposition, and intelligence were highly valued almost universally.

Certain gender differences in the preferred characteristics of a mate were similar across cultures—findings that have been confirmed by other surveys (e.g., Sprecher, Sullivan, & Hatfield, 1994). Men, more than women, prefer a potential marriage partner who is physically attractive. In contrast, women, more than men, prefer a potential spouse who is ambitious and industrious.

One explanation for cross-cultural similarities in gender differences rests on evolutionary factors. According to psychologist David Buss and colleagues (Buss et al., 1990), it is advantageous for human beings, as a species, to seek out certain characteristics in order to maximize the availability of beneficial genes. He argues that males in particular are genetically programmed to seek out mates with traits indicative of high reproductive capacity. Consequently, physically attractive, younger women might be more desirable because they are more capable of having children over a longer time period.

TABLE 14-3

MOST DESIRED CHARACTERISTICS IN A MARRIAGE PARTNER

	China		South African (Zulu)		United States	
	Males	Females	Males	Females	Males	Females
Mutual Attraction—Love	4	8	10	5	1	1
Emotional Stability and Maturity	5	1	1	2	2	2
Dependable Character	6	7	3	1	3	3
Pleasing Disposition	13	16	4	3	4	4
Education and Intelligence	8	4	6	6	5	5
Good health	1	3	5	4	6	9
Sociability	12	9	11	8	8	8
Desire for Home and Children	2	2	9	9	9	7
Refinement, Neatness	7	10	7	10	10	12
Ambition and Industriousness	10	5	8	7	11	6
Good Looks	11	15	14	16	7	13
Similar Education	15	12	12	12	12	10
Good Financial Prospects	16	14	18	13	16	11
Good Cook and Housekeeper	9	11	2	15	13	16
Favorable Social Status or Rating	14	13	17	14	14	14
Similar Religious Background	18	18	16	11	15	15
Chastity (no prior sexual intercourse)	3	6	13	18	17	18
Similar Political Background	17	17	15	17	18	17

Note: numbers indicate rank ordering of characteristics.
(*Source:* Buss et al., 1990.)

In contrast, women are genetically programmed to seek out men who have the potential to provide scarce resources in order to increase the likelihood that their offspring will survive. Consequently, they are attracted to mates who offer the highest potential of providing economic well-being (Feingold, 1992; Walter, 1997).

Although the evolutionary explanation makes logical sense, not everyone agrees. For instance, critics suggest that the similarities across cultures relating to different gender preferences may simply reflect similar patterns of gender stereotyping that have nothing to do with evolution. Such critics point out that, although some differences in what men and women prefer are consistent across cultures, there are several inconsistencies as well.

Filtering Models: Sifting Out a Spouse.   Although surveys assist in identifying the characteristics that are highly valued in a potential spouse, they are less helpful in determining how a specific individual is chosen as a partner. One approach that helps explain this is the filtering model developed by psychologists Louis Janda and Karen Klenke-Hamel (1980). They suggest that people seeking a mate screen potential candidates through successively finer-grained filters, just as we sift flour to remove undesirable material (see Figure 14-4).

The model assumes that people first filter for factors relating to broad determinants of attractiveness. Once these early screens have done their work, more sophisticated types of screening are used. The end result is a choice based on compatibility between the two individuals.

What determines compatibility? Pleasing personality characteristics are not the only factors; several cultural factors also play an important role. For instance, people often marry according to the principle of homogamy. **Homogamy** is the tendency to marry someone who is similar in age, race, education, religion, and other basic demographic characteristics. Homogamy is a dominant standard in most marriages in the United States (Kalmijn, 1991; Surra, 1991).

The marriage gradient represents another societal standard that determines who marries whom. The **marriage gradient** is the tendency for men to marry women who are

homogamy   the tendency to marry someone who is similar in age, race, education, religion, and other basic demographic characteristics

marriage gradient   the tendency for men to marry women who are slightly younger, smaller, and lower in status, and women to marry men who are slightly older, larger, and higher in status

---

FIGURE 14-4

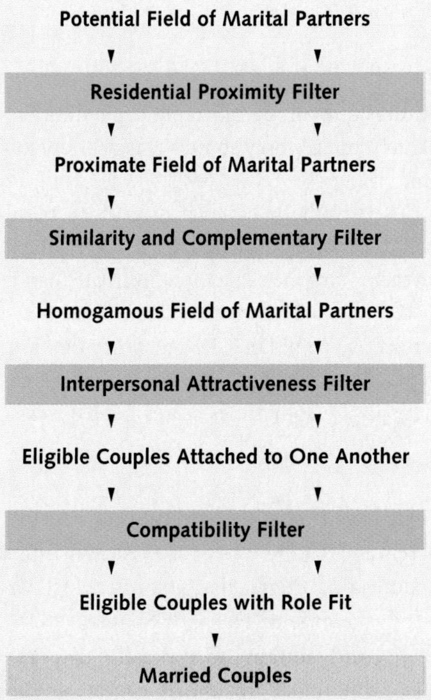

Potential Field of Marital Partners
↓   ↓
Residential Proximity Filter
↓   ↓
Proximate Field of Marital Partners
↓   ↓
Similarity and Complementary Filter
↓   ↓
Homogamous Field of Marital Partners
↓   ↓
Interpersonal Attractiveness Filter
↓   ↓
Eligible Couples Attached to One Another
↓   ↓
Compatibility Filter
↓   ↓
Eligible Couples with Role Fit
↓
Married Couples

FILTERING POTENTIAL MARRIAGE PARTNERS

According to one approach, we screen potential mates through successively finer-grained filters to settle on an appropriate spouse.

(*Source:* Adapted from Janda & Klenke-Hamel, 1980.)

slightly younger, smaller, and lower in status, and women to marry men who are slightly older, larger, and higher in status (Bernard, 1982).

The marriage gradient, which has a powerful influence on marriage in the United States, has important, and insidious, effects on partner choice. For one thing, it limits the number of potential mates for women, especially as they age, and allows men a wider choice. Furthermore, some men do not marry because they cannot find women of low enough status to meet the demands of the gradient, or cannot find women of the same or higher status who are willing to accept them as mates. Consequently, they are, in the words of sociologist Jessie Bernard (1982), "bottom of the barrel" men. On the other hand, some women will be unable to marry because they are higher in status than anyone in the available pool of men—"cream of the crop" women, in Bernard's words.

The marriage gradient makes finding a spouse particularly difficult for well-educated African American women. Fewer African American men attend college than African American women, making the potential pool of men who are suitable—as defined by society—relatively small. Consequently, relative to women of other races, African American women are more apt to marry men who are less educated than they are—or not marry at all (Taylor et al., 1991; Tucker & Mitchell-Kernan, 1995; Kiecolt & Fossett, 1997).

Attachment Styles and Romantic Relationships: Do Adult Loving Styles Reflect Attachment in Infancy?

Is the nature of attachment that people display during infancy reflected in their adult romantic relationships?

Increasing evidence suggests that it very well may be. As you may recall, attachment refers to the positive emotional bond that develops between a child and a particular individual (see Chapter 6). Infants generally are seen as falling into three attachment categories: *securely attached* (children with a healthy, positive, trusting relationship); *avoidant* (infants who are relatively indifferent to caregivers and who avoid interactions with them); and *anxious-ambivalent* (infants who show great distress when separated from a caregiver, but who appear angry upon the caregiver's return).

According to psychologist Phillip Shaver and colleagues, the influence of infants' attachment styles continues into adulthood and affects their romantic relationships (Hazan & Shaver, 1987; Shaver, Hazan, & Bradshaw, 1988; Shaver, 1994; Koski & Shaver, 1997). For instance, consider the following statements:

(1) I find it relatively easy to get close to others and am comfortable depending on them and having them depend on me. I don't often worry about being abandoned or about someone getting too close to me.

(2) I am somewhat uncomfortable being close to others; I find it difficult to trust them completely, difficult to allow myself to depend on them. I am nervous when anyone gets too close, and often love partners want me to be more intimate than I feel comfortable being.

(3) I find that others are reluctant to get as close as I would like. I often worry that my partner doesn't really love me or won't want to stay with me. I want to merge completely with another person, and this desire sometimes scares people away. (Shaver, Hazan, & Bradshaw, 1988)

According to Shaver's research, agreement with the first statement reflects a secure attachment style. Adults who agree with this statement readily enter into relationships and feel happy and confident about the future success of their relationships. Most young adults—just over half—display the secure style of attachment (Hazan & Shaver, 1987).

In contrast, adults who agree with the second statement typically display the avoidant attachment style. These individuals, who make up about a quarter of the population, tend to be less invested in relationships, have higher break-up rates, and often feel lonely.

Finally, agreement with the third category is reflective of an anxious-ambivalent style. Adults with an anxious-ambivalent style have a tendency to become overly invested in relationships, have repeated break-ups with the same partner, and have relatively low self-esteem. Around 20 percent of adults fall into this category (Simpson, 1990).

Recent research indicates that attachment style is also related to caregiving that adults give to their romantic partners. For instance, secure adults tend to provide sensitive caregiving, whereas anxious adults are more likely to provide compulsive, intrusive caregiving to partners who require assistance (Shaver, 1994; Feeney & Noller, 1996).

It seems clear that there are continuities between infants' attachment styles and their behavior as adults. People who are having difficulty in relationships might well look back to their infancy to identify the root of their problem (Brennan & Shaver, 1995).

Developmental Diversity

Gay and Lesbian Relationships: Men with Men and Women with Women

Most research conducted by developmental psychologists has examined heterosexual relationships, but an increasing number of studies have looked at relationships involving gay men and those involving lesbian women. The findings suggest that, compared to relationships between heterosexuals, there are both similarities and differences.

For example, gay men describe successful relationships in ways that are similar to heterosexual couples' descriptions. For example, successful relationships involve greater appreciation for the partner and the couple as a whole, less conflict, and more positive feelings toward the partner. Similarly, lesbian women in a relationship show high levels of attachment, caring, intimacy, affection, and respect (Peplau, Padesky, & Hamilton, 1982; Brehm, 1992).

Furthermore, the age preferences expressed in the marriage gradient for heterosexuals also extend to partner preferences for homosexual men. Like heterosexual men, homosexual men prefer partners who are the same age or younger. On the other hand, the age preferences of homosexual women fall somewhere between those of heterosexual women and heterosexual men (Kenrick et al., 1995).

Still, there are differences among gay, lesbian, and heterosexual couples. For example, lesbian women place greater emphasis than gay men on the importance of equality in their ideal relationships. Furthermore, labor is divided more evenly in homosexual households than in heterosexual households. Although gay and lesbian couples who adopt children become

Homosexuals value similar attributes in their partners as do heterosexuals, and most seek to form loving, long-term, and meaningful relationships.

more specialized in their household chores, working out a less egalitarian arrangement, the same shift typically occurs in heterosexual couples upon the arrival of children (Deutsch, Lussier, & Servis, 1993; Kurdek, 1993, 1994, 1995; Patterson, 1992, 1994; Flaks et al., 1995).

Despite the stereotype that gay males, in particular, find it difficult to form relationships and are interested in only sexual alliances, the reality is different. Most gays and lesbians seek loving, long-term, and meaningful relationships that differ little qualitatively from those desired by heterosexuals (Caldwell & Peplau, 1984; Peplau & Cochran, 1990; Kurdek, 1991, 1992).

REVIEW AND RETHINK

REVIEW

- According to Erikson, young adults are facing the intimacy-versus-isolation conflict, which, if resolved successfully, enables intimate physical, intellectual, and emotional relationships.

- The course of relationships typically follows a pattern of increasing interaction, intimacy, and redefinition. SVR theory regards relationships as passing successively though stimulus, value, and role stages.

- According to the labeling theory of passionate love, people experience love when intense physiological arousal is accompanied by situational cues that the experience should be labeled "love."

- Types of love include passionate and companionate love. Sternberg's triangular theory identifies three basic components (intimacy, passion, and decision/commitment), which in combination can form eight types of love.

- Attachment styles in infants appear to be linked to the ability to form romantic relationships in adulthood.

- In general, the values applied to relationships by heterosexual, gay, and lesbian couples are more similar than different, in that all couples seek loving, long-term, and meaningful relationships.

RETHINK

- What has to change for a relationship to move from passionate to companionate love? From companionate to passionate love? In which direction is it more difficult for a relationship to move? Why?

- Through which of Sternberg's eight types of love do relationships tend to pass if they proceed from first acquaintance to a lifelong marriage?

- Do you accept the evolutionary explanation of gender differences in mate preferences proposed by Buss and colleagues? Why or why not? How would you test this theory?

- How do the principles of homogamy and the marriage gradient work to limit options for high-status women? How do they affect men's options?

THE COURSE OF RELATIONSHIPS

> He wasn't being a chauvinist or anything, expecting me to do everything and him nothing. He just didn't *volunteer* to do things that obviously needed doing, so I had to put down some ground rules. Like if I'm in a bad mood, I may just yell: "I work eight hours just like you. This is half your house and half your child, too. You've got to do your share!" Jackson never changed the kitty litter box once in four years, but he changes it now, so we've made great progress. I just didn't expect it to take so much work. We planned this child together and we went through Lamaze together, and Jackson stayed home for the first two weeks. But then—wham—the partnership was over. (Cowan & Cowan, 1992, p. 63)

Relationships, like the individuals who make them up, face a variety of challenges. As men and women move through early adulthood, they encounter significant changes in their lives as they work at starting and building their careers, having children, and establishing, maintaining, and sometimes ending relationships with others. One of the primary questions young adults face is whether and when to marry.

Marriage, POSSLQ, and Other Relationship Choices: Sorting Out the Options of Early Adulthood

For some people, the primary issue is not identifying a potential spouse, but whether to marry at all. Although surveys show that most heterosexuals say they want to get married, a significant number choose some other route. For instance, the past three decades have seen a dramatic rise in couples living together without being married, a status known as **cohabitation** (see Figure 14-5). These people, whom the census bureau calls *POSSLQs*, or *persons of the opposite sex sharing living quarters*, now make up around 4 percent of all couples in the United States—almost 7.5 million people (Miller, 1997a).

POSSLQs tend to be young: Almost 40 percent are under 25. Although most are white, African Americans are more likely to cohabit than whites. Other countries have even higher cohabitation rates. In Sweden, for instance, around a quarter of all couples cohabit (Bianchi & Spain, 1986; Popenoe, 1987; Tucker & Mitchell-Kernan, 1995).

Why do some couples choose to cohabit rather than to marry? Some feel they are not ready to make a lifelong commitment. Others feel that cohabitation provides "practice" for marriage. Some reject the institution of marriage altogether, maintaining that marriage is outmoded and that it is unrealistic to expect a couple to spend a lifetime together (Sarantakos, 1991; Hobart & Grigel, 1992; Cunningham & Antill, 1994).

However, those who feel that cohabiting increases their subsequent chances of a happy marriage are incorrect. On the contrary, the chances of divorce are somewhat higher for those who have previously cohabited, according to data collected in both the United States and western Europe (McRae, 1997). However, it's unclear why this is true. It may be that people who decide to cohabit have personal characteristics that would already predispose them to marriage problems (DeMaris & Rao, 1992).

Despite the prevalence of cohabitation, marriage remains the preferred alternative for most people during early adulthood. Although some prefer egalitarian marriages in which

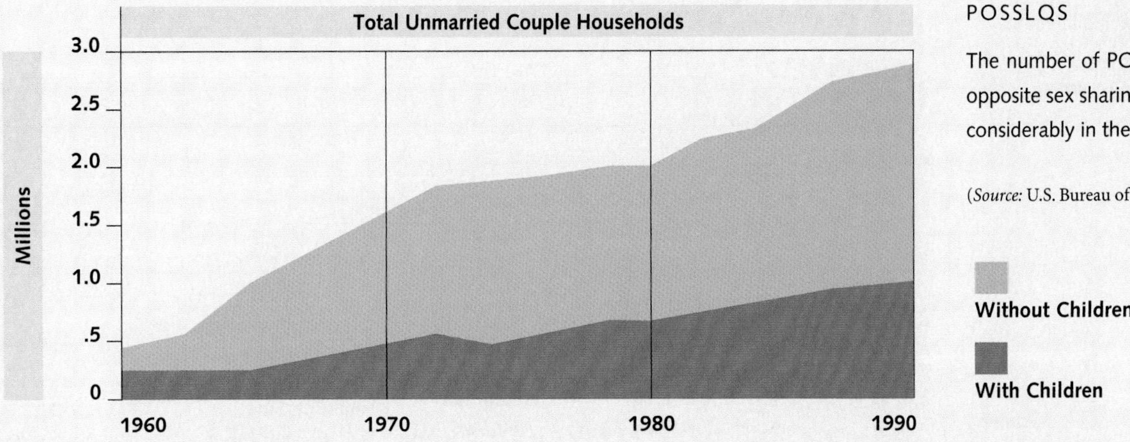

cohabitation *couples living together without being married*

FIGURE 14-5

POSSLQS

The number of POSSLQs, or persons of the opposite sex sharing living quarters, has risen considerably in the last three decades.

(*Source:* U.S. Bureau of the Census, 1993.)

▪ **Without Children**

▪ **With Children**

Total Unmarried Couple Households

Millions

3.0
2.5
2.0
1.5
1.0
.5
0

1960   1970   1980   1990

Although it takes many forms, marriage is a central societal institution. Here we see a traditional wedding on the left, while the photo on the right shows 20,000 grooms and brides at a mass wedding ceremony conducted by the Unification Church.

men and women share responsibilities equally, others prefer more traditional marriages; only a few people say they wish to remain single (see Figure 14-6).

Many see marriage as the appropriate culmination of a loving relationship, whereas others feel it is the "right" thing to do after reaching a particular age in early adulthood. Others seek marriage because of the various roles that a spouse can fill. For instance, a spouse can play an economic role, providing security and financial well-being. Spouses also fill a sexual role, offering a means of sexual gratification and fulfillment that is fully accepted by society. Another role is therapeutic and recreational: Spouses provide a sounding board to discuss one another's problems and act as partners for activities. Marriage also offers the only means of having children that is fully accepted by all segments of society. Finally, being married provides significant emotional, financial, and even health benefits, compared with remaining single or cohabiting. For example, married men and women have a lower incidence of alcohol-related problems and other health risks than divorced and widowed people (Clarkberg, Stolzenberg, & Waite, 1995; Furstenberg, 1996).

FIGURE 14-6

LOVE LEADS TO MARRIAGE

Most people still see marriage as the appropriate culmination of a loving relationship, although they differ on whether they are seeking an egalitarian or traditional marriage.

(*Souce*: American Demographics, June 1996, p. 40.)

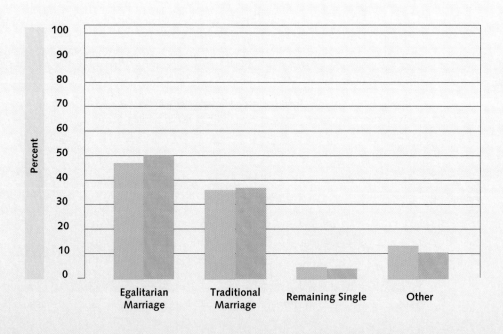

Although marriage remains important, it is not a static institution. For example, fewer U.S. citizens are now married (62 percent) than at any time since the late 1890s. Part of this decline in marriage statistics is attributable to higher divorce rates (which we discuss in Chapter 16), but the decision of people to marry later in life is also a contributing factor. The median age of first marriage in the United States is now 26 for men and 24 for women—the oldest age for women since national statistics were first collected in the 1880s (see Figure 14-7; Landers, 1990; Usdansky, 1992; Furstenberg, 1996).

Does this mean that marriage is losing its viability as a social institution? Probably not. Most people—some 90 percent—eventually do marry, and national polls find that almost everyone endorses the notion that a good family life is important. In fact, almost nine out of ten 18 to 29-year-olds believe that a happy marriage is an ingredient of a good life (Roper Starch Worldwide, 1997).

Why are people getting married later in life? The delay in part reflects economic concerns and the commitment to establishing a career. Choosing and starting a career presents an increasingly difficult series of choices to young adults, and some young adults feel that until they get a foothold on a career path and begin to earn an adequate salary, marriage plans should be put on hold (Dreman, 1997).

FIGURE 14-7

POSTPONING MARRIAGE

The age at which women and men first marry is the highest since national statistics were first collected in the late 1800s.

(*Souce:* Landers, 1990.)

■ Men
■ Women

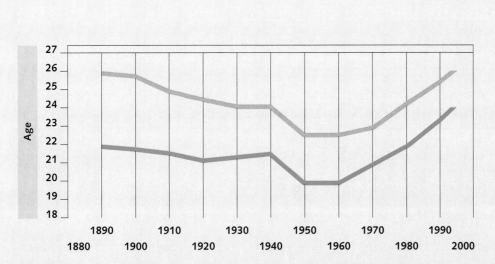

What Makes Marriage Work?

Partners in successful marriages display several characteristics. They visibly show affection to one another, communicate relatively little negativity, and tend to perceive themselves as part of an interdependent couple, rather than as one of two independent individuals. They also experience *social homogamy*, a similarity in leisure activity and role preferences. They hold similar interests, and they agree on a distribution of roles—such as who takes out the garbage and who takes care of the children (Gottman, Katz, & Hooven, 1996; Houts, Robbins, & Huston, 1996; Wallerstein & Blakeslee, 1996).

However, our awareness of the characteristics displayed by husbands and wives in successful marriages has not helped prevent what can only be called an epidemic of divorce. The statistics on divorce are grim: Only about half of all marriages in the United States remain intact. Over a million marriages end in divorce each year, and there are 4.7 divorces for every 1,000 individuals. This figure actually represents a decline from the peak in the mid-1970s of 5.3 divorces per 1,000 people, and most experts think that the rate is leveling off (Edwards, 1995).

Furthermore, divorce is not a problem just in the United States. Countries around the world, both rich and poor, have shown increases in divorce during the last several decades (see Figure 14-8).

Although we discuss the consequences of divorce in greater detail in Chapter 16 when we consider middle age, divorce is a problem that has its roots in early adulthood and the early years of marriage. In fact, most divorces occur during the first 10 years of marriage.

Early Marital Conflict. According to some statistics, nearly half of newly married couples experience a significant degree of conflict. One of the major reasons is that partners may initially idealize one another, perceiving each other through the proverbial "starry eyes." However, as the realities of day-to-day living together and interacting begin to sink in, they become more aware of flaws (Pauker & Arond, 1989).

For instance, before marriage a man may take pride in his partner's frequent business trips to exotic locations. After their marriage, however, he may view the trips as a way for his wife to avoid responsibility at home, and he may become resentful of the time that she is absent (Bird & Melville, 1994).

Other factors may lead to marital conflict. For example, husbands and wives may have difficulty making the status transition from children of their parents to autonomous adults. Others have difficulty developing an identity apart from their spouses, and some

FIGURE 14-8

DIVORCE AROUND THE WORLD

Increases in divorce rates are not just a U.S. phenomenon: Data from other countries also show significant increases.

(*Source:* Population Council, 1995.)

Divorce Rates: Divorces per 100 Marriages

THE FAR SIDE By GARY LARSON

*"Look, marriage is OK—but I also want my own
identity. . . . I mean, how would you like it if everyone
referred to you as 'Chocolate Bar and Chocolate Bar'?"*

struggle to find a satisfactory allocation of time to share with the spouse, compared with time spent with friends and other family members (Tucker & Aron, 1993; Cohan & Bradbury, 1997; Fincham et al., 1997).

On the other hand, most married couples view the early years of marriage as deeply satisfying. For them, marriage can be a kind of extension of courtship. As they negotiate changes in their relationship and learn more about each other, many couples find themselves more deeply in love than before marriage. In fact, the newlywed period is for many couples one of the happiest of their entire married lives (Melville & Bird, 1994; Orbuch et al., 1996).

Can Divorce Be Predicted? Researchers are obtaining increasing evidence that certain factors very accurately predict a later divorce. For instance, according to psychologist John Gottman, the accuracy of predicting divorce using certain variables can be higher than 90 percent (Gottman, Buehlman, & Katz, 1992; Gottman, 1993, 1995; Gottman et al., 1998).

According to Gottman, the crucial factors that affect whether a marriage ends in divorce include the following:

- affection displayed toward the spouse
- amount of negativity communicated to the spouse
- expansiveness or expressivity in communicating information about the relationship
- a sense of "we-ness," or perceiving oneself as part of an interdependent couple, rather than as one of two separate, independent individuals
- traditionality in gender roles
- volatility regarding the intensity of feelings in conflict situations

■ a sense of control over one's life, as opposed to feelings of chaos

■ pride in successfully getting through previous difficulties in the relationship

■ disappointment and disenchantment with the marriage

The greatest likelihood of subsequent divorce occurred in cases in which husbands were low in affection, "we-ness," and expansiveness, but high in negativity and disappointment. Wives, on the other hand, displayed a different pattern. For them, the best predictors of divorce were low "we-ness" and high disappointment scores. The best single predictor of divorce was the degree of disappointment the husband felt about the marriage.

Other factors enter into the equation. For instance, divorce is more likely if spouses habitually attribute negative events to their partners. In this situation, when unpleasant things happen—even those that aren't necessarily the spouse's fault—they are seen as connected to negative, unchangeable qualities of the spouse.

For example, consider the case of a husband who forgets to pick up a prescription for his wife at the drugstore. Wives who view such a mistake as an example of habitual forgetfulness, thoughtlessness, and irresponsibility are more prone to divorce than those who see the error as a one-time mistake, unrelated to enduring personality flaws. Generally, in solid marriages attributions about negative events tend to minimize the spouses' responsibility (Bradbury & Fincham, 1992; Fincham & Bradbury, 1992; Honeycutt, 1993).

Although it is clear that the nature of attributions differs in marriages that are at risk and those that are not, it is not clear whether the different attributional styles found in distressed marriages are the cause or the effect of the distress. Specifically, it may be that more dysfunctional attributions occur as a result of marital distress. On the other hand, it is also plausible that negative attributional styles produce marital distress. If a man or woman continually misinterprets the causes of a spouse's behavior, seeing it in the worse possible light, it is likely that the result will be an increase in marital discord.

Parenthood: The Arrival of Children

> We had no idea what we were getting into when our first child was born. We certainly prepared for the event, reading magazine articles and books and even attending a class on childcare. But when Sheanna was actually born, the sheer enormity of the task of taking care of her, her presence at every moment of the day, and the awesome responsibility of raising another human being weighed on us like nothing else we'd ever faced. Not that it was a burden. But it did make us look at the world with an entirely different perspective.

Like many parents, this couple was unable, before the fact, to grasp fully the tremendous, and sometimes overwhelming, nature of childrearing. The arrival of a child alters virtually every aspect of family life, in positive and, sometimes, negative ways.

Deciding to Have Children.   What makes a couple decide to have children in the first place? Childrearing certainly isn't economically advantageous: According to one estimate, a middle-class family with two children spends around $100,000 for each child by the time the child reaches the age of 18. Add in the costs of college and the figure comes to over $200,000 per child (Belkin, 1985; Cutler, 1990).

Instead, young adults typically cite psychological reasons for having children. They expect to derive pleasure from watching their children grow, fulfillment from their children's accomplishments, satisfaction from seeing them become successful, and enjoyment from forging a close bond with their children. But there also may be a self-serving element in the decision to have children. For example, parents-to-be may hope that their children will provide for them in their old age, maintain a family business or farm, or simply offer companionship. Others have children because to do so is such a strong societal norm: More than 90 percent of all married couples have at least one child (Mackey, White, & Day, 1992).

For some couples, the decision to have children is inadvertent. Due to the failure of birth control methods, some children are born without the benefit of being planned. In some cases, the family had been planning to have children at some point in the future, and so the pregnancy is not regarded as particularly undesirable and may even be welcomed. But in families that had actively *not* wanted to have children, or already had what they considered "enough" children, the pregnancy can be viewed as problematic (Clinton & Kelber, 1993).

The couples who are most likely to have unwanted pregnancies are often the most vulnerable in society. Unplanned pregnancies occur most frequently in younger, poorer, and less educated couples. On the other hand, there has been a dramatic rise in the use and effectiveness of contraceptives, and the incidence of undesired pregnancies has declined in the last several decades (Pratt et al., 1984).

The availability and use of effective contraceptives has also dramatically decreased the number of children in the average American family. As shown in Figure 14-9, almost 70 percent of Americans polled in the 1930s agreed that the ideal number of children was three or more, but by the 1990s the percentage had shrunk to less than 40 percent. Today, most families seek to have no more than two children—although most say that three or more is ideal if money is no object (CNN/USA Today/Gallup Poll, 1997; Kate, 1998).

These preferences have been translated into changes in the actual birth rate. In 1957, the *fertility rate* reached a post-World War II peak in the United States of 3.7 children per woman and then began to decline. Today, the rate remains below 2.0 children per woman, which is less than the *replacement level*, the number of children that one generation must produce to be able to replenish its numbers.

What has produced this decline in the fertility rate? In addition to the availability of more reliable birth control methods, one reason is that increasing numbers of women have joined the workforce. The pressures of simultaneously holding a job and raising a child have convinced many women to have fewer children. Furthermore, many women who work outside the home are choosing to have children later in their childbearing years in order to develop their careers. In fact, women between the ages of 30 and 34 are the only ones whose rate of births has actually increased over earlier decades. Still, because women who have their first children in their 30s have fewer years in which to have children, they ultimately cannot have as many children as women who begin childbearing in their 20s.

Finally, some of the traditional incentives for having children—such as their potential for providing economic support in old age—may no longer be as attractive. Potential parents

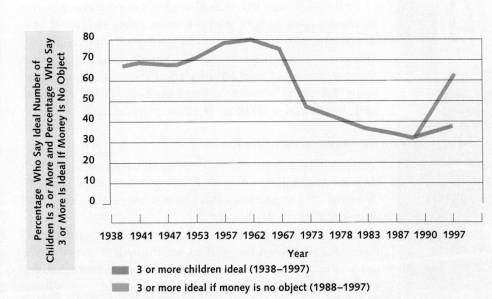

FIGURE 14-9

SHRINKING FAMILIES

In the 1930s close to 70 percent of Americans felt the ideal number of children was three or more. By the late 1990s that figure dropped to less than 40 percent.

(*Source:* CNN/USA Today/Gallup Poll, 1997.)

Percentage Who Say Ideal Number of Children Is 3 or More and Percentage Who Say 3 or More Is Ideal If Money Is No Object

Year

■ 3 or more children ideal (1938–1997)

■ 3 or more ideal if money is no object (1988–1997)

may view Social Security and other pensions as a more predictable means of support when they are elderly. Furthermore, the sheer cost of raising a child, particularly the well-publicized increase in the cost of college, may act as a disincentive for bearing larger numbers of children (Bird & Melville, 1994).

The Impact of Children on Parents: Two's a Couple, Three's a Crowd? How do couples react to the birth of a child? One fact is well established: For many couples, marital satisfaction takes a dive (Figley, 1973; Tucker & Aron, 1993). Before the birth of children, spouses are able to focus their attention on each other. They are able to respond to one another's needs, and they see their partners, as well as themselves, as autonomous individuals.

The birth of a child brings about a dramatic shift in the roles spouses must play. They are suddenly placed in new roles—"mother" and "father"—and these new positions may overwhelm their ability to respond in their older, although continuing, roles of "wife" and "husband" (Clulow, 1991). As one new father expressed his frustration with what he saw as his wife's willingness to allow their child to take precedence over him, "I keep asking her to get a sitter so we can go out for a quiet dinner, but she always finds a reason not to. It's like being turned down for a date week after week" (Cowan & Cowan, 1992, p. 61).

For many couples, the strains accompanying the birth of a child produce the lowest level of marital satisfaction of any point in their marriage. This is particularly true for women, who tend to be more dissatisfied than men with their marriages after the arrival of children. The most likely reason for this gender difference is that wives typically experience a greater increase in their responsibilities than husbands do (Glenn & Weaver, 1990).

Wives' perception that men expend less effort in childrearing than they do is an accurate reading of reality. Even when both spouses hold jobs outside the home and work similar hours, the wife generally spends more time taking care of the children than the husband does (Huppe & Cyr, 1997). And even though men are spending more time with their children than in the past (the amount of time has increased by one-quarter in the last 20 years), wives still spend more time with their children than husbands do (Families and Work Institute, 1998).

Furthermore, the nature of husbands' contributions to the household are often different from those of wives. For instance, husbands tend to carry out chores that are more easily scheduled in advance (such as mowing the lawn or house repairs), whereas women's household chores tend to be devoted to things that need immediate attention, such as child care and meal preparation. As a result, wives experience greater levels of anxiety and stress (Biernat & Wortman, 1991; Kurdek, 1993; Barnett & Shen, 1997; see Figure 14-10).

On the other hand, not all couples experience a decrease in marital satisfaction upon the birth of a child. Some, in fact, feel greater satisfaction during the years when they are most involved in childrearing. This is true primarily for couples who harbor realistic expectations regarding the extent of childrearing effort and other household responsibilities they face when children are born (Cowan & Cowan, 1988; Belsky, Ravine, & Fish, 1989; Hackel & Ruble, 1992).

Gay and Lesbian Parents

In increasing numbers, children are being raised in families in which there are two Moms or two Dads. Rough estimates suggest that some 20 percent of gay men and lesbian women are parents (Falk, 1989; Turner, Scadden, & Harris, 1990).

How do lesbian and gay households compare to heterosexual households? To answer the question, we first need to consider some characteristics of gay and lesbian couples without children. According to studies comparing gay, lesbian, and heterosexual couples, labor

Parenthood expands the roles of both husbands and wives into that of fathers and mothers, a process that can have profound effects on couples' relationships.

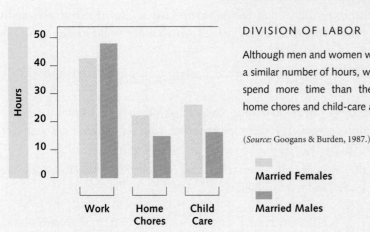

FIGURE 14-10

DIVISION OF LABOR

Although men and women work at their jobs a similar number of hours, women are apt to spend more time than their husbands in home chores and child-care activities.

(*Source:* Googans & Burden, 1987.)

■ Married Females

■ Married Males

tends to be divided more evenly in homosexual households than in heterosexual households. Each partner in a homosexual relationship is more likely to carry out approximately the same number of different chores, compared with heterosexual partners. Furthermore, gay and lesbian couples cling more strongly to the ideal of an egalitarian allocation of household work than heterosexual couples do (Deutsch, Lussier, & Servis, 1993; Kurdek, 1993; Patterson, 1992, 1994).

However, as with heterosexual couples, the arrival of a child (usually through adoption or artificial insemination) changes the dynamics of household life considerably in homosexual couples. As in heterosexual unions, a specialization of roles develops. According to recent research on lesbian mothers, for instance, childrearing tends to fall more to one member of the couple, whereas the other spends more time in paid employment. Although both partners usually say they share household tasks and decision making equally, biological mothers are more involved in child care. Conversely, the nonbiological mother in the couple is more likely to report spending greater time in paid employment (Patterson, 1995).

In short, research appears to indicate that the evolution of homosexual couples when children arrive is more similar to that of heterosexual couples than dissimilar, particularly in the increased role specialization occasioned by the requirements of child care. Of course, such research does not answer the question of what the consequences are for children being raised by homosexual parents. However, most research suggests that children raised in households in which the parents are homosexual show no differences in terms of eventual adjustment from those raised in heterosexual households. Although they may face greater challenges from a society in which the roots of prejudice against homosexuality are deep, children who have two Moms or two Dads ultimately seem to fare well (Flaks et al., 1995; Patterson, 1992; Patterson & Redding, 1996; Tasker & Golombok, 1997).

REVIEW AND RETHINK

REVIEW

■ Cohabitation is an increasingly popular option for young adults, but most still choose marriage. The median age at which both men and women marry for the first time is rising, however.

■ Divorce is prevalent in the United States, particularly within the first 10 years of marriage. The shift from an idealized view of married life to the reality can cause early discord.

■ Factors that predict divorce include the levels of affection, negativity, and expressivity in the marriage.

■ Couples overwhelmingly desire to produce children, although the availability of contraception and changes in women's roles in the workplace have combined to decrease average family size.

■ Children bring pressures to both heterosexual and homosexual relationships, causing changes in focus, roles, and responsibilities.

RETHINK

■ In what ways do you think cognitive changes in early adulthood (e.g., the emergence of postformal thought and practical intelligence) affect how young adults deal with questions of marriage, divorce, and childrearing?

■ Why do you think society has established such a powerful norm in favor of marriage? What effects might such a norm have on a person who prefers to remain single?

■ Why might spouses view each other's behaviors differently before and after marriage?

■ Do the changes that children bring to a relationship affect husbands and wives equally? Do they affect each partner in a gay or lesbian relationship equally? Why or why not?

WORK: CHOOSING AND EMBARKING ON A CAREER

> Why did I decide that I wanted to be a lawyer? The answer is a bit embarrassing. When I got to my senior year of college, I began to worry about what I was going to do when I graduated. My parents were asking, with increasing frequency, what kind of work I was thinking about, and I felt the pressure rising with each phone call from home. So I began to think seriously about the problem. At the time, the O.J. Simpson trial was in the news all the time, and it got me to thinking about what it might be like to be an attorney. I had always been fascinated by *L.A. Law* when it had been on television, and I could envision myself in one of those big corner offices with a view of the city. For these reasons, and just about none other, I decided to take the law boards and apply to law school.

For almost all of us, early adulthood is a period of decisions with lifelong implications. One of the most critical is choosing a career path. The choice we make goes well beyond determining how much money we will earn; it also relates to our status, our sense of self-worth, and the contribution that we will make in life. In sum, decisions about work go to the very core of a young adult's identity.

Identity During Young Adulthood: The Role of Work

According to psychiatrist George Vaillant, young adulthood is marked by a stage of development called career consolidation. During **career consolidation**, a stage that begins between the ages of 20 and 40, young adults become centered on their careers. Based on a comprehensive longitudinal study of a large group of male graduates of Harvard begun when they were freshmen in the 1930s, Vaillant found a general pattern of psychological development (Vaillant, 1977; Vaillant & Vaillant, 1990).

career consolidation *a stage that is entered between the ages of 20 and 40, when young adults become centered on their careers*

In their early 20s, the men tended to be influenced by their parents' authority. But in their late 20s and early 30s, they started to act with greater autonomy. They married and began to have and raise children. At the same time, they started and began to focus on their careers—the period of career consolidation.

Based on his data, Vaillant drew a relatively uninspiring portrait of people in the career consolidation stage. The participants in his study tended to be rule-followers, worked very hard, were working their way up the corporate ladder, and sought to conform to the norms of their professions. Rather than showing the independence and questioning that they had displayed earlier, while still in college, they threw themselves unquestioningly into their work.

Vaillant argues that work played such an important role in the lives of the men he studied that the career consolidation stage should be seen as an addition to Erikson's intimacy-versus-isolation stage of psychosocial identity. In Vaillant's view, career concerns come to supplant the focus on intimacy, and the career consolidation stage marks a bridge between Erikson's intimacy-versus-isolation stage and Erikson's next period, that of generativity versus stagnation. (Generativity refers to an individual's contribution to society, as we discuss in Chapter 16).

People enter the period of career choice in early adulthood, and seek information about specific career choices, as at this job fair.

However, the reaction to Vaillant's viewpoint has been mixed. Critics point out, for instance, that Vaillant's sample, although relatively large, comprised a highly restricted, unusually bright group of people, all of them men. It is hard to know how generalizable the results are. Furthermore, societal norms have changed considerably since the time the study was begun in the late 1930s, and people's views of the importance of work may have shifted. Finally, the lack of women in the sample, and the fact that there have been major changes in the role of work in *women's* lives, make Vaillant's conclusions even less generalizable.

Still, it is hard to argue about the importance of work in most people's lives, and current research suggests that it makes up a significant part of both men's and women's identity—if for no other reason than many people spend more time working than they do on any other activity (Deaux et al., 1995). We turn now to how people decide what careers to follow—and the implications of that decision.

Picking an Occupation: Choosing Life's Work

Some people know from childhood that they want to be physicians or firefighters or go into business, and they follow invariant paths toward that goal. For others, the choice of a career is very much a matter of chance, of turning to the want ads and seeing what's available.

Ginzberg's Career Choice Theory.   According to Eli Ginzberg (1972), people typically move through a series of stages in choosing a career. The first stage is the **fantasy period**, which lasts until a person is around 11. During the fantasy period, career choices are made, and discarded, without regard to skills, abilities, or available job opportunities. Instead, choices are made solely on the basis of what sounds appealing. Thus, a child may decide she wants to be a veterinarian—despite the fact that she is allergic to dogs and cats.

People begin to take practical considerations into account during the tentative period. During the **tentative period**, which spans adolescence, people begin to think in pragmatic terms about the requirements of various jobs and how their own abilities might fit with them. They also consider their personal values and goals, exploring how well a particular occupation might satisfy them.

Finally, in early adulthood, people enter the realistic period. In the **realistic period**, young adults explore specific career options either through actual experience on the job or through training for a profession. After initially exploring what they might do, people begin to narrow their choices to a few alternative careers and eventually make a commitment to a particular one.

Although Ginzberg's theory makes sense, critics have charged that it oversimplifies the process of choosing a career. Because Ginzberg's research was based on subjects from

fantasy period   *according to Ginzberg, the period, lasting until about age 11, when career choices are made, and discarded, without regard to skills, abilities, or available job opportunities*

tentative period   *the second stage of Ginzberg's theory, which spans adolescence, when people begin to think in pragmatic terms about the requirements of various jobs and how their own abilities might fit with them*

realistic period   *the third stage of Ginzburg's theory, which occurs in early adulthood, when people begin to explore specific career options either through actual experience on the job or through training for a profession, and then narrow their choices and make a commitment*

middle socioeconomic levels, it may overstate the choices and options available to people in lower socioeconomic levels. Furthermore, the ages associated with the various stages may be too rigid. For instance, a person who does not attend college but begins to work immediately after high school graduation is likely to be making serious career decisions at a much earlier point than a person who attends college.

Holland's Personality Type Theory.   Other theories of career choice emphasize how an individual's personality affects decisions about a career. According to John Holland, for instance, certain personality types match particularly well with certain careers. If the correspondence between personality and career is good, people will enjoy their careers more and be more likely to stay in them; but if the match is poor, they will be unhappy and more likely to shift into other careers (Holland, 1973, 1987; Gottfredson & Holland, 1990).

According to Holland, six personality types are important in career choice:

- *Realistic.* These people are down-to-earth, practical problem solvers, and physically strong, but their social skills are mediocre. They make good farmers, laborers, and truck drivers.

- *Intellectual.* Intellectual types are oriented toward the theoretical and abstract. Although not particularly good with people, they are well suited to careers in math and science.

- *Social.* The traits associated with the social personality type are related to verbal skills and interpersonal relations. Social types are good at working with people, and consequently make good salespersons, teachers, and counselors.

- *Conventional.* Conventional individuals prefer highly structured tasks. They make good clerks, secretaries, and bank tellers.

- *Enterprising.* These individuals are risk takers and take-charge types. They are good leaders and may be particularly effective as managers or politicians.

- *Artistic.* Artistic types use art to express themselves, and they often prefer the world of art to interactions with people. They are best suited to occupations involving art.

Although Holland's enumeration of personality types is sensible, it suffers from a central flaw: Not everyone fits neatly into particular personality types. Furthermore, there are certainly exceptions to the typology, with jobs being held by people who don't have the particular personality that Holland would predict. Still, the basic notions of the theory have been validated, and they form the foundation of several measures designed to assess the occupational options for which a given person is particularly suited (Randahl, 1991). (See "Speaking of Development" box).

Gender and Career Choices: Women's Work

WANTED: Full-time employee for small family firm. DUTIES: Including but not limited to general cleaning, cooking, gardening, laundry, ironing and mending, purchasing, bookkeeping and money management. Child care may also be required. HOURS: Avg. 55/wk but standby duty required 24 hours/day, 7 days/wk. Extra workload on holidays. SALARY AND BENEFITS: No salary, but food, clothing, and shelter provided at employer's discretion; job security and benefits depend on continued good will of employer. No vacation. No retirement plan. No opportunities for advancement. REQUIREMENTS: No previous experience necessary, can learn on the job. Only women need apply. (Unger & Crawford, 1992, p. 446)

Just two decades ago, many women entering early adulthood assumed that this admittedly exaggerated job description matched the work for which they were best suited and to which they aspired: housewife. Even those women who sought work outside the home were relegated to certain professions. For instance, until the 1960s employment ads in

SPEAKING OF DEVELOPMENT

Henry Klein, Career Counselor

Education: .... University of Pennsylvania, B.A. in English; University of Pennsylvania, M.A. in sociology; Temple University, Ph.D. in psychoeducational processes

Position: .... Founder and director, American College and Career Counseling Center

Home: .... Philadelphia, Pennsylvania

At one time or another everyone has pondered the question of which career to pursue, or whether to change a current job. For those facing that decision there are people like Henry Klein.

In 1962 Klein founded the American College and Career Counseling Center in Philadelphia. Its purpose is to help people find professions that are right for them.

A former columnist who wrote for 20 years on careers and education for several Philadelphia newspapers, Klein has also published a book that answers questions about getting into, and staying in, college.

Career counseling at Klein's center, which lasts about five sessions, begins with a basic interview and proceeds to the point at which the counselor and the client have identified specific companies to pursue and outlined concrete strategies for approaching them.

"Before people come to me for career counseling I ask them to send me their résumés, and if they're close to graduation, copies of their transcripts," Klein explains. "I look through the transcript to find the strongest subject areas and try to get a baseline from that. I then look over the résumé to get a sense of the progression of jobs the person has passed through, as well as the functions and skills that the person has practiced.

"I look for a particular trend in a field, and if there are no negatives, we go in that direction," he adds.

Although a fairly clear trend line is easier to work with, the person with a scattered, inconsistent history is more of a challenge, according to Klein.

"If the person's experience is scattered and there's no particular trend, we almost have to start from zero. In that case we have to ask a lot of basic questions, such as 'What kind of person are you?' and 'Where are you in your development?'

"We won't throw away all the things a person has been doing. We will try to find out if there's any common thread, no matter how small, that runs through each of the jobs—and there is usually *something* there that I can grab onto," he notes. "There might be a clue inside each job. It could be only a part of each of the jobs people have had, but they couldn't see it because they were always looking at the job as a whole."

Although it is important to look at academic and work background, Klein points out that a person's character and development are equally important, if not more so.

"A person with a fairly stable life, who hasn't moved around a lot or job-hopped, produces a trend in careers and vocations that we can use," he says. "You have to work on personal development before you can commit to something in the longer term.

"Even if you fell into the perfect job, your personal development might push you out sooner or later if you were not up to a long-term career commitment. You can't talk in terms of just one occupation; you have to think in terms of a career."

"We will try to find out if there's any common thread, no matter how small, that runs through each of the jobs—and there is usually something there that I can grab onto."

"You can't talk in terms of just one occupation; you have to think in terms of a career."

communal   professions   *occupations that are associated with relationships*

agentic professions   *occupations that are associated with getting things accomplished*

newspapers throughout the United States were almost always divided into two sections: "Help Wanted: Male" and "Help Wanted: Female." The men's job listings encompassed such professions as police officer, construction worker, and legal counsel; the women's listings were for secretaries, teachers, cashiers, and librarians.

The breakdown of jobs deemed appropriate for men and women reflected society's traditional view of what the two genders were best suited for. Traditionally, women were considered most appropriate for **communal professions**, occupations associated with relationships. In contrast, men were perceived as best suited for agentic professions. **Agentic professions** are associated with getting things accomplished. It is probably no coincidence that communal professions typically have lower status and pay less than agentic professions (Eagly & Steffen, 1984, 1986).

Although discrimination based on gender is far less blatant today than it was several decades ago—it is now illegal, for instance, to advertise a position specifically for a man or a woman—remnants of traditional gender role prejudice persist (Pratto et al., 1997). As we discussed in Chapter 13, women are less likely to be found in traditionally male-dominated professions such as engineering and computer programming. As shown in Figure 14-11, women in many professions earn significantly less than men in identical jobs. In fact, in 97 percent of the occupations for which data have been collected, women's weekly earnings are less than men's earnings (U.S. Bureau of Labor. Women's Bureau, 1998).

Despite status and pay that are often lower than men's, more women are working outside the home than ever before. Between 1950 and 1990, the percentage of the female population (aged 16 and over) in the U.S. labor force increased from around 35 percent to nearly 60 percent, and women today make up around 55 percent of the labor force. Almost all women expect to earn a living, and almost all do at some point in their lives. Furthermore, in about one-half of U.S. households, women earn about as much as their husbands (Lewin, 1995).

Furthermore, opportunities for women are in many ways considerably greater than they were in earlier years. Women are more likely to be physicians, lawyers, insurance

FIGURE 14-11

THE GENDER-WAGE GAP

The median wages of women in a given profession is shown here as a proportion of the wages that men receive.

(*Source:* U.S. Bureau of Labor Statistics, 1998.)

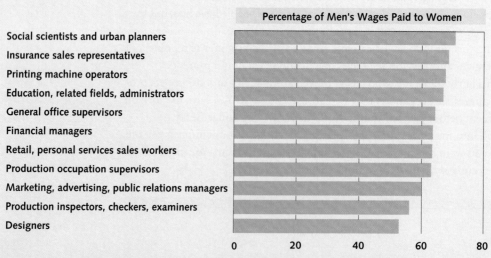

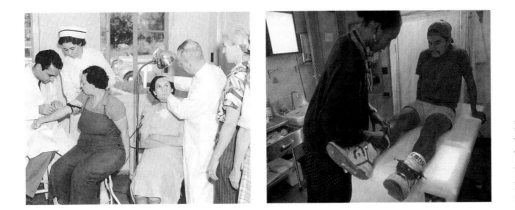

In the 1930s, it was the rare woman who would even consider becoming a doctor. Today, however, the story is different, and women make up an increasing proportion of physicians. Even so, women often earn less than men do, even in identical professions.

agents, and bus drivers than they were in the past. However, within specific job categories, sex discrimination still occurs. For example, female bus drivers are more apt to have part-time school bus routes, whereas men hold better-paying full-time routes in cities. Similarly, female pharmacists are more likely to work in hospitals, whereas men work in higher-paying jobs in retail stores (England & McCreary, 1987; Unger & Crawford, 1996).

In the same way, women (and minorities, too) in high-status, visible professional roles may hit what has come to be called the *glass ceiling*. The glass ceiling is an invisible barrier within an organization that, because of discrimination, prevents individuals from being promoted beyond a certain level. It operates subtly, and often the people responsible for keeping the glass ceiling in place are unaware of how their actions perpetuate discrimination against women and minorities (Larwood, Szwajkowski, & Rose, 1988; Morrison & von Gilnow, 1990; Snyder et al., 1992; Kilborne, 1995).

extrinsic motivation   *motivation that drives people to obtain tangible rewards, such as money and prestige*

Why Do People Work? More Than Earning a Living

This may seem an easy question to answer: People work to earn a living. Yet the reality is different, for young adults express many reasons for seeking a job.

Intrinsic and Extrinsic Motivation.   Certainly, people work to obtain various concrete rewards, or out of extrinsic motivation. **Extrinsic motivation** drives people to obtain tangible rewards, such as money and prestige (Singer, Stacey, & Lange, 1993).

Lawyers are high on the status hierarchy of professions, and some lawyers—such as Marcia Clark, prosecutor at the O.J. Simpson murder trial—achieve even greater status as a result of media exposure.

On the other hand, people also work for factors relating to intrinsic motivation. **Intrinsic motivation** causes people to work for their own enjoyment, not for the rewards work may bring. For instance, people in many Western societies tend to subscribe to the *Puritan work ethic*, the notion that work is important in and of itself. According to this view, working is a meaningful act that brings psychological and (at least in the traditional view) even spiritual well-being and satisfaction (Stohs, 1992; Serow, 1994).

Work also brings a sense of personal identity. Consider, for instance, what people say about themselves when they first meet someone. After mentioning their names and where they live, they very typically tell what they do for a living. What people do is a large part of who they are.

Work also may be a central element in people's social lives. Because so much time is spent in work settings, work can be a source of young adults' friends and social activities. Social relationships forged at work may spill over into other parts of people's lives. In addition, there are often social obligations—dinner with the boss, or the annual seasonal party in December—that are related to work.

Finally, the kind of work that people do is a factor in determining status. **Status** is the evaluation by society of the role a person plays. Various jobs are associated with a certain status, as indicated in Table 14-4. For instance, physicians and college teachers are near the top of the status hierarchy, whereas ushers and shoe shiners fall to the bottom.

Satisfaction on the Job. The status associated with particular jobs affects people's satisfaction with their work. As might be expected, the higher the status of the job, the more satisfied people tend to be (Yankelovich, 1974). Furthermore, the status of the job of the major wage-earner can affect the status of the other members of the family.

Of course, status isn't everything: Worker satisfaction depends on a number of factors, not the least of which is the job itself (Ting, 1997). For example, consider the plight

TABLE 14-4

STATUS HIERARCHY OF VARIOUS PROFESSIONS

Occupation	Score	Occupation	Score
Physician	82	Bank teller	50
College teacher	78	Electrician	49
Lawyer	76	Police officer	48
Dentist	74	Insurance agent	47
Bank officer	72	Secretary	46
Airline pilot	70	Air traffic controller	43
Clergy	69	Mail carrier	42
Sociologist	66	Owner of a farm	41
Secondary school teacher	63	Restaurant manager	39
Registered nurse	62	Automobile mechanic	37
Pharmicist	61	Baker	34
Elementary school teacher	60	Salesclerk	29
Accountant	56	Gas station attendant	22
Painter	56	Waiter and waitress	20
Librarian	55	Laundry operator	18
Actor	55	Garbage collector	17
Funeral director	52	Janitor	16
Athlete	51	Usher	15
Reporter	51	Shoe shiner	12

(*Source:* NORC, 1990.)

of Patricia Alford, who worked at the Equitable Life Assurance Company. Her job consisted of entering data into a computer 9 hours each day except for two 15-minute breaks and an hour off for lunch. She never knew how much she was earning, because her salary depended on how many insurance claims she entered into the computer each day. The pay standards were so complicated that her pay varied from $217 to $400 a week, providing her with a weekly surprise at paycheck time (Booth, 1987).

Other people who work at computers are monitored on a minute-by-minute basis; supervisors can consistently see how many keystrokes they are entering. In some firms in which workers use the telephone for sales or to take customer orders, their conversations are monitored by supervisors. Not surprisingly, such forms of management produce worker dissatisfaction.

On the other hand, job satisfaction increases when workers have input into their jobs. Furthermore, variety is the spice of job life: People enjoy jobs that require several different types of skills more than those that require only a minimal number. Finally, the more influence employees have over others, either directly as supervisors or more informally, the greater their job satisfaction (Katzell & Guzzo, 1983; Steers & Porter, 1991).

Welfare and Jobs.   During the last decade, the idea of welfare reform struck a deep political chord with many voters in the United States. Many citizens articulated the belief that the welfare system, which provided benefits to some 5 million families and almost 10 million children, trapped people in poverty and dependency, ultimately hurting recipients of welfare more than it helped them.

Few people believe that living on welfare benefits is a desirable state, particularly in a society in which work plays such a central role in people's identity and sense of self-worth. However, what was often lost in the calls for welfare reform was the fact that the most numerous—and vulnerable—welfare recipients are children, frequently being cared for by single parents (Larner, Terman, & Behrman, 1997). As we consider in the "Directions in Development" box, welfare reform raises substantial issues relevant to both adults and children.

Directions in Development

Welfare Reform: The Difficulties of Moving from Welfare to Work

Shirley Eshelman is physically disabled, but she manages to work small miracles for her 12-year-old son Jonathan, who is emotionally disturbed and has learning difficulties. And she does it on a family income of just $241 a week. She stretches a $30-a-month grocery budget by planting a large vegetable garden outside her home in rural Middletown, Maryland, and by taking Jonathan to a food pantry where they volunteer in exchange for food. She sets aside money in meticulous expense ledgers for Jonathan's outings with a local teacher, who teaches him socialization skills, and a little more for his twice-monthly speech therapy. (Cohen, 1997, p. 50)

The transition from welfare to work is difficult due to the many obstacles to overcome.

The Eshelmans' life may be on the edge of disarray, however, because of new rules stemming from the 1996 overhaul of the U.S. federal welfare system. As part of the legislation, the check that the Eshelman family receives each week—some $74—may be terminated.

Welfare reform legislation was passed as a result of widespread agreement that the U.S. welfare system was in disarray. Polls showed that most U.S. citizens were impatient with welfare recipients, believing that they had become trapped into a state of dependency (Blendon et al., 1995). The problem was how to encourage people to move off the welfare rolls and into the workforce, while still providing a safety net for those who truly needed assistance, particularly the most vulnerable individuals—children.

Perhaps the most significant (or, according to critics, harshest) features of the new law are requirements obliging mothers to enter the workforce if they receive cash assistance for more than 2 years, and the imposition of a 5-year lifetime limit on the receipt of assistance. Furthermore, individual states will receive full federal funding only if half of the adults receiving federal assistance work at least 30 hours each week by the year 2002. Legal immigrants arriving in the United States later than the passage of the 1996 legislation will be prohibited from receiving aid.

Although the long-term outcomes of welfare reform are far from clear, research suggests that it may produce some difficulties for families. For instance, most welfare recipients have relatively poor job skills. Their education is limited—almost half lacking a high school diploma—and they typically score poorly on standardized tests. Ten percent have a physical disability that restricts employment, and an additional 4 percent have a serious psychological or mental disability (Maynard, 1995).

Even when previous welfare recipients are able to get jobs, the jobs they find typically pay poorly. The average mother who has been on welfare earns only around $6.00 an hour, with prospects for an increase minimal. Because single mothers often face significant transportation and child-care costs, their actual net incomes may be quite small, rarely rising above the poverty line (Burtless, 1997).

Mothers who previously were on welfare and who subsequently enter low-paying and stressful jobs also suffer psychological costs. In fact, mothers who work for low wages and whose jobs are routine, repetitive, and heavily supervised, providing little autonomy—as is most commonly the case in jobs held by unskilled workers who have previously received welfare—are less likely to provide optimal home environments for their children than mothers who earn higher wages and have more challenging jobs.

In short, mothers face a dilemma. If they do not work, they have few economic and interpersonal resources, potentially damaging the quality of the home environment. However, if they enter the workforce, they have less time with their children and for their home responsibilities, and they still have few economic and interpersonal resources—given the likelihood that they hold low-wage, high-stress jobs (Parcel & Menaghan, 1997).

Clearly, there are no simple solutions to helping people to move from welfare to work. The Center for the Future of Children, in conjunction with the American Academy of Arts and Sciences, makes the following recommendations:

■ Policies to support employment in low-income families should not single out welfare recipients, but should provide broad access to affordable health insurance, child-care subsidies, wage supplements, and unemployment and temporary disability insurance. These supports should be independent of the welfare system, cover all families with children who meet income eligibility criteria, and require parents to share the cost of benefits as their incomes rise.

■ Good child-care alternatives are needed to fit the schedules, preferences, and residence patterns of low-income working families. Measures that strengthen the quality of child care include regulatory oversight, training, access to capital for facilities, networks of professional support, and steps to attract and keep skilled providers.

■ To facilitate entry into the labor force, and to smooth transitions between jobs, short-term welfare-to-work supports and services, such as job training, cash stipends, and child-care subsidies, should be provided during training and job search to both unemployed mothers and unemployed fathers.

■ Families headed by parents who are unable to find or keep employment should receive special attention from trained case managers to ensure that the needs of their children are met. The skilled case manager can assess family problems, observe the child's well-being, make referrals for services, and follow up with the family.

■ New information should be gather immediately to assess the short-term and long-term impact of new policies. Studies are needed that track the experiences of poor children and families as reforms are implemented, and that document the community conditions that support successful welfare reform.

■ Welfare reform plans should emphasize the core values of work, independence, fairness, and responsibility for family. Plans should focus on long-term rather than short-term costs and benefits, especially those related to children. (The Future of Children, 1997, p. 4)

The Informed Consumer of Development

Choosing a Career

One of the greatest challenges people face in early adulthood is making a decision that will have lifelong implications: the choice of a career. Although there is no single correct choice—most people can be happy in any of several different jobs—the options can be daunting. Here are some guidelines for at least starting to come to grips with the question of what occupational path to follow.

■ Systematically evaluate a variety of choices. Libraries contain a wealth of information about potential career paths, and most colleges and universities have career centers that can provide occupational data and guidance.

■ Know yourself. Evaluate your strengths and weaknesses, perhaps by completing a questionnaire at a college career center that can provide insight into your interests, skills, and values.

■ Create a "balance sheet," listing the potential gains and losses that you will incur from a particular profession. First, list the gains and losses that you will experience directly, and then list gains and losses for others. Next, write down your projected self-approval or self-disapproval from the potential career. Finally, write down the projected social approval or disapproval you are likely to receive from others. By systematically evaluating a set of potential careers according to each of these criteria, you will be in a better position to compare different possibilities.

■ "Try out" different careers through paid or unpaid internships. By seeing a job firsthand, interns are able to get a better sense of what an occupation is truly like.

■ Remember that if you make a mistake, you can change careers. In fact, people today increasingly change careers in early adulthood and even beyond. No one should feel locked into a decision made earlier in life. As we have seen throughout this book, people develop substantially over the course of their lives.

■ It is reasonable to expect that shifting values, interests, abilities, and life circumstances might make a different career more appropriate later in life than the one chosen during early adulthood.

REVIEW AND RETHINK

REVIEW

■ Choosing a career is an important step in early adulthood, so important that George Vaillant considers career consolidation a developmental stage on a par with Erikson's intimacy-versus-isolation stage.

■ According to Eli Ginzberg, people pass through three stages in considering careers: the fantasy period, the tentative period, and the realistic period.

■ Other theories of career choice, such as John Holland's, attempt to match personality types to suitable careers.

■ Gender stereotypes and traditional societal views regarding women's and men's work are changing, but women still experience subtle prejudice in career choices, roles, and wages. Even in high-status jobs, women—and minorities, too—may hit an impenetrable "glass ceiling."

■ People work because of both extrinsic and intrinsic motivation factors. Job satisfaction results from characteristics such as status, control, job variety, and influence over others.

RETHINK

■ If Vaillant's study were performed today on women, in what ways do you think the results would be similar to or different from those of the original study?

■ How good do you think the match is between personality characteristics and career choices? What issues relating to gender, ethnic, or cultural bias would be of concern to you in designing a career-oriented personality inventory?

■ How does the division of jobs into communal and agentic relate to traditional views of male–female differences?

■ How does the issue of motivation apply to workers of low socioeconomic status performing low-status jobs? How might opportunities for promotion and advancement be affected by low motivation?

LOOKING BACK

■ **How do young adults form loving relationships, and how does love change over time?**

• Young adults face Erikson's intimacy-versus-isolation stage, with those who resolve this conflict able to develop intimate relationships with others.

• According to stimulus-value-role theory, relationships pass through a stage based on surface characteristics, values, and finally the roles played by the participants.

• Passionate love is characterized by intense physiological arousal, intimacy, and caring, while companionate love is characterized by respect, admiration, and affection.

• Psychologist Robert Sternberg suggests that three components of love (intimacy, passion, and decision/commitment) combine to form eight types of love, through which a relationship can dynamically evolve.

■ **How do people choose spouses, and what makes relationships work and cease working?**

• Although in Western cultures love tends to be the most important factor in selecting a partner, other cultures emphasize other factors.

• According to filtering models, people filter potential partners initially for attractiveness factors, and then for compatibility factors, generally conforming to the principle of homogamy and the marriage gradient.

• Gay men and lesbian women generally tend to seek the same qualities in relationships as heterosexual men and women: attachment, caring, intimacy, affection, and respect.

• In young adulthood, cohabitation is popular, marriage remains the most attractive option. The median age of first marriage is rising for both men and women.

• Divorce is prevalent in the United States, affecting nearly half of all marriages. Spouses who attribute negative events to unchanging personal characteristics in the spouse are more likely to divorce.

■ **How does the arrival of children affect a relationship?**

• More than 90 percent of married couples have at least one child but the size of the average family has decreased due partly to birth control and partly to the changing roles of women in the workforce.

• Children bring pressures to any marriage, shifting the focus of the marriage partners, changing their roles, and increasing in their responsibilities. Gay and lesbian couples with children experience similar changes in their relationships.

■ **Why is choosing a career such an important issue for young adults, and what factors influence the choice of a career?**

• According to George Vaillant, career consolidation is a developmental stage in which young adults are involved in defining their careers and themselves.

• A model developed by Eli Ginzberg suggests that people typically move through three stages in choosing a career: the fantasy period of youth, the tentative period of adolescence, and the realistic period of young adulthood.

- Other theories attempt to match people's personality types with suitable careers. This sort of research underlies most career-related inventories and measures used in career counseling.

- Gender role prejudice and stereotyping remain a problem in the workplace and in preparing for and selecting careers. Women tend to be pressured into certain occupations and out of others, and they earn less money for the same work.

■ **Why do people work, and what elements of a job bring satisfaction?**

- People are motivated to work by both extrinsic factors, such as the need for money and prestige, and intrinsic factors, such as the enjoyment of work and its personal importance. Work helps determine a person's identity, social life, and status.

- Job satisfaction is the result of many factors, including the nature and status of one's job, the amount of input one has into its nature, the variety of one's responsibilities, and the influence one has over others.

- The full implications of the welfare reform movement have not yet been assessed. Regulations that force welfare recipients into jobs—typically low-paying, stressful jobs—may have negative effects on home life and families.

EPILOGUE: DANCE

In this chapter we looked at the major issues of early adulthood: relationships, love, marriage, and careers. We explored the factors that lead to loving relationships, the considerations that affect the choice of whether and whom to marry, and the characteristics of good—and not so good—marriages. We also discussed factors that people consider in choosing careers and the features of careers that make them satisfying.

Recall the prologue in this chapter, about the highly significant dance that John and Alison performed at their wedding. Answer the following questions.

1. Do you think the pattern by which people fall in love was any different for John and Alison than it is for other couples? Why or why not?

2. Do you find evidence of social homogamy in John and Alison? What signs of a successful marriage do you see?

3. Do you think John and Alison are any more or less likely to divorce than other couples? Why or why not?

4. If John and Alison decide to have children, will they face unique challenges and opportunities, or will they encounter the same ones that all other new parents encounter? Why?

5. Do you foresee any particular challenges for John and Alison as they embark on their careers?

KEY TERMS AND CONCEPTS

intimacy-versus-isolation stage (p. 478)
stimulus-value-role (SVR) theory (p. 479)
passionate (or romantic) love (p. 480)
companionate love (p. 480)
labeling theory of passionate love (p. 480)
intimacy component (p. 481)
passion component (p. 481)
decision/commitment component (p. 481)
homogamy (p. 485)
marriage gradient (p. 485)

cohabitation (p. 489)
career consolidation (p. 498)
fantasy period (p. 499)
tentative period (p. 499)
realistic period (p. 499)
communal professions (p. 502)
agentic professions (p. 502)
extrinsic motivation (p. 503)
intrinsic motivation (p. 504)
status (p. 504)

CHAPTER 15

MIDDLE ADULTHOOD

Physical and Cognitive Development

PROLOGUE: A SECOND CHANCE TO SHINE

The challenges of school multiply when older people return to obtain an education.

Hazel Robinson just wanted to change her hairstyle, but one trip to a hairdresser in Amherst brought her a new lifestyle as well. A chance meeting with associate dean of studies Ruth Bass Green at the hairdresser's led Robinson, who is forty-seven, to stop thinking of Mount Holyoke College only as a place her daughter might attend and start thinking of it as a place where she could finish her degree.

"I'd drive by the campus many times, but always thought of it as Harvard: totally out of my reach even though I was a good student," Robinson recalls. But Green planted the seed of an idea, and soon Robinson was thinking, "I survived all these other things, why can't I go to this school?"

Green's encouragement to apply helped boost Robinson over the last of many hurdles between her and a diploma. At eighteen, she was too busy helping her mother raise her siblings to consider college. She took several courses over the next twenty-seven years, although rearing two kids in a dangerous inner city Boston neighborhood, coping with a drug-addicted husband, and supporting the family didn't leave much time for study. (Weir, 1997, pp. 1, 4)

LOOKING AHEAD   Today, Robinson is enrolled at Mount Holyoke, completing the degree that earlier circumstances prevented. Although her age sets her apart from her classmates, she certainly lacks none of the cognitive abilities required to excel.

In this chapter, we consider both physical and cognitive development during middle adulthood, roughly defined as the period from 40 to 60 years of age. For many people, it is a period when the passage of time becomes increasingly conspicuous as their bodies and, in slight ways, their cognitive abilities begin to change in unwelcome ways, perhaps for the first time in their lives. Yet at the same time, as we see in this and the following chapter, it is a period when many individuals are at the height of their capabilities, when they are engaged in the process of shaping their lives as never before.

We begin the chapter by considering physical development. We consider changes in height, weight, and strength, and discuss the subtle decline in acuity of the senses. We also look at the role of sexuality in middle adulthood.

Next, we consider health. We examine both wellness and illness during middle age, and pay particular attention to two of the major health problems of the period, heart disease and cancer.

Finally, the chapter focuses on cognitive development in middle age. We ask whether intelligence declines during the period, and we consider the difficulty of answering the question fully. We also look at memory, examining the ways in which memory capabilities change during middle adulthood.

In sum, after reading this chapter, you will be able to answer these questions:

Q

- What sorts of physical changes affect people in middle adulthood?

- What changes in sexuality do middle-aged men and women experience?

- Is middle adulthood a time of health or disease for men and women?

- What sorts of people are likely to get coronary heart disease?

- What causes cancer, and what tools are available to diagnose and treat it?

- What happens to a person's intelligence in middle adulthood?

- How does aging affect memory, and how can memory be improved?

PHYSICAL DEVELOPMENT

It crept up gradually on Sharon Boker-Tov. Soon after reaching the age of 40, she noticed that it took her a bit longer to bounce back from minor illnesses such as colds and the flu. Then she became conscious of changes in her eyesight: She needed more light to read fine print, and she had to adjust how far she held newspapers from her face in order to read them easily. Finally, she couldn't help but notice that the strands of gray hair on her head, which had begun to appear gradually in her late 20s, were becoming a virtual forest.

Physical Transitions: The Gradual Change in the Body's Capabilities

Middle adulthood is the time when most people first become aware of the gradual changes in their bodies that mark the aging process. Of course, physical changes occur throughout the entire life span. Yet these changes take on new significance during middle adulthood, particularly in Western cultures that place a high value on youthful appearance. For many people, the psychological significance of such changes far exceeds the relatively minor and gradual changes that they are experiencing.

People's reactions to the physical changes of middle adulthood depend, in part, on their self-concepts. For those whose self-image is tied closely to their physical attributes—such as highly athletic men and women or those who are physically quite attractive—middle adulthood can be particularly difficult. On the other hand, because most people's views of themselves are not so closely tied to physical attributes, middle-aged adults generally report no less satisfaction with their body images than younger adults (Berscheid, Walster, & Bohrnstedt, 1973).

Still, physical appearance plays an important role in determining how people view themselves, as well as how they are viewed by others. This is particularly the case for women, for whom societal pressures to retain a youthful appearance are especially strong in Western cultures. In fact, society applies a double standard to men and women in terms of appearance: Whereas older women tend to be viewed in unflattering terms, aging men are more frequently perceived as displaying a maturity that enhances their stature (Nowak, 1977; Katchadourian, 1987; Harris, 1994).

Height, Weight, and Strength: The Benchmarks of Change

For most people, height reaches a maximum during their 20s and remains relatively stable until around age 55. At that point, people begin a "settling" process in which the bones attached to the spinal column become less dense. Although the loss of height is very slow, ultimately women average a 2-inch decline and men a 1-inch decline over the rest of the life span (Rossman, 1977).

Women are more prone to a decline in height because of their greater risk of osteoporosis. **Osteoporosis**, a condition in which the bones become brittle, fragile, and thin, is often brought about by a lack of calcium in the diet. As we discuss further in Chapter 17, women can reduce the risk of osteoporosis by maintaining a diet high in calcium (which is found in milk, yogurt, cheese, and other dairy products) and by exercising regularly (Prince et al., 1991).

Both men and women continue to gain weight during middle adulthood, and the amount of body fat likewise tends to grow in the average person. Because height is not increasing, and actually may be declining, these weight and body fat gains lead to an increase in obesity. "Middle-age spread" is a visible symptom of this problem, as even those who have been relatively slim all their lives may begin to put on weight.

The typical gains in weight that occur during middle adulthood are hardly preordained by genetic factors. In fact, people who maintain an exercise program during middle age tend to avoid obesity, as do individuals living in cultures in which the typical life is more active and less sedentary than that of many Western cultures.

Changes in height and weight are also accompanied by declines in strength. Throughout middle adulthood, strength gradually decreases, particularly in the back and leg muscles. By the time they are 60, people have lost, on average, about 10 percent of their maximum strength. Still, such a loss in strength is relatively minor, and most people are easily able to compensate for it (Troll, 1985).

The Senses: The Sights and Sounds of Middle Age

One of the signs of middle age that most people find unmistakable is a change in the sensitivity of the sense organs. Although all the organs seem to shift at roughly the same rate, the changes are particularly noticeable in vision and hearing.

osteoporosis: *a condition in which the bones become brittle, fragile, and thin, often brought about by a lack of calcium in the diet*

Beginning at around the age of 40, visual acuity, the ability to discern fine spatial detail, begins to drop. Most people begin to suffer from presbyopia, a decline in near vision.

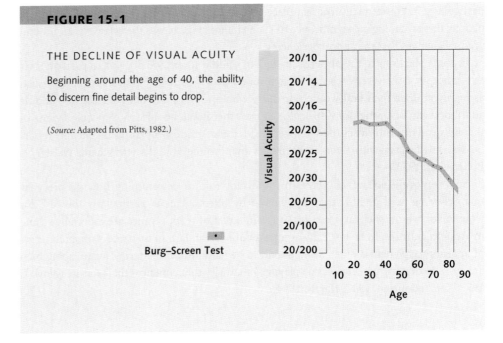

FIGURE 15-1

THE DECLINE OF VISUAL ACUITY

Beginning around the age of 40, the ability to discern fine detail begins to drop.

(*Source:* Adapted from Pitts, 1982.)

Vision. Starting at around age 40, *visual acuity*—the ability to discern fine spatial detail in both close and distant objects—begins to decline (see Figure 15-1). One major reason is a change in the shape and elasticity of the eye's lens, which makes it harder to focus images sharply onto the retina. Furthermore, the lens becomes less transparent, which reduces the amount of light that passes through the eye (Pitts, 1982; DiGiovanna, 1994).

A nearly universal change in eyesight during middle adulthood is the loss of near vision, called **presbyopia**. Even people who have never needed glasses or contact lenses find themselves holding reading matter at an increasing distance from their eyes in order to bring it into focus. Eventually, they need reading glasses. For those who were previously nearsighted, presbyopia may require bifocals or two sets of glasses (Kline & Schieber, 1985).

Other changes in vision also begin in middle adulthood. For instance, declines occur in depth perception, distance perception, and the ability to view the world in three dimensions. Furthermore, adaptation to darkness, which allows people to see in dimly lit environments, also declines. Such visual reductions may make it more difficult to climb stairs or to navigate around a dark room (Artal et al., 1993; Spear, 1993).

Although changes in vision are most often brought about by gradual aging processes, in some cases disease is involved. One of the most frequent causes of eye problems is glaucoma—which may, if left untreated—ultimately produce blindness. **Glaucoma** occurs when pressure in the fluid of the eye increases, either because the fluid cannot drain properly or because too much is produced. Around 1 to 2 percent of people over the age of 40 are afflicted by the disorder, and African Americans are particularly susceptible (Wilson, 1989).

Initially, the increased pressure in the eye may constrict the neurons involved in peripheral vision and lead to tunnel vision. Ultimately, the pressure can become so high that all nerve cells are constricted, which causes complete blindness. Fortunately, glaucoma can be treated if it is detected early enough. Medication can reduce the pressure in the eye, as can surgery to restore normal drainage of eye fluid.

Hearing. Like vision, hearing undergoes a gradual decline in acuity starting in middle adulthood. For the most part, however, the changes are less evident than those involving eyesight.

The primary sort of loss is for sounds of high frequency, a problem called **presbycusis**. About 12 percent of people between 45 and 65 suffer from presbycusis. There is also a gender difference: Men are more prone to hearing loss than women, starting at around age 55.

presbyopia *a nearly universal change in eyesight during middle adulthood that results in some loss of near vision*

glaucoma *a condition in which pressure in the fluid of the eye increases, either because the fluid cannot drain properly or because too much fluid is produced*

presbycusis *loss of the ability to hear sounds of high frequency*

Finally, because the two ears are not equally affected by hearing difficulties, *sound localization*, the process by which the origin of a sound is identified, is diminished (Schneider, 1997). This is true because sound localization depends on comparing the discrepancy in sound perceived by the two ears (DiGiovanna, 1994).

Some of the hearing losses of middle adulthood result from environmental factors. For instance, people whose professions keep them near loud noises—such as jet airplane mechanics and construction workers—are more apt to suffer debilitating and permanent hearing loss.

However, many changes are simply related to aging. For instance, age brings a loss of *hair cells* in the inner ear, which transmit neural messages to the brain when vibrations bend them. Furthermore, the eardrum becomes less elastic with age, further reducing sound sensitivity (Olsho, Harkins, & Lenhardt, 1985).

Despite these physiological changes, declines in sensitivity to sounds do not markedly affect most people in middle adulthood. Most people are able to compensate for the losses that do occur relatively easily—by asking people to speak up, turning up the volume of a television set, or paying greater attention to what others are saying.

Reaction Time: Not-so-slowing Down

One common concern about aging is the notion that people begin to slow down once they reach middle adulthood. How valid is such a worry?

In most cases, not very. Although there is an increase in reaction time (meaning that it takes longer to react to a stimulus), usually the increase is fairly mild and hardly noticeable (Nobuyuki, 1997). For instance, reaction time on simple tasks increases by around 20 percent from age 20 to 60. More complex tasks, which require the coordination of various skills—such as driving a car—show less of an increase. Still, it takes a bit more time for drivers to move the foot from the gas pedal to the brake when they are faced with an emergency situation. Increases in reaction time are largely produced by changes in the speed with which the nervous system processes nerve impulses (DiGiovanna, 1994).

On the other hand, because complex skills are often heavily practiced, or rehearsed, major drops in actual performance are generally avoided. In fact, middle-aged drivers tend to have fewer accidents than younger ones. Although part of the reason for their better performance is that older drivers tend to be more careful and to take fewer risks than younger ones, much of the cause is older drivers' greater amount of practice in the skill. In the case of reaction time, then, practice may indeed make perfect (Birren, Woods, & Williams, 1980; Siegler & Costa, 1985).

Can increases in reaction time, as well as other physical consequences of aging related to the muscle systems of the body, be slowed down? In many cases, the answer is yes. Specifically, involvement in an active exercise program retards the effects of aging, producing several important outcomes (see Figure 15-2). "Use it or lose it" is an aphorism with which developmental psychologists would agree.

Sex in Middle Adulthood: The Ongoing Sexuality of Middle Age

Common wisdom, particularly among those under 40, suggests that sex is an activity of youth and early adulthood that generally fades away with age.

Most middle-aged people would tell a different story. Although it is true that the frequency of sexual intercourse declines with age (see Figure 15-3 on page 517), sexual activities of various sorts remain a vital part of most middle-aged adults' lives (Whitbourne, 1990; Smith, 1991; Michael et al., 1994; Shaw, 1994; Sipski & Alexander, 1997).

In fact, many people experience a kind of sexual enjoyment and freedom that they lacked during their earlier lives. With their children grown and away from home, middle-aged couples may have more time to engage in uninterrupted sexual activities. Furthermore, if the female partner has passed through menopause, they may be liberated from the fear of pregnancy and may no longer need to employ birth control techniques (Sherwin, 1991; Lamont, 1997).

FIGURE 15-2

THE BENEFITS OF EXERCISE

There are many benefits from maintaining a high level of physical activity throughout life.

(*Source:* DiGiovanna, 1994, p. 159.)

The advantages of exercise include

Muscle System

Slower decline in energy molecules, muscle cell thickness, number of muscle cells, muscle thickness, muscle mass, muscle strength, blood supply, speed of movement, stamina

Slower increase in fat and fibers, reaction time, recovery time, development of muscle soreness

Nervous System

Slower decline in processing impulses by the central nervous system

Slower increase in variations in speed of motor neuron impulses

Circulatory System

Maintenance of lower levels of LDLs and higher HDL/cholesterol and HDL/LDL ratios

Decreased risk of high blood pressure, atherosclerosis, heart attack, stroke

Skeletal System

Slower decline in bone minerals

Decreased risk of fractures and osteoporosis

Certainly there are differences in the sexual experiences of women and men during middle adulthood. For instance, a man typically needs more time to achieve an erection, and it takes longer after an orgasm to have another. The volume of fluid that is ejaculated declines. Finally, the production of *testosterone*, the male sex hormone, declines with age (Hyde, 1994).

For women, the walls of the vagina become thinner and less elastic. The vagina shrinks and its entrance becomes compressed, potentially making intercourse painful.

Contrary to popular opinion, sexuality continues to be a vital part of most couples' lives in middle adulthood.

FIGURE 15-3

FREQUENCY OF SEXUAL INTERCOURSE

As people age, the frequency of sexual intercourse declines.

(*Source:* Adapted from Michael et al., 1994.)

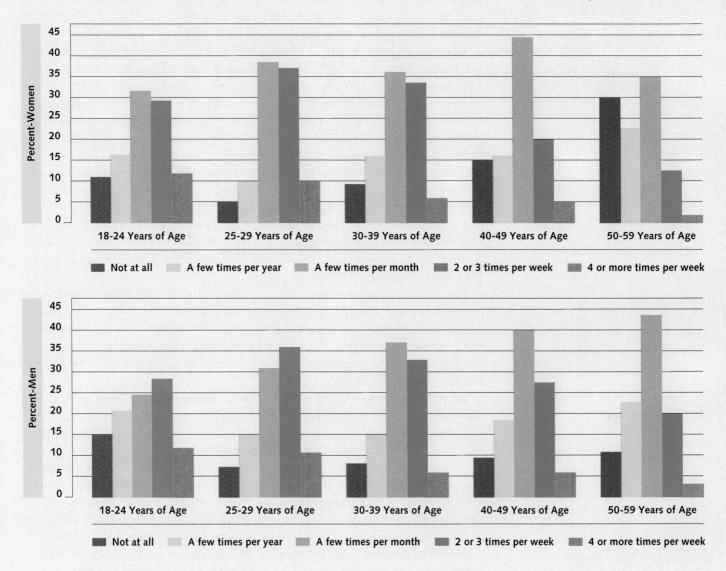

The Female Climacteric and Menopause.   Starting at around age 45, women enter a period known as the climacteric that lasts for some 15 to 20 years. The **female climacteric** marks the transition from being able to bear children to being unable to do so.

The most notable sign of the female climacteric is menopause. **Menopause** is the cessation of menstruation. For most women, menstrual periods begin to occur irregularly and less frequently during a 2-year period starting at around age 47 or 48, although this process may begin as early as age 40 or as late as age 60. After a year goes by without a menstrual period, menopause is said to have occurred.

Menopause is important for several reasons. For one thing, it marks the point at which a traditional pregnancy is no longer possible (although, as we will discuss later, eggs implanted in a postmenopausal woman can produce a pregnancy). In addition, the

female climacteric   *the period that marks the transition from being able to bear children to being unable to do so*

menopause   *the cessation of menstruation*

production of estrogen and progesterone, the female sex hormones, begins to drop, producing a variety of hormone-related age changes (Hyde, 1994; DiGiovanna, 1994; Wise, Krajnak, & Kashon, 1996).

The changes in hormone production may produce a variety of symptoms, although the degree to which a woman experiences them varies significantly. One of the best known and most prevalent symptoms is "hot flashes," in which a woman senses an unexpected feeling of heat from the waist up. A woman may get red and begin to sweat when a hot flash occurs. Afterwards, she may feel chilled. Some women experience hot flashes several times a day; others, not at all.

Other symptoms may mark menopause. For instance, headaches, feelings of dizziness, heart palpitations, and aching joints are relatively common during the period. However, such complaints are far from universal. In one survey, for instance, only half of the women reported experiencing hot flashes. In general, only about one-tenth of all women experience severe distress during menopause. And many—perhaps as many as half—have no significant symptoms at all (McKinlay & Jeffreys, 1974; Hyde, 1994).

For women who do experience significant distress, one treatment is to take substitute hormones. In *estrogen replacement therapy* (ERT), estrogen and progesterone are administered to alleviate the worst of the symptoms experienced by menopausal women. ERT reduces a variety of problems, such as hot flashes and loss of skin elasticity, and it may help prevent osteoporosis, heart disease, colon cancer, and stroke. However, the use of estrogen replacement therapy poses several risks, and it has become controversial, as we consider in the accompanying "Directions in Development" box (Schover & Jensen, 1988; Elias, 1990; Wallis, 1995).

Does menopause produce psychological problems? Traditionally, experts, as well as the general population, believed that menopause was linked directly to depression, anxiety, crying spells, lack of concentration, and irritability. In fact, estimates of the incidence of severe depression ran as high as 10 percent of menopausal women. It was assumed that physiological changes in menopausal women's bodies brought about such disagreeable outcomes (Schmidt & Rubinow, 1991).

Today, however, most researchers view menopause from a different perspective. It now seems more reasonable to regard menopause as a normal part of aging that does not, by itself, produce psychological symptoms. Certainly some women experience psychological difficulties, but they do at other points in life as well.

Furthermore, research indicates that the expectations women have about menopause make a significant difference in their experience of it. Women who expect to have difficulties during menopause are more likely to attribute every physical symptom and emotional swing to it. On the other hand, those with more positive attitudes toward menopause may be less apt to attribute physical sensations to menopausal physiological changes. A woman's attribution of physical symptoms, then, affects her perception of the rigors of menopause—and ultimately her actual experience of the period (Leiblum, 1990).

The nature and extent of menopausal symptoms also differ according to a woman's ethnic and cultural background. For instance, an ongoing large-scale study involving some 10,000 women in the United States is finding clear ethnic differences in menopausal symptoms. By identifying ethnic differences, researchers may be able to target health programs to specific groups.

In preliminary findings from the research, dubbed the "Study of Women's Health Across the Nation (SWAN), Asian American women report that menopause produces relatively few symptoms of any sort. On the other hand, although they are less likely to experience such symptoms as sleep difficulties and headaches, African American women report relatively high levels of estrogen-related symptoms such as night sweats and hot flashes. Hispanic women are more likely to experience racing heart and urinary leakage than members of other groups. Regardless of ethnicity, smokers have more symptoms than nonsmokers (DeAngelis, 1997).

Directions in Development

The Estrogen Dilemma

On February 13, 1963, a new patient strode into the office of New York City gynecologist Robert A. Wilson. To Wilson, she was nothing less than a revelation or, to be more precise, a walking, talking confirmation of his most deeply held medical convictions. Wilson was a leading proponent of treating menopausal women with the female hormone estrogen. He was convinced that, given early enough and continued throughout life, hormone treatment could actually prevent what he called the "staggering catastrophe" of menopause and the "fast and painful aging process" that attended it.

Wilson's new patient, "Mrs. P.G.," as he later called her, said she was 52 years old, but her body told another story. "Her breasts were supple and firm, her carriage erect; she had good general muscle tone, no dryness of the mucous membranes and no visible genital atrophy. Above all," Wilson noted, "her skin was smooth and pliant as a girl's." When asked about menopause, she laughed and replied, "I assure you, Dr. Wilson, I have never yet missed a period. I'm so regular, astronomers could use me for timing the moon." (Wallis, 1995, p. 46)

Mrs. P.G.'s secret, according to Wilson: For years, she had been taking birth-control pills that contained a combination of estrogen and progesterone, two female hormones. According to Wilson, these drugs not only would delay the onset of menopause, but would act as a veritable fountain of youth.

Although Wilson's claims were challenged from the start, later research has shown that estrogen does help relieve the symptoms of menopause and may, as a side effect, slow some aspects of aging. These findings have been enough to make estrogen the most widely prescribed drug in the United States.

Is estrogen a wonder drug? In many ways, research shows that it has positive effects well beyond menopausal-related symptoms. For instance, there is some suggestion that it reduces coronary heart disease by changing the ratio of "good" cholesterol to "bad" cholesterol. In addition, it decreases the thinning of the bones related to osteoporosis, a problem for many people in late adulthood. Furthermore, some studies show that the risk of stroke declines, and there may be a decreased risk of colon cancer. Estrogen may even slow the mental deterioration found in people suffering from Alzheimer's disease. Finally, estrogen may lead to an increased sex drive (Nachtigall & Heilman, 1995; Stahl, 1997).

But what is also clear is that estrogen replacement therapy may have a dark side, and that the positive results may come at a price that some women may find too high to pay. The most daunting problem is research suggesting that the risk of breast cancer rises with estrogen use. For instance, some studies, such as one involving 70,000 nurses, indicate that there is a greater risk of breast cancer in women taking replacement hormones. Other risks include increases in the incidence of cancer of the uterine lining and an increase in benign fibroid tumors in the uterus (Colditz et al., 1995).

Other research suggests that ERT is associated with additional health risks, including abnormal blood clots and cancer of the uterine lining. These uncertainties make the routine use of ERT controversial, and many women face difficult choices in deciding whether the benefits of the treatment outweigh the potential dangers (Steinberg et al., 1991; LaVecchia, 1996; Sheffield, 1997; Swan, 1997).

Learning that there are ethnic differences in menopause within the United States is consistent with research that women in non-Western cultures often have vastly different menopausal experiences. For instance, women of high castes in India report few symptoms of menopause. In fact, they look forward to menopause because being postmenopausal produces several social advantages, such as an end to taboos associated with menstruation and a perception of increased wisdom due to age. Similarly, Mayan women have no notion of hot flashes, and they generally look forward to the end of their childbearing years (Flint, 1982, 1989; Beck, 1992; Koster & Davidsen, 1993).

Pregnancy After Menopause: What Are the Ethics?

Sophia sits in a booth in a dimly lighted Chinese restaurant, reluctantly talking about the details of her life. She is beyond tired, as she has been for several months, and as she is likely to be for several more. The weathered brown of her hair, the weary brown shadows under her eyes, even the muted brown of her maternity dress over her very pregnant lap—all of these things somehow magnify her exhaustion.

male climacteric *the period of physical and psychological change relating to the male reproductive system that occurs during late middle age*

The number of women over 50 giving birth is increasing.

It is a Friday night, and she did not leave the office until nearly 6:30, working until the last moment, tying up the loose ends in her high-powered job. On Monday, she will have a Caesarean section, which she scheduled months ago because her doctor did not think her body could withstand the rigors of labor....

Sophia is having her first baby. She is 51 years old. (Belkin, 1997, p. 35)

Sophia is not the oldest woman to become pregnant—not by a long shot. That record belongs to a 63-year-old woman, who gave birth to a healthy baby girl in 1997 (Kolata, 1997).

Despite earlier thinking that the environment of the uterus of post-menopausal women was inhospitable to eggs even from much younger women, the successful pregnancy of the 63-year-old suggests that any woman, no matter her age, may be able to become pregnant with a donated egg, providing the donor is young enough. If the sperm used to fertilize the egg is from the husband or partner of the woman seeking to be pregnant, then the baby will receive half its genetic endowment from him.

The possibility of older women becoming pregnant raises both medical and ethical questions. One is whether the pregnancy will be too physically taxing for the woman, and whether—once the baby is born—she will have the energy to care for the child adequately. Furthermore, there is the issue of who should determine whether an older woman should be implanted with a younger egg: the woman, physicians, medical boards, or legislatures? The source of an egg also raises issues, particularly when younger women are paid a fee for providing an egg. Furthermore, it is unclear whether the woman who donates the egg should have any legal or financial responsibility or ties to the child. Because the technology that allows for pregnancies in older women is so new, none of these questions has been sorted out (Belkin, 1997; Kolata, 1997).

The Male Climacteric. Do men experience the equivalent of menopause? Not really: Because they have never weathered anything akin to menstruation, they would have difficulty experiencing its discontinuation. On the other hand, men experience some changes during middle age that are collectively referred to as the male climacteric. The **male climacteric** is the period of physical and psychological change in the reproductive system that occurs during late middle age.

Because the changes happen gradually, it is hard to pinpoint the exact period of the male climacteric. For instance, despite progressive declines in the production of testosterone and sperm, men continue to be able to father children throughout middle age. Furthermore, it is no easier in men than in women to attribute psychological symptoms to subtle physiological changes.

One physical change that does occur quite frequently is enlargement of the *prostate gland*. By the age of 40, around 10 percent of men have enlarged prostates, and the percentage increases to half of all men by the age of 80. Enlargement of the prostate produces problems with urination, including difficulty starting urination or a need to urinate frequently at night.

Although the physical changes associated with middle age are unequivocal, whether they are the direct cause of any particular psychological symptoms or changes is unclear. Men, like women, clearly undergo psychological development during middle adulthood, but the extent to which psychological changes—which we discuss more in the next chapter—are associated with changes in reproductive capabilities remains an open question.

REVIEW AND RETHINK

REVIEW

■ People in middle adulthood experience changes in physical characteristics and appearance. Although most changes are gradual and minor, they can trouble people whose self-images are closely tied to physical attributes.

- The acuity of the senses, particularly vision and hearing, and speed of reaction also decline during middle age, but the losses are usually slight and produce few real problems.

- Sexuality in middle adulthood changes slightly, but not as dramatically as common wisdom supposes. Middle-aged couples, freed from concerns about children, can often progress to a new level of intimacy and enjoyment.

- Physiological changes relating to sexuality occur in both men and women. Both the female climacteric, which includes menopause, and the male climacteric seem to have physical and psychological symptoms.

RETHINK

- Do you think a woman of 45 who works hard "not to look her age" combats or contributes to a cultural bias against middle-aged women? Why?

- What cultural factors in the United States might contribute to a woman's negative experience of menopause? How?

- Would you rather fly on an airplane with a middle-aged pilot or a young one? Why?

- Why do you think consistent exercise has positive effects not only on strength and agility, but on general health and psychological state as well?

HEALTH

It was an average exercise session for Jerome El-Neel. After the alarm went off at 5:30 A.M., he climbed onto his exercise bike and began vigorously peddling, trying to maintain, and exceed, his average speed of 14 miles per hour. Stationed in front of the television set, he used the remote control to tune to the morning business news. Occasionally glancing up at the television, he began reading a report he had not finished the night before, swearing under his breath at some of the poor sales figures he was finding in the report. By the time he had completed exercising a half-hour later, he had gotten through the report, had managed to sign a few letters his secretary had typed for him, and had even left two voice-mail messages for some colleagues.

Most of us would be ready to head back to bed after such a packed half-hour. For Jerome El-Neel, however, it was routine: He consistently tried to accomplish several activities at the same time. Jerome thought of such behavior as efficient. Developmental psychologists might view it in another light, however: as symptomatic of a style of behavior that makes Jerome a likely candidate for coronary heart disease.

Although most people are relatively healthy in middle adulthood, they also become increasingly susceptible to a variety of health-related concerns. We will consider some of the typical health problems of middle age, focusing in particular on coronary heart disease and cancer.

Wellness and Illness: The Ups and Downs of Middle Adulthood

For most people, middle age is a period of health. According to census figures, the vast majority of middle-aged adults report no chronic health difficulties and face no limitations on their activities (U.S. Bureau of the Census, 1990b).

In fact, in some ways people are better off, healthwise, in middle adulthood than in earlier periods of life. For instance, they are less apt to be involved in accidents, and people between the ages of 45 and 65 are less likely than younger adults to experience infections, allergies, respiratory diseases, and digestive problems. In part, their relative protection from such diseases is due to the fact that they may have already experienced them and built up immunities during younger adulthood (Siegler & Costa, 1985; Sterns, Barrett, & Alexander, 1985).

On the other hand, during middle adulthood people can become particularly susceptible to chronic diseases. Arthritis typically begins after the age of 40, and diabetes is most likely to

TABLE 15-1

SELECTED PREVENTION AND SCREENING RECOMMENDATIONS FOR OLDER ADULTS

Blood pressure	Every exam, at least every 1–2 years
Mammogram	The American Cancer Society recommends annually after age 40, although other groups say every other year is OK*. From 70 to 85, screening can be every 1–3 years of a doctor deems it appropriate. Screening is unnecessary after that.
Physician breast exam	Annually after age 40
Pelvic exam/Pap	Every 2–3 years after 3 negative annual exams. Can decrease or discontinue after age 65–69.
Prostate/PSA	The American Cancer Society recommends annually after age 50, but other groups say this is only an option that should be discussed between patient and physician.
Cholesterol	Adults every 5 years; less certain for elderly
Rectal exam	Annually after age 40
Fecal occult blood test	Annually after age 50
Sigmoidoscopy	Every 3–5 years after age 50
Thyroid function	Prudent for elderly, especially women
Electrocardiogram	Periodically from 40s onward
Tetanus vaccine	Booster every 10 years

*This controversy is addressed later in this chapter.
(*Source:* Adapted from Journal of the American Geriatrics Society, March 1997.)

occur in people between the ages of 50 and 60. Hypertension (high blood pressure) is one of the most frequent chronic disorders found in middle age. Sometimes called the "silent killer" because it is symptomless, hypertension, if left untreated, greatly increases the risk of strokes and heart disease. For such reasons, a variety of preventive and diagnostic medical tests are routinely recommended for adults during middle adulthood (see Table 15-1).

Health concerns become increasingly important to people during middle adulthood. In fact, surveys asking adults what they worry about show health—as well as safety and money—to be an issue of concern. For instance, more than half of adults surveyed say they are either "afraid" or "very afraid" of having cancer (see Figure 15-4).

As a result of this greater susceptibility to disease, the death rate among middle-aged individuals is higher than it is in earlier periods of life. Still, the figures are not particularly grim: Statistically, only 3 out of every hundred 40-year-olds would be expected to die before the age of 50, and 8 out of every hundred 50-year olds would be expected to die before the age of 60. Furthermore, the death rate for people between 40 and 60 has declined dramatically over the past 50 years. For instance, the death rate now stands at just half of what it was in the 1940s (U.S. Census Bureau, 1991c).

The A's and B's of Coronary Heart Disease: Linking Health and Personality

More men die in middle age from diseases relating to the heart and circulatory system than from any other cause. Each year such diseases kill around 200,000 people under the age of 65, and they are responsible for more loss of work and disability days due to hospitalization than any other cause (American Heart Association, 1988).

FIGURE 15-4

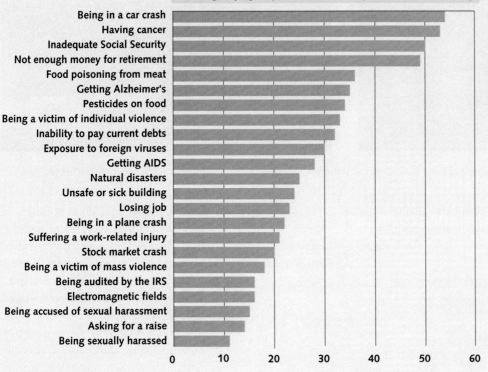

Percentage Saying They Are "Afraid" or "Very Afraid" of the Following:

- Being in a car crash
- Having cancer
- Inadequate Social Security
- Not enough money for retirement
- Food poisoning from meat
- Getting Alzheimer's
- Pesticides on food
- Being a victim of individual violence
- Inability to pay current debts
- Exposure to foreign viruses
- Getting AIDS
- Natural disasters
- Unsafe or sick building
- Losing job
- Being in a plane crash
- Suffering a work-related injury
- Stock market crash
- Being a victim of mass violence
- Being audited by the IRS
- Electromagnetic fields
- Being accused of sexual harassment
- Asking for a raise
- Being sexually harassed

0   10   20   30   40   50   60

WORRIES OF ADULTHOOD

As people enter middle adulthood, health and safety concerns become increasingly important, followed by financial worries.

(*Source: USA Weekend*, August 22–24 1997, p 5. Copyright 1997, USA Weekend. Reprinted with permission.)

Developmental Diversity

Individual Variation in Health: Ethnic and Gender Differences

Masked by the overall figures describing the health of middle-aged adults are vast individual differences. Although most people are relatively healthy, some are beset by a variety of ailments. Part of the cause is genetic. For instance, hypertension often runs in families.

Some of the causes of poor health are more insidious, however; they are related to social and environmental factors. For instance, the death rate for middle-aged African Americans in the United States is twice the rate for Caucasians. Why should this be true?

The answer seems to lie not in race per se, but in socioeconomic status (SES) differences between majority and minority groups. For instance, when whites and African Americans of the same SES level are compared, the death rate for African Americans actually falls below that of whites. Furthermore,

the lower a family's income, the more likely it is that a member will experience a disabling illness. Similarly, people living in lower SES households are more apt to work in occupations that are dangerous, such as mining or construction work. Ultimately, then, a higher incidence of accidents and poor health, and ultimately a higher death rate, are linked to lower levels of income (Hall, 1982; U.S. Bureau of the Census, 1990b; Fingerhut & MaKuc, 1992; Dahl & Birkelund, 1997; see Figure 15-5).

Gender, like ethnicity and race, also makes a difference in health. Even though women's overall mortality rate is lower than men's—a trend that holds true from the time of infancy—the incidence of illness among middle-aged women is higher than among men.

Why are women more apt to be sick, but at the same time less likely to die? The answer is that women are more likely to experience minor, short-term, and non-life-threatening diseases, and men are more apt to experience more serious illnesses. Furthermore, the rate of cigarette smoking is lower among women than men, which reduces their susceptibility

The discrepancies in the lives of people of higher and lower socioeconomic status are associated with differences in death rates between the two groups.

to cancer and heart disease; women drink less alcohol than men, which reduces the risk of cirrhosis of the liver and auto accidents; and they work at less dangerous jobs (Verbrugge, 1985; Schaefer & Lamm, 1992).

One might reason that the higher incidence of illness in women would be accompanied by greater medical research targeted toward the types of disorders from which they suffer. However, this is not the case. In fact, the vast majority of medical research money is aimed at preventing life-threatening diseases faced mostly by men, rather than at chronic conditions that may cause disability and suffering, but not necessarily death. Even when research is carried out on diseases that strike both men and women, much of it has focused on men as subjects, rather than women. Although this bias is specifically being addressed in new initiatives announced in the mid-1990s by the U.S. National Institutes of Health, the historical pattern has been one of gender discrimination by the traditionally male-dominated research community (Shumaker & Smith, 1994).

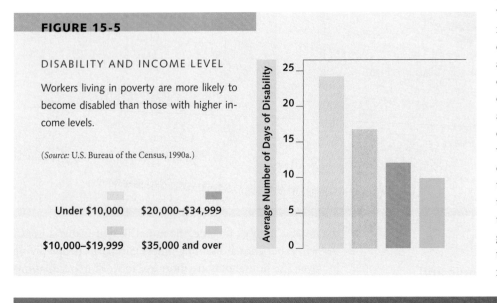

FIGURE 15-5

DISABILITY AND INCOME LEVEL

Workers living in poverty are more likely to become disabled than those with higher income levels.

(*Source:* U.S. Bureau of the Census, 1990a.)

Under $10,000 $20,000–$34,999

$10,000–$19,999 $35,000 and over

(Y-axis: Average Number of Days of Disability — 0, 5, 10, 15, 20, 25)

   Risk Factors for Heart Disease.   Although heart and circulatory diseases are a major problem, they are not equally deadly to all people. In fact, some people have a much lower risk than others. For instance, the death rate in some countries, such as Japan, is only a quarter the rate in the United States (see Figure 15-6). Why should this be true?

The answer is that both genetic and experiential characteristics are involved. Some people seem genetically predisposed to develop heart disease. If a person's parents suffered from it, the likelihood is greater that she or he will, too. Similarly, sex and age are risk factors: Men are more likely to suffer from heart disease than women, and the risk rises as people age.

   However, several risk factors are a function of environmental and behavioral factors. For instance, cigarette smoking, a diet high in fats and cholesterol, and a relative lack of physical exercise all increase the likelihood of heart disease. Such factors may explain

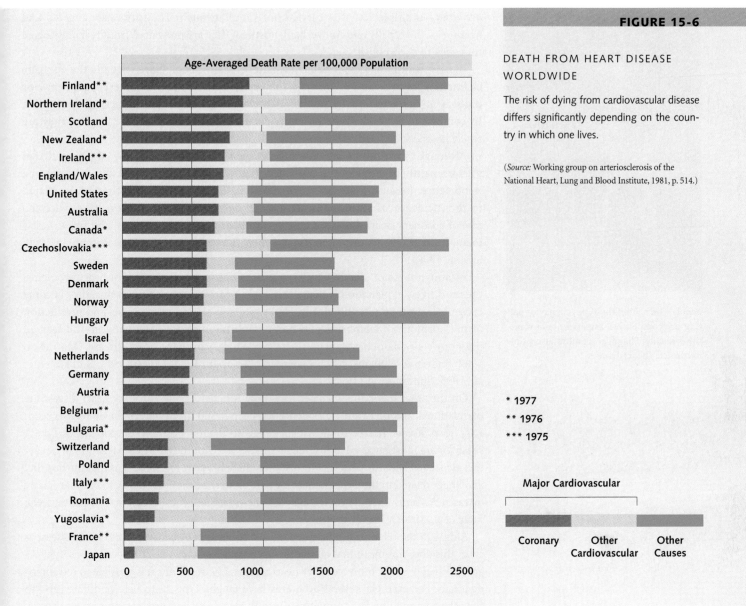

FIGURE 15-6

DEATH FROM HEART DISEASE
WORLDWIDE

The risk of dying from cardiovascular disease differs significantly depending on the country in which one lives.

(*Source:* Working group on arteriosclerosis of the National Heart, Lung and Blood Institute, 1981, p. 514.)

* 1977
** 1976
*** 1975

Major Cardiovascular

Coronary   Other Cardiovascular   Other Causes

country-to-country variations in incidence. For example, the relatively low death rate attributable to heart disease in Japan may be due to differences in diet: The typical diet in Japan is much lower in fat than the typical diet in the United States.

In addition, increasing evidence suggests that psychological factors may be associated with heart disease. In particular, a set of personality characteristics appears to be related to the development of coronary heart disease—the Type A behavior pattern.

Type A's and Type B's.   For a certain proportion of adults, waiting patiently in a long line at the grocery store is a near impossibility. Sitting in their cars at a long red light makes them seethe. And an encounter with a slow, inept clerk at a retail store turns them furious.

People like this—and those similar to Jerome El-Neel, who uses his exercise program as an opportunity to accomplish more work—have a set of personality characteristics known as the Type A behavior pattern. The **Type A behavior pattern** is characterized by competitiveness, impatience, and a tendency toward frustration and hostility. Type A people are driven to accomplish more than others, and they engage in *polyphasic*

Type A behavior pattern behavior characterized by competitiveness, impatience, and a tendency toward frustration and hostility

People who exhibit the Type A behavior pattern are competitive, impatient, and sometimes hostile. They also are more susceptible to coronary heart disease.

activities—multiple activities carried out simultaneously. They are easily angered and become both verbally and nonverbally hostile if they are prevented from reaching a goal they seek to accomplish.

In contrast to the Type A behavior pattern, many people have virtually the opposite characteristics in a pattern known as the Type B behavior pattern. The **Type B behavior pattern** is characterized by noncompetitiveness, patience, and a lack of aggression. In contrast to Type A's, Type B's experience little sense of time urgency, and they are rarely hostile.

Although most adults are not purely Type A's or Type B's, they do tend to fall predominantly into one of the two categories. Which category they fall into is of some importance, because a great deal of research suggests that the distinction is related to the incidence of coronary heart disease. Specifically, Type A men have twice the rate of coronary heart disease, a greater number of fatal heart attacks, and five times as many heart problems overall as Type B men (Rosenman et al., 1976; Rosenman 1990; Strube, 1990).

Although it is not certain why Type A behavior increases the risk of heart problems, the most likely explanation is that when Type A's are in stressful situations, they become excessively aroused physiologically. Heart rate and blood pressure rise, and production of the hormones epinephrine and norepinephrine increases. Undue wear and tear on the body's circulatory system ultimately produces coronary heart disease (Matthews, 1982; Suarez & Williams, 1992; Blascovich & Katkin, 1993; Lyness, 1993; Raikkonen et al., 1995; Sundin, et al., 1995).

On the other hand, the links between Type A behavior and coronary heart disease are correlational, and no definitive evidence has been found that Type A behavior *causes* coronary heart disease. In fact, some evidence suggests that only certain components of Type A behavior are most involved in producing disease, and not the entire constellation of behaviors associated with the pattern. For instance, there is a growing consensus that the hostility and anger related to the Type A behavior pattern may be the central link to coronary heart disease (Williams, 1993, 1996; Lassner, Matthews, & Stoney, 1994; Siegman & Smith, 1994; Jiang et al., 1996; Miller et al., 1996).

Although the relationship between at least some Type A behaviors and heart disease is clear, this does not mean that all middle-aged adults who can be characterized as Type A's are destined to suffer from coronary heart disease. For one thing, it is possible to retrain individuals. For example, several programs have taught Type A's to behave differently—to slow their pace, to be less competitive, and in general to be more patient and less hostile with others. Such training is linked to declines in the risk of coronary heart disease (Cottreaux, 1993; Williams, 1993; Thoresen & Bracke, 1997).

In addition, almost all the research conducted to date has focused on men, primarily because the incidence of coronary heart disease is much higher for males than for females. Consequently, until more research involving women is done, the findings that link the Type A behavior pattern to coronary heart disease apply primarily to men.

The Threat of Cancer

Few diseases are as frightening as cancer, and many middle-aged individuals view a cancer diagnosis as a death sentence. Although the reality is different—many forms of cancer respond quite well to medical treatment, and 40 percent of people diagnosed with the disease are still alive 5 years later—the disease raises many fears. And there is no denying the fact that cancer is the second-leading cause of death in the United States (American Cancer Society, 1992).

The precise trigger for cancer is still not known, but the process by which cancer spreads is straightforward. For some reason, particular cells in the body begin to multiply

Type B behavior pattern *behavior characterized by noncompetitiveness, patience, and a lack of aggression*

uncontrollably and rapidly. As they increase in number, these cells form tumors. If left unimpeded, they draw nutrients from healthy cells and body tissue. Eventually, they destroy the body's ability to function properly.

Like heart disease, cancer is associated with a variety of risk factors, some genetic and others environmental. Some kinds of cancer have clear genetic components. For example, a family history of breast cancer—which is the most common cause of cancer death among women—raises the risk for a woman.

However, several environmental and behavioral factors are also related to the risk of cancer. For instance, poor nutrition, smoking, alcohol use, exposure to sunlight, exposure to radiation, and particular occupational hazards (such as exposure to certain chemicals or asbestos) are all known to increase the chances of developing cancer.

After a diagnosis of cancer, several forms of treatment are possible, depending on the type of cancer. One treatment is *radiation therapy*, in which the tumor is the target of radiation designed to destroy it. *Chemotherapy* involves the controlled ingestion of toxic substances meant, in essence, to poison the tumor. Finally, surgery may be used to remove the tumor (and often the surrounding tissue). The exact form of treatment is a function of how far the cancer has spread throughout a patient's body when it is first identified.

Because early cancer detection improves a patient's chances, diagnostic techniques that help identify the first signs of cancer are of great importance. This is particularly true during middle adulthood, when the risk of contracting certain kinds of cancer increases. Consequently, physicians urge that women routinely examine their breasts, and men regularly check their testicles, for signs of cancer. Furthermore, mammograms, which provide internal scans of women's breasts, also help identify early-stage cancer. However, the question of when women should begin to routinely have the procedure is highly controversial.

Routine Mammograms: At What Age Should Women Start?   Consider the following case:

> I found the lump in February, 1990. Buried deep in my left breast, it was rock-hard, the size of a BB and it hurt. I wondered if it might be cancer. Like blue eyes and a sense of humor, the disease runs in my family. But not breast cancer. And not me. I was too young. OK. I had recently turned 40, but I was healthy. I worked out three times a week and I was *almost* a vegetarian. My next physical was only a month away. I'd have it checked then. (Driedger, 1994, p. 46)

For Sharon Driedger, feeling healthy, exercising, and eating a good diet was not enough: She did have cancer. But she was also lucky. After aggressive treatment with radiation therapy, she stands a good chance of a full recovery.

In part, her good luck is a result of the early identification of her cancer. Statistically, the earlier breast cancer is diagnosed, the better a woman's chances of survival. But just how to accomplish early identification has become a major source of contention in the medical field, pitting one medical expert against another, and sometimes patients against physicians. Specifically, the controversy surrounds the use of mammograms, pictures produced by a process called mammography, and among the best means of detecting breast cancer in its earliest stages.

In mammography, a weak X-ray is used to examine breast tissue. The technique allows for the early identification of tumors while they are still very small, which permits treatment before the tumor has had time to grow and spread to other parts of the body. In short, mammograms have the potential for saving many lives, and both the National Cancer Institute and the American Cancer Society suggest that women over the age of 50 routinely obtain them.

Sharon Driedger survived a bout of breast cancer following aggressive treatment with radiation therapy.

FIGURE 15-7

AGE AND THE RISK OF BREAST
CANCER

Starting around the age of 30, the risk of
breast cancer becomes increasingly likely, as
these annual incidence figures show.

(*Source:* Adapted from Kaplan, Sallis & Patterson, 1993.)

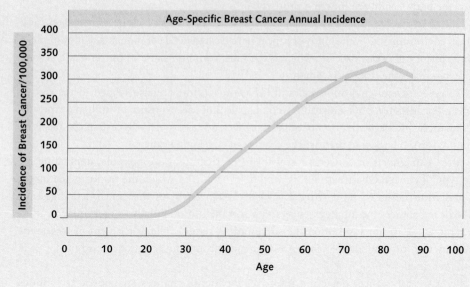

But what about younger women? As shown in Figure 15-7, the risk of breast cancer does not suddenly rise at the age of 50. Instead, it begins to grow at around the age of 30 and then becomes increasingly more likely. For instance, the incidence of breast cancer in women between the ages of 40 and 44 is 112 out of 100,000, and the number almost doubles between the ages of 50 and 54 (Sondik, 1988). What, then, is so special about the age of 50?

To many observers, nothing much. According to them, women should have routine mammograms beginning at age 40, and some advocate the routine use of mammography even earlier. However, others dispute this advice because of two considerations. First, there is the problem of *false positives,* instances in which the test suggests something is wrong when in fact there is no problem. Because the breast tissue of younger women is denser than that of older women, younger women are more likely to have false positives. In fact, some estimates suggest that as many as a third of all younger women who have repeated mammograms are likely to have a false positive that necessitates further testing or a biopsy. Furthermore, the opposite problem also may occur: *false negatives*, in which a mammogram does not detect indications of cancer (Miller, 1991; Baines et al., 1997).

A second problem with routine mammograms for women under 50 is cost. The average mammogram costs $100. If the incidence of breast cancer at age 40 is 112 cases out of 100,000, this means that it will cost $10 million to detect just 112 cases. Although one can argue that even one life saved is worth any financial cost, the medical establishment, plagued with increasing costs, is unlikely to find such reasoning compelling (Kaplan, Sallis, & Patterson, 1993).

In sum, the use of mammograms raises some difficult issues, involving medical, developmental, and societal considerations. It pits one medical group against another: for instance, the American Cancer Society and the American Medical Association both recommend annual mammograms for women aged 40 to 49, but the American College of Physicians and the National Cancer Institute do not recommend them. Whether the current recommendation that only those over 50 undergo routine mammograms will evolve remains to be seen (Taubes, 1997).

Psychological Factors Relating to Cancer: Mind Over Tumor?   Increasing evidence suggests that cancer is related not only to physiological causes, but to psychological factors as well (Edelman & Kidman, 1997). In particular, some research indicates that the emotional responses of people with cancer can influence their recovery. In one study, for instance, a group of women who recently had had a breast removed as part of their treatment for breast cancer were categorized according to their attitudes. Some felt their situation was hopeless, whereas others stoically accepted their cancer, voicing no complaints. Other women expressed a "fighting spirit," contending that they would lick the disease. Finally, some simply denied that they had cancer, refusing to accept the diagnosis.

Ten years later, the researchers looked again at the group of women. They found clear-cut evidence that initial attitude was related to survival. A larger percentage of the women who had stoically accepted their cancer or had felt hopeless had died. The death rate was much lower for those who had a "fighting spirit" or who had denied that they had the disease (Pettingale et al., 1985; see Figure 15-8).

Other studies suggest that the degree of social support people experience may be related to cancer. For example, some research finds that people with close family ties are less likely to develop cancer than those without them (Thomas, Duszynski, & Schaffer, 1979). Other studies show links between personality and cancer. For instance, cancer patients who are habitually optimistic report less physical and psychological distress than those who are less optimistic (Baltrusch, Stangel, & Tirze, 1991; Carver & Scheier, 1993; Bolger et al., 1996).

Finally, recent evidence suggests that participation in psychological therapy may give cancer patients an edge in treatment success. According to the preliminary results of a study done by psychologist David Spiegel, women in the advanced stages of breast cancer who participated in group therapy lived at least 18 months longer than those who did not participate in therapy. Furthermore, the women who participated also experienced less anxiety and pain (Spiegel et al., 1989; Spiegel, 1993, 1996).

Such evidence, assuming it is valid, raises the question of the link between psychological state and cancer. One possibility is that patients who have the most positive attitudes and are involved in therapy might be more likely to adhere to intricate, complex, and often unpleasant medical treatments for cancer. Consequently, such patients are more likely to experience treatment success (Holland & Lewis, 1993).

However, there is another possibility. It may be that a positive psychological outlook benefits the body's *immune system*, the natural line of defense against disease. According to this perspective, a positive emotional outlook bolsters the immune system, energizing the production of "killer" cells that fight the cancerous cells. In contrast, negative emotions and attitudes may impair the ability of the body's natural killer cells to fight off the cancer (Kiecolt-Glaser & Kiecolt-Glaser, 1991, 1993; Andersen, Kiecolt-Glaser, & Glaser, 1994; Fawzey, 1994; Seligman, 1995).

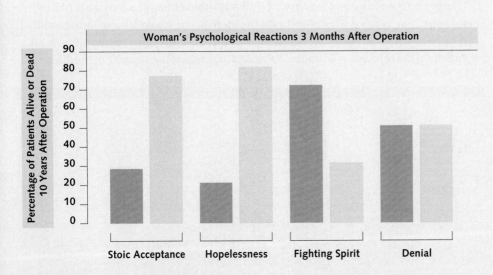

FIGURE 15-8

ATTITUDE AND SURVIVING CANCER

Fighting spirit pays off. A woman's psychological reaction 3 months after her cancer operation was clearly associated with whether she was alive 10 years later.

(*Source:* Pettingale et al., 1985.)

■ **Alive**

■ **Dead**

"Serious illness puts a lot of pressure on the social system of the family."

"The crisis points of cancer are when most people need the most support. It is most important for the clinician at all stages to seek and understand the meaning of the disease."

SPEAKING OF DEVELOPMENT

Allen Levine, Cancer Counselor

Education: .... Long Island University, B.A. in sociology; New York University, M.A. in social work; Long Island Institute for Mental Health, degree in psychoanalytic psychotherapy

Position: .... Assistant director of social work at Cancer Care, Inc.

Home: .... New York City, New York

As a child of the 1960s, Allen Levine had a desire to help people in whatever profession he chose. This desire led him not only to academic degrees in social work, but also to his life's vocation at Cancer Care, Inc., in New York City.

Levine has worked at the care facility for 17 years, counseling people who have cancer. He has served as assistant director of social work for the past 2 years.

"In treatment it is important to get a good assessment of how a person has coped with serious issues in his or her life prior to the disease," he says. "By the time people have reached middle age, they have had to deal with a lot of life issues. You want to know how they coped before, and then find out how they are coping now.

"A person may have personal factors or a personal history that would make moving on with treatment difficult," Levine adds. "You don't want to treat a person for cancer-related depression and then find out he or she has been depressed since adolescence. It's a different diagnosis in that case."

Levine notes that facing an illness such as cancer in middle age can affect a person's functioning at four basic levels.

"The first is the physical," he explains. "You have to look at the physical experiences the person has had with the disease. Is there disfigurement, weight loss or weight gain? Has there been surgery, chemotherapy? How is the cancer—and its treatment—affecting daily living, working, intimacy, playing with the kids? All of these factors need to be looked at.

"Second are the financial aspects of the disease. In middle age, many people are saving for retirement or college for their children. A chronic illness can be very expensive, and insurance doesn't cover everything. Financially, a major disease can really upset the apple cart.

"The third level is social. How deep is the family in terms of providing support for a person with a chronic illness? There's also the issue of parents having to deal with chronically ill children who may not survive them. Serious illness puts a lot of pressure on the social system of the family.

"The psychological aspect of cancer as a possibly life-threatening disease is the final level," Levine notes. "For instance, what does the disease mean to one's womanhood or manhood?

"The crisis points of cancer are when most people need the most support. It is most important for the clinician at all stages to seek and understand the *meaning* of the disease."

time slows with age, as we discussed earlier in the chapter—then their poorer performance on IQ tests may be a result of physical, rather than cognitive, changes (Schaie, 1991; Nettlebeck & Rabbit, 1992).

To complicate the picture even further, many researchers believe that there are two kinds of intelligence: fluid intelligence and crystallized intelligence (Cattell, 1967, 1987). As we first noted in Chapter 9, **fluid intelligence** is the ability to deal with new problems and situations. For instance, a person who is asked to arrange a series of letters according to some rule or to memorize a set of numbers uses fluid intelligence. In contrast, **crystallized intelligence** is the store of information, skills, and strategies that people have acquired through education and prior experiences, and through their previous use of fluid intelligence. Someone who is solving a crossword puzzle or attempting to identify the murderer in a mystery story is using crystallized intelligence, relying on his or her past experience as a resource.

Initially, researchers believed that fluid intelligence was largely determined by genetic factors, and crystallized intelligence primarily by experiential, environmental factors. However, they later abandoned this distinction, largely because they found that crystallized intelligence is determined in part by fluid intelligence. For instance, a person's ability to solve a crossword puzzle (which involves crystallized intelligence) is a result of that person's proficiency with letters and patterns (a manifestation of fluid intelligence).

When developmental psychologists looked at the two kinds of intelligence separately, they arrived at a new answer to the question of whether intelligence declines with age. Actually, they arrived at two answers: yes and no. Yes, because in general, fluid intelligence does show declines with age; no, because crystallized intelligence holds steady and in some cases actually improves (Baltes & Schaie, 1974; Anstey, Stankov, & Lord, 1993; Schaie, 1993; Wang & Kaufman, 1993; Heidrich & Denney, 1994; Isingrini & Vazou, 1997; see Figure 15-9).

In fact, according to developmental psychologist K. Warner Schaie (1994), who has conducted extensive longitudinal research on adult intellectual development, the broad division of intelligence into the fluid and crystallized categories masks true age-related differences and developments in intelligence. He argues that researchers should instead consider many particular types of ability, such as spatial orientation, numeric ability, verbal ability, and so on.

When looked at in this way, the question of how intelligence changes in adulthood yields yet another answer, but a more specific one. Schaie finds that certain abilities, such as inductive reasoning, spatial orientation, perceptual speed, and verbal memory, start a gradual decline at around age 25 and continue to decline through old age. On the

fluid intelligence the ability to deal with new problems and situations

crystallized intelligence the store of information, skills, and strategies that people have acquired through education and prior experiences, and through their previous use of fluid intelligence

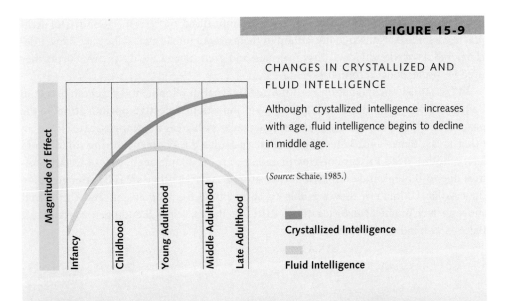

FIGURE 15-9

CHANGES IN CRYSTALLIZED AND FLUID INTELLIGENCE

Although crystallized intelligence increases with age, fluid intelligence begins to decline in middle age.

(*Source:* Schaie, 1985.)

■ **Crystallized Intelligence**

▨ **Fluid Intelligence**

other hand, numeric and verbal abilities show a quite different pattern. For instance, numeric ability tends to increase until the mid-40s, is lower at age 60, and then stays steady throughout the rest of life. Verbal ability rises until about the start of middle adulthood, around age 40, and stays fairly steady throughout the rest of the life span (Schaie, 1994).

Reframing the Issue: What Is the Source of Competence During Middle Adulthood?
Clearly, the question of whether intelligence declines during middle and later adulthood does not have a simple answer. The issue remains controversial; we will return to it when we consider older people in Chapter 17.

What is apparent is that even though overall IQ, as measured by traditional intelligence tests, drops in middle adulthood, almost all people in middle age show no apparent decline in general cognitive competence (Cunningham & Hamen, 1992). In fact, it is during the middle part of the life span that people come to hold some of the most important and powerful positions in society. How can we explain such continuing, and even growing, intellectual competence in the face of apparently ongoing declines in certain cognitive skills?

One answer comes from psychologist Timothy Salthouse (1989, 1990, 1994a), who suggests that there are four reasons why this discrepancy exists. For one thing, it is possible that typical measures of cognitive skills tap a different type of cognition than what is required to be successful in particular occupations. Recall the discussion of practical intelligence in Chapter 13, in which we considered the position that traditional IQ tests fail to measure cognitive abilities that are related to occupational success. Perhaps we would find no discrepancy between intelligence and cognitive abilities in middle adulthood if we used measures of practical intelligence rather than traditional IQ tests to assess intelligence.

A second factor also relates to the measurement of IQ and occupational success. It is possible that the most successful middle-aged adults are not representative of middle-aged adults in general. It may be that only a small proportion of people are highly successful, and the rest, who experience only moderate or little success, may have changed occupations, retired, or become sick and died. If we look at highly successful people, then, we are examining an unrepresentative sample of individuals.

It is also conceivable that the degree of cognitive ability required for professional success is simply not that high. According to this argument, people can be quite successful professionally and still be on the decline in certain kinds of cognitive abilities. In other words, their cognitive declines are not all that important.

Finally, it may be that older people are successful because they have developed specific kinds of expertise and particular competencies. Whereas IQ tests measure reactions to novel situations, occupational success may be influenced by very specific sorts of well-practiced abilities. Consequently, although their overall intellectual skills may show a decline, middle-aged individuals may maintain and even expand the distinctive talents they need for professional accomplishment.

In fact, this last explanation is supported by what developmental psychologists Paul Baltes and Margaret Baltes call selective optimization. **Selective optimization** is the process by which people concentrate on particular skill areas to compensate for losses in other areas. Baltes and Baltes suggest that cognitive development during middle and later adulthood is a mixture of growth and decline. As people begin to lose certain abilities due to biological deterioration, they also advance in other areas by strengthening their skills. Ultimately, they are able to compensate for their losses, and they avoid showing any practical deterioration (Baltes & Baltes, 1990; Staudinger, Marsiske, & Baltes, 1993; Baltes, 1987, 1993, 1995).

selective optimization the process by which people concentrate on particular skill areas to compensate for losses in other areas

For instance, recall that reaction time lengthens as people get older. Because reaction time is a component of typing skill, we would expect that older typists would be slower than younger ones. However, this is not the case. Why? The answer is that while their reaction time is increasing, older typists look further ahead in the material they are to type. This allows them to compensate for their lengthier reaction time (Salthouse, 1984).

In short, even minor declines in particular intellectual abilities are compensated for during middle adulthood. Overall cognitive competence, then, remains quite intact.

Memory: You Must Remember This

Whenever Mary Donovan can't find her car keys, she mutters to herself that she is "losing her memory."

However, if she fits the pattern of most people in middle adulthood, her assessment is not necessarily accurate. According to research on memory changes in adulthood, most people show only minimal memory losses, and many exhibit none at all, during middle adulthood.

Types of Memory.   To understand memory changes, it is necessary to consider the different types of memory. Memory is traditionally viewed in terms of three sequential components: sensory memory, short-term memory, and long-term memory. *Sensory memory* is an initial, momentary storage of information that lasts only an instant. Information is recorded by an individual's sensory system as a raw, meaningless stimulus. Next, information moves into *short-term memory*, which holds it for 15 to 25 seconds. Finally, if the information is rehearsed, it is moved into *long-term memory*, where it is stored on a relatively permanent basis.

The different types of memory storage vary with age in different ways. Both sensory memory and short-term memory show virtually no weakening during middle adulthood. The story is a bit different for long-term memory, which, for some people, shows some decline with age. However, the reason for the decline does not appear to be a fading or a complete loss of memory, but rather that the initial registering of the information and its storage become less efficient with age. Furthermore, memory declines may also be related to a reduction in the efficiency of information retrieval from memory. In other words, even if the information was stored efficiently in long-term memory, it may become more difficult to locate or isolate it (Hultsch, Masson, & Small, 1991; Schieber, et al., 1992; Salthouse, 1994b).

It is important to keep in mind that memory declines in middle age are relatively minor, and most can be compensated for by various cognitive strategies. For instance, paying greater attention to material when it is first encountered can aid in its later recall. Losing one's keys, for instance, may have relatively little to do with memory declines; instead, it may be the result of inattentiveness at an earlier moment. Furthermore, because of societal stereotypes about aging, people in middle adulthood may be prone to attribute their absent-mindedness to aging, even though they have been absent-minded throughout their lives. Consequently, it is the *meaning* they give to their forgetfulness that changes, rather than their actual ability to remember (Erber, Rothberg, & Szuchman, 1991).

Memory Schemas.   During adulthood, we recall material through the use of schemas. **Schemas** are organized bodies of information stored in memory. Schemas help people represent the way the world is organized, and allow them to categorize and interpret new information (Rumelhart, 1984; Fiske & Taylor, 1991).

People hold schemas for particular individuals (such as a mother, a wife, or a child) as well as for categories of people (mail carriers, lawyers, or professors). People's schemas

schemas *organized bodies of information stored in memory*

Understanding a tale told by Native American story-tellers requires familiarity with the culture, due to the existence of particular schemas.

serve to organize their behavior into coherent wholes, and help them to interpret social events. For instance, psychologists Susan Fiske and Shelley Taylor (1991) give an example of an old Native American folktale in which the hero participates with several companions in a battle and is shot by an arrow. However, he feels no pain from the arrow. When he returns to his home and tells the story, something black emerges from his mouth, and he dies the next morning.

This tale is puzzling to many people because they are unschooled in the particular Native American culture to which the story belongs. People from Western societies tend to add, change, and omit details to fit their own existing schemas. However, to someone familiar with the Native American culture, the story makes perfect sense. The hero feels no pain because his companions are ghosts, and the "black thing" coming from his mouth is his departing soul.

In short, people's previous experiences within the context of a particular culture allow them to construct schemas in memory. In turn, their schemas allow them to comprehend and interpret new encounters. Furthermore, memory schemas influence people's recall of new information to which they are exposed. Material that is consistent with existing schemas is more likely to be recalled than material that is inconsistent (Laszlo, 1986; Hansen, 1989; VanManen & Pietromonaco, 1993).

mnemonics *formal strategies for organizing material in ways that make it more likely to be remembered*

The Informed Consumer of Development

Effective Strategies for Remembering

All of us, at one time or another, are forgetful. However, there are techniques that can enhance our memories and make it less likely that we will forget things that we wish to remember. **Mnemonics** (pronounced "nee-MON-iks") are formal strategies for organizing material in ways that make it more likely to be remembered. Among the mnemonics that work not only in middle adulthood but at other points of the life span are the following (Mastropieri & Scruggs, 1991; Bellezza, Six, & Phillips, 1992; Guttman, 1997).

■ *Get organized.* For someone who has trouble keeping track of where they left their keys or remembering appointments, the simplest approach is to become more organized. Using an appointment book, hanging one's keys on a hook, or using Post-it notes can help jog one's memory.

■ *Encoding specificity phenomenon.* According to the encoding specificity phenomenon, people are most likely to recall information in environments that are similar to those in which they initially learned ("encoded") it (Tulving & Thompson, 1973). For instance, people are best able to recall information on a test if the test is held in the room in which they studied.

■ *The keyword technique.* Anyone who has attempted to learn a foreign language knows that one of the greatest challenges is remembering vocabulary. To overcome the difficulty posed by long lists of unfamiliar words, memory experts have developed the keyword technique (first described in Chapter 9), in which a foreign word is paired with a common word in the learner's native language that has a similar *sound* to the foreign word. The native language word is known as the keyword. For example, the keyword for the Spanish word for horse (*caballo,* pronounced *cob-eye-yo*) might be "eye."

Once a keyword has been identified, the procedure is simple: The learner forms a mental picture in which the keyword is envisioned as "interacting" with the foreign word's translation (such as a horse with big eyes). Psychologists who study memory have found the keyword procedure to be effective, producing better recall than traditional techniques for memorizing lists of vocabulary words (Pressley & Levin, 1983; Pressley, 1987; Pressley & VanMeter, 1993).

■ *Rehearsal.* In the realm of memory, practice makes perfect, or if not perfect, at least better. Adults of all ages can improve their memories if they expend more effort in rehearsing what they want to remember. By initially paying attention when they are exposed to new information, by purposefully thinking that they wish to recall it in the future, and by practicing what they wish to recall, people can substantially improve their recall of the material.

REVIEW AND RETHINK

REVIEW

- The question of whether intelligence declines in middle adulthood is complicated by limitations in the two main methods of answering it: cross-sectional studies and longitudinal studies.

- Another complication in answering this question is the fact that intelligence appears to be divided into components, some of which decline while others hold steady or even improve.

- In general, cognitive competence in middle adulthood holds fairly steady despite declines in some areas of intellectual functioning.

- Memory may appear to decline in middle age, but in fact sensory and short-term memory are unaffected, and long-term memory deficits are probably due to ineffective strategies of memory storage and retrieval, which can be consciously improved.

- Mnemonics help people enhance their recall of information from memory, generally by forcing greater attention during memory storage.

RETHINK

- How might crystallized and fluid intelligence work together to help middle-aged people deal with novel situations and problems?

- How do you explain the apparent discrepancy between declining IQ scores and continuing cognitive competence in middle adulthood?

- How do memory schemas help people interpret social situations and novel events? How do you think people deal with elements of such situations that don't fit into existing schemas?

- How would you advise someone who complains of being unable to remember people's names? What strategies might be helpful?

LOOKING BACK

- **What sorts of physical changes affect people in middle adulthood?**
  - During middle adulthood, roughly the period from 40 to 60, people typically decline slowly in height and strength and gain in weight. Height loss, especially in women, may be associated with osteoporosis.
  - Visual acuity, hearing acuity, and reaction time deteriorate during this period. The incidence of glaucoma, a disease that can cause blindness, increases.

- **What changes in sexuality do middle-aged men and women experience?**
  - Adults in middle age experience changes in sexuality, but these are less dramatic than commonly supposed. Women experience the female climacteric, an end to the child-bearing period, manifested in menopause, which is often accompanied by physical and emotional discomfort.
  - Estrogen replacement therapy (ERT) is a popular but controversial therapy that aims to decrease symptoms related to menopause and slow the deterioration associated with aging by replacing the female body's estrogen.
  - Men also undergo changes in their reproductive systems, sometimes referred to as the male climacteric. Generally, the production of sperm and testosterone declines and the prostate gland enlarges, causing difficulties with urination.

■ **Is middle adulthood a time of health or disease for men and women?**

- Middle adulthood is generally a healthy period, but people become more susceptible to chronic diseases and have a higher death rate than before. Overall health in middle adulthood varies according to socioeconomic status and gender. People of higher SES are healthier and have lower death rates than people of lower SES. Women have a lower mortality rate than men, but a higher incidence of illness.

■ **What sorts of people are likely to get coronary heart disease?**

- Genetic characteristics, such as age, gender, and a family history of heart disease, are associated with the risk of heart disease, as are environmental and behavioral factors, including smoking, a diet high in fats and cholesterol, and a lack of exercise. Psychological factors also play. A pattern of behaviors associated with competitiveness, impatience, frustration, and hostility—called the Type A behavior pattern—is associated with a high risk of heart problems.

■ **What causes cancer, and what tools are available to diagnose and treat it?**

- Like heart disease, cancer becomes a threat in middle adulthood and is related to genetic and environmental factors. Treatments include radiation therapy, chemotherapy, and surgery. Psychological factors appear to play a role in the treatment of cancer and even in the chances of developing cancer.

- Breast cancer is a significant risk for women in middle adulthood. Mammography can help identify cancerous tumors early enough for successful treatment, but the age at which women should begin to have routine mammograms is a matter of controversy.

■ **What happens to a person's intelligence in middle adulthood?**

- In general, fluid intelligence slowly declines through middle adulthood while crystallized intelligence holds steady or even improves. Dividing intelligence into greater numbers of components produce an even more complicated pattern.

- People in middle adulthood generally display a high degree of overall cognitive competence focusing on specific areas of competence that generally compensate for areas of loss, a strategy known as selective optimization.

■ **How does aging affect memory, and how can memory be improved?**

- Problems with long-term memory in middle adulthood appear to relate to storage and retrieval strategies rather than to overall memory deterioration, and the problems are minor and relatively easy to overcome.

- People interpret, store, and recall information in the form of memory schemas, which organize related bits of information to set up expectations and add meaning to phenomena. Mnemonic devices can help people improve their ability to recall information by forcing them to pay attention to information as they store it to use cues to enable retrieval or to practice information retrieval.

EPILOGUE: A SECOND CHANCE TO SHINE

We began our consideration of middle adulthood with a look at physical development, health, and sexuality. We noted the increasing incidence of chronic and life-threatening diseases, and we paid special attention to two of them: heart disease and cancer. In the cognitive realm, we noted very gradual declines in some areas of intelligence and memory, but compensatory strategies and gains in other areas. We concluded with a look at some ways to improve memorization.

Return to the prologue of this chapter, about Hazel Robinson's return to college, and answer these questions.

1. In what ways might changes in her sensory functions affect Hazel's classroom and homework experiences? What adjustments should she expect to make in compensation?

2. Will Hazel's physical development more directly affect her performance on untimed essay tests or timed classroom quizzes? How might Hazel deal with a professor who seems to favor tests that happen to address weaknesses that are due to aging?

3. How can Hazel deal with an assignment that calls for her to memorize a long list of factual information (e.g., the Periodic Table of Elements or the names of the presidents of the United States)? Will this assignment most likely be more difficult for her than for younger students?

4. Compared with younger students, what advantages will Hazel most likely have in completing her studies in college? Why?

5. What benefits for her fellow students will Hazel be able to bring to her classes? In general, do you think older students are an asset or a liability in college classes? Why?

KEY TERMS AND CONCEPTS

osteoporosis (p. 513)
presbyopia (p. 514)
glaucoma (p. 514)
presbycusis (p. 514)
female climacteric (p. 517)
menopause (p. 517)
male climacteric (p. 520)

Type A behavior pattern (p. 525)
Type B behavior pattern (p. 526)
fluid intelligence (p. 533)
crystallized intelligence (p. 533)
selective optimization (p. 534)
schemas (p. 535)
mnemonics (p. 536)

CHAPTER 16

MIDDLE ADULTHOOD

Social and Personality Development

P R O L O G U E: NANCY BROADWAY'S WINDING JOURNEY TO SUCCESS

Nancy Broadway

Flexibility became a means of survival for Nancy Broadway. At 55, she has experienced many of the ups and downs of women in her age group: divorce, rearing a child alone, a layoff from a good job. Now she is struggling to get back to work, unwilling to give up on regaining her career as a well-paid hospital administrator—but ready, she says, to take a lesser job, if she is forced to do so.

Divorced at age 30, Ms. Broadway supported herself with a full-time job while rearing a child. Her salary rose through a series of administrative positions to $51,000 a year as associate director of Bellevue Hospital's AIDS program. But she lost that job in February in a management reorganization, her first layoff in nearly 30 years of constant employment. Like so many college-trained women in their 50s, she acted quickly to prepare herself for another job.

Ms. Broadway enrolled for a master's degree in public administration, training she considers essential in her quest for a new job as a hospital or clinic manager. "I am just kicking myself for not listening to my friends, who told me for years, 'Go back and get your master's,'" Ms. Broadway said. . . .

Having come out of college with a Peace Corps mentality, as Ms. Broadway puts it, she tries to help others even as she hunts for a job for herself. She is the unpaid vice president of Forty Plus Inc., a support group mostly for people over 40 who are out of work.

As for herself, contingency plans are beginning to form. "I love supervising and working with staff," she said. But if such a job does not materialize, she would take a lesser one. "I cannot imagine myself out of the work force." (Uchitelle, 1994, p. B8)

LOOKING AHEAD   The twists and turns in Nancy Broadway's life path are not unusual: Few lives follow a set, predictable pattern through middle adulthood. In fact, one of the remarkable characteristics of middle age is its diversity, as the paths that different people travel continue to diverge.

This chapter focuses on the personality and social development that occurs in midlife. We begin by considering personality development. We examine the changes that typify this period, according to various stage theorists, and the ways people's "social clocks" continue their countdown through life's milestones. We also explore some of the controversies that underlie developmental psychologists' understandings of midlife, including whether the midlife crisis, a phenomenon popularized in modern society, is fact or fiction.

We then turn to the relationships that evolve during middle adulthood. We consider the various familial ties that bind people together (or come unglued) during this period, including marriage, divorce, the empty nest, and grandparenting. We also look at a bleaker side of family relations: family violence, which is surprisingly prevalent.

Finally, the chapter considers the role of work and leisure during middle adulthood. We will examine the changing role of work in people's lives and some of the difficulties associated with work, such as burnout and unemployment. The chapter concludes with a discussion of leisure time, which gains increasing importance during middle age.

In short, after reading this chapter, you will be able to answer the following questions:

Q

- In what ways does personality develop during middle adulthood?
- What are some current controversies in personality development?
- What are typical patterns of marriage and divorce in middle adulthood?
- What changing family situations do middle-aged adults face?
- What are the causes and characteristics of family violence in the United States?
- What are the characteristics of work and career in middle adulthood?

PERSONALITY DEVELOPMENT

My 40th birthday was not an easy one. It's not that I woke up one morning and felt different—that's never been the case. But what did happen during my 40th year was that I came to the realization of the finiteness of life, and that the die was cast. I began to understand that I probably wasn't going to be president of the United States—a secret ambition—or even a captain of industry. Time was no longer on my side, but something of an adversary. But it was curious: Rather than following my traditional pattern of focusing on the future, planning to do this or do that, I began to appreciate what I had. I looked around at my life, was pretty well satisfied with some of my accomplishments, and began to focus on the things that were going right, not the things that I was lacking. But this state-of-mind didn't happen in a day; it took several years after turning 40 before I felt this way. Even now, it is hard to fully accept that I am middle-aged.

As this 47-year-old man suggests, the realization that one has entered middle adulthood does not always come easily. In many Western societies, the age of 40 has special meaning, bringing with it the inescapable fact that one is now middle-aged—at least in the view of others—and the suggestion, embodied in everyday common wisdom, that one is about to experience the throes of a "midlife crisis" (Gergen, 1990).

However, as we will see, the midlife crisis is far from inevitable, and many—perhaps most—people sail through middle age with little or no crisis or psychological turmoil. On the other hand, midlife does bring with it new psychological concerns, and those concerns do influence the nature and course of personality development.

In Western society, turning 40 represents an important milestone.

Erikson's Stage of Generativity Versus Stagnation

As we first discussed in Chapter 12, psychoanalyst Erik Erikson suggests that middle adulthood encompasses the period of **generativity versus stagnation**. Generativity refers to an individual's contribution to family, community, work, and society as a whole. Generative people strive to play a role in guiding and encouraging future generations. They may work directly with younger individuals, acting as mentors, or they may satisfy their need for generativity through creative and artistic output, seeking to leave a lasting contribution. The focus of those who experience generativity, then, is beyond themselves, as they look toward the continuation of their own lives through others (Bradley, 1997; McAdams & de St. Aubin, 1998).

On the other hand, a lack of psychological success in this period means that people become stagnant. Focusing on the triviality of their own activity, people may come to feel that they have made only limited contributions to the world, that their presence has counted for little. In fact, some individuals find themselves floundering, still seeking new, and potentially more fulfilling, careers. Others become frustrated and bored.

Although Erikson provides a broad overview of personality development, some psychologists have suggested that we need a more precise look at changes in personality during middle adulthood. For example, adult developmental psychologist George Vaillant (1977) has suggested that an important period during middle adulthood is "keeping the meaning versus rigidity." *Keeping the meaning versus rigidity* occurs between about ages 45 and 55. During that period, adults seek to extract the meaning from their lives, and they seek to "keep the meaning" by developing an acceptance of the strengths and weaknesses of others. Although they recognize the shortcomings of the world, they strive to preserve their world, and they are relatively content. On the other hand, those who are rigid become increasingly isolated from others.

Levinson's Seasons of Life

According to psychologist Daniel Levinson (1986, 1992), the early 40s are a period of transition and crisis. He based his contention on a comprehensive study of 40 men. Despite the relatively small sample size, and the fact that the study included no women, Levinson's view has been influential. It provided one of the first, and most far-reaching, descriptions of the stages through which people pass during adulthood.

Levinson suggests that adult men pass through a series of stages beginning with their entry into early adulthood at around age 20 and continuing into middle adulthood (see

generativity versus stagnation ac-cording to Erikson, the stage during middle adulthood in which people consider their contributions to family and society

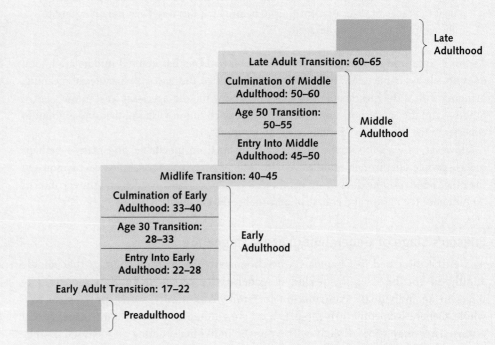

FIGURE 16-1

MEN'S STAGES OF ADULTHOOD

According to Levinson, men pass through a series of stages and crises. However, not everyone accepts the universality of these stages, and their applicability to women has not been established.

(*Source:* Adapted from Levinson, 1978.)

Figure 16-1). The beginning stages have to do with leaving one's family and entering the adult world. During this time of early adulthood, people construct what Levinson calls "The Dream," a broad, comprehensive vision of the future. The dream encompasses an individual's goals and aspirations, whether they entail becoming a captain of industry, a parent, or an elementary school teacher.

In early adulthood people make, and sometimes discard, career choices as they come to grips with their capabilities and ultimately commit to long-term decisions. This process leads to a period—the late 30s—of settling down. They establish themselves, throwing themselves into their chosen roles and moving toward the vision they created earlier in "The Dream."

However, at around age 40 or 45, people move into a period that Levinson calls the midlife transition. The *midlife transition* is a time of questioning. People begin to focus on the finite nature of life, realizing and even growing obsessed with the fact that they will not live forever. They concentrate on the present rather than looking toward the future, and they begin to question some of their everyday, fundamental assumptions. They experience the first signs of aging, and they may begin to doubt the value of their accomplishments, finding them lacking in real meaning. More importantly, they confront the knowledge that they will be unable to accomplish all their aims before they die.

In Levinson's view, this period of assessment may lead to a midlife crisis. The **midlife crisis** is a stage of uncertainty and indecision brought about by the realization that life is finite. Facing signs of physical aging, people may also discover that even the accomplishments of which they are proudest have brought them less satisfaction than they expected. Looking toward the past, they may seek to define what went wrong and look for ways to correct their past mistakes. The midlife crisis, then, is a painful and tumultuous period of questioning.

What happens next depends on how successfully people deal with the midlife crisis. In Levinson's study, those men who came to grips with their aging found the remainder of their 40s productive and satisfying. Some took on new roles, such as mentors to

midlife crisis *a stage of uncertainty and indecision brought about by the realization that life is finite*

younger persons, and some even changed careers. On the other hand, those who were less successful in dealing with the midlife crisis entered a period of stagnation or even decline for the rest of their 40s. Such individuals were still struggling to find their places in the world well into their 50s.

For most people, though, the turmoil of the midlife crisis was resolved by the mid-40s. As they moved into their 50s, they felt secure in their worlds, comfortably looking forward to the future with a feeling of fulfillment.

Levinson's view of middle adulthood, then, clearly suggests that most people are susceptible to a fairly profound midlife crisis. But before accepting his view, we need to go back to some critical drawbacks to his research. First, his theorizing was based on a group of only 40 men. Although he interviewed them extensively, findings based on such a small sample of only one gender are difficult to generalize, particularly to women. Furthermore, the results of Levinson's interviews are not consistent. Some subjects had quite smooth midlife transitions, with little apparent turmoil, whereas others experienced psychological crises at ages when, according to the theory, crises should be relatively unlikely (McCrae & Costa, 1990).

In short, Levinson may have overstated the consistency and generality of the patterns he found in the sample of men he used to derive his theory. On the other hand, Levinson (1992), on the basis of more recent research, has argued that women generally go through the same stages as men, although with certain differences. For example, he suggests that women have greater difficulty than men in "The Dream" stage, experiencing trouble clearly articulating what their futures will encompass. The reason, he argues, is that women are more subject than men to conflict between the goals of having a career and raising a family.

The Social Clocks of Women's Lives: Marking Time

Having children. Receiving a promotion. Getting divorced. Changing jobs. Becoming a grandparent. Each of these events marks a moment on what has been called the social clock of life. The **social clock** is an expression used to describe the psychological timepiece that records the major milestones in people's lives. Each of us has such a social clock; it provides us with a sense of whether we have reached the major benchmarks of life early, late, or right on time in comparison to our peers.

Developmental psychologist Ravenna Helson and colleagues suggest that people have several social clocks from which to choose, and the selection they make has substantial implications for personality development during middle adulthood. Focusing on a sample of women who graduated from college during the early 1960s, Helson's longitudinal research has examined women whose social clocks were focused on their families, on careers, or on a more individualistic target (Helson & Moane, 1987).

Helson found several broad patterns. Over the course of the study, which assessed participants at the ages of 21, 27, and 43, the participants generally became more self-disciplined and committed to their duties. They also felt greater independence and confidence, and they were able to cope with stress and adversity more effectively.

Measures of traditional feminine behavior changed over time. Although traditional feminine behavior increased from age 21 to age 27, it showed a decrease between the ages of 27 and 43. Helson speculates that the increase was related to a rise in sex-role specialization as the women became more involved in mothering. In contrast, the subsequent decline was likely a result of a decrease in child-care responsibilities as the women's children became older.

Helson's work also identified some intriguing similarities in personality development between women who chose to focus on family and those who focused on career. Both groups tended to show generally positive changes. In contrast, the women who had no strong focus on either family or career tended to show either little change or more negative shifts in personality development.

social clock the psychological timepiece that records the major milestones in people's lives

Helson's conclusion is that the particular social clock that a woman chooses may not be the critical factor in determining the course of personality development. Instead, involvement in some socially acceptable and justifiable social-clock pattern may be the key. Furthermore, it is important to keep in mind that social clocks are culturally determined. For instance, as we consider next, the patterns of development are quite different when we consider other cultures (Helson, Stewart, & Ostrove, 1995).

Developmental Diversity

Middle Age: In Some Cultures It Doesn't Exist

There's no such thing as middle age. At least one can draw that conclusion by looking at the lives of women living in the Oriya culture in Orissa, India. According to research carried out by developmental anthropologist Richard Shweder, who studied how high caste Hindu women viewed the process of aging, a distinct period of middle age does not exist. These women view their life course not on the basis of chronological age, but on the nature of one's social responsibility, family management issues, and moral sense at a give time (Shweder, in press).

The model of aging of the Oriyan women is based on two phases of life: life in her father's house (*bapa gharo*), followed by life in her husband's mother's house (*sasu gharo*). These two segments make sense in the context of family life, which consists of multigenerational households in which marriages are arranged. After they are married, husbands remain with their parents and wives are expected to move into the husband's parents' household. At the time of marriage, a wife is seen as having changed social status from a child (someone's daughter) to a sexually active female (a daughter-in-law).

The shift from child to daughter-in-law typically occurs around the ages of 18 or 20. However, chronological age, per se, does not mark significant boundaries in life for Oriyan women, nor do physical changes, such as the onset of menstruation or its cessation at menopause. Instead, it is the change from daughter to daughter-in-law that brings about a significant alteration in social responsibility. For instance, women must shift their focus from their own parents to the parents of their husband, and they must become sexually active in order to reproduce the (husband's) family line.

Indian women view their life course not on the basis of chronological age, but on the nature of one's social responsibility, family management issues, and moral sense at a given period.

Although a description of the life course of these Indian women suggests that they might perceive their lives as restricted, because in most cases they have no careers outside the home, they do not see themselves in this light. In fact, in the Oriya culture, domestic work is highly respected and valued. Furthermore, Oriyan women perceive themselves as more cultured and civilized than men, who must work outside the home.

In short, the notion of a separate middle age is clearly a cultural construction. The significance of a particular age range differs significantly depending on the culture in which one lives.

Controversies in Personality Development During Middle Adulthood

Although they are also of concern at other stages of life, several controversies regarding personality development are particularly pronounced during middle adulthood. One issue is the reality of the midlife crisis. Another controversy is whether personality development proceeds through a series of age-related stages with associated crises or is instead tied to particular life events. Finally, a third basic issue relates to the degree of stability and change found in personality during adulthood.